GENESIS 1–25A

Smyth & Helwys Bible Commentary: Genesis 1–25A

Publication Staff

Publisher & Executive Vice President
Keith Gammons

Book Editor
Leslie Andres

Graphic Designers
Daniel Emerson
Dave Jones

Assistant Editors
Katie Brookins
Kelley F. Land

Smyth & Helwys Publishing, Inc.
6316 Peake Road
Macon, Georgia 31210-3960
1-800-747-3016
© 2018 by Smyth & Helwys Publishing
All rights reserved.
Printed in the United States of America.

Library of Congress Cataloging-in-Publication Data

Names: O'Connor, Kathleen M., 1942- author.
Title: Genesis / by Kathleen M. O'Connor.
Description: Macon : Smyth & Helwys, 2018. | Series: Smyth & Helwys Bible
commentary ; vol. 1 | Includes bibliographical references and index.
Contents: [V. 1a]. 1-25a -- [v. 1b]. 25b-50.
Identifiers: LCCN 2018010501 | ISBN 9781641730525 (alk. paper)
Subjects: LCSH: Bible. Genesis--Commentaries.
Classification: LCC BS1235.53 .O26 2018 | DDC 222/.11077--dc23
LC record available at https://lccn.loc.gov/2018010501

SMYTH & HELWYS BIBLE COMMENTARY

GENESIS 1–25A

KATHLEEN M. O'CONNOR

SMYTH&HELWYS
PUBLISHING, INCORPORATED · MACON, GEORGIA

ADVANCE PRAISE

By any measure Kathleen O'Connor is among the best readers of text of her generation. She brings to her interpretive work a lively imagination, a playful sense of the dramatic, a keen awareness of the urgent crises of the day, and grounding in deep faith. She brings, moreover, two particular gifts to the commentary that serve in compelling ways to redefine the work and capacity of a commentary. First, she is steeped in "trauma study" and so sees how texts are responses to disaster. Second, she offers an artistic sensibility about language so that in her hands the text continues to be generative. This is a most welcome commentary that summons the reader to rich and probing interpretation that effectively finesses the gap between ancient and contemporary. It is a work of art.

—*Walter Brueggemann*
Columbia Theological Seminary

A beautifully written commentary that captures the literary and theological essence of the book of Genesis. O'Connor skillfully demonstrates how Genesis responded to a people's trauma by reframing the traditions of their ancestors as stories of survival. She reveals how, through the aid of their Creator God, the people could cope with the disaster they faced and move beyond it to a new life.

—*Gale A. Yee*
Nancy W. King Professor of Biblical Studies Emerita
Episcopal Divinity School

Finally, an altogether fresh reading of Genesis which will delight seasoned interpreters and beginning students. Informed by disaster and survival studies, Kathleen O'Connor's work brings breathtaking clarity and theological insight to the biblical text and its afterlife.

— *Louis Stulman*
University of Findlay

Kathleen O'Connor possesses the enviable combination of rigorous exegetical precision and innovative engaging interpretation. She reminds those who look to Genesis for history that that collection of stories actually "intervenes in history," offering a theological view of beginnings to those who fear that they might be facing the end. She employs features of the present to encourage insight into the historical and cultural context of the biblical past, and she weaves artistic expressions of values and sentiments to throw light on universal concerns. Her sensitivity to ecological, gender, and multicultural matters will speak to a broad readership. And all of this is accomplished in a reader-friendly compositional style. This book is a gem!

—*Dianne Bergant*
Carroll Stuhlmueller, CP Distinguished Professor Emerita
of Old Testament Studies
Catholic Theological Union, Chicago

Elegantly written and thoroughly engaging, Professor O'Connor's Genesis commentary is treasure of insights whose breadth is unmatched by any other commentary available. Moreover, her particular focus on trauma and restoration offers a groundbreaking perspective on Genesis. As the book of Genesis addresses the deep issues of life within its ancient context, so Dr. O'Connor finds remarkable relevance in Genesis for the pressing issues of today.

—*William P. Brown*
William Marcellus McPheeters Professor of Old Testament
Columbia Theological Seminary

Beautifully written and filled with exegetical and hermeneutical insights, O'Connor's commentary is ideal for classroom use, Bible study, and sermon preparation. The rich sidebar essays explore interpretive cruxes and provoke new conversations. By framing the final form of Genesis as a response to the trauma of national defeat and exile, O'Connor sheds new light on the power of the book to address loss and provide hope.

—*Carol A. Newsom*
Candler School of Theology
Emory University

DEDICATION

In honor of
Louis Stulman,
Christine Roy Yoder, and
Walter Brueggemann,
and in memory of A. R. Pete Diamond
for years of creative inspiration
and collaborative friendships.

CONTENTS

ABBREVIATIONS USED IN THIS COMMENTARY

Books of the Old Testament, Apocrypha, and New Testament are generally abbreviated in the Sidebars, parenthetical references, and notes according to the following system.

The Old Testament

Genesis	Gen
Exodus	Exod
Leviticus	Lev
Numbers	Num
Deuteronomy	Deut
Joshua	Josh
Judges	Judg
Ruth	Ruth
1–2 Samuel	1–2 Sam
1–2 Kings	1–2 Kgs
1–2 Chronicles	1–2 Chr
Ezra	Ezra
Nehemiah	Neh
Esther	Esth
Job	Job
Psalm (Psalms)	Ps (Pss)
Proverbs	Prov
Ecclesiastes	Eccl
or Qoheleth	Qoh
Song of Solomon	Song
or Song of Songs	Song
or Canticles	Cant
Isaiah	Isa
Jeremiah	Jer
Lamentations	Lam
Ezekiel	Ezek
Daniel	Dan
Hosea	Hos
Joel	Joel
Amos	Amos
Obadiah	Obad
Jonah	Jonah
Micah	Mic

Nahum	Nah
Habakkuk	Hab
Zephaniah	Zeph
Haggai	Hag
Zechariah	Zech
Malachi	Mal

The Apocrypha

1–2 Esdras	1–2 Esdr
Tobit	Tob
Judith	Jdt
Additions to Esther	Add Esth
Wisdom of Solomon	Wis
Ecclesiasticus or the Wisdom of Jesus Son of Sirach	Sir
Baruch	Bar
Epistle (or Letter) of Jeremiah	Ep Jer
Prayer of Azariah and the Song of the Three	Pr Azar
Daniel and Susanna	Sus
Daniel, Bel, and the Dragon	Bel
Prayer of Manasseh	Pr Man
1–4 Maccabees	1–4 Macc

The New Testament

Matthew	Matt
Mark	Mark
Luke	Luke
John	John
Acts	Acts
Romans	Rom
1–2 Corinthians	1–2 Cor
Galatians	Gal
Ephesians	Eph
Philippians	Phil
Colossians	Col
1–2 Thessalonians	1–2 Thess
1–2 Timothy	1–2 Tim
Titus	Titus
Philemon	Phlm
Hebrews	Heb
James	Jas
1–2 Peter	1–2 Pet
1–2–3 John	1–2–3 John
Jude	Jude
Revelation	Rev

Other commonly used abbreviations include:

AD	*Anno Domini* ("in the year of the Lord") (also commonly referred to as CE = the Common Era)
BC	Before Christ (also commonly referred to as BCE = Before the Common Era)
C.	century
c.	*circa* (around "that time")
cf.	*confer* (compare)
ch.	chapter
chs.	chapters
d.	died
ed.	edition or edited by or editor
eds.	editors
e.g.	*exempli gratia* (for example)
et al.	*et alii* (and others)
f./ff.	and the following one(s)
gen. ed.	general editor
Gk.	Greek
Heb.	Hebrew
ibid.	*ibidem* (in the same place)
i.e.	*id est* (that is)
LCL	Loeb Classical Library
lit.	literally
n.d.	no date
rev. and exp. ed.	revised and expanded edition
sg.	singular
trans.	translated by or translator(s)
vol(s).	volume(s)
v.	verse
vv.	verses

Selected additional written works cited by abbreviations include the following. A complete listing of abbreviations can be referenced in *The SBL Handbook of Style* (Peabody MA: Hendrickson, 2014):

AB	Anchor Bible
ABD	*Anchor Bible Dictionary*
ACCS	Ancient Christian Commentary on Scripture
ANF	*Ante-Nicene Fathers*
ANTC	Abingdon New Testament Commentaries
BA	*Biblical Archaeologist*
BAR	*Biblical Archaeology Review*
CBQ	*Catholic Biblical Quarterly*
HTR	*Harvard Theological Review*

HUCA	*Hebrew Union College Annual*
ICC	International Critical Commentary
IDB	*Interpreters Dictionary of the Bible*
JBL	*Journal of Biblical Literature*
JSJ	*Journal for the Study of Judaism in the Persian, Hellenistic, and Roman Periods*
JSNT	*Journal for the Study of the New Testament*
JSOT	*Journal for the Study of the Old Testament*
KJV	King James Version
LXX	Septuagint = Greek Translation of Hebrew Bible
MDB	*Mercer Dictionary of the Bible*
MT	Masoretic Text
NASB	New American Standard Bible
NEB	New English Bible
NICNT	New International Commentary on the New Testament
NIV	New International Version
NovT	*Novum Testamentum*
NRSV	New Revised Standard Version
NTS	*New Testament Studies*
OGIS	*Orientis graeci inscriptiones selectae*
OTL	Old Testament Library
PRSt	*Perspectives in Religious Studies*
RevExp	*Review and Expositor*
RSV	Revised Standard Version
SBLSP	*Society of Biblical Literature Seminar Papers*
SP	Sacra pagina
TDNT	*Theological Dictionary of the New Testament*
TEV	Today's English Version
WBC	Word Biblical Commentary

AUTHOR'S PREFACE

For several years I set aside efforts on this Genesis commentary to complete a book about Jeremiah. This delay proved beneficial because my Jeremiah work gave me a surprising new lens with which to interpret Genesis; I had discovered trauma and disaster studies. To my astonishment, aspects of the national catastrophe so evident in that prophetic book—the fall of Judah and Jerusalem to the Babylonian Empire—left unmistakable traces across the book of Genesis and provided it with new urgency. The beautiful, perplexing, and astonishing accounts of the beginnings that make up Genesis serve the "pastoral" purpose to help the people begin again in the face of the impossible.

This commentary would not exist were it not for the dogged devotion of librarians in the John Bulow Campbell Library of Columbia Theological Seminary. When asked a question about sources or references, they do not stop until they find answers. I wish to thank, in particular, Erica Durham, Mary Martha Kline Riviere, and Bob Cragmile. Equally, the kind and patient IT experts at this seminary, Chris Sidor and Vince Greco, deserve credit for keeping me connected and almost sane. I'm grateful as well to former students R. C. Griffin and Sheldon Steen for research assistance on some early chapters and to Columbia Theological Seminary faculty and students for years of theological conversation and debate about texts, faith, and life in our global world.

Special gratitude goes to my editors, Samuel Balentine and Mark Biddle, first, for their patience, and second, for their probing, generous editorial work.

—*Kathleen M. O'Connor*
May 2018

SERIES PREFACE

The *Smyth & Helwys Bible Commentary* is a visually stimulating and user-friendly series that is as close to multimedia in print as possible. Written by accomplished scholars with all students of Scripture in mind, the primary goal of the *Smyth & Helwys Bible Commentary* is to make available serious, credible biblical scholarship in an accessible and less intimidating format.

Far too many Bible commentaries fall short of bridging the gap between the insights of biblical scholars and the needs of students of God's written word. In an unprecedented way, the *Smyth & Helwys Bible Commentary* brings insightful commentary to bear on the lives of contemporary Christians. Using a multimedia format, the volumes employ a stunning array of art, photographs, maps, and drawings to illustrate the truths of the Bible for a visual generation of believers.

The *Smyth & Helwys Bible Commentary* is built upon the idea that meaningful Bible study can occur when the insights of contemporary biblical scholars blend with sensitivity to the needs of lifelong students of Scripture. Some persons within local faith communities, however, struggle with potentially informative biblical scholarship for several reasons. Oftentimes, such scholarship is cast in technical language easily grasped by other scholars, but not by the general reader. For example, lengthy, technical discussions on every detail of a particular scriptural text can hinder the quest for a clear grasp of the whole. Also, the format for presenting scholarly insights has often been confusing to the general reader, rendering the work less than helpful. Unfortunately, responses to the hurdles of reading extensive commentaries have led some publishers to produce works for a general readership that merely skim the surface of the rich resources of biblical scholarship. This commentary series incorporates works of fine art in an accurate and scholarly manner, yet the format remains "user-friendly." An important facet is the presentation and explanation of images of art, which interpret the biblical material or illustrate how the biblical material has been understood and interpreted in the past. A visual generation of believers deserves a commentary series that contains not only the all-important textual commentary on Scripture, but images, photographs, maps, works of fine art, and drawings that bring the text to life.

The *Smyth & Helwys Bible Commentary* makes serious, credible biblical scholarship more accessible to a wider audience. Writers and editors alike present information in ways that encourage readers to gain a better understanding of the Bible. The editorial board has worked to develop a format that is useful and usable, informative and pleasing to the eye. Our writers are reputable scholars who participate in the community of faith and sense a calling to communicate the results of their scholarship to their faith community.

The *Smyth & Helwys Bible Commentary* addresses Christians and the larger church. While both respect for and sensitivity to the needs and contributions of other faith communities are reflected in the work of the series authors, the authors speak primarily to Christians. Thus the reader can note a confessional tone throughout the volumes. No particular "confession of faith" guides the authors, and diverse perspectives are observed in the various volumes. Each writer, though, brings to the biblical text the best scholarly tools available and expresses the results of their studies in commentary and visuals that assist readers seeking a word from the Lord for the church.

To accomplish this goal, writers in this series have drawn from numerous streams in the rich tradition of biblical interpretation. The basic focus is the biblical text itself, and considerable attention is given to the wording and structure of texts. Each particular text, however, is also considered in the light of the entire canon of Christian Scriptures. Beyond this, attention is given to the cultural context of the biblical writings. Information from archaeology, ancient history, geography, comparative literature, history of religions, politics, sociology, and even economics is used to illuminate the culture of the people who produced the Bible. In addition, the writers have drawn from the history of interpretation, not only as it is found in traditional commentary on the Bible but also in literature, theater, church history, and the visual arts. Finally, the *Commentary* on Scripture is joined with *Connections* to the world of the contemporary church. Here again, the writers draw on scholarship in many fields as well as relevant issues in the popular culture.

This wealth of information might easily overwhelm a reader if not presented in a "user-friendly" format. Thus the heavier discussions of detail and the treatments of other helpful topics are presented in special-interest boxes, or Sidebars, clearly connected to the passages under discussion so as not to interrupt the flow of the basic interpretation. The result is a commentary on Scripture that focuses on the theological significance of a text while also offering the reader a rich array of additional information related to the text and its interpretation.

An accompanying CD-ROM offers powerful searching and research tools. The commentary text, Sidebars, and visuals are all reproduced on a CD that is fully indexed and searchable. Pairing a text version with a digital resource is a distinctive feature of the *Smyth & Helwys Bible Commentary.*

Combining credible biblical scholarship, user-friendly study features, and sensitivity to the needs of a visually oriented generation of believers creates a unique and unprecedented type of commentary series. With insight from many of today's finest biblical scholars and a stunning visual format, it is our hope that the *Smyth & Helwys Bible Commentary* will be a welcome addition to the personal libraries of all students of Scripture.

The Editors

HOW TO USE
THIS COMMENTARY

The *Smyth & Helwys Bible Commentary* is written by accomplished biblical scholars with a wide array of readers in mind. Whether engaged in the study of Scripture in a church setting or in a college or seminary classroom, all students of the Bible will find a number of useful features throughout the commentary that are helpful for interpreting the Bible.

Basic Design of the Volumes

Each volume features an introduction that provides a brief guide to information necessary for reading and interpreting the text: the historical setting, literary design, and theological significance. Each introduction also includes a comprehensive outline of the particular text under study.

Each chapter of the commentary investigates the text according to logical divisions. Sometimes these divisions follow the traditional chapter segmentation, while at other times the textual units consist of sections of chapters or portions of more than one chapter. The divisions reflect the literary structure of the text and offer a guide for selecting passages that are useful in preaching and teaching.

An accompanying CD-ROM offers powerful searching and research tools. The commentary text, sidebars, and visuals are all reproduced on a CD that is fully indexed and searchable. Pairing a text version with a digital resource also allows unprecedented flexibility and freedom for the reader. Carry the text version to locations you most enjoy doing research while knowing that the CD offers a portable alternative for travel from your office, church, classroom, and home.

Commentary and Connections

As each chapter explores a textual unit, the discussion centers around two basic sections: *Commentary* and *Connections*. The analysis of a passage, including the details of its language, the history reflected in the text, and the literary forms found in the text, are the main focus of the *Commentary* section. The primary concern of the *Commentary* section is to explore the theological issues presented by the Scripture passage. *Connections* presents potential applications of the insights provided in the *Commentary* section. The *Connections* portion of each chapter considers what issues are relevant for teaching and suggests useful methods and resources. *Connections* also identifies themes suitable for sermon planning and suggests helpful approaches for preaching on the Scripture text.

Sidebars

The *Smyth & Helwys Bible Commentary* provides a unique hyperlink format that quickly guides the reader to additional insights. Since other more technical or supplementary information is vital for understanding a text and its implications, the volumes feature distinctive sidebars, or special-interest boxes, that provide a wealth of information on such matters as:

• Historical information (such as chronological charts, lists of kings or rulers, maps, descriptions of monetary systems, descriptions of special groups, descriptions of archaeological sites or geographical settings).

• Graphic outlines of literary structure (including such items as poetry, chiasm, repetition, epistolary form).

• Definition or brief discussions of technical or theological terms and issues.

• Insightful quotations that are not integrated into the running text but are relevant to the passage under discussion.

• Notes on the history of interpretation (Augustine on the Good Samaritan, Luther on James, Stendahl on Romans, etc.).

• Line drawings, photographs, and other illustrations relevant for understanding the historical context or interpretive significance of the text.

• Presentation and discussion of works of fine art that have interpreted a Scripture passage.

Each sidebar is printed in color and is referenced at the appropriate place in the *Commentary* or *Connections* section with a color-coded title that directs the reader to the relevant sidebar. In addition, helpful icons appear in the sidebars, which provide the reader with visual cues to the type of material that is explained in each sidebar. Throughout the commentary, these four distinct hyperlinks provide useful links in an easily recognizable design.

Alpha & Omega Language

This icon identifies the information as a language-based tool that offers further exploration of the Scripture selection. This could include syntactical information, word studies, popular or additional uses of the word(s) in question, additional contexts in which the term appears, and the history of the term's translation. All non-English terms are transliterated into the appropriate English characters.

Culture/Context

This icon introduces further comment on contextual or cultural details that shed light on the Scripture selection. Describing the place and time to which a Scripture passage refers is often vital to the task of biblical interpretation. Sidebar items introduced with this icon could include geographical, historical, political, social, topographical, or economic information. Here, the reader may find an excerpt of an ancient text or inscription that sheds light on the text. Or one may find a description of some element of ancient religion such as Baalism in Canaan or the Hero cult in the Mystery Religions of the Greco-Roman world.

Interpretation

Sidebars that appear under this icon serve a general interpretive function in terms of both historical and contemporary renderings. Under this heading, the reader might find a selection from classic or contemporary literature that illuminates the Scripture text or a significant quotation from a famous sermon that addresses the passage. Insights are drawn from various sources, including literature, worship, theater, church history, and sociology.

Additional Resources Study

Here, the reader finds a convenient list of useful resources for further investigation of the selected Scripture text, including books, journals, websites, special collections, organizations, and societies. Specialized discussions of works not often associated with biblical studies may also appear here.

Additional Features

Each volume also includes a basic bibliography on the biblical text under study. Other bibliographies on selected issues are often included that point the reader to other helpful resources.

Notes at the end of each chapter provide full documentation of sources used and contain additional discussions of related matters.

Abbreviations used in each volume are explained in a list of abbreviations found after the table of contents.

Readers of the *Smyth & Helwys Bible Commentary* can regularly visit the Internet support site for news, information, updates, and enhancements to the series at **www.helwys.com/commentary**.

Several thorough indexes enable the reader to locate information quickly. These indexes include:

• An *Index of Sidebars* groups content from the special-interest boxes by category (maps, fine art, photographs, drawings, etc.).

• An *Index of Scriptures* lists citations to particular biblical texts.

• An *Index of Topics* lists alphabetically the major subjects, names, topics, and locations referenced or discussed in the volume.

• An *Index of Modern Authors* organizes contemporary authors whose works are cited in the volume.

INTRODUCTION

Beginnings are the subject of the book of Genesis: beginnings of the cosmos, its inhabitants, and most particularly the people of Israel. The book's memorable characters, tumultuous events, and repeated appearances of new life witness to divine creativity amid chaos, barrenness, and destruction. The Creator God is the book's principal character, the One who brings order from disorder, turns a barren couple into parents of countless children, and promises land to a wandering, displaced, and conflicted people. [Outline of Introduction]

Because Genesis is the Bible's first book, it serves as introduction to the Pentateuch, to the Old Testament/ Hebrew Bible, and to the Christian Bible. The term "Pentateuch" refers to the first five books: Genesis, Exodus, Leviticus, Numbers, and Deuteronomy. [The Pentateuch] Known among Jews as the Torah, the Pentateuch tells of Israel's origins from the creation of the cosmos until Israel arrives at the edge of the promised land under the leadership of Moses. Genesis opens this long national narrative with an unquestionable affirmation of God's creative power that is implanted in creation. Every aspect of the book testifies to God as Life-giver who repeatedly brings the ancient ancestors back to life.

The Pentateuch

The five books of the Pentateuch—Genesis, Exodus, Leviticus, Numbers, and Deuteronomy—are associated closely with Moses. Together they tell the story of Israel from before the times of Israel's ancestors in Genesis, through their escape from slavery in Egypt, and on to the reception of the law in Exodus. They provide contents of the Law in Leviticus and Numbers, report Israel's wandering in the wilderness, and, finally, bring the wandering peoples to the edge of the promised land in Deuteronomy.

Among Jews, the Pentateuch is called Torah, "the law" or "instruction." Although the Pentateuch contains much legal material, Jews understand it as their communal constitution of faith—a blessed, grace-filled "instruction" for life with God and humans. The Torah is the primary source of Jewish identity and way of life.

For further reading, see Mark McEntire, *Struggling with God: An Introduction to the Pentateuch* (Macon GA: Mercer University Press, 2008) 1–43, and Terence E. Fretheim, *The Pentateuch* (IBT; Nashville: Abingdon, 1996) 19–38.

COMMENTARY

Why Tell Stories of Beginnings?

It is a common human experience to be curious about the past. From generation to generation and culture to culture, people want to know where they come from, how they came to be on earth, who they are, who their ancestors are, why they die, and what joins them together, anchors them in the world, and connects them to God and other peoples. Genesis responds to these deeply human questions with ancient stories of origins, but its purposes are both larger and more concrete than responding to general human curiosity about beginnings. The purposes are larger because the book tells these stories to assure its audience that the God who created, ordered, and gave life in the ancient past can recreate them now. The purposes are more concrete because Genesis addresses specific historical struggles of the people of Judah in the aftermath of the nation's destruction under the Babylonian Empire. [Why Beginnings?]

Genesis does not ask about beginnings from general inquisitiveness regarding the world and its inhabitants. It does not probe the past for its own sake as do modern historians, nor does it explore precise scientific knowledge of the cosmos like modern scientists.[1] Rather, the book draws on the past to address particular needs of its ancient audience. In doing so, it reveals the living God who continues to create and recreate. [Ancient Audiences and Modern Readers]

More than recording history, Genesis intervenes in history. It speaks of beginnings to incite hope among Israel's remnant that they too might begin again. The book offers a theology of beginnings to a people flattened by invasions, displacements, and the strong possibility that they will disappear among the prevailing empires. Its overarching

Why Beginnings?

It is self-evident that Genesis focuses on origins, but why? Is it

- to tell what actually happened or what the book's writers thought actually happened?
- to answer universal questions about the meaning of life?
- to preserve oral traditions in fidelity to Israel's past?
- to unify the twelve tribes of Israel into one people by joining their stories together?
- to assert the divine election of Israel?

Many of these matters are important in the book's interpretation, but they support larger purposes of the book. This commentary points to ways Genesis aided Judah in reconstituting itself after the historical disasters of the Babylonian and early Persian periods. (See "The Crisis that Gave Rise to the Book of Genesis" on page 3.)

Ancient Audiences and Modern Readers

When I use the term "audience" in this commentary, I am referring to the Judean people, survivors of the nation's fall and their descendants living in the early Persian Period for whom the book was composed. When, by contrast, I refer to "readers," I mean you and me, contemporary readers of Genesis seeking to make sense of it and to discover in it a word of life. The distinction between readers and audience is important because we modern readers live in different times than the original audience did and have vastly different understandings of the world. The gap between the two requires interpretation for our times and contexts. Christian, Jewish, and Islamic communities have long traditions of interpretations that find God speaking anew in later cultural contexts.

For further reading, see Ian Provan, *Discovering Genesis: Content, Interpretation, Reception* (Discovering Biblical Texts; Grand Rapids MI: Wm B. Eerdmans, 2015).

purpose is to convince its audience that the Creator of the cosmos and of all that exists is recreating them now.

The Crisis that Gave Rise to the Book of Genesis

Genesis became a work of literature sometime during the early Persian Period (539–330 BCE). [Persian Empire] During that time, the nation of Judah continued to struggle with long-term consequences of earlier events that took place during the Babylonian Period, also called the "Exilic Period" (587–538 BCE). [Babylonian Empire] A broad consensus among interpreters places the book's composition after the Persian defeat of the Babylonian Empire.[2] In this commentary I attend to the vibrant dialogue between the book and the historical struggles of Judah during that time. Looking at Genesis from this angle illuminates many interpretive difficulties and brings the book itself to life in new ways.

Persian Empire

In the context of biblical studies, the term "Persian period" refers to the time when the ancient Persians were in power throughout the Near East. They established the first world empire with Cyrus II's conquest of his fellow Iranians, the Medes, in about 550 BCE. They stayed in power until 330 BCE with the death of Darius III, following defeat by Alexander and the Greeks. Cyrus's victory over Babylon in 539 BCE and the eventual release "of Hebrews from Babylonian exile gave him significant standing in several biblical books, which also refer to subsequent Persian kings and rule. These texts include Deutero-Isaiah, Haggai, Zechariah (1–8), I and II Chronicles, Ezra, Nehemiah, Esther, and Daniel."

For further reading, see Erhard S. Gerstenberger, *Israel in the Persian Period: The Fifth and Fourth Centuries B.C.E.*, trans. Siegfried S. Schatzmann (Leiden, Netherlands: Brill, 2012).

Jenny Rose, "The 'Persian' Period," http://www.oxfordbibliographies.com.

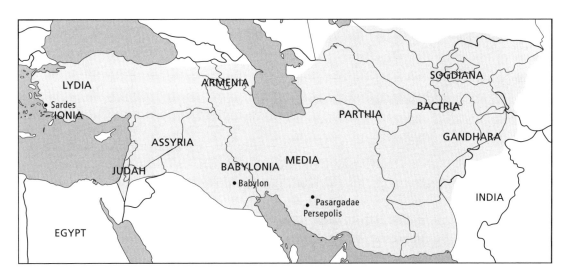

Babylonian Empire

Prior to the rise of Persia, the Babylonians gained control by defeating the Assyrians in the year 612 BCE, and eventually took over their conquered territory. King Cyrus of Persia defeated them in 538. David Vanderhooft, a historian of the Babylonian Period, has argued that their military and governing tactics were as cruel and disruptive as the notorious Assyrians before them.

For further reading, see Jill Middlemas, *The Templeless Age: An Introduction to the History, Literature and Theology of the Exile* (Louisville KY: Westminster John Knox, 2007) 22–27.

David Vanderhooft, "Babylonian Strategies of Imperial Control in the West: Royal Practice and Rhetoric," in *Judah and the Judeans in the Neo-Babylonian Period*, Oded Lipschitz and Joseph Blenkinsopp, eds. (Winona Lake IN: Eisenbrauns, 2003) 104–14.

Cyrus the Great monument at Sydney Olympic Park. (Credit: Wikimedia Commons; Siamax, CC-BY-SA-3.0)

A Long History of Destruction by Invading Empires

A brief overview of Israel's turbulent history shows why stories of beginnings were necessary to help Israel/Judah begin life together again. To imagine being part of this tragic history is to set oneself among struggles and fears of the ancient audience of Genesis. An historical imagination invites reflection not only on the known facts of military invasion, occupation, and deportation but also on their long-term consequences for survivors.

The crisis confronting Judah during the early Persian Period was long in the making. After a short time of national unity during the tenth century BCE, the kingdom of Israel divided into two nations, Israel in the north and Judah in the south. These two kingdoms existed side by side with varying degrees of cooperation and conflict until an invasion by the Assyrian army effectively destroyed the northern kingdom of Israel, absorbed the population into the Assyrian Empire, and cruelly occupied the land (722 BCE).[3] Except for a small remnant, the northern kingdom effectively disappeared. Assyria also attacked the southern kingdom of Judah but then mysteriously withdrew (Isa 36–37 and 2 Kings 18–19). Judah survived and became heir to the name Israel.[4] More than one hundred years later, the neo-Babylonian Empire defeated Assyria and, in a series of military invasions, attacked Judah, nearly destroyed the nation, and threatened the people's future.

The Babylonians brought with them widespread and enduring upheaval. They invaded Jerusalem for the first time in 597 BCE, after which they put a puppet Judean king on the throne. They deported elite religious and government leaders and heavily taxed the conquered nation.

Ten years later the appointed king rebelled—probably by withholding tribute—and provoked a second, more disastrous invasion of Judah and Jerusalem. This siege lasted for nearly two years and devastated the city. When famine and exhaustion weakened resistance, the Babylonian army finally broke through the city walls. They deported the king, burned the temple and the king's palace, killed many, and exiled elite groups in a forced march to Babylon.

These tactics of empire destroyed the nation's leadership, undermined its economy, displaced people internally, sent others away, and finally left a swath of destruction in their wake. Yet this cascading series of calamities was still not over. A small group of Judeans assassinated the Babylonian-appointed governor, which provoked a third invasion and more deportations.

The people left in the land underwent varying degrees of dislocation and loss, while the exiles lost nearly everything but their lives. [Degrees of Destruction] Life did continue in parts of Judah outside Jerusalem, and some exiles eventually prospered in Babylon, but the nation was decimated and its future was profoundly uncertain.[5] Judah was in danger of disappearing into the invading empire like the northern kingdom after the Assyrian attacks. Later, after nearly five decades of Babylonian control, a change occurred. The Persian Empire defeated Babylon, took over its occupied territories, and eventually allowed exiles to return to Judah. This is the historical context that produced Genesis.

Degrees of Destruction

Biblical archaeologists and historians argue over the extent of Judah's destruction during the Babylonian Period. At the least, the Babylonians decimated the nation. They deported the leadership, destroyed much of the capital city of Jerusalem, removed the king, burned down the temple, undermined the economy, and occupied the land. Debates have centered on how far and wide the disruption of life was for people who remained in the land under the Babylonian occupation (see Lipschits).

Destruction was not limited to death and physical destruction of the habitat. Of most importance for biblical books, warfare and imperial occupation tended to produce profound theological crises (cf., Lam 5). For Israel, long-held traditions collapsed under the weight of Babylonian imperialism. God had promised, for example, to dwell with them in the Jerusalem temple, but the Babylonians burned it down. God had declared that a son of David would sit on Judah's throne forever, but Babylonians sent the king into captivity in Babylon. God had promised the land to Abraham, but the Babylonians and then the Persians controlled it. In the face of these losses, God seems powerless, indifferent, or absent. How can faith survive? How can the Judean people survive? Are the gods of the empire the true gods?

Oded Lipschits, "Shedding New Light on the Dark Years of the 'Exilic Period': New Studies, Further Elucidation, and Some Questions Regarding the Archeology of Judah and an 'Empty Land,'" in *Interpreting Exile: Displacement and Deportation in Biblical and Modern Contexts*, ed. Brad E. Kelle, Frank Ritchel Ames, and Jacob L. Wright (AIL; Atlanta: SBL, 2011) 57–90. For further reading, see David M. Carr, *Holy Resilience: The Bible's Traumatic Origins* (New Haven CT: Yale University Press, 2014) 11–90.

Reading Genesis with this history in view shows the stories, lives of characters, and theological insights of the book to be mirroring tableaus of historical suffering and of beginning again. The literature not only reflects aspects of Judah's catastrophe but also helps the community cope with, understand, and move beyond it. That these historical events were traumatic and bore haunting consequences for the people is increasingly clear.[6] Genesis addresses descendants of survivors for whom the effects of the nation's

Inspiration through a Living Process

Recognizing that Genesis underwent a long process of development might cause some readers to doubt notions of biblical inspiration. This is especially true among faith communities who believe that revelation was a fully formed divulgence of God to one individual or community. Although both Jews and Christians traditionally credit Moses with authorship of the entire Pentateuch, Moses could hardly have written them, particularly since Deuteronomy reports his death. Moses does loom over the Pentateuch as the spiritual leader who brings the people out of slavery in Egypt and receives the Law on Mount Sinai. He is author of the nation if not of the literature.

Understanding, instead, that Genesis springs from a centuries-long process of transmission and composition expands and democratizes the notion of inspiration. Rather than being restricted to a few individuals, inspiration takes place among the people from generation to generation. They search for God, struggle amid human experiences of all sorts, and act both badly and magnificently. Gifted poets, storytellers, sages, elders, priests, parents—ordinary people contributed indirectly or directly to the book's composition. In this way, biblical texts have become the refined and treasured testimony of the people in search of their God. Genesis, therefore, is a work of the people. There, in the community of struggling believers and seekers, the Spirit works and reveals God in human language.

collapse continue to inhibit their future together and their life as God's people. The Judeans bear the scars of this history, and to become a nation again, they require new life because the old life is gone. [Inspiration through a Living Process]

Warfare, Disaster, Trauma, and Their Effects

Contemporary study of traumatic violence and communal disaster illuminates circumstances that prompted the writing of Genesis. [Trauma and Disaster Studies] Warfare and military occupation typically have devastating long-term effects for survivors. They leave communities of people with crippling memories of assault and death; they destroy ways to talk about what happened; they shut down emotion and trust. Of most importance for biblical literature, they destroy faith in God and in traditions and institutions that had sustained them as a people in the first place.

Genesis is not the first biblical book to intervene in the aftermath of the nation's disintegration under the Babylonians. Other biblical books serve as theological first responders, including the weeping book of Lamentations and the prophetic books of Jeremiah, Ezekiel, and Second Isaiah.[7] I believe that the book of Job belongs in this list, too. These are theological works of great power that mirror destruction, loss, and the chaotic existence that typically follow disasters.[8] They serve the survivors by providing language for and interpretations of destructive events that defy both language and interpretation. In many respects, the Judean people survive because of the "pastoral care" these books provide. Their creativity reawakens the community, reframes Judean identity, and shows a path forward. Surprisingly, their sometimes harsh theologies keep trust in God alive when God seems weak, ineffective, and altogether absent. By a generation or two later, memories of this violent history continue to mix with profound doubts about God, and the nation's future remains a vast, murky impossibility.

Trauma and Disaster Studies

Trauma and disaster studies examine the effects of violence and warfare on individuals and communities. The studies arise from an interdisciplinary conversation among many fields, including psychology, psychiatry, medicine, pastoral care, history, sociology, anthropology, and literature. Biblical interpreters have increasingly appropriated trauma studies to understand some biblical texts (see the list below). Insights from trauma and disaster studies are "heuristic," from the Greek word "to find"; they are like "glasses" that help us see aspects of the literature that had not been so evident before. Trauma theories have illuminated books from the Babylonian Period, namely, Jeremiah, Ezekiel, Second Isaiah, and Lamentations. The loss, grief, harsh rhetoric, and fire and brimstone found in these books appear as ways to help the people of Judah survive after cascading catastrophes. After studying Jeremiah from this angle, I was startled to find similar elements of literary and theological processes of survival also present in Genesis (see O'Connor, *Jeremiah*, esp. 19–24).

Trauma and disaster studies help us consider what the text says, how it says it, and how texts might have functioned to aid the recovery of the people. Typically, for example, violence and disaster destroy faith and trust in the world, people, and God. In the aftermath of various kinds of cataclysms, communities and individuals have a profound need to "know" why these things happened to them, that is, to interpret and reframe them. How can they understand destruction all around them and within them? Without explanations, they are left in a terrifying world of random chaos. In such circumstances, any explanation turns out to be better than none. An interpretation that gives meaning to events suggests that there is order in the universe; something or someone caused it. Often survivors place responsibility on themselves, their leaders, communities, and God.

These interpretations challenge modern readers because they frequently portray God as a violent and punishing deity, a terrorist who accuses the people of bringing catastrophes upon themselves by their sinful idolatry and betrayal. Yet such interpretations arise from the experience of violence itself. They understand God as involved in destruction, and often when they hold God accountable, they keep God in their lives. This is because Babylonian deities did not overpower the God of Israel nor did God lose the war to them, but instead God brought disaster to punish them and set them on the right path.

This theology is not acceptable today. It takes a historically conditioned ancient view and freezes it as if it were a full and permanent insight into God's very being. But the biblical texts are not attempting to do that; they offer insight for their times out of the thinking of their times.

At the same time, interpretations that locate causes of cataclysms in human sin and divine punishment also help survivors. Understanding disaster as divinely sent punishment for sin, for example, keeps God connected to their lives. It provides a sense that cause and effect are still at work in a world that has fallen apart and offers a way to avoid disaster in the future by avoiding more sin. When people believe that their sin caused catastrophe, they can prevent future catastrophes by changing their behavior. This is no small benefit as we know from trauma theory, domestic abuse, and child abuse, even when self-blaming and images of a punishing deity create mighty challenges for modern believers and require qualification.

For further reading, see "Trauma and Faith," *Int* 69/1 (January 2015): 7–75.

Most recently, see Samuel E. Balentine, "Legislating Divine Trauma," in Elizabeth Boase and Christopher Frechette, eds., *Bible through the Lens of Trauma* (Semeia Studies 86; Atlanta: Society of Biblical Literature Press, 2016) 161–76; David G. Garber, Jr., "Trauma Theory and Biblical Studies, Currents in Biblical Research 14 (2015): 24–44; David Carr, *Holy Resilience: The Bible's Traumatic Origins* (New Haven CT: Yale University Press, 2014); Eve-Marie Becker, Jan Dochorn, and Else Krageland Holt, eds., *Trauma and Traumatization in Individual and Collective Dimensions: Insights from Biblical Studies and Beyond* (Studia Aarhusiana Neotestamentica 2; Göttingen: Vandenhoeck & Ruprecht, 2014); Kathleen M. O'Connor, *Jeremiah: Pain and Promise* (Minneapolis: Fortress, 2011).

How Genesis Contributes to the Nation's Rebuilding

The book of Genesis continues work begun by these earlier books. It interprets and reframes the disaster, rebuilds national identity, and revives confidence in God for the fractured nation. It does this by presenting terrors of accumulated disasters in symbolic stories of destruction, and it portrays the hopelessness through themes of

Creation and Recreation

It may seem strange to speak of the recreation of Judah/Israel in Genesis when, according to the biblical story, Israel does not yet exist. The nation's historical birth occurs much later in the canon, debatably from the time of the Judges through Kings. One way to appreciate the many levels of meaning in biblical books is to attend to historical circumstances that produced the literature—in the case of Genesis, the early Persian Period. When I study stories in Genesis, I see not simply one level of meaning but also a reflection of events that have happened during and after the nation's fall. That means that the stories have symbolic power. They tell of the past in light of the present world of the ancient audience.

impossibility. Yet Genesis differs sharply from the earlier biblical books from the time because, beyond depicting disaster and survival, it glories in the Creator who overcomes endings and promises future blessings beyond imagining. [Creation and Recreation]

The book's outline shows that the lives of the ancestors are a major subject of the book (Gen 12–50), yet these accounts are set within the larger arena of the creation of the cosmos and all its inhabitants (Gen 1–11). This literary organization makes clear that Israel does not exist in isolation from other life but within a web of ecological, political, cultural, and human relationships. Of more importance, however, chapters 1–11 establish that God is the Creator of everything, the Life-giver who makes all things and sustains them in harmony and, by implication, will do so again.

I. Beginnings of the Cosmos and Its Inhabitants: The Primeval History (chs. 1–11)
II. Beginnings of Israel: The Ancestral Stories (chs. 12–50)
   A. First Generation, Abraham and Sarah (chs. 12–25)
   B. Second Generation, Isaac and Rebekah (chs. 21–28)
   C. Third Generation, Jacob and Leah, Rachel, Bilhah and Zilpah (chs. 25–36)
   D. Fourth Generation, Joseph and Asenath (chs. 37–50)

Mirroring Disaster and Promising Life

Memories of past violence find symbolic expression in Genesis in three ways: through stories that I call "disaster narratives," themes of impossibility, and promises of new life.

Disaster narratives indirectly evoke Judah's experiences of warfare and destruction. Themes of futurelessness portray a persistent background of conditions inhospitable to life, yet God repeatedly overturns these impossible situations and promises overwhelming abundance. The divine promises provide the primary energy in Genesis. They carry the book's major import, its creative force, its pledge that bountiful, brimming life will come from the potent word of the Creator. Genesis moves beyond tragedy and death to proclaim that the God who brought all things into being will recreate the people of Judah.

Disaster Stories

Disaster shows up in a variety of ways across the book but receives special attention in a group of stories that present collapse and violent destruction within a largely mythic world. [Mythic World] The stories do not depict the nation's collapse in any literal way such as describing warfare and invasions. Rather, they tell about other cataclysms that happened to

Mythic World

Myths are stories about gods and humans that tell the truth in settings and events beyond normal human experience. Myth is a literary genre that narrates divine-human relationships as a way to explain the world. To speak of a mythic world is not to speak of a false one but of an imagined, symbolic one with levels of meaning beyond the literal account itself. Ancient Israel was surrounded by other peoples with rich myths that they borrowed and adapted for their own theological purposes.

other people in the distant past. Such stories work like memory trails conveying similar experiences of destruction for the ancient audience. Terrors unfold at a distance, in a literary world, as if on a screen or a stage where events happen to others. By transposing cataclysm to other domains—like floods that destroy the world or fire and brimstone that fall upon a city—the disaster stories dip into memories of violence and loss without re-traumatizing the people. Narratives like these interpret and reframe former traumas and re-anchor people in a world that is otherwise paralyzingly chaotic.

Disaster stories in Genesis "refract" disaster and point to survival.[9] Some of the book's more memorable and puzzling episodes share a similar pattern. They relate catastrophic events, massive destruction of life, and the possibility of extinction of the characters, often brought about by God. Yet in every story some people survive and begin again. Always a remnant escapes. For the book's audience—a people faced with the consequences of destruction, displacement, and occupation—this narrative plotline conveys aspects of their own immediate past. In the process, the disaster stories give shape to frightful, chaotic events and, of no little importance, interpret why terrible things have happened.

I call the stories listed below "disaster narratives." They along with others in Genesis follow a similar narrative pattern. Characters face some form of catastrophe and the end of existence; causes are confounding, mythic, provoked by human or divine behavior, yet always God provides a way for some to survive. The list of disasters begins with the expulsion of the first couple from the garden (ch. 3). They are told that if they eat of the fruit, they will die, but they do not die. They are cast out of Paradise instead and experience pain, suffering, and dislocation. God helps them, and they begin again, chastened but alive. Similar patterns of catastrophe and survival, prompted by inexplicable causes, appear in the Cain and Abel story (Gen 4:1-16); the flood events that report the end of nearly all living things (Gen 6–9); the story of Babel (11:1-9); and the fiery destruction of Sodom (Gen 18:16–19:19). Perhaps the most important disaster story in Genesis is the binding/sacrifice of Isaac (ch. 22), where God commands Abraham to kill his long-awaited son. The family of promise almost disappears, but Isaac survives and the generations begin again.

These disaster narratives serve the book's ancient audience by reflecting indirectly the nation's historical disasters and offering hope of survival, since repeatedly God saved some in the past. Together, these stories encode Judah's history of destruction in symbolic form.

Besides mirroring catastrophe, disaster episodes in Genesis aid Judah's survival in other ways. They contain inexplicable, "irrational" elements in the mode of disasters themselves. The causes of the catastrophes are opaque, incomparable to actual destruction, and generally come from outside ordinary human interactions, like failed leadership or imperial aggrandizement. They share mythic, unclear, strange features that create interpretive problems for modern readers: for example, the sons of God and daughters of humans having intercourse (6:1-4), people building a city and tower in order to stay together (11:1-9), eating from a tree that seems like a good and beautiful thing (ch. 3), the binding/sacrificing of the child of the promise whose birth has driven the plot for ten chapters beforehand (ch. 22).

Trauma theories allow us to see these strange, catastrophic narratives in Genesis as constructive of life after calamity. They enact the nation's troubled memories in a literary realm, through similar disasters happening to someone else. They help the community come to terms with the end of their world and move beyond it. They insist on God's involvement, but about this they do not agree.[10]

The Power of the Literature

Genesis continues the unfinished and unfinishable quest to find language for Judah's disasters begun by the earlier biblical books, such as Jeremiah, Ezekiel, Second Isaiah, and Lamentations. I am not claiming that disaster episodes in Genesis were composed to "represent" Judah's traumatic history in any factual sense; rather they *function* within a literary arena as distant echoes of similar destructions. Disasters happened to Israel's ancestors among the nations in the shadowy past, and they survived. This is one way the sacred literature opens toward new life. Disaster stories guide the ancient audience and modern readers to approach their suffering indirectly, gently. Without such processes to reclaim and reinterpret their history, Judah is certain to disappear among the conquering empires.

Themes of Impossibility

A second way in which Judah's historical disaster finds symbolic expression in Genesis is through themes of impossibility. Barrenness, famine, and landlessness are limiting situations that gravely challenge the people and their future.

A. Barrenness. Barrenness is a persistent condition of matriarchs in Genesis, beginning with ancient Sarai for whom conception is physically impossible and continuing with both the youthful Rebekah and Rachel. The condition of the mothers' wombs conveys the nation's futurelessness, for without offspring Judah/Israel is dead. Yet, beginning with an elderly woman ridiculously beyond childbearing age, God brings about the impossible, opening wombs and giving the women children. [Barrenness and Contemporary Women]

B. Famine. Famines occur in the life of each patriarch—Abraham (12:10), Isaac (26:1), and Jacob/Joseph (41:56–42:5)— and function like barrenness in Genesis, for neither land nor people can reproduce. [Famines] Famines create a backdrop of catastrophe where the old and very young die first, and where humans are helpless to control conditions of life or health. Death of the people is a likely result, except that God provides food and nourishment in every generation from Abraham to Joseph. Each reference to famine in Genesis stands on its own, but together they create a continuing crisis of survival, and each time God provides.

C. Landlessness. The only land the family owns in Genesis is a grave, a cave that Abraham buys to bury his wife, plus a small plot

Barrenness and Contemporary Women

The barrenness of the matriarchs is an important theme in Genesis because it points to God alone as the source of new life for Israel. It demonstrates that God creates the future; the matriarchs, by implication, must trust God in the midst of all forms of barrenness. Genesis often portrays birth as a divine decision, one not controlled by human desires.

For modern women and couples facing fertility issues, these texts can cause deep pain, for it can seem that God withholds conception from them because they are somehow unworthy or unloved by God. Genesis, however, does not make universal statements about divine intervention in biological processes. Instead, it locates in women's bodies the place of future life for Israel after death and destruction. The theme is a literary and theological one formulated for the particular realities of ancient Israel rather than a universal theological claim about biological conception and birthing.

Famines

Famines occurred in the ancient world due to drought or crop failure. In Genesis they create a motif of life-ending lack, a threat to the very existence of the people. It is the famine in Jacob's time that brings the family to Egypt, a journey anticipated by Abram and Sarai (12:10–13:1). It may be true that the frequency of famines in Genesis indicates that the patriarchal period was drier than later times in the region, but the famines in the book symbolize threats to the life of the nation.

William H. Shea, "Famine," *ABD* 2:770–71.

that Jacob purchases when he returns to the land after his sojourn in Laban's household in Mesopotamia. Even when they are in the land, Israel's ancestors are wanderers, dislocated people who neither own nor control their native soil. Without the land, they lack rootedness in their own culture and their identity melts away, for they stand under the control of the empires. The ancestors in Genesis, with the exception of Isaac, are displaced from the land, seek it, and return to it again and again but only in promissory fashion. They live in perilous conditions, facing armies, neighbors who stop up wells, and hostile people who see them as threats to survival. Displacement from the land also signifies the situation of the book's audience, some exiled and some displaced within the land.

The Promises of God

The promises that God makes to Abraham and his descendants create a stunning contrast to the disaster stories and themes of impossibility (12:1-3). They offer more than survival of a remnant, instead, pressing toward unimaginable abundance that will recreate the Judean people. The divine promises form the major structuring device in the body of Genesis (chs. 12–50). They are not merely connective threads to hold disparate stories together; they are the book's main concern.[11] God's promises to Abraham—extravagant numbers of offspring, land, blessings, and a great name—are "over the top" in their profligate generosity and contain the exact gifts that a destroyed nation requires to begin again.

A. Promise of Offspring. Sarai's barrenness is twice-told: "she was barren; she had no child" (11:30). Barrenness is the starting point of the promise, the condition of divine action. Across the chapters, the birth of children to Abram and Sarai becomes increasingly impossible (12–20). It is precisely because they cannot possibly have children nor engineer an heir that God pledges to give them phenomenally more: more descendants than the stars of the heaven and the sands of the sea. So impossible does it seem, so against human logic, that nothing remains but to laugh.

The rest of Genesis slowly unfolds accounts of how God fulfills the promise of offspring as the numbers of offspring increase. First, Isaac is born and survives his father's attempt on his life; he in turn has two sons, Isaac and Ishmael, who continually fight and nearly kill each other yet survive; and then Jacob's four wives produce thirteen children. Throughout the book, Abram's family confronts disintegration and death that endangers the promise "at nearly every turn in the narrative."[12] For the audience whose recent ancestors faced death from warfare, invasion, and dislocation under Babylon, and who surely wondered if they had come to the end of the family tree, God's promises of uncountable children augur a future of unthinkable joy. [Generations and Genealogies]

B. Promise of Land. Babylonian invasions result in people displaced within the land and exiles deported from the land. Wherever they are, Judeans live under the control of foreign empires. Given these circumstances, the promise of land is central to Judah's reconstitution as a people. For the ancient audience, returning to life there may seem as impossible as children being born to barren women. Yet control of the land matters greatly, for there they can again be one people who worship their God and not the gods of the empires.

Generations and Genealogies

These "the generations of" formulations are an important structuring device in Genesis (*tōlĕdōt* formula), serving as a heading for major sections in the book. Their frequent presence draws attention to God's command "to be fruitful and multiply" (1:28) and to the continuity of generations from creation onward. They also imply that the generations will continue in the same way, for God and humans will continue to create.

These are the generations of heavens and earth (Gen 2:4)
These are the generations of Adam (5:1)
These are the generations of Noah (6:9)
These are the generations of Shem, Ham, and Japheth (10:1)
These are the generations of Shem (11:10)
These are the generations of Terah (11:27)
These are the generations of Ishmael (25:12)
These are the generations of Isaac (25:19)
These are the generations of Esau (36:1 and 36:9)
These are the generations of Jacob (37:2) (Thomas, 72)

Both the generational headings and the genealogies stand in service of the promises to Abraham. Instead of a heading or a genealogy, Abraham has the promise of offspring (12:1-3), a promise repeated again and again from chapters 12–50. The genealogies and the headings support the promises and portray the fertility that God bestows upon humans. They demonstrate that the family of Abraham has a future in continuity with the pre-ancestors.

Oddly, Abram, the father of the nation, receives no generational (*tōlĕdōt*) heading. He is instead subsumed under his father Terah's generation. This is a puzzle because he is the first and primary recipient of the promises of offspring; from him descends all Israel. Perhaps the heading is omitted because it would ruin the uncertainty created by the couple's inability to bear children. Three generations later, Joseph also lacks the heading and also appears under his father's generation. My hunch is that because the Joseph story more directly reflects the situation of the book's audience than that of his ancestors, the future of the family tree is still uncertain (see Gen 37–50 in vol. 2 of this commentary; Löwisch, 26–42).

These generational headings sometimes introduce genealogies in Genesis. Genealogies are also structuring devices, presented as lists that trace the ancestry of various individuals, usually from father to son, with very occasional mention of mothers or daughters. Genealogies in Genesis narrow the text's focus to particular individuals. They pass rapidly over multiple generations, speeding up the narrative and opening out to stories about a particular generation in slow narrative time. By including disparate groups in the list, they reinforce international connections among all the peoples, for everyone descends from Adam and Eve (Römer, 1151). They preserve blood connections among members of the larger human family and depict an orderly sequence of fertility and life.

Matthew A. Thomas, *These are the Generations: Identity, Covenant, and the 'Toledot' Formula* (London: T & T Clark, 2011).

Ingeborg Löwisch, *Trauma Begets Genealogy: Gender and Memory in Chronicles* (Sheffield, UK: Sheffield Phoenix Press, 2015).

Thomas Römer, "Genesis, Book of," *EBR*.

Land in Perpetuity

The promise that God will give land to Israel's offspring in perpetuity is immensely controversial today. Those Christians and Jews who insist on modern Israel's right to the land over against the Palestinian residents take the promise as a literal statement for all time, but the Bible does not make political or land-related promises for all time. The Bible, for example, also accepts slavery and the subordination of women as unquestioning modes of life because these were the unquestioned suppositions of the ancient world; they are not a prescription for all cultures at all times.

When Genesis insists on God's promise of land to Abraham and his descendants, it is to assure the ancient audience that it has a future, that exiles will return, and that life will begin again in their land. It neither endorses nor denies modern Israel's right to the land. That matter relates to modern geo-political history, the outrageous treatment of Jews throughout the ages, and the particular efforts to destroy the Jewish people by the Nazis in the twentieth century. The modern fate of the Palestinian people on their land was not settled in the ancient times with the composition of Genesis.

The book's emphatic attention to land results from the fact that Judeans no longer own or control it. Even those who remain in Judah are sojourners like Isaac, unable to leave yet not in possession of their heritage. Others like Jacob and Joseph, indentured or enslaved to others, also encode the history of Judeans, for they are forced from the land. In Genesis the land is the place of worship and altar building, the terrain where the people best know God, covenant with God, and live together as God's people. The promise of land, therefore, focuses largely on the offspring, the book's audience alienated from their home. [Land in Perpetuity]

The ancestors are strangers and migrants from beginning to end. Wanderings are continual, settlements temporary, and displacement a characterization of their existence—but not forever. Abraham's children, the book's ancient audience, are the ultimate recipients of the promises. The land is theirs but not yet.

C. Promise of Blessings. Blessings in Genesis are multifaceted and include material goods and mutual relationships.[13] "God's activity of blessing entails creating and giving life, health, progeny, and the means to sustain a harmonious life as a society."[14] Blessings refer in part to material necessities of life that God provides to Abraham, Isaac, Jacob, and later to Joseph in overflowing amounts. Divine bestowal of wealth of animals, large households, and silver upon each generation in Genesis fulfills the blessing. These goods herald more than subsistence and survival; they promise fullness, "a gracious plenty." Material blessings function in Genesis to encourage hope for new life, a seeming impossibility under imperial domination.

Blessings also have "intangible" dimensions. In the ancient Near East, blessings refer to relationships between rulers and subjects. Even though such relationships are asymmetrical (the ruler has power over the subjects), they are also "personal, favorable, and reciprocal."[15] "To bless" is an affirmation of commitment between ruler and subject. God's promise of blessing to Abraham ensures continued commitment between the people and the God of their ancestors despite the seeming break between them caused by nation's defeat.

D. Promise of a Great Name. God's promise to give Abram a great name tells the defeated people that they will have dignity and honor, status and respect. A great name in the ancient world means that Judah will no longer be a dishonored, humiliated nation crushed by foreign empires. [Culture of Honor and Shame] Divine promises are assured in Genesis because God says so (Gen 1). The word of Judah's God is powerful and creative. That word has created all that is, and now it recreates Israel from the waste and void of destruction. Genesis tells about beginnings so that the people might begin again.

Origins of Genesis

Composers of Genesis did not start from scratch; they did not invent stories out of whole cloth to convince the Judean people that God could create them anew. Instead, they drew from the deep well of Israel's sacred memories and wove them together in a long, bumpy narrative about the ancient past. Among modern interpreters of Genesis, broad questions about the book's origins have largely been settled for many decades, although specifics are still under study. [Authorship in the Ancient World]

Culture of Honor and Shame

The ancient culture from which Genesis emerged differed vastly from modern Western culture and, not unlike some modern Mediterranean and African cultures, is often characterized as a culture of honor and shame. In such cultures, honor and shame establish principles of human behavior and interaction.

Anxiety, shame (along with its correlative, honor), guilt are three control patterns of human personality that exist in all cultures. . . . All cultures contain these three strategies for controlling human behavior but tend to stress one more than others. . . . Honor is a public claim to worth and value and a public acknowledgement of that claim. Positive shame is a concern for maintaining and protecting one's worth, value, and reputation. Negative shame is loss of one's honor. Refusing to be concerned about one's honor is shameless. Honor and shame are thus external controls on human behavior that depend on the opinion of others. (Pilch)

To have honor is to have positive social status and to have shame is to be of low social status. Honor is necessary for the good of the family and the well-being of society itself. Since biblical societies were community oriented rather than individual oriented, the society bestowed honor, or it was inherited from the status of one's father or gained from one's place in the family and society. Men had honor, for example, by being heads of households, being the firstborn, being warriors, or exercising other roles in the wider community. Women gained honor from connection to their men and as wives and mothers. The honor/shame distinction controlled behaviors that were important or to be avoided in society. The honor of a community provided a sense of worth, dignity, and well-being. Defeated nations and communities lost honor.

For further reading, see Johanna Stiebert, *The Construction of Shame in the Hebrew Bible: The Prophetic Contribution* (JOTSS 346; Sheffield, UK: Sheffield Academic Press, 2002).

John J. Pilch, "Honor and Shame," in *Oxford Bibliographies*, Biblical Studies, http://www.oxfordbibliographies.com.

Authorship in the Ancient World

In antiquity, literature emerged from different processes than in it does in modern Western societies. In industrialized countries today, individual authorship is of great importance, protected by copyright law as the intellectual property of the author, but in the ancient world authors were generally anonymous members of a community. Often they attached their writings to the names of great figures from the past to give their work the authority of tradition and to stand in line with the wisdom of great ancestors. The Bible, for example, ascribes many biblical books to Moses, David, and Solomon, even though the books came into being long after these figures lived.

For further reading, see Simon B. Parker, "The Ancient Near Eastern Literary Background of the Old Testament" (*NIB* 1; Nashville: Abingdon, 1994) 228–43.

Who Wrote Genesis?

Although theories that Genesis had only one human author prevailed until the Enlightenment, modern scholarship has recognized that Genesis and the other books of the Pentateuch are products of a complicated history of composition.[16] [Ancient Traditions about the Authorship of Genesis] Interpreters began to notice literary inconsistencies, duplications, contradictions, and a confusing variety of names for God, and they worked toward understanding them. Eventually it became evident that one writer could not have composed all five books.

Ancient Traditions about the Authorship of Genesis

Although the figure of Moses looms over the Pentateuch, biblical interpreters have widely agreed for nearly two centuries that these five books were not written by one inspired author, neither the traditional Moses nor Ezra (Neh 8:1-12) nor any other single writer. Rather than a unified work created by one person, the five books are a compilation of writings from a variety of authors and times that came together slowly in a centuries-long process.

Genesis is a long, complex work composed of various types of literature and containing many different styles and forms of writing. Modern commentators generally agree that the book comprises oral and written pieces gathered from different periods in Israel's history. Even a cursory reading shows that it is not one smooth literary composition but an amalgamation of materials gathered to form its present shape.

Modern understandings about the beginnings of Genesis arose from a broad sense of the ways ancient peoples typically produced literature. When only a few could read or write, material was passed along as oral compositions. Storytellers, artists really, told about events, put them into memo-

Oral Traditions

The ability to read was a rare skill in antiquity. In the ancient Near East, literacy rates were low and access to written texts was reserved for the privileged few. In such societies, oral speech was the way culture and tradition were passed along. Oral tradition refers to the transmission of stories, customs, business transactions, and other types of knowledge by word of mouth. Many Genesis stories surely originated in oral form and went through significant development before being written down and compiled into the book. Even when Genesis took written form, most of the audience heard it rather than read it. As a result, it is difficult if not impossible to determine earlier and later texts on the basis of supposed oral clues.

For further reading, see Robert D. Miller II, SFO, *Oral Tradition in Ancient Israel* (Biblical Performance Criticism 4; Eugene OR: Cascade, 2011).

rable shapes and patterns, and passed them from generation to generation.[17] [Oral Traditions] [Folkloric Traditions] These oral performers

Folkloric Influences

Folkloric influences appear in many Genesis stories. These include the sneaky ways of the underdogs and tricksters, emphasis on action, ways of making fun of enemies, and legendary forms. These and other elements may have their roots in oral storytelling, borrowings from other cultures, and amazing literary artistry.

For further reading, see Susan Niditch, "Folklore and Biblical Interpretation," in *Oxford Encyclopedia of Biblical Interpretation*, vol. 1, ed. Steven McKenzie (Oxford and New York: Oxford University Press, 2013) 313–21.

Susan Niditch, *Prelude to Biblical Folklore: Underdogs and Tricksters* (Chicago: University of Illinois Press, 2000) 1–22.

drew from stories they already knew and from others that circulated among neighboring peoples. [Influences of Ancient Near Eastern Literature] They adapted, expanded, and wrote documents or "sources" that were later incorporated into the book. [Documentary Theory of Composition]

This understanding of the book is known as the documentary or source-critical theory of composition. It goes a long way to explain the book's many inconsistencies. Interpreters have distinguished four separate documents in the production of the Pentateuch. These are often referred to as the Yahwist (J), the Elohist (E), the Deuteronomist (D), and the Priestly Writer (P). Since the Deuteronomic (D) source appears largely in the book of Deuteronomy, it has little importance for Genesis.[18] It is generally agreed that the people who made Genesis into a book were a group of anonymous priests, called simply the Priestly or P writer. It was they who selected, assembled, and added to the great store of traditions that were at their disposal. Lately, however, distinctions between the Yahwist and Elohist sources seem less clear so that some refer simply to the Priestly Writer (P) and Non-Priestly Writer (non-P or pre-P), lumping everything that is not P into one large collection of documents.[19]

This extended process of composition may seem to be purely literary and historical in nature, but it is also theological. Rather than understanding Genesis as dictated directly to one writer such as Moses or Elijah, the theory of many sources points to the role of the faith community in receiving and expressing divine revelation. Genesis and the whole Bible exist because of long processes of human interactions with God that are discovered, struggled with, and expressed in the languages, cultures, and experiences of generations of Israel and later Christianity. Rather than limiting divine power, the theological process recognizes that God reveals the divine self in the midst of the created world and of human history and culture. God speaks to the people in the context of their lives.

Influences of Ancient Near Eastern Literature

Creation accounts, or "cosmogonies," abounded in the ancient world, and some had bearing upon Gen 1–11 and other biblical texts. A cosmogony is an account of how creation came into being. To study them helps place biblical creation accounts in their historical and cultural contexts. Old Testament interpreter Richard J. Clifford has provided an overview of how ancient understandings of creation differ from modern ones.

1. Ancient Near Eastern people imagined creation as a personal conflict among divine will of the gods, with one party defeating another. Moderns, by contrast, see the process as impersonal.

2. The process of creation in the ancient Near East produced society and culture in the service of the gods, while moderns focus on the physical world. (Clifford, 7–10)

Biblical texts borrow some of this worldview even as they differ from it. Gen 1, for example, appears to rebut the story of the violence among the gods that produced the cosmos in the *Enuma Elish*.

The Old Testament (including the Book of Genesis) was not composed in a cultural vacuum. Israel borrowed and adapted material from other nations, creating its own creation stories from existing myths. This is also evident when comparing the primordial history in Gen 1–9 (especially the stories of creation and the account of Noah and the flood) with the *Enuma Elish* (a Babylonian creation myth), *The Epic of Gligamesh* (a Mesopotamian creation and flood myth), and the *Atrahasis* (another Mesopotamian flood myth).

We can see significant overlap in these texts' depictions of the creation. Specifically, water features prominently in both the creation account of Gen 1 and in the *Enuma Elish*; it is a force of chaos that must be bound (Genesis) or defeated (*Enuma Elish*). Whereas the Babylonian myth depicts the storm god Marduk slaying the salt-water sea goddess Tiamat, slicing her in two in order to create the skies and the seas (or the waters above and the waters below), in Genesis God simply speaks a word to put bounds around the chaotic seas.

The creation of humankind is another area of overlap between the book of Genesis and other ancient Near Eastern accounts. Like the creation of the first man in Gen 2, the *Epic of Gilgamesh* depicts the gods forming Enkidu—a wild, naked, hairy man—out of dirt (the *Atrahasis* depicts humans as made from clay). Moreover, after an epic flood, King Gilgamesh undertakes a heroic quest to find the magic garden with the secret to eternal life only to discover that the gods have created humans with death in mind (Clifford, 137–50).

Parallels between Genesis and other ancient Near Eastern texts also involve flood narratives. The *Epic of Gilgamesh* and *Atrahasis* depict floods, and Atrahasis builds a boat to save himself and the animals.

For further reading, see Christopher B. Hays, *Hidden Riches: A Sourcebook for the Comparative Study of the Hebrew Bible and the Ancient Near East* (Louisville KY: Westminster John Knox, 2014).

Richard J. Clifford, *Creation Accounts in the Ancient Near East and in the Bible* (CBQMS26; Washington, DC: The Catholic Biblical Association of America, 1994).

Neo-Assyrian clay tablet. Epic of Gilgamesh, Tablet 11: Story of the Flood. Known as the "Flood Tablet" from the Library of Ashurbanipal, 7th century BCE. British Museum, London. (Credit Wikimedia Commons, babelstone, CC0)

Cuneiform tablet with the Atrahasis Epic. Babylonian, about 17th century BCE. From Sippar, southern Iraq. British Museum. (Credit Wikimedia Commons, Jack1956*, PD)

Documentary Theory of Composition

A number of literary features of Genesis indicate that it contains preexisting elements that do not fit together easily. These include

1. Variation in style and language. The first creation account is solemn and repetitive (Gen 1:1–2:4a), but the second account is lively narrative (Gen 2:4b–3:25).

2. Variation in the name for God. God's name is Elohim (Gen 1:1–2:4a), YHWH God (2:4b–3:24), and YHWH (4:1-16), to mention only a few names for God in the book.

3. Variation in theologies. God appears distant and powerful (Gen 1:1–2:4a), human-like and immersed in human life (2:4b–4:16), or largely hidden in the background (chs. 37–50).

4. Repetitions and doublets. Events repeat with only slight variation, such as the three stories of the near-loss of Sarah and Rebekah to foreign rulers due to their husbands' deception (12:10-20; ch. 20; 26:1-11).

5. Internal contradictions. The text identifies Joseph's slave traders as Ishmaelites and then as Midianites (38:25-28, 36).

6. Episodic nature of the stories. The stories seem like a series of diverse accounts rather than a smooth continuous narrative. (Brodie, 5–6)

Literary inconsistencies such as the above lead interpreters to propose that many authors composed Genesis and the Pentateuch. The theory known as the Documentary Hypothesis solved some problems by proposing that four literary sources were used to compose the books of the Pentateuch: the "Yahwist" or J Source (from the German "Jahwist"), the "Elohist" or E Source, the "Deuteronomist" or D Source (not present in Genesis). and the "Priestly" or P Source—J, E, D, P for short.

Current scholarship has not abandoned the belief that multiple sources are present in Genesis, but clear-cut distinctions between J and E have been discredited (see Joel Baden's *Composition of the Pentateuch*, however, for a reassertion of the four-source theory). Today there is increasing doubt that J and E can be distinguished from one another, resulting in new nomenclature of the sources as P and non-P (Carr, 318–26).

This scholarly question is important because it recognizes that Genesis contains many preexisting pieces of writing from a long history. Priests joined these sources and added their own material to produce the book in the late sixth or early fifth century BCE.

For further reading, see David Carr, *Reading the Fractures of Genesis: Historical and Literary Approaches* (Louisville KY: Westminster John Knox, 1996).

Thomas L. Brodie, *Genesis as Dialogue* (New York: Oxford University Press, 2001).

Joel S. Baden, *The Composition of the Pentateuch: Renewing the Documentary Hypothesis* (AYBRL; New Haven CT: Yale University Press, 2012).

David M. Carr, "Source Criticism," in *The Oxford Encyclopedia of Biblical Interpretation*, vol. 2, ed. Steven L. McKenzie (Oxford and New York: Oxford University Press, 2013).

Cohesion of Genesis

Despite its episodic, uneven character, Genesis is not a confusing hodgepodge of unrelated pieces. Its strong literary structure—built around divine promises, genealogies, and stories of beginnings—provides a unifying plot in the service of new life. Overlapping events, themes, and characters come together in a large narrative web of stories about the creation of the people Israel.

In this commentary, I explore the question of why Genesis was put together in the first place. I assume that biblical books emerge to intervene in crises in the community—to challenge, encourage faith, or provide answers to urgent questions of life and death. I assume the same about the composition of Genesis. The forces that prompted priestly writers to compose the book came from a historical crisis that threatened the nation's existence. The book tells of beginnings to insist that the Creator who made them can and will remake them anew. At the book's heart is its multifaceted portrait of the Creator. Genesis is essentially a book about God.

The Search for God in Genesis

Genesis looks for ways to find God, to relate to God, and to claim God at the beginning of the nation's rebuilding, and it does so in enormously varied ways. [God and Human Language] With more insistence and thoroughness than other biblical books, Genesis conceives of God as Creator, author of life, giver of fertility, and companion of the displaced. God is so creative that mere words bring forth life. God is the Source of everything, Orderer of Existence, Promise Maker, Community Builder, God of All Nations, and the One alone who makes a future in the face of the impossible.

These glimpses of God emerge with heightened intensity from Judah's un-creation by invading empires. Hope that God is still with them in their scattered, landless lives gives birth to clear articulation that God creates, makes, forms, orders, and builds in the face of the impossible, and has always done so from the beginning. The gods of the empires are not God. Israel's God is such an intensely powerful Creator that the divine word alone makes life leap forth.

God and Human Language

In trying to understand God in the Bible, we cannot get beyond or around the limitations of human language. The task is impossible not because of God but because we are human, and human understanding comes in the form of language, and language is always limited. This is not only because the book's sources depict God in different ways with different names but also finally because God eludes full definition. God cannot be contained in one set of images or ways of speaking. Ultimately, many portraits, images, and themes provide glimpses of the Holy One who exceeds all human categories of expression, a point repeatedly affirmed in Christianity and other world religions. Yet human words remain a primary albeit limited tool to express encounters with the divine.

Language is metaphoric. We use metaphors to capture many different aspects of life. We "fall in love," and love "is a red, red rose." Metaphor is not simply religious language. It is human language for all areas of human life. "Because metaphor is a primary tool for understanding our world and ourselves," write George Lakoff and Mark Turner, "entering into an engagement with powerful poetic metaphors is grappling in an important way with what it means to have a human life. Like so much of the Bible, creation texts use human language to convey who God is" (3).

Genesis presents story worlds that depict God and humans at work, that derive from life in the ancient world, and that are preserved, remembered, and elaborated in efforts to present theological truth in terms humans of the time understood. We live in different times, have different languages, and have different historical and cultural realities. Biblical interpretation requires the study of the ancient text in its own context and its translation and reinterpretation for our times.

For further reading, see William P. Brown, *The Ethos of the Cosmos: The Genesis of Moral Imagination in the Bible* (Grand Rapids MI: Wm. B. Eerdmans, 1999) 19–27.

George Lakoff and Mark Turner, *More than Cool Reason: A Field Guide to Poetic Metaphor* (Chicago: University of Chicago Press, 2004), cited in Mark S. Smith, *How Human Is God? Seven Questions about God and Humanity in the Bible* (Collegeville MN: Liturgical Press, 2014) 75.

CONNECTIONS

Stories and characters from Genesis infuse Western culture. From "Let there be light" to the great flood; from the famine in Egypt to characters like Adam, Eve, the serpent, Noah, Abraham, Sarah, Hagar, Esau, Jacob, Rachel, Leah, and Joseph—the book is a source of art, literature, music, archetypal figures, and even cartoons. If that were not enough, the stories themselves make memorable pieces of literature. They contain tragedy, pathos, psychological insight, love and sex, and life-threatening dangers survived and overcome.

For Jews, Muslims, and Christians, however, Genesis is much more. It is sacred literature, inspired word of God, "a lamp to our feet and a light to our path" (Ps 119:105). Communities of faith find their lives shaped and reflected here and their God revealed here. [Interpretive Traditions]

Because God does the impossible in Genesis, bringing life where obstacles are insurmountable, the book invites hope in the midst of international catastrophe and global terrorism; ugly, frightening politics; and the vast movements of people. The book affirms that God creates life where there is no life. Genesis is a political document as well as a theological one, a counter-argument to belief that the gods of Babylon or Persia control life as rulers of the

Interpretive Traditions

Muslims, Jews, and Christians claim Abraham as the progenitor of their faiths, and each has developed its own rich, deep, and extensive interpretive traditions.

For further reading, see, for example, Ian Provan, *Discovering Genesis: Content, Interpretation, Reception* (Discovering Biblical Texts; Grand Rapids MI: Wm B. Eerdmans, 2015); Jacob Neusner, *The Genesis Rabbah: The Judaic Commentary on the Book of Genesis*, A New American Translation (BJS 104–106; Atlanta: Scholars Press, 1985); and John Kaltner, *Ishmael Instructs Isaac: An Introduction to the Qur'an for Bible Readers* (Collegeville MN: Liturgical Press, 1999); and "Genesis, Book of: articles I-V on the New Testament, Judaism, and Christianity, Islam," *EBR* 9:1153–86.

cosmos. It offers a radical challenge to claims of empires ancient and modern by insisting that Judah's God is not a weak national deity defeated in battle by stronger gods. In Genesis, God is the sole Creator of whole cosmos, of the sacred web of all life. God is the maker of all peoples and also the One who chooses Israel from all the peoples of the world.

To insist that the Creator God continues to do the impossible sounds naïve, Pollyannaish, even ridiculous in a world torn apart by warfare, hatred, and environmental destruction. God seems not to interfere in history, in despotic governments, or in individual suffering except after the fact, when we look back over our shoulders. Even then, after frightful events human life can seem empty and meaningless. When people of faith look back on their struggles and tragedies, however, they can sometimes discover the sense of a guiding presence, a providential thread that kept them going and enabled them to survive, even if it was not evident at the time.

Such reflection can set events into a larger web of life by setting past events in a new light.

NOTES

1. For analysis of similarities between Genesis creation accounts and modern science, see William P. Brown, *The Seven Pillars of Creation: The Bible, Science, and the Ecology of Wonder* (Oxford: Oxford University Press, 2010).

2. See Andre Le Cocque, *The Trial of Innocence: Adam, Eve, and the Yahwist* (Eugene OR: Cascade, 2006) 17–19; and David Carr, *Holy Resilience: The Bible's Traumatic Origins* (New Haven CT: Yale University Press, 2014); and see essays in Thomas B. Dozeman and Konrad Schmid, eds., *A Farewell to the Yahwist? The Composition of the Pentateuch in Recent European Interpretation* (Symposium; Atlanta: Society of Biblical Literature, 2006).

3. For the history of the Assyrian Empire see Marti Nissinen, "Assyria in the Bible" and "Assyria and the Bible" in *EBR* 2:1072, and 1086–91.

4. For further reading, see David Carr, *Holy Resilience: The Bible's Traumatic Origins* (New Haven CT: Yale University Press, 2014) 41–66.

5. See Jill Middlemas, *The Templeless Age: An Introduction to the History, Literature and Theology of the Exile* (Louisville KY: Westminster John Knox, 2007) 10–27.

6. The degree of destruction wrought by the Babylonians finds no agreement among historians. See essays in Oded Lipschits and Joseph Blenkinsopp, eds., *Judah and the Judeans in the Neo-Babylonian Period* (Winona Lake IN: Eisenbrauns, 2003). Increasingly scholars recognize the traumatic effects on Judah and are investigating the consequences for biblical interpretation.

7. See Louis Stulman and Hyun Paul Kim, *You Are My People: An Introduction to Prophetic Literature* (Nashville: Abingdon, 2010) 1–23.

8. See Kathleen M. O'Connor, *Jeremiah: Pain and Promise* (Minneapolis: Fortress, 2011) 19–34; David Carr, *Holy Resilience: The Bible's Traumatic Origins* (New Haven CT: Yale University Press, 2014); David G. Garber, Jr. "Trauma Theory and Biblical Studies," *CBR* 14/1 (2015): 24–44; Eve-Marie Becker, Jan Dochorn, and Else Krageland Holt, eds., *Trauma and Traumatization in Individual and Collective Dimensions: Insights from Biblical Studies and Beyond* (Studia Aarhusiana Neotestamentica 2; Göttingen: Vandenhoeck & Ruprecht, 2014); Brad E. Kelle, Frank Rictehl Ames, and Jacob L. Wright, eds., *Interpreting Exile: Displacement and Deportation in Biblical and Modern Contexts* (AIL 10; Atlanta: SBL, 2011); see also "Trauma and Faith," *Int* 69/1 (January 2015): 7–75; Shelly Rambo, *Spirit and Trauma: A Theology of Remaining* (Louisville KY: Westminster John Knox, 2010); and Rambo, *Resurrecting Wounds: Living in the Afterlife of Trauma* (Waco TX: Baylor University Press, 2017).

9. David M Carr ("Reading into the Gap: Refractions of Trauma in Israelite Prophecy," in Kelle et al., *Interpreting Exile*, 295–308) speaks of "refractions" of trauma in biblical texts, meaning that horrific events are present but not fully representable.

10. O'Connor, *Jeremiah*, 19–34.

11. According to John Anderson, "The central theme and organizing principle is the protection and passing of the promise given Abraham in Gen 12:1-3" (*Jacob and the Divine Trickster* [Siphrut 5; Winona Lake IN: Eisenbrauns, 2011] 41). See also Joel S. Baden, *The Promise to the Patriarchs* (New York: Oxford University Press, 2013).

12. Anderson, *Jacob and the Divine Trickster*, 41.

13. See Paul D. Vrolijik, *Jacob's Wealth: An Examination into the Nature and Role of Material Possessions in the Jacob Cycle (Gen 25:19–35:29)* (Leiden: Brill, 2011), Appendix B, 310–23.

14. Christopher Frechette, "Why Bless God?" in *Reading the Old Testament: Pastoral Essay in Honor of Lawrence Boadt, CS.*, ed. Corrine L. Carvalho (Mahwah NJ: Paulist, 2013) 11–119, 114.

15. Ibid., 116.

16. The various approaches and methods for studying Genesis and the Old Testament have been well documented, beginning with historical criticism and presently expanding to include a wide range of approaches. For a clear, succinct overview of historical criticism that began modern approaches, see Megan Bishop Moore, "Historical Criticism: Hebrew Bible," in *The Oxford Encyclopedia of Biblical Interpretation*, vol. 1, ed. Steven L. McKenzie (Oxford and New York: Oxford University Press, 2013) 391–400.

17. See Raymond F. Person, Jr., "Orality Studies and Oral Tradition: Hebrew Bible," in *The Oxford Encyclopedia of Biblical Interpretation*, vol. 2, ed. Steven L. McKenzie (Oxford and New York: Oxford University Press, 2013) 55–63.

18. For a brief, clear overview of sources, see Gerhard von Rad, *Genesis*, rev. ed. (OTL; Philadelphia: Westminster, 1972) 24–43. Von Rad extends the appearance of the sources to include Joshua.

19. See David Carr, "Source Criticism," in *The Oxford Encyclopedia of Biblical Interpretation*, vol. 2, ed. Steven L. McKenzie (Oxford and New York: Oxford University Press, 2013) 321.

IN THE BEGINNING

Genesis 1–4

Genesis does not divide easily into subsections. More like a multi-threaded tapestry than a building made of distinct boards and bricks, its parts, themes, literary forms, and even generations overlap and intertwine from the beginning to the end of the book. Chapters 1–4 contain two distinct accounts of original creation (1:1–2:4a and 2:4b–3:24) and a genealogical account of Eve's children and the first murder (4:1-26). Genesis 1–4, therefore, is something of an arbitrary literary unit, for the next division (chs. 5–9) contains Adam's genealogy and the story of the flood.

Yet these introductory chapters (Genesis 1–4) lay out important theological themes for the rest of the book. They reach back to the creation of everything by the power of God's word alone (1:1–2:4a), to the planting of a paradisial garden from which the first couple is exiled (2:4b–3:25), and they show life beginning again when all seems lost (4:1-26). In these ways they establish for the book's audience, struggling to survive in the aftermath of the nation's fall to Babylon, that the God who spoke all creatures into existence, who exiled them from their past life and commanded them to be fruitful and multiply, can and will create them anew.

CREATION BY WORD

Genesis 1:1–2:4a

This first of two creation accounts provides a bracing introduction to the story of Israel's origins (chs. 12–50). It anchors the creation of the people of Israel inside the larger arena of the cosmos and all its inhabitants. Events related in it take place in seven days—six days plus a day of rest (2:1-4a). Taking the form of a poetic narrative, this version of creation proclaims the potency of the divine word that alone brings order from chaos, turns waste and void into beauty and form, and gives birth to all living things. [Poetic Narrative] God's word is the powerful force that brings everything into existence. [Prologue to the Gospel of John (1:1-18)] God's creative word is the bedrock on which the book's ancient audience can rely for the nation's recreation after the destruction of their world during the Babylonian Period.

Contemporary battles around scientific and historical meanings of the first creation account often obscure the intense power of the literature even in translation. [Genesis and Modern Science] Yet the passage's pleasing shape and literary beauty cannot be separated from its meaning. The tight arrangement of creation into seven days creates a rhythmic unfolding of life in the style of a hymn of praise. [Creation Psalms] Within the orderly week, the Creator works step by step to bring forth the cosmos, and so the narrator implicitly invites all living things to join in awe and wonder, and like God, to rest in the blessing of the Sabbath day (2:1-4a). [Wonder]

Creation takes one week. Six days occur in chapter 1, while the seventh day overflows into chapter 2 (vv. 1-4a).[1] The seven-day structure is a literary device that highlights order; the ordering of time portrays creation in incremental steps in which each set of events fills in and builds upon previous ones.

Poetic Narrative

By poetic narrative, I mean a story told in concise, balanced sentences with carefully chosen language. The first creation account is poetic like a hymn of praise (Gen 1:1-2:4a). It contains vivid imagery and rhythmic arrangements. To quickly see its differences from a prose narrative, read the second creation account (Gen 2:4a–3:24). There the story flows smoothly from event to event, and although it contains poetic elements (2:23 and 3:14-19), it has characters, dialogue, and a plot with a beginning, a middle, and an end. For further reading, see Yairah Amit, *Reading Biblical Narratives: Literary Criticism and the Hebrew Bible* (Minneapolis: Fortress, 2001).

Prologue to the Gospel of John (1:1-18)

The Prologue to the Gospel of John (1:1-18) uses the first chapter of Genesis to reflect on the meaning of the good news of Jesus Christ. In the process, John reinterprets Genesis.

In the beginning was the Word, and the Word was with God. He was in the beginning with God. All things came into being through him, and without him nothing came into being. What has come into being in him was life and the life was the light of all people. The light shines in the darkness and the darkness shall not overcome it (John 1:1-5).

On the one hand, Genesis provides John with language and theology to probe the meaning of the incarnation, life, and death of Jesus. For him, Jesus is the Word of God present from the beginning of everything. He is the light of the world threatened by darkness, yet darkness cannot destroy him for he is risen.

On the other hand, John reinterprets Genesis 1, finding hidden meaning in it. He declares, "What has come into being in him was life and the life was the light of all people" (1:4). For John, Jesus is the Word, the active creative agent who brings the world into being. "He was in the world, and the world came into being through him" (1:10). In John, the figure of Jesus gathers elements of the first creation account and grants it new depth from a Christian viewpoint. Jesus is both the Word of God and the light that darkness cannot destroy. He created the world and continues to create it anew.

"God Creates," in Martin Luther (1483–1546), *Kirchen Postilla, das ist, Auslegung der Episteln vnd Euangelien an Sontagen vnd furnemesten Festen / D. Mart. Luth* (1554). (Courtesy of the Pitts Theology Library, Candler School of Theology, Emory University)

Genesis and Modern Science

The first creation account of Genesis does not answer questions of modern science. It does not address evolution and the Big Bang theory or present a literal account of the emergence of the cosmos itself. The ancient writers did not know these things. They were, instead, writing for the people of their time and using their own cultural, religious, and scientific traditions. They borrowed a bit from other ancient creation stories to create their version of beginnings. They used the material available to them to cultivate trust in God, who brings forth life and brings order from chaos.

Rather than a work of modern science, the first creation account is proclamation, an act of faith, an inducement to hope; it is, as Walter Brueggemann has insisted about biblical texts, "testimony" (117–44). Biblical texts are not in opposition to the modern pursuit of knowledge about the cosmos. They draw from ancient understandings of the physical world to speak of God's relationship to the world and its people. The people of Israel, for example, partake of the ancient world's interest in celestial science to understand the times, but they do not deify the stars or the planets or the lamps of the heavens that separate light from darkness. They reject the luni-solar calendar of their neighbors and replace it with the Sabbath Calendar with its seven-day week, culminating in the seventh day of rest and worship (see Cooley, esp. 225–87, 313–20).

The unfolding of creation in Genesis 1 does exhibit some similarities to the insights of modern science, but modern scientists bracket theological concerns to investigate the origins of matter on their own terms (Brown, 66–77). This, too, can lead to praise of course, but its first purpose is to understand the physical world.

For further reading, see William P. Brown's *Seven Pillars of Creation*, 33–77, and, more recently, his *A Handbook to Old Testament Exegesis* (Louisville KY: Westminster John Knox, 2017) 201–27.

Walter Brueggemann, *Theology of the Old Testament: Testimony, Dispute, Advocacy* (Minneapolis: Fortress, 1997).

Jeffrey L. Cooley, *Poetic Astronomy in the Ancient Near East: The Reflexes of Celestial Science in Ancient Mesopotamia, Ugaritic, and Israelite Narrative* (Winona Lake IN: Eisenbrauns, 2013).

William P. Brown, *The Seven Pillars of Creation: Bible Science, and the Ecology of Wonder* (New York: Oxford University Press, 2010).

Creation Psalms

A number of psalms praise the God of creation. These include Psalms 8; 19:1-7; 95:1-7; 104; 145–50 and others that contain creation themes. Like Gen 1, Ps 8:5 exalts God's creation of humans as little less than gods, Ps 104 celebrates the world's order and fecundity, and Ps 150 invites a great symphony of praise for God in "his mighty firmament" (v. 1), for the world itself is the temple of the Creator. Gen 1 joins this tradition of hymnic praise.

Wonder

Old Testament interpreter William P. Brown has made "wonder" as a response to God's creation into a major theological category. In attending to biblical accounts of the cosmos's beginnings, he insists with much eloquence that they invite us to experience wonder and awe at divine power, creativity, and creation itself:

"Wonder is an emotional response; it cannot be willed into existence. It is a response to something unexpected, and that response reflects a potent mix of curiosity and perplexity." The experience of wonder includes bewilderment, curiosity, and the desire to know.

William P. Brown, *Sacred Sense: Discovering the Wonder of God's Word and World* (Grand Rapids MI: Wm. B. Eerdmans, 2015) 4.

COMMENTARY

The first creation story uses vocabulary artfully. A limited number of words and phrases repeat day by day, also contributing to the order and beauty of the passage. [Seven-day Structure] Repeated language describes the days, one from one another, so that the course of events is nearly the same each day. Yet variations in the formulaic structure of repeated phrases—sometimes with expansions and sometimes alterations—make certain events stand out in importance from the rest, such as the creation of humans (1:26-30) and the establishment of Sabbath day (2:1-4a). [Outline of Genesis 1:1–2:4a]

Seven-day Structure

The structure of the first creation account is both beautiful and intricate, and that literary arrangement cannot be separated from the meanings of the passage. The seven-day arrangement, extending from 1:1 to 2:4a, provides a progression from the creation of a habitat (days 1 through 3) to the creation of its vegetal, animal, and human residents (days 4 to 6) and concludes with divine rest on the seventh day. In addition to the week-long set of creative events, repeated words and phrases create a strong similarity among the days, with important variations to add emphases. Also important to the passage's structuring are the interrelationships among the days. Each day builds upon the previous day, manifesting interdependence between habitat and inhabitants. The arrangements of the literature express order emerging from chaos and integration of beings within the cosmos.

Chaos and Formlessness, 1:1-2

The first two verses of the book draw readers into an ambiguous and complex domain:

Outline of Genesis 1:1–2:4a

1. Chaos and Formlessness, 1:1-2
2. God Creates the Cosmos, 1:3-13
   First Three Days of Creation
3. God Creates Inhabitants of the Cosmos, 1:14-31
   Second Three Days of Creation
4. God Rests, 2:1-4a

In the beginning when God created the heavens and the earth,
the earth was a formless void
and darkness covered the face of the deep,
while a wind from God swept over the face of the waters (1:1-2).
[Translation Challenges of Genesis 1:1]

Translation Challenges of Genesis 1:1

Here are possible translations of Genesis 1:1:

In the beginning when God created the heavens and the earth . . . (NRSV)

When God began to create heaven and earth . . . (JPS)

At the beginning of God's creating of the heavens and the earth . . . (E. Fox)

In the beginning God created the heavens and the earth. (NIV)

In the beginning God created the heaven and the earth. (KJV)

These examples of different translations might seem of minor importance, but they yield different theological understandings of the text. Did God create the cosmos from scratch (*ex nihilo*, "from nothing")? "In the beginning God created the heavens and the earth" (NIV, KJV). Or was the work of God to put order into preexisting chaos? Was something already existent "When God created the heavens and the earth and the earth was a formless void" (NRSV, JPS, Fox)?

The first three translations above (NRSV, JPS, Fox) understand verse 1 as a temporal clause, that is, it provides the start of the divine actions that take place in the rest of the chapter, starting with God's voice ("And God said . . . ," v. 3). God spoke at the beginning of the work of creation, when the earth was formless and darkness was everywhere. Similarly, Gen 2:4 and 5:1 begin this way and so does the ancient Mesopotamian creation account, the *Enuma Elish* (see Sarna, 5), strengthening the case for this translation.

The last two translations (NIV and KJV), by contrast, understand verse 1 as a complete sentence, a declarative statement that introduces the whole chapter. Nothing existed until God got to work immediately. When "God said," waste and void appeared.

I think, however, that the composers of Genesis would not have asked the questions either way. They lived in an ancient world abounding in creation myths. Everett Fox has put it well:

Most of the cultures surrounding ancient Israel had elaborate creation stories, highlighting the birth, sexuality and violent uprising of the gods. . . . The concept of God presented here militates against such ideas, arguing chiefly out of omission and silence. (It should be noted that in poetic books such as Isaiah, Job, and Psalms, a tradition about violent conflict has been preserved). The Genesis narrative has taken such old mythological motifs as battle with the primeval (female) waters or with sea monsters and eliminated or neutralized them. What remains is both utterly simple and radical in it is time. (Fox, 1:12)

The composers of Genesis were not creating doctrine, writing modern science, nor reporting history. The text does draw from the ancients' particular understandings of the cosmos, but it is not a scientific statement; it is a hymn of praise, a poetic confession of truth, a liturgy of wonder. To read it as a literal account of the events of creation or an omniscient grasp of the origins of life is to do violence to the text and to mistake praise for history, poetry for science, liturgy for scientific analysis.

With their temporal ambiguity, the opening verses of Genesis invite readers into time before time, into a reality of formless chaos and seething energy. Humans cannot know material reality that has no form. We require shape and other knowledge of the senses to see and know. Hence, the translation, "in the beginning when God created the heavens and earth," urges us to imagine a time and space that is unrecognizable, mystifying, and inexplicable. Before photographs and videos, these verses invited readers into a shadowy, enigmatic, and fluid materiality in sharp contrast to the ordered world and swarming life to follow.

Nahum M. Sarna, *Genesis* (JPS Torah Commentary; Philadelphia: The Jewish Publication Society, 1989).

Everett Fox, *The Five Books of Moses: Genesis, Exodus, Leviticus, Numbers, and Deuteronomy* (Schocken Bible; Dallas: Word, 1995).

These verses announce both time and setting for creation, but neither is clear. The time is vague—"in the beginning, when"—and the setting is amorphous—a formless void, deep covered by darkness, and waters swept by the wind.

Rather than pinpointing the time and place in which God sets to work, the introduction provides only nebulous hints about them.

Earthly realities do appear but only as allusions to the solid, more substantial world that humans know. The "formless void" (*tōhû wābōhû*) or the "wild and waste"[2] is mystifying, while the darkness covering "the face of the deep (*tĕhôm*)" adds to the impenetrable strangeness of the scene. How can eyes pierce this obscured world or minds grasp a shapeless emptiness? Yet the time and setting are not inert, for the "wind (*rûaḥ*) from God swept over the face of the waters" (1:2). In Hebrew, the "wind (*rûaḥ*) from God" increases the scene's inscrutability. The *rûaḥ* might refer to the wind as a climate event, or to "breath," or to "the spirit" "hovering" over the waters (NIV). The *rûaḥ* invites readers to imagine all these possibilities at once. Each alludes mysteriously to divine presence at the beginning of everything.

Questions about the time and place of creation have provoked many interpretive battles, but they cannot be answered from these verses. [Conversation with Modern Science] Instead of determining the setting in a definitive way, the verses conjure an atmosphere, a world of beginnings before beginnings, of time before time. In a style typical of poetic narratives, they use vocabulary with an abundance of meanings to arouse curiosity, imagination, reflection, and expectation. Linguistic wealth encourages readers to dwell in the scene and participate in the play of many meanings. Instead of hammering down later doctrinal insights, this account of creation begins in the shadows with unfathomable deeps and chaotic waters that can be seen only in the mind's eye. [Haydn's *Creation*] With their many implied questions, these introductory verses draw readers toward what follows in the next verse: "Then God said" (v. 3).

God Creates the Cosmos, 1:3-13

When God speaks, the cosmos emerges from chaotic waste and void. Step by step the days build upon one another, moving

Conversation with Modern Science

Alert readers might notice that darkness and waters already exist before God begins to speak creation into existence (1:1-3). Composers of Genesis 1 drew from their knowledge of the physical world to suggest an unfathomable scene of dark chaos and pulsing energy in these verses. They were writing a hymn of praise with persuasive purposes—to convince the Judean people that God who created everything was still creating them. Yet the chapter does not exclude conversation with modern science.

Genesis 1 brings into conversation a number of scientific disciplines. Its coverage of creation is vast and for good reason. This ancient report provides the most comprehensive account of creation anywhere in the Bible. . . . Genesis 1 attempts to chart the rise of form out of formlessness, the emergence of structure and life from "chaos," no mean feat! What Genesis touches upon so briefly, science has explored with great depth, detail, an ongoing investigation. Like Genesis 1, science charts the course of the cosmos from the initially amorphous character of the universe to the wealth of structure we see today. To explain cosmic evolution today, one must plunge into quantum physics, astronomy, and biology, and that's only the tip of the iceberg. In all its specialized discipline, science puts flesh on the skeletal account of Genesis, but not without out surgical rearrangement. (Brown, 66)

For further reading on the relationship of Genesis and science, see William P. Brown's *The Seven Pillars of Creation* (cited below) and his *A Handbook to Old Testament Exegesis* (Louisville KY: Westminster John Knox, 2017) 200–27.

William P. Brown, *The Seven Pillars of Creation: The Bible, Science, and the Ecology of Wonder* (New York: Oxford University Press, 2010).

Haydn's *Creation*

Austrian composer Joseph Haydn wrote his oratorio, *The Creation* (*Die Schöpfung*, 1798), during the Enlightenment with its emphasis on order and scientific understanding. This great musical work for instruments and voice interprets Gen 1:1–2:3 in that light. Haydn depicts a rationally ordered universe, seeing creation and its inhabitants as good and harmonious. He omits the second creation account with its conflicts. Above all, he celebrates his faith in the Creator and offers the work as praise of God. The oratorio opens with mysterious, evocative instrumental music, suggestive of the mood of Gen 1:1-2. The language about creation of the heavenly lights on day four shows the sense of order and joy that dominate his interpretation:

And God said: Let there be lights in the firmament of heaven, to divide the day from the night, and to give light upon the earth; and let them be for signs and for seasons, and for days, and for years. He made the stars also. [Gen 1:14-16]

In splendour bright is rising now the sun
And darts his rays; a joyful, happy spouse,
A giant proud and glad

To run his measured course.
With softer beams and milder light,
Steps on the silver moon thro' silent night;
The space immense of azure sky.
In num'rous host of radiant orbs adorns,
The sons of God announced the fourth day,
In song divine, proclaiming thus his power—

For further reading, see Pierpaolo Polzonetti, "Haydn, (Franz) Joseph," in the *Oxford Encyclopedia of the Bible and the Arts*, ed. Tim Beal (Oxford: Oxford University Press, 2015) 401–405.

A contrasting musical interpretation of creation in Genesis is a work by French composer Darius Milhaud, *La Création du Monde Op. 81* (1922–1923). Milhaud encountered Harlem jazz and ragtime when visiting New York and drew from it to create a musical composition for ballet. The exuberance of the 1920s era, blended with the disruptiveness and bursting life of the then-new American music, resulted in an interpretation of the creation of the world as an explosive irruption of energy and beauty.

Joseph Haydn, *Haydn's Oratorio, The Creation*, arr. Vincent Novello (London: London Sacred Music Warehouse, Novello, Ewer & Co., n.d.) iv.

Darius Milhaud, *La Création du Monde Op. 81*, http://www.warnerclassics.com/shop/3253679,0094634580823/ballet-edition-milhaud-la-creation-du-monde-le-boeuf-sur-le-toit.

from the darkness of the deep to a fully occupied world bursting with light and life. The sense of an orderly process emerges from the format of each individual day. The days are "remarkably symmetrical,"[3] revealing something like an architectural plan for the emergence of the heavens, the earth, and its residents. [Shape of Each Day] On the first three days of the week, God constructs the cosmic household (Gen 1:3-13). On the next three, God creates inhabitants to dwell within it (1:14-31). Each day and each creation interweaves inseparably with the others in an integrated process that forms a living organism.

Shape of Each Day

Each day, created by repeated words and phrases, follows the same general pattern:

And God said, "Let . . ."
God saw that it was good
God separated
God called
God made
God created
And it was so
And there was evening and morning, the [x] day.

This list of repeated phrases reminds readers that God alone is the acting subject. God is the doer who speaks, sees, separates, calls, makes, and creates. God's word creates the world.

Day One, 1:3-5

"Then God said, 'Let there be light,' and there was light" (v. 3). This simple command startles; God's voice alone brings light into being and shadowy chaos begins to subside. Now work can be done, the earth can be made, and living things can live. A God who can do this merely by speaking is clearly God not only of one people, nation, or powerful empire; this is the God of everything that is. To declare the power of God's word and evoke confidence in God's creative power is a major concern of the first creation account.

After the light comes, God expresses appreciation: "God saw that it was good" (1:4). Then God separates light from darkness. Separating things is a way to put them in order. Although

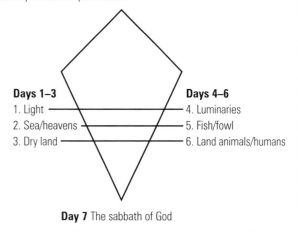

Chart of Relationships among Days
See Samuel E. Balentine, *The Torah's Vision of Worship* (OBT; Minneapolis: Fortress, 1999) 85, for a balanced chart of the days' relationships to one another. Chart reprinted with permission.

Days 1–3
1. Light
2. Sea/heavens
3. Dry land

Days 4–6
4. Luminaries
5. Fish/fowl
6. Land animals/humans

Day 7 The sabbath of God

darkness was already there (v. 2), God now divides it from newly created light. After speaking, seeing, evaluating, and separating the light, God then names this elusive element and calls it "day"; the darkness God names "night." Naming may be a form of showing divine control, establishing power over things, but naming also recognizes the essence of something, reveals its identity, and sets it apart from other things in its uniqueness. The act of naming establishes relationship with a person or thing. When God names day and night, God identifies the most fundamental structuring devices of time in human experience, visible elements of movement and alteration in the environment. These are gifts of the Creator. The first day ends as will all the days: "it was evening and morning, the first day" (1:5, paraphrase).

Day Two, 1:6-8

No transitional words tell readers that the second day has begun. The only indications of a new day are the announcement of the previous day's end and the fact that God again speaks: "Let there be a dome in the midst of the waters." With slight variations, the structure of the first day repeats itself on the second. The command for the appearance of the dome, for example, involves an additional command that explains the dome's purpose: "Let it separate the waters from the waters." According to cosmologies of the ancient Near East, the sky was a dome or, in an earlier translation, "a firmament" that held up waters above it. [Ancient Near Eastern Cosmology] The ancients believed that the earth was completely

Ancient Near Eastern Cosmology

Key to representation below: 1) waters above the firmament; 2) storehouses for snow; 3) storehouses for hail; 4) chambers of winds; 5) firmament; 6) sluice; 7) pillars of the sky; 8) pillars of the earth; 9) fountain of the deep; 10) navel of the earth; 11) waters under the earth; 12) rivers of the nether world.

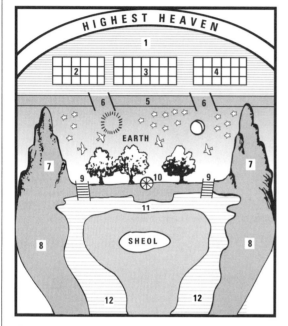

(Credit: Barclay Burns)

surrounded by water, as if the world were set into something like a snow globe or terrarium, protected all around from watery inundation. Without the dome to keep the waters away, the earth would never emerge. By separating the waters, the dome makes a place that can support earthly, non-watery life. In another slight addition to the format, God also "makes the dome" after commanding it to come into being, as if God's saying and making are one (1:7). "And it was so" (v. 7). God calls the dome "sky," and it was evening and morning, day two.

Day Three, 1:9-13

Two creative events take place on the third day, as they also will on the sixth day in another form of symmetry in the chapter. Here on day three, God both gathers the waters (1:9-10) and creates vegetation (1:11-13). Like darkness, waters existed before God spoke. When God commands them to gather in one place, dry land appears. God names the dry land "earth," and the gathered waters God calls "seas." God sees that the results are good.

On the same day, God speaks again: "Let the earth put forth vegetation" (v. 11). The dry land obeys and green things sprout, things that contain seeds, plants, and fruit trees of every kind bearing fruit. All of these appear in the first springtime of life. In a new element of the days, God sets reproductive powers into the structure of the growing things themselves in a great "greening" of the earth. [Hildegard of Bingen] God sees that it is good. Day three ends, evening and morning.

God Creates Inhabitants of the Cosmos, 1:14-31

After three days the cosmic habitat is ready for occupants, the living beings appear during the second set of three days. The things God creates on a given day stand upon previous acts of creation, so that nothing and no creature exists apart from the rest.

Creative Power of the Word: Jacob Lawrence's *Genesis Series*

Jacob Lawrence's *Genesis Series* (1990) describes a passage from the book of Genesis in the King James Version of the Bible. The series reflects Lawrence's youthful memories of passionate sermons about the Creation given by ministers at the Abyssinian Baptist Church in Harlem where he was baptized in 1932.

Jacob Lawrence (1917–2000) © ARS, NY. Eight Studies for the Book of Genesis. 1. *In the beginning, all was void*. 1989. Gouache on board. (Credit: The Jacob and Gwendolyn Lawrence Foundation / Art Resource, NY)

Jacob Lawrence (1917–2000) © ARS, NY. Eight Studies for the Book of Genesis. *3. And God said, "Let the earth bring forth the grass, trees, fruits, and herbs."* 1989. Gouache on board. (Credit: The Jacob and Gwendolyn Lawrence Foundation / Art Resource, NY)

Jacob Lawrence (1917–2000) © ARS, NY. Eight Studies for the Book of Genesis. 6. *And God created all the beasts of the earth*. 1989. Gouache on board. (Credit: The Jacob and Gwendolyn Lawrence Foundation / Art Resource, NY)

Because chapter 1 introduces Genesis, it also introduces everything biblical—the creation accounts (Gen 1–3), the Primeval History (Gen 1–11), the whole of Genesis (1–50), the entire Hebrew Bible or Old Testament, and the Christian Bible. The word of God that bursts forth in Genesis 1 is creative—it creates the cosmos, creates Israel, and creates the biblical books that follow.

This series of paintings by African-American artist Jacob Lawrence brings the theme of the powerful divine to life with amazing interpretive skill. In them, he depicts sermons by the famous preacher Adam Clayton Powell and other ministers from the Abyssinian Baptist Church in Harlem. The simplified figures of preacher and congregants are set against the backdrop of the church windows. In each painting the windows change according to the days of the Genesis account. The windows in the first painting are dark and blank. Each subsequent day depicts the creative events of that day brought into being by the power of the preacher's words. Lawrence implies that the preacher shares in and extends the power of God's word to bring forth form, beauty, and new life. Such is the intimidating and challenging task of preaching: to create the world anew.

Hildegard of Bingen

Although the twelfth-century Christian theologian, artist, and mystic Hildegard of Bingen did not directly quote Genesis, her symbolic theology echoes the creative power that God shares with vegetation and living beings in Genesis 1. She wrote in Latin to develop her insights about *viriditas*, the "greening" of all life. The absence of *viriditas* is *ariditas*, "aridity" or "barrenness." At the literal level, God sets *viriditas* or greening loose in creation. Symbolically, greening refers to the human body as a microcosm of the fertility of the cosmos. Beyond that, for Hildegard, the greening of the cosmos points to the presence of the Risen Christ in history and creation, and comes to fulfillment in the revelation of the cosmic Christ who brings all things together.

Hildegard's Christian ecological vision of the "greening" of the cosmos could never have been imagined by the composers of Genesis 1, but her thinking captures the power of creativity that God places within the world itself. Typical of medieval theology, she sees all reality to be multi-layered and overflowing with meanings that interrelate and build upon one another. Perhaps modern readers can borrow her sense of the interconnectedness of earth, human bodies, and the larger cosmos flowing together toward the God of life. Her language of the "greening" of the cosmos highlights the fluidity of boundaries between physical and spiritual, human and animal, vegetation and soil on which we all live together. In this sense, Hildegard provides an ecological ethic that accords well with Genesis 1.

For further reading, see Renate Craine, *Hildegard, Prophet of the Cosmic Christ* (New York: Crossroad, 1997) 75–78.

Saint Hildegard of Bingen (1098–1179). "The Four Seasons." From *De Operatione Dei*. Rupertsburg, Germany, 1200 CE. Codex Latinum 1942. Biblioteca Statale, Lucca, Italy. (Credit: Scala / Art Resource, NY)

Day Four, 1:14-19

"And God said, 'Let there be lights in the dome of the sky to separate the day from night.'" Yet God had already created light on the first day, independent of sun, moon, and stars (1:15). It might seem that ancient peoples were unaware that light comes from heavenly bodies, but the sparkling residents of the sky have other roles to play in addition to giving light (v. 15). They signify time and distinguish days, seasons, and years from one another. In this sense, they "rule" days and nights by controlling light and darkness and by heating and cooling land and seas. With the heavens populated, God sees that it is good. It was evening and morning, day four.

Day Five, 1:20-22

Waters continue to play a role on day five. God commands them to reproduce by giving birth to swarms of living creatures and birds to fly across the dome of the sky. The once-empty seas and skies are suddenly alive with swimming creatures and flying creatures, including sea monsters, fish, and birds of every kind who dwell in the waters and the sky. Like vegetation, waters participate in the production of life, but something new also takes place on day five. God names reproduction itself as a blessing with this command: "Be fruitful and multiply and fill the waters of the seas and let birds multiply upon the earth" (v. 22). The blessing of swimming and flying creatures shows biological reproduction to be a participation in divine creativity that humans also share (cf. Gen 1:28; 9:1). The sea monsters and everything that moves share in divine fecundity, and God again sees goodness.

Day Six, 1:23-30

The sixth day, like the third, involves two creative acts, the making of animals and of humans. Again God enables created things to reproduce. God commands the earth to bring forth cattle, creeping things, and wild animals. Then God makes living creatures of every kind and sees that it is good (1:23-25).

God's second act on this last working day is to create humans (1:16-31). Because humans do not have their own day but share it with other animals and creeping things of all sorts, the text signals that humans are co-members of a larger community of life. Yet in the creation of humans, variations in the daily literary format are extensive. God speaks at length rather than in short commands, makes humans in the divine likeness, gives them dominion over other creatures, and speaks to an unidentified "us." Then the narrator reports the creation of humans and repeats the divine deliberation. Finally, after the addition of humans to the cosmos, God sees that it is "very good." The effect of these alterations and additions is to highlight the human creation and to single them out from other creatures:

> Then God said, "Let us make humankind in our image,
> According to our likeness,
> And let them have dominion over the fish of the sea,
> And over the birds of the air,
> And over the cattle,
> And over every creeping thing that creeps upon the earth" (1:26).

["Adam" Means "Human"]

"Adam" Means "Human"

AΩ "Adam" is not a proper name in this passage. The Hebrew word is a generic noun meaning humankind. It includes all human beings no matter their sex. The noun takes on the role of a personal name when the human names Eve at the end of the second creation account (3:20).

Heavenly Beings

Other divine beings besides God appear in Genesis. In the first creation account, God appeals to a heavenly community, perhaps a heavenly council (1:26). In Gen 1:28, the "we" whom God addresses may be the heavenly council. These are heavenly beings, lesser gods, or perhaps divine messengers or angels who surround God in the heavenly court. They appear also in Job 1–2 and in 1 Kings 22:19-23. A cherub, a heavenly angel, appears in Gen 3:24 with the task of barring the way to the tree of life and thereby ensuring that humans are not able to eat of the tree and live forever. In many other places, the Angel of the Lord appears to characters at important moments. The Angel of the Lord at first seems to be a heavenly messenger, but in Genesis it transforms into a manifestation of God's own self, revealed slowly over the course of events.

Trinitarian Language?

Some in the early Christian church interpreted the phrase "Let us make humans in our image" as anticipation of the Christian doctrine of three persons in God. Such a view rests on later dogmatic developments in Christian belief. Modern interpretations have rightly understood the text to be addressed to a specific historical audience in ancient Israel, not to later Christian believers. Of course, Christians can look back at the ancient texts and find meanings hidden there, but for the priestly composers of Genesis, the Trinity was not a known way of thinking about God.

Claus Westermann, *Genesis 1–11* (Minneapolis: Augsburg, 1984) 144.

The first change in the daily format is that God uses a first-person plural form of address ("us," "our") in forming a plan to create humans. To whom is God speaking? The text does not tell us. God may be speaking to other lesser gods or members of a heavenly council. [Heavenly Beings] Alternatively, God may be using the royal "we," that is, the formal speech of a king or other notable that adds solemnity to the words and underlines the speaker's authority. [Trinitarian Language?] Although the precise meaning of the plural forms is unclear, they have a strong literary effect. They draw attention to humans and set them apart from the creation of other beings.

The text highlights the creation of humans in other ways. They are the only creatures that God makes in the divine likeness. No others receive this honor, nor are any other creatures commissioned to have dominion over anything as humans are: "Let them have dominion over other living creatures, fish, birds, cattle, wild animals, and creeping things" (1:26, 28; cf. 1:22). Then the narrator draws still further attention to human creation by reporting the fulfillment of divine intentions:

So God created humankind in his image
In the image of God he created them
Male and female he created them (Gen 1:27).

This short verse says two more times that humans are somehow like God; they are created in the divine image; in the image of God, God created them.

But what does it mean for humans to be made in the divine image? Clearly, and against ancient cultural expectations of male dominance, male and female form equal parts of this creation. [Male and Female] Remarkably, men alone are not divinely created in God's image. Much biblical interpretation has sought to explain the exact nature of the divine image in humans. What sets humans apart from animals, fish, and vegetation in the image of God? Is it

Male and Female

 The cultures of the ancient Near East largely set men and women apart in dualistic understandings of sex and gender roles. Males were nearly universally persons of privilege, power, and authority in a hierarchical arrangement. The patriarch presided over lower-status men, women, and slaves. Women had important roles in the maintenance and survival of the family, but the family was patrilineal, that is, women joined the man's household, households were identified with the authority of the father, and women were generally dependent on fathers, husbands, or sons for economic survival (see Berquist, Zsolnay, and Grabill).

Nor has equality of identity between male and female creatures always been assumed in the history of biblical interpretation. In Christian tradition, Augustine recognized that human nature itself is made in the image of God, but he believed that the woman alone is not in God's image, yet the man alone is. She is in the divine image only when joined to him. Thomas Aquinas agreed and went further. In his opinion, since God made man first, man is the glory of God, while woman is the glory of man (see Lucas, 5–7). These views are but a tiny sampling of a long interpretive tradition that is still being challenged and corrected in the twenty-first century.

Jon L. Berquist, "Family Structures: Hebrew Bible," 1:199–205; Ilona Zsolnay, "Gender and Sexuality: Ancient Near East," 1:275–87; and Rhiannon Grabill, "Male-Female Sexuality: Hebrew Bible," 445–50, in *The Oxford Encyclopedia of the Bible and Gender Studies*, ed. Julia M. O'Brien (Oxford/New York: Oxford University Press, 2014).

Angela M. Lucas, *Women in the Middle Ages: Religion, Marriage, and Letters* (New York: St. Martin's, 1983).

---

maleness and femaleness together, walking upright, the capacity to speak, to think, to choose, to love, to procreate, to act in free will, to form a covenant?

The composers of Genesis leave this question completely open. [Image of God] What they do insist upon is that all humans share some divine-like quality, some participation in the life of the deity. Humans are images, icons, reflections that reveal something of God, perhaps the way an artistic image reflects the subject portrayed in it. The text implies, suggests, and points toward the

---

Image of God

The creation of humans in God's image and likeness is a prominent interpretive crux. Genesis uses this language in 1:26-28; 5:3; and 9:6. From these texts we can conclude that male and female humans alone among God's creatures are made in the divine image and that this iconic status grants humans unique dignity. The text does not explain the meaning of this status, and subsequent interpretation has attempted to become more precise about it. Noreen L. Herzfeld has provided a helpful summary of three interpretive approaches: substantive, functional, and relational. The substantive notion holds that humans are like God in their substance, that is, in their ability to reason. "In all Christian writers up to Aquinas we find the image of God conceived of as man's [sic] power to reason" (16). This view draws on Augustine's broad interpretation of reason as including "memory, understanding, and will." Reinhold Niebuhr follows this understanding by pointing to human self-consciousness and ability to transcend themselves. (See Herzfeld's discussion of works by Neibuhr, von Rad, and Barth, 10–32.)

The functional understanding of humans made in the image of God arises from God's commission for the humans to have dominion. Gerhard von Rad articulated the view that humans act on earth as God's agents and function like regents in God's place.

Finally, Karl Barth believed that the plural speech used by the Creator, "Let us create humans in our image," points to the divine relationship within God's self and with humans, but see [Trinitarian Language?].

While each of these interpretations has some theological appeal, the text supports none of them. Nowhere does Genesis explain what it means that humans are made in God's image. For this reason, I think the purpose of the claim is to insist on human dignity for all humans. It is poetic and evocative in its intentions, insisting on shared human worthiness without definition. In this regard, the effect is not unlike the statement in 2:5 that God breathed into Adam's nostrils "the breath of life."

Noreen L. Herzfeld, *In our Image: Artificial Intelligence and the Human Spirit* (Theology and the Sciences; Minneapolis: Fortress, 2002). Also see pp. 10–32.

Imago Dei

That humans are at the top of the hierarchic arrangement of creation seems indisputable from this passage. The assertion that all human life is of the utmost importance reverences human life and grants dignity to everyone, from the loftiest to the most vulnerable, shunned, and demeaned of people. At the same time, the belief that humans are made in the divine image has become an excuse for the violation and despoliation of the earth and its others denizens, as if the text gives humans divinely approved freedom to destroy the earth and its non-human creatures at will. This interpretation contributes to the current ecological crisis (see Habel, 1:29).

Such a view, however, ignores others elements of the text. A more inclusive, less agonistic way of seeing human relationship with the earth is possible. According to Ellen Davis, instead of teaching conquest and submission, the hierarchical relationships in the text envision a chain of being, a set of relationships in which humans participate with the rest of the created beings. It is within this chain of relationships that humans, whose lives are "of inestimable value," live and are able to find food (Gen 1:29; Davis, 57).

Norman C. Habel, *Readings from the Perspective of Earth, The Earth Bible* (Sheffield, UK: Sheffield Academic Press, 2000). Also see his *The Land Is Mine: Six Biblical Land Ideologies* (OBT; Minneapolis: Fortress, 1995).

Ellen C. Davis, *Scripture, Culture, and Agriculture: Agrarian Readings of the Bible* (Cambridge UK: Cambridge University Press, 2009).

mysterious, unknowable, ineffable quality of human life without explaining exactly what that is. While it asserts that humans made in the divine image have immense dignity, it simultaneously invites readers to probe, reflect, and imagine how every single human is an image of God and to affirm that it is so. [*Imago Dei*]

The human vocation to fill the earth, "to subdue it," and have "dominion over" other creatures is a vocation of relationship "to every living thing that moves on the earth" (1:28). [Have Dominion and Subdue] Then God gives plants and fruit with seeds to humans to be their food, and to all the other living creatures God gives green plants (1:29-30). Animals, fish, and birds are not part of the human diet, and the animals in turn eat only of green plants.

This exquisitely composed account gives honor and dignity to humans, male and female, but not as isolated, dominating creatures to lord it over the rest of the created world. Even as this hymn of praise singles out humans alone as made in the divine image, the very literary structures of the chapter integrate humans with other beings, making them part of each other and dependent on one another. The verbal repetitions, the linking

Have Dominion and Subdue

The divine commission to have dominion over the earth has brought a great deal of controversy in contemporary times because it has been used as permission to exploit, rape, and harm the earth and its creatures for human aggrandizement and greed. The two verbs in question, "to have dominion" and "to subdue," accurately convey the Hebrew. Humans are charged with rulership over other creatures and are to subdue the earth. Without question, humans have found in this passage a divine warrant for violent subjection of other creatures and mindless misuse of the earth. We have seen ourselves as God's special agents, centers of the universe, governors of and separated from all that is. From this perspective, creation is utterly subservient to humans who freely dominate and destroy it. Yet many

features of Genesis 1 and of other texts qualify that assumption, including the fact that humans do not have their own day of creation but share it with other animals (Tull, 15–29).

In the ancient world, the difficulties of acquiring food from the ground and living with animals would surely have required some forms of conquest. The text may reflect the difficulties of agriculture in the dry lands (Gen 3:17-19).

For further reading, see Ellen F. Davis, *Scripture, Culture, and Agriculture: An Agrarian Reading of the Bible* (Cambridge UK; Cambridge University Press, 2007) 53–65; and Norman C. Habel, *The Land Is Mine: Six Biblical Land Ideologies* (OBT; Minneapolis: Fortress, 1995).

Patricia K. Tull, "Jobs and Benefits in Genesis 1 and 2," in *After Exegesis Feminist Biblical Theology: Essays in Honor of Carol A Newsom*, ed. Patricia K. Tull and Jacqueline E. Lapsley (Waco TX: Baylor University Press, 2015).

of events on days one to three with events on days four to six, the fact that all creation occurs in the one block of time of a single week, plus God's summarizing appraisal that all things are good contribute to the recognition that creation is organically united, a wondrous whole, a living organism of interrelated beings. From this flow ethical consequences. We cannot survive if we do not live in harmony with the world around us. We cannot sustain our life without the thriving life of plants and animals, of soil and water, of sea and air.[4] Our uniqueness in the cosmos results in responsibility for respect and stewardship.

At the end of the sixth day, "God saw everything that he had made, and indeed it was very good" (1:31). God looks upon creation in its orderliness, its increasing complexity, its celestial, biological, and human components, each located in their proper place, and declares it all to be very good. [Goodness] Creation is good; the earth is good; animals, birds, trees, and plants are good. The humans, made in the divine image, are good. Everything is very good. Yet there is still one more day left in this creative week.

Goodness

When God sees that creation is "very good," the text offers no definition of goodness (Gen 1:31). At the least, the reader can know that creation is not in itself evil. Beyond that, what is good? I do not think we can settle the matter, but the history of interpretation includes many approaches to the topic. Augustine, for one, claimed that while individual created things are good, the entire creation together is very good:

> For if prudent observers consider the single works of God, they find that individually in their own species, they have praiseworthy measures, numbers, and orders. How much more then will this be true of them together, that is of the universe that is filled with these individual things gathered into a unity. For every beauty that is composed of parts is much more praiseworthy in the whole than in the part. (Louth, 43)

In this reflection, Augustine does not limit interpretation to one meaning but elsewhere affirms that God's own self is the "primal good" and that creation and created things are similar to God who created them in power and wisdom; some things are like God by the simple fact that they are alive (see Louth, 44).

Later, Ambrose affirms that creation reveals God, for God's goodness is evident in the divine works (see Louth, 44).

The goodness of creation is not a fixed or static reality, and the blanket statement of Genesis that God sees everything as good invites reflection. All of creation is good, and all is worthy of respect and appreciation by humans who are part of it. The text invites ecological awareness, a recognition that we too are part of the living organism that is the cosmos.

William Brown has noted that God sees goodness in creation six times in the course of Genesis 1, and so it is not limited to or dependent on humankind. It includes the structure and order of creation and above all refers to creation as the cosmic temple, the sacred place of worship that includes all living things and our habitat (pp. 235–36).

For the book's ancient audience in the early Persian Period, God's assertion that the creation is very good is of immense import. God created all things and will continue to create them as a people. That too is goodness.

Augustine, *Two Books on Genesis Against the Manichaeans*, I.21.32, quoted in *ACCS*, Old Testament I, Genesis 1–11, ed. Andrew Louth (Downers Grove IL: Intervarsity Press, 2001).

William P. Brown, *A Handbook to Old Testament Exegesis* (Louisville KY: Westminster John Knox, 2017).

**Jewish and Christian
Interpretations of the Seventh Day**

Traditionally, Jewish interpretation has understood the climax of the first creation account to be seventh day, whereas Christians have found the high point to be the creation of humans and the seventh day to be a denouement, the rest that brings events to the end. Yet it is not necessary to decide between these two perspectives, for they represent different interpretive traditions developed within two communities of faith over many centuries of life and practice. The text itself, however, drives toward the Sabbath day: "The seventh day is the Lord's day through which all the creativity of the preceding days achieves fulfillment" (14). God celebrates the Sabbath, inviting audience and readers to do the same. To do so in liturgical form brings the community together both in rest from labor and in worship of the Creator. Christians have made Sunday the Lord's Day, the first day of the week in commemoration of Easter, itself seen as the first day of the new creation in the Risen Christ.

Nahum M. Sarna, *Genesis* (JPS Torah Commentary; Philadelphia: The Jewish Publication Society, 1989) 14.

God Rests, 2:1-4a

Each day of God's labors, with small variations, follows the same general linguistic structure until the creation of humans when the change in format marks humans as the climax of creation. The seventh day, however, concludes the week with the biggest structural and linguistic variation of all. The seventh day is a day unto itself.

The narrator first summarizes events of the previous days: "The heavens, the earth and their multitudes were finished" (2:1). The multitudes of living creatures, absent from the summary statement that began chapter 1 (1:1), are present now and filling the earth. Even though God rests from all the work, creation is not over on the seventh day. Creation and blessing are of a different order from the previous days; God creates and blesses the seventh day itself, the Sabbath day. God blesses, hallows, and makes sacred the seventh day; then God rests from all labor of creation. The Sabbath is also God's creation.

Chapter 1 builds up to the seventh day as the grand conclusion of the creative acts of God. [Jewish and Christian Interpretations of the Seventh Day] The blessing of a sacred and hallowed day means that God invents and authorizes the Sabbath day, the day of rest from labor and the day of worship and praise. On that day, humans praise God and worship God apart from the days of intense labor over the course of the week.

In the blessing of the seventh day, the priestly composers of Genesis reveal their intentions. God institutes the Sabbath. The text credits God with the origins of the Sabbath, the day when the people of Israel gather to worship the Creator, to remember their identity as God's people, and to renew their relationship with their God that forms them into a people. [The Seventh Day]

CONNECTIONS

Human Dignity

If the exact ways humans represent the divine image and are "made in the image and likeness of God" were the point of the passage, it

---

The Seventh Day

The seventh day of creation (Gen 2:1-4a) provides an account of origins for the commandment to "remember the Sabbath day and keep it holy" (Exod 20:8-11). That the first creation account of Genesis concludes with God celebrating a divine Sabbath encourages the scattered community of Judah to practice it, to take action, to join together in what matters most—the worship of God. The Sabbath liturgy not only brings people together but also serves as *a symbolic act of social construction* (Balentine, 90, italics in original). That means that liturgy can change participants. Ritual can unite them, encourage faith, and bring order to the world as it also "repairs and restores" order where it is absent (Balentine, 90). By lifting people temporarily into a transcendent reality, liturgical ritual can reconstitute them as a community. It renews them as people created by God and brings to life the Creator who is recreating them.

For further reading, see Samuel E. Balentine, The *Torah's Vision of Worship* (OBT; Minneapolis: Fortress, 1999).

---

would probably be clearer about it. What is clear from these verses is the divine assertion that humans—all humans—possess a particular dignity, a divine-like quality belonging to them alone among God's creatures. At the same time, humans are one with animals and integrated into the rest of creation. God blesses them as God blesses swarming fish, and commands them also "to be fruitful and multiply and to fill the earth." Like the animals to which they are integrally joined, humans are to continue divine creativity by procreating and filling the earth. The passage ascribes to them honor and dignity and presents them with a unique role in the cosmos, but not as isolated beings. [The Sanctity of the Black Body]

Creation and Survival

Within the seven-day arrangement, the heavens, the earth, and their inhabitants come into being simply because God speaks. For the audience during the Persian Period (see the Introduction to this commentary), the opening chapter of Genesis invites them to remember who they are, to accept their dignity as human creatures invited to join in praise of their Creator, and to gather again as God's people in the midst of all creation. The text points more than anything to the wondrous power of their God, the God who created the world, who took the waste and void and gave it order, beauty, and life. It is this God whom they are to worship on the Sabbath. This God created everything that is. This God merely speaks to create, and this God gives to live creatures the creative power to reproduce.

These claims are precisely what the audience of Genesis needs to survive the nation's fall. Those who have survived those days, along with their offspring, bear memories of death, destruction, and humiliation. Displaced and fearful, their future as a people is

The Sanctity of the Black Body

American journalist and memoirist Ta-Nehesi Coates has written a public letter to his son about his experience of being a black man growing up in a white, racist society. With fiercely powerful writing, he tells his son of the dignity of blackness in a society where their own black bodies endanger their lives. Coates resists religious language, yet as he speaks from inside the suffering caused by white racism, he evokes Genesis 1's exaltation of all human life made in the divine image. He reflects on Malcolm X's injunction that blacks must protect their lives:

"Don't give up your life, preserve your life," he would say. "And if you got to give it up, make it even steven." This was not boasting—it was a declaration of equality rooted not in better angels or the intangible spirit but in the sanctity of the black body. You preserved your life because your life, your body, was good as anyone's, because your blood was precious as jewels, and it should never be sold for magic, for

spirituals inspired by the unknowable hereafter. You do not give your precious body to the billy clubs of Birmingham sheriffs nor to the insidious gravity of the streets. Black is beautiful—which is to say the black boy is beautiful, that black hair must be guarded against the torture of processing and lye, that black skin must be guarded against bleach, that our noses and mouths must be guarded against modern surgery. We are all our beautiful bodies and so must never be prostrate before barbarians, must never submit our original self, our one of one, to defiling and plunder.

When Coates expresses the dignity of the black body from within the African-American experience in the United States, he provides insight from one community of suffering about what it means to be made in the image of God.

Ta-Nehesi Coates, *Between the World and Me* (New York: Spiegel & Grau, 2015) 35–36.

uncertain even in the Persian Period (see "The Crisis that Gave Rise to the Book of Genesis" in the Introduction above). Within a community that has lost nearly everything through wars and imperial oppression, the text's assertions of human dignity grants them honor, reminders of the divinely given power to reproduce that is shared with all creation, the command to be fruitful and multiply—these resonate with their deepest needs and promise them a future. The text's conclusion on the seventh day of hallowed rest provides a communal practice to bring the divided community together and to worship the God who can recreate them.

NOTES

1. Verse 2:4a, "These are the generations of the heavens and the earth when they were created," is ambiguous. Does it serve as an ending to the first creation account, or does it introduce the second account (2:4b–3:25)?

2. Translation of Everett Fox, *The Five Books of Moses* (Schocken Bible; Dallas: Word, 1995) 11.

3. Walter Brueggemann, *Genesis* (IBC; Louisville: Westminster John Knox, 2010) 30.

4. For further reading, see William P. Brown, *A Handbook to Old Testament Exegesis* (Louisville KY: Westminster John Knox, 2017) 229–45.

CREATION BY DEED

Genesis 2:4b-25

A second story of creation follows the first and differs from it in a number of ways. [Ancient Near Eastern Creation Accounts] This version, a drama in prose narrative, appears in two acts that take place in the Garden of Eden (Gen 2:4b–2:25 and 3:1-24). [Relationships between the Two Creation Accounts] The first act of the drama opens on a barren landscape that blossoms into an oasis, an island utopia where creation exists in interconnected, balanced relationships (2:4b-25). The first act prepares for the second act that depicts the gradual unraveling of the peaceful relationships established in this chapter.

Conflict and disharmony occur in the garden because humans disobey the divine prohibition against eating from the tree of knowledge. Despite much subsequent theological tradition, however, these two chapters never use vocabulary of sin. That language appears for the first time only in chapter 4 when Cain murders his brother Abel. Curiosity drives the infraction and yields painful consequences. Yet human willfulness in the garden is clearly at odds with the divine prohibition against eating of the tree, even if the deed is not labeled as sinful. The drama ends when God casts the humans out of the garden into pain, suffering, and the perils of mortal existence.

In subtle ways, the garden story evokes the historical catastrophe of the Judean people in the Babylonian Period and after (see Introduction, "Warfare, Disaster, Trauma, and Their Effects"). Indirectly it calls to mind the near death of Judah and the doubtful

Ancient Near Eastern Creation Accounts

The people of Israel lived in the midst of ancient cultures that had their own multiple creation accounts, and Israel borrowed from those stories. The borrowings probably occurred from general cross-cultural conversations and local knowledge of neighbors' stories rather than directly from written texts (Hays, 69). See [Oral Traditions]. Nevertheless, some texts from Babylon, Egypt, and other places do exist and provide evidence of similarities and differences with Israel's stories of creation.

The Babylonian *Enuma Elish*, for example, is a theogony, that is, a story of the origins of the gods themselves. In this case, the universe preexisted the gods who were formed by the union of Apsu, the watery chaos, and Tiamat, the mother goddess who gave birth to them all. The gods fought among one another and one of them, Marduk, slayed Tiamat and split her body in two to make the heavens and the earth. In Genesis 1, by contrast, the cosmos emerges peacefully by the power of the divine word, while in Genesis 2 creation occurs slowly and peacefully by the power of divine actions. Biblical versions of creation both borrowed from and altered ancient Near Eastern creation stories. Israel borrowed from and changed the Babylonian account to build their identity in relation to the one God YHWH.

Christopher B. Hays, *Hidden Riches: A Sourcebook for the Comparative Study of the Hebrew Bible and the Ancient Near East* (Louisville KY: Westminster John Knox, 2014). See the detailed study of these texts and comparison with Genesis on pp. 41–73.

Relationships between the Two Creation Accounts

Common themes join the two versions of beginnings that introduce Genesis. Both Gen 1:1–2:4a and 2:4b–3:24 tell of the beginnings of life. Both present God as the Creator. Both portray a world of beauty and interconnection among all created beings. Both portray humans as uniquely related to God among all creatures. Finally, both make humans responsible for and in service to the rest of creation.

Reading the chapters sequentially might suggest that the first account of seven days of creation presents the beginnings of the cosmos, while the second focuses on the creation of humanity, as if it were zooming in on the sixth day of creation reported in Genesis 1. Yet differences between the two versions show that the stories come from two different sources, now connected by the book's composers.

These differences include the use of different names for God. In the first chapter God is called Elohim (*'ĕlōhîm*), the general Semitic name for God. In the second account, God is called YHWH God, the specific name of Israel's God revealed to Moses at the burning bush (Exod 3:14). The deity in the first account is a transcendent, hidden Other portrayed primarily as One who speaks and performs limited actions that produce creation. In the second account, God is anthropomorphic—that is, human-like—immersed physically in the process, taking the roles of an artisan, a surgeon, a scientist, and a stroller in the garden. The Lord God performs physical deeds and experiments to find a partner that is right for the human. The literary style and genre of the two versions of creation also sharply differentiate them from one another. Gen 1 is a tightly structured hymn to the God of creation, whereas Gen 2–3 is prose narrative, containing only brief poetic passages at key moments in the story.

Together, however, these differing approaches to beginnings introduce important themes of the book. Genesis begins with a magnificent claim that the God who brings life to the world and gives birth to Israel is neither a limited local god, nor the god of one nation, nor weak and powerless. The God of Gen 1 brings all things into being merely by speaking. The second account underscores sexuality as a divinely ordained gift to humankind that by implication will ultimately yield offspring. The fulfillment of God's promises of offspring is in one sense the goal of Genesis, for the children become evidence of the fulfillment of God's fidelity to Abraham (12:1-3) and, hence, to the audience.

The two accounts have different but related theological goals. Gen 1 assures Judah/Israel that the word of their God is more than reliable; it is potent and creative beyond human imagining. It brings all things into being and so will create them anew. The second account (Gen 2–3) assures Judah/Israel that they will not disappear among the nations despite their present reality of conflict, loss, and the threat of death that characterizes not only life in a world but also their very life as a people.

nature of its future. In that sense it "refracts trauma."[1] (See [Trauma and Disaster Studies].) The first man and woman live in paradise, but because they are disobedient, God casts them out into a dangerous world. Yet the couple survives because God helps them and cares for them, and life begins anew. This drama, along with the rest of Genesis, invites the book's audience to trust this God who enables survival and creates new beginnings so that they might begin again. [Disaster Stories in Genesis]

COMMENTARY

Act One: Harmony in the Garden

Genesis 2 sets the scene, introduces characters, and foreshadows events that occur in the following chapter. Unlike the poetic hymn

Disaster Stories in Genesis

The Garden story sets out a narrative of catastrophe, death, and survival. It begins with the creation of a peaceful time and place, a golden era when everything is provided and exists in quiet harmony. Human disobedience brings that world to an end; the first couple faces death, but even after being cast out, they survive because God cares for them. The basic elements of this plot appear again and again in various episodes of the book of Genesis. Every time the end of life for the people, the family, or the children of Abraham is at hand, survivors live because God intervenes for them in some unexpected fashion.

These stories include the murder of Abel by his brother Cain (4:1-16), Noah and the flood (chs. 6–9), the destruction of Babel (11:1-9), the casting out of Hagar and Ishmael (chs. 16 and 21), the destruction of Sodom (18:16–19:21), the near death of Isaac (ch. 22), and the many threats to Jacob especially from his brother Esau (chs. 25–33). These and other near-death events bring the characters to the point of extinction through violent means, yet every single time divine intervention enables survival and new beginnings. Although these strange episodes exhibit a great deal of variety, the general pattern of violent threat, divine intervention, and survival of a remnant appears in each.

Because, in veiled form, these stories reflect the disasters experienced during the Babylonian Period, they bring hope to the book's Judean audience. (See Introduction, [Trauma and Disaster Studies] and [Famines].) Survivors of traumatic violence typically need to reenter past catastrophes again and again, slowly, indirectly, partially, gradually, and perhaps for generations. These stories help the people slowly to come to terms with what has happened to their parents and grandparents, to give chaotic events shape and form, and to interpret them. Events in such stories call to mind their memories without repeating their experiences literally and driving them back into traumatic violence. They tell the "truth at a slant" (Frost, in Benfey, 49) and set it at a distance, as if on a screen and happening to someone else from the ancient past. In this way they avoid re-traumatizing the community and help it gradually move forward into life.

Catastrophe stories can help in further ways. They present causes for the violent events that place responsibility on the humans in some fashion. Some portray God as the Punisher who brings on the disaster. Such theology enables survival. Victims of traumatic violence need interpretations to help them go forward in life. Without an explanation, the world would be unlivable; a world of complete chaos leaves people paralyzed by fear and impossibility. That God appears as the Punisher is an effort to make sense of the senseless. It is not, however, a thoroughgoing understanding of the Holy One; it is not a theology that fully reveals the Divine. It is, instead, a "momentary stay against confusion" (Frost), that is, an effort to interpret the situation in a way that interprets divine involvement human life.

For further reading on biblical texts as literature of survival, see Kathleen M. O'Connor, *Jeremiah: Pain and Promise* (Minneapolis: Fortress, 2011) and Brad E. Kelle et al., eds., *Interpreting Exile, Displacement, Deportation in Biblical and Modern Contexts* (AIL 10; Atlanta: SBL, 2011).

Robert Frost, "The Figure a Poem Makes" (1939, quoted by Christopher Benfey, "The Storm over Robert Frost," *The New York Review of Books*, 4 December 2008).

of praise that forms the first creation account (1:1–2:4a), this version of beginnings in prose narrative uses short poetic elements for emphasis (2:23; 3:14-19). To be a proper story, a narration requires a conflict, a problem, or some difficulty to be overcome or goal to be achieved in an unfolding plot. The tension made by the difficulty raises curiosity and draws readers into events to find out what might happen. Like most good stories, chapter 2 introduces a scene, a problem arises, tension mounts, and finally resolution is reached. [Outline of Genesis 2]

The first act of the second creation account establishes a world in perfect harmony, a garden paradise where all live together in organic unity. Only the mention of two forbidden trees—a foreshadowing of the next chapter—hints at a mysterious and dangerous reality beyond.

God Plants a Garden, 2:4b-9

An introductory statement hints that readers are entering a different understanding of beginnings from that in chapter 1. Chapter 2 mentions only one day rather than seven: "In the day that God made the heavens and the earth" (Gen 2:4b). Other differences between the two versions of events appear in the next verse. Rather than opening on a formless void, watery energy, and darkness of the deep, chapter 2 begins in a barren desert, and rather than say what is already there, the narrator reports what is missing from the landscape. There is no plant, no herb, no rain, and no one to till the ground. The reason for this lifeless void is that "the LORD God had not yet caused rain to fall upon the earth" (v. 5; English Bibles use LORD instead of YHWH). A further clue that the chapter provides a different version of creation from chapter 1 is that God has a different name, the "LORD God" (YHWH *elohim*), not simply "God" (*elohim*) as in chapter 1. [Names of God in Genesis]

Action begins when a stream mysteriously rises and waters the whole face of the ground, altering the lifeless terrain. Only now does the LORD God set to work, not with words as in chapter 1 but with hands-on actions. "Then the LORD God formed the human (*hā'ādām*) from the dust of the ground" (*hā'ādāmāh*) (2:7). More like a Divine Workman than a Heavenly Speaker, the Lord God sculpts, cuts, forms, and builds the first human. Humanity rather than the whole cosmos is the focus of this version of events (1:3). [Adam the Human]

Attention to the Hebrew of the text brings out the clever artistry of the story with its frequent use of wordplay. [Wordplay in the Garden] God creates the human (*hā'ādām*) from the dust of the ground (*hā'ādāmāh*). Hebrew wordplay conveys more than the music and amusement made by similar sounds and spellings of words. The play on words subtly underscores connections among people and things in the garden. The fact that Adam is taken from the dust of the ground, for example, links him to the ground from which he is taken, which he will soon till, upon which he will depend for food and nourishment, and to which he will finally return (3:19).

Yet the human is not simply a sculpted two-legged creature made solely from the ground. The breath of life, an essential ingredient added to the other raw material, animates him. To make the

Names of God in Genesis

AΩ One cannot read too far into Genesis before encountering different names for the deity. In the first creation account (1–2:4a), God is called *elohim*, the general Semitic term for God, while in the second creation story (2:4b–3:24), God is most often called YHWH *elohim*, or the Lord God. English translations can be deceiving, simply translating a multiplicity of Hebrew terms into the single English word, "God."

The use of various names for the divine in the book led scholars to distinguish one literary source from another (see [Documentary Theory of Composition]). In other words, various names of God suggest the presence of multiple sources on the assumption that writers from various times and places called God by different names. The use of YHWH (or YHWH *elohim*) is an especially important signifier of source theory because God does not self-identify as YHWH until Exod 3:14-15, yet the second creation story uses the name freely to describe the Creator (Gen 2:4b–3:24). The different names have been used in the past to distinguish the J and E sources from one another, but it is no easy task to differentiate J source from E source on this or any other basis, hence the contemporary preferences for

referring to P (priestly source) and non-P. The P source regularly utilizes the term *el/elohim* to name God. Other names for God include "God Almighty" or "God the Almighty" (*el shaddai*); God who sees (*el roi*, Gen 16:13); Everlasting God (*el olam*, 21:33); God of heaven/God of earth (*elohi hashmayim/elohi haaretz*, 24:3, 7), and more.

One theological consequence of this multiplicity of divine names is that neither any single term nor any single experience is adequate to describe God. The multiplicity of names in Genesis encourages reflection on the often narrow limits of our language for worship. Using the same few names all the time in prayer, worship, and theology places limits on God and closes down possibilities of other ways of knowing God who remains beyond all language.

Muslims can teach us appropriate humility before the Divine. One practice holds that God has 100 hundred names, but we only know ninety-nine of them. None contain God and there is even more to know, but we do not know. Similarly, Jews often refuse to say the name of God, sometimes using "The Name," or G-D, or Adonai (my lord) in place of the name revealed to Moses. These traditions respect the inability of language to fully express experiences of God who transcends all human speech.

human a living being, the Lord God "breathed into his nostrils the breath of life" (2:7). Humans, therefore, possess the breath of life because God breathes it into them. This breath of life distinguishes them from animals though it does not make them gods. Instead, it affirms in poetic language a special place in creation and relationship with the Creator. Humans contain both the earth itself and the pulsing life of the Creator. Whereas the first creation account announces that humans are made in the divine image (1:28), the second also grants humans special status using different imagery.

Adam the Human

AΩ The creation of humanity frames the chapter. The Lord God begins creation by forming the first human and concludes it by creating the woman. Humanity rather than the cosmos is the chapter's main concern. The Hebrew noun "adam" with the article "the" (*hāʾādām*) simply means "human" or "humankind." Adam becomes the personal name of the first male (*ʾîš*) at the end of the chapter when God differentiates the sexes (2:23). To keep the focus on humanity, I refer to the first human as the human, the earthling, or the groundling. That word "human" accurately translates the Hebrew and emphasizes the common identity of all human beings, no matter the

sex, race, or ethnic origins. Women, among others, care about this interpretation because it recognizes that they are not a divine afterthought, a concession in the service of male needs for companionship and assistance. In light of women's oppression throughout history and across the globe today, this is a helpful distinction. Yet it seems unlikely to me that the ancient storytellers actually thought in this way, since maleness was judged to be the dominant form of humanity, while femaleness has been considered secondary, a lesser creation. Still, the Hebrew term does mean "humanity," not male person. The Lord God creates humanity and then diversifies it.

Wordplay in the Garden

AΩ   Wordplay is a frequently used literary device of the Garden story and of other passages in Genesis, but it is hard to translate into English. Hebrew words play on one another through spelling and sound across the two chapters:

• The man (*hā'ādām*) is made from the dust of the ground (*hā'ādām*).
• The woman (*'iššāh*) is made from the man (*'iš*) or, in one version, her man (*'iššāh*, 2:23).
• The couple is naked (*'arummîm*, 2:25) and the serpent is clever (*'arum*, 3:1).
• Eve (*ḥayyāh*) is the mother of the living (*ḥay*, 3:20).

Listeners to and readers of the Hebrew may have found the frequent repetition of similar sounds amusing. At the least, though, the wordplays signal how carefully crafted and artistic this ancient story is, while they also point to the interrelated nature of creatures in the Garden. Wordplay is a literary instrument used here to express a theology of interconnection among God's creatures. Wordplay connects humans to the ground from which they come, the naked couple to the clever animal, and the woman to her offspring. The literary device shows that God created a closely joined world.

Humans, "groundlings" or "earthlings,"[2] live because God breathes life into them, something that does not happen with other creatures. Humans are not God; they remain human, but God creates a special relationship with them by breathing life into their nostrils.

After forming the human, the Lord God plants a garden as a habitat and puts the earthling there among trees of all kinds. Trees are key elements of the second creation account—sources of beauty, shade, nourishment, and also of the taboo that becomes important in chapter 3. Of all the trees, the narrator gives particular importance to two: the tree of life and the tree of the knowledge of good and evil. Mysteriously named, the trees appear briefly here, twice in chapter 2 (vv. 8, 16-17), both times foreshadowing events in the next act where they take on potent ambiguity. [Two Trees]

Rivers Surround the Garden, 2:1-14

Encircling the newly planted garden is a single river that divides into four rivers. It might be tempting to read through theses verses quickly, since their description is like a parenthesis that interrupts the action of the story. Yet they affect the plot of the drama because their presence turns the garden into an island apart, an oasis surrounded by rivers on all four sides. Two of the four rivers, the Tigris and the Euphrates, provide geographical concreteness to the location of garden because they are known. Yet the other two, the Pishon and the Gihon, exist only in the story, giving mythic dimensions to this island oasis. The garden is at once of the earth and not of it. Perhaps even more important, water is the *sine qua non* of life in the desert-like region of the ancient Near East (contemporary Middle East), and it is always in short supply. To create a paradise in such typography is to imagine a lush oasis, a verdant island in a mythic world.

Two Trees

The most obvious feature of the trees in Gen 2–3 is that they are mysterious. The first mystery concerns the number of trees, since the syntax of 2:9 is unclear. The narrator reports that "the tree of life stands in the midst of the garden, and the tree of knowledge of good and evil." That sounds like two, but the tree of knowledge of good and evil may be a second attribute of the tree of life. Then God prohibits the human only from eating of "the tree of knowledge of good and evil" (2:17). In the next act, the woman refers to a prohibition against eating of the tree in the middle of the garden (3:3), as if there were only one forbidden tree. Later, after the couple eats fruit from the tree, God asks the man if he ate from the forbidden tree (3:10). At the end of the story, however, God fears that the humans may eat from the tree of life, as if that were distinct from the tree of knowledge (3:22-24).

The second mystery is the nature of the trees. The tree of knowledge of good and evil is symbolic (2:9, 17). "God knows good and evil, and humans attain that knowledge upon eating of the tree" (Fretheim, 350). Rather than representing sexual knowledge, or knowledge of evil itself, the knowledge the woman and man gain is of the limitations of human life. They gain wisdom and learn complexities of adult human life itself. (See chapter 3, Creation Unravels.) Hence, the tree symbolizes knowledge of limitations of life outside the paradisial garden. The tree of life (2:9, 22-24) symbolizes immortality. To eat of it would grant humans a world without death, like the shrub that Gilgamesh seeks in the Babylonian Epic of Gilgamesh.

The trees gain their meanings from their role in the story itself. They establish boundaries that the humans are not to pass. In eating the fruit, the couple gains wisdom but they never gain immortality. Of these, however, the tree of life alone reappears in the Old Testament in the wisdom book of Proverbs (3:18; 11:30; 13:12; 15:4). Woman Wisdom herself is identified with the tree of life, one to whom humans should cling to find happiness (3:18).

For further reading, see Claus Westermann, *Genesis 1–11: A Commentary* (Minneapolis: Augsburg, 1984) 211–15.

Terence E. Fretheim, "Genesis" (*NIB* 1; Nashville: Abingdon, 1994).

Adam Is Given Care of the Garden, 2:15-17

After the interlude about the rivers, the Lord God resumes creative action, putting the human in the garden with specific responsibilities to till and to care for it. The Hebrew word translated "to till" is actually a broader, more resonant word that means "to serve" (*'bad*). The earthling has a vocation to work, a commission to till the ground in respectful, close relationship with it, to labor as an act of service to the earth itself. The human is both laborer and protector who serves and "keeps the garden." [Work] Although the Lord God gives the human the work of caring for the garden, there are limits to human control, related to the tree mentioned in verse 9. The human is free to eat of every tree in the garden except for the tree of knowledge of good and evil, "for in the day that you eat of it you shall die" (2:17). With this ominous announcement of danger and threat, the narrative becomes more intriguing. The narrator has pointed to the tree of knowledge already (2:9), but now the Lord God forbids eating from it. Given the suspense building around the tree and the psychological reality that the forbidden becomes attractive, humans may be unable to avoid eating from it. In this chapter, however, only briefly does the divine prohibition interrupt the harmonious accord of paradise, again to anticipate things to come.

Work

In the Old Testament, work originates as a blessing closely associated with God. Such a view of work lies in stark contrast to Mesopotamian *Enuma Elish* that depicts labor as the result of a dispute among the gods who impose manual labor upon humankind as a form of slavery, or Atrahasis in which humans work so that the gods do not have to do the labor. In these texts, labor is punishment and subservient activity. In Genesis, though, human labor involves a vocation to stewardship, and the human serves the Garden as God's representative (Hays, 71).

The Bible does not differentiate manual from non-manual labor. At times, non-manual labor is burdensome (see Exod 18:13-27; Eccl 12:12b), and at other times, working with one's hands is understood to be an offering to God (Exod 35:20–36:7). Divine dignity infuses both human identity and human labor. The rhythms of work are set forth in light of the first creation narrative and involve rest on the seventh day (Gen 1:1–2:4a; Janzen, 121).

According to this chapter of Genesis, human labor is not only closely associated with God but also connects to the earth itself as a form of service to the ground. In an eschatological vision, Isaiah emphasizes this intimate interconnectedness as well as the blessing that ensues from a properly ordered world (Isa 65:21-23).

Since work is not punishment but an aspect of the human vocation, a gift of God to all humans, one implication is that all humans have a right to work, are called to work, and need to work, not as a punishment but as an essential part of being human. Modern concerns about labor are multiple. How can work be created to sustain individuals and families in their daily lives? How can work be found that enhances human dignity and builds community rather than demeaning it through various forms of slave labor and meaningless repetitive activities, or belittling human people and depleting them body and spirit?

For further reading see Christopher Hays, *Hidden Riches*, 41–73, and William P. Brown, "Whatever Your Hand Finds to Do: Qoheleth's Work Ethic," *Int* (July 2001): 271–84.

Christopher B. Hays, *Hidden Riches: A Sourcebook for the Comparative Study of the Hebrew Bible and the Ancient Near East* (Louisville KY: Westminster John Knox, 2014).

Waldemar Janzen, "The Theology of Work from an Old Testament Perspective," *The Conrad Grebel Review* 10 (1992).

A Problem Arises in the Garden, 2:18-23

The initial problem that arises in the garden is not yet about the tree. A difficulty appears that God alone notices, announces, and immediately sets about solving: "It is not good that the man [human] should be alone." Although the human has not noticed any lack, nor has yet spoken any words, God proposes a solution to the dilemma: "I will make him a helper as partner" (2:18). [Helper as Partner] To find the right partner for the human will require two attempts. The animals will not solve the problem; only the woman makes a fitting partner for this solitary creature.

Helper as Partner

The Hebrew word for "helper" (*'ēzār*) frequently specifies God as helper (Pss 33:20; 70:6; 115:19; 121:2; 124:8; 146:4; Exod 18:4; Deut 33:7, 26, 29; see Brown, 82 n.23). Highlighted by Phyllis Trible and echoed by many since then, the term does not subordinate the woman to the man but places her in a role similar to God (Trible, 90, n.13).

William P. Brown, *The Seven Pillars of Creation: The Bible, Science, and the Ecology of Wonder* (New York: Oxford University Press, 2010).

Phyllis Trible, *God and the Rhetoric of Sexuality* (OBT; Philadelphia: Fortress, 1978).

A. Animals Do Not Solve the Problem, 2:18-20. In the first divine search for a solution to human aloneness, the Lord God repeats the process used to create the human in the first place. God takes raw material from the ground to form animals and birds, and then, curious about the result, brings them to the human to see what he will name them. [Naming] The names that the human gives to living creatures become their names and join the human to them. [Mark Twain's Version] Yet "there was not found a helper as his partner" (2:20).

Although the creation of animals and birds does not yield a suitable partner for the human, the creatures do play a critical role in the narrative. The Lord God's unsuccessful effort to find a partner for the human delays the resolution of the problem, creates tension, builds expectation, and turns the actual solution into a dramatic climax. The delay also makes space for the arrival of new creatures in the garden. They may not be partners, but they are co-inhabitants of the garden, made from some of the same raw material as the human. Although God makes the animals and birds directly from the ground as God made Adam, they do not suit because

Naming

AΩ The capacity to name creatures involves the authority to designate in some sense their character, essence, or unique ways of being in the world, to interpret who and what they are. In that sense, when Adam names the animals and birds, he exercises a power over them, for the animals do not get to name him. Some have found in Adam's act of naming a catalyst for human exploitation of the earth and its creatures. Yet naming can also be an act of recognition and connection. Parents name children to connect them to themselves, to their ancestors, to their culture and society, and as acts of hope for the future. Horticulturalists name flowers to honor significant people or as symbols of particular historical events.

Names create relationships, establish linkages, and join people and things with one another. In some traditions, the one who names recognizes the essence or character of the thing or person being named and so establishes identity or realm of connection with the named. To name does not necessarily mean to subject or exploit. The namer knows who the creatures are, honors their identity, and lives in relationship with them.

Mark Twain's Version

In *The Diaries of Adam and Eve*, the great American humorist Mark Twain playfully reimagined the naming in the Garden of Eden. Eve speaks:

During the last day or two I have taken all the work of naming things off his hands, and this has been a great relief to him, for he has no gift in that line, and is evidently very grateful. He can't think of a rational name to save him, but I do not let him see that I am aware of his defect. Whenever a new creature comes along, I name it before he has time to expose himself by an awkward silence. In this way I have saved him many embarrassments. I have no defect like his. The minute I set eyes on an animal I know what it is. I don't have to reflect a moment; the right name comes out instantly, just as if it were an inspiration, as no doubt it is, for I am sure it wasn't in me half a minute before. I seem to know just by the shape of the creature and the way it acts what animal it is.

When the dodo came along he thought it was a wildcat—I saw it in his eye. But I saved him. And I was careful not to do it in a way that could hurt his pride. I just spoke up in a quite natural way of pleased surprise, and not as if I was dreaming of conveying information, and said, "Well, I do declare if there isn't the dodo!" I

explained—without seeming to be explaining—how I knew it for a dodo, and although I thought maybe he was a little piqued that I knew the creature when he didn't, it was quite evident that he admired me. That was very agreeable, and I thought of it more than once with gratification before I slept. How little a thing can make us happy when we feel we have earned it. (5)

Adam speaks:

Been examining the great waterfall. It is the finest thing on the estate, I think. The new creature calls it Niagara Falls—why, I am sure I do not know. Says it *looks* like Niagara Falls. That is not a reason; it is mere waywardness and imbecility. I get no chance to name anything myself. The new creature names everything that comes along, before I can get in a protest. And always the same pretext is offered—it *looks* like the thing. There is the dodo, for instance. Says the moment one looks at it one sees at a glance that it "looks like a dodo." It will have to keep that name, no doubt. It wearies me to fret about it, and does no good, anyway. Dodo! It looks no more like a dodo than I do. (31–33)

Mark Twain, *The Diaries of Adam and Eve*, ed. Shelley Fisher Fishkin (New York: Oxford University Press, 2010).

Breath of Life

AΩ "The uniqueness of the Hebrew phrase *nishmat xayyim* matches the singular nature of the human body, which, unlike the creatures of the animal world, is directly inspirited by God . . . ." Like humans being made in the divine image, the breath of life breathed by God is poetic language. It makes no claim that humans are even partly divine by nature, only that they are unique among creatures because God breathed life into them.

Nahum M. Sarna, *Genesis* (JPS Torah Commentary; Philadelphia: The Jewish Publication Society, 1989) 17.

another ingredient is missing. They do not receive the same "breath of life" that animates the human. The fact of origins from the ground unites the human with animals and birds, but non-human living creatures do not possess the breath of life in the same way as humans. [Breath of Life]

B. Woman Solves the Problem, 2:21-23. To ensure success on the second attempt to provide the human with a partner, the Lord God puts the human into a deep sleep, performs surgery on him, removes his rib (side), and then closes up his flesh. From this human body, God creates another human body, shaping human substance into a woman. There is no mistake this time, for God makes her from Adam's very body. She has his flesh and, like him, she too is animated by the breath of life given directly by God, for she is taken from his flesh that is already animated by the breath of life. She is "a helper corresponding to him."[3] God makes a partner for the first human by creating sexuality.

To see what will happen, God brings this new creature before the man. When Adam sees her, he bursts into speech for the first time. In poetry, he sings of his delight, "This at last is bone of my bone and flesh of my flesh" (2:25). Immediately, Adam recognizes the woman as his own helper/partner.

Adam celebrates what readers already know, that this new human and he are equal beings, made from the same bone and flesh. The doubling of the words, "bone of my bone, flesh of my flesh" not only emphasizes the couple's shared humanity but also highlights kinship (Gen 29:14) and covenant connection between them.[4] Adam's lyrical expression of delight comments on the physical identity between them; they are the same bone and flesh, but they also share covenant bonds. In other texts, the words bone and flesh "are used together to speak about a person in his total relation to another."[5] Here the doubling of the terms implies ecstatic appreciation of the man for the woman.

Poetry often draws attention to what is important in the stories of Genesis, and Adam's poetic outburst is no exception. The Lord God's creation of the woman solves the problem of human aloneness, for she finally is his helper and partner. As Adam's exclamation continues, he names his newfound partner, not yet with a personal name but with a generic category that further connects the couple with one another.

Creation of Eve

Maria Denman's depiction of the creation of Eve makes an interesting contrast to Michelangelo's *Creation of Adam* below. In Denman's work, God gently reaches toward Eve as if to lift her into the world while Eve reaches back with both arms as if to embrace her Creator. In Renaissance artist Michelangelo's classic work, *Creation of Adam*, God touches the hand of Adam, who reaches back in an active manner. Michelangelo interprets the divine-human connection not as a shared breath but as if an electric charge of life passed between them.

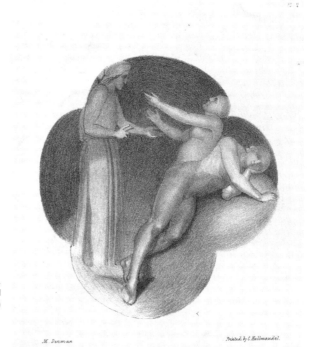

Maria Denman (after John Flaxman). *The Creation of Eve*, from Wells Cathedral. 1829. Lithograph. (Credit: National Gallery of Art, Rosenwald Collection, Washington, DC)

Michelangelo (1475–1564). *Creation of Adam* (detail). 1591. Fresco. Sistine Chapel. (Credit: Wikimedia Commons, PD-1923)

This one shall be called Woman (*ʾiššāh*)
For out of Man (*ʾîš*)[6] this one was taken (2:23).

By means of another play on words, the Hebrew introduces distinctions between the sexes for first time in the chapter. The word for woman (*ʾiššāh*) shares the same root as the word meaning "man" (*ʾîš*). This verbal connection identifying biological differences may imply that the woman is linguistically derivative of man, or of the same substance as man, or both. No longer is *adam* (the groundling) a term for unspecified humanity; it is now a proper name for this particular male, Adam.

Moral of the Story, 2:24-25

Commenting on Adam's words, the narrator provides "the moral of the story" and the consequence of the man's delight in the woman: "Therefore a man leaves his father and his mother and clings to his wife and the two become one flesh."[7] This verse explicitly turns the chapter into an etiology, an explanation of how sexuality comes into being. [Etiology] Sexual attraction comes from God and leads to living together. The story explains and celebrates the origins of sexual differences and similarities and concludes with a reference to co-habitation, for a man leaves his parents and clings to his wife/woman, but not as a legal or religious practice or explicitly as a reason to procreate (that will come later). [Sexual Differentiation] [Who Leaves their Parents' Household?]

Although Genesis 2 provides an account of the origins of sexuality, the moral with its focusing effect does not exhaust the chapter's meaning. The last verse returns to the vision of the garden as a place where harmony and peace prevail in every dimension of creation, including in Adam and Eve. They are "both naked and feel no shame" (2:25). In this paradise, there is no such thing as body shame, self-hatred, lust, or discontent with oneself or the other. Both male and female are whole beings, integrated, self-accepting, and free. They do not

---

Etiology

This is the first of several etiologies in the book of Genesis. An etiology is a narrative or writing in which events explain the origins of something. The book of Genesis itself might be considered an etiology of Israel in the sense that it tells how the nation came to be.

Sexual Differentiation

The ancient story understands sexuality as demarcated between two versions of human bodies manifested in dualistic terms, male and female. In modern times it has been widely recognized that sexual differences fall along a continuum not always determined by biology and anatomy alone. The biblical text does not address the insistence of the lesbian, gay, bisexual, and transgender (LGBT, more recently including further additions to the acronym to name those who identify as queer, intersex, and more) communities that there are many ways to inhabit sexual bodies, but neither does Genesis 2 make a permanent moral claim about sexual identity. It speaks within the limits of the understanding of the ancient time and centers on the creation of partnership and help in this text. It never refers to children. The chapter honors the human need for community, love, and care expressed through physical bodies. Genesis 2–3 does not settle the question of gay marriage one way or the other. The chapter, like all biblical texts, reflects the insights and limits of its time. New moral questions require new insights in light of the larger canon and the issues of one's time, a process often carried out in pain and conflict within believing communities and within the wider society.

For further reading, see Robert E. Shore-Goss, "Gay Liberation," in *Oxford Encyclopedia of the Bible and Gender Studies*, ed. Julia M. O'Brien (New York: Oxford University Press, 2014) 1:257–64.

Who Leaves their Parents' Household?

The first couple's living arrangements are peculiar. In ancient Israel, a man did not leave his paternal household to join the woman's household. Women in Genesis and in Israel typically join the man's family rather than the other way around, except in the case of Jacob, who moves into the household of Laban to obtain four wives.

Other biblical texts, however, suggest that matriarchal arrangements may have existed. The woman in the Song of Songs, for example, desires to bring her beloved into her mother's house. It is not clear, however, whether the Song expresses the woman's imagination or reveals practices in some parts of ancient Israel and its neighbors (Song 3:4; 8:2).

disparage their beautiful bodies but accept them like innocent children. [Song of Songs]

On the way to the chapter's appreciative delight in sexuality, it builds a vision of harmony and interconnection among all things great and small. The Hebrew wordplays and the relationships among the creatures portray a peaceful world where all beings live together without conflict. Everything exists in ecological balance and in properly ordered relationships, that is, in paradise. With its vision of perfect existence, Act One sets the stage for Act Two. In the second half of the drama, these relationships come undone in reverse order from their development in chapter 2. From a literary point of view, this depiction of paradise is a setup, a preparation for the second act of the drama (ch. 3). There paradise unravels, humans foil divine intentions for peaceful coexistence, and, in the end, reality replaces paradise.

Song of Songs

The Song of Songs is a lyrical celebration of sexuality and love that Phyllis Trible has interpreted as a reversal of Gen 2–3, which she calls "a love story gone awry." She interprets the Song as "love lyrics redeemed," "a symphony of eroticism" in which all the senses of the couple participate in the celebration of sexual love that the text declares to be "stronger than death" (Song 8:6).

For further reading, see J. Cheryl Exum, *Song of Songs: A Commentary* (Louisville KY: Westminster John Knox, 2005).

CONNECTIONS

Web of Life

Genesis 2 envisions creation in which each element interconnects with others in peaceful harmony. Attention to literary details of the text reveals the garden to be a living organism, an island paradise where the earth and inhabitants are inextricably joined to one another, depend on one another, and require one another for flourishing life. [The Garden as a Living Organism] The garden expresses ecological, psychological, and spiritual balance so that no part can operate alone or hurt or destroy another part. This vivid web of inter-threaded life stands as God's intention for creation, a vision echoed in both Old and New Testaments.

This chapter does not describe humans as images of God (Gen 1:26-28), but it does honor humans in a similar fashion, for the breath of life breathes in them. Without this breath given to them by God, they are not human but made only of the earth like the animals. The story gives humans a higher place than other creatures in hierarchical fashion.

The Garden as a Living Organism

In Act One, all are one in the garden, united in their source, the Lord God who makes them.

The human is made from the earth and in turn is charged to serve and keep it.

The humans are joined to God who made them and whose breath they share.

The animals and birds are linked to the earth from which they are made and to the human who names them.

The woman is united with the man from whom she is made by his song of recognition of their shared humanity and by their shared life together as one flesh.

These relationships come apart in the next chapter.

Unfortunately, we have used that status not to serve the earth and other creatures as called to do here but to lord it over them, disrupting the fragile balance of the living organism. Human desire to control, to acquire for ourselves alone at any cost, and to live as if we are not integrally dependent on the earth and other creatures has destroyed relationships vital to our lives, never more apparently than now in the post-industrial and neo-colonial age.

Yet the text invites a reengagement of human connections with the earth and non-human creation. It calls for renewed recognition of our mutual bonds with creation to serve the earth, to guarantee a future for the planet, and to restore breath to our own souls. The story of this garden paradise serves as a call, an invitation, to recognize our place in all humility within this ecologically balanced organism of which we are only a small part. This world does not exist for us alone. [Ecojustice Principles of Biblical Interpretation] It is not to be brutalized, raped, or poisoned for our comfort, aggrandizement, or our exclusive benefit. It is to be served and protected, tilled and nourished that it may continue to care and feed life in return. [An Ecological Web]

Children Implied

Genesis 2 also implies that sexual intercourse is a central and sacred activity of human life, a gift of God, a participation in divine creativity, and a matter for celebration and joy. Sexuality contributes to the ongoing life of our earthy home. By highlighting and rejoicing in sexual attraction, the chapter portrays sexuality as a divine gift to humans and a form of participation in the creative

---

Ecojustice Principles of Biblical Interpretation

The Earth Bible is an international project led by Norman Habel, Flinders University, Adelaide, South Australia. The project includes volumes on ecojustice readings of major sections of the Bible, published by Sheffield Press in 5 vols., 2000–2002. This version interprets the books of the Bible from the perspective of the earth itself according to the following six principles:

1. The Principle of Intrinsic Worth, meaning that the whole of the cosmos has value unto itself without regard to its worth to humans.

2. The Principle of Interconnectedness by which all created things are mutually interdependent.

3. The Principle of Voice whereby the earth is a subject capable of raising its voice in celebration, lament, and resistance.

4. The Principle of Purpose by which all things have a place in the cosmic design.

5. The Principle of Mutual Custodianship though which humans, as responsible custodians, function as partners rather than rulers.

6. The Principle of Resistance, meaning that the earth suffers from injustice and actively resists it. (adapted from Jones, 1:453).

For further reading, see Arthur Walker Jones, "Ecological Biblical Criticism," in *The Oxford Encyclopedia of Biblical Criticism*, 2 vols., ed. Steven L. McKenzie (Oxford: Oxford University Press, 2013) 1:249–59. Jones's principles were adapted from Norman C. Habel, ed., *Readings from the Perspective of Earth*, vol. 1 (Cleveland OH: Pilgrim, 2000).

life of God. The chapter never mentions children, but it celebrates sexual intimacy for its own sake, for its benefits to the couple. It is not good for humans to be alone. In the ancient world, of course, children were surely an implied and expected gift of sexuality. The gift of children promises parents, tribes, and nations that they and their memory will not disappear but survive through their offspring.

For the book's audience, deeply uncertain about its survival as a people, God's creation in the garden culminating in sexuality serves as a promissory note of their own future. The chapter celebrates implicitly the production of offspring. It anticipates God's promise to Abraham that he will have numerous offspring, more numerous than he can count, a major theme of the body of the book (chs. 12–50). This chapter prepares for that promise to Abraham and his descendants. [Embodiment]

The earthling is made from the dust of the earth, placed in the garden, and given the vocation of serving the garden. Genesis 2 imagines how humans and the earth might live as part of one organism, related to one another yet separate. Indeed humans have a special and privileged relationship to the earth and its other inhabitants. They are of the earth and also of God, for they alone possess the breath of life given by God.

An Ecological Web

Biblical interpreter Ellen Davis has written about humans made in the image of God (Gen 1:26-28) in ways that apply equally well to chapter 2, where humans are endowed with the breath of life. Borrowing her words, these depictions indicate "that human life has both value and form: inestimable value and a form that is uniquely and richly expressive of divine intentions." Yet, she continues,

the form of human life is fundamentally *ecological* . . . . We are enmeshed in a harmonious web of relationships, infinitely complex in their intersections, that have in God their origins and their point of cohesion . . . . The understanding that the world is ordered as a comprehensive series of interconnected and interdependent structures is of fundamental importance . . . for the food chains. Seminal to the agrarian discussion is Leopold's notion of land as a fountain of energy flowing through a circuit of soils, plants, and animals. Food chains are the living channels which conduct energy upward, death and decay return it to the soil. (56–57)

Ellen F. Davis, *Scripture, Culture and Agriculture: An Agrarian Reading of the Bible* (Cambridge: Cambridge University Press, 2009), citing Aldo Leopold, "The Land Ethic," in *A Sand County Almanac* (New York: Oxford University Press, 1966) 253.

Embodiment

Genesis 2 affirms the human need for companionship. It focuses on human bodies as an instrument by which people create bonds with each other and with God. Although much Jewish and Christian practice urges believers to place their trust in and to love God above all others, for most people that trust and love are mediated through other human bodies, whether of couples, parents and children, the sick and their caregivers, or friendships of all kinds. There is no space here for a Gnostic sense of life that denies, denigrates, or ignores the body in favor of intellectual and spiritual connection alone. The chapter affirms the goodness of humans as embodied creatures who come to know God through intimacy with other embodied beings.

NOTES

1. An expression of David Carr, "Reading into the Gap: Refractions of Trauma in Israelite Prophecy," in Brad E. Kelle, Frank Ritchel Ames, and Jacob Wright, *Interpreting Exile: Displacement and Deportation in Biblical and Modern Contexts* (AIL 10; Atlanta: SBL, 2011) 295–308.

2. William P. Brown's terms for the human in *The Seven Pillars of Creation: The Bible, Science, and the Ecology of Wonder* (New York: Oxford University Press, 2010) 81.

3. As translated in Everett Fox, *The Five Books of Moses: Genesis, Exodus, Leviticus, Numbers, and Deuteronomy* (Schocken Bible; Dallas: Word, 1995).

4. "Bone of my bone and flesh of my flesh" is a covenantal formula that does not speak about derivation in a biological sense but means to speak about commonality of concern, loyalty, and responsibility as expressed in the texts accepting David as king (Judg 9:2; 2 Sam 5:1; 1 Chr 1:11; 2 Sam 19:13). See Walter Brueggemann, "Of the Same Flesh and Bone, Gn 2:23a," *CBQ* (1970): 532–42.

5. Brueggemann, "Of the Same Flesh and Bone," 533.

6. Some ancient Greek manuscripts read "her man," a nearly identical word in Hebrew.

7. This *NRSV* translation creates further gender imbalance in identifying the woman by her role, wife, and the man as a male person. The Hebrew should be translated, "the man clings to his woman" to indicate equivalent dignity.

CREATION UNRAVELS

Genesis 3:1-24

The idyllic harmony that slowly emerges in the first act of the garden story comes apart relationship by relationship in chapter 3. Peaceful coexistence among earth and its creatures unravels here in reverse order and concludes with the expulsion of the humans and a decree of death, the ultimate unraveler. Despite their splintered relationships, the humans do not die immediately, for God preserves them outside the garden. [Outline of Genesis 3]

Outline of Genesis 3
1. Persuasion, 3:1-6
2. Consequences, 3:7-13
3. Punishment or Reality, 3:13-19
4. Expulsion, 3:20-25

COMMENTARY

A new character quietly appears in the garden, one who was not mentioned in the previous chapter but on whom the plot turns.

Persuasion, 3:1-6

The serpent is "more crafty (*'arum*) than any other wild animal that the LORD God had made" (3:1). Although this animal represents the apex of "craftiness," it is still one of God's creatures, a citizen of the garden rather than a being from another world. The Hebrew word translated "crafty" (NRSV) has several possible English translations that complicate interpretation of the serpent's purposes. The serpent could be "clever" or even "sensible," making its nature ambiguous. [Who Is the Serpent?]

Action begins when the serpent starts talking to the woman: "Did God say that you shall not eat from any tree in the garden?" Perhaps the snake asks his question innocently, not having heard the earlier divine prohibition. Or perhaps, clever and independent-minded himself, he simply wants the woman to think and so to see a larger reality. Or maybe the serpent truly intends to disrupt the divine-human relationship. Readers must decide from the story if this amazing, speaking serpent is sensible or deceptive. Yet simply by asking what God said, the reptile fractures all relationships in the garden and gives snakes everywhere a bad name.

Who Is the Serpent?

AΩ Whatever the serpent represents, it is related closely with humans by Hebrew wordplay. The serpent is "crafty" (*'arum*, NRSV), "shrewdest of all" (JPS), or "most cunning" (Alter, *Genesis*), whereas the humans are "naked" (*'arummîm*, 2:25). English translations of the serpent's major quality imply deviousness. The long history of interpretation that sees the serpent as evil personified, the one who introduces sin into the cosmos, and the devil himself undoubtedly influenced these translations. Although this is an honorable, long-standing tradition deeply embedded in Christian thinking, other translations of *'arum* are possible. The word can mean clever in the sense of "subtle" rather than wicked (NJB), or "sensible" (Prov 12:23; 14:15; 22:3; 27:12; see BDB, 791). Does interrupting the status quo in the garden by asking questions qualify to make the serpent wicked?

The story itself is a crafty composition, leaving uncertainty about its purposes and the serpent's role. There is growing appreciation of this chapter as a mythic account of human maturation. Hebrew has several words for sin, but none appear until Cain murders Abel outside the garden (4:7). Nor does the chapter use the Hebrew word for the Satan (*śāṭān*, cf. Job 1:6); instead it uses the word referring to the animal (*nāḥāš*). Already proclaimed to be one of God's creatures, the serpent convinces the woman of the joys of eating from the tree of knowledge. The serpent is wise enough to realize that the forbidden tree provides true knowledge. He even interprets the divine prohibition as evidence of the Lord God's worries that humans will become like gods (3:4). Meanwhile, the woman's motives appear "sensible," for the tree offers a form of life, beauty, and wisdom (3:6). The serpent turns out to be right. The humans' eyes open, but they do not die immediately and they do know good and evil. Yet they transgress boundaries and disobey the Creator. By pointing to nuances of language and writing, I am not proposing that traditional interpretations of this chapter as the story of original sin are wrong. I am, rather, noting complexities of the clever writing that seem designed precisely to provoke questions about the text and life.

For further reading, see Ellen van Wolde, "Facing the Earth: Primeval History in a New Perspective," ed. Philip R. Davies and David J. A. Clines, *The World of Genesis: Persons, Places, Perspectives* (Sheffield UK: Sheffield Academics Press, 1998) 22–47.

Robert Alter, *Genesis* (New York: W. W. Norton, 1996).
BDB, 791.

The woman answers the serpent's question truthfully, though her reply expands God's words. They can eat from all the trees in the garden, but they must neither eat nor "touch" the one in the middle, or, she adds, they will die.[1] [Woman as Theologian] Boldly denying what God said, the serpent responds, "You shall not die" (3:4). His claim turns out to be partially true, for they live. God "knows," the serpent continues, that if they eat of the tree they will be like God, "knowing good and evil," and their "eyes will be opened" (3:5). The serpent argues that if the woman eats, she will become like God, knowing both good and evil, seeing reality in its many dimensions. Who would not want to eat of this fruit?

The serpent and the woman are talking about what it means to know, to live consciously, and to have judgment. According to the serpent, the most important thing about God is knowledge, the capacity to distinguish between good and evil. The text does not tell us what it

Woman as Theologian

The woman in the garden is the Bible's first theologian. She speaks with the serpent about God. She understands the divine command not to eat of the tree and expands on it in the rabbinic practice of "putting a fence around the law," that is, adding a less serious prohibition to discourage breaking the big one: to avoid the tree, avoid touching it (Gen 3:3). She "contemplates" the tree, decides for herself that it will provide true knowledge to make her like God. If knowledge of right and wrong characterize divinity, and they do in this chapter, then the woman chose well.

For further reading see, Phyllis Trible, *God and Rhetoric of Sexuality* (OBT; Philadelphia: Fortress, 1978) 72–144.

means by good and bad, whether the couple is about to discover moral, spiritual, physical, or psychological goodness and badness. Until this point in the story, the snake implies, humans have lived in a uniform world, unaware of distinctions between good and bad. Humans are to the serpent no more than naive children. The woman listens to this with heightened awareness; she sees that the tree is a delight to look at, edible, and desirable to make her wise. The fruit attracts her for its goodness, beauty, and truth, so she eats from it. [The Fruit] Then she gives it to the man "who was with her" all along, "and he ate" (3:6). Both man and woman disobey God's prohibition. [Blaming the Woman]

Consequences, 3:7-13

Knowledge has consequences. The first thing the couple knows when their eyes are opened is that they are naked. They know their own bodies. Nakedness was simply a fact at the end of the first act in the garden, a sign of the perfect harmony within and between them. Now nakedness brings shame and the loss of bodily integrity

---

The Fruit

There is no apple mentioned in the Garden of Eden, only the generic Hebrew word for "fruit." Yet the apple is such an entrenched detail in art and tradition that it seems futile to fight it. Consider the oil painting *The Temptation of Adam* (1551–1552) by Italian Renaissance artist Tintoretto.

Eve offers an apple to Adam, who shrinks back, as if shocked and reluctant to take it. In this interpretation, the woman is the culprit and Adam her reluctant but easily swayed companion. Fig leaves are already in place in the painting, undoubtedly due to religious piety rather than faithfulness to the text, for the couple has not yet discovered their nakedness.

Though both images show an apple, the Hebrew word "fruit" covers a wide range of possibilities common in the ancient Near East, such as pomegranates, apricots, olives, and lemons (Yee, 43–55).

Gale A. Yee, "What Is Culture Criticism of the Old Testament?" in *Pastoral Essays in Honor of Lawrence Boadt, CSP: Reading the Old Testament*, ed. Corrine L. Carvalho (Mahwah NJ: Paulist, 2013).

Jacopo Tintoretto (1518–1594). *Adam and Eve: The Fall of Man.* Gallerie dell'Accademia, Venice, Italy. (Credit: Alfredo Dagli Orti / Art Resource, NY)

Blaming the Woman

Unlike later artistic and theological interpretations, Gen 3 does not blame the woman alone for the introduction of sin and alienation into the world. The man is there with her and accepts the fruit from her with no comment and no resistance. Interpretation throughout Christian history, however, has made the woman the scapegoat for all the world's evils. This view is deeply fixed in popular culture and has long provided an excuse for sexism, misogyny, and all forms of abuse and oppression of women.

When women interpreters began to do biblical studies, however, interpretations began to shift. Women noticed features of the text previously overlooked or misinterpreted (Yee, 47–49).

Women interpreters have insisted that God made women and men equally in the divine image (1:26-28), that the subordination of women is not uniformly taught in the Bible, and that where it is present, it is an artifact of ancient culture that should go the way of slavery as utterly unacceptable to God. Modern biblical studies by

women and for women have yielded an enormous bibliography, beginning with editor Elizabeth Cady Stanton's *The Woman's Bible* (1895–1898), extending to editors Carol A. Newsom and Sharon Ringe's *The Woman's Bible Commentary* (1992), and moving on to the currently appearing Wisdom Bible Commentary with a volume on every book of both Testaments by women interpreters from around the globe.

For further reading, see Kathleen M. O'Connor, "The Feminist Movement Meets the Old Testament," in *Engaging the Bible in a Gendered World*, ed. Linda Day and Carolyn Pressler (Louisville KY: Westminster John Knox, 2006) 3–24.

Gale A. Yee, "What Is Culture Criticism of the Old Testament?" in *Pastoral Essays in Honor of Lawrence Boadt, CSP: Reading the Old Testament*, ed. Corrine L. Carvalho (Mahwah NJ: Paulist, 2013).

Elizabeth Cady Stanton, ed., *The Woman's Bible*, 2 vols. (New York: European Publishing Co., 1895–1898); Carol A. Newsom and Sharon Ringe, eds., *The Woman's Bible Commentary* (Louisville KY: Westminster/John Knox, 1992); Barbara Reid, ed. (Wisdom Bible Commentary Series; Collegeville MN: Liturgical Press, 2015–).

or inner wholeness. With the couple's new knowledge comes inner turmoil and alienation, so they hide their naked bodies with fig leaves. No longer do they accept themselves or each other.

The couple cannot bear their exposure so they hide from God. When they hear the Lord God walking in the garden, they hide again. God, however, looks for them and asks, "Where are you?" [God in Human Terms] "I was afraid," the man tells God, as if the woman is not there. Adam's shame about his naked body alienates him from God as well as from his partner. Because God is not all-knowing in this story, God wants to know what happened: "Have you eaten from the tree of knowledge from which I told you not to eat?" (3:11). In response, Adam turns defensive and accusatory. He denies responsibility and

God in Human Terms

An "anthropomorphic" God is a description of God with human qualities. This way of presenting the deity, considered typical of the J source, is evident in Gen 2–3. In chapter 2, for example, God creates the woman only after trial and error. In chapter 3, God walks around the garden searching for humans and does not they know they are naked. The practice of using human experiences to talk about God is an important theological practice of Genesis. To speak of God, the ancient writers, as well as modern thinkers, draw from their experiences of the realities around them, their cultures, their worldviews, and particular human experiences.

Gen 1, by contrast, portrays a truly powerful Creator who brings all things into being simply by speaking. These are just two of many approaches the Bible uses to name the unnamable, to speak of God who transcends all human language, for God is beyond humans, veiled by our world, our realities, and our limitation.

Interpreters have often credited the anonymous writer known as J or the Yahwist with authorship of Gen 2–3 and the Priestly writer (P) with chapter 1, which describes a more transcendent deity. Neither approach exhausts God, contains God, or adequately names God. See [Documentary Theory of Composition].

For further reading, see Mark S. Smith, *How Human Is God? Seven Questions about God and Humanity in the Bible* (Collegeville MN: Liturgical, 2014).

blames the woman, the "bone of his bone and flesh of his flesh," and even incriminates God. "The woman whom you gave me to be with me, she gave me fruit from the tree, and I ate" (3:12). It was her fault, it was God's fault, but it was not his own fault.

Alienation spreads from the couple's bodies to their relationship with God, and it ruptures their relationship even further. When God interrogates the woman, she behaves no better than Adam. "The serpent tricked me and I ate," she responds (3:13). Disharmony and estrangement pass now from them to other living creatures. Humans and the serpent speak with each other no more.

Consequences or Reality, 3:14-19

The Lord God responds to the fractured relationships in the garden with the poetry of consequences. The switch from prose narrative to poetry gives formal solemnity to the outcomes of the choice to eat of the fruit and draws attention to the consequences of the humans' knowledge of good and evil. Beginning with the serpent and moving to the woman, the man, and finally to the ground, consequences unfold in reverse order of creation in the previous chapter. Curses of serpent and ground create a literary frame around the consequences of the humans. ["Curse" in Biblical Hebrew]

The poetry of consequences contributes something further to the garden story; it depicts the world as it is or has become, that is, a place of human limitations, of creatureliness. Reality is what they come to know, and this is how reality came to be as it is. (See [Etiology].)

"Curse" in Biblical Hebrew

There are many words for "curse" in biblical Hebrew. In general, to curse means "to predict, wish, pray for, or cause trouble or disaster on a person or thing" (Stuart, 1:1218–19). Any curse in the ancient world gains its power only from God or the gods. When humans curse, they call upon the deity to bring disaster. God utters curses in the garden against both the serpent and the ground, permanently altering their status. The serpent crawls on the ground of the lush island and the ground becomes barren (Gen 2:5).

Douglas Stuart, "Curse," *ABD*.

• Why do serpents crawl in the dust of the ground in lethal combat with humans? "Because you have done this, cursed are you among all animals," God announces to the serpent (3:14). It will crawl on its belly and live in conflict with human beings. For instigating human disobedience, snakes and humans will become deadly enemies. The woman's offspring will crush the heads of the serpent's offspring, who, in turn, will bite the heels of humans.

• Why do women have pain in childbirth? [Childbirth] Being able to give birth is the very capacity that gave a woman identity in the ancient world, and the consequence of her choice to eat of the fruit is to suffer mightily while giving birth. [Motherhood and Agrarian Labor] Despite the pain of birth, the woman will still desire her man

Childbirth

Childbirth made women valuable, necessary, and vulnerable in ancient societies. The pain of childbirth captured the attention of the prophets and poets, who used it as a metaphor to describe terrible suffering and a cause of great fright (Isa 13:8; 21:3; Jer 4:31; 48:41). Women typically died by the age of thirty and "had to become pregnant nearly twice for every child that lived to age five" (Ebeling, 101). We read that midwives and birth stools or birth bricks assisted women in labor (Exod 1:16-20), but little is known about birth processes in ancient Israel, perhaps because few men attended births and so could not write about them.

Childbirth Scene. Stone Relief. Roman. Museo Ostiense, Ostia, Italy. (Credit: Scala / Art Resource, NY)

For more, see Carol Meyers, *Rediscovering Eve: Ancient Israelite Women in Context* (New York: Oxford University Press, 2013) especially 80–101; Phyllis A. Bird, *Missing Persons and Mistaken Identities: Women and Gender in Ancient Israel* (OBT; Minneapolis: Fortress, 1997) 23; and Jennie Ebeling, *Women's Lives in Biblical Times* (New York: T & T Clark, 2010).

sexually, become pregnant again, and experience repetition of pain. To make things even more difficult, the man will "rule over" her (3:16). She will desire him, love him, want to please him, and experience his love in return, but, after eating the fruit, mutuality and equality disappear. Power between them becomes asymmetrical. [Childbirth and Male Dominance] As the undisputed ruler of the family, the man has power over his woman and can do as he pleases with her. [Patriarchal Social Arrangements]

• Why do men suffer while working the ground? The consequence for the man as for the woman strikes at his identity in the ancient world. He is the tiller of the ground who must labor mightily to produce food from the earth. Just as the woman's fate is tied to the man's, so his fate is tied to the ground. [Original Sin] After chiding him for listening to her, God curses the ground on his account. Food production and human survival itself are now both onerous and precarious. God punishes the man by making the ground return to barrenness, yielding thistles and thorns. The man will work on this

Motherhood and Agrarian Labor

Carol Meyers has shown that women's fecundity was necessary for the subsistence farming practiced by most Israelites during the Iron Age (1200–586 BCE)—the period possibly reflected in what is often called the Yahwist or J source:

Genesis 3:17-19 mandates exhausting labor for men and 3:16 orders women to work hard and have multiple pregnancies. Together these passages reflect the Israelite environmental and demographic context. They explain and validate the hardships of agrarian life in Iron Age Israel. (Meyers, 101)

In this commentary, I propose that this ancient theme of women's fertility and capacity to give birth had added importance for the book's Judean audience in the early Persian Period because the birth of children was critical for the nation's survival after the Babylon destruction and the scattering of the nation.

Carol Meyers, *Rediscovering Eve: Ancient Israelite Women in Context* (New York: Oxford University Press, 2013).

Childbirth and Male Dominance

 Childbirth in ancient Israel was fraught with difficulties, and the mortality rate of infants and mothers was high. Carol Myers has argued that the famous passage about the woman's punishment neither teaches nor authorizes total male dominance. Instead, men must dominate women sexually because women resist sexual relations due to the dangers of childbirth. In her view, women held power and status akin to men who tilled the ground because in households during the Iron Age (1200–586 BCE), women managed the home, raised and educated children, prepared food, and oversaw matters of health. They had power in the household.

For further reading, see Carol Meyers, *Rediscovering Eve: Ancient Israelite Women in Context* (New York: Oxford University Press, 2013).

unyielding soil all his days and eat plants coaxed from it under the sweat of his efforts. This is his life until he dies. [Interdependence]

• How did death enter the world? Knowledge of death is the final consequence of eating the fruit. The human will die and will return to the dust of the earth from which he was made. ["O Human, You Are Dust"]

Expulsion, 3:20-25

To depict the aftermath of the divine consequences, the chapter returns to more mundane prose narrative. Now living in the world of human limitation and creatureliness, of suffering and pain, the man gives the woman a personal name without receiving a new name from her in return. He rules over her and interprets her being. With a final wordplay, he names her Eve (*ḥayyáh*), for she is the mother of the living (*ḥáy*, 3:20). [Eve in Interpretive Tradition]

God casts the couple from the garden and bars the way back, but God does not abandon them. Making garments from skins to clothe them, God continues to interact with them. Yet God's own life seems out of kilter, as if fear has even entered divinity. To unnamed others, God says, "See the man has become like one of us, knowing good and evil"

Patriarchal Social Arrangements

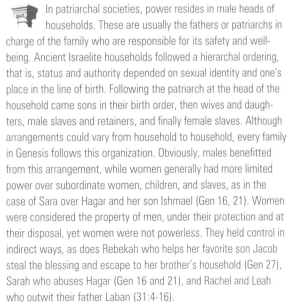 In patriarchal societies, power resides in male heads of households. These are usually the fathers or patriarchs in charge of the family who are responsible for its safety and well-being. Ancient Israelite households followed a hierarchal ordering, that is, status and authority depended on sexual identity and one's place in the line of birth. Following the patriarch at the head of the household came sons in their birth order, then wives and daughters, male slaves and retainers, and finally female slaves. Although arrangements could vary from household to household, every family in Genesis follows this organization. Obviously, males benefitted from this arrangement, while women generally had more limited power over subordinate women, children, and slaves, as in the case of Sara over Hagar and her son Ishmael (Gen 16, 21). Women were considered the property of men, under their protection and at their disposal, yet women were not powerless. They held control in indirect ways, as does Rebekah who helps her favorite son Jacob steal the blessing and escape to her brother's household (Gen 27), Sarah who abuses Hagar (Gen 16 and 21), and Rachel and Leah who outwit their father Laban (31:4-16).

Genesis disrupts some patriarchal and hierarchical relationships of the ancient world by consistently giving priority to the second-born son over the firstborn and by portraying the Egyptian slave woman Hagar to be highly favored by God and the matriarch of the Bedouins.

Patriarchal thinking today continues around the globe and in the United States. It is deeply intertwined with racism and classism and all forms of social organization that grant authority and privilege to the few. Typically, patriarchal thinking values men over women, whites over peoples of color, and rich over poor. Although global challenges to these entrenched ways of living are emerging, these systems still prevail in both blatant and subtle ways.

Original Sin

Language of original sin is a New Testament concept developed by Paul's creative exegesis (Rom 5:12-21). Walter Brueggemann has pointed out that Paul deviates from the text of Genesis. Paul is not interested in abstract questions of the origins of sin or in the origins of the world, but in proclaiming the Gospel. Rom 5 draws its ideas largely from the theological thinking about sin and death of Paul's time (see the apocryphal book 2 Esd). He proposes a chain of connections, starting with sin. Sin enters the world through one man and death enters through sin. That one man, the old Adam, Paul contrasts with the new Adam, Jesus Christ. He sets the old Adam's trespass against the new Adam's righteousness, the old Adam's disobedience against the new Adam's obedience. Grace brought by the new Adam replaces sin brought by the old.

In seeking to understand the life, death, and resurrection of Jesus Christ, Paul uses Gen 3 in his letter to the Romans. He draws from intertestamental literature (Wis 2:24 and 2 Esd 3:2), and his thought later becomes the basis for the Christian doctrine of original sin. "Just as sin came into the world through one man, and death came through sin, and so death spread to all because all have sinned . . . ."

Paul's interpretation has influenced subsequent interpretations for centuries. Reinterpretation of the ancient tradition remains the responsibility of every time and every culture, including our own.

For further reading, see Mark E. Biddle, *Missing the Mark: Sin and Its Consequences in Biblical Theology* (Nashville: Abingdon, 2005).

Walter Brueggemann, *Genesis* (Interpretation; Atlanta: John Knox, 1982) 40–44.

Interdependence

The consequences of eating the fruit are imbalanced relationships. The man lords it over the woman, and both lord it over the earth (1:26), yet the humans are utterly dependent on the earth for their lives.

For further reading, see Ellen van Wolde, "Facing the Earth: Primeval History in a New Perspective," in *The World of Genesis: Persons, Places, Perspectives*, ed. Philip R. Davies and David J. A. Clines (Sheffield, UK: Sheffield Academic Press, 1998) 22–47.

"O Human, You Are Dust"

"O Human, you are dust and to dust you shall return"—a statement derived from Gen 3:19—is the verbal reminder that traditionally accompanies the liturgical practice of marking foreheads with ashes on Ash Wednesday among some Christian communities. The declaration calls Christians to remember their mortality, repent of sin, and be faithful now. Each believer will die sooner or later and return to the earth from which he or she came. They have come from the earth and will soon be united with it again.

So we must love while these moments are still called today
Take part in the pain of this passion play
Stretching our youth as we must, until we are ashes to dust
Until time makes history of us.

This reflection on the brevity of life and the need to live with full intensity now in the midst of our own suffering, our own "passion play," comes from singer and songwriter Emily Saliers of the folk-rock group the Indigo Girls, in her song, "History of Us."

Saliers quoted in Don Saliers and Emily Saliers, *A Song to Sing, A Life to Live: Reflections on Music as Spiritual Practice* (The Practices of Faith Series; San Francisco: Jossey-Bass, 2005) 92.

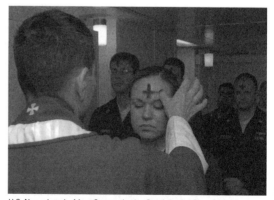

U.S. Navy photo by Mass Communication Specialist 3rd Class Brian May. Atlantic Ocean (Feb. 6, 2008). Electronics Technician 3rd Class Leila Tardieu receives the sacramental ashes during an Ash Wednesday celebration aboard the amphibious assault ship USS Wasp (LHD 1). (Credit: Wikimedia Commons/ Released PD)

Eve in Interpretive Tradition

It may surprise readers to learn that Eve never appears again in the Hebrew Bible. She turns up later in Tobit (8:6) and Ecclesiasticus (25:24, also known as Jesus ben Sirach) during the intertestamental period. Both books are considered apocryphal in the Protestant tradition and deutero-canonical in Roman Catholic and Orthodox traditions, that is, they are sacred works but of secondary importance. Ben Sirach wrote, "From a woman sin had its beginning and because of her we all die" (25:24). From this late book, Eve became the source of sin in Jewish and Christian thinking throughout the centuries.

For further reading, see Carol Meyers, *Rediscovering Eve: Ancient Israelite Women in Context* (New York: Oxford University Press, 2013) 60–65.

(3:22). Just as the serpent predicted, the humans have become like gods, knowing good and evil. The Lord God fears that they will eat of the tree of life and live forever. God's fear of humans here (cf. 11:1-9) is less an explanation of the divine character as it is a primitive explanation of why humans do not live forever. God will not allow them to gain divine status.

This chapter, like chapter 2, ends with a "therefore," that is, a moral of the story: "Therefore the LORD God sent him forth from the garden of Eden to till the ground from which he was taken" (3:23). Adam's work is the same work that God gave him before (2:15), but now serving the ground is laborious and wearisome. A final verse reports that humans will never gain access to the tree of life, for "God places the cherubim and a sword flaming to guard the way to the tree of life." [Eden Revisited]

CONNECTIONS

Reality Again

The story of the garden paradise and its disintegration is mythic, truthful, and remarkably insightful. [A Mythic Story] In paradise, all creatures live together with integrity and wholeness, without hatred or bitterness, without greed or threat. That, however, is not the way it is now. We humans are divided within ourselves, among ourselves, from other creatures, and from our Creator. The garden of perfect peace, harmony, and immortality is inaccessible to us. Eden is a perfect world, except that the people in it are not yet adults. They do not know the deep layers of life and struggle around them. Knowing nothing, the couple cannot make proper judgments, cannot critique or assess, and cannot have moral or intellectual lives. Perhaps, then, they cannot love, but merely live without awe or wonder, without gratitude or faith. When they eat the fruit, they gain knowledge they lacked, and life becomes

Eden Revisited

The Eden narrative captured the attention not only of later artists and authors but also of other biblical authors. They often used the rich imagery of Eden to describe their world and to imagine God's future, sometimes obliquely and sometimes explicitly. The Song of Songs, for instance, can be read as a response to what went wrong in Eden. According to Phyllis Trible, if we understand the story of the Eden as "a love story gone awry," we can then see the Song as "love's lyrics redeemed" (Trible, 72, 144). The Song is saturated with garden and creation imagery such as when the female lover euphemistically refers to herself as a vineyard (1:6), the male lover calls her "a garden locked" (4:16), and the woman declares that her lover has "gone down to his garden . . . to gather lilies" (6:2). Moreover, the lovers use a wide array of nature metaphors to describe each other, themselves, and their desire such that all of creation is invited to participate in the redemption of the "love story gone awry."

Other echoes of Eden, however, center on the expulsion from the garden in Gen 3. The prophet Ezekiel makes explicit reference to Eden in an oracle against the king of Tyre. God, speaking through the prophet, connects the king to the first human. He proclaims, "You were in Eden, the garden of God" (Ezek 28:12), and laments, "you were filled with violence and you sinned; so I cast you as a profane thing from the mountain of God" (28:16). Second Isaiah imagines Israel's restoration in the land after the exile as a return to Eden (Isa 51:3).

Evoking Eden becomes a common theme in the New Testament as well, often as an expression of eschatological hope. The author of the book of Revelation promises the faithful that they will "have permission to eat from the tree of life that is in the paradise of God" (2:7). Later in the beatific vision of the New Jerusalem descending from heaven to earth, John the seer describes a river running through the middle of the city, and "on either side of the river is the tree of life with its twelve kinds of fruit, producing its fruit each month; and the leaves are for the healing of nations" (22:2). According to the vision, the end looks much like the beginning, except that in this new Eden, "nothing accursed will be found there anymore" (22:3). John's vision of the end thus involves a return to the Edenic harmony, except the threat of danger has been removed. As God makes all things new (Rev 21:5), the presence of God once again dwells on earth as in Eden.

Some interpreters have also suggested parallels to the Eden story in Gospel of John's resurrection account. John's narrative is the only account to situate the tomb in a garden (John 19:41), and while the Synoptic Gospels list other women who came to the tomb, John names only Mary Magdalene. As Mary peers into the empty tomb, she sees two angels who ask her why she is weeping. Before she can answer, she turns and sees the risen Jesus, who asks her the same question. Yet she does not immediately recognize him and instead thinks he is the gardener (20:15), until he speaks her name and she then recognizes him and reaches out to him. At that point, Jesus sends her back to share the good news with the other disciples.

Potential allusions to the Garden of Eden abound. Jesus and Mary may symbolize the new Adam and new Eve. The garden setting and apparent misidentification of Jesus as the gardener may be an intentional form of "symbolic communication" through which the Evangelist hints to the reader that the resurrection garden is actually the garden of new creation. When Mary assumes that Jesus is the gardener, her ironic misidentification is more right than she realizes. In John, Jesus is the very presence of God in the garden, the gardener who plants the new creation in the original creation of the garden (Gen 2:8).

Phyllis Trible, *God and the Rhetoric of Sexuality* (Philadelphia: Fortress Press, 1978).

Hermann Spieckermann, "Eden, Garden of," "I. Ancient Near East and Hebrew Bible," *EBR* 7:362–63.

Ruben Zimmerman, "Symbolic Communication between John and His Reader: Garden Symbolism in John 19–20," *Anatomies of Narrative Criticism: The Past, Present, and Futures of the Fourth Gospel as Literature*, ed. Tom Thatcher and Stephen D. Moore (Atlanta: SBL, 2008) 221–36.

Adele Reinhartz, *Befriending the Beloved Disciple: A Jewish Reading of the Gospel of John* (New York: Continuum, 2001).

intriguing and dramatic, full of challenges to cause them to grow or to die.

To see how this story depicts psychic, spiritual, ecological life in our time, one need only hear the news, follow social media, attend a meeting, or reflect on one's sins and foibles to find similar tensions and brokenness today. Humans are wounded, sinful, and imperfect. We wound, betray, and violate in return. Human life

A Mythic Story

"The Garden story is unapologetically 'mythic.' But as William Sloan Coffin aptly notes, 'The truth of a myth is not literally true, only eternally so'" (64).

Myths have immense power for individuals and cultures. As narratives, they shape imagination and life beyond doctrinal statements, philosophical propositions, or religious rules. They invite readers to enter the story, ask their own questions, reflect on memorable characters and events portrayed there, and finally glimpse truth in unforgettable ways. In these ways, myths shape the identities of peoples.

William Sloan Coffin, *Letters to a Young Doubter* (Louisville KY: Westminster John Knox, 2005), quoted in William P. Brown, *The Seven Pillars of Creation: The Bible, Science, and the Ecology of Wonder* (New York: Oxford University Press, 2010) 107.

includes estrangement from one's self, separation from others, alienation from the environment. It includes conflicts, violence, abuse, enslavements, violations of the earth, failure, dysfunction, mental illness—the list seems infinite.

Yet this place of alienation and brokenness, of pain and death, that is, the real world we live in now, is the arena wherein God meets and interacts with all creation. God manifests the divine self within this fractured, disfigured domain. To seek God, believers need not first find a perfect paradise, a lush oasis of agreeable people, a sinless, harmonious inner self, an ideal church or family, or utopian political and religious institutions. None of these exist, or, when they seem to, they are momentary, fragile, and fleeting. [*Paradise Lost* by John Milton] Christians believe that "the Word became Flesh and dwelt among us" in precisely such a world (John 1:14). Jesus' own body was beaten, tortured, and killed because the world is as it is—broken, evil, cruel, wounded, and alienated. It is in the place of wounds that the Christian God is most vividly recognized.

The First Disaster Narrative

The garden story is the first of many disaster stories, "refractions of trauma,"[2] in Genesis. [Refractions of Trauma] Despite its mythic setting in time before time, intimations of Judah's history appear in it. The basic narrative pattern of troubles, displacement, and near death ends with

Paradise Lost by John Milton

Popular understandings of the Genesis story in the garden rely heavily on *Paradise Lost*, the seventeenth-century poem by English poet John Milton. In his interpretation, the serpent is the Satan cast out from heaven into hell who then tempts the woman "to fall off from their Creator." Milton surrounds the Genesis story with accounts of heavenly angels at war in the cosmos and involved in human behavior. His interpretation of the event sees Eve as a lesser creature to Adam. A classic of English poetry, *Paradise Lost* greatly embroiders the Genesis story and has influenced much subsequent interpretation:

Th' infernal Serpent; he it was, whose guile
Stirred up with envy and revenge, deceived
The mother of mankind, what his pride
Had cast him out from Heav'n, with all his host
Of rebel angels . . .

For Milton, only Adam is made in the image of God, while Eve is made in Adam's image. She, made for softness, is the weak link, easily persuaded to eat from the tree of knowledge. Milton, along with Paul and Augustine, looks to the coming of Christ as the overturning the sin of Adam.

Of man's first disobedience, and the fruit
Of that forbidden tree, whose mortal taste
Brought death into the world, and all our woe,
With loss of Eden, till one greater man
Restore us, and regain the blissful seat . . .

John Milton, in John Leonard, ed., *John Milton: Selected Poems*, Penguin Classics (London UK: Penguin, 2007) 72–73.

Refractions of Trauma

"Refractions of trauma" is an apt phrase to apply to disaster stories in Genesis because Judah's historical disaster appears in glimpses in the literature, scattered and separated like rays of light through a prism, yet shining through unmistakably in the bones of the story. For victims of traumatic violence, the benefits of revisiting disaster through such literary refractions are multiple. To see characters who have also undergone the collapse of their world enables victims to regain hope for themselves. They can see it from afar, interpret it, find cause and effect that "explain" it and restore some sense of security. The world no longer appears to be an utterly chaotic and randomly terrifying place. An explanation that arises often after disasters is "It was our fault; we did this to ourselves." Taking responsibility, even if wrongly so, helps people go forward because it ascribes cause and effect to past suffering. To put it overly simply, we caused this trouble; God punished us; now we can go forward for there is order in the world. (See Introduction and [Trauma and Disaster Studies].)

divine help and the survival of some. This pattern roughly outlines the dilemma of the Judean people during the early Persian Period. After the nation's destruction from Babylonian invasions, deportation, and displacements, Judeans were cut off from their origins and their identity. Doubt remained about whether they had any future as the people of God, for an angel barred the way back to their former paradise.

Immigrants, displaced people, and their descendants often think of the lost past as a golden time barely marred by troubles, a lost paradise. Like Adam and Eve, the Judeans faced a world fraught with struggles, alienation, and loss. They needed an etiology of their own catastrophe, an interpretation of its causes, and an understanding of how they could go forward. [Who Is Responsible?] Genesis 3 provides one explanation of disaster. Humans disobey God and God punishes them. This perspective helps theologically because it says that the divine-human relationship is not severed nor is God a powerless being. Such an explanation suggests that they may survive with help from God, with animal skins replacing fig leaves to cover their nakedness and provide protection. God does not abandon Adam and Eve but helps them survive (3:21). God protects and preserves, even in the face of death.

Who Is Responsible?

Gen 3 gives humans the responsibility for the loss of paradise, for bringing alienation and disharmony into the world, and for bringing about their own mortality. Encouraged by the serpent, human disobedience "explains" the origins of human suffering and mortality.

After the nation of Judah fell to Babylon, arguments flared among survivors and descendants over why this happened and who was responsible. Similar questions of interpretation haunted the Judean community for generations after the nation's collapse in the sixth century BCE. Why did the promised land fall under the control of foreign empires? Did God abandon the beloved community of Judah to Babylon and its deities? The theological problem of how the nation fell pervades the prophetic literature of that time. Prophets such as Jeremiah and Ezekiel, along with the book of Lamentations, contain a variety of clashing explanations, including the frequently expressed view that the nation's sin brought divine punishment down upon it.

Such interpretations actually help victims of warfare and traumatic violence to survive. This is because, after disasters of any sort, most survivors require explanations to make sense of what has become a senseless world. Although taking responsibility for the nation's fall may only partially or minimally explain catastrophe, to do so provides a reason for events that are beyond reason. Traumatic violence almost always destroys trust in God, the world, and other people. Random chaos appears to govern events, and God appears absent or powerless. In such conditions, people search for any interpretation to help reduce fears and to put some sense of order back into the world. Placing responsibility on human failure and seeing suffering as divine punishment are helpful ways to cope with such suffering. Doing so gives meaning to what has happened, defends God as neither whimsical nor absent, and gives people a sense that they can avoid catastrophe in the future by living in right relationship with God.

While such interpretations of violence assist survival on a temporary basis, they do not adequately explain human suffering. Although people may bear some responsibility for troubles, these matters are largely beyond their control. Causes and effects of disasters are far more complicated, and when individuals or communities get stuck in such self-blaming and God-the-Punisher theologies, they limit God and limit themselves. (See Introduction and [Trauma and Disaster Studies].)

In a veiled way, the story of the Garden of Eden reflects similar theological questions, but it adds an important conclusion to the story of human failure and expulsion. The first couple survives their sojourn into the larger world because the Creator God protects them.

For further readings about effects of disaster on Judah, see Kathleen M. O'Connor, *Jeremiah: Pain and Promise* (Minneapolis: Fortress, 2011) 19–27.

NOTES

1. Phyllis Trible, *God and the Rhetoric of Sexuality* (OBT; Philadelphia; Fortress, 1978) 110 has strongly influenced my interpretation of Gen 2–3.

2. David M. Carr, "Reading into the Gap: Refractions of Trauma in Israelite Prophecy," in *Interpreting Exile: Displacement and Deportation in Biblical and Modern Contexts*, ed. Brad E. Kelle, Frank Richtel Ames, and Jacob L. Wright (AIL 10; Atlanta: SBL, 2011) 295–308.

EVE'S GENEALOGY

Genesis 4:1-26

Initially, at least, life outside Eden appears hopeful because two sons are born to Adam and Eve at the chapter's beginning and more offspring at the chapter's conclusion. Yet what seems to be a straightforward narrative of Adam and Eve's obedience to the divine command to "be fruitful and multiply" (1:28) quickly becomes complicated by the sin of murder. Outside Eden, violence, suffering, and death mark the lives of Adam and Eve's children, but relationship with God and life itself continue despite many troubles.

[Original Violence]

COMMENTARY

Genesis 4 takes the form of a genealogy, elaborated by short narratives in three smaller literary units about the first couple's offspring; Cain and Abel (vv. 1-16), Cain's children (vv. 17-24), and more children of Eve and Adam (vv. 25-26). The genealogies portray in short-hand fashion both the passage of time and the interconnections from generation to generation. Yet unexpectedly in genealogies where women have minor or no roles, Eve is the ancestor of importance here. The chapter tells more about conceiving and bearing than of begetting (vv. 1, 2, and 25), and her words frame the chapter (vv. 1 and 25). An opening genealogical notice (vv. 1-2) introduces a prose narrative about the murder of second son Abel by firstborn son Cain (vv. 3-16). The fratricide runs like a toxic stream through the chapter,

Original Violence

Perhaps this chapter is about original violence, not simply original sin. Regina Schwartz writes, "We do not kill one another *because* Cain did; rather, we kill one another for similar reasons" (2). The truth of this statement is hard to contest. Schwartz has proposed that monotheism is the problem because the brothers offer sacrifices to the one God of wrath. In this view, it is no wonder that Cain is devastated by not being accepted, making the real problem in the text to be the character of God. What she does not consider fully is the mythic nature of the story and its purposes. It does not portray a full picture of the divine so much as it provides an account of why relationships are the way they are—broken, alienated, and prone to violence. In doing so, the chapter portrays death, exile, loss, grief, and finally survival. It is not offering a complete theology, a portrait of God that is always and everywhere expressive of the way God is. It is searching for understandings of disaster. Genesis portrays God as powerful, decisive, and surprising, a God who gives grace, chooses against human expectations, and is involved even in horrifying events. The theologies of Genesis serve to call the people to new life after disaster by keeping God present and actively recreating them after catastrophes.

Regina M. Schwartz, *The Curse of Cain: The Violent Legacy of Monotheism* (Chicago: University of Chicago Press, 1997).

for Cain's brutal sin both affects his own genealogy (vv. 17-24) and motivates more births to Adam and Eve (vv. 25-26). [Outline of Genesis 4:1-16]

The murder takes place in a self-contained narrative about the first children, but the conflict between brothers and the question it raises foreshadow family battles to come later in Genesis. Bitter disputes among family members repeatedly call into question human survival and the future of the family of Abraham. The Cain and Abel story anticipates conflicts between the brothers Jacob and Esau (25:19-34; 27:1-46), between the sisters Leah and Rachel (29:1–30:22), and most shockingly between Joseph and his brothers (chs. 37–45).

Comparison of Adam and Eve/Cain and Abel Stories

📖 The story of Cain and Abel follows closely the pattern of the Adam and Eve story (Gen 2–3).

Both include a divine prohibition/warning (Gen 2:17; 4:7), misdeed (3:1-6; 4:8), divine interrogation of humans (3:8-13; 4:9-10), punishment involving alienation from the ground (3:17-19; 4:11-12), softening of condition (3:21; 4:13-15), and the final expulsion of the humans eastward (Gen 3:24; 4:16). The main difference is that the dynamics played out with husband and wife in Genesis 3 are now being played out with the two brothers in Genesis 4. (Carr, 69–70)

In this sense, both stories are what I name "disaster" stories. (cf. Introduction) They convey the end of life, threaten the family's future, and conclude with survival. The narrative pattern echoes in a remote fashion the plight and the interpretive questions of the Judean community after the nation's collapse in the early Persian Period.

David Carr, *Reading the Fractures of Genesis: Historical and Literary Approaches* (Louisville KY: Westminster John Knox, 1996).

For the first time in Genesis, language of sin becomes part of the story. Compared to the overpowering force that leads to murder, Adam and Eve's disobedience in the garden seems like mere youthful indiscretion. [Comparison of Adam and Eve/Cain and Abel Stories] But even after Cain's heinous deed, God protects him and ensures his life.

Like the story of the Garden of Eden, the Cain and Abel narrative is also an etiology. It tells of the origins of the sin of murder, of hatred between brothers, and of violent disruption of family life by jealousy and competition for honor. The chapter extends the theme of alienation introduced in Genesis 3, for here discord and disagreement have infected the next generation, spreading from parents to offspring. When Cain desires to dominate his brother and murders him, he further severs the original accord between humans and the earth.

Introduction, 4:1-2

The first two verses about the birth of offspring augur a promising future for the human race. Adam "knew his wife Eve and she conceived and she bore Cain" (v. 1). The Hebrew verb meaning "to know" often carries the sense of knowing intimately, sexually, as it clearly does here, for "she conceived and she bore."[1] After Adam and Eve's expulsion from the garden, double verbs of conceiving and bearing point to a new beginning. [She Conceived and She Bore]

Amazed at her pregnancy and the birth of her child, Eve exclaims, "I have produced a man with the help of the LORD" (v. 1). "LORD" is the English translation for "YHWH," Israel's particular name for God. Remarkably, Eve is the first human to use God's name in the Bible.[2] Considered from the point of view of the larger narrative of the Pentateuch, that she does so is surprising, for God reveals that name for the first time later to Moses at the burning bush (Exod 3:13-15). Yet the Priestly composers of Genesis, that is, the book's final editors (see [Ancient Traditions about the Authorship of Genesis]), know Israel's personal name for God and connect it back to the very beginnings of the human race as a way to show that Israel's God is God of all peoples.

What is more surprising is that the final editors of Genesis place the sacred name on the lips of the first woman. Although the verse gives no reason for this, Eve's knowledge of God's name implies an intimate relationship between them, a mutual knowing and cooperation outside the garden. Her exclamation of surprised joy at Cain's birth in collaboration with Yahweh underscores her participation in the creative life of the Creator. God gave humans, and in the case of childbirth women especially, a share in the production of life that is already anticipated in the divine command to be fruitful and multiply (1:28). By producing children, the people cooperate with God, participate in the making of life, and continue filling the earth with other humans. Eve's sexuality gives life, participates in divine life, and models human creativity in all domains of human life.

Conceiving, giving birth, and producing offspring is a central theme of Genesis, begun here and given prominence later in the body of the book (chs. 12–50). Eve has produced a man-child. She plays on words, following a Hebrew style usually associated with the Yahwist (J writer, or non-P material), found also in the garden story. The verb translated in the NRSV as "I have produced" (*qānîtî*) looks and sounds like the name of her son Cain (*qāyin*), a wordplay that stresses Cain's importance as firstborn son.

She Conceived and She Bore

The doubled birthing verbs of conceiving and bearing serve as a formula of hope to announce births across the book. They emphasize new life and convey the miracle of childbirth, here carried to successful completion. Such completion was not to be assumed either in the ancient world or in parts of our world today. The more pregnancies a woman had, the greater the chance she would die in childbirth. Adult life spans in ancient Israel, estimated from skeletal remains, suggest that men lived from 30–40 years and women for 20–30 years. Risks from pregnancy, childbirth, and lactation contributed to women's high mortality rates. Ancient populations had few medical solutions for the complications of labor and delivery, such as hemorrhage, pelvic deformation, disproportion between the sizes of the child's head and pelvis, eclampsia, and more. In Genesis, Rebekah has a troubled pregnancy (25:22-26), and Rachel dies in childbirth (35:16-18). The many dangers to a woman's life may have contributed to her reluctance to conceive children, perhaps explaining why men ruled over women sexually (3:16).

For further reading, see Carol Myers, *Rediscovering Eve: Ancient Israelite Women in Context* (New York: Oxford University Press, 2013) 97–102.

Status of the Firstborn

Firstborn sons hold special status in the Old Testament (Exod 13:12-15; Num 18:15-16). They are dedicated to God partly in remembrance of the exodus when God saved Israel's firstborn sons during the slaughter of Egypt's firstborn. "Firstborn son" is the title given to Israel (Exod 4:22; Jer 2:3; 31:9), showing it to be a title of honor and responsibility. The firstborn son inherits a double portion of the family estate, gains the father's blessing, and becomes the patriarch of the extended family, the one charged with providing for and protecting the rest. In Genesis, these social expectations are reversed by God's frequent election of the second-born son, such as Abel over Cain and Jacob over Esau.

[Status of the Firstborn] Strangely, Eve describes her male baby as "a man," as if before the story even begins Cain has symbolically reached adulthood.

Compared to the attention the chapter gives Eve's words about Cain's birth (v. 1), the very simple mention of Abel's birth hints of a foreshortened existence. "Next she bore his brother Abel" (v. 2). No further comment accompanies the occasion. The name "Abel" itself suggests brevity of life. It resembles the word *hebel*, a favorite word of Ecclesiastes that conveys a sense of vapor, vanity, or short duration (v. 2). [*Hebel* in Ecclesiastes] Although Abel takes up little space in the narrative, the narrator is careful to identify him as Cain's brother rather than Adam and Eve's son. The fraught relationship among siblings is at issue in the story and across the book.

Hebel in Ecclesiastes

Abel's name intimates that his life will be short, for it relates to a frequent term found in the Old Testament wisdom book known as Ecclesiastes ("Qoheleth," Hebrew). Ecclesiastes looks at human endeavors and concludes that "all is vanity (*hebel*) and chasing after the wind" (Eccl 1:14). He investigates wisdom, accomplishment, and the acquisition of great wealth and fame and concludes that human endeavors are *hebel*, that is, vapor that arrives quickly and disappears (Eccl 1:2; 2:11, 17, 23, 26; 3:19; 4:4, 7, 16; 5:10; 6:2, 4,7; 8:14; 11:8; 12:8). Abel's life is brief, itself disappearing like vapor.

The introduction succinctly identifies the varying labors of the two brothers. Beginning with the second born, verse 2 notes that Abel is a keeper of sheep, whereas Cain is a "tiller of the field" or, more literally, a "servant of the ground" like his father Adam. The sentence's syntax reverses the brothers' birth order, perhaps to anticipate God's choice of second-born Abel over his firstborn brother. Some interpreters have seen the brothers' differing labors as a reflection of an ancient conflict between herdsman and agriculturalists and, therefore, also as an explanation of farmer Cain's animosity toward his shepherd brother,[3] but the narrator makes no such point.

Sacrifices, 4:3-5

Rather than offering one sacrifice, the brothers present two separate offerings that become the cause of conflict (vv. 3-5). [Sacrifices and Worship] Cain offers fruit of the ground, while Abel brings the "firstlings of his flock, their fat portions." Whether Abel's offering is superior because it is the firstborn of the flock while Cain brings produce of the field rather than "first fruits" is not clear. Perhaps ancient readers heard superiority in Abel's offering, but the text does not make that judgment. "God's response to Cain gives no indication that there was a specific problem with

Sacrifices and Worship

Each brother offers something from his line of work, one of meat and the other of plants, perhaps suggesting conflict between shepherds and agri-culturalists. The text assumes that readers know something about worship in ancient Israel, so it does not explain the offerings. All that can be told from the text is that Abel is a shepherd who brings "the firstlings of the flock, and the fat portions," while Cain is a farmer who offers "fruit from the ground" (4:3). The narrator provides no reason for God to prefer either one offering or one brother over the other. By choosing Abel's sacrifice, perhaps God shows preference for animal offerings and shepherds over agriculturists. If so, that preference may be due to the influence of the priests who edited the final form of the Pentateuch. Priests presided over animal sacrifices in ancient Israel, and they understood that Israel's vocation was to become a priestly people set apart for the worship of God.

Sacrifices were part of ancient Israel's worship practices that showed reverence for and gratitude to God and served as gifts for God, whether comprised of animals or cereal and plant offerings (Rattray, 1143–47). Priests presided over animal and other sacrifices (Lev 3:5, 11), for which instructions appear in Exodus, Leviticus, and Numbers. Animals were ritually sacrificed, not merely slaughtered, and blood was offered on the altar, although that process is not mentioned here. The fat of the animal was most precious and belonged to God. All animals were to be unblemished. Burnt offerings were a common animal sac-rifice for atonement or thanksgiving from which the priests received some meat while the people bringing the sacrifice received the rest (Lev 1; Num 28–29). Cereal or plant offer-ings could be wheat, barley, olive oil, wine, frankincense, or a variety of other cereal offerings.

For further reading, see Joseph Blenkinsopp, *Creation, Un-creation, Re-Creation: A Discursive Commentary on Genesis 1–11* (London and New York: T & T Commentary, 2011) 82–105.

Susan Rattray, "Worship," *HBD*

his sacrifice."[4] The two brothers simply work in different modes of food production, leaving the divine choice of Abel unexplained here as elsewhere in stories of divine election. God chooses Isaac, for example, over firstborn Ishmael and Jacob over firstborn Esau. Divine choice reverses human expectations and social arrange-ments, and that reversal may well be the point of God's choice of Abel over Cain. This is the first of many instances where God over-turns Israel's cultural and legal preference for firstborn sons.

For unexplained reasons, God prefers Abel's offerings, "but for Cain and his offering God had no regard" (4:5). God's preference sets in motion the calamity that follows, for Cain's "face fell" and he became "very angry" (v. 5). He may well have expected to be favored because he was the elder. [Divine Preference]

Distorted Desires, 4:6-7

Outside the garden, alienation becomes unfettered and unre-strained. Despite Cain's angry pouting, God is attentive to him, notices his furious, crestfallen appearance, and addresses him directly. God asks him questions. The first repeats language of the previous verse and draws attention to Cain's response: "Why are you angry and why has your countenance fallen?" (v. 6). The second question is more like a declaration to the effect that neither disgrace nor rejection is a necessary result of these events: "If you

Divine Preference

The story of the first murder portrays God as an arbitrary acceptor and rejecter of humans without explanation. Why does God have "no regard" for Cain's offering, "even as the LORD had regard for Abel and his offering" (4:4)?

The trouble comes not from Cain but from Yahweh, the strange God of Israel. Inexplicably Yahweh chooses—accepts and rejects. Conventional interpretation is too hard on Cain and too easy on Yahweh. It is Yahweh who transforms a normal report into a life/death story for us and about us. Essential to the plot is the capricious freedom of Yahweh. Like the narrator, we must resist every effort to explain it. (Brueggemann, 56)

Perhaps God's choice concerns the tension between God's "ungrounded divine preference for Israel over the rest of humanity" (Brett, 37).

Yet the heart of divine choice may lie elsewhere. The Cain and Abel story reflects the dilemma of the survivors of the nation's destruction under Babylon and the problems of why some survived, some were exiled, and some died. For survivors and their offspring, the inscrutability of the divine choice of Abel may be a theological reflection after the fact, a search for explanation and comfort if the inscrutable God chose the survivors. Such theological reflections often emerge from tragic conditions where some few make it through alive but are unable to explain how that happened unless God chose them.

Walter Brueggemann, *Genesis* (Interpretation; Atlanta: John Knox, 1982).
Mark Brett, *Genesis: Procreation and the Politics of Identity* (OTR; New York: Routledge, 2000).

do well, will you not be accepted?" (v. 7, NRSV). [Translation Problem] God's acceptance of Cain is a given, but Cain has responsibility. He must do well, perhaps meaning he must overcome his jealousy and accept that he is not chosen despite being the firstborn.

Translation Problem

AΩ   The Hebrew of v. 7 is not clear because words seem to be missing. Cain has to bear God's failure to appreciate his offering: "Surely if you do well, then you will [be able to] bear it." "Be able to" seems to be implied (Smith). In Hebrew, the "then" clause of the verse "is a single word, *śĕ'ēt*. Normally a Hebrew clause would have a main verb, and a form such as this one would have a main verb to govern it. For the corresponding negative form "not to be able to bear," see Prov 30:15. Another translation is, "Surely if you do good, is there not a lifting up [of your face]?" (Westermann, 281, 299). Still another is "you will find acceptance," following the NRSV (Bandstra, 239). Although translated differently, these suggestions agree that the text is obscure and that God does not abandon Cain but counsels him that he has responsibility for his future.

Mark S. Smith, private email to author, 2/14/16.
Claus Westermann, *Genesis 1–11* (Minneapolis: Augsburg, 1984).
Barry Bandstra, *Genesis 1–11: A Handbook on the Hebrew Text* (Waco TX: Baylor University Press, 2008).

The literary skill evident here results from restraint. The text omits clear insight into motivations of either God or Cain. Yet Cain's apparent desire for superiority or at least equivalent status drives him and distorts his thinking. He cannot see that what he longs for and believes has been denied to him is already a reality, that is, God accepts him, includes him in divine care, and counsels him to live better. Then God asks why he is acting so angrily and speaks with him, as if divine care still embraces him. Because God does not favor his sacrifice, Cain seems to think that God loves only his brother in a kind of a zero-sum game, a competition where one receives everything and the other nothing. In this sense, Cain is a quintessential human whose false perceptions warp his relationships, alienating him from both God and his brother.

God's questions quickly dissolve into warning and show Cain's perilous situation. If he fails to do well, then "sin is lurking at

Language of Sin

AΩ Sin in the Old Testament involves a wide vocabulary relating to unacceptable behavior. The most important terms are "to miss the mark" (*ḥāṭāʾ*), "to transgress," (*pāšaʿ*), "to be evil" (*rʿa*), and the noun "iniquity" (*ʿāwôn*). In the Old Testament, all carry the theological sense of violation against God, against the covenant, and against others. Sin is a profoundly religious notion for it is always against God even when directed against other people.

Cain's murder of his brother seems to involve more than missing the mark, which is the verb used here (4:7). He takes a life, a supreme act of moral transgression; the deed is iniquitous and transgressive as it misses the mark of basic respect for the life of another and simultaneously offends God. The noun "iniquity" (*ʿāwôn*) has a wide range of meanings including sin, guilt, and punishment. In Gen 4:13, Cain tells God that his punishment or guilt (*ʿāwôn*) is more than he can bear (Cover, 4:31–40; Attridge, 263–79).

For further reading, see Mark E. Biddle, *Missing the Mark: Sin and Its Consequences in Biblical Theology* (Nashville: Abingdon, 2005).

Robin Cover, "Sin, Sinners (OT)," *ABD*.

Harold W. Attridge, "Sin, Sinners" (*NIDB* 5; Nashville: Abingdon, 2009).

---

the door; its longing is for you but you must rule over it" (v. 7, my translation). The elder brother's faulty understanding and emotional confusion opens the door to sin. Sin is a living force in this story, imagined metaphorically as a voracious animal or a potent power with its own qualities of desire and intention. Sin lurks, waiting to pounce like a lion longing to devour Cain. Cain has the capacity to rule over it, to master it, to remain free of it, and he must do so. But in the very next scene, sin rules over Cain.

This story is the Bible's first introduction to sin as an explicit way to speak of human behavior. [Language of Sin] In this dramatic scene, sin involves neither rule-breaking nor sexual irregularities. It refers, rather, to the taking of another's life and perhaps, even further, refusing to respect, care for, and protect the life of the other. In the symbolic world of the text, sin is not merely an evil human deed; the text *imagines* it as if it were a compelling energy outside Cain waiting to attack and enslave him. This way of articulating the experience of sin captures deep struggles humans often have governing their desires, emotions, and behaviors. Cain can resist sin and can master it, yet like most humans he does not.[5]

Murder and Its Aftermath, 4:8-16

Abel's murder happens in sharp bursts of speech and action that end quickly. "Cain said," "let us go,"[6] "Cain rose up," and "he murdered him" (v. 8). Lest the reader forget the relationship that unites the two sons of Adam and Eve, the verse mentions Cain the elder first and twice identifies Abel as "his brother." Cain is the subject of the action, the doer of the crime against his younger brother. The murder's aftermath (vv. 9-16), however, not the murder itself (v. 8), is the focal point of the text. Just as God appears immediately after the fruit-eating scene in the garden, so God comes forth after Cain's crime to interrogate him about "your

Cain and Abel by Titian

An Italian artist of the 16th century, Titian painted the first murder with Cain and Abel portrayed as two adult brothers, thereby capturing the iconic nature of the killing, of brothers against brothers, men against other men, throughout history.

Titian changed Western art partly by using dramatic arrangements of light and shadow to create highly dramatic scenes. He portrays Cain and Abel as robust, muscular men attired similarly. The light falls on Abel's leg and upper body, foregrounding the victim, while his murdering brother recedes into darkness. Cain's powerful leg, raised arm, and barely visible weapon convey overpowering hatred and might. With both faces obscured, the brothers depict in a single picture the crushing power of violence of the stronger against the weaker.

Titian (Tiziano Vecellio) (c. 1488–1576). *Cain and Abel*. 1576. S. Maria della Salute, Venice, Italy. (Credit: Erich Lessing / Art Resource, NY)

brother": "Where is your brother?" [*Cain and Abel* by Titian]

Cain answers God's question with a lie and with a question of his own: "I do not know; am I my brother's keeper?" (v. 9). This cold, brutal reply reverberates through the rest of Genesis and through history itself. The word traditionally translated "keeper" can mean one who "tends" "guards," or "protects." "Am I my brother's/sister's protector?" Am I his guard? Am I to tend her? Am I to serve him in the same way that I am servant of the soil? It is the relationship of brotherhood that Cain refuses to assume. He not only fails to keep and guard his younger brother but also becomes the very one from whom Abel needs protection. Cain replies to God with a defensive lie, a diversionary tactic, a denial of what he has done. In the process, Cain shows callous indifference toward his brother and the destruction of family that follows from it. Sin rules over Cain.

God demands to know, "What have you done?" as if God cannot absorb this violence among human creatures. God's question is a rhetorical strategy to underscore the horror of what Cain has done. Cain remains silent, but God insists that Cain attend to the consequences of his actions, that he reflect on them and face what he has done: "Listen; your brother's blood calls out to me from the ground" (v. 10). Literary devices in this verse highlight the sin's enormity. The very earth on which Cain stands has received his brother's blood, and that blood rises up from the ground in a cry of outrage to God. The words blood (*děmě*) and ground (*'adāmāh*) sound somewhat alike in Hebrew, and both assume nearly human status in this verse. The ground has a mouth to absorb Abel's blood, and the blood has a voice to cry out to God [The Blood and the Ground]

God, in turn, acts as observer, witness, commentator, prosecutor, and judge, taking all the parts in a lawsuit against the murderer (vv. 9-16). After the killing, God's first act is to speak on behalf of the victim, the younger one, the one betrayed and overpowered by the elder and stronger. It is the blood of the martyr that makes the claim upon God and to which God attends (cf. Job 16:18).

Taken aback by Cain's cruel refusal to be his brother's keeper, God punishes Cain or, more accurately, announces the consequences of his sinful actions. A curse comes upon him, not from God but from the ground itself. The ground has "opened its mouth to receive your brother's blood" (v. 11). Cain's crime against his brother is also a crime against the ground that he serves (tills), a relationship now broken because of the murder. His father before him had to work the ground by the sweat of his brow, but for Cain the ground will yield nothing. To survive, he will be forced to become a "wanderer" upon the earth.

God punishes Cain but does not curse him. [The So-Called Curse of Cain] In an appeal for clemency, like Abel's blood, he cries out to God, for he cannot bear his punishment (v. 13). Gerhard von Rad noticed what is missing from Cain's appeal.

> **The Blood and the Ground**
>
> The Cain and Abel episode emphatically asserts the strong interconnection among all God's creation. Abel's blood cries out from the ground, and the ground curses Cain, so his very livelihood—his vocation to be a servant of the soil like his father Adam—will no longer be possible. Blood carries life (Lev 17:11), so spilling it is pouring away life. The ground receives it, takes it in, and cries out on Abel's behalf. The earth witnesses against Cain and will no longer "yield its strength" to him, no longer produce food to feed him, nor share its life with him. "The earth itself will deny him its power of blessing" (von Rad, 106). Cain believes that only by working the land will he see the face of God, but now he must become a nomad, a wanderer. His curse is his exclusion from land, from community, and now he believes he will be prey to anyone who sees him.
>
> Cain's violation of his brother's body violates the earth itself, for killing his brother disrupts the divine ecology of the cosmos. The earth absorbs Abel's blood, cries out in pain, and witnesses on his behalf. When the earth receives his martyr's blood, it becomes his voice. The earth as the voice of the voiceless, the innocent, and the murdered continues to receive the blood of the innocent—those slain in war, gunned down on the streets, raped and stabbed in their homes. The ground becomes Abel's voice, "gagged during his short existence . . . . And goes up unencumbered to God (4:10)" (Lacocque, 65).
>
> Gerhard von Rad, *Genesis* (OTL; Philadelphia: Westminster, 1972).
> André Lacocque, *Onslaught against Innocence: Cain, Abel, and the Yahwist* (Eugene OR: Cascade, 2008).

He expresses no remorse for murdering his brother, no grief over his death, no sorrow for his bereaved parents; instead, he "goes to pieces" over his own fate.[7] He cares only for himself, and whether he repents later, we never learn. When he does raise a lament that becoming a wanderer will separate him from God and perhaps from divine protection, making him prey for anyone he meets, he is still thinking only of himself.

Some readers may wonder from whom the danger to Cain could possibly come, since Genesis implies that there are only three humans remaining upon the earth. Genesis, however, shows no such concern because it is not offering an account of the facts of human population. It is instead presenting a theological account of human sin and perhaps an etiology to explain why some people wander in search of food rather than live settled agrarian lives.

Fear now overwhelms Cain just as jealousy had previously. Still with a self-serving attitude, he lists the deprivations that will

---

The So-Called Curse of Cain

The mark that God placed on Cain figured prominently among Christian arguments to support the
institution of slavery in the United States during the nineteenth century. With absolutely no basis in the text,
Christian slaveholders used interpretations that associated
Cain with evil either because he married a "black wife" or
because they theorized that the mark of Cain was dark
skin. They called dark skin "the curse of Cain" (Haynes, 15).
God's mark on Cain is first in a list of misread biblical
images justifying slaveholding by Christians in the United
States.

Nowhere does Gen 4:15 say that God cursed Cain;
rather the ground curses him, making his work of tilling
the ground more difficult than it was for Adam. The ground
will produce nothing for him; therefore, he will wander
from place to place in search of food to survive as the first

nomad. God's mark on Cain is actually the reverse of the
dehumanization that slaveholders misconstrued it to be.
The mark of Cain is a protection, a mark to preserve his life
against other people who might want to harm or kill him.

Both Testaments of the Bible accept slavery as a cultural
institution beyond question, so embedded was it in ancient
societies, biblical or otherwise. Ancient practices were,
however, not based on skin color. The Judean people
were generally brown-skinned. Slaves were obtained as
prisoners of war (with women and children being the booty
from war) or as debtors from the community who had to
sell themselves or family members into servitude to pay
debts.

For further reading, see Stephen R. Haynes, *Noah's
Curse: The Biblical Justification of American Slavery* (New
York: Oxford University Press, 2002).

---

accompany his alienation from the ground and forced wandering:
"I will be hidden from your face, I shall be a fugitive and a
wanderer on earth, and anyone who meets me may murder me"
(v. 14). Cain dreads life without divine protection, for then anyone
could treat him as he treated his brother. He assumes unquestion-
ingly that wandering will distance him from the divine presence.

God does not take Cain's life or allow anyone else to do so but
promises instead to protect him by a sevenfold vengeance against
attackers. By not executing the ancient law of "an eye for an eye
or a tooth for a tooth," and demanding his life in reparation for
Abel's, God overturns Cain's perceptions and the reader's expectations. To seal the promise, God puts a mark on Cain that will
make clear to anyone he meets that he is not to be harmed (4:15).
The mark is protective, a tattoo or tribal marking to identify him
to others.

The murder story concludes when Cain leaves the divine presence and has "settled in the land of Nod," east of Eden (v. 12).
Since Nod is related to the Hebrew word for "wanderer," André
LaCocque proposed that Nod means "Nowhere" and that Cain
moves to the "land of Roaming," further east than Adam and
Eve were sent when they were cast out of Eden (3:24).[8] That he
"settled" there, however, is puzzling, since settling seems to be the
opposite of the punishment meted out to him. Yet he does settle,
even becoming the founder of a city (v. 17).

The remaining units of chapter 4 tell of Cain's descendants
(vv. 17-24) and additional births to his parents (vv. 25-26). Both
units are genealogical in form and quickly move the text through

the generations. Both bring fulfillment to God's command to "be fruitful and multiply" (1:28), and both continue to speak of the murder that runs like a scarlet thread through the chapter.

Cain's Offspring, 4:17-24

The second unit begins with the conception and birth formula that announces the spread of humanity throughout Genesis. The wanderer Cain "knew his wife and she conceived." Like many women in the book, Cain's wife has neither name nor role beyond childbearing, yet this is a crucial contribution for a people facing possible extinction. The text does provide the male child's name, Enoch, and just as abruptly tells us that when Cain built a city, he named it after his son, the third generation of humans. The wandering father ironically cements his place as the patriarch of a settled people. A rhythmic listing of the five generations of Cain's lineage follows (v. 18).

The list of Cain's descendants pauses six generations after Cain with a brief narrative about Lamech (vv. 19-24). Lamech has two wives who have both names and important children. The first wife, Adah, has two sons: Jabal lives in tents and raises animals, and Jubal is a foreparent of musicians. Lamech's second wife, Zillah, is mother of Tubal-Cain, maker of bronze and iron tools, and of a daughter Naamah with a name but no mentioned contribution. Besides bearing children who help to develop civilization, Lamech's two wives are important witnesses to their husband's cruelty, for they are the audience to his poetry.

Again Genesis draws attention to important content by using poetry (2:23; 3:14-19). In his poem, Lamech says everything twice: Adah and Zillah, you wives of Lamech, "hear my voice . . . listen to what I have to say." Then with a doublet of violence he brags, "I have killed a man for wounding me, a young man for striking me" (v. 23). [Motivations] He ends with a comparison that accentuates and expands the violence: "If Cain is avenged sevenfold, truly Lamech seventy-seven fold" (v. 24).

After Cain killed Abel, God dispensed with the ancient practice of "an eye for an eye" by showing mercy. [An Eye for an Eye] Lamech dispenses with it, too, not to forgive someone but to retaliate against minor offenses with "seventy-sevenfold" vengeance. He kills for a wound, murders for a blow. His poem celebrates horrific reprisal, multiplying by ten the sevenfold vengeance with which God promises to protect Cain from harm (v. 15). God's announcement of vengeance warns against further violence, while Lamech's

Motivations

📖 Whatever may be the ostensible reason for Lamech to boast before his wives, it ultimately covers up a deep anxiety about his own significance. . . . In this sense the song of Lamech is not just repulsive, it is also pitiful. As is characteristic of narcissistic self-assertion, it is made at the expense of others. Self-feeling creates a desert around the illusion, *"l'enfer, c'est les autre"* (hell is other people). That is why the figures of Cain and Lamech are so similar and complementary. It is not just because the one and the other are killers, but also because the motivation for killing and for boasting is so much the same in both: self-aggrandizement and outshining of others.

André LaCocque, *Onslaught against Innocence: Cain, Abel and the Yahwist* (Eugene OR: Cascade, 2008) 137.

William Blake (1757–1827). *Lamech and His Two Wives*. 1795. Color print finished in ink and water-color on paper. Acquisition presented by W. Graham Robertson, 1939. Tate Gallery, London, Great Britain. (Credit: © Tate, London / Art Resource, NY)

announcement enacts extreme violation in retaliation for minor offenses.

Interpreters have seen in Lamech's poem the acceleration of sin and the multiplication of violence to contribute to the "story of cursing" that weaves throughout the first eleven chapters of Genesis. That broad theme is surely present, for alienation and violence spread to the whole world, but the bragging, violent Lamech also threatens his wives. Public brutality often manifests itself in the domestic sphere.

More Offspring of Eve and Adam, 4:25-26

In the chapter's final unit, the murder rises again like an infection resurfacing after a brief dormancy. Cain's murder of Abel motivates the birth of a third son after Eve's unspeakable loss. This time when she comments upon the birth of her child, it is without obvious emotion: "God has appointed for me another child instead of Abel,

An Eye for an Eye

📖 To contemporary Western thinkers, "an eye for an eye" as a response to violent attack seems unjust, and to Christians it is utterly unforgiving. In the ancient world, however, the principle known as *lex talionis*, the law of extraction of payment, controls and reduces vengeance. Found in the book of Exodus, the law prescribes "an eye for an eye, a tooth for a tooth, a hand for a hand, a foot for a foot, a burn for a burn, a wound for

a wound" (21:22-25). By allowing only for punishment equivalent to the crime rather than wholesale slaughter in retaliation for a singular offense, the legal principle regulates vengeance and helps to contain it.

For further reading, see Trevor W. Thompson, "Punishment and Restitution," in *The Oxford Encyclopedia of the Bible and Law*, 2 vols., ed. Brent Strawn (New York: Oxford University Press, 2015) 183–93.

because Cain killed him" (v. 25). God's action and the resulting child are one and the same. Despite the tragic losses of the second generation, death does not triumph here and the family does not come to an end.

The last verse creates a frame around the chapter: "At that time people began to invoke the name of the LORD" (v. 26). This line either ignores or corrects Eve's call upon God's name at the chapter's beginning (v. 1). Although many critical interpreters attempted to explain Eve's archaic use of the name YHWH since it does not follow our understanding of Israel's history, I do not find a problem here. The writer locates intimate relationship with Israel's God within the primordial beginnings of human life. Rather than using *elohim*, the general Semitic term for God or gods, the writer understands close relationship with the God of Israel to be available to all humans, to Eve the first woman, and to all people who are her offspring.

CONNECTIONS

Eve as Spiritual Model

Eve's role in chapter 4 is surprising, complicated, and also helpful to modern believers. Her words open the story of life outside the garden, and since women rarely speak in Genesis, her words are worth noticing. She begins with an ecstatic cry of delight at the birth of her first son "with the help of Yahweh" and ends with a subdued announcement that "God has appointed for me another child instead of Abel because Cain killed him." Her words heighten the murder's tragedy, for she has lost both sons, the one who was murdered as well as the murderer who now wanders far from her. Her expression captures the bitter, unfathomable grief of parents whose children die before them. [William Blake's *The Body of Abel Found by Adam and Eve*] Eve's loss results not from the physical threats of nature or from the precariousness of childbirth in the ancient world but from bitterness, violence, and hatred within the family.

Eve's speech also draws attention to the critical role women played in the ancient world by producing offspring for the survival of society. She reminds us of the perilous circumstances of birth, the strong possibility that children would not survive to adulthood due to complications of pregnancy, infant diseases, hunger, and many other dangers that made life precarious. Although women

William Blake's *The Body of Abel Found by Adam and Eve*

Blake's painting captures in stark clarity the tragedy of Abel's murder and the human emotions hidden in the scene. To the left, the horrified Cain puts his hands to his head in shock and runs vigorously away from the horror of his brother's dead body and the results of his own violence. Blake paints Cain in dark gray color, as if he were nearly dead himself. Both the parents and the dead Abel are a slightly lighter color of gray, creating the effect of a family remnant also facing the end of its common life.

The bodies of Adam and Eve blend into one another against the solid dark rock behind them. With his hands lifted in shock, Adam kneels upright and his gaze follows his escaping elder son, Cain. Eve bends over Abel with arms encircling his face while her body forms a canopy of grief over him. Clouds as dark as the granite rocks extend over the scene and appear to be following Cain away from the family from which he has excluded himself. Crosshatching and horizontal lines convey a darkening world, and a black grave awaits Abel's body. The mortality that came from being barred from the tree of life in the garden now comes upon the couple with full force. They lose one son to death and lose the other to consequences of his violent hatred. Their future appears to be over.

William Blake (1757–1827). *The Body of Abel Found by Adam and Eve*. 1826. Ink, tempera, and gold on mahogany. Tate Gallery, London. (Credit: Wikimedia Commons, PD-1923)

were generally subordinate to men in the ancient world, their role in childbearing was essential for the future of the people.

Eve is the first human character in the Bible to speak God's name, just as she is the Bible's first theologian when she speaks about God with the serpent in the garden. By claiming her own spiritual experiences within the embodied circumstances of her existence, she provides a glimpse of adult faith that finds God in her own unique life. She recognizes herself as God's partner in the generative work of producing life, in the co-creation of her child "with the help of the LORD." Rarely noted by interpreters, the brief role assigned her in this chapter portrays something essential in divine human partnership. Calling on the name of God, living in the presence of the divine, and cooperating with divine power is the source of new life and of all genuine creativity. The first woman recognizes God's power coursing through her own body—not a power to fight, subdue, or dominate but to bring life into being that, in turn, brings forth more life. Eve's words invite women and men to recognize the source of all creativity in relationship with God.

Ways to Murder

As metaphors of the strong and the weak, Cain and Abel reappear in every generation. Cain's murder of Abel is the archetype of all murders, all killings of the innocent, the weaker, the younger, the more vulnerable, the more naive. [Abel as Iconic Martyr] Cain's refusal to be his brother's "keeper" resonates in our day whenever rich nations exploit poorer ones, a cleric abuses a member of the flock, a ruler kills his own people, a parent kills a child's soul with neglect or harm, the employed fail to aid the unemployed, the settled refuse to welcome the displaced, or the violent use guns against ordinary people going about their daily lives.

The list of sins of domination and violence is endless so that sadly this story reverberates among us. The truth emerges from a seemingly simple tale. One person or group hates others because they appear to have more honor, more love, more wealth, more glory—because they are chosen. The first group enacts fear and jealousy to exclude and dehumanize the other. Murder is the ultimate dehumanization. It may not be surprising, therefore, that the context of this conflict is worship itself—religion as battleground in conflict over God's favor. [Liturgy as Place of Blasphemy]

Abel as Iconic Martyr

New Testament interpretations find in Abel's blood a symbol or type of innocent suffering, of spilled blood that takes on meaning far beyond itself. When Jesus is under siege from lawyers and Pharisees in the Gospel of Luke, for example, he mentions Abel as the first in a long list of innocent martyrs. He accuses religious leaders of burdening the people and not lifting a finger to help them. They kill and persecute the prophets and the apostles and bring guilt upon the present generation "charged with the blood of all the prophets since the foundation of the world," beginning with the blood of Abel (Lk 11:46-52).

The letter to the Hebrews, in turn, expands the meaning of Abel's death by associating Jesus' martyrdom on the cross with the blood of Abel. For the anonymous writer of Hebrews, Jesus is the mediator of the new covenant, the perfect sacrifice who perfects the blood of Abel. Jesus embraces the blood of the innocent, to pour it out in a perfect sacrifice to God (Heb 12:22-24).

Abel's bloody death, therefore, signifies the death of innocent martyrs, Christian and otherwise, who lose their lives to violent hatred. His blood cries out today from the earth on every continent in the blood of martyrs crying out from the ground of Central America, Syria, Yemen, Baltimore, Orlando, and Nice. Their blood cries out from and with the earth in an appeal for compassion and an end to all conditions that make it possible for violence to destroy human life. Their bodies, already despised by some, cry out for acceptance, for a witness, and for justice. The blood of Abel points to the blood of Jesus Christ.

Human Sin

The Cain and Abel story has its own integrity as an etiology about the beginnings of murder and nomadism, but it also reflects conditions of the scattered people of Judah in its ongoing struggle to survive in the early Persian Period. To have a future as a people,

Liturgy as Place of Blasphemy

Worship is the context of the murder of brother by brother. Against the backdrop of honoring the creator, the ultimate hatred expressed by the killing of another made in the divine image emerges as a double blasphemy. William T. Cavanaugh has told of a scene that took place in Chile during the early days of the Pinochet regime that expresses the depth of the offense.

In the early days of the military regime, Chile was driven indoors. Behind some doors, champagne corks popped; behind others, there was only an anxious silence. In the streets the military patrols sped by on their hungry search for enemies. Those labeled enemies faced a terrible dilemma. They could stay at home and await capture, or they could attempt to flee, a choice that would take them out into the streets ruled by the regime. Among those who chose to run was a pair of young leftists who, three days after the coup, arrived panicked at the doorstep of a priest's residence in the center of Santiago. They were received, but they were not allowed to stay. Back out into the street, they would have to try their luck elsewhere. That evening as the community prepared for Mass, a seminarian spoke up and objected to the celebration of the Eucharist under the circumstances. He said Christ had been turned away at the door of the residence. Communion in the body of Christ had already been denied in the denial of the two seeking asylum.

William T. Cavanaugh, *Torture and the Eucharist* (Challenges in Contemporary Theology; Malden MA: Blackwell, 1998) 205.

they need children, peace, and cooperation among themselves, and they need to understand how God is involved in the catastrophe. Echoing these needs, the chapter highlights childbirth as co-creation with God and celebrates Eve, mother of the living. It depicts a God of new life who protects the wanderer and provides him with a home. It portrays internal conflict among brothers as a major impediment to their future together.

The story of the first murder locates the source of violence in humans and in the feral power of sin. It understands the murdered one as innocent victim and, in some oblique fashion, as the chosen one. Rather than causing the violence, God is outraged by it, is appalled by human failure, and punishes the killer. [Punishment]

Yet God also protects Cain and even promises to avenge him sevenfold if others assault him. After the tragedies of murder and exile, the chapter concludes with the birth of more children, first to Cain and then to Adam and Eve. Set in the primal past, the chapter functions as a muted echo of issues with which the Judean audience is struggling, and, like all the disasters that nearly bring extinction in the book, it ends in the creation of new life and anticipates the promises of life to come.

Punishment

📖 Cain interprets his expulsion as punishment greater than he can bear (4:13). His exile is the consequence of the murder. Actions bring consequences, but frequently Genesis understands God as the one who issues the consequences, that is, punishes. I understand that assessment to be the way the book's composers make sense of catastrophes that have befallen them rather than as a full-blown theological expression of the nature or actions of God. This text and others where divine punishment of humans occur aim to explain disruption and catastrophe and keep God near during the process of survival and recovery.

God's involvement as punisher is human interpretation, human expression to make sense of life gone amuck. By contrast, for modern readers in the west, cause and effect are complex and multifaceted. We do not hold that God rains down hurricanes, causes wars, brings on genocides, infects people with cancer. We bring consequences upon ourselves.

To say that suffering and disruption are divine punishment can, nevertheless, help survivors of disasters. It keeps God in their lives, creates order in the midst of turmoil, and makes sense out of no sense. Language of divine punishment is biblical speech appropriate to the time and place of the book's composition. My effort, however, is to understand how it helps survivors despite its theological inadequacies. See [Trauma and Disaster Studies] and [Disaster Stories in Genesis].

Pastors, care-givers, counselors, and spiritual directors see this process at work all the time. People need explanation and so often blame God or blame themselves to find the cause of tragedy and loss. The problem, theologically and personally, is getting stuck in that view.

NOTES

1. Cf. Gen 4:17, 25; 38:26.

2. André LaCocque, *Onslaught Against Innocence: Cain, Abel, and the Yahwist* (Eugene OR: Cascade, 2008) 80.

3. Robert Alter, *Genesis: Translation and Commentary* (New York: W. W. Norton & Company) 16; LaCocque, *Onslaught Against Innocence*, 18–21.

4. Mark McEntire, *Struggling with God: An Introduction to the Pentateuch* (Macon GA: Mercer University Press, 2008) 58.

5. For full discussion of the nature of sin in the Bible and subsequent tradition see Mark E. Biddle, *Missing the Mark: Sin and Its Consequences in Biblical Theology* (Nashville: Abingdon, 2005).

6. The Hebrew reads "and when they were in the field," but many ancient versions including the Septuagint and the Targum read, "Come, let us go into the field."

7. Gerhard von Rad, *Genesis*, rev. ed. (Philadelphia: Westminster, 1973) 107.

8. LaCocque, *Onslaught Against Innocence*, 31.

NOAH AND THE FLOOD

Genesis 5–9

Genesis 5–9 continues the form of genealogy begun in chapter 4, but this time the descendants are explicitly offspring of Adam rather than Eve. A disaster narrative again interrupts the genealogical frame (Gen 6–8). This time it is not limited to two brothers but involves the destruction of all living creatures with exception of Noah, his family, and animals he saves from the flood. Embedded within the extended list of Adam's progeny, the flood again brings the family line almost to extinction. These chapters threaten Adam's family in drastic ways, and when life resumes in a new creation, Noah and his family alone are left of Adam's descendants. [Outline of Genesis 5–9] Only then does the list of Adam's offspring conclude with Noah's death (9:28).

The story of Noah with its ark, spectacular waters, charming animals, and

Outline of Genesis 5–9
1. Genealogy of Adam Begins, 5:1-32
2. Stories of Times before the Flood, 6:1-8
3. Stories about the Flood, 6:9–8:19
4. New Creation after the Flood, 8:20–9:28

vivid rainbow is widely known, loved by children, and frequently depicted in popular art. Yet the story's simplicity is deceptive. Its four chapters contain literary echoes of other ancient flood stories as well as the first creation account (Gen 1:1–2:4a). More than one version of events appears in the chapters, and some episodes do not seem immediately connected to the narrative, yet they have the important purpose of struggling with causes of catastrophe. Gaps, repetitions, and inconsistencies disrupt the story, but the plot line is clear, artfully constructed, and unforgettable.

By focusing somewhat myopically on analysis of the story's complexities, modern critical interpretation has often missed the power and beauty of these chapters, even as this analysis has helped to explain why the story is choppy, episodic, and repetitive. [Literary Problems and the Two-source Theory] Perhaps ancient readers were not disturbed by conflicts of details and causes within the story because it is basically a coherent and powerful tale. Yet the modern two-source theory of the story's composition understands the problems of the text to be the result of editorial work that combined older sources without smoothing them out. The important theory helps

Literary Problems and the Two-source Theory

Because the flood story's many difficulties are evident to most readers, it is best to start by noting them:

• The text supplies two reasons for the flood: the wickedness of the human heart (6:5) or the corruption of all life and the presence of violence (6:11-12, 13).
• God commands Noah to bring varying numbers of animals aboard: one pair of each animal (6:19-20), or seven pairs of clean animals and one pair of unclean animals (7:2).
• The duration of the flood differs: forty days and nights (7:4, 12) or a whole year (7:6, 11: 8:13, 14).
• There are two sources of the waters: rain (7:12; 8:2b) or the opening of the springs of the deep and the windows of heaven (7:11; 8:1-2a).
• There are two occasions for leaving the ark: when the dove returns with an olive branch indicating the emergence of land (8:6-12) or when God commands it (8:15-17).
• There are different divine names interspersed across the story: YHWH or God (*'elôhîm*).

How is it possible to explain these repetitions and contradictions? Most interpreters hold that the flood story combines two previously written versions of the story called "sources" into the final version of the text. David Cotter offers a helpful chart of the two sources that he calls Source A and Source B. The A source is equivalent to the Priestly source or P and the B source is non-P.

Story Detail	A [P]	B [non-P]
The evil of humanity	6:5	6:11-12
God decides to destroy the universe	6:7	6:13
The announcement of the flood	7:4	6:17
The order to enter the ark	7:1	6:18
The command concerning animals	7:2	6:19-20
The aim to save them from the flood	7:3	6:19
Entering the ark	7:7-9	7:13-16
The beginning of the flood	7:10	7:11
The rising of the waters	7:17	7:18
The destruction of all living things	7:22-23	7:20-21
The end of the flood	8:2b	8:2a
The waters recede	8:3a	8:3b, 5
Preparations for leaving the ark	8:6-12	8:15-17
God promises never to send another flood	8:20-22	9:16-17

Whether each source can be identified this precisely is surely open to question, in part because neither one provides the complete story. Yet the analysis suggests that the writer of the flood story drew from more than one version and artistically created the memorable tale from works available in the culture.

For further reading, see David Carr, *The Fractures of Genesis: Historical and Literary Approaches* (Louisville KY: Westminster John Knox, 1996) 52–62; and Christopher B. Hays, *Hidden Riches: A Sourcebook for the Comparative Study of the Hebrew Bible and the Ancient Near East* (Louisville KY: Westminster John Knox, 2014) 75–95.

From p. 50, *Berit Olam: Genesis* by David W. Cotter, OSB

us appreciate the long and complicated process of speaking and writing that produced the narrative as we have it.

Still there is much more to see. [Outline of Genesis 6–9] The story of Noah and the flood is a remarkable work of literary art. Its language, pacing, and plot rise slowly and fluidly and then escalate, as if to carry readers into the thick of the storm and to convey the experience of the havoc wrought by the flood. Its structure mimics events told within it, building toward the disaster slowly and haltingly, in a bumpy style, anticipating the approaching tragedy (ch. 6). Terrors rise as waters increase and swell like an enormous, unstoppable tsunami, a giant outburst of water that overtakes everything and everyone (ch. 7). The turning point comes at the crest of the waters, when God remembers Noah (8:1). From that point forward, the torrent recedes little by little in a quieting of nature and an eventual return of dry land (ch. 8). At last, Noah offers sacrifice on dry ground and God covenants with him as life begins again in a new creation (9:1-17). Then, in a curious symmetry with events prior to the flood (6:1-9), the flood cycle ends where it began, with hints of renewed disharmony and wickedness among humans (9:18-27).

A concentric structure unites elements of the story.[1] [Concentric Structure of the Flood Story] The buildup to the flood is incremental; instructions and preparations take place, followed by gradually mounting waters that flood in a torrent of death. When the text tells of receding waters, it uses language and structure that closely parallel the buildup, only now moving in a downward direction as waters subside like a tide leaving a beach. Only when God remembers Noah do the waters begin to recede (8:1). The story of the flood is one of the major disaster accounts in Genesis, and it echoes and evokes historical disasters that afflicted Judah in the aftermath of the Babylonian Period (see Introduction). In light of the

Outline of Genesis 6–9
1. Pre-Flood Wickedness, 6:1-22
2. The Waters Rise, 7:1-24
3. The Waters Fall, 8:1-22
4. Creation Again, 9:1-28
5. Post-Flood Wickedness, 9:20-28

Concentric Structure of the Flood Story

The following chart of the text's structure borrows from and adapts a more detailed chart by David Cotter.

6:1-8, Pre-flood wickedness
   6:9-10, Genealogical note—Noah's three sons
      6:11-12, God sees the earth is ruined, all flesh corrupted
         6:13-22, God's instructions to Noah
            7:1-9, They enter the ark
               7:10-16, Flood begins, ark is closed
                  7:17-20, Waters rise, mountains covered
                  7:21-24, Death
               8:1-5, Waters recede, mountains uncovered
            8:6-14, Flood ends, ark's window opened
            8:15-22, They exit the ark
         9:1-7, God's instructions to Noah
      9:8-17, God promises never again to ruin the earth
   9:18-19, Genealogical note—Noah's three sons
9:20-28 Post-flood wickedness

The text's literary symmetry creates a narrative wave that rises to a zenith (7:17-24) and then recedes, mimicking the water's onslaught and its aftermath.

Cotter's chart attends to repeated language and literary shape. He has noticed how each phase leads up to the swelling crest of waters and furious death, and each phase finds its near match on the way down. To Cotter's chart I add observations about parallels between pre-flood (6:1-8) and post-flood wickedness (9:20-28). These two episodes extend the structure of the flood like wings attached to the main event. Turned on its side, a modified chart would show how the text piles up words, structures, and events to portray the flood. Although probably composed of two sources, the story's present structure dramatically performs the flood and invites readers to enter that experience through the pure power of language.

Literature of Resilience

It may seem strange to speak of the flood story, as well as of the book of Genesis, as literature of resilience, but both flood and book address people who lived in the early Persian Period aftermath of massive destruction of their nation and their lives (see Introduction). To read of a catastrophe that happened to their ancestors, where the family nearly came to an end but from which some survived and began again because God remembered them, enables them to hope for their own revival. In the ancient narrative, they could see themselves indirectly. More than anything, they could see that the future depended on their re-creation by their God. The new creation at the conclusion of the flood story is one expression of book's theological heart. The Creator creates life and re-creates life and continues to do so now.

---

circumstances of the ancient audience, the flood story and the book of Genesis emerge as literature of resilience. [Literature of Resilience]

NOTE

1. My structural analysis relies on the literary work of David Cotter, *Genesis* (Berit Olam; Collegeville MN: Liturgical Press, 2003) 49–58. I expand Cotter's arrangement by adding 6:1-8 and 9:18-28.

ADAM'S GENEALOGY

Genesis 5:1-32

Chapter 5 leads up to the birth of Noah and his sons, setting the stage for the story of the flood with its destruction of creation as well as the new creation that follows with only Noah's family as survivors.

The version of the family tree that appears in chapter 5 tells of descendants extending from Adam through Seth. Eve receives no mention, even though this chapter names some of the same offspring who appear as Cain's descendants in chapter 4 where Eve is the prominent ancestor. [Comparison of Genealogies in Chapters 4 and 5] Her family tree gives repeated attention to the story of the first murder and lists seven generations of Eve's offspring and their various contributions to civilization. Chapter 5, by contrast, announces itself as a scroll or book, giving it solemnity and authority as a discrete document about the descendants of Adam (v. 1). Unlike Eve's genealogy (ch. 4), this one omits contributions and characteristics of most of its family members, and it does not even refer to Cain and Abel, as if that episode in family life were over and done with or had never happened at all. Adam's offspring expands to ten generations, adding new characters up to the time of Noah and his sons.

These differences between the two genealogies might simply be variations that arise from two different sources about descendants of the first couple, but the differences are telling and suggest that

---

Adam and Seth

In compensation for Abel's death (background), God gives Adam Seth and other children.

Author unknown. "Adam and Seth." Engraving. *Afbeeldingen der voornaamste historien, soo van het Oude als Nieuwe Testament*. 1700[?]. Netherlands. (Courtesy of the Pitts Theology Library, Candler School of Theology, Emory University)

Comparison of Genealogies in Chapters 4 and 5

Gen 4	Gen 5
The man and Eve	Adam
Cain (and Abel)	*Seth*
Enoch	Enosh
Irad	Kenan
Mehujael	Mahalel
Methusael	Jared
Lamech by Adah and Zillah	*Enoch*
Jabal, Jubal, Tubal-Cain,	*Methuselah*
Naaman	*Lamech*
Seth (born to Adam and	Noah
Eve)	Shem, Ham and Japheth

The repeated names in italics are few, although a few others may represent variant spellings of the same names.

Adapted from Mark McEntire, *Struggling with God: An Introduction to the Pentateuch* (Macon GA: Mercer University Press, 2008) 59.

different purposes drive the two chapters. [Two Versions of the Family Tree] Eve's genealogy (ch. 4) is like a microcosm of Adam's (chs. 5–9), yet both concern the destruction of life and its renewal. Eve's genealogy focuses on the breakdown of the first family caused by the murder and ends with the birth of another child. Adam's genealogy also concerns breakdown, but of all creation due to human violence and corruption, and it culminates in a new command to be fruitful and multiply (8:17 and 9:1). [Types of Genealogies]

COMMENTARY

Besides moving the timeline of Genesis forward through ten generations, chapter 5 funnels attention toward Noah and the disastrous events of his time, in part by including narrative interruptions of the family tree. A double reprise of God's creation of humankind in the divine image from the first creation account (1:28) encloses the whole of Adam's genealogy. Chapter 5 begins with those words (5:1), and chapter 9 uses them again when Noah's family of survivors leaves the ark (9:6). Continuation of the species is a major concern of the section. [Outline of Genesis 5]

Two Versions of the Family Tree

The similarities and differences between the genealogies of chapters 4 and 5 are "difficult to explain by viewing one genealogy as an extension or revision of the other. Instead they appear to be two parallel versions" (Carr, 69). Chapter 4 continues the non-P tradition in chapters 2–3, whereas chapter 5 is typical of the P tradition.

David Carr, *Reading the Fractures of Genesis: Historical and Literary Approaches* (Louisville KY: Westminster John Knox, 1996).

Theological Introduction, 5:1-2

Before Adam's genealogy begins, the introductory verses proclaim the chapter's theological significance by borrowing creation language from chapter 1: "This is the book of the generations of Adam (*ʾādām*) on the day God created humankind (*ʾādām*), in the image of God he made him" (my translation, 5:1). When v. 1 reiterates human creation in the divine image and likeness, it asserts

Types of Genealogies

The genealogy of Adam, like the genealogies in the previous chapter, follows a linear form. Linear genealogies list only one descendant for each generation: "Adam became the father of Seth . . . ," "Seth became the father of Enoch" (5:3, 6). Linear genealogies show the speedy passage of time and focus only on the family patriarch for each generation. Segmented genealogies, by contrast, identify several members of each generation, such as various brothers and their multiple offspring. Chapter 10, often called "the Table of the Nations" (10:1-32), for example, lists Noah's sons—Shem, Ham, and Japheth—and their offspring.

Both types of genealogies create narrative order through biological continuity and family relationships. Both move time through the generations, but linear genealogies move

quickly, while segmented ones slow down narrative time as they linger within each generation.

Both types of genealogies connect the generations to God's original creation in the garden, for they reach back to the beginning when God commands humans to be fruitful and multiply (1:28). The promises of God to Abram and Sarai (12:1-3) anchor the body of the book and continue this creation of life with the amazing numbers of uncountable offspring. The genealogies, therefore, serve to stir up confidence among the book's audience that the Creator God of the ancestors persists in creating new generations and will do so for them.

For further reading, see Matthew A. Thomas, *These Are the Generations: Identity, Covenant, and the 'Toledot' Formula* (London: T & T Clark, 2011) 83–104.

that the first generation of humans was not an anomaly among God's creatures; being made in the image of God was not a dignity reserved for the first couple alone. Like their foreparents, God also creates these descendants in the divine image.

Outline of Genesis 5
1. Theological Introduction, 5:1-2
2. Genealogy from Adam to the Sons of Noah, 5:3-32

Nor is being in God's image and likeness a status limited to males: "Male and female he created them, and he blessed them, and named them 'humankind' (*'ādām*), when they were created" (5:2). Being made in God's image "presupposes a relationship of a person to God that is given by the very fact of human existence . . . ."[1] Yet despite the inclusive claim at the beginning of these chapters, the text focuses on Adam's begetting of children, not Eve's bearing of children.

Genealogy from Adam to the Sons of Noah, 5:3-32

For the majority of the genealogical entries in chapter 5, the list of Adam's offspring follows a literary pattern or formula with great precision. [Pattern of Adam's Genealogical List] The very rhythm of the pattern's repetition—"When X had lived Y number of years, he became the father of Z"— suggests a stable process of births across the generations and illustrates the fulfillment of God's first command to Adam and Eve to be fruitful and multiply (1:28).

Pattern of Adam's Genealogical List

With three exceptions (Adam, Enoch, Lamech), each entry in the genealogy of chapter 5 follows the same formula:

When X had lived Y number of years, he became the father of Z. X lived after the birth of Z for Y number of years more and had other sons and daughters. Thus all the days of X were Y number of years and he died.

The formula organizes and standardizes the flow of life. The orderliness created by the genealogies contributes to the larger purposes of Genesis. It insists that God brings order out of chaos; it implies that communal chaos experienced in the Persian Period will not dominate the future.

In the first chapter, that command follows human creation in the divine image (1:26-27). To be made in the divine image at the beginning of this chapter means to produce children (5:1).

One purpose of the patterned entries in Adam's genealogy is to move the narrative thread of Genesis through time across ten generations. Another is to suggest the orderliness of creation among humans, naming one man in each generation who contributes to the people's identity and whose name they should know as their important ancestor. Generation after generation, each man lives a long number of years, begets children, and then dies in the ever-repeating cycle of birth and death.

Yet disruptions of the formulaic pattern attract attention and carry explicit theological weight. Adam's notation, for example, is distinct from those that follow in that he alone begets a son "in his likeness, according to his image" (5:3). Adam, like Eve when she produces Cain with "the help of the LORD" (4:1), also participates in God's creative acts when he begets Seth. Seth, not born until the end of Eve's genealogy (4:25-26), is first in Adam's. That Seth is born in Adam's image emphasizes that being born outside the garden does not deprive the offspring of Adam and Eve of their rank as images of God. Adam's iconic role as creator of offspring in his likeness needs to be mentioned only once at the top of the genealogy, for, by implication, the participation in the divine work of procreation continues throughout the generations.

The second disruption to the genealogical pattern in chapter 5 concerns the mysterious figure of Enoch (5:21-24). Enoch is the father of the Methuselah, the oldest human ever, and twice the text mentions that Enoch is set apart because "he walked with God" (vv. 22, 24). Besides his close relationship with God on earth, the text mysteriously announces, "he is no more because God took him" (v. 24). Everyone else on the list is said to die. Whether God's taking of Enoch means he was spared death and carried directly into the divine presence, as much later interpretation assumes, or whether God's taking of Enoch is a way to speak euphemistically of his death is not clear. Whatever the clause means, Enoch represents a pinnacle of human intimacy with the divine because he "walked with God." These variations in the genealogical formula, combined with puzzling statements about Enoch, created a great deal of speculation among ancient interpreters. [Traditions about Enoch]

The third disruption of the pattern brings Lamech to the fore again (5:28-31). In Eve's genealogy we learn of his wives, offspring, and violent character (4:18-24). In Adam's genealogy, neither Lamech's wives nor his wickedness appear. Rather his

Traditions about Enoch

The mysterious nature of Enoch's being taken "has been linked to God's 'taking' of Elijah in 2 Kgs 2:1," and perhaps led to later traditions that Enoch escaped death and received divine secrets (Sir 44:16; 1-2 Enoch; Jubilees; Heb 11:5; Jude 14-15; see Fretheim, 1:380).

In the Septuagint translation of Genesis into Greek, Enoch does not die: "And Enoch was pleasing to God; and he was not dead, for God had *transferred* him" (Septuagint Gen 5:24; Kugel, 101).

In the first century CE, the Jewish historian Josephus wrote, "However, concerning Elijah and Enoch, who lived before the flood, is it written in the sacred books that they became invisible, and no one knows of their death" (*Jewish Antiquities*, 1:85, 9:28; Kugel, 101).

In addition, lacunae in the Genesis text gave birth to apocryphal books ascribed to Enoch. Of these a complete version exists only in Ethiopic (1 Enoch). Isaac writes, "The tradition of Enoch's spiritual relocation gave rise to many haggadic stories, including one that Enoch, son of Jared, when he was taken away by God, saw the secrets of the mysteries of the universe, the future of the world and the predetermined course of human history" (Isaac, 1:5).

For further reading see James L. Kugel's *The Bible as It Was* and E. Isaac's "I (Ethiopic Apocalypse of) Enoch," esp. 5–315.

Terence Fretheim, "Genesis" (*NIB* 1; Nashville: Abingdon, 1994).

James L. Kugel, *The Bible as It Was* (Cambridge MA: The Belknap Press of Harvard University Press, 1997).

E. Isaac, "I (Ethiopic Apocalypse of) Enoch," *The Old Testament Pseudepigrapha: Apocalyptic Literature and Testaments*, ed. James H. Charlesworth (ABRL; New York: Doubleday, 1983).

This engraving depicts the clouds carrying Enoch away.

Jan Goeree (1670–1731) and Jan Baptist (1670–1731). "Enoch Walks with God." From David Martin (1639–1721), *Historie des Ouden en Nieuwen Testaments: verrykt met meer dan vierhonderd printverbeeldingen in koper gesneeden* (1700). (Courtesy of the Pitts Theology Library, Candler School of Theology, Emory University)

main contribution is fathering Noah, who was absent from the previous chapter and whose special mention here leads forward to the flood story to follow (chs. 6–8). Lamech marks Noah's birth with a puzzling declaration about his son's future role. Noah will bring "relief" or "comfort" to human labors in the soil that God has cursed. Noah's name sounds something like the Hebrew word meaning "to comfort" or "console." Since Noah and his family alone survive the impending flood, his work of comforting presents another puzzle. Whom does Noah comfort if nearly everyone else dies? One proposal is that he comforts by cultivating vines to make wine from the cursed ground, and the drink soothes humans after painful labor.[2] For the book's audience during the Persian Period, his story may ultimately bring comfort because he survives catastrophe and begins anew.

Perhaps the most intriguing aspect of chapter 5 is the very ripe old ages to which Adam's offspring live. Methuseleh is the longest living human, making it to 969 years, but even Enoch, the youngest of Adam's long-lived offspring, survives for more than 300 years. Although ancient Sumerian king lists report kings living to even more preposterous ages, it is not clear that the Genesis list depends on those literary precedents. [Sumerian King Lists] In the king lists, long lives indicated heightened glory of the kings. The long lives of Adam's children may suggest enormous vitality or perhaps some greater goodness of the ancestors for which they were rewarded with long life spans.

Sumerian King Lists

"The Sumerian King List is a text composed between the end of the third and the beginning of the second millennium BC as a clearly propagandistic text aimed at unifying the tradition of Sumerian power in southern Mesopotamia" (Ascalone, 10). The text features the names of kings from each Sumerian city and the years of their respective reigns. The purpose of the text was to link each king to a time when royalty was descended from heaven, thus justifying the various kings' dominions. The list functions to create a single, unified people (or a single, unified political entity) from a vast geographical territory with regional differences.

Enrico Ascalone, *Mesopotamia*, trans. Rosanna M. Gianmmanco Frongia (Berkeley CA: University of California Press, 2005).

The chapter ends where it has been heading all along, with the climax of Noah's birth and life. He becomes the father of three sons—Shem, Ham, and Japheth (5:32)—in fulfillment of the divine command "to be fruitful and multiply." The sons mentioned here by name contribute to another frame around the flood story, for they will play key roles in the flood's aftermath (9:18-28) and later become the fathers of all humanity (ch. 10).

The main purpose of Adam's genealogical list is to arrive at Noah, born ten generations after Adam. Adam's family tree is now established, but his genealogical list splits open into a lengthy expansion about Noah and the flood and does not close until Noah's death (9:28).

CONNECTIONS

One of the oft repeated but perhaps least honored of biblical claims is that humans are made in the image and likeness of God. Yet throughout history, that teaching has been little observed. It is a radical vision that roots all humanity in a common identity of dignity and honor, no matter any hidden or precise meaning left unstated in the sacred text. I have argued in chapter 1 of this commentary that because the text refuses to explain what it means to be "made in the image and likeness of God," the phrase is more important for how it functions than for specific content. To be made in the image of God, like receiving the "breath of life" directly from God (2:6), confers high stature, unique identity, and participation in divine relationship as the identifying mark of all humans. Its importance is that human dignity and honor are universal, not reserved for any one people, nation, race, sex, level of ability, economic status, or religious identity.

In this genealogy, however, the creation of humans in God's image and likeness appears to focus particularly on human participation in divine creativity by bringing forth children. Being in God's image focuses on male and female, while the next verse announces that Adam begets a son in his own likeness:

> When God created humankind,
> he made them in the likeness of God,
> Male and female he created them
> and he blessed them
> and named them humankind. (5:1-2)

Then follows Adam's genealogy in which he becomes "the father of a son in his likeness" (5:3).

Likeness of fathers and sons surely is implied for the rest of the generations in the genealogy, but the juxtaposition of Adam and Seth's likeness with the likeness of humans to the Creator focuses that similarity on sexual differences and the command and the power to produce offspring.

Surprisingly to modern Western sensibilities, Adam's genealogy, along with others in the book, has theological importance. It manifests the creativity of God and of human collaboration in the creative process through the continuing cycle of reproduction. Adam, Eve, and their offspring participate in this process, as do their descendants.

For the book's audience in the early Persian Period, scattered and threatened by their possible disappearance as a people, the command to be fruitful and multiply through generation after generation hints at the possibility of an unseen future. By focusing on the continued stream of births from generation to generation in continuity with the divine command and blessing of being fruitful, Adam's genealogy creates an ordered account of the ancestral generations. It suggests that divine productivity will continue in them and enable them to begin again after destruction. The God who set this reproductive and ordered continuity in place will continue to do so for them because this is what the Creator of all things does.

NOTES

1. Claus Westermann, *Genesis 1–11* (Minneapolis: Augsburg, 1984) 361.

2. Robert Alter, *Genesis* (New York: W. W. Norton, 1996) 25; Herman Gunkel, *Genesis* (Macon GA: Mercer University Press, 1997) 55.

PRE-FLOOD WICKEDNESS

Genesis 6:1-22

Two short units (vv. 1-8 and vv. 9-10) in chapter 6 set the stage for the flood. [Outline of Genesis 6] One falls outside the carefully balanced structure that begins at 6:9 and extends to 9:19, but it contributes to the rising turbulence while its disharmony matches that in Noah's family after the flood (9:20-28).

God's "seeing" is the main subject of chapter 6, and it prompts subsequent events. God sees the wickedness of humankind (v. 5) and the corruption of the earth (vv. 11, 12). God's seeing motivates the decision to "blot out" the earth and its inhabitants. By contrast, God also sees Noah's righteousness, and that seeing (v. 8) leads to Noah's commission to build the ark (vv. 14-22).

The first unit of the chapter "explains" why the flood must occur (6:1-8); that is, it presents causes for it, although the causes are strange and inconsistent. The wickedness arises when the sons of God who inhabit the spirit world cross over the boundaries of the human world to select mates from the daughters of humans (6:1-4). The following verses comment by identifying wickedness among humans alone (6:5-8). The largest unit provides genealogical information about Noah, reminding readers that Noah's story belongs within the larger framework of Adam's genealogy (5:1–9:17), and it concludes in the broken world of family troubles (9:18-28).

Outline of Genesis 6

1. Wickedness in the cosmos, 6:1-8
2. Genealogical note—Noah's three sons, 6:9-10
3. God sees the earth is ruined, all flesh corrupted, 6:11-12
4. God's instructions to Noah, 6:14-22

6:1-8, Pre-flood wickedness
    6:9-10, Genealogical note—Noah's three sons
        6:11-12, God sees the earth is ruined, all flesh corrupted
            6:13-22, God's instructions to Noah
                7:1-9, They enter the ark
                7:10-16, Flood begins, ark is closed
                    7:17-20, Waters rise, mountains covered
                    7:21-24, Death
                  8:1-5, Waters recede, mountains uncovered
                8:6-14, Flood ends, ark's window opened
                8:15-22, They exit the ark
            9:1-7, God's instructions to Noah
         9:8-17, God promises never again to ruin the earth
      9:18-19, Genealogical note—Noah's three sons
9:20-28 Post-flood wickedness

COMMENTARY

Wickedness in the Cosmos, 6:1-8

The most intriguing and difficult unit of chapter 6 is the first one where creatures from another sphere of existence, called "the sons of God," invade the domain of humans to take away some of their daughters as sexual partners. Told in a short vignette, this tale of wife seizing takes place at the intersection between the heavenly world and the earthly one. The important theme of procreation from earlier chapters continues here. Human daughters attract the attention of the sons of God, who find them "fair" and select mates from among them. This mixing of spirit beings and human females produces giants.

Limited to eight verses, the story creates multiple unsolvable puzzles, including questions of translation, syntax, meaning, and purposes within Adam's genealogy. The first difficulty to face readers concerns the identity of its characters, including the sons of God [Who Are the Sons of God?], the daughters of humans [Who Are the Daughters of Humans?], as wells as the giants or Nephilim, seemingly produced by the mating of the sons and the daughters. [Who Are the Nephilim?]

A second difficulty is that the passage does not easily connect with the stories that precede and follow it. The opening verse ignores the genealogies of chapters 4 and 5 by setting events in the beginnings of life, "when people began to multiply on the face of the ground" (6:1), even though at least ten generations of children have already been born. The vague timing links these verses to chapter 5 rather than locating them chronologically. Nor do the verses that follow fit well with preceding verses (vv. 5-8). In those verses, God accuses humans of wickedness, but it was the spirit beings who initiated the boundary crossing in the first place, not the humans.

A third difficulty is that connections between verses and phrases within the passage are not clear. Speakers and subjects change abruptly, leaving readers to deduce the sense of things. A narrator reports the "facts" of the tale—the sons of God select human daughters as sexual partners (vv. 1-2). God, however, speaks in the next verse, changing the subject abruptly to the matter of the human lifespan. Then the narrator reports the existence of Nephilim in "those days—and also afterward." Finally, the narrator announces that the Nephilim were born "when the sons of God went into the daughters of humans" (v. 4). The peculiar syntax of the time notation, in "those days—and also afterward," does not

Who Are the Sons of God?

The first challenge in identifying the sons of God is to decide how to translate the Hebrew phrase *běnê hā'*, for it can be legitimately rendered either "sons of the God" or "sons of the gods." *Ĕlohîm* is the Semitic term that can refer either to God or to the polytheistic gods of Israel's neighbors. The latter translation may suggest that the story comes from Israel's neighbors and was then incorporated into Genesis. Yet many biblical interpreters have preferred the former translation because the phrase "sons of God" appears elsewhere in a number of texts (1 Kgs 22; Pss 29:1; 82:6; 89:7; Job 38:7). They are creatures that occupy a space between the divine world and the human one, perhaps some kind of "demi-gods" (Towner, 79–80). They occupy God's heavenly court and include intermediaries, messengers, or, more commonly, angels. In Job, the satan is such a figure; he goes to and fro upon the earth as God's overseer (Job 1–2). Yet a third interpretation understands the sons as human males descended from Seth, Adam and Eve's third son (see Fretheim, 1:382).

Donald E. Gowan, *Genesis 1–11: From Eden to Babel* (ITC; Grand Rapids MI: Eerdmans, 1988) 84.

Sibley Towner, *Genesis* (WBC; Louisville KY: Westminster John Knox, 2001).

Terence E. Fretheim, "Genesis" (*NIB* 1; Nashville: Abingdon, 1994).

Julius Schnorr von Carolsfeld (1794–1872). *God's Children Mingle with the Children of the Earth: that the sons of God saw the daughters of men that they were fair; and they took them wives of all which they chose.* Gen. 6:2. Plate 15, from *Die Bibel in Bildern [The Bible in Pictures]*. Leipzig (Georg Wigand), 1853–1860. (Credit: Alfredo Dagli Orti / Art Resource, NY)

Who Are the Daughters of Humans?

Daughters of humans are earthbound creatures, the females of the human species from whom the sons of God make choices of mates. Interpretations claiming that the sons were human offspring of Seth often also claim that the daughters were the offspring of Cain.

That means the sons were descended from the good ancestor and the daughters from their evil murderer ancestor, laying guilt upon them by their alleged place on the family tree. This interpretation finds no support in the text of 6:1-4.

specify whether the Nephilim are the offspring of the two groups or are simply born at the time of the union of the two. Moreover, although most interpreters believe this passage to be about some form of evil action, the narrator goes on to praise the Nephilim, honoring them as "heroes and renowned warriors of old" (6:4) rather than as the spawn of wickedness.

For these and other reasons, contemporary interpreters have theorized that the passage is a fragment of an ancient Near Eastern text borrowed from Israel's neighbors, although inadequately adapted or partly lost. Archaeologists have not found an

Who Are the Nephilim?

The Hebrew word "Nephilim" in Gen 6 probably denotes giants. They appear to be offspring of the sons of God and the daughters of humans, although the strange syntax of the sentence leaves room for wonder: "The Nephilim were on the earth in those days—and also afterwards—when the sons of God went into the daughters of humans, who bore children to them." Fretheim thinks that rather than being offspring of the mixing of heavenly and human mating, they were warriors of old, born to the sons of God and daughters of humans, and here compared to the Nephilim mentioned in Num 13:33 (see Fretheim, 382). There Hebrew spies cross into the land of Canaan and bring back a report of terrifying giants occupying the land. The Hebrew root for Nephilim is the verb "to fall," hence these giants are sometimes called "fallen ones." There are other giants mentioned in Deut 1:28; 2:20-21; Ezek 32:21, 27; Amos 2:9; and Josh 11:21-22.

Archie Chi Chung Lee maintained that the entire account of the sons of God and daughters of humans might be viewed as a myth that provides "an explanation of the birth of a special breed of human being," namely the giants (93). Towner added to the discussion: "Like other traditional cultures, the ancient Israelites seemed to have imagined that the aboriginal peoples were bigger and stronger than anyone around in their own time" (79).

For further reading, see Archie Chi Chung Lee, "When the Flood Narrative of Genesis Meets Its Counterpart in China," in *Genesis*, ed. Athalya Brenner, Archie Chi Chung Lee, Gale A. Yee (Texts @ Contexts; Minneapolis: Fortress, 2010) 81–97.

Terence E. Fretheim, "Genesis" (*NIB* 1; Nashville: Abingdon, 1994).

Sibley Towner, *Genesis* (WBC; Louisville KY: Westminster John Knox, 2001).

Similarity to Other Primal Myths

Modupẹ Oduyoye studied African and Asian primal myths and drew comparisons with Genesis 1–11:

In mythologies of creation through birth, the male partner comes from the sky (rain from the sky = semen), while the female partner comes from the earth (Mother Earth = womb): hence sons of the gods (in heavens) and daughters of men (on earth). It will be hard to find the opposite in mythology anywhere: sons of men marrying daughters of gods. Egyptian cosmogony is one exception.

Modupẹ Oduyoye, *The Sons of the Gods and the Daughters of Men: An Afro-Asiastic Interpretation of Genesis 1–11* (Maryknoll NY: Orbis, 1983) 23.

exact literary precursor, yet ancient texts do portray divine beings invading from another sphere in pursuit of human women.[1] [Similarity to Other Primal Myths]

In its present location in Genesis, the story's purpose is to build a case about wickedness as the cause of the flood. Yet the aggressors in the story are not the daughters of humans but the sons of God, so even this explanation fails to make the puzzle pieces stick together. Von Rad concluded that the sons "let themselves be enticed by the beauty of human women to grievous sin; they fall from their ranks and mix with them in wild licentiousness."[2]

This interpretation sees beautiful women and wild sex to be the problem. Yet the women do no enticing and have no role except to be selected, as in something like a modern beauty contest or, even more disturbingly, sexual assault by strangers. [Abusive Relationships] Still, the story highlights the importance of daughters, who are critical for procreation of offspring and seemingly threatened here. The larger wickedness seems to be the crossing of boundaries between the spirit and human world, a mixing of species, human and non-human.

When God interrupts the narrator in an "artless transition,"[3] God has grown impatient with humans, not with the sons of God: "My spirit will not abide in mortals forever, for they are flesh;

their days shall be one hundred twenty years" (6:3). Human life clearly involves abiding with the divine spirit, perhaps alluding to the breath of life from the creation of Adam (Gen 2:7), but human mortality has boundaries, even if by our standards they are long indeed. This new limit on life alters expectations from the preceding chapter where some ancestors lived to nearly one thousand years. The new limit may be a punishment for the breaking of boundaries between the spirit world and the human one, but it is human flesh and its weakness that disturbs God rather than the spirit residents of the cosmos.

Modern critical scholars have generally agreed that precise meanings of the passage remain opaque but that its juxtaposition with the next unit (vv. 5-8) indicates that some transgression has occurred. Perhaps we can agree that without more information the text remains largely indecipherable, and its very opaqueness may explain why it has generated such interest over the centuries. "The fact that the text presents ambiguity may be exactly the point . . . : the mode of telling matches the nature of the message."[4] The way the story unfolds is confused and broken, and its implied "message" is that the earth and its occupants live in such a world. In this way, the first signs of turbulence augur the storm ahead.

Abusive Relationships

John Goldingay used the story of a friend's sexual abuse to reflect on power relations between the sons of God and the daughters of humans:

We had a friend in England who had been sexually abused on an ongoing basis by her uncle, who was a minister. The abuse had happened when she was a little girl (she was then in her forties), but all her life she had been trying to come to terms with the effects of that experience. She had indeed done much coming to terms, but the awfulness of the experience, the pain of it, and the effects of it still lived with her. The coming to terms continued. The grim thing is that her story is not an unusual one. . . . The other day one of my colleagues declared casually that a third of the people in the average congregation have been abused in some way. It seemed an unlikely statistic, but then I remembered the two occasions when men made advances on me when I was a teenager. I was older than our friend, and these were not members of my family or ministers (though one was my math teacher), so that made it easier to resist. My colleague was protesting that people who write about the Bible don't mention this fact about abuse, which will have affected many of their readers. So here I am mentioning it, because the Bible mentions it . . . . Linked with abuse is the question of power. "Whether the women in Genesis 6 are victims of supernatural or human males, they are victims of people much more powerful than they . . . ." The sons' action in taking these women and having sex with them brings to a culmination the story of resistance to God's vision of the world. The story leads to God's decision to abort the whole project.

John Goldingay, *Genesis for Everyone: Part One, Chapters 1-16* (Louisville KY: Westminster John Knox, 2010) 90–91.

God Proposes to Blot Out the Earth, 6:5-8

The second unit of the chapter (6:5-7) comments on the previous story (6:1-4) simply by being set next to it. [Parataxis] "God saw that the wickedness of humankind was great upon earth . . ." (v. 5). For God, human evil has a stunning totality: "Every

Parataxis

Parataxis is the literary practice of setting different written materials next to one another without indicating how the parts are connected, yet by proximity the texts comment on one another. Because 6:5-8 talks about human wickedness, it appears to comment on the story of the sons of God and the daughters of humans that precedes it.

inclination of the thoughts of their hearts was only evil continually" (v. 5). [The Human Heart] The verse falls over itself to condemn human beings whom God called "very good" only four chapters before (1:31). God sees that the propensities of humans are evil. Divine accusations against humans are absolute. God does not charge them with occasional wickedness; in this verse they have no redeeming qualities; they incline toward evil fully. [Evil] The picture is one of total human depravity.

Overbearing human wickedness grieves God, who regrets having made them in the first place. "And the Lord *was sorry* that he made humankind upon the earth, and it *grieved him* to his heart" (6:6). Although human hearts are evil (v. 5), God's heart, by contrast, is grieved, pained, and regretful.5 The narrator daringly claims to have insight into God's inner life and finds there justification for the coming flood. Divine dismay is emotional and disturbing.

The Hebrew root translated "grieved" (*ʿāṣab*) emphasizes divine pain. Elsewhere the word refers to Eve's pain in childbirth (3:16), Adam's pain in tilling the earth (3:17), and the pain of human labor (5:29). God was sorry about creation, rued having created humans at all, and God's own heart was "pained" to its center. This portrait of the inner world of God serves as a defense of God, who suffers on account of humans, does not want to destroy them, and does so only with the deepest sorrow. [Theodicy]

By imagining God's inner life, the writer protects God from charges of callous indifference to suffering. God did not want to send the flood, but human wickedness forced the decision. Yet regret aside, God resolves to "blot" them out, together with all living things, animals, creeping things, and birds of the air, for again God says, "I am sorry that I made them" (v. 7). God's proposal to blot out the earth, in the form of a divine soliloquy, comes without a plan of execution. The tension heightens as "the narrator purposefully does not yet state the means Yahweh intends to use to annihilate humanity."6

The Human Heart

To assert that the thoughts of the human heart were "only evil" means the entire orientation of human beings is wicked. The Hebrew notion of heart is more expansive than modern western understandings of the term. The ancients did not readily divide the humans into separate parts of thinking and feeling. Instead, terms like heart and mind described the whole of the human person from a particular aspect. The heart serves "as the source of thought and reflection, involving intellectual capacities of wisdom and discernment (Isa 6:10; Deut 8:5; Isa 42:5). It is the center of emotions, feelings, moods and passions," and perhaps primarily the heart "represents the idea of volition and conscience." The heart is closer to our concept of "will" as the "center for decisions, obedience, devotion and intentionality" (1 Sam 24:5; 2 Sam 7:21).

Douglas R. Edwards, *HarperCollins Bible Dictionary*, ed. Paul J. Achtemeier (San Francisco: HarperCollins, 1996) 408.

Evil

The Hebrew root for evil (*ra'a*) encompasses a vast array of meanings, extending from being unpleasant to behaving wickedly. Nouns and adjectives from this root are equally expansive. In v. 5 God ascribes to humans moral wickedness that extends from their actions to the source of action, the very inclinations of their hearts. God provides no evidence of human evil except for the incident of intercourse between the sons of God and the daughters of humans.

The great Protestant reformer John Calvin finds in this verse evidence for his view of humankind as utterly depraved, as opposed to being "good" from the time of God's creation in Gen 1:26-31. He uses this verse to interpret the Adam and Eve's disobedience in the garden and finds depravity as the human condition from birth. He develops this notion in his Genesis commentary when he comments on the word "continually" at the end of v. 5.

Some expound this particle to mean from commencing infancy; as if he would say, the depravity of men is very great from the time of their birth. But the more correct interpretation is, that the world had then become so hardened in its wickedness, and was so far from any amendment, or from entertaining any feeling of penitence, that it grew worse and worse as time advanced; and further that it was not the folly of a few days, but the inveterate depravity with the children, having received, as by hereditary right, transmitted from their parents to their descendants. (Calvin, 248)

By contrast, other Christian communities such as Roman Catholic and Episcopalian stress God's words at the end of the sixth day of creation that all within sight is good. Humans are basically good with a propensity toward evil but not "hardened in wickedness."

For further reading, see David Penchansky, "Good and Evil," in the *Oxford Encyclopedia of the Bible and Theology*, ed. Samuel E. Balentine (Oxford/ New York: Oxford University Press, 2015) 1:426–32.

John Calvin, *A Commentary on Genesis*, trans. and ed. John King (London: The Banner of Truth Trust, 1965).

The threat looming over the world is generic and unspecified. The unit, nonetheless, closes with a hint of hope. In sharp contrast to all his contemporaries, Noah "finds favor in the sight of God" (v. 8).

Theodicy

The range of questions that the flood story and other disaster narratives in Genesis (see Introduction) raise falls under the theological subject known as "theodicy," a Greek term for the "justice of God." Across the biblical canon, questions about God's involvement in disasters and suffering arise again and again. When life collapses and the world spins out of control, people of faith ask insistently where is God, how could God let this happen, did God send devastation, is God punishing us, has God abandoned us, or is our God defeated by other stronger deities?

These questions of theodicy haunt the biblical corpus. Genesis sets the question at the beginning of the Old Testament. Before the destruction of Sodom, Abraham asks God, "Will you indeed sweep away the righteous with the wicked?" (Gen 18:23), and "Shall not the Judge of all the earth do what is just?" (18:25). The Psalmist asks "how long" God will look on suffering, remain silent, and batter the victim (Pss 6:3; 13:1-2; 35:17; 62:3). Lamentations suspects that God has forgot the nation forever, and the prophets, most particularly Jeremiah and Ezekiel, depict God variously as indifferent to human suffering and punisher of the community who sends the enemy to destroy them (Barton, 12:593). The book of Job most particularly explores the matter of God's involvement in the suffering of the innocent human being (Balentine, esp. 668–74). These questions receive no fully satisfying answer anywhere. And Jesus' death on the cross raises them again for Christians.

For further reading, see Walter Brueggemann, *Theology of the Old Testament: Testimony, Dispute, Advocacy* (Minneapolis: Fortress, 1997) 359–72.

John Barton, "Theodicy: 11. Old Testament," in *Religion Past & Present; Encyclopedia of Theology and Religion*, ed. Hans Dieter Betz et al. (Boston: Brill, 2012).

Samuel E. Balentine, *Job*, SHBC.

Noah's Place in the Family Tree, 6:9-10

A genealogical statement interrupts the narrative to remind readers that Noah's story forms a part of Adam's genealogy and presents a subset of that family. "These are the generations (*tōlĕdot*) of Noah" (6:9). God's seeing remains key to unfolding events, but here divine seeing marks a critical turn toward hope for the family survival, for Noah and his household will be the sole children of Adam to survive the disaster. Described in formulaic language, in three ways Noah emerges as a chosen and exalted figure. Like Job (Job 1:1, 8; 2:3), he "was a righteous man, blameless in his generation," and like Enoch, he "walked with God" (v. 9). [Noah in the Qur'an] Using the same genealogical formula as the previous chapter, "These are the descendants of . . ." (5:1), the next verse announces that Noah had three sons, Shem, Ham, and Japheth, who will have important roles in the flood's aftermath (9:18–10:32).

Noah in the Qur'an

The Qur'an elaborates on Noah's righteousness in these verses:

We sent Noah to his people,
and he said: "O people worship God;
you have no other god but He; for I fear
the retribution of the great Day may fall upon
you."
The elders of his people replied:
"We see clearly you have gone astray."
"I have not gone astray, O my people," he said,
"but have been sent by my Lord,
the creator of all the worlds.
I bring to you the messages of my Lord,
and give you sincere advice,
for I know from God what you do not know."

Al-Qur'an: A Contemporary Translation, Ahmed Ali, trans. (Princeton: Princeton University Press, 1993) 7:59–63.

God Decides, 6:11-13

After the brief genealogical interlude, the narrative buildup to the flood resumes with heightened force (vv. 11-13). Evidence of sin is cumulative, even if vague, and God's own decision foreshadows what is to come in the horrendous chapter to follow (Gen 7). Throughout chapter 6, God is the speaker, designer, and coordinator of the action, even though God's inner life is fraught with sorrow (see [Outline of Genesis 6] for an outline of God's decision).

If the first two units of chapter 6 have built conditions of conflict between God and humans, those rifts in the relationship now reach the breaking point. Corruption and violence that prevail among humans grow and spread, and God sees that even the earth is "corrupt . . . and filled with violence" (v. 11). Triple repetitions of the root for "corrupt" (*šāḥat*) portray the acceleration of divine anger:

"Now the earth was corrupt in God's sight"
"God saw that the earth was corrupt"
"For all flesh had corrupted its ways upon earth" (6:11-13)

The writer imagines God's inner decision-making process in which God saw that "all flesh had corrupted its ways upon the earth." Language of human "flesh" and God's impatience with it appear in the first unit of this chapter (6:3), but here the flesh is "all flesh," animal flesh as well. At the least, corruption and wickedness have flourished, and all the earth is filled with violence, as if God's own creation has rebelled or has been infected with evil. God then announces to Noah the decision to end all flesh, for "The earth is filled with violence because of them. Now I am going to destroy them along with the earth" (v. 13).

The object of God's anger appears to be humans alone, yet their corruption and violence affects and corrupts the whole earth and its other inhabitants.

Preparations, 6:14-22

Once God makes the final decision to destroy the earth, preparations to survive its collapse involve a division of labor. There are preparations to be made by Noah (vv. 14-16 and 19-22) and preparations to be made by God (vv. 17-18). God commissions Noah to build an ark, [The Ark] but the assignment fosters more suspense and anxiety by providing no reason for the ark's building. The commission comes with a careful listing of steps and precise architectural directions for the building, including the kind of wood with which to make it—gopher wood (perhaps cypress); the shape of the interior—with rooms; the application of pitch to cover the ship and so prevent sinking; plus its length to be 300 cubits with three properly arranged decks, a roof, and a door (6:14-15).

While Noah works on the ark, God declares, "For my part, I am going to bring a flood of waters upon the earth to destroy from under heaven all flesh in which is the breath of life; everything on the earth will die" (v. 17). The word order in Hebrew is emphatic: "and I, look, (*hinnēh*) I am bringing a flood of waters," that is, my task will be to execute punishment, and I will definitely do it, no one else (cf. 9:6). ["Look!"] The text sharply underscores God's action. The decision

The Ark

AΩ   Two Hebrew words mean "ark," "box," or "chest." The word naming Noah's ark (*tēbah*) appears again only for the basket or ark of bulrushes that served as Moses' safe conveyance through the treacherous waters of the Nile (Exod 2:3, 5). Like Noah, Moses survives the waters because of the providential provision of an ark. A different Hebrew word (*'ārôn*) appears for the Ark of the Covenant (Deut 10:8; Num 4:5).

Joshua R. Porter, "Ark," *Harpers Dictionary of the Bible*, 1:63.

"Look!"

AΩ   The Hebrew word *hinnēh* is often left un-translated in the New Revised Standard Version of Genesis. Older translations such as the King James Version translated it with the archaic English terms "Alas" or "Behold." Yet as an exclamation of surprise or a request for attention, it highlights significant speech or action. Its frequent appearance in Genesis narratives provides clues to important moments in story of Israel, such as here.

is made and announced beforehand, and now the results are inevitable.

Yet in the thick of preparations for the worst possible destruction, God promises to make a covenant with Noah (6:18). This cryptic announcement anticipates the formal establishment of the covenant in the flood's aftermath (9:8-17). At this bleak moment in the story, the promise of the covenant brings a glimmer of hope that God will not abandon Noah, that he will survive, and that life will go on. The covenant anticipated here is of major importance to the overall story.

Noah's commission extends beyond ark building to keeping and preserving animal life and types of food for humans and animals. God's instructions about the creatures appear in a set of commands, repeated with variations and expansion at the beginning of the next chapter (6:19-22; see 7:1-5). These commands make concrete and immediate the divine plan to save a remnant of animals and humans (6:19-22). Noah and his family are to come into the ark and bring two of "every living thing, of all flesh" (v. 19). These pairs include male and female birds, animals, creeping things: two of every kind "shall come to you to keep them alive." For the benefit of all on board, Noah must also bring and store food of every kind. From Noah the text reports no words, only his complete obedience; Noah "did this; he did all that God commanded him" (6:22). Noah's righteousness and obedience will save him, his family, and the animals.[7]

CONNECTIONS

Disaster Story as Helpful for the Book's Audience

The story of Noah and the flood is a fully formed disaster narrative (see Introduction). A more complete destruction cannot be imagined unless the entire world itself would end. I propose in this commentary that the many depictions of disaster in Genesis contribute to the book's larger intentions: to empower the people of Judah to begin again after the nation's fall to the Babylonian Empire. First, however, lingering memories of the past must be confronted and reframed and God's role in the catastrophe must be "explained." Without that work of theodicy, they cannot be Israel/ Judah, God's people but will likely disappear among the nations. They must "explain" how the God who chose them and promised to be with them on Mount Zion, to govern them through a son of David on the throne, and to dwell with them in the land had failed to protect them. Without giving their historical experiences a narrative framework and rediscovering their theological traditions in new ways, they would disappear among the nations and the God of Israel would disappear as well.

The portrait of God as one who becomes furiously angry at human flesh, who is "sorry that I made them, humans, animals, creeping things and birds of the air" (6:7), and who determines to blot them out, to un-create all creation, the creation deemed "very good"—that theological portrait "explains" catastrophe and defends God from charges of injustice. It interprets the collapse of Judah's world. Like Noah's world, their world as they knew it came to an end, and like Noah's family, some have survived, but can their God survive with them? [Does God Repent?]

By attributing the flood to God as punishment for human sin, the text claims without explicitly saying it that Israel's God is in charge of the cosmos, its weather, its animals and humans, its creation, and later its recreation. The destruction by flood was not the work of any other deity, neither the machinations of uncontrolled chaos nor of unbridled primal forces. It was a decision of Israel's own God. Humans became wicked and infected all of creation with their wickedness and, for that, God brought punishment. This theological vision leaves God freely connected to the cosmos. It gives victims a way to feel less powerless in the face of chaos, for if they behave righteously, avoid violence and sin, perhaps they can avoid similar disasters in the future.

The flood story along with others raises basic theological questions about the nature of God-language. Is every way the text

Does God Repent?

The ancient Greeks held that God was immutable and unchangeable: God never makes a plan in one direction and then changes it to go in another direction. That view of God is simply not very biblical. In the story of the flood, God regrets making humans and so decides to blot them out and start afresh with Noah and his family. In the book of Jonah, God sends Jonah to announce the destruction of Nineveh in forty days (3:4), but when the people of Nineveh repent, including their cattle, God changes the decision about the calamity to be brought upon the Ninevites, and "he did not do it" (3:10). In the Old Testament, God is not a fixed or frozen character but a deity represented by sometimes contradictory characteristics.

Terence E. Fretheim has seen in God's "regret" (repentance) another theological dimension:

God knows what might have been and profoundly desires that things had not come to this! Here the past of God, what might have been, seems to stand in disjunction with the present of God, what actually is, and the collision of past and present in God occasions a deep divine regret and accompanying suffering for God. (58)

God is in crisis in this text, according to Walter Brueggemann: "The crisis is not the much water, which now becomes only a dramatic setting. Rather, the crisis comes because of the resistant character of the world which evokes hurt and grief in the heart of God" (78).

For the book's audience, divine repentance suggests that God remains involved in the world, suffers with the suffering community, and has neither dismissed them from thought nor abandoned them to other gods.

Terence E. Fretheim, *Creation Untamed: The Bible, God, and Natural Disasters* (Grand Rapids MI: Baker Academic, 2010).

Walter Brueggemann, *Genesis* (Interpretation; Atlanta: John Knox, 1982).

speaks of God somehow a literal depiction of who God is and how God acts, or is each one an effort to name God in the midst of complex, changing historical circumstances? The Bible's "unsettled" speech about God reflects ancient struggles to name God in the midst of human realities.[8]

The language is symbolic, that is, it tells of God indirectly, in terms that have many meanings that contradict one another, that are paradoxical and suggestive. God can never fully be named. James Crenshaw rightly has insisted that all language about God is inferential, that is, the inspired human writers infer who God is from their experiences of the world. This is different than saying that all language about God is referential, meaning that it all refers to God in absolute ways denoting one clear meaning. The Holy One eludes all speech and cannot be reduced to a final word, image, or experience. Put another way, God "is seen through a glass darkly" (1 Cor 13:12), glimpsed momentarily and partially. [Problematic Theology and Struggle for Meaning]

Problematic Theology and Struggle for Meaning

To understand the cause of disaster as unspecified human wickedness oversimplifies cause and effect and blames victims in harmful ways. What precise sins caused the massive destruction of life brought about by the flood? Perhaps it is best to recognize that major cataclysms usually have multiple causes, human and natural, and that theologically, sin as cause is at best a partial explanation. The text tries to explain the unexplainable. Where it succeeds theologically is by insisting that human actions have consequences and that God does not desire death and destruction; rather God regrets it mightily. Whereas modern Western believers may find natural causes of catastrophe such as climate imbalances like disruptions of wind and cloud, the ancients believed, by contrast, that events have their direct source in divine decisions. This approach both kept God alive in their lives and gave some sense of safety. They could be righteous like Noah to prevent such a cataclysm again in the future.

A problem arises for modern believers in turning theological interpretation into a literal explanation of events rather than recognizing it as evidence of the theological struggle to find meaning in turbulent and overwhelming historical circumstances. After every natural and human-caused disaster, humans seek to understand it, to contain the chaos, and to anchor themselves again in the world.

To understand catastrophe as divine punishment for sin is a temporary survival strategy, a way to go forward in a senseless world, but it does not tell us who God is always and everywhere.

For further reading see Kathleen M. O'Connor, *Jeremiah: Pain and Promise* (Minneapolis: Fortress, 2011).

Does God Send Catastrophes?

Does God send catastrophes to punish sin? Why was God angry enough at original creation to destroy it almost totally after having declared it all to be "very good" (1:31)? What is the Creator's relationship to contemporary catastrophes from natural disasters and military calamities? While it is certainly true that most ancient peoples understood natural disasters and other catastrophes to be the result of direct divine actions in the world, it is also the case that the text tries to interpret terrible catastrophes and to make sense of senseless experiences.

Such thinking raises many theological questions that bear upon present-day issues.[9] The Bible gives no firm answer to questions of human suffering. As difficult as it is for modern believers to accept, a theology that places responsibility on humans for the flood can help believers keep their connections to God alive and to survive themselves as a people. This theology asserts that God is neither powerless nor ineffective; instead, God is the direct cause of all things (see [The Punishing and Saving God]). No other gods of the ancient world caused this to happen; only their God could do this. This thinking is a form of theodicy, for it defends God from charges of ineptness, powerlessness, and indifference. For modern readers, however, such efforts to make sense of catastrophe as punishment for human sin are deeply problematic. Yet we can appreciate it as an attempt to make sense of the senseless, to put order into chaotic existence by finding cause and effect, and, above all, to keep God connected to the lives of the people in the aftermath of nearly total destruction of their nation.

NOTES

1. Joseph Blenkinsopp, *Creation, Un-creation, Re-creation: A Discursive Commentary on Genesis 1–11* (New York: T & T Clark, 2011) 121–30, discusses connections of the Genesis sons of God and daughters of humans episode with traditions about Enoch such as in the Book of the Watchers, but he finds more direct connections with an account in Jub 5:1-11 and other ancient sources. Blenkinsopp, however, sees the episode as a conclusion to pre-diluvian history rather than as a contributing cause of the flood.

2. Gerhard von Rad, *Genesis*, rev. ed. (OTL; Philadelphia: Westminster, 1972) 114.

3. Ibid., 113.

4. Terence E. Fretheim, "Genesis" (*NIB* 1; Nashville: Abingdon, 1994) 382.

5. David Cotter, *Genesis* (Berit Olam; Collegeville MN: Liturgical Press, 2003) 53.

6. Herman Gunkel, *Genesis*, trans. Mark E. Biddle (Macon GA: Mercer University Press, 1997) 61.

7. Several ancient texts contain flood stories that may have influenced the Genesis account of Noah and the flood. These include the Epic of Gilgamesh, Atrahasis, and other texts from world literature. Christopher B. Hays has prepared a careful study of similarities and differences of these, especially Gilgamesh, with Genesis 6–9. See his *Hidden Riches: A Sourcebook for the Comparative Study of the Hebrew Bible and the Ancient Near East* (Louisville KY; Westminster John Knox, 2014) 75–95.

8. See Walter Brueggemann, *An Unsettling God: The Heart of the Hebrew Bible* (Minneapolis: Fortress Press, 2009) on the complexity of language for God.

9. For further reading, see Terence E. Fretheim, *Creation Untamed: The Bible, God, and Natural Disasters* (Theological Explorations for the Church Catholic; Grand Rapids MI: Baker, 2010).

THE WATERS RISE

Genesis 7:1-24

Before the American film *The Perfect Storm*, there was the Genesis story of the flood. The biblical story probably functioned like a film in the ancient world where oral storytelling shaped life and taught people who they were in the world. Stories of destructive floods sent by the gods remain extant from the ancient world, and chapter 7 is a literary performance of high drama that draws from other ancient flood stories. [Gilgamesh and Atrahasis] It follows chapter 6 in a continuous flow even with its repetitions and contradictions. Threats to life begun in chapter 6 become increasingly ominous in chapter 7; tensions mount, more solemn preparations unfold, and the waters swell and rise, killing everything "in whose nostrils was the breath of life" (7:22).

Although chapter 7 begins with divine speech, it focuses primarily on earthly creatures and their fate. [Outline of Chapter 7] So artfully does it bring readers into the thick of catastrophe that it is easy to forget that more than one version of the story weaves through the account. As if God had not uttered instructions to Noah about stocking the ark with animals and food in chapter 6, those commands are partly

---

The Perfect Storm
The Perfect Storm, a film based on a novel by Sebastian Junger, tells of an unusually intense storm off the Coast of New England in the fall of 1991 in which six fishermen die at sea in a fishing boat, the *Andrea Gale*. Video depictions show the tiny boat like an ark as it rises and falls on mountains of water, its human cargo subject to the storm's forces but not protected like Noah's family by a solicitous hand of God. The film is hauntingly memorable, terrifying, and, unlike the Genesis story, computer generated.

Ivan Konstantinovich Aivazovsky (1817–1900). *Among the Waves*. Aivazovsky Gallery, Feodosya (Crimea), Ukraine. (Credit: Scala / Art Resource, NY)

Gilgamesh and Atrahasis

The ancient Sumerian Gilgamesh Epic has many connections to the biblical story of Noah and the flood. Gilgamesh was a ruler of the city-state Uruk around 2700 BCE. Sumerians and later Assyrians and Babylonians told his story. Several versions exist today, though not all are complete. Gilgamesh seeks immortality, becomes discouraged, and journeys to the end of the world to find a wise man known as Utnapishtim, "the Babylonian Noah," and asks him how to avoid death. Utnapishtim tells him about his own life and how the gods finally grant him status among them (see Moran, ix–x).

Here are excerpts from David Ferry's poetic rendering of the story:

"The gods in heaven decided in their council to bring the flood down on the fortunate city."
The god Ea warns Utnapishtim:
"Abandon your house and build a boat instead . . . .
Take with you on the boat you build, an instance
of each living thing so that they may be
safe from obliteration in the flood.

The god gives precise instructions about the boat's construction pertaining to the roof, wood, pitch, decks, and number of cabins. On the seventh day, Utnapishtim finishes building and loads the boat with his possessions, all the people of his household, and "all instances of living things to be saved from obliteration in the flood."

The god addresses him, "Abundance will rain down, get yourself inside and close the hatch." Then the gods bring about a terrible storm: Annunaki "blazed terrible light," Nergal "opened the earth," Ninurta "opened the dikes and other floods burst forth." When Utnapishtim opened the hatch, nothing was moving and all the humans on earth "had turned to clay." Ea had saved him from the flood because "the punishment should always fit the crime," and the flood apparently was larger and far out of proportion. Eventually, Utnapishtim and his wife are "admitted into the company of the gods."

The Genesis account of the flood resembles the Gilgamesh story of Utnapishtim in that its hero Noah is also righteous, is saved by a deity who commands him to build a boat with a hatch or door to be closed, and brings along living creatures. Once Utnapishtim survives the storm and abundant floodwaters, he opens the hatch to find himself in a landscape of death, after which the gods bless him by letting him join their company as an immortal.

The epic of Atrahasis, of which we have fragments in Babylonian and Assyrian, also provides parallels with the biblical flood story. The epic deals with human sin that the gods punish with plagues and a deluge. In one version, the gods are trying to sleep and become annoyed by the noise humans make, so they send plagues upon them. In a Babylonian fragment, a god threatens to send a flood and orders Atrahasis to build a ship.

The Ship shall be an ark, and its name shall be
"Preserver of Life." . . .
Into the ship thou shalt take the beasts of the field,
the fowl of the heavens. (X, 9, 10)

An Assyrian version tells of divine commands to close the door of the ship, to bring grain, possessions, family, and beasts of various kinds. The god promises to send the beasts to him and that "they shall guard the door" (C, 10; *ANET*, 104–105).

The existence of these ancient texts indicates that the Genesis writers knew the literature of their ancient Near Eastern neighbors in written or oral form. They borrowed from old stories, adapted them, and made a new story of their own. Plot similarities are obvious, but the Genesis version contains important differences. Noah is a mortal and remains mortal after the flood. Noah's God is the one God who shows extra care for Noah by shutting him into the ship. Perhaps most important, the motive of Noah's God is to punish evil, not to express irritation at the noisy humans who disturb sleep. When Noah's flood ends, God makes a covenant with him and life begins anew.

For further reading, see Nahum M. Sarna, *Understanding Genesis: The Heritage of Biblical Israel* (New York: Schocken Books, 1966) 37–62; and more briefly Mark G. Brett, *Genesis: Procreation and the Politics of Identity* (London: Routledge, 2000) 40–42.

William L. Moran, "Introduction" to David Ferry, *Gilgamesh: A New Rendering in English Verse* (New York: Farrar, Strauss and Giroux, 1992).
David Ferry, *Gilgamesh: A New Rendering in English Verse* (New York: Farrar, Strauss and Giroux, 1992) 65–75.
ANET, 104–105.

Akkadian cylinder-seal and impression of the flood epic, showing Uta-Napaishtim in a boat, Gilgamesh with a bull. (Credit: HIP / Art Resource, NY)

repeated and further developed at the beginning of chapter 7. The second half (7:1-5) of this two-part set of instructions summarizes and adds detail to the first half (6:19-22). The next units of chapter 7 do something similar by doubling accounts of Noah's obedient preparations (7:6-10 and 11-16). The overall effect of these doublings is to build expectations of doom, both delaying the arrival of the flood and simultaneously escalating apprehension and anxiety. Meanwhile, the plot moves inevitably toward disaster, tying the separate units together in ascending waves of turbulence. [Watery Story Line of Chapter 7]

A third unit depicts the flood and its macabre consequences, bringing the story to a climax (7:17-24). This time the doubling is subtler. Although each part carries different content, the two are alike in that each repeats language within it, first in multiple rises of the waters (vv. 17-20) and then with layers of death that the waters cause (vv. 21-24).

Outline of Chapter 7

1. Divine Instructions, 7:1-5
2. Entering the Ark, 7:6-16
   a. Growing Threat, vv. 6-10
   b. Massive Danger, vv. 11-16
3. Overwhelming Waters, 7:17-24
   a. The Ark, vv. 17-20
   b. Beneath the Waters, vv. 21-24

Watery Story Line of Chapter 7

The chart shows how the chapters build to a climax of death in chapter 7.

6:1-8, Pre-flood wickedness
  6:9-10, Genealogical note—Noah's three sons
    6:11-12, God sees the earth is ruined, all flesh corrupted
      6:13-22, God's instructions to Noah
        7:1-9, They enter the ark
          7:10-16, Flood begins, ark is closed
            7:17-20, Waters rise, mountains covered
            7:21-24, Death
          8:1-5, Waters recede, mountains uncovered
        8:6-14, Flood ends, ark's window opened
      8:15-22, They exit the ark
    9:1-7, God's instructions to Noah
   9:8-17, God promises never again to ruin the earth
  9:18-19, Genealogical note—Noah's three sons
9:20-28 Post-flood wickedness

COMMENTARY

Divine Instructions, 7:1-5

At first glance God's instructions to Noah (7:1-5) seem merely to repeat events leading to the flood at the end of chapter 6, but the two sets of directives are not identical. [Literary Doublings] Here God orders Noah to board the ark and reminds him why he and his family alone are singled out to be saved: "I have seen that you alone are righteous in this generation" (7:1). Previously, God commanded him to bring on board both male and female examples of all living things, but now God requires an increased number of creatures to be brought aboard: seven pairs of all clean creatures and only one pair of unclean creatures. Seven pairs of clean animals means there will be an abundant supply of creatures for sacrifice in the future,[1] and one of the unclean means that animal life in all its vast diversity will continue. [Clean and Unclean Creatures] The original

Literary Doublings

📖 From 6:19 until 7:23, the story unfolds in a series of repetitions or doublings. Information from 6:19-22 appears again with additions and expansions at the beginning of chapter 7. Interpreters found in these repetitions evidence of the merging of the Priestly and non-Priestly sources, but the effect of this mixing is to increase the drama of the narrative. Whatever differences between the two units tell us about the sources of the book, the repeated and expanded information has important literary effects within the larger narrative. Repetitions create a slow, steady buildup to the flood by prolonging preparations and accelerating anticipation and dread. Here is an example of such repetitions:

End of Chapter 6
God commands Noah to bring all living things,
all flesh,
two of every kind into the ark,
"to keep them alive with you,
male and female."
birds,
animals,
"to keep them alive."
"And Noah did as God commanded." (6:19-22)

Beginning of Chapter 7
God commands Noah
to take seven pairs of clean animals,
male and female,
and of unclean, male and female,
and of birds to keep them alive on the face of the earth.
Noah did all that God commanded. (7:1-5)

ecologist, God strives for some continuity of original creation by planning "to keep their kind alive on the face of all the earth" (7:3).

Now, for the first time, God finally tells Noah what all the preparations are for and names the deadline by which he must complete them: "In seven days I will send rain on the earth for forty days and forty nights" (7:4). The one-week time limit magnifies the urgency of Noah's work and adds further apprehension to the scene. There is not some indefinite number of days to do everything, for in one short week "every living thing I have made I will blot out from the face of the ground." The seven days evoke the seven days of creation, of course (Gen 1:1–2:4a), but here the week progresses backward from the lush, inhabited world toward its un-creation as in the original watery chaos (1:6-7).

Entering the Ark, 7:6-16

Growing Threat, vv. 6-10

Rather than marking the time of the storm's beginning by stating the years of a king's rule or by noting astrological events, as were typical dating techniques among ancient cultures, the narrator dates the storm by Noah's auspicious age of 600 years "when the flood of waters came upon the earth" (v. 6). These short verses repeat information, no longer as preparations but in the form of Noah's obedient execution of divine commands. The effect of the repetition is to increase apprehension. At the end of seven days, "the waters of the flood came upon the earth" (v. 10).

Noah's prompt obedience stands out in these verses because an inclusio draws attention to it. An inclusio is a literary framing device wherein a text ends with similar words or phrases with which it begins.[2] The same clause with slight variations—"the waters of the flood came upon the earth" (vv. 6 and 10)—surrounds the account of Noah's obedient actions in vv. 7-9. He and his family

Clean and Unclean Creatures

The terms "clean" and "unclean" refer not to physical cleanliness but to aspects of creatures, persons, or objects that make them suitable or unsuitable to participate in or to be offered in ritual sacrifice (Lev 11:1-47; Deut 14:3-21). The Priestly writer includes seven pairs of each clean animal and one pair of the unclean on the ark in anticipation of Noah's sacrifice at the end of the flood (8:20).

Purity regulations of Leviticus and of God's command to Noah concerning clean and unclean animals serve at least three purposes. First, "ideas about separating, purifying, demarcating and punishing transgressions have as their main function to impose a system on an inherently untidy experience" (*Purity and Danger*, 4). They help people make sense of the world. Second, these distinctions also serve a liturgical purpose for the people of Judah. They reflect not only what types of sacrifices they could offer their God but also the foods of which they themselves could partake. "Body for altar, altar for body, the rules which protect the purity of the tabernacle are paralleled by rules which protect the worshipper. What one can eat without contracting impurity and what can be offered to God in sacrifice are the same" (Douglas, 138–39). Thus, humans are allowed to eat what God eats and vice versa. Finally, the language of cleanliness creates social identity; that is, the Judean people define themselves as people who do certain things while abstaining from other things. Such practices set them apart from their neighbors.

Mary Douglas, *Purity and Danger: An Analysis of the Concepts of Pollution and Taboo* (New York: Ark Paperbacks, 1984).

Mary Douglas, *Leviticus as Literature* (Oxford: Oxford University Press, 1999).

---

complete divine instructions to enter the ark, moving as if in solemn procession, first the sons, then Noah's wife, then the son's wives. Then follow the living creatures, clean and not clean, "as God commanded Noah" (v. 9). "Two and two, male and female," they also process into the ark, and the days of preparation are over. [Zora Neal Hurston's Hurricane]

Massive Danger, vv. 11-16

The next unit repeats events from the previous one about entering the ark, but it alters details, adds information, and builds further fear. [Instructions Repeated] Again the unit begins with Noah's age, but now the date of the flood is more precise: it happened in the second month and the seventeenth day of his 600th year. On that very day, chaos returned. Now the "waters of the flood" come from everywhere. The "fountains of the great deep and the windows of heaven were opened" (7:11). This highly dramatic language tells of overwhelming catastrophe, of engulfing waters that rise out of fountains under the earth and pour down as through sluice gates from the skies where the windows of the heavens are open. When waters flood up from beneath and fall down from above, there is no escaping, for the whole earth has returned to its pre-creation condition. [Waters from Beneath and Above the Earth] The dangers to life are massive, and the mythic terms of this verse express the totality of destruction. Then cosmic language abruptly gives way to more plain speech: "The rain fell on the earth for forty days and forty nights" (v. 12).

Again as in 7:6-10, the narrator reports that the family enters the ark in order, but this time Noah's sons, Shem, Ham, and Japheth,

Zora Neale Hurston's Hurricane

In the novel, *Their Eyes Were Watching God*, Zora Neale Hurston writes one of the best storm stories in literature, drawing from the Genesis story of animals processing toward the ark (see 229–30). As a hurricane and its massive flooding approach, she begins describing unusual movements of people and animals in the world of the main characters, Janie and Tea Cake, who have no knowledge of what is about to happen. First, Janie watches Seminole Indians pass in a kind of solemn procession, and then animals begin to depart in a similar fashion.

Some rabbits scurried through the quarters going east. Some possums slunk by and their route was definite. One or two at a time, then more. By the time the people left the fields the procession was constant. Snakes, rattlesnakes began to cross the quarters. The men killed a few, but they could not be missed from the crawling horde. People stayed indoors until daylight. Several times during the night Janie heard the snort of big animals like deer. Once the muted voice of a panther. Going east and east. That night the palm and banana trees began that long distance talk with rain. Several people took fright and picked up and went into Palm Beach anyway. A thousand buzzards held a flying meet and then went above the clouds and stayed.

A few pages later, Hurston describes the storm's onslaught as Janie and Tea Cake try to leave the quarters. Hurston's storm, resembling the style of the Genesis flood, is mythic, assaulting the senses and transforming itself into a beast that rages against the cosmos:

Zora Neale Hurston. Portrait. (Credit: Library of Congress, Prints & Photographs Division, Carl Van Vechten Collection)

They had to fight to keep together to keep from being pushed the wrong way and to hold together. They saw other people like themselves struggling along. A house down, here and there, frightened cattle. But above all the drive of the wind and the water. And the lake. Under its multiplied roar could be heard a mighty sound of grinding rock and timber and wail. They looked back. Saw people trying to run in the raging waters and screaming when they found they couldn't. A huge barrier of the makings of the dike to which the cabins had been added was rolling and tumbling forward. Ten feet higher and as far as they could see the muttering wall advanced before the braced-up waters like a road crusher on a cosmic scale. The monstropolous beast had left his bed. The two hundred miles an hour wind had loosed his chains. He seized hold of his dikes and ran forward until he met the quarter; uprooted them like grass and rushed on after his supposed-to-be conquerors, rolling the dikes, rolling the houses, rolling the people in the houses along with other timbers. The sea was walking the earth with a heavy heel. (238–39)

Zora Neale Hurston, *Their Eyes Were Watching God* (1937; rev. ed., Urbana: University of Illinois Press, 1978).

appear by name and the living creatures no longer divide by their status as clean and unclean. They form one mass instead, marching all together in pairs—every kind of animal, domestic animals, creeping things, birds and every winged creature. "Two and two of all flesh," male and female, they embark in orderly fashion as God had commanded. [Male and Female Animals in the Genesis Rabbah] Noah and every living creature with him are safe and their survival assured because God protects them from the waters. God "shuts him in" (v. 16). [Chrysostom Interprets God's Shutting the Ark's Door]

Instructions Repeated

The chart below shows repetitions regarding the beginning of the flood and God's protection of Noah and his family. These repetitions have long served as evidence of the presence of two separate literary sources in the telling of the flood story. These repetitions plus additions in vv. 11-16 add intensity to events and build further tension as flooding waters expand beyond imagining, Noah's sons acquire names, more animal types appear, and finally God intervenes directly by personally shutting them into the ark. Whether these two versions existed separately or not does not change the effects of the present composition. Repetition creates drama, invites readers to experience the mounting fears of the scene, and strengthens theological hope for survival of the remnant under divine protection.

Genesis 7:6–10	Genesis 7:11–16
[6]Noah was six hundred years old	[11]In the six hundredth year of Noah's life, in the second month, on the seventeenth day of the month,
when the flood of waters came on the earth.	on that day all the fountains of the great deep burst forth, and the windows of the heavens were opened. [12]The rain fell on the earth forty days and forty nights.
[7]And Noah with his sons and his wife and his sons' wives went into the ark to escape the waters of the flood.	[13]On the very same day Noah with his sons, Shem and Ham and Japheth, and Noah's wife and the three wives of his sons entered the ark, [14]they
[8]Of clean animals, and of animals that are not clean, and of birds, and of everything that creeps on the ground, [9]two and two, male and female,	and every wild animal of every kind, and all domestic animals of every kind, and every creeping thing that creeps on the earth, and every bird of every kind—every bird, every winged creature. [15]They went into the ark with Noah, two and two of all flesh in which there was the breath of life.
went into the ark with Noah, as God had commanded Noah. [10]And after seven days the waters of the flood came on the earth.	[16]And those that entered, male and female of all flesh, went in as God had commanded him; and the Lᴏʀᴅ shut him in.

Repetitions to this point in the story suggest a conflation of sources, yet the units flow into one another and build on one another, fashioning narrative waves of increasing alarm and suggesting a stunned need to tell and retell a story, to express the drama of catastrophe and paint a picture of disaster. The scenes of preparing and entering the ark replay themselves, not in rote repetition but with addition and variation, as if more voices were remembering with rising trepidation something about God's commands as the narrative advances.

Waters from Beneath and Above the Earth

Right on God's announced schedule the flood begins, with water pouring in from below and above. The bursting forth (or splitting open) of the deep (Heb. *tĕhôm*, v. 11; cf. Ps 78:15; Isa 51:10) suggests a breakdown of the division between the waters above and below (1:6-7). The windows of the heaven, however, seem simply to be the source of rain (Mal 3:10, but see Isa 24:18). The presence of the event within a timeframe remains important, for it keeps the destruction within created temporal limits.

Terence E. Fretheim, "Genesis" (*NIB* 1; Nashville: Abingdon, 1994). 392.

Male and Female Animals in the Genesis Rabbah

In the Genesis Rabbah, a midrashic commentary on Genesis completed by rabbis around 400 CE, the rabbis commented on Gen 7:16, first giving the translation and then noting gaps and difficulties in the text. The material in brackets represents the translator's efforts to make the comments clearer. The comments below show both careful attention to the Hebrew text and creative imagination to explain a logical problem for anyone who may have taken the details of the story at face value. How, for example, could Noah learn the sex of the all the animals that were to come aboard? Wild animals would surely not submit to examination. The discussion is amusing and, for modern readers, highlights the importance of appreciating the genre of the account. Is it a story to tell what happened exactly or to convey the experiences of disaster and hope in divine protection?

A. "And they that entered, male and female [of all flesh, went in as God had commanded him, and the Lord shut him in]" (Gen 7:16).

B. [Since Noah was supposed to bring a male and a female of each species], he said to [God], "Am I a hunter? [How am I supposed to know male from female in all cases?]"

C. He said to him, "What difference does it make to you! What is written is not, 'Those that were *brought* in,' but, 'Those that *entered*,' meaning they came on their own [so you do not have to bring them]."

Genesis Rabbah: The Judaic Commentary to the Book of Genesis, 3 vols., trans. Jacob Neusner (Atlanta: Scholars Press, 1985) 1:335.

Kaspar Memberger (1555–1618). Detail of *Noah's Ark Cycle 2: Entering the Ark*. 1588. Kunsthistorisches Museum, Vienna. (Credit: Erich Lessing / Art Resource, NY)

Chrysostom Interprets God's Shutting the Ark's Door

One of the fathers of the early church and the Bishop of Constantinople, Chrysostom preached on the verse with awareness of traumatic elements in the story.

"The Lord God shut the ark from the outside." Notice . . . the considerateness in the expression "God shut the ark from the outside" to teach us that he had insured the good man's complete safety. The reason for adding "from the outside" to "he shut" was that

the good man might not be in the position of seeing the disaster occur and suffering even greater distress. I mean, that if he brooded over that terrible flood and set indelibly in his mind the destruction of the human race, the complete annihilation of all brute beasts, and the disappearance of, as it were of people, animals and the earth itself, he would have been disturbed and anguished.

"HOMILIES on Genesis 25:12," *ACCS* 1:38.

Overwhelming Waters, 7:17-24

The third and final unit of the chapter also divides into two interlocking parts, but here repetition occurs within each part, not across the two sections. In them, the horror that has been brewing since the beginning of chapter 6 comes to its terrible climax. Its subject is the rising waters (vv. 17-20) and its effects (vv. 21-24).

The Ark, vv. 17-20

It rains for forty days and forty nights and the waters accumulate to bear up the ark that rises higher and higher above the earth (vv. 17-18). With each increase in the depth of the water, the ship ascends, then ascends again high above the known world. It floats on the face of the waters above the mountains, while the waters still rise even farther by more than fifteen cubits. In some sense, the mounting up of the ark measures the flood's extremity, even as it also shows God's particular care for Noah and all the living creatures on board the ark with him floating above the world.

The ark strangely drops out of focus in vv. 19-20, and only the ever-higher piling waters interest the narrator. The flood grows more towering, beyond even the highest mountain, nearly beyond human capacity to imagine. Waters multiply until the cosmos itself is flooded, as if the fountains of the deep have exploded from below and the windows of the heavens have imploded from above. The flood continued forty days and forty nights, a point so unbelievable it needs frequent repeating.

Verbs of increasing and swelling track the waters' ascent and engulf readers' sense of safety under their force:

Waters increased (*rābāh*)
Waters swelled (*gābar*) and increased (*rābāh*) greatly
Waters swelled (*gābar*) so mightily that the mountains were covered
Waters swelled (*gābar*) above the mountains more than fifteen cubits deep (vv. 17-20)

Repetition of the Hebrew verbs of "increase" (*rābāh*) and "swelling" (*gābar*) creates a tumultuous scene of waters overtaking the earth. The first verb (*rābāh*) means "to multiply," "increase," or "become more," and the second (*gābar*) further intensifies the increase because it means to "be strong," "be mighty," and hence, in the case of waters, to "swell." The KJV translates the verb as "prevail," suggesting that each increase in the flood's dimensions was a triumph in the struggle of watery chaos over orderly creation. [Fox's Translation]

Beneath the Waters, vv. 21-24

A climactic scene announces the consequences of the enlarging waters. The narrator's attention shifts from the height of the waters to plummet beneath them and reveal their effects: "All flesh died that moved on the earth, every creature, birds, animals and all human beings" (v.

Fox's Translation

Everett Fox's translation of the verbs captures how the "structure here mirrors the action: the surging and growing of the waters"—"increased . . . swelled and increased exceedingly . . . swelled exceedingly . . . swelled."

Everett Fox, *The Five Books of Moses: Genesis, Exodus, Leviticus, Numbers, and Deuteronomy* (Schocken Bible; Dallas: Word, 1995) 1:39.

Layers of Death

📖 These verses portray the overriding vision of total destruction. Again a series of repetitions characterize the telling. The narrator piles up language to convey the enormity of loss and the end of creation. The agent of the action is God.

All flesh died that moved on the earth,
birds, domestic animals, wild animals,
all swarming creatures that swarm on the earth,
and all human beings;
Everything on dry land in whose nostrils was the breath of life died.
He blotted out every living thing that was on the face of the ground,
human beings and animals and creeping things and birds of the air;
they were blotted out from the earth.
Only Noah was left, and those that were with him in the ark.

21). Lest the totality of the cataclysm be missed, the narrator reiterates the extent of the destruction: "everything on dry land in whose nostrils was the breath of life"—all these died (v. 22). Yet a third time, the narrator adds layers of death similar to the heaping up of the waters in the previous section. [Layers of Death] God "blotted out every living thing on the face of the earth"—humans, animals, creeping things, birds--"they were blotted out from the earth" (v. 23). It all happened as God promised, for God was "sorry to have made them" (6:7).

Of all of God's creation, only a tiny remnant of living things, the creatures on board the ark with Noah, remain alive from the original creation of the world. The rest of its inhabitants and the rest of the people born through ten generations of being fruitful and multiplying are dead (v. 23). As the chapter ends, the waters still "swell"—they continue to do so for 150 days.

CONNECTIONS

Any people who have undergone personal or communal disasters might recognize their experiences in the turbulence of this chapter as it unleashes destruction by water. The story is told in a straight-forward way, building toward cosmic destruction with waters engulfing and drowning out life from all around, as if language cannot express or contain the inundation or the blotting out of nearly all life. The artfully told chapter intends to evoke terror and to create a sense of overwhelming loss and destruction. Here God un-creates the world with water, life ends, and the original creation of all the earth's inhabitants is wiped away.

Although literary memories of actual floods in antiquity surely influence the telling, the purposes of this story in Genesis are to reflect the Judean people's own overwhelming memories of military and political disaster and to interpret the survival of some. In this "refraction of disaster,"[3] they can find their experiences told in oblique fashion, recalling memories, showing them their reality indirectly, and inviting them into the horrors of their past both

The World Destroyed by Water

Gustave Doré was a French printmaker and illustrator. His art often sought to portray violent, troubling biblical events in an art folio known as the *Bible de Tours*. Here, rather than portraying cuddly animals marching onboard the ark, Doré depicts tragic aspects of the flood as humans and animals attempt to escape the waters. This illustration of Gen 7:24 depicts the horrific aftermath of the flood that destroys life over the whole world.

Gustave Doré (1832–1883).
The World Destroyed by Water. 19th C. Engraving.
(Credit: www.creationism.org/images/
DoreBiblelllus/)

intimately and at a distance. The flood happened to other people in the ancient past, so they can attend to it without being retraumatized by direct historical retellings of events.

Some escape with their lives, even though their whole world has collapsed. The survival of Noah and his family interprets theologically the survival of a remnant; God protected them. Many believers in the past and the present see their own survival of violence and cataclysm as the result of the beneficent care of a loving God who kept them alive for a reason. Yet this overwhelming destruction with the survival of a few happened to people in the ancient past. The book's ancient audience can see their experience of fear, of colossal destruction, of the death of their own past life in Judah mirrored here.

Simultaneously, the chapter portrays God as the Bringer of Destruction, the Un-Creator of their world. This picture seems to be its own horror to some modern believers and neo-atheists alike.

The Punishing and Saving God

Some communities of faith hold that if the biblical text says God is punishing, violent, wrathful, then God *is* punishing, violent, and wrathful. The words directly reveal the character of God. Yet other communities and interpreters, including me, hold that divine revelation is indirectly, inferentially embedded in human language, human limitations, human efforts to live in particular historical and cultural circumstances. The text speaks of God within the viewpoints and limitations of its time. This is also the general viewpoint of modern critical biblical studies.

Viewed this way, the biblical portrait of an angry God who destroys creation because of human wickedness provides words for the human effort to understand God in relation to disaster. Humans require explanation to survive after traumatic experience. They need to know why these events happened. Interpretation seeks to put order into what is otherwise random chaos. To say that God caused the flood is to keep God alive and in relationship with the survivors, but it provides neither full insight into the being of the Holy One nor an adequate explanation of events.

From a faith perspective, this theological approach recognizes that God is ultimately beyond human words, that any naming of God is partial, temporary, and a way to understand human experience of the divine. God is beyond our language. Through biblical speech we gain glimpses of the God whom we worship, yet we are always seeking ways to speak of God that suit new situations and reveal God anew. The biblical canon itself witnesses to these efforts from generation to generation throughout the centuries, for the books of the Bible speak of God in amazingly diverse ways.

For further reading, see Kathleen M. O'Connor, *Jeremiah: Pain and Promise* (Minneapolis: Fortress, 2011) 41–45.

Yet it is a theological survival strategy, a way of thinking that keeps God in their lives amid the swirling chaos they have experienced. If God sends the flood or any disaster, that means to the ancients that God is neither powerless nor defeated by other gods. God still relates to them. In these and other ways, the flood narrative connects the Judean people to the God who saves lives and will do so again in a new creation. [The Punishing and Saving God]

NOTES

1. See Nahum M. Sarna, *Genesis* (JPS Torah Commentary; Philadelphia: The Jewish Publication Society, 1989) 54, n. 2.

2. For further reading, see Victor M. Wilson, *Divine Symmetries: The Art of Biblical Rhetoric* (New York: University Press of America, 1997) 38–41.

3. A helpful phrase of David Carr, "Reading the Gap: Refractions of Trauma in Israelite Prophecy," in *Interpreting Exile: Displacement and Deportation in Biblical and Modern Contexts* (AIL 10; Atlanta: SBL, 2011) 295–308.

THE WATERS FALL

Genesis 8:1-22

While the literary arrangement of chapter 7 swells toward an apex of flooding and death, chapter 8 moves in the opposite direction. Everything slides downward toward the flood's diminishment until dry land appears. The previous chapter presents a vocabulary of increasing, multiplying, and enlarging waters, but this chapter abounds in language of abatement and restraint, of waters drying up and turning back. In reverse order, its literary structure generally retraces the buildup to the flood. Reduction replaces magnification at the moment when God remembers Noah and all the animals with him in the ark (8:1). [Outline of Genesis 8]

> **Outline of Genesis 8**
> 1. The Flood Subsides, 8:1-5
> 2. The Flood Ends, 8:6-19
> 3. Noah Sacrifices, 8:20-22

COMMENTARY

The Flood Subsides, 8:1-5

Although God and Noah alternate as primary actors in this chapter, God initiates the action, whereas Noah's role is always responsive. He is an executor of divine wishes. The chapter leaves no doubt about who enables survival and causes new life to emerge on the earth. God merely "remembers" Noah and things begin to change (8:1).

To remember (*zākār*) means more than simply to call to mind or to stop forgetting. With God as the subject, to remember is to attend to someone with kindness, as in granting requests or delivering and protecting someone. When God remembers Noah, the earth begins to dry and to heal. When God remembers Noah, God makes "a wind blow over the earth, and the waters subsided" (8:1). When God remembers Noah, creation begins all over again.

The movement of the wind (*rûaḥ*) evokes God's first creation of the world: "In the beginning when God created the heavens and the earth and the earth was a formless void and darkness covered the face of the deep, while a wind from God swept over the face of the waters . . ." (Gen 1:1). [*Rûaḥ 'elohîm*] The wind of God can also be translated as "breath" or "spirit." In God's first act of creation, God's *rûaḥ* passes

Rûaḥ 'elohîm

AΩ The Hebrew word translated "wind," "spirit," or "breath" (*rûaḥ*) is not easily reduced to one meaning. As the wind of God, it accords well with the material chaos of the introductory verses (Gen 1:2), and the term reappears here to dry up the waters; God creates again. The precise choice of English nouns may not matter as much as the fact that the *rûaḥ* is God's creative, life-giving energy and an expression of divine presence. The breath of God transforms the inert, disorganized matter to animate it with his spirit (see Sarna, 6). This language of the spirit of God is elusive rather than precise, combining agency and presence in a search for vocabulary to express the inexpressible.

Nahum M. Sarna, *Genesis* (JPS Torah Commentary; Philadelphia: The Jewish Publication Society, 1989).

over the waters and the churning chaos becomes a place of order and life. In this new creation, God's breath or spirit again passes over the waters, and with that "the waters [subside]" (8:1), chaos diminishes, and humans and animals find solid land on which to live.

The reappearance of "the breath of God" (Gen 1:1) is a clear signal that the flood account is a creation or, more accurately, a recreation narrative. Like Genesis 1–3, it too is a story of origins, this time of starting over after a broken past. Noah becomes the new ancestor, the new Adam from whom all humans descend.

After the spirit of God blows upon the waters, a sequence of events turns down the waters in the reverse order from which they streamed forth. [Waters Reverse] Again the literary structure and language of the chapter imitate the action, in this case, of draining away. The receding waters follow a narrative line so tight that the source theory that more than one version of the story appears here is nearly lost upon readers, until one considers the complicated and confusing use of numbers to mark events. [Numbers]

When God blows upon the waters, they begin to subside in nearly the same amount of time it took for them to submerge the world, half a year. First, the fountains of the deep and the windows of the heavens—previously opened for the waters to pour out from the top and flow up from bottom of the world—are closed; then, the rain is "restrained" (8:2). The Hebrew verbs translated "closed" and "restrained" occur in the passive voice because God acts upon them. The waters do not disappear of their own accord or close themselves down; God acts upon them. The triple sources of water—mythic fountains, heavenly windows, and the more mundane rain—respond to divine action and "the waters [recede] from the earth" (8:3).

By contrast to the mounting overflow of waters in 7:17-21, the flood vocabulary in chapter 8 is language of shrinkage. The waters "subsided" (*šākak*, v. 1); the fountains of the deep and the windows of heaven were "closed" (*sākar*, v. 2), the rain was "restrained" (*kālʾa*, v. 2); the waters "receded" (*ḥāsar*, vv. 3, 5) and "abated" or, more literally, "turned back" (*šûb*, v. 3, two times). The waters do this continually (*hālok*, vv. 3, 5),[1] steadily returning to their proper place in creation.

Waters Reverse

6:1-8, Pre-flood wickedness
   6:9-10, Genealogical note—Noah's three sons
      6:11-12, God sees the earth is ruined, all flesh corrupted
         6:13-22, God's instructions to Noah
            7:1-9, They enter the ark
            7:10-16, Flood begins, ark is closed
               7:17-20, Waters rise, mountains covered
               7:21-24, Death
            8:1-5, Waters recede, mountains uncovered
         8:6-14, Flood ends, ark's window opened
         8:15-22, They exit the ark
      9:1-7, God's instructions to Noah
   9:8-17, God promises never again to ruin the earth
   9:18-19, Genealogical note—Noah's three sons
9:20-28 Post-flood wickedness

The pattern of swelling and multiplying waters is gradual, step by step, and ineluctable. In chapter 7, when the flood begins,

   The fountains of the deep burst forth, and the windows the heavens were opened (7:11)
   The rain fell on the earth forty days and forty nights (7:12)
   The flood continued for forty days and forty nights (7:17)
   The flood continued and the waters increased, swelled (7:18)
   The waters swelled so mightily on the earth
   All the high mountains were covered (7:19)

The same pattern occurs in chapter 8 in reverse order in a gradual step-by-step diminishment that mirrors the rising waters in chapter 7. When the flood ends in chapter 8,

   The fountains of the deep and the windows of heaven were closed,
   The rain from the heavens was restrained,
   The waters gradually receded from the earth
   At the end of 150 days the waters had abated
   And the ark came to rest on the mountains of Ararat
   The waters continued to abate until the tops of the mountains appeared (8:2-3)

The balanced arrangement of the two chapters again underscores the way Genesis both tells of and mimics the arrival and departure of the flood.

In the midst of this step-by-step abatement, the ark rests on the mountains of Ararat. [Mountains of Ararat] Poised there, the ark perched on a mountaintop signifies the water's gradual disappearance, since previously the waters had "swelled above the mountains, covering them fifteen cubits deep" (7:20). In chapter 8 the mountains first function like a sandbar that stays the ship in the midst

Numbers

The numbers in chapters 7 and 8 present complicated markers of the flood's timing. Seven days lead up to the flood (7:4, 10), the 600th year of Noah's life (7:11), 40 days and 40 nights (7:12, 17), 150 days (8:1, 3, 4), the 10th month, the first day (8:6-7), waiting for 7 days for 3 times (8:10-12), the 601st year of Noah's life (8:13), and, finally, the 2nd month, on the 27th day. The duration of the flood is one year, but the numbers of days it rains and floods vary between 40 and 150 (Cotter, 57). It is not clear if the rains were limited to 40 days and nights and the flood persisted for 110 days after the rain ended, and then began to recede taking approximately another 150, or, as scholars generally believe, the time arrangements merely point to alternate versions of the same flood story combined in this narrative.

David Cotter, *Genesis* (Berith Olam; Collegeville MN: Liturgical Press, 2003).

Mountains of Ararat

Ararat is the "biblical name for the region around Lake Van (southeast Turkey, extending into northwest Iran) and the people and state established there from the ninth through the sixth centuries, BC." The ark settles on the mountains because they "were evidently conceived as the highest part of the world. The modern 'Mt. Ararat' is a later appellation." (See Parker, 43.)

Ararat, mentioned in 2 Kings 19:37 and Jer 51:37, is "most likely in extreme northeastern Turkey near the sources of the Tigress and Euphrates Rivers" (Fretheim, "Genesis," 392). This possibility has led some interpreters to propose that these rivers gave rise to the flood story, but more recently Fretheim has noted the proposal that the flood involved the Mediterranean Sea, pouring into the Black Sea through the Bosporus. The story of the flood might have spread from there (Fretheim, *Creation*, 43–44). These theories are enormously speculative. That means, for this and other reasons, modern archaeological sleuths will not find the ark there.

Simon B. Parker, *HBD*.

Terence Fretheim, "Genesis" (*NIB* 1; Nashville: Abingdon, 1994).

Terence Fretheim, *Creation Untamed: The Bible, God, and Natural Disasters* (Grand Rapids MI: Baker, 2010)

of the still-flooded world. As mountaintops begin to reappear, they continue to mark the flood's diminishment (8:5). [Gilgamesh Again]

The Flood Ends, 8:6-19

After God remembers Noah and blows upon the waters, they fall away but only slowly. All the inhabitants remain on the ark while Noah tests conditions to learn whether or not there is dry land on which to disembark. In traditional storytelling form, the test occurs multiple times before it succeeds. Clever Noah sends out birds as his emissaries in search of evidence that somewhere the land is dry and life is reviving. He begins by dispatching a raven that keeps flying around, to and fro, back

Gilgamesh Again

Composed around 2100 BCE, about 1600 years before Genesis, the Gilgamesh Epic exhibits many similarities to the Genesis account of the flood, both in regard to the ship resting on the mountains, the subsequent search for dry land by sending out birds, and the story of sacrifice that follows. When Utnapishtim tells Gilgamesh the story, he recounts that his ship was held fast on a mountaintop in the midst of the flood. The mountain was Mount Nisir and the ship was stuck there motionless for six days. Then, like Noah, Utnapishtim sends out birds: "When the seventh day arrived, I sent forth and set free a dove. The dove went forth but came back since no resting place for it was visible . . . . Then I sent forth and set free a swallow and finally I sent forth and set free a raven." After that, Utnapishtim offers sacrifice and the gods "smelled the savor, smelled the sweet savor" (XI, 140–60).

These similarities in plot and structure strongly suggest that the Genesis account builds upon this ancient flood story and adapts it for its own theological purposes.

ANET 94–95.

and forth, presumably circling near the ark until waters dry up. The raven brings no helpful news to Noah because the accumulated waters force it into a holding pattern.

Noah tries again, this time sending out a dove, an act he must repeat three times to obtain the needed results. The first time the dove returns, "for the waters were still on the face of the whole earth" (v. 9). Noah waits for seven days, this time not for rains to begin but for the waters to diminish further, but the dove is unsuccessful and returns to his hand. When he sends out the dove a third time, anticipation builds for a good result, but though weakening, the crisis is not completely over. The dove comes back with an olive leaf in its mouth: this was how "Noah knew the waters had subsided from the earth" (v. 11). Only when Noah waits yet another week and sends the dove out for the fourth time does a fully satisfying situation emerge. The dove does not return to the ark, so Noah must assume the bird has settled safely on dry land.

Will Noah and every living creature on the ark survive? Noah's multiple attempts to get news of the waters' depth by sending out the ever-circling raven and the to-ing and fro-ing dove build suspense and delay the climax of the chapter until the dove finally escapes for good.

Noah Sends Forth the Dove from the Ark
The dove in the center of the painting is the focal point of attention. It forms a vivid spot of light amid the drowned humans and beasts left in the wake of the waters. Doré again attends to the underside of the story, the actual consequences of floods with death covering the reappearing dry land. See [The Flood].

Gustave Doré (1832–1883). *Noah Sends Forth the Dove from the Ark*. 19th C. Engraving. (Credit: www.creationism.org/images/DoreBibleIllus/)

One year and one day after the beginning of the rains, the flood ends and "the waters were dried up from the earth" (8:13), but still not entirely. The drying process itself is as incremental as the recession of waters. Noah took the covering off the ark and "looked and saw that the face of the ground was drying." Presumably the ark is no longer on the mountains and only at the twenty-seventh day of the second month is the earth dry enough for the ark's occupants to leave the ship at last.

Now God commands Noah in terms as emphatic as the commands to enter the ark, only in the opposite direction: "Go, you, out of the ark" (8:16). For emphasis, the Hebrew uses the independent personal pronoun, highlighting God's direct, personal address to Noah. Maybe Noah would have left the ark anyway because the land was dry, but for the composer of the story, Noah's exit from the ark is God's will, God's plan, God's order, articulated as a formal commission to Noah. All humans are to leave the ark—Noah, his wife, his sons, and their wives. Noah is also to bring "every living thing that is with you of all flesh—birds and animals and every creeping thing." The purpose of their rescue and release is clear, that "they may abound on the earth and may be fruitful and multiply" (8:17). A summary statement reports Noah's obedience to the divine command. He and his family and every creature went out of the ark, no longer two and two but now grouped together by families (vv. 18-19). [Do Historical Memories Underlie the Flood Story?] The cycle of procreation resumes, living creatures again participate in creation of life, and God begins again.

Noah Sacrifices, 8:20-22

Noah's first act is not to build a house for himself and his family but to build an altar to the Lord. Perhaps for the Priestly writer this is the grand climax of the story, the point in the narrative wherein the role of

Do Historical Memories Underlie the Flood Story?

It seems likely that a memory of at least one great flood somewhere, sometime in the ancient Near East lies behind the various ancient stories about floods extant today. These include the Epic of Gilgamesh, the Atrahasis Epic, and the biblical story of Noah. Fretheim observed that "The existence of numerous flood stories has stimulated efforts to discern the basis of the story. The above-noted stories are set in the Tigris Euphrates River valley; alluvial deposits show that it was periodically flooded in ancient times. There are no such deposits in the land of Canaan, and archeological and geological remains provide no evidence of a worldwide flood" ("Genesis," 388).

Although some believing communities understand this story and the rest of the primeval history (Gen 1–11) as a literal accounting of events, at the heart of that perception is a misunderstanding of the complex and multiple genres of biblical literature. The chapters about the flood are not a history in any modern sense but a literary rendering of a story about God's rescue of a remnant of animals and humans from a massive catastrophe in order to begin life anew. The exact genre of the story is not certain, but it is an epic tale, built on other ancient stories and adapted to provide hope of new life after catastrophe for the people of Judah in the early Persian Period. The more interesting historical question is not what really happened to Noah or where the story originated but rather how this story addressed the historical plight of its early audience who survived the Babylonian destruction of their nation.

For further reading, see Terence E. Fretheim, *Creation Untamed: The Bible, God, and Natural Disasters* (Grand Rapids MI: Baker, 2010).

Terence Fretheim, "Genesis" (*NIB* 1; Nashville: Abingdon, 1994).

the aforementioned clean animals comes to the foreground. It is from among them that Noah selects his sacrifices and offers burnt offerings on the altar. Their aroma rises up to God, maybe as the sacrifices of Utnapishtim pleased the gods in the Gilgamesh Epic. (See [Gilgamesh and Atrahasis] and [Gilgamesh Again].) Afterwards, God makes a promise to Noah: "I will never again curse the ground because of humankind, for the inclination of the human heart is evil from youth: nor will I ever again destroy every living creature as I have done." [Noah's Sacrifice and God] This is an odd promise. Are not the wicked inclinations of the human heart the cause of the flood in the first place? [The Purifying Flood] God swears to protect the earth and its living creatures, but will God again blot out humans? A beautiful line of poetry completes the promise: "As long as the earth endures, seedtime and harvest, cold and heat, summer and winter, day and night shall not cease" (8:22).

The poetic verse adds depth to the divine promise of "never again." God grounds the promise in the seeming eternal solidity of

Sacrifice of Noah

After the flood, Noah builds an altar and sacrifices some clean animals that he saved from drowning earlier. The Michelangelo fresco presents Noah's family working busily together to prepare the animals for sacrifice and gather wood for the fire. Noah, his wife, and one of the daughters-in-law stand behind the altar. The elliptical composition made by the arms and heads of family members in front of and behind the altar suggests the family is a harmonious circle joining together in the work of worship, a form of unity that will disappear at the end of chapter 9.

Michelangelo Buonarroti (1475–1564). Sistine Chapel ceiling (1508–1512). *The Sacrifice of Noah*. Fresco, pre-restoration. (Credit: Vatican Museums and Galleries, Vatican City / Alinari / Bridgeman Images)

Noah's Sacrifice and God

"On exiting the ark, Noah's first act is to build an altar to YHWH (the first such altar mentioned in the Hebrew Bible) and to offer sacrifices. The scene describes an act of worship that combines both ritual and spontaneity. There is an altar, but it rests on common ground; there is a whole burnt offering of ceremonially clean animals but no priest to mandate or to supervise its implementation. Instead, Noah's offering is presented as a natural and immediate response of thanksgiving to God that emerges out of the concrete experience of deliverance from the consuming waters of the flood.

"Noah's spontaneous ritual of speechless thanks has an enormous effect on God. Where before there was grief in God's heart (Gen 6:6) now there is new resolve (8:21). Twice God turns away from previous decisions. 'I will not again curse . . .'; 'I will not again destroy . . . .'"

Samuel E. Balentine, *The Torah's Vision of Worship* (OBT; Minneapolis: Fortress, 1999) 101.

The Purifying Flood

James Kugel has gathered interpretations of Genesis from early Jewish and Christian sages and scholars. Some interpreters in the post-biblical period understood God's choice of a flood to destroy the world to have served as a purifying bath. That would mean that the flood cleansed and prepared the earth for the new creation that follows. Kugel pointed out that baths played a crucial role in everyday life and are prescribed in the Bible for many occasions. Here is a sampling of these interpretations:

[God says to the angel Michael:] Destroy all wrong from the face of the earth . . . and **cleanse** the earth from all wrong, and from all iniquity, and from all sin, and from all impiety, and from all uncleanness which brought about on the earth; **remove** them from the earth. —*1 Enoch* 10:20

When the Creator took it to mind to cleanse the earth by means of water and decide that the soul [symbolized by the earth] should be purged of its unmentionable ill deeds and have its uncleanness washed away in the manner of a sacred purification. —Philo, *The Worse Attack the Better* 170

You have heard, my son Seth, that a flood is come and will wash the whole earth. —*Testament of Adam* 3:5

Christians build on these ideas and not surprisingly find in the flood an anticipation of baptism:

God's patience waited in the days of Noah, during the building of the ark, in which a few, that is, eight persons were saved through the water. Baptism, which corresponds to this, now saves you, not as a removal of dirt but as an appeal to God for a clear conscience. —1 Pet 3:20-21, RSV

Alternatively, in Matthew's Gospel and the second letter of Peter, the flood anticipates the end of days. Matthew takes an interest in the shock the flood would have been for people who were carrying on with their normal lives until the very minute of the catastrophe with no awareness of their peril. The second letter of Peter draws a contrast between the waters of the flood and the fires still to come, presumably because God's promise never to destroy the earth again pertains only to the end by water, not by fire.

For further reading, see James L. Kugel, *The Bible as It Was* (Cambridge MA: Belknap Press of Harvard University Press, 1997) 118–20.

the earth and its circadian rhythms, kept in proper working order by the Creator and Re-Creator of all things. Despite the thoroughgoing evil of the human will, God promises not to curse the ground or to destroy every living thing again. God will protect the ground as long as the earth endures and the times and seasons flow into one another, yet who determines the endurance of the earth but the Creator? [Other Early Christian Interpretations of the Flood]

CONNECTIONS

Ecological Destruction and Recovery

The story of the flood offers many avenues for reflection about living things. Like most "natural" disasters, this one affects not only human life but also the life of living creatures and of the earth itself. In that sense, the flood in Genesis is an iconic cataclysm. Symbolically, it gathers up experiences of destruction and loss of life throughout history—floods, earthquakes, fires, and other natural disasters. Nearly everything dies; every creature suffers. This story focuses on the devastation of human and animal life, but implicit in the tale is massive damage to their habitat. The land, too, needs to recover and heal, and the earth's waters need to recalibrate and balance themselves in relation to the land.

Almost modern in its sensibilities, the story reveals the profound relationship between human behavior and the well-being of the rest of creation. Human wickedness, its violence and corruption, provokes the flood. Even if, in scientific terms, human behavior does not exclusively cause floods, human greed and disregard for other created beings continue to have devastating effects on the created world in this story and today. [Inflicting Harm]

Paradoxically, even though God summons the rains and engineers the flood, God emerges as the Supreme Ecologist in the story, for God cares for the continuity of species upon earth. God commissions Noah to save two of each kind of creature, "to keep them alive with you" (6:19-22), and singles out clean animals, adding seven of each to Noah's cargo (7:1-5). God requires Noah to make adequate preparations to feed the animals as well as the humans (6:21). God promises never again to "curse the ground" because of humans. Finally, God celebrates the enduring rhythms

---

Other Early Christian Interpretations of the Flood

The flood story has an important place in Christian reflection.

The New Testament most often views the flood story typologically. The flood, for example, was viewed as a prefiguring of the end times (e.g., Matt. 24:37-39:2; 2 Pet. 3:5-10). As Noah was saved from the deluge by means of the ark, so will believing Christians be saved by God when the end unexpectedly comes. In early Christian interpretations, the ark came to symbolize the church, built on such texts as 1 Peter 3:20-21, where the saving of Noah and his household through water prefigured Baptism and being saved through the waters. From another angle, Noah was viewed as the exemplar of one who was faithful to God: in the words of 2 Peter 2:5, Noah was a "herald of righteousness" (see Heb 11:7 on the faith of Noah. Noah even became a type of Christ in some interpretation, prefiguring the resurrection). (Fretheim, 44–45)

Each of the above Christian perspectives has some metaphoric basis in the Genesis account. The deluge is a story of catastrophic endings suggesting the end times. Noah is brought through the waters to safety and renewed relationship with God as Israel will be in the book of Exodus and Christians will be in the experience of baptism. Although we know little of Noah's righteousness except for the claims that he was so and that he was obedient to divine commands, the perception of Noah as "herald of righteousness" has some basis in Genesis.

Terence E. Fretheim, *Creation Untamed: The Bible, God, and Natural Disasters* (Grand Rapids MI: Baker, 2010).

Inflicting Harm

"Overflowing landfills, befouled skies, eroded soils, polluted rivers, acidic rain, and radioactive wastes suggest ample attainments for admission into some intergalactic school for learning-disabled species."

David Orr, *Earth in Mind: On Education, Environment, and the Human Prospect* (Washington, DC: Island Press, 1994) 50, cited in Sam Hamilton Poore, *Earth Gospel: A Guide to Prayer for God's Creation* (Nashville: Upper Room Books, 2008) 85.

of nature, growth, and circadian cycles of the days and the seasons (vv. 21-22). At the flood's end, God orders all the humans who disembark from the ark to be "fruitful and multiply," to repopulate the earth (9:1). The character of God presented in the flood narrative symbolically interprets the historical disaster experienced by the book's audience. God brings the disaster, saves a remnant, declares loyalty to humans, and orders Noah and family to be fruitful and multiply. God the Creator is even more importantly the Recreator.

Yet if human relationship with God is reestablished, the human relationship with animals is altered. Although humans may eat of them, dread exists for the nonhumans; they have become prey. "God will require a reckoning" of the blood of life (9:2-7), but even where there is conflict and disharmony, underlying this story rests a reverence for the life of all creatures. God restrains wanton destruction of animal and human life.

Destruction of Creation

Christian discipleship for twenty-first-century North American Christians "means cruciform living," an alternative notion of the abundant life that will involve a philosophy of "enoughness," limitations on energy use, and sacrifice for the sake of others. For us privileged Christians, a "cross-shaped life" will primarily be not what Christ does for us but what we can do for others. We do not need so much to accept Christ's sacrifice for our sins as we need to repent of a major sin—our silent complicity in the impoverishment of others and the degradation of the planet. In Charles Birch's pithy statement, "The rich must live simply so that the poor may simply live."

In Sallie McFague, *Life Abundant: Rethinking Theology and Economy for a Planet in Peril* (Minneapolis: Fortress, 2001) 14, cited in Sam Hamilton Poore, *Earth Gospel: A Guide to Prayer for God's Creation* (Nashville: Upper Room Books, 2008) 154.

For modern readers, the biblical command to subdue the earth cannot be obeyed in a wanton spoilage of the earth and all its creatures. The Supreme Ecologist demands from humans rightful respect and participation in keeping the animals "alive with you," feeding and caring for them, and respecting the blood of all life. "Basic to understanding the God of this story is that God has entered into a basic relationship with humans and the world."[2] [Destruction of Creation]

A Remnant Survives

Because the flood presents the un-creation of the world, it stands as a distant mirror of the destruction of Judah under the Babylonians for the book's earliest audiences. Not in military or political terms but as mythic narrative, the flood symbolizes overwhelming catastrophe, ecological destruction, and the loss of almost all that is solid on which to live. Yet not all is lost; a small remnant of people and animals remain. This chapter interprets survival as an act of God who remembers the righteous Noah. For Judean survivors, it calls forth memories of the nation's catastrophe and interprets causes of the survival of some. The story proposes that some survive because God favored the righteous. The flood story augurs hopes for new beginnings rooted in worship of the Creator of new life. [Cosmic Hope]

The portrait of God in this chapter assumes divine agency in bringing about the flood. After major catastrophes and personal traumas, survivors often think that God has abandoned them or has punished them. This is a way to make sense of a world that has spun out of control, and such views are not limited to ancient peoples. This view also keeps God connected to them because it sees the flood not as random chaos loose in the world but as a purposeful event in relation to God. [Catastrophic Theology]

Although Genesis 8 accepts divine agency behind disaster, it also challenges it. God responds to Noah's act of worship with promises to abstain from bringing such disasters again: "I will never again curse the ground because of humankind . . . nor will I ever again destroy every living creature as I have done" (v. 21). This, too, is a theology that arises from the circumstances of the community, of the book's ancient audience living in the aftermath of destruction. Such a God is their security, their future, the solid root that binds them together as they are created anew.

The narrative of the flood does not seek to provide a definitive word about the being of God; it is not a complete theological definition of the Holy One, as if that were possible. Instead, the flood narrative shows the Judean people their own history in mythic terms; it finds in God's own life One who makes the ground solid, protects them, and presses toward a new creation. This biblical theology is an act of pastoral care.

Cosmic Hope

"The greatest image of the world destroyed is, of course, in the flood story, which is undoubtedly borrowed from Mesopotamian sources. God resolves to blot out all who have turned to evil, preserving the only one righteous man, his family and animals so as to preserve all species of living creature(s). The story is not of world destruction (God lets in the powers of chaos, but does not actively destroy his creation) but rather of the purging of the world so as to restore it, while bearers of God's blessing are preserved to continue life on Earth. Thus the story is a great paradigm of warning but also of hope. As a narrative it has the character of myth rather than history. God reaffirms the 'cosmic order' (Gen 8:22) with an 'eternal covenant' which he makes with both humans and animals (9:8-18). The inclusion of the animals is characteristic of the cosmic vision of a covenant with God that represents a different mode of symbolic religious thought from the Mosaic covenant of law, and points to an origin of a different kind of milieu."

Robert Murray, "The Cosmic Covenant," *The Ecologist* 30/1 (Jan/Feb 2000): 26.

Catastrophic Theology

The *New York Times* quoted a survivor of an earthquake in Mexico that happened the day before. This survivor cited another disaster narrative of Genesis (see Introduction): "It's like Sodom and Gomorrah, like God is angry at us."

Kirk Semple, Paulina Villegas, Elisabeth Malkin, "Mexico Earthquake Kills Hundreds, Trapping Many under Rubble," *New York Times*, 19 September 2017, p. 1.

NOTES

1. This verb is the infinitive absolute of the verb "to walk" and here intensifies the action of the main verbs in the style of an adverb. See Bruce Waltke and M. O'Connor, *An Introduction to Biblical Hebrew Syntax* (University Park PA: Eisenbrauns, 1990) 587–88.

2. Terence E. Fretheim, *Creation Untamed: The Bible God and Natural Disasters* (Grand Rapids MI: Baker Academic, 2010) 55–56.

CREATION AGAIN

Genesis 9:1-28

By the end of chapter 8, the waters are gone, and God promises to desist from destroying the earth by flood. Chapter 9 concludes the story of the flood and launches a new creation. From a literary perspective, the chapter continues the falling literary wave that begins when God remembers Noah in 8:1. [Outline of Genesis 9] The tight structural arrangement made by repeated language and plot development begins in 6:9 and ends at 9:17. Although some interpreters think the story about Noah's sons (9:18-28) is a separate unit,[1] there are indications that these events belong to the larger flood story.

Outline of Genesis 9
1. Recreation, 9:1-7
2. The Covenant and Its Sign, 9:8-17
3. Wickedness Persists, 9:18-28

One reason to understand the debacle among Noah's sons to be the end of the flood narrative is that it exhibits similarities to the story of the mating of the sons of God with the daughters of humans that gave rise to the flood in the first place (6:1-4, 5-9). As balancing pieces at the beginning and end, the two stories extend the flood's literary structure. [The Watery Line of the Narrative] Both involve "an outrage . . . and its punishment."[2] In both, the nature of the outrage is opaque and the punishment seems not to fit the crime. Both contain an odd combination of literary parts, and both are puzzles that omit something important for understanding. The sons of God episode begins the gradual buildup to the flood, and the sons of Noah portion ends with a return to normal life where wickedness resumes. A final reason to include the sons of Noah story with the flood material is that only at its end does Adam's genealogy come to a conclusion (5:1–9:28).

The Watery Line of the Narrative
The rise and fall of action and of water come back to the starting point of this disaster narrative in this chapter.

6:1-8, Pre-flood wickedness
  6:9-10, Genealogical note—Noah's three sons
    6:11-12, God sees the earth is ruined, all flesh corrupted
      6:13-22, God's instructions to Noah
        7:1-9, They enter the ark
          7:10-16, Flood begins, ark is closed
            7:17-20, Waters rise, mountains covered
              7:21-24, Death
            8:1-5, Waters recede, mountains uncovered
          8:6-14, Flood ends, ark's window opened
        8:15-22, They exit the ark
      9:1-7, God's instructions to Noah
    9:8-17, God promises never again to ruin the earth
  9:18-19, Genealogical note—Noah's three sons
9:20-28 Post-flood wickedness

COMMENTARY

Recreation, 9:1-7

God begins creation again in chapter 9, yet the new beginning that follows the flood stands in continuity with the original creation. The earth itself remains ready to be re-inhabited. A remnant of animals, birds, and creeping things as well as Noah's small family of humans are still alive. From them, all subsequent generations of humans and living creatures will descend, implicitly turning Noah into a new Adam. Heightening the connection with the original creation, these verses draw explicitly on events and language from the first two chapters of Genesis. God again blesses humans and commands them to "be fruitful and multiply" (9:1, 7; cf. 1:22, 28), solidifies their dominion over animals (v. 2; cf. 1:28), resupplies them with food (v. 3; cf. 1:29-30), presents them with a prohibition (vv. 4; 2:16-17), and, of most importance, reiterates their status as images of God (v. 6; cf. 1:26-27). (See [Image of God].) The command to "be fruitful and multiply" frames the unit (vv. 1 and 7) and further emphasizes connections with the first creation story.

In v. 7, Noah and his sons become recipients of God's blessing as well as of the command to reproduce, in words nearly identical to Genesis 1:28: "God blessed them, and God said to them, 'Be fruitful and multiply, and fill the earth . . . .'" In Genesis 1, however, the command to procreate extends to all humans, male and female (1:27). One reason women do not find a place here may be because the verse's exclusive attention to Noah's sons anticipates their difficulties at the end of the chapter and the conflicts ahead (9:18-28).

In Genesis 1, God grants humans "dominion over the fish of the sea and over the birds of the air and over every living thing that moves on earth" (1:28). Human relationship with other living creatures established as one of dominion and subservience takes a turn for the worse in chapter 9. The same animals listed in reverse order will now relate to humans in "dread and fear" (9:2). Every bird of the air, everything that creeps on the ground, and all the fish of the sea "will be delivered into your hand" (v. 2). Relations of domination and absolute control implied in chapter 1 become harshly clear here. "To be delivered into someone's hands" is an idiomatic expression that means to be left in their power, and this power creates fear and dread among non-human creatures. [Delivered into the Hands]

For the first time, God gives animals to humans for food. The former vegetarian diet of plants (1:29) expands here to include meat: "Every moving thing that lives shall be food for you . . . I give you everything" (v. 3). Yet with divine generosity also comes a limit in the form of a prohibition (9:4-6) akin to the prohibition in the garden. In Eden, God was permissive and generous—"You may freely eat of every tree in the garden"— but then set a limit on the food that can be eaten—"Of the tree of knowledge of good and evil you shall not eat for in the day you eat of it you shall die" (2:17). Similarly, after the flood, God resupplies Noah and his family with edibles, but now God adds a new restriction. You can eat everything, "Only you shall not eat flesh with its life, that is, with its blood" (9:4). [Blood] [Inclusive Translation]

The first requirement of the prohibition is to rid meat of its blood before eating it. This is a dietary provision of Hebrew law in legal texts (Lev 17:10-14; Deut 12:15-27). [Jewish Dietary Law] Although dietary law may come from a different historical time, its spirit may be behind this passage and surely would be an interest of Priestly editors of Genesis. The law urges care and respect for animal life even when it is killed for food. Yet the text quickly pushes beyond dietary concerns (9:3-4) toward concern for the shedding of human blood (9:5-6). The ancients would find animal and human blood to be inseparable because blood is life. [Killing Animals] That means that "restrictions they place on the shedding and use of blood were continual reminders of the conviction that all life belongs to God and under no circumstances may it be treated in a random or arbitrary way by human beings."[3] If blood is life and life belongs to God, only God can seek a reckoning for it.

God's role notwithstanding, the next verse seems to place responsibility for such reckoning on human beings. The line's compact,

Delivered into the Hands

AΩ The motif of being delivered from/into someone's hands appears in three primary ways in the Old Testament. Most often, authors use the phrase to connote God's power in determining the outcome of battles between warring factions. After favorable outcomes in war, the Israelite people praise God for "deliverance" (see Gen 14:20; Judg 7:2; 1 Chr 22:18; Ps 31:8). Of course, they also frame their defeats in terms of God's activity (Lev 26:25; 2 Chr 24:24; Lam 2:7; Ezek 23:9; 1 Macc 5:50). This sense of conflict and antipathy finds expression in Gen 9:2-5, for humans now have complete power over animals.

Second, the phrase can depict generosity. During the construction of the temple, the king pays the builders by delivering money into their hands—"for they dealt honestly" (1 Kgs 12:15; see also 22:7, 9; 2 Chr 34:17). It also describes Jacob's reconciling gift to his estranged brother Esau (Gen 32:16).

Finally, the phrase describes the abstract powers of sin, transgression, and disobedience in later tradition. Both Job and Isaiah describe people as having been delivered into the hand of their transgression/iniquity (Job 8:4; Isa 64:7).

Human domination of animals expressed here does not support abuse and exploitation of animals without regard to their well-being. The verses are etiological in intention, interpreting life in the ancient world where animals and humans were often at odds with one another. The situation forms part of the alienation within creation that begins in Gen 3 and extends throughout the world across chapter 3–11.

For further reading, see Yael Shemesh, "Vegetarian Ideology in Talmudic Literature and Traditional Biblical Exegesis," in *Genesis*, ed. Athalya Brenner, Archie Chi Chung Lee, Gale A. Yee (Texts @ Contexts; Minneapolis: Fortress, 2010) 107–27.

Blood

AΩ The Hebrew stresses the proscription against eating flesh with its blood by repeating, "only" (*'ak*) at the beginning of both vv. 4 and 5: "Only (*'ak*) you shall not eat flesh with its life, that is, its blood . . . For (only, *'ak*) your own blood I will surely require a reckoning."

The double use of the term, not visible in most translations, establishes a contrast between the two clauses. The sense is that you can eat everything except what follows, that is, "you shall not eat flesh with its life force (i.e., its blood) in it" (Waltke and O'Connor, 670). The prohibition appears in two verses, one in prose (v. 5) and one in poetry (v. 6). The NRSV translates the prose verse, "For your own life blood, I will require a reckoning (*dāraš*): from every animal I will require it (*dāraš*), and from human beings, each one for the blood of another [his brother], I will require a reckoning (*dāraš*) for human life" (v. 5). Repeated three times, the Hebrew root means to "seek," "require," or "demand," sometimes with the idea of avenging something (Deut 18:19 and Ezek 34:10; BDB, 205). Its repetition stresses God's insistence on establishing blood justice by "seeking out" the spilling of human blood. Justice is so important that God actively seeks a reckoning, "each one for the blood of his brother," as the Hebrew literally reads. The "blood of his brother" calls to mind the blood of Abel murdered by his brother Cain, blood that cried out to God from the ground (4:10).

That blood is essential for life seems obvious. For the ancients, blood along with breath were life itself. Blood was where life resided in the body, for to see a living creature lose its blood was to watch death take up residence and life slip away.

The statement about blood (v. 4) is not now an isolated statement. Though it may originally have been a cultic rule, it now stands as part of a formidable barrier against dehumanization. An old statement on blood has now been transformed into an affirmation of human life and human worth. This decree urges human enhancement and the valuing of human persons (Brueggemann, 83).

Bruce K. Waltke and M. O'Connor, *An Introduction to Biblical Syntax* (Winona Lake IN: Eisenbrauns, 1990).

Walter Brueggemann, *Genesis* (Interpretation; Atlanta: John Knox, 1982) 83.

Inclusive Translation

AΩ Where possible, the NRSV laudably avoids using the exclusive male terms of the Hebrew text where male terms sometimes implicitly include women. In contemporary Western cultures that claim equality between the sexes as images of God, inclusive translations are immensely important. Particularly in liturgy and prayer, preaching and teaching, translations that include women explicitly remind us that all people, male and female, are icons of God.

In this inclusive translation of 9:5, however, nuances are lost: ". . . From every animal I will require it and from human beings, each one for *the blood of another* . . . ." In an effort to be gender inclusive for modern readers, the English translation substitutes the inclusive "blood of another" for the "the blood of his brother." The likely reference to the Cain and Abel story becomes lost in translation, yet the inclusive language does make clear that the prohibition includes any taking of human blood by any another human.

Jewish Dietary Law

"Dietary law" is the collective term for the Jewish laws and customs pertaining to the types of food permitted for consumption and preparation. They establish what is kosher, meaning suitable or proper. The Bible does not explain the laws nor is it clear that they were in place as Genesis was composed. Exodus 22:30 connects them to "holiness," that is, being set apart for God. Some interpreters believe the laws arose for hygienic and sanitary reasons. Others find an ethical base in abstaining from eating blood as a taming of violence. Still others suggest that the laws are primarily markers of Jewish identity and the willingness to adopt that identity in a multicultural society.

For further reading, see Harry Rabinowicz and Rela Mintz Geffen, "Dietary Laws," *EncJud*, 650–59.

chiastic style adds solemnity to its claim, and like other uses of short lines of poetry embedded in narratives in Genesis (1:27; 2:23; 3:14-19; 4:23-24), it draws attention to the verse as an important theological point:

Whoever sheds the blood of a human,
By a human shall that person's blood be shed;
For in his own image God made humankind.
(9:6)

The first two lines of the chiasm are apparent even in English translation. [Chiasm] Words of the first line reoccur in reverse order in the second line; "sheds," "blood," "human" in the first line become "human," "blood," "sheds" in the second. At the center of the words is the human, first the one killed and second the one who avenges the blood of the first, seemingly in another killing, perhaps as a form of capital punishment or as simple retribution.

What is in dispute in the interpretation of this verse is not its translation as much as its genre, a decision about which affects the weight of the verse. Is the verse a legal statement, a juridical mandate from God requiring blood vengeance for the killing of one human by another? Alternatively, does the verse's rhythmic style and chiastic form suggest, instead, that the verse is akin to a prophetic warning, a threat of punishment to discourage the spilling of human blood? Does the style indicate that the line is a proverb, a saying that describes things as they are? This decision is difficult to make with certitude, yet of immense moral import. Does God endorse capital punishment? [Capital Punishment?]

Whatever decision is made regarding the genre, on its own the verse cannot stand as God's strong support for capital punishment because other texts challenge it. First, God authors the commandment given to Moses at Sinai, seemingly contradicting Genesis 9:6: "You shall not kill" (Exod 20:13, my translation). Second, God demands a reckoning of human beings, "each one for the blood of his brother," in a likely allusion to the Cain and Abel story (4:1-16), but God does not demand the blood of Cain after he killed his brother. God punishes Cain, instead, by banishing him from the community and even while protecting him from blood vengeance with a special mark (4:15).

The third line of v. 6 provides the critical reason for God's special concern for human life: "for in his own image God made humankind" (9:6c). As images of God, humans represent divine life in some unspecified way; they possess dignity and beauty; they deserve reverence and respect. (See [Image of God].) To kill another

Killing Animals

Terence Fretheim made an important observation about the link between respect for animal life and respect for human life:

This proscription regarding blood—and the attention needed to fulfill it—stands as a sharp reminder that killing animals ought not to be taken lightly, for God is the source of their life. As such, it guards against brutality, carelessness, and needless killing. Concern for the life of animals immediately leads into concern for human life.

Terence Fretheim, "Genesis" (*NIB* 1; Nashville: Abingdon, 1994) 399.

Chiasm

A chiasm or chiastic literary device is a "crisscross figure of speech: a verbal pattern in which the second half of an expression is balanced against the first with the parts reversed."

From Richard Nordquist, "Chiasmus Figure of Speech," *ThoughtCo*, updated 18 April 2017, http://grammar.about.com/od/c/g/chiasmusterm.htm.

Capital Punishment?

Some interpreters believe that the verse about blood shedding, "Whoever sheds the blood of a human, by a human shall that person's blood be shed" (9:6), urges the death penalty for the offense of killing another (i.e., Westermann, *Genesis 1–11*, 467).

The verse provides a challenge to revenge cycles common in antiquity. In their place, this text demands "fitting, blood-shedding punishment. . . . God, it seems, expects human bloodshed to continue, but it must not be tolerated; homicide must no longer go unpunished. Indeed, human bloodshed even by an animal must be avenged, and *a fortiori*, bloodshed by a man's own brother—a clear reference to Abel" (Kass, 181). The divine instruction insists upon a life for a life, granting no one superior status or exemption (Kass, 183).

However, "This text does not advocate or authorize or justify capital punishment; rather it recognizes the way in which human beings would participate in the moral order

as executors of the divine judgment . . ." (Fretheim, 1:399). Similar resistance to viewing the text as a warrant for capital punishment relates to the draining of the blood in ritual sacrifices only. Any who practice ritual human sacrifice will be punished by death (Hanks, 4).

In the United States today, capital punishment remains a controversial issue. In part this is because judgments of juries and judges alike can be based on faulty evidence, racial bias, and political opinions. Many people of faith believe rightly that life belongs to God, so human life is sacred, not to be taken lightly by murderers or by the state for there are other ways to mete out justice.

For further reading, see Gardner C. Hanks, *Capital Punishment and the Bible* (Scottsdale PA: Harald, 2002).

Claus Westermann, *Genesis 1–11: A Commentary* (Minneapolis: Augsburg, 1984).

Leon Kass, *The Beginning of Wisdom: Reading Genesis* (Chicago: University of Chicago Press, 2003).

Terence Fretheim, "Genesis" (*NIB* 1; Nashville: Abingdon, 1994).

human being is akin to killing an image of God in a kind of blasphemy. A call to show reverence for all life flows from this passage, but its primary focus is respect for human life.

Parallels with Genesis 1–3

The flood story deliberately echoes Gen 1–3 to remind readers that the flood narrative is also a story of chaos followed by recreation. These parallels include

• references to the "breath of life" (1:30; 2:7; 6:17; 7:22) and to God's wind over the waters (1:2; 8:1).
• lists of animals (1:20-26, 28, 30; 2:20; 6:20; 7:14, 21, 23; 9:2).
• humans created in God's image (1:2; 9:6), given dominion and food (1:26, 28-30; 9:2-3), prohibited from eating (2:17; 9:4), and charged to reproduce (1:28; 8:17; 9:1, 7).

List adapted from John Kaltner, *Ishmael Instructs Isaac: An Introduction to the Qu'ran for Bible Readers* (Collegeville MN: Liturgical, 1999) 82.

Reminding us that time after the flood is a time of recreation, God again commissions the humans to "be fruitful and to multiply" (v. 7). In Genesis 1:28 their task is to participate in divine creativity by creating offspring to populate the earth. They are told, "Now be fruitful and multiply to re-populate the earth." They must begin again to fill the earth. [Parallels with Genesis 1–3]

The Covenant and Its Sign, 9:8-18

After restoring creatures to dry land and commanding them to reproduce, God makes a covenant with them as promised in 6:18. [Covenants] Most striking about these verses in Hebrew is the number of active first-person verbs with God as their subject: "I am establishing" (v.9); "I establish" (v. 11); "I make" (v. 12); "I have set" (v. 13); "I bring" (v. 14); "I will remember" (v. 15); "I will see and remember" (v. 16); "I have established" (v. 17). This verbal density draws attention to the making of the covenant and especially to the "I" who establishes it. It is clear that God inaugurates it, authorizes it, and gives

Covenants

A covenant is an agreement between two parties, often in the form of a treaty, contract, or formal pact. Covenants, a common fact of life in the ancient Near East, arose in political, social, and commercial exchanges. In the Old Testament they serve as a central metaphor of Israel's relationship with God.

Covenants were made when a clan or tribe sought the protection of an overlord or sovereign of a more powerful clan or city-state from an enemy group. In return, the tribe acted as vassal to the overlord, promising loyalty, military support, or tribute in the form of taxes or a percentage of harvests. A covenant agreement demanded absolute loyalty of each party to the other and usually involved responsibilities or legal stipulations on both sides.

The covenant enacted on Mt Sinai when Israel escaped from Egypt and God began a formal relationship with Israel through Moses looms over the rest of the Old Testament (Exod 19–24). The Priestly writers' narrative of Israel's beginnings, including the covenants with Noah and subsequently with Abraham (Gen 15), anticipate the Sinai covenant at the narrative level, for the Priestly editors know it and reflect it as they present earlier covenants. The covenant God makes with Israel comes to its fullest theological expression in the book of Deuteronomy. That fifth book follows the format of typical ancient Near Eastern covenants but Deuteronomy also reflects theologically on the Sinai event, insisting that the covenant began at God's initiation to form mutual relationship with Israel. Covenants include a self identification of the suzerain and the history of the good things the suzerain has done for the covenant partner followed by lists of stipulations and witnesses, and ending with curses and blessings.

In the covenant with Noah, by contrast, God establishes a relationship with all creation and its inhabitants, a covenant sealed by the sign of the rainbow. God alone has responsibility and promises never to destroy the world again by flood. The Noachic covenant encompasses more than Noah and his family; God's promise extends to "all flesh that is on the earth" (9:17) and, by proxy, to all of creation.

For further reading see, Steven L. McKenzie, *Covenant* (Understanding Biblical Themes; St. Louis MO: Chalice, 2000).

Christoph Koch, "Covenant," *EBR* 900–901.

Michael Coogan, *The Old Testament: A Historical and Literary Introduction to the Hebrew Scriptures* (New York: Oxford University Press, 2006) 107–17.

Noah stands before the altar as a rainbow appears and the animal pairs leave the ark. From *Scenes of the principal histories of the Old and New Testaments and other books. . .* (18th C.). Engraving from the design of Gerard Hoet (1648–1733). (Courtesy of the Pitts Theology Library, Candler School of Theology, Emory University)

Genesis. VIII. 20.

נח במזבח העלה עלות ליהוה / NOACHUS IN ALTARI VICTIMAS DOMINO OFFERT.

Noé offre à Dieu des victimes sur un autel. / Noah offerd burnt offerings on an altar to the Lord.

Noah opfert dem Herrn Brandopfer auf einem Altar. / Noach offert den Heere brandofferen op eenen altaar.

G. Hoet del. / F. van Nianen fecit.

it solidity (vv. 9, 11, 17). The unit begins with God as the subject of a participle, "I am establishing" (v. 9), and it ends with God as the subject of a verb of completed action, "I have established" (v. 17).

In this alone of the Old Testament covenants, there are not stipulations or requirements from the covenant partners. This is a covenant where God declares divine loyalty as free gift, grace, for the earth and all its inhabitants. Benefactors include not only Noah and his sons but also his descendants after him (vv. 9 and 12), as if to assure the book's readers of their own inclusion in God's covenanting act. The announcement is solemn, a declaration of God's deliberate action: "Then God said to Noah and to his sons, 'As for me, I am establishing my covenant with you and your descendants after you and with every living creature'" (vv. 8-10). Now God expands the list of those benefiting from the covenant to include every living creature; all living creatures receive the covenant as divine gift.

The declaration begins with the introductory phrase that the NRSV translates, "As for me" (*wĕʾanî hinnî*) (v. 9; cf. 6:17). The word (*hinnēh*) is a particle of exclamation, meaning "behold" (KJV) or, less archaically, "look." (See ["Look!"].) It is an attention-getter that occurs frequently in Genesis. The Hebrew might be rendered more literally as "I, look, I am establishing my covenant," The first person pronoun draws attention to God's self-disclosure to emphasize that God is the *one* "establishing my covenant with you, and your descendants (your seed) after you." The covenanting one is not some other god or sovereign. It is the Creator acting on their behalf and on behalf of the cosmos after all the death and destruction wrought by the flood.

Human partners in the covenant—Noah and also "your descendants after you" (v. 9)—include Noah's children and point toward chapter 10 where another genealogy names their descendants. Yet by including "all future generations" (v. 12), the text addresses the "implied" readers or earliest readers of Genesis, the ancient audience whose struggles to survive shape the story.[4] (See Connections below.)

The passage insists repeatedly that even though humans are made in the divine image, the covenant with Noah is unlike every other biblical covenant because it is not restricted to humankind. Noah's covenant is cosmic and includes "birds, domestic animals, and every animal of the earth with you" (9:10), that is, all the creatures Noah saved from perishing by bringing them onto the ark. The NRSV supplies the adjective "domestic" to modify animals, perhaps as a way to distinguish the animals and all living things or because in Hebrew the same word can mean "cattle." Other translations read "wild beasts" (JPS).

Noah's covenant (the Noahic covenant) differs from other biblical covenants in still more ways than in its inclusion of all creation. The provisions and requirements come entirely from divine initiative, requiring nothing of humans, and the covenant is eternal.

Attention to the typical covenant patterns of the ancient Near East shows this covenant's uniqueness. Covenants often begin by identifying the "overlord," the powerful sovereign and agent who makes the agreement. In this case, that is God: "I, look, I am establishing my covenant with you" (v. 9). Typically there follows a statement of good things the overlord has done for the covenant partners in the history of their relationship, but here the good things are not about past deeds already performed. They are about what God will *not* do in the present and the future: "Never again shall all flesh be cut off by the waters of a flood and never again shall there be a flood to destroy the earth" (9:11). This covenant with the whole earth is an "everlasting covenant" (9:16). Its unbreakable and everlasting nature signifies divine commitment to the cosmos and its inhabitants.

Ancient covenants often include stipulations to remind covenant partners of their obligations to the suzerain, but the covenant with Noah completely lacks actions for the humans to perform, and it does not demand their loyalty. The burden of commitment falls entirely on God, while the sign of that commitment is the rainbow, a burst of beauty after a storm. The rainbow functions like another provision of ancient covenants where the partners put a written copy in a temple and read it publicly to remind them of their obligations. In the covenant with Noah, the sign is written in the temple of the cosmos where God will "read" it and remember to be faithful (9:12-17). God announces the sign three times, making it as important as the covenant itself (vv. 12, 13, and 17):

- "This is *the sign of the covenant* that I make between you and every living creature that is with you and for all future generations" (v. 12).
- "I have set my bow in the clouds and it shall be *a sign of the covenant* between me and the earth" (v. 13).
- "This is *the sign of the covenant* of that I have established between me and all flesh that is on the earth" (v. 17).

Verses 14-16 tell how the sign will work. The bow in the clouds, a rich symbol that evokes divine grace, secures "the stability of the orders of nature."[5] When God brings the clouds, the rainbow will follow a post-storm event that surprises, delights, and signifies in a fitting celebration that the storm is over. The rainbow may signify that "God has put aside his bow,"[6] a weapon of war, hung high for all to see. The Hebrew word for "rainbow" does refer to a weapon, yet according to the text, the rainbow's purpose is to remind God—something like a string around the finger—never again to destroy the earth with a flood. [The Rainbow]

The eternal cosmic covenant with Noah and all creation communicates hope and security after the chaos and turbulence of disaster. It makes the ground firm again so new life might spring forth from the earth for all its inhabitants. It reaffirms relationship with God as stable and permanent; it has existed from the time of Noah. It proclaims that the earth itself has become solid again because it rests entirely within the oversight of the covenant-making Creator. Yet, in the final unit of chapter 9, the moral condition of the world seems little altered by the watery cataclysm.

The Rainbow

The rainbow, a sign inherent in climate and weather conditions of the earth, is a rich and exceedingly beautiful sign of God's covenant care of the world:

One can imagine it variously: for example, as a bridge between earth and heaven (akin to Jacob's ladder, see Gen 28:10-22), or as the bow of the divine warrior now laid aside. It usually appears after a time of heavy rain when the sun comes out and shines again but while dark clouds are still in the sky; and often the dark clouds are backdrops for the many colors of the rainbow. Thus when the rainbow is viewed in the light of the preceding Flood narrative, its appearance at the very moment when one can see both darkness and light in the sky comes to symbolize God's commitment to light over darkness, to beauty over chaos, to life over death.

R. W. L. Moberly, *Old Testament Theology: The Theology of the Book of Genesis* (Cambridge UK: Cambridge University Press, 2009) 110–11.

Malcah Zeldis (b. 1931) © ARS, NY.
Noah's Ark. Private Collection.
(Credit: Malcah Zeldis / Art Resource, NY)

For the book's ancient audience in the early Persian period, the covenant with Noah is a reassurance that God has always been faithful, unilaterally good, and therefore cares for them despite the destruction of their world (cf. Isa 54:6-10).[7] The God who calls them to repopulate the earth is eternally faithful and will never again destroy all the earth. They have a future.

Wickedness Persists 9:18-28

From one point of view, the story of Noah and his sons breaks off from the flood story by moving to a new epoch. The next generation comes to the fore and the tightly constructed rise and fall of language that occurs in the flood material disappears (6:9–9:17). Puzzling events here remind readers that the human condition involves sinfulness, the precise nature of which is no clearer than in the case of the sons of God and the daughters of humans (6:1-8). Yet this story forms a balancing literary panel with that story. The episode with Noah's sons in the flood's aftermath "alludes cryptically to the narrative material that may have been familiar to the ancient audience but must have seemed to the monotheistic writer dangerous to spell out."[8] It reveals that recreation does not return humans to paradise. Humans persist in their wicked ways, even if that wickedness involves an opaque set of actions. [Jonah and Noah]

Genealogical notices mark the episode's beginning and end. The first notice names Noah's sons who went out from the ark, and the last reports Noah's death (vv. 18 and 28). Noah's three sons presumably appear according to their birth order—Shem, Ham, and Japheth—yet later Noah identifies Ham as his youngest, and so he should come last in the list (v. 24). An additional note about Ham amplifies his importance among the sons, naming him as the father of Canaan. All the people of the earth descend from Noah's three sons

Jonah and Noah

Judy Klitsner has found parallels between the Noah and Jonah stories. She concluded that the book of Jonah begins to "dismantle and revise" the Noah story even as it questions many of its assumptions. Although never named as prophets, both Noah and Jonah receive the word of God and convey it to others.

Both navigate perilous waters aboard their boats apart from the doomed populations they might have saved. Names, words, and themes are shared freely by their narratives. In both, rampant injustice, *hamas*, threatens to seal the people's fate; both speak of a forty-day period preceding a planned annihilation. Each story prominently features a *"yonah"*—Jonah's Hebrew name is identical to that of the winged messenger sent by Noah, the dove. Both stories highlight rare locations such as Tarshish and Nineveh [and Ararat]. Both narratives focus on personal chronicles of the prophets themselves, while presenting the barest minimum in the way of the actual prophecy they deliver. And both prophets escape . . . Noah through alcohol and Jonah through a coma-like slumber. (1–2)

The stories are also different in important ways. Noah's people continue in their wickedness until their fate is sealed, whereas Jonah's Ninevite audience repents immediately, thoroughly—even the cattle repent—and thereby avert the disaster. Jonah retells the Noah story and presents a God who gives people a second chance.

For further reading, Judy Klitsner, "The Wings of the Dove: Noah and Jonah in Flight from Self," in *Subversive Sequels in the Bible: How Biblical Stories Mine and Undermine Each Other* (Philadelphia: Jewish Publication Society, 2009) 1–29.

The Canaanites

Canaan is primarily a geographical name, fluidly applied to Palestine/Israel. Canaan is the eponymous forefather of the native peoples (Gen 10:6, 15-16), Ham's son cursed by Noah (9:25). Canaanite is an inclusive term for the inhabitants of the land that became Israel (Gen 12:6; Deut 7:1), including many groups, such as the Amorites, Hivites, Jebusites, and others. In Gen 15 God promises to give Abram the land that belongs to the Kenites, the Kenizzites, the Kadomites, the Hittites, the Perrizites, the Rephaim, the Amorites, the Canaanites, the Girgashites, and the Jebusites (15:19-21). Canaan is also an ancient the name for the land of Palestine/Israel. Although in other biblical texts, the Canaanites are enemies of the Israelites, Gen 9 insists they are connected by blood, offspring of Noah, yet set against each other by primal missteps among the ancestors.

In some texts, Canaanite becomes an ideologically loaded term, a metaphor for the native peoples against whom Israel often identifies itself. Israel finds Canaanite religion to be despicable and Deuteronomy calls for its eradication (Deut 20:16-18). Yet some biblical historians and archaeologists argue that the Israelites and Canaanites were closely related, that some Israelites were Canaanites who became worshipers of YHWH, and that the hostility between the two cultures was the result of later competition for land. At the least, the relationships between the two were complicated and fraught with tensions over land and worship.

For further reading, see Brian Schmidt, "Canaanites," in *EBR* 4:871–73.

Vineyards and Drinking

"Verse 21 cannot be interpreted as a negative comment on drinking, alcohol, or drunkenness. Indeed, the Old Testament is not preoccupied with such 'a moral issue.' It is aware of the potential destructiveness of excess, but Lev. 10:9 is an exception to the general acceptance of wine. The drunkenness of Noah is only presented as a context for what follows."

Walter Brueggemann, *Genesis* (Interpretation; Atlanta; John Knox, 1988) 89.

(9:19; 10:1-31), but it is the relationship with Canaan that matters in these verses. [The Canaanites]

After the deluge, Noah reengages with the earth. Despite his experience as the helmsman of a boat and as keeper of animals, Noah is primarily a tiller of the soil, and thus in another way, a new Adam (9:20; cf. 1:28). He advances civilization by planting a vineyard and making wine, but when he becomes drunk, he falls asleep and lies naked in his tent. [Vineyards and Drinking] While he sleeps it off, Ham sees his father's nakedness and tells his two brothers about their father's condition. The text offers no hints about the meaning of this news broadcast, whether it was motivated by concern for his father's well-being, shock at his drunkenness, or mocking disrespect. Whatever the offense may be, Shem and Japheth protect their father and carefully avoid looking at him. [Nakedness] The passage insists that the brothers refuse to look, suggesting that just the looking is the wickedness here. They put a garment on their shoulders, walk backwards, keep their faces turned away, and cover Noah (9:23). It all appears as a kind of bumbling farce except that the consequences are so severe.

When Noah came back to consciousness, he somehow "knew" what his youngest son had done, even though readers are not at all sure what that was. What matters are Noah's words, set apart from the story by their parallel construction, wordplay, and concision. Complicating the story, Noah's words do not curse Ham, the offending son; they curse Ham's son Canaan. To his brothers, Canaan will be "slave of slaves," that is, the lowliest of slaves.

A clearly articulated curse against Canaan permeates Noah's speech, but the blessings are fairly unspecified because the curse is what matters:

1. "Cursed be Canaan, lowest of slaves shall he be to his brothers" (v. 25).

Nakedness

Nakedness was a cause of shame in Genesis ever since the first couple ate of the fruit in the garden (3:7). That a father's nakedness before his son would cause such a terrible consequence, not for Ham who looked upon his father's nakedness but for Noah's grandson not yet born, seems like punishment out of proportion to the crime. But what is the crime?

Alter noted that no one has figured out what the crime is. He observed, though, that early Jewish Midrash "sees here a Zeus-Chronos story in which the son castrates the father, or alternatively penetrates him sexually" (40). In Leviticus, "uncovering nakedness" means to have sex with someone: "None of you shall approach anyone near of kin to uncover their nakedness. You shall not uncover the nakedness of your father" (18:6). The text goes on to include "your mother," or "your father's wife; it is your father's nakedness." Other family members then follow in the long list of prohibited sexual relationships, all portrayed as "uncovering the nakedness" (vv. 6-19).

The suggestion of incest between son and father Noah is shocking, but the purpose of the passage is to comment negatively on later relationships among peoples. If there is sexual infraction here, the intent is to demean the Canaanites. Ham is not important in the passage except as the conduit of the curse upon the more important figure of Canaan, often portrayed as an enemy Israel (Deut 20:16-18). The cursed Canaan is shamed by the actions of his father Ham, whatever they were, and condemned to be a slave to his brothers. His slavery may refer to the book of Judges where some Canaanites are subjected to Israel (Judg 1:28).

The story of Ham's offense is not unlike a similar account concerning Moab and Edom, offspring of Lot, whose daughters have sex with him while he is drunk (Gen 19:30-38), a story intended to show disdain for enemies even while asserting a blood relationship with them.

Robert Alter, *Genesis* (New York: W. W. Norton, 1996) 40.

Christoph Weigel (1654–1725). "Noah's Drunkenness" from *Biblia ectypa: Bildnussen auss Heiliger Schrifft Alt und Neuen Testaments*. (Courtesy of the Pitts Theology Library, Candler School of Theology, Emory University)

2. "Blessed . . . be Shem" and "let Canaan be his slave" (v. 26).

3. "May God make space (*yaptĕ*) for Japheth (*yepet*)" in Shem's tents and "let Canaan be his slave" (v. 27).

The curse of Canaan is the primary point of Noah's last will and testament (9:25-27). His words encode geopolitical relationships among Israel's neighbors later in the nation's history (Gen 10). [Racial Curse] This episode is etiological; it explains antagonisms between Israel and the people of the land when Israel conquers Canaan as recorded in the books of Joshua and Judges. Shem is the ancestor of Semites and the father of Israel, and Japheth is the father of Israel's neighbors the coastland peoples. In an ideal

Racial Curse

Rodney S. Sadler, Jr., advocates a critical reading of Gen 9:18-27. It is a dangerous proof text that can be used to continue to support nationalism, racism, sexism, heterosexism, and other oppressions. A proof text refers to a mode of interpretation that selects a text to support a previous viewpoint without regard to its literary and historical context. Proof-texting rips a text from the story and adds it to others to prove a point. Proof-texting does violence to the story itself by chopping it into pieces and ignoring the larger context.

Because the curse of Ham and Canaan "was used to justify the disenfranchisement of one group by another [the loss of land by the Canaanites to the Israelites], it established a precedent for the abuse of an 'Other' by a favored group and can easily be adopted as a proof text by subsequent groups seeking to legitimate theologically their superiority over or oppression of another 'othered' group" (Sadler, 73).

Rodney S. Sadler, Jr., "Genesis," *The Africana Bible: Reading Israel's Scriptures from Africa and the African Diaspora*, ed. Hugh R. Page, Jr. (Minneapolis: Fortress, 2010).

world, they should be allies with Ham's offspring, the Canaanites. Yet the Canaanite children of Ham are to be their slaves. [Noah's Curse and American Slavery]

Adam's genealogy that began in Genesis 5 resumes with the announcement of Noah's death 350 years after the flood at the age of 950 (9:28). Adam's family tree provides the overarching structure of the story of the flood (6:10–9:17), its antecedent causes (6:1-9) and aftermath (9:18-28). Looking backward from chapter 9, it becomes evident that the genealogical framework portrays the first ten generations of Adam through time in an orderly cycle of births and deaths. Most of the interruptions and narrative expansions of the genealogies of both Adam (chs. 5–9) and Eve (ch. 4) concern the breakdown of creation. These disruptions of the otherwise steady flow of births and deaths climax in the flood, after which creation begins anew and the long line of begetting, living, and dying resumes.

CONNECTIONS

Why Focus on the Flood?

Why does Genesis single out the story of Noah from Adam's long line of descendants? Why pause at this juncture and tell of a disaster

Noah's Curse and American Slavery

Nineteenth century American advocates of slavery used Gen 9:20-27 to defend the institution of slavery. "Proslavery Southerners were drawn to Genesis 9:20-27 because it resonated with the deepest cultural values," namely, matters of honor and shame. According to Stephen R. Haynes, Noah's curse was proof to slaveholders that "the enslavement of black people was God's will." In the history of interpretation, Ham has been associated with sexual license, perversion, tyranny, theft, rebellion, and many other crimes. But in the American South, Ham's crime and that of his descendants "was a transgression of family loyalty that made them utterly devoid of honor and thus fit for slavery" (Haynes, 66–67).

This interpretation of slaveholders and slavery supporters seriously misreads Genesis because it is Canaan, not Ham or his African descendants, who is cursed. This sinful interpretation sees in the Bible an authorization for the enslavement of African peoples. The argument is an example of proof texting and shows the danger of ignoring the actual words of the text and its historical context. Such a way of interpreting violates Scripture and leaves no room for the power of God to challenge the culture.

Stephen R. Haynes, *Noah's Curse: The Biblical Justification of American Slavery* (Oxford UK: Oxford University Press, 2002).

from which only a tiny portion of the previous creation survives? Why even remember those ancient people whose offspring disappeared in the flood? One puzzling feature of the flood story is that it takes up more space than any other part of the primal history, even more than the first two creation accounts together (chs. 1–3), as if it were somehow more important.

One purpose of the story may have been to teach righteousness and warn against evil. Throughout the history of interpretation, Noah has been raised up as a righteous man, along with Daniel and Job (Ezek 14:14, 20). In the New Testament he is a model of faith (Heb 11:7) and a "herald of righteousness" (2 Pet 2:5), and early church fathers found in him a type of Christ. Yet Genesis itself merely asserts that Noah was righteous and portrays him as obedient to divine commands. Because the text spends little effort elaborating on Noah's goodness, teaching righteousness does not seem to be the main concern of the material.

Another reason the book devotes so much attention to the flood material is that the story opens new theological worlds, complicating the picture of God and God's relationship to the world. The flood passages show another face of God than what appears in the book's previous chapters. God becomes not only a world builder but also a world destroyer. God punishes in ways that do not seem to fit the crime, determinedly blots out all living things, and regrets ever creating humans and all flesh. In the flood story, God creates fear and dread among humans (just as humans create fear and dread among animals), for they are in God's power. In the flood narrative, God is violent, capricious, and vindictive even while God is also regretful, grieving, and a covenant-making Creator. Even as these chapters underline divine power, freedom, violence, and awesomeness, the divine portrait is deeply problematic for us.

The Flood as Disaster Narrative

I think the reason the flood chapters outweigh other sections in size and dramatic intensity is that they concern the reality of the first audiences of the book who had survived the Babylonian period. These chapters form the heart of the primeval history (Gen 1–11) and matter the most to the book's composers because they interact with the national disaster that lingers in the memories of the book's audience. The deluge is "comparable in its destructive power to the recent experiences of the exiles"[9] and the experiences of the displaced people who remained in the land under Babylonian control. The Babylonian period (597–537 BCE) saw the destruction of Judah through three invasions, deportations, and internal occupation and control. (See Introduction.) The prophetic books of the time, namely Jeremiah and Ezekiel, and also Lamentations, portray the devastation as a massive disaster that crushes the nation, its government, economy, and daily life, and that leaves in shambles trust in God's fidelity and protection.

The theology of the flood story reflects the horrors of history. People who live through traumatic violence reside in a world unmoored from previous traditions and from faith in God. Chaos continually threatens them and the future remains uncertain. [Ongoing Chaos] Studies of the effects of trauma show that, to go forward, survivors require interpretation and reframing of events. They need ways to make sense of the past and to create new forms of stability and order. Jeremiah, Ezekiel, and Lamentations help the people interpret the national collapse, face it, and find language to talk about it. Those books and others struggle to find ways to cling to God through it all. The prophets explain the disaster in several ways, one of which, not unlike the flood story, is that the destruction happened as divine punishment for human sin.

Ongoing Chaos

"The reality of chaos is not an ancient memory of peoples too primitive to think otherwise. It is as contemporary as human experience today. The community of faith is invited to participate in the story and to be identified with the new humanity which will preside over the new creation. It is important to recall that it was the experience of Israel's exile that made the flood an existential reality. Exile is indeed the collapse of the known world."

Walter Brueggemann, *Genesis* (Interpretation; Atlanta: John Knox, 1988) 87.

The exilic prophets make it possible for the people of Judah to survive by lifting the violence of warfare and its consequences into the symbolic worlds of poetry and imagery. To retell the violence in a literal way would invite further traumatic disruption. To tell it in the terms of a massive flood that leaves only a remnant of survivors whom God saves, recreates, and with whom God covenants, however, is to evoke their situation in a symbolic world. Seeing another disaster that calls up their difficulties can help them come to terms with all they have lost and to find God again. When the flood ends in a covenant with all creation, it assures them of divine commitment to life, stability, and protection in a recreation of the world (cf. Jer 31:31-37; Ezek 34:25; 37:26). The flood story can reunify the destroyed nation after their near extinction by reviving faith in God, who more than anything is a powerful Creator, a renewer of the cosmos, a rebuilder of human community, an eternally faithful covenant partner. In other words, God never abandoned them and instead held on to them so they could begin again.

The portrait of a punishing God asserts that the disaster was not a result of God's defeat by superior Babylonian gods or the result of divine weakness or indifference. The national disaster, like the flood, was the result of God's action, but that action was filled with regret and grief. God was reluctant.

The whole of the flood story bears similarities to the historical plight of Judah overtaken by Babylon from which only a remnant survived. To the human eye, it seemed as if the God of Israel was powerless and lost the war to the gods of Babylon, but the flood story shows an involved, active God, still seeking relationship, still present through destruction and ruin. It affirms that Israel's God is the Creator God of the whole world. The covenant God makes with Noah and all the earth is cosmic and everlasting, a recreation and a new commission to survive as a people who are to be fruitful and to multiply. The flood story is a work of art that calls survivors and their descendants to go toward the future in confidence that God wants them to live and wants to live with them. [Art and Disaster] In the wake of disaster, the story reassures readers that new beginnings are possible. [Theology as Partial]

Commentators speak of God's covenant with Noah and all living creatures as a comfort to survivors of the flood, but that may not be right. Survivors of disasters are rarely ready to receive comfort after enduring traumatic violence of any kind. Rather, this covenant may represent a first step toward reestablishing a sense of safety, a basic prerequisite for any future at all. The God who promises never again to destroy every living creature by flood "as long as the earth endures" (8:22) now makes that promise official in a covenant for which God alone takes responsibility. After disaster, life can go on because God promises protection, a world with a certain amount of order, and an assurance that the very same disaster will not happen again. These words also portray the divine covenant-maker as ruler of the world, its weather, and its stability, something survivors of any disaster might welcome. Re-commissioned to be fruitful, to multiply, they will survive as a people. [Isaiah and Noah]

Art and Disaster

Music, literature, poetry, drama, storytelling, and other artistic expressions sustain us in the worst of times. Art and atrocity, perhaps counter-intuitively, belong together and create a matrix for survival, whether the artistic expressions take the form of a poem by Garcia Lorca, a sermon by Oscar Romero, a sculpture by Julio González, a painting by Picasso, a lyric by Leonard Cohen, or arts and crafts by victims of xenophobia. Indeed, art steps forward on behalf of victims of unspeakable violence. Art steps forward to imagine a world in and through and beyond the traumatic violence (see Stulman, 177–92, 183).

Stulman rightly sees this process of interpretation as the work of the prophetic books from the Babylonian Period. Genesis engages in the same process of interpretation, and although it contains disaster narratives, its larger purpose is to lead the people of Judah beyond their tragic past to confidence in the Creator who will remake them.

For further reading, see Daniel L. Smith-Christopher, "Trauma and the Old Testament: Some Problems and Prospects," in Backer et al., eds., *Trauma and Traumatization*, 223–43.

Louis Stulman, "Reading the Bible Through the Lens of Trauma and Art," in Eve-Marie Backer, Jan Dochhorn, Else K. Holt, eds., *Trauma and Traumatization in Individual and Collective Dimensions: Insights from Biblical Studies and Beyond* (Studia Aarhusiana Neotestamentica 2; Göttingen: VandenHoeck & Ruprecht, 2014).

Theology as Partial

Some Christians dismiss the entire Old Testament because from its disaster narratives (see Introduction) comes a picture of God who is punishing, vengeful, angry, intolerant of human weakness. Yet recognizing the likely source and role of this theology as a product of and an attempt to deal with the nation's destruction shows that such theologies are survival strategies to help people through the most dire of times. Biblical texts are not trying to provide us with a full and complete theology, a picture of God that gives fixed, permanent, and total insight into the nature of God that stands forever in some universal fashion.

The text is not a compendium of all that can be said about God. It functions the way Emily Dickinson says poetry functions: "Tell the whole truth, but tell it slant." Tell it symbolically, mythically, poetically, for then it can lift the people beyond their own narrow perceptions and open them to the surprising presence of the Creator in the depth of their suffering. Genesis along with other biblical books seeks to revive the community by clinging to God and making sense of the historical tragedies that the people of Israel/Judah have endured. That means the divine freedom and power Genesis projects comprise a partial theology, a glimpse of divine life that continues to hold the people together and press them forward. The book arises in the context of their experience in conversation with the tradition.

For further reading, see Kathleen M. O'Connor, *Jeremiah: Pain and Promise* (Minneapolis: Fortress, 2011) 29–58.

Isaiah and Noah

Second Isaiah wrote at the end of the Babylonian Period and continued the "recovery" work begun by Jeremiah and Ezekiel (see Introduction). For Second Isaiah (Isa 40–55), the story of God's covenant of peace with Noah involves the rebuilding of Jerusalem and the re-enlivening of God's compassion for the people (Westermann, 479). In full conversation with themes present in Genesis, Second Isaiah also claims that the God of life can create life anew. This anonymous prophet of the exile finds in Noah, the flood, and the cosmic covenant of peace a divine promise of fidelity and compassion.

This is like the days of Noah to me:
Just as I swore that the waters of Noah
Would never again go over the earth,
So I have sworn that I will not
Be angry with you.
For the mountains may depart
And the hills be removed,
But my steadfast love shall not depart from you,
And my covenant of peace,
Shall not be removed,
Says the LORD who has compassion on you. (Isa 54:9-10)

Claus Westermann, *Genesis 1–11: A Commentary* (Minneapolis: Augsburg, 1984).

NOTES

1. Claus Westermann, *Genesis 1–11: A Commentary* (London: SPCK, 1984) 483.

2. Ibid.

3. Donald E. Gowan, *From Eden to Babel: A Commentary on the Book of Genesis 1–11* (Grand Rapids MI: Wm B. Eerdmans, 1988) 103.

4. Gerhard von Rad, *Genesis*, rev. ed. (Philadelphia: Westminster, 1973) 130.

5. Ibid.

6. Ibid., 134.

7. See Terence E. Fretheim, "Genesis" (*NIB* 1; Nashville: Abingdon, 1994) 400.

8. Robert Alter, *Genesis* (New York: W. W. Norton, 1996) 40.

9. Gowan, *From Eden*, 101.

THE FAMILY OF NATIONS AND THEIR LANGUAGES

Genesis 10–11

Chapters 10–11 belong together even though they comprise four genealogies (10:1-32 and 11:10-32) and one narrative interruption not directly linked to the characters in the genealogical lists (11:1-9).[1] In different ways, both chapters address the reality that many peoples with many languages fill the earth. Chapter 10 tells of the spread of cultures, languages, and peoples in a genealogical list often called the "Table of Nations," perhaps "a kind of ancient linguistic map"[2] or, more precisely, a cultural one. The table charts peoples and their lands as sociopolitical groups rather than as ethnic ones (10:6, 20, 31).[3] Only because chapter 11 begins with the story of Babel from which multiple tongues originate and spread across the world does the Table of Nations appear to center on language (11:1-9). That story of Babel is another narrative of disaster and survival. [Echoes of Destruction] After the city's abandonment, chapter 11 provides a second genealogy of Shem that narrows the focus from all the peoples of the world to his offspring the Semites (11:10-26). Finally, attention narrows further in the genealogy of Terah, father of Abram and the people of Israel (vv. 27-32). Their struggles take up the rest of the book (chs. 12–50).

Echoes of Destruction

It is not far-fetched to see that whatever contributions the Babel story makes to the book's understanding of the spread of people and languages across the globe, the narrative of abandonment of a city also stands as reflection on and interpretation of the destruction of Jerusalem by the Babylonians for the ancient audience. Lingering memories of a lost place from which the people are forcibly dispersed come to the foreground, while both human responsibility and divine responsibility are simultaneously evoked and strangely unclear. Yet survival ensues and a divine plan for populating the earth is implicit in the catastrophe.

NOTES

1. Joseph Blenkinsopp, *Creation, Un-creation, Re-creation* (London: T & T Clarke, 2011) 168.

2. Tremper Longman, *How to Read Genesis* (Downers Grove IL: Intervarsity, 2005) 121.

3. Mark G. Brett, *Genesis: Procreation and the Politics of Identity* (OTR; London and New York: Routledge, 2000) 46.

THE NATIONS AND PEOPLES

Genesis 10:1-32

COMMENTARY

Chapter 10 often receives the title "Table of Nations" because it both classifies people by ancestry and establishes relationships among them.[1] Yet the table makes a profound theological claim: from Noah and his three sons descend all peoples, cultures, languages, and nations. Every human comes from one father, yet each of his sons becomes the father of different peoples according to lands, languages, families, and nations. In this vision, bodies of flesh and blood unite all human groups into one community, yet the groups are also simultaneously distinct from one another from the earliest beginnings of human life. Perhaps of most importance, the genealogies attest to the new creation that follows the destruction by flood in chapters 6–9.

Herman Gunkel has called the list of Noah's offspring "naïve" and "childish" because it reveals a limited historical and geographic perspective in relation to the larger world.[2] The list or table is neither complete nor accurate in representing language groups as they come to be known in modern times. It may not even contain ancient traditions about the national origins but instead reflect subsequent relationships among Israel's neighbors. [Genealogies and Traumatic History] Noah's genealogy, however, does not attempt to describe relations among peoples in any modern

Genealogies and Traumatic History

 Genealogies arise in times of crisis when people lose a sense of identity and place in the world. They do not simply report the past but give design to it. Ingeborg Löwisch has shown how genealogies respond to traumatic events in Genesis and Chronicles. The genealogy of Gen 5, for example, comes as a relief after the murder of Abel by Cain in chapter 4; "It reassures us that the line of life was not broken but is still passed on from generation to generation" (see Löwisch, 215–29). Like music with repetitive formats and rhythmic, clear-cut structures, the genealogies soothe and reassure about life's continuation.

Genealogies perform or enact memories of the past, and breaks in the repetitive patterns can interrupt social structures. The rare introduction of female figures or additions of narrative fragments, for example, interrupt patrilineal succession from father to son. Genealogies are not rote lists of historic people but purposeful constructions of the past to affect life in the present. When they select some figures and omit others, they shape the community such as in the Table of Nations that uses the ancient past to shape relationships in the present.

Ingeborg Löwisch, *Trauma Begets Genealogy: Gender and Memory in Chronicles*, Amsterdam Studies in the Bible and Religion (Sheffield UK: Sheffield Phoenix Press, 2015).

literary or anthropological sense. Rather, it sets forth God's designs for the spread of peoples across the earth in light of later events in Israel's history.

Like most genealogies in Genesis, the ones in these two chapters make clear the need to read them on multiple levels at once. The people in the lists are not simply individuals remembered from the past. Each of them represents peoples who receive their specific identity from one of Noah's sons. The composers of Genesis, of course, are Israelites, so the list understandably groups human communities in relation to them. Despite its ethnocentric principle of organization, however, the Table of Nations is expansive in its understanding of the world and the multiplicity of peoples. It surprisingly breaks away from an exclusive focus on Israel as might be expected in any national literature. In doing so, it expresses a vision of Israel as a citizen of the globe, a nation among nations under the one God, the God of Israel and God of all nations. In Gunkel's more appreciative view, the writers "who speak here are no longer bound to the confined boundaries of their own people. Rather, their vision seeks to encompass and incorporate all the nations of the world."[3] Prompted by the fall of Israel and its dispersion among the nations, this broad understanding of God as the God of all nations emerges most fully in the late Babylonian and Persian Periods. Biblical witnesses of the exilic and postexilic times testify that their God is not subservient to the gods of the empires. Their God is lord over all human governments and the cosmos itself. [The Nations Are a Drop from the Bucket]

The Table of Nations follows a fairly simple pattern. It divides into three major sections, one for each son of Noah. [Outline of Genesis 10] Each lists the descendants of one son and concludes with the antiphon-like statement, "These are the descendants of X, by their families, languages, their lands, and their nations" (vv. 5, 20, 31). Enclosing the entire genealogy is the

---

The Nations Are a Drop from the Bucket

Second Isaiah, prophet of the exile, articulates forcefully the clear monotheism that emerged during the exilic period:

Who has measured the waters in the hollow of his hand and marked off the heavens with a span, enclosed the dust of the earth in a measure, and weighed the mountains in scales and the hills in a balance?
Who has directed the spirit of the LORD, or as his counselor has instructed him?
Whom did he consult for his enlightenment, and who taught him the path of justice?
Who taught him knowledge and showed him the way of understanding?
Even the nations are like a drop from a bucket, and are accounted as dust from the scales. (Isa 40:12-15)

The transcendent singularity of Judah's God is the subject of the rhetorical questions of this beautiful passage. This God is a giant who measures the waters, marks off the heavens, encloses dust in a measure, and weighs mountains and hills in a balance. Judah's God has no counselor, no director, and no advisor, but stands alone above the entire cosmos. Moreover, to this just, wise, knowledgeable Being nations and empires are utterly insignificant, as if a drop from the bucket. Assyria and Babylon who have destroyed Israel and Judah, and now Persia that governs Judah and its exiles—these will have no real power and will surely dry up like a splash of water. Isaiah's questions are actually answers. They assert that the Creator of the world is beyond human imagining.

Outline of Genesis 10

1. Introduction, 10:1
2. Descendants of Japheth, 10:2-5
3. Descendants of Ham and Canaan, 10:6-20
4. Descendants of Shem, 10:21-31
5. Conclusion, 10:32

reminder of the sons: "These are the descendants (*tolĕdot*) of Noah's sons, Shem, Ham, and Japheth" (10:1, and see v. 32). [These Are the Generations] The opening verse places Noah's sons according to their birth order from eldest to youngest, but unexpectedly, the genealogical lists set them in the reverse order of their birth. Shem, the eldest, comes last rather than first, probably to allow the chapter to conclude by centering on the Hebrews and the family of Abraham (Eber, 10:21, 11:16). [Eber, Father of Hebrews?]

Noah's genealogy is a branched genealogy, that is, it mentions several siblings in each generation rather than simply following one offspring from parent to child in a linear style. [Types of Genealogies] The value of the branched format is that it allows room to name a multiplicity of peoples in each family group as they spread across the world rather than driving toward a single important figure from generation to generation. The result is that Noah has seventy descendants through his sons, a perfect biblical number,[4] a complete fulfillment of the command to be "fruitful and multiply" (Gen 1:28).

Introduction, 10:1

The chapter's introductory verse forms a literary frame with the chapter's last verse that repeats it in slightly modified form: "These are the descendants of Noah's sons" (10:1, 32).[5] The repetition highlights the genealogy by enclosing it, but its larger purpose is to remind the book's audience that human fruitfulness has burst forth again after the watery disaster. The offspring of Noah, the new Adam, [Noah, the New Adam] and his three sons repopulate the whole earth. The Table of Nations separates and divides peoples from one another in a fashion akin to God's separating and dividing the elements

These Are the Generations

AΩ The *tolĕdot* formula ("these are the generations") appears in chapters 10–11 three times, following upon three previous uses in Genesis:

> These are the generations of the heavens and the earth (2:4–4:26)
> These are the generations of Adam (5:1–6:8)
> These are the generations of Noah (6:9–9:28)
> These are the generations of Noah's sons, Shem, Ham, and Japheth (10:1–11:9)
> These are the generations of Shem (11:10-26)
> These are the generations of Terah (11:27–25:11)

The triple appearance of the formula points to the pivotal nature of these two chapters. Noah's descendants spread across the world, taper down to the descendants of Shem, and finally turn to Terah the father of Abram.

Eber, Father of Hebrews?

AΩ It is not clear whether the name Eber (*Ēber*, 10:24; 11:16) is an early form of the name of the Hebrew people. Westermann has denied the possibility (526), but Oduyoye has argued that the Hebrews are, indeed, sons of Eber, whose name relates to the Hebrew verb "to pass over" (*'ābar*) (63–64). The name "Hebrews" may derive from the nomadic life of the people as they "passed" by cities, never settling among the Canaanites. Blenkinsopp called Eber the proto-Hebrew, a secondary formation from *Ēbrî* (159). Alter agreed that Eber "is the eponymous father of the Hebrews, *'ibrim*. Whatever the original meanings of the names, there is a clear tendency in the Table to intimate exemplary meanings in the names of the mythic founders . . ." (44; also see Blenkinsopp, 159).

Claus Westermann, *Genesis 1–11: A Commentary* (Minneapolis: Augsburg, 1984).

Modupẹ Oduyoye, *The Sons of the Gods and the Daughters of Men: An Afro-Asiastic Interpretation of Genesis 1–11* (Maryknoll NY: Orbis, 1983).

Joseph Blenkinsopp, *Creation, Un-Creation, Re-Creation: A Discursive Commentary on Genesis 1–11* (New York: T & T Clark, 2011).

Robert Alter, *Genesis* (New York: W. W. Norton, 1996).

Types of Genealogies

Genealogies are not monolithic in either form or purpose. Two types appear in Genesis, the linear genealogy and the branched or segmented genealogy. Linear genealogies may be the more familiar type, following the pattern "so and so begot so and so" from generation to generation, such as in Adam's genealogy (ch. 5). This type forms a chain of descendants in orderly form, focusing on one important individual in each generation, and it speeds up the passage of time as it links narratives in the books.

Branched or segmented genealogies, by contrast, slow down time by presenting more than one figure in each generation as here in the Table of Nations (Gen 10). Several siblings born in each generation show the multiplication, dispersion, and relationships of the three lines of the family after the flood. By means of the many branches of offspring, the table establishes that God created peoples of many nations, not simply Israel alone. Consequently, the people of Israel exist in relationship to the nations; they are part of the same human family and do not exist apart from it.

All the genealogies of Genesis reach back to creation and remind the ancient audience of the divine imperative to be fruitful and multiply. Birthing children, therefore, continues divine creativity and participates in the survival and flourishing of the human race. This implicit theme also reminds the book's ancient audience of the creative power of their God who can create them again them after the destruction of the nation. Löwisch's insight that trauma begets genealogy seems confirmed again. The Table of Nations follows the flood and marks new human beginnings after the widespread destruction of animal and human life. Life can thrive again beyond imagining amid the nations in the shared blood and common DNA of all people.

For further reading, see Matthew A. Thomas, *These are the Generations: Identity, Covenant, and the 'Toledot' Formula* (London: T & T Clark, 2011) 82–104.

Ingeborg Löwisch, *Trauma Begets Genealogy: Gender and Memory in Chronicles* (Sheffield UK: Sheffield Phoenix Press, 2015).

Noah, the New Adam

Just as Adam and Eve had three sons after their expulsion from the garden—Cain, Abel, and Seth—so Noah has three sons from whom everyone else descends. Both Adam and Noah till the soil, one a garden, the other a vineyard, and both confront forms of disaster. Adam eats the fruit of the forbidden tree and knows his nakedness as shame, while Noah drinks too much wine and his nakedness creates shame and disruption before his son Ham. Curses follow both incidents, on the serpent and then on Canaan.

See Joseph Blenkinsopp, *Creation, Un-creation, Re-creation: A Discursive Commentary on Genesis 1–11* (New York: T & T Clark, 2011) 154–55.

Medieval Map

Saint Isidore Bishop of Seville. Illustration of a medieval T and O map showing the three continents as originated by the sons of Noah. (Credit: © British Library Board / Robana / Art Resource, NY)

of the entire creation from one another (Gen 1). Appearing here for the fourth time, the descendants (*tolĕdot*) formula marks the genealogy as a new beginning in continuity with the older acts of creation (cf. 2:4; 5:1; 6:9).

Descendants of Japheth, 10:2-5

The Table of Nations begins with the offspring of Noah's youngest son, Japheth, father of the sea or coastland peoples. Japheth has the fewest descendants, seven sons of which two, Gomer and Javan, also have named offspring. Jewish historian Josephus has said that the "Japhethites settled in Asia as far as the river Tanain (the Don) and in Europe as far as Gaerira (Cadiz)."[6] The peoples in question are Israel's neighbors to the far north and west, at least those on the list whose names stand for known places referred to in Ezekiel (38:1, 6, 18; 27:7, 12, 13).[7] Noah "blessed" them by putting them under the protection of their older brother Shem, father of Semites and direct ancestor of Abraham (9:27). This means that Japhethites, Israel's neighbors, are under the protection of Israel, that is, they are Israel's vassals. The closing refrain provides them with a unique identity: "These are the descendants of Japheth in their lands, with their own language, by their families in their nations" (v. 5).[8]

Descendants of Ham and Canaan, 10:6-20

Ham's descendants comprise the longest of the three lists and cover the widest terrain. Ham becomes father of African peoples "south of the first cataract of the Nile," including present-day Egypt, Sudan, Ethiopia, Eritrea, and Somalia.[9] The single narrative interruption of Ham's genealogy concerns Nimrod, son of Cush (vv. 8-12). With Nimrod's entry, the passage of time hurried by the simple listing of names slows to describe his exploits. These include Nimrod's founding of two empires that invaded and controlled Israel from the eighth to the sixth centuries, Assyria and Babylon. Nimrod is a mighty warrior, hunter, and empire builder in Mesopotamia who, like Cain, builds cities, including Babel (11:1-9). He rules all the land of Shinar, another name for Babylon, known in Mesopotamia as the land of Sumer and Akkad and corresponding to the portion of modern Iraq south of Baghdad.[10]

[Nimrod]

From city-building, Nimrod moves on to found the two enemy empires. He is a hunter, mighty man, and possibly king who evokes Israel's own history of destruction, first by Assyria (721 BCE) and then Babylon (587 BCE). His fierce presence in this list of Ham's descendants remarkably proposes that the very people who nearly removed Israel from the face of the earth are their ancient kinfolk. Pie receives no mention in the Tower of Babel story, but his presence here links him to the next chapter. It also reinforces connections between disaster and the rise of genealogical memories in Genesis and elsewhere.[11]

Also descended from Ham are Arabian peoples. As in Noah's strange curse (9:25-27), however, attention falls prominently on Ham's son Canaan. His offspring occupy "all the region west of the Jordan, Syria, the coastal region and the Phoenician cities."[12]

Nimrod

Nimrod, grandson of Ham, does not have a good reputation. In Mic 5:6, the "land of Nimrod" is Assyria, the invader and destroyer of the northern kingdom of Israel. The Wisdom of Solomon (10:1-5) connects Nimrod's crime with Cain's, and Josephus calls him "the worst of tyrants." Rabbi Simon agreed with this negative assessment: "Nimrod rebelled when he was a mighty one on earth" (Gen 10:8; Genesis Rabbah).

Dutch painter of the sixteenth century Pieter Bruegel also connects Nimrod with the story of the Tower and city of Babel and sees him as a tyrant who destroyed the city. (See illustration by Pieter Bruegel the Elder, *The Tower of Babel*.) This artist interprets the destruction of city and tower as the result of Nimrod's cruel and oppressive rule of its poor.

In the Table of Nations, Nimrod is a minor character present in a narrative fragment that connects him to the city of Babel in the next chapter (Blenkinsopp, 160–64). Although almost nothing is known about him, a vast legend of his evil-doing has risen around him. In the matter of American slavery, as descendant of Ham, father of African peoples, Nimrod became a symbol of disorder and disruption employed to promote the enslavement of black peoples (Haynes, *Noah's Curse*, 41–61, 105–21).

For further reading, see Stephen R. Haynes, *Noah's Curse: The Biblical Justification of American Slavery* (Oxford and New York: Oxford University Press, 2002).

Gen. Rab. XXXIII:VII.

Joseph Blenkinsopp, *Creation, Un-creation, Re-creation* (London: T & T Clark, 2011).

"Oh senseless spirit! let thy horn for thee
Interpret: therewith vent thy rage, If rage
Or other passion wring thee."

Canto XXXI, lines 64-66.

Gustave Doré (1832–1888). "Nimrod" engraving from Dante Alighieri, *Dante's Inferno; Translated by the Rev. Henry Francis Cary, M.A. from the original of Dante Alighieri, and illustrated with the designs of M. Gustave Doré.* Dante and Virgil appear as tiny shadows behind the massive form of Nimrod, shown here as one of the giants guarding the gate to the Ninth Circle of Inferno. Nimrod was responsible for the Tower of Babel and thus speaks in a tongue unknown to either Virgil or Dante. The engravers, Stéphane Pannemaker (1847–1930) and Ad Ligny (active 1855–1876), have placed their signature at the bottom left, while the artist Gustave Doré has placed his signature at the bottom right. (Courtesy of the Pitts Theology Library, Candler School of Theology, Emory University)

The genealogy combines two ways Ham's family spreads across the earth. First, they expand through the work of potentates (Nimrod, vv. 8-12), and second through growth and migration (Canaan's sons, v. 15).[13] The celebratory refrain closes Ham's branch of the family, summarizing his offspring by families, languages, lands, and nations (v. 20).

Descendants of Shem, 10:21-31

Noah's eldest son Shem appears last in the Table of Nations rather than first as custom dictates. This placement narrows the many branches of Noah's family to Semites from whom Abram's children will spring. "Shem has given his name to the Semitic peoples (*šēm*)," although not all in the list are Semites.17 Shem is important, for he is father of all the children of Eber (v. 21). Eber appears in v. 24 not as Shem's son but as Shelah's son, making him Shem's great-great-grandson. Eber's place as the first son of Shem may simply serve to highlight his importance as the father of the Hebrews. He is the "standout" in the family tree. In the same manner as the two lists of his brother's offspring, the list of Shem's offspring closes by heralding them as his children according to "their families, their languages, their lands, and their nations" (v. 31).

Conclusion, 10:32

The genealogy ends where it began: "These are the families of Noah's sons according to their genealogies (*lĕtolĕdotām*) in their nations; and from these the nations spread abroad on the earth after the flood." Absent from this closing statement is any mention of language because it is only one mark of diversity among peoples descended from Noah and his sons. The family tree embraces unity and diversity together. It stresses common identity, one blood, one set of ancestors for all peoples, even as it honors their distinctions of language, nations, and cultures.

A major function of the genealogies in this chapter is to show that after the flood with its massive destruction of life, humans begin again in fruitful multiplication throughout the whole earth. These genealogical lists soothe and comfort by their repetitive forms, and they provide hopeful reminders of divine creativity manifested through human reproduction. From chapter 12 forward, the book deals with the children of Eber, the Hebrews, but the Table of Nations insists that they reside firmly within the family of nations. All are blessed.

CONNECTIONS

With their strange names and places, genealogies often confound modern Western readers. Giving what seem to be bare facts of birth and begetting, genealogies do not arouse interest, but in Genesis their role is central for a number of reasons. They portray human survival in the fulfillment of God's first commandment to "be fruitful and multiply" (1:28). They provide order and regularity to the passage of time. They insist that after the catastrophic destruction of life ("after the flood," vv. 1 and 32), creation begins again to produce the entire family of nations. They point beyond themselves to a God who makes the human race grow and flourish.

The Table of Nations depicts a complex international reality within which Israel lived. Diversity among nations and peoples is God's design, God's desire, God's doing. [From One Ancestor] Both unity and difference among humans find expression here and belong together from the beginning. God's universal care for all people has social and political consequences for the ancient audience and for modern readers. Because the Creator manifests the divine self in this diversity and multiplicity, the text invites mutual respect and acceptance. Diversity of cultures, languages, nations, personalities, and capabilities is not something to be overcome in a false effort at unity; rather, unity must be found in the midst of this diversity itself.

The Table of Nations affirms indirectly that Judah's God transcends the gods of every nation ancient and modern. The deities of ancient empires may have seemed powerful, but the God of Judah brought people of these lands into existence in the first place. For the ancient audience of the Table of Nations, the God of order, creativity, and fertility infuses the world with new life and energy. Set against the backdrop of the nation's destruction, the genealogical lists offer the possibility that they too can be created anew.

For modern readers, these genealogies lead to reflection about who is in and who out, who matters and who is to be excluded. Everyone matters. No one is to be excluded. [The Present Crisis of Displaced Persons] Moral consequences flow from the Table of Nations because it expands our imaginations about who is in our family. All people belong, all have dignity, all are members of the family of nations. Enemies and allies alike belong, natives and foreigners, the disabled and the temporarily able-bodied, the old and the very young—all are members of the global family.

Although used as a warrant for slavery, the text actually undermines racism. [Race and the Family of Nations] Here there is one race, one stream of flesh and blood; there is a fundamental respect for difference and no regard whatsoever to skin color. One race of humans descended from Noah. The challenge facing this very diverse society of the United States, families, and churches is how

From One Ancestor

In the Acts of the Apostles, Paul draws on the vision of common ancestry in Gen 10 when he tries to persuade the Athenians that God is the one God of all peoples:

From one ancestor he made all nations to inhabit the whole earth, and he allotted the times of their existence and the boundaries of the places where they would live, so that they would search for God and perhaps grope for him and find him—though he is not far from each one of us. For "In him we live and move and have our being"; as even some of your own poets have said, or we too are his offspring. (Acts 17:26-28)

The Present Crisis of Displaced Persons

We live in a time of massive displacement of persons from nations in the Southern Hemisphere and in the Middle East. Old Testament interpreter Louis Stulman has lamented the situation of Syrian refugees, one example among many of the violent displacement of persons in our time.

Syria's civil war is the worst humanitarian crisis of our time. Over 400,000 people have died. Almost 7 million have been internally displaced. And over four million Syrians are refugees, half of whom are women and children (https://www.worldvision.org/wv/news/Syria-war-refugee-crisis-FAQ#sthash.CuJwsBWw.dpuf). The scale of the suffering is beyond imagination [see elaboration in Stulman's footnote below.] Who can even grasp the suffering of millions, except perhaps in the face of a child?

You would think that such a disaster would generate an outpouring of sympathy but instead it has generated a frenzy of hostility. Some would simply tell Syrian refugee children "you can't come here." "We don't know where your parents come from. You have no documentation . . . You may be from Syria, you may be ISIS, you may be ISIS-related" (Donald Trump, February 8, 2016). Maybe you have even said or thought to yourself: "these people aren't like us. They have a different religion, language, and culture. They're from the Middle East; they could be dangerous. Don't let them come here. Send them elsewhere, anywhere but here." By and large, I think these thoughts are based on fear, not ill-will; but they are still disturbing given that this is what we said to surviving Jews after World War II, and that is what we are now saying to Mexicans and Muslims. Who knows who is next?

Ideologies of exclusion may calm our fears momentarily; they may make us feel safe for a short time, but they do little to address our moral obligation to improve the lives of those in need, to heal the broken world. They do little to make us human or fulfill the great commandment (loving God and loving your neighbor as yourself). Dividing our worlds into "us and them" appeals to our worst selves, our fearful selves, not to the people we want to be. As Pope Francis said not long ago, "building walls . . . and not building bridges, is not Christian. It's not the Gospel."

USAID Assistant Administrator for Democracy, Conflict, and Humanitarian Assistance Nancy Lindborg interacts with Syrian refugees at Islahiye Refugee Camp in Turkey on January 24, 2013. (Credit: State Department photo/Wikimedia Commons/public domain)

This is a footnote in Stulman's article:

"The UN High Commission for Refugees (UNHCR) reports that there are more than 60 million refugees and internally displaced persons (IDPs) as of the end of 2014, the largest number since World War II. Syria is only the most visible crisis, affecting some four million refugees and about eight million internally displaced persons." Susan F. Martin, "The Global Refugee Crisis," *Georgetown Journal of International Affairs* 17/1 (Winter/Spring 2016): 5. Martin observes that the "solidarity expressed in . . . earlier crises appears to be in abeyance today" (7) and she concludes that "Political leadership is greatly needed to reverse today's trends and find new approaches." (10)

Louis Stulman, "'My Father Was a Syrian Refugee' (Deut 26)," The DeBow and Catherine Freed Contemporary Lecture, 26 September 2016, Findlay OH.

to embrace difference rather than squelch it or fight it. The Table of Nations affirms the immense dignity of all and is the seedbed of the wholeness that God intends for the world.

Race and the Family of Nations

 Rodney S. Sadler, Jr. wrote about Gen 10,

When the concept of race came into vogue during the so-called Enlightenment (circa seventeenth century), Scripture was employed in ways that supported the theories that emerged during that period . . . . The story of Noah's sons was reinterpreted as the passage demonstrating the origins of "race" in the Bible . . . .

Although the Table of the Nations provides biblical testimony to the divine origins of three distinct human groups, the passage shows no concept of skin-based racism; "The familial linkage of all humanity is the key to understanding this passage and indeed Genesis itself." Indeed, slaves are acquired in antiquity by being taken prisoner in war, from debt slavery or indenture and other forms of social troubles not related to ethnicity or skin color.

Rodney Sadler, *The Africana Bible: Reading Israel's Scriptures from Africa and the African Diaspora*, ed. Hugh R. Page (Minneapolis: Fortress, 2010) 74.

NOTES

1. Herman Gunkel, *Genesis*, trans. Mark E. Biddle (Macon GA: Mercer University Press, 1997) 86.

2. Ibid., 87.

3. Ibid., 88.

4. Nahum M. Sarna, *Genesis* (JPS Torah Commentary; Philadelphia: The Jewish Publication Society, 1989) 69, observed that "the total number seventy is a literary device to convey the notion of the totality of the human race."

5. For further details of the names in the chapter, see Sarna, *Genesis*, 70–80.

6. From *Jewish Antiquities* I:122-29, cited by Blenkinsopp, *Creation*, 158.

7. Claus Westermann, *Genesis 1–11: A Commentary* (Minneapolis: Augsburg, 1984) 509, discusses all the names in the genealogy in much detail with an eye to distinguishing P and J sources (see pp. 504–28). See also Blenkinsopp, *Creation*, 155–64.

8. The Masoretic or Hebrew text omits the phrase "These are the sons of Japheth." The scribes may have inadvertently left it out and corrected it to follow vv. 20 and 31, or perhaps because Japheth is of minor importance, the usual formula appears in shortened form.

9. Blenkinsopp, *Creation*, 158–59.

10. James R. Davila, "Shinar," *ABD* 5:1220.

11. Ingeborg Löwisch, *Trauma Begets Genealogy: Gender and Memory in Chronicles* (Sheffield UK: Sheffield Phoenix Press, 2015).

12. Blenkinsopp, *Creation*, 159.

13. Westermann, *Genesis 1–11*, 520.

14. For further readings, see Blenkinsopp, *Creation*, 159.

SPREADING ABROAD

Genesis 11:1-32

The story of Babel, nearly as popular in Western culture as Noah and the flood, has sparked a long history of conflicting interpretations. Besides the narrative of the city and tower of Babel (11:1-9), chapter 11 also contains a second genealogy of Noah's oldest son Shem (11:10-26), followed by a short genealogy of Shem's descendant Terah (11:27-32). These two lists set the stage for the stories of Abraham's family that take up the rest of the book. [Outline of Genesis 11]

Outline of Genesis 11
1. The Tower of Babel, 11:1-9
   a. Humans Act, vv. 1-4
   b. God Acts, vv. 5-9
2. Genealogy of Shem, 11:10-26
3. Genealogy of Terah, 11: 27-32

COMMENTARY

The Tower of Babel, 11:1-9

The Babel story tells of the abandonment of a city and the spread of both peoples and languages across the world. The placement of this episode after genealogies of Noah's three sons according to "their lands, languages, families, and nations" is puzzling because diversity of language and lands already exists in chapter 10 (vv. 5, 20, 32). More logically, the Babel story (11:1-9) would come before the Table of Nations, for, located here, its explanation of the rise of multiple languages comes after the fact. Source critics have explained the narrative order as a consequence of combining different literary sources in the book's composition.[1]

Yet the strong focus on language in chapter 11 has new purposes not found in chapter 10. This chapter narrows concerns from multiple markers of human diversity found in chapter 10—"lands, languages, families, and nations"—to the subject of speech itself. It also serves as another disaster narrative (see Introduction) set between two genealogies of Shem, for it is his descendants for whom the book is composed and who must survive the catastrophes wrought by the occupying powers. The ruins of the unfinished city evoke lingering memories of Jerusalem's destruction and the dispersion of some of its occupants. Like other disaster stories in Genesis, it exhibits

Pieter Bruegel the Elder, *The Tower of Babel*

Dutch Renaissance painter Pieter Bruegel the Elder, known for painting peasants and their circumstances, depicts Nimrod in the left foreground of the painting. For Bruegel, the tyrant, that is, the invading Protestant merchant class, represents the cause of the turmoil of his time in Antwerp. In his view, his Roman Catholic city and its simple life of fidelity was being destroyed by wealthy Protestants. He depicts the tower as an amalgamation of architectural styles that cannot hold together, and so the tower is left to molder. Its massive size ruins the old cityscape characterized by smaller buildings. A small dark cloud in the upper left corner may symbolize divine anger coming to destroy the city as the poor and the oppressed bow before the king.

Pieter Brueghel, the Elder (c. 1526/1530–1569). *The Tower of Babel*. 1563. Oil on panel. Kunsthistorisches Museum, Vienna, Austria. (Credit: Wikimedia Commons, PD-1923)

strange mythic features, opaque causes, and, of most importance, following massive disruption it ends with survivors.

The story's setting in Babel and Shinar (11:2) links it to chapter 10 where Nimrod appears. He is the hunter, mighty warrior, builder of empires, and founder of Babel (10:8-12). The narrative takes place in the heart of the Babylonian Empire to which Judeans had been deported, and hence the story of a city's collapse indirectly speaks to the book's Judean audience.

The first verse announces the theme of the passage: "Now the whole earth has one language and the same words" (11:1). A balanced literary composition, the story divides into two parts determined by the actions of the characters, human and divine. Humans act in part 1 (11:1-4), while God responds in part 2 (11:5-9). The story conveys its appreciation of speech in an echo chamber of significance. [Language Unites the Parts] Nearly every verse admits of multiple meanings created by vocabulary repeated first within each unit and then across each in a tapestry of sound and meaning. The one original language of the people creates their unity, but God's words turn everything upside down, baffling and confusing their words. The story is a work of art that refuses reduction to a single meaning. [Words and Sounds]

Language Unites the Parts

AΩ Words and phrases repeat *across* the two units to fashion a unified whole:

"All the earth" (vv. 1, 4, and vv. 8, 9)
"Upon the face of" (v. 4, and vv. 8, 9)
"One tongue" (v. 1 and v. 6)
"Scattered" (*nāpûṣ*, v. 4) and (*hĕpîṣām wayōpeṣ*, vv. 8, 9)

"Said" "And they said" (vv. 3, 4 and v. 6)
"Build" (v. 4 and v. 8)
"City" (v. 4 and v. 8).
"Name" (v. 4 and v. 9)
"There" (v. 2 and vv. 7, 8, 9, 2 times)

Humans Act, vv. 1-4

In contrast to the many differences among peoples set forth in chapter 10, chapter 11 begins by imagining the opposite—uniformity of speech: "Now the whole earth has one (*'eḥāt*) language."

Lest we miss the point that the language is "one," the verse repeats the point in typical Hebrew style with a parallel phrase "the same (*ăḥadîm*) words" (v. 1). Because the people speak only one "tongue," they are able to act as a homogeneous community, migrating and settling together in the land of Shinar (v. 2). They urge themselves to take common action: "Come (*hābah*), let us make bricks and burn them thoroughly." The words "come let us" translate a Hebrew verb in the cohortative mood, which expresses self-command or encouragement; that is, they exhort themselves to brickmaking. They use stone for bricks and bitumen for mortar, ancient materials for building, but they do not identify the reason for their labor. The next verse repeats the self-command and reveals their purpose: "Come let us (*hābah*) build a city and a tower" (v. 4).

> **Words and Sounds**
>
> AΩ In addition to repeated Hebrew vocabulary within and across the two units of the passage, sounds also repeat to create a rhythmic quality across the text: The words for "Let us make bricks" (*nilbenah levenim*) resemble those for "bake them thoroughly" (*nisrefah lisrefah*), and the word for "tar" resembles the one for "mortar" (*hemar* and *homer*). There is also alliteration between "brick" (*lebenah*) and "for stone" (*le'aben*)" and assonance with "The place" (*sham*), "heavens" (*shamayim*) and "name" (*shem*).
>
> J. P. Fokkelman, *Narrative Art in Genesis* (Amsterdam: Van Gorcom, 1975) 11–45, as cited in (and transliterated by) Tremper Longman, *How to Read Genesis* (Downers Grove IL: Intervarsity, 2005) 119–20.

Although the builders set out to construct both a "city and a tower" (11:4, 5, and in v. 8 only a city), the tower alone has gleaned the most interpretive attention, undoubtedly because it receives elaboration in the plans to build a tower with its "top in the heavens" (v. 4). [A Ziggurat?] Building a city and a tower is not the only motivation, however; they intend to "make a name" for themselves. [Making a Name] The reason for name-making, the goal of the entire enterprise, is to prevent being "scattered abroad upon the face of the whole earth" (v. 4). They want safety and security in their own closed world. What they most fear is to be dispersed across the face of the earth. Fear drives their building projects and their aspiration for a name.

God Acts, vv. 5-9

The second part of the story shifts attention from human action to divine action. God comes down to earth to see the city and tower that "mortals had built" (v. 5). What God sees, though, is neither city nor tower. Instead, God explicitly notices the people's unity and the oneness of their language, as if the building were not the issue but merely a pointer to an underlying problem. Rather than rejoicing in human solidarity and human community, God expresses alarm, announcing with high drama the divine plan to deal with human unity: "Look!" (*hēn*). "They are one (*'eḥād*) people, and they have all one (*'eḥāt*) language" (v. 6). Humanity's oneness prompts God's fear of them, or at least divine resistance,

A Ziggurat?

Gen 11:1-9 offers little in determining the nature of the tower of Babel about to be built. Perhaps the tower is a ziggurat, that is, a stepped structure or building. Help comes from archaeology:

The ziggurat was part of the religious architecture found at the centre of Mesopotamian settlements and was probably a feature of most cities after c.2000 B.C. Millions of sun-dried mud bricks were used in their construction. Layers of bricks were often separated by layers of reeds, perhaps helping to spread the load or allow drainage. Baked bricks and bitumen were used to protect the exterior from rain and wind. In Babylonia, ziggurats had a shrine on the top-most stage but it has been suggested that in Assyria there were no buildings on the summit.

Cuneiform texts from 2100 B.C. onwards refer to temples with seven storeys, and are described as being like mountains linking earth and heaven. However, depictions on cylinder seals, boundary stones, stone reliefs and clay tablets show buildings with either four or five storeys. Some of the seals date to the mid-third millennium B.C. which shows that the idea of a ziggurat predates the best known and best preserved example at Ur (c. 2100 B.C.). (British Museum)

Still, the narrative offers no explanation of the tower's shape, meaning, or purpose, despite also exhibiting knowledge of Babylonian building techniques (Sarna, 64).

In the sixth century BCE, the Babylonian king Nabonidus rebuilt the ziggurat, making it much taller.

The British Museum, "Ziggurats," http://www.mesopotamia.co.uk/staff/resources/background/bg22/teachersheet.html.
Nahum M. Sarna, Understanding Genesis: The Heritage of Biblical Israel (New York: Shocken, 1986).

Ziggurat of Ur. (Credit: Wikimedia Commons, Kaufingdude, CC BY-SA 3.0)

---

for "this is only the beginning of what they will do" (v. 6). Nothing will "be impossible to them." [Divine Fear of Humans]

Then, as on the sixth day of creation when God created humans (Gen 1:26), God again calls on the heavenly council, using the same first-person plural cohortative verb that humans use twice in making their plans: "Come, let us (*hābah*) go down and confuse (*bālal*) their language" (v. 7). [Fox's Translation of Genesis 11:7]

"One language and the same words" are central to human power, human collectivity, and human planning in this text. God responds by confusing their speech, baffling it, turning it into babble, so they have to stop building because they cannot understand one another. If confusing human communication

Making a Name

To modern Western ears, the impulse to make a name for oneself sounds like arrogant self-promotion or, at least, ambition that unacceptably diminishes other human values. In a culture of honor and shame (see [Culture of Honor and Shame]) such as that of ancient Israel, however, to make a name has a different meaning. It is to acquire the honor, respect, and status needed to gain resources and community connections for the sake of the survival and well-being of one's family or tribal group. In the case of nations and peoples, to make a name is to acquire honor and influence among other peoples and nations. Such influence aids in keeping relationships smooth and secure, always needed for safety and prosperity.

is God's first response to human oneness, the second is to bring about the very thing humans fear: "God scattered them abroad over the face of the earth" (v. 8). They are forced to abandon the city, only partly built.

Clearly the narrative is an etiology of language. The source from which flow the many languages of the world is God, who again sends the people out to fill the earth (1:28). God comes down, sees, speaks, confuses language, and disperses the people. The story could end here, but a conclusion adds a moral or consequence that summarizes and interprets it:

> "Therefore,
> [1] The city will be called Babel (Babble).[2]
> [2] There the tongue of all the earth is baffled.
> [3] From there, God scattered humans upon the face of all the earth (v. 9)."

Divine Fear of Humans

Does God fear humans as if they would gang up against the deity? This question brings up matters of interpretation. In this story, God responds to the aspirations of the city and the empire to be mighty and shows that God "is mightier" (Gunkel, 98). The text is not attempting to provide a full theology to define divine essence or divine action. Instead, its purposes are to explain many languages and many nations, and to do so it presents a dramatic tale where God controls human efforts and plans.

Herman Gunkel, *Genesis*, trans. Mark E. Biddle (Macon GA: Mercer University Press, 1997).

Fox's Translation of Genesis 11:7

AΩ Everett Fox's translation captures the sound and wordplay of the verse, where the Hebrew word for "confuse" (*bālal*) echoes the name "Babel": "Come-now! Let us go down and there let us baffle their language."

Everett Fox, *The Five Books of Moses: Genesis, Exodus, Leviticus, Numbers, and Deuteronomy* (Schocken Bible; Dallas: Word, 1995) 1:49.

Events of the plot flow from a single, common tongue, settled life, and uniform activity. God disrupts this settled life. Multiplicity of languages, scattered and dispersed lives, and incomprehension among peoples displace community based on sameness and unanimity. Divine discontent, even alarm, with humans is the catalyst for change.

The Babel story tells of the origin of many languages and diverse peoples and why peoples fail to understand one another as they spread over the earth. Divinely built into human life is the difficulty of comprehending one another across differences. If the garden story provides origins of human failure to live together as a couple within the environment, the Babel story explains the failure of the world's peoples to understand one another and live together. The source of this complexity and diversity is God. These are indisputable claims of the text, conveyed by its plot, verbal fireworks, and summarizing conclusion (v. 9).

Yet the passage, like other works of literary art, allows for many interpretations. Why, for example, does God resist settled human life and sow misunderstanding? Ancient interpreters justified divine actions as punishment for sin in the prideful building of the tower, perhaps as a form of idolatry. [The Tower as an Attack on God]

The Tower as an Attack on God

Most ancient interpretations of the story of Babel have understood the proliferation of language as the consequence of human sinfulness. The Book of Jubilees, our oldest commentary on Genesis, is one example. It attributes words to the humans as they prepare to build the tower that add arrogance to the building effort. Jubilees understands the tower as a vehicle for invading the heavens: "They built the city and the tower saying, 'Let us ascend on it into heaven'" (Jub 10:19; Kugel, 124).

Other ancient witnesses see the tower as a weapon of war against God. The apocryphal book 3 Baruch puts it succinctly: "[An angel said to Baruch], 'These are the ones who built the tower of the war against God, and the Lord removed them'" (3 Baruch [Greek] 2:7; Kugel, 124).

For further reading, James L. Kugel, *The Bible as It Was* (Cambridge MA: Belknap Press of Harvard University Press, 1997) 123–30.

Augustine on Nimrod

Augustine believed that the passage condemns human sin under the leadership of Nimrod (10:8-12):

It is humility that builds a safe and true path to heaven, raising aloft the heart towards God—not *against* God, in the way that that same giant Nimrod was said to be a hunter "against God [Gen 10:9] . . . . He and his people erected a tower against God, by which is signified irreligious arrogance. (Augustine, *City of God* 16.4)

Most based their readings on the tower, so tall that its top reached the heavens, and they assumed that its height was an offense against God, an act of hubris or an attack on the heavenly realm. St. Augustine, for example, was among those who charged Nimrod (10:8-14) with rebellion against God that brought punishment upon the city. [Augustine on Nimrod] Yet the passage itself never evaluates the moral status of either the tower or its builders. A tower with "its top in heaven" is merely a way to describe a very tall structure in ancient Mesopotamia.[3] Some modern interpreters have agreed that the text is a crime and punishment story, [Modern Interpretations—Part 1] but others have found in it a celebration of languages or a critique of the life-flattening effects of empire building. [Modern Interpretations—Part 2]

The story of Babel does still more than celebrate language. For the ancient Judean audience, this episode joins other disaster narratives to evoke and reflect on memories of the nation's own collapse. It narrates the abandonment of a beloved city, ironically located in the Babylonian Empire, and the dispersion of a once-unified people among the nations. It leaves uncertain the nature of human offense and whether or not the result is punishment. Even as it clearly understands God to have directed the end of the city and the dispersion of the people, it offers a murky explanation of divine thinking. This mythic interpretation of catastrophe rests in divine fear of a unified humanity able to do whatever it wants, as if, in retrospect, Jerusalem itself had lost its way and needed correction.

Like other disaster stories in Genesis, the Babel story does not present history in any literal sense but instead uses indirection to prompt reflection on catastrophe seen at a distance. The narrative idealizes the harmony of past life and conjures memories of the razing of Jerusalem. Causes of the city's demise are unclear, the exact problem uncertain. Of most importance, as in all the Genesis disaster narratives, survivors live to begin again. Although Babel's inhabitants are cast out like Adam and Eve, they do not die in their new worlds. Under divine command, they survive and spread across the earth. [Caring for the Earth]

Modern Interpretations—Part 1

Modern interpretations have picked up ancient themes, accepting or disagreeing with them. Some agree with ancient witnesses that the Babel story is a tale of crime and punishment based on ziggurats as evidence of idolatry and hubris (Strong, 625–34). Lacocque, for example, sees the tower building as the climax of the growth of sin depicted in Gen 1–11, beginning with disobedience in the garden, through the first murder, to the human wickedness that prompted the flood. Babel is the climax of wickedness (Lacocque, 29).

Neither Ellen van Wolde nor Theodore Hiebert thinks that the multiplication of languages is punishment for sin. Van Wolde has proposed an ecological reading wherein the Babel story builds to its climax by forcing compliance with God's command to "fill and cultivate the earth" (1:28; see van Wolde, 80–109). Hiebert has found a celebration of diverse cultures in which God rejoices, and cultural appreciation of Babylon as the cradle of civilization (see 625–34).

Each of these perspectives has merit, but in this commentary, I see these elements of the text to be part of its larger function as a disaster story, wherein details such as these echo experience of disaster and point toward survival within a changed reality.

John T. Strong, "Shattering the Image of God: A Response to Theodore Hiebert's Interpretation of the Story of the Tower of Babel," *JBL* 127 (2008).

André Lacocque, "Whatever Happened in the Valley of Shinar? A Response to Theodore Hiebert," *JBL* 128 (2009): 29–41.

Ellen van Wolde, *When Words Become Worlds: Semiotic Studies of Genesis 1–11* (BIS 6; Leiden: Brill, 1994).

Theodore Hiebert, "The Tower of Babel and the Origin of the World's Cultures," *JBL* 127 (2008).

Modern Interpretations—Part 2

Three modern interpreters from the two-thirds world have agreed with ancient interpretations that the story is about sin, not the sins of universal humanity but of the ancient Babylonian Empire and, by implication, of modern neocolonialist empires. These approaches bring out important aspects of the text and show how the context of interpreters illuminates the text from new angles.

The late J. Severino Croatto, a biblical scholar from Argentina, proposed that Gen 11 is a crime and punishment tale, but the prideful sinner is the Babylonian Empire of the sixth century. Babylon held a concentration of power, wielded oppressive control, and imposed uniform language, a normative worldview, and culture on the colonized. Imperial aggression is the problem that God sees and punishes by destroying city and tower.

José Míguez-Bonino has expanded Croatto's interpretation and reflected on the importance of diverse native languages in light of Ecuadoran history. Seven years after Pizarro arrived in the new land, the population of native Incans was reduced from 7 million to 700,000. The Spanish Conquest forcefully imposed a new language that eradicated native tongues. Loss of their languages denied to the people everything that gave life meaning—stories, traditions, songs, words of music, words of family, and words of love. Míguez-Bonino has also connected Nimrod, warrior and founder of Babel in chapter 10 (vv. 8-12), with the text's attention to imperial oppression. Yet God goes down "to thwart the empire's project of false unity and to destroy the tyranny of one language, one culture, one economic system."

C. S. Song has argued something similar from his context of Taiwan. Gen 11 is not about conflict within God, as if God were threatened by human building. It is about conflict within the human community caused by dictators, religious authorities, and the economically powerful whose towers and cities have created untold miseries. God demolishes this tower because God stands with women and men who suffer and endure hardship under such towers (Song, see 27–36).

For further reading, see Kathleen M. O'Connor, "Let All the People Praise You: Biblical Studies and a Hermeneutics of Hunger," *CBQ* 72 (2010): 1–14.

J. Severino Croatto, "A Reading of the Story of the Tower of Babel from the Perspective of Non-Identity: Gen 11:1-9 in the Context of Its Production," *Teaching the Bible: Discourses and Politics of Biblical Pedagogy* (ed. Fernando F. Segovia and Mary Ann Tolbert; Maryknoll NY: Orbis, 1998) 203–23.

José Miguez-Bonino, "Genesis 11:1-9: A Latin American Perspective," and Choan-Seng Song, "Genesis 11:1-9: An Asian Perspective," in *Return to Babel: Global Perspectives on the Bible*, ed. Priscilla Pope-Levison and John R. Levison (Louisville: Westminster John Knox, 1999) 17–26; 27–36.

Genealogy of Shem, 11:10-26

The genealogies of Shem and Terah convey theological purposes through their literary forms: Shem's is linear, while Terah's branches out for one generation. Shem's family tree rushes directly to Terah,

Caring for the Earth

"God thus counters their efforts to remain an isolated community by acting in such a way that they have no choice but to obey the command [to fill the earth]. God does this by making their languages so diffuse that they can no longer communicate, having to leave off what they are doing, move apart from one another, and establish separate linguistic communities. The confusing that leads to their scattering (confusion is the only means cited by which God does this) thus becomes a means to another end: the filling of and caring for the earth in fulfillment of the creational command. God thereby promotes diversity at the expense of any form of unity that seeks to preserve itself in isolation from the rest of creation."

Terence Fretheim, "Genesis" (*NIB* 1; Nashville: Abingdon, 1994) 321–673, here 413.

leaving aside the nations, while Terah's branches out again like Noah's in preparation for the divine promises to Terah's son Abram. These will be people of the promises.

In contrast to Shem's branched genealogy in chapter 10 (vv. 21-31), this second linear version of his family tree opens with a new heading, the *tôlĕdot* formula, "these are the generations of Shem." (See [These Are the Generations].) For each of nine generations, it mentions one person, although it acknowledges that each patriarch had other sons and daughters beyond the one mentioned. Rather than focusing on the spreading out of the nations, this reduction to one enables Genesis to move directly to Terah and his son, Abram, the tenth generation of Shem and the first of Terah. Terah receives special attention with his own *tôlĕdot* notation ("these are the generations of Terah," 11:27).

Although Terah continues Shem's line to the ninth generation, his genealogy starts anew in the tenth. His offspring are the prime concern of the rest of Genesis and where the linear form has been heading rapidly from Noah's three sons to the family of Abraham (Abram's name changes to Abraham in 17:5).[4] Noah's sons have been fruitful, have multiplied, and have spread across the earth (ch. 10), but the genealogies of Shem and Terah (ch. 11) leave relationships with other peoples behind to hone in on one family line.

The format of Shem's family line is nearly identical to Adam's in chapter 5 except for the absence of a death announcement and age of death for each figure. [Pattern of the Genealogy] Because it follows the same pattern as that of the first human, Shem's genealogy participates in a continuous line of fathers and sons from the beginning of creation who are born, beget, live long lives, and die.[5] Shem's family tree connects as far back as Adam and forward to humanity's new beginnings after the flood: "Shem became the father of Arpachshad two years after the flood" (11:10). Names in Shem's list, however, only partially overlap with his descendants in the Table of Nations (10:21-31). New here are Reu, Serug, Nahor, and Terah, the last four generations that culminate in Terah's sons Abraham, Nahor, and Haran.[6]

Pattern of the Genealogy

The pattern of the genealogy is repetitive and abrupt to do the work of moving time forward and narrowing the text's focus to one family: "When X had lived Y number of years, he became the father of Z. X lived after the birth of Z for Y number of years more and had other sons and daughters."

Other differences in Shem's two genealogies point to other purposes of chapter 11. The segmented family list in the Table of Nations (ch. 10) slows time down, while this one condenses time and speeds up the action, heading directly to Abraham. Life spans of characters in chapter 11 are half those in Adam's genealogy, and they reduce by half again in the family of Terah.[7] The shortening of lives suggests a literary movement from the mythic world of primeval history (chs. 1–11) toward a reality where humans might live less than a century, rather than nine centuries as in the case with Methuselah (5:25) and others in Adam's genealogy.

The shift back to a branched narrative with the birth of Terah's three sons, Abram, Nahor, and Haran, identifies the new generation as more than an "ordinary link in the genealogical chain, like the preceding generations, but one of intrinsic and outstanding significance."[8] Terah's genealogy expands like Noah's to three sons, for they too will be fruitful and multiply beyond imagining (v. 26).

Genealogy of Terah, 11:27-32

The final unit of chapter 11 follows a different genealogical format even though it, too, begins with the *tôlĕdot* heading, signifying another beginning. To bring greater attention to the family who will appear in the narratives to follow, Terah's genealogy includes unexpected brief narrative additions about his sons. The first verse repeats the names of his three sons who concluded Shem's genealogy: Abram, Nahor, and Haran. These are also place names. [Places in Terah's Genealogy] Haran becomes the father of Lot, but Haran dies earlier than his father Terah in their homeland of Ur of the Chaldeans, before the family journey even begins.

Women appear here, for Terah's two remaining sons take wives, foremothers of Israel. Rare in Genesis genealogies, their names are included in this list. Sarai, spouse of Abram, appears first, then her sister-in-law, Milcah, along with her pedigree. (See [From Abram to Abraham and Sarai to Sarah].) Milcah is Haran's daughter and sister to Iscah. The genealogy, however, returns to Sarai with a critical, show-stopping detail: Sarai is barren. After long lists of people who have been fruitful, multiplied, and filled the earth from Eve to ten generations after the flood, Sarai's barrenness is startling. It disrupts the story line, reproduction comes to a sudden halt, and fertility ends. Abram's wife cannot bear children. Then, for unexplained reasons, Terah takes his family—Abram, Lot, and Sarai—on a journey. They leave Ur of the Chaldeans and head for Canaan. They intend to go to the land of promise before it is promised, but

Places in Terah's Genealogy

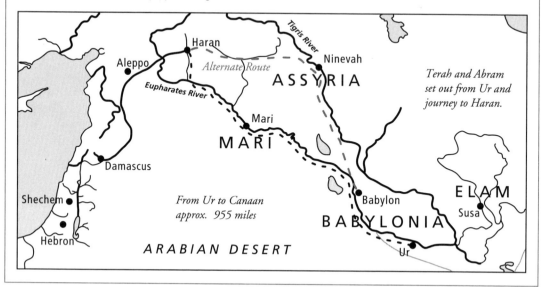

Ur of the Chaldeans (present-day Iraq) is the starting point of this family's long sojourning (11:31). Ur was an important commercial and religious urban center in Mesopotamia. From there the family moved to Haran, a caravan site located in northern Syria. Haran is also the name of one of Terah's sons. He dies, however, in Ur, before the family sojourn begins and before the family reaches the city that shares his name. The map below traces two possible routes through the Fertile Crescent from Ur to Haran, a distance of about one thousand miles. The family's movements were part of large migrations of peoples during troubled times.

they do not make it. They settle, instead, in Haran where Terah dies (v. 32). Haran is where Abram will grow up, and this is the beginning of the ceaseless migrations of the ancestors in Genesis.

CONNECTIONS

Many Languages

Diversity of languages is recognized today as a central component of the vast cultural differences among the world's population. Language carries the history and experiences of a people, gives power to its poetry, lyrics to its songs, and strength to its love-making. Language carries traditions, faith, and cultural memory. No language is fully translatable into another, so when a language disappears through assimilation or force, some part of the soul dies. [Languages of Clarkston, Georgia]

The story of Babel leaves open the question of whether language multiplicity is punishment or blessing, but the source of this abundance of speech is God. Proliferation of languages and cultures over the earth is neither a fluke of evolution nor a random happening. It is the result of divine intervention in the world. Just as events in the Garden of Eden represent a move from naïve innocence toward the difficulties of reality and adulthood, so the people of Babel move from communal sameness and isolation to the glorious and difficult multiplicity of human languages and cultures. [Pentecost and Many Languages]

Language domination amid a global economy, electronic tyrannies, and churches, communities, and families that exclude, reject, and harm others because they are different all violate the biblical claim that every person is made in God's image. We all share the breath of life no matter the language we speak.

> **Languages of Clarkston, Georgia**
>
> Clarkston, Georgia, is a small town of 7,500 that has gone from being 90 percent white in the 1980s to less than 14 percent white today. It is a microcosm of the United Nations, where diversity of language and culture flourish. In the shadow of Stone Mountain, once a gathering place for Ku Klux Klan cross burnings, today Clarkston is home to thousands of refugees from Vietnam, Somalia, Iraq, Bhutan, Syria, and some 40 other countries. *Time* magazine has called this town in the American South the most diverse square mile in America. Sixty different languages are spoken within this one square mile, and the Clarkston public high school has students from more than 54 countries who speak more than 47 languages. Clarkston represents the changing face of America built on respect for difference and the energy that immigrants continue to bring here.
>
> For further information, watch "Politics of the New South," episode 5 of *America by the Numbers*, available on PBS in some areas: http://www.pbs.org/wgbh/america-by-the-numbers/episodes/episode-105/.
>
> City of Clarkston, "Clarkston Facts," http://clarkstonga.gov/about/clarkston-facts.html (accessed 20 February 2018).

At the heart of American racism is a rejection of peoples of color, often from unconsciously held attitudes that see them as inferior, unworthy, as less human than people of Caucasian identity. The deep history of black slavery and white privilege has left a community that is not broken for we were never fully together. It often seems as if we are speaking different languages arising from our different experiences of the world and each other. [A Test of Faith]

God of New Life

The hopelessness and powerlessness experienced by barren couples desiring children find reflection in Sarai's barrenness. Efforts of modern science to enable conception and birth astonish and, to some, even suggest that science is trying to take the place of God. Yet science and medicine cannot guarantee that a couple will become fertile, conceive, and have children. The mystery of conception and birth, although sometimes moved to a further limit of human effort, remains a central horizon in the birth of a child, an awe-producing and often faith-renewing experience for parents. For those couples who wish to have children yet cannot despite enormous efforts and faith in a God of life, immense and enduring grief can haunt them for a long time.

Pentecost and Many Languages

The Pentecost scene in the Acts of the Apostles (2:1-13) is often thought to be a reversal of the tower of Babel story. Yet Acts does not reverse the "linguistic disunity of Babel" (Pervo, 61). When the Spirit descends upon the disciples, they preach the good news to all assembled from around the Mediterranean world, and miraculously each can understand in their own language. The Babel story leads to the baffling of language and the confusion of speech, but here in Acts all receive the word and understand: "The crowd gathered and was bewildered because each one heard them speaking in the native language of each" (Acts 2:6). Acts does not overturn the tower story; it fulfills it and finds unity in the presence of the Spirit rather than in uniformity of language or culture.

Richard I. Pervo, *Acts: A Commentary* (Hermeneia; Minneapolis: Fortress, 2008).

Mosaic representing Pentecost in St. Louis Cathedral, St. Louis, Missouri. (Credit: Wikimedia Commons, Pete unseth, CC BY-SA 4.0)

Couples who cannot conceive or, having conceived, give birth to a stillborn child or who lose a child from other causes know loss in profound and life-altering pain. The text's affirmation that God brings life out of death does not ensure physical fertility or miracles of birth. It does not mean that having faith in God will yield a child, as happens eventually for Abram and Sarai. The literal story of barren ancestors bears metaphoric meanings. It asserts that God brings life from sterility, lifelessness, and death and creates out of that wild and hopeless place a life-giving future beyond human expectation. New life in Genesis begins in barrenness. [A Barren People]

A Test of Faith

Rabbi Jonathan Sacks, chief rabbi of the United Hebrew Congregations of Britain and the Commonwealth, has reflected deeply on the implications of the story of Babel in relation to modern life, international politics, and by implication to issues of racism:

The test of faith is whether I can make space for difference. Can I recognize God's image in someone who is not in my image, whose language, faith, and ideals are different from mine? If I cannot then I have made God in my image instead of allowing him to remake me in his. Can Israeli make space for Palestinian, and Palestinian for Israeli? Can Muslins, Hindus, Sikhs, Confucians, Orthodox, Catholics and Protestants make space for one another in India, Sri Lanka, Chechnya, Kosovo and the dozens of other places in which ethnic and religious groups exist in close proximity? Can we create a paradigm shift through which we come to recognize that we are enlarged, not diminished, by the 6,000 languages that exist today, each with its unique sensibilities, art forms and literary expressions? This is not the cosmopolitanism of those who belong nowhere, but the deep human understanding that passes between people who, knowing how important their attachments are to them, understand how deeply someone else's different attachments matter to them also. (201–202)

Jonathan Sacks, *The Dignity of Difference: How to Avoid the Clash of Civilizations* (New York: Continuum, 2002).

A Barren People

Sarah's barrenness is the critical starting point for the ancestral stories in Gen 12–50. Her barrenness not only creates a narrative of hopelessness regarding the family's future at the narrative level but also serves as a metaphor for the circumstances of the book's ancient audience. Without offspring, the destroyed nation of Judah also has no future as a people. After invasions and deportations, Judeans face the possibility of extinction or of absorption into other nations. That the foremother of Israel is barren makes her a symbol of lifelessness, but God will turn the seeming death into life. Hemchand Gossai writes,

If . . . it would take divine initiative to bring creation out of nothing or order out of chaos, then it would involve equally divine initiative to bring about a people out of barrenness. Such is the dramatic reminder in Genesis 11:30, that indeed it would take nothing less than a divine working. In both Genesis 1 and 12, God employs barrenness both literally and metaphorically as a point of beginning. Without ever stating the obvious, the text establishes that God is able to bring creation into being from any source—including from a source unimaginable to human beings. (5)

Hemchand Gossai, *Barrenness and Blessing: Abraham, Sarah, and the Journey of Faith* (Eugene OR: Wipf and Stock, 2008).

NOTES

1. The combined documents most likely come from non-Priestly sources (Yahwist) and the P source (Priestly) according to Herman Gunkel, *Genesis*, trans. Mark E. Biddle (Macon GA: Mercer University Press, 1997) 94.

2. Translated by Everett Fox, *The Five Books of Moses: Genesis, Exodus, Leviticus, Numbers, and Deuteronomy* (Schocken Bible; Dallas: Word, 1995) 49. The name "Babel" means "gate of the god," perhaps as a reference to the city as a religious center. Here the term is ironic. See also Nahum M. Sarna, *Understanding Genesis: The Heritage of Biblical Israel* (New York: Shocken, 1986) 69–70.

3. Robert Alter, *Genesis* (New York: W. W. Norton, 1996) 46.

4. Matthew A. Thomas, *These Are the Generations: Identity, Covenant, and the 'Toledot' Formula* (London: T & T Clark, 2011) 90–91.

5. Claus Westermann (*Genesis 1–11* [Minneapolis: Augsburg, 1984] 560) has disagreed because Adam's genealogy is about the whole human race while Shem's concerns only one branch of the family.

6. The differences in the two versions of Shem's family tree suggest the existence of separate traditions about it.

7. Alter, *Genesis*, 48.

8. U. Cassuto, *Genesis*, 2:266–67, cited in Thomas, *These Are the Generations*, 91.

THE FIRST GENERATION
OF ISRAEL

Genesis 12–25:18

Chapter 12 introduces God's promises to Abram (12:1-3). These promises are the throbbing heart of the book, the major theological themes that structure the chapters and articulate the book's overarching purpose. Genesis seeks to encourage its ancient audience to trust the Creator of life to enable them to begin again. It seeks to buoy up the destroyed nation by anticipating a future of more than simple survival. By means of God's promises, it anticipates a future life of abundance unbounded and beyond the ordinary needs of a community. Yet the path to the fulfillment of these promises is rocky, uncertain, and repeatedly marked by threats to the life of the family itself. The first generation of Israel comprises Abram and his wife Sarai, but they are not alone in the family. Abram's nephew Lot; Hagar, the African slave and concubine; and Eliezer, servant from Damascus are also members of the household and greatly complicate the narrative of the fulfillment of the promises.

THE PROMISES TO ABRAM

Genesis 12:1-20

Presented briefly at the beginning of chapter 12, the promises to Abram come out of nowhere. There is no preparation for them since the previous chapter ends with all the people of the world in exile. In chapter 12, however, the narrative focuses on one people singled out from all the rest. What distinguishes them from the very beginning is the surprising revelation to Abram and his family that God wants them to go, to begin again, and to live amid blessings beyond comprehension. At every turn, Abram and his progeny face extinction, childlessness, famine, and attacks by both enemies and brothers as well as other life-threatening crises. The promises move beyond survival and endurance; they anticipate plentiful, unimaginable abundance, more children, more blessings than needed, given by a God of prodigal generosity. God's promises are the glue that holds the episodic lives of the ancestors together. The rest of Genesis concerns their fulfillment, delays in their fulfillment, or whether they will be fulfilled at all.

COMMENTARY

God's Promises to Abram, 12:1-3

Chapter 12 divides into three units. [Outline of Genesis 12:1-20] "God's Promises to Abram (12:1-3)" is the shortest of the three, but its role in the book is central. It depicts in microcosm Israel's relationship with God, who pledges to make a people of them by giving them progeny, blessing, honor, and land. The second scene reiterates the promise of land, provides Abram with an overview of the land's future boundaries, and seals that promise with a divine appearance (12:4-9). The final unit narrates the abduction of Abram's wife Sarai, the first of many threats to the fulfillment of the promises (12:10-20). [From Abram to Abraham and Sarai to Sarah]

> **Outline of Genesis 12:1-20**
> 1. God's Promises to Abram, 12:1-3
> 2. Holy Pilgrimage through the Land, 12:4-9
> 3. First Threat to the Promise, 12:10-20

From Abram to Abraham and Sarai to Sarah

Abram and Sarai are the names of two main characters in the story of Israel from Genesis 12–17. In chapter 17, God changes their names to Abraham and Sarah. These shifts in spelling may reflect linguistic variations arising from different sources used in the book's composition. Yet the changed spelling alerts readers to a major turning point in the story: the couple's new status related to the birth of their son Isaac (see Speiser, 126). Abram (Abraham) means "the father is exalted" or the "father is of high status" (17:5; Coogan, 65). Sarai's name changes when God tells Abraham that she will become mother of a son (17:15). Her names, Sarai and Sarah, mean "princess."

E. A. Speiser, *Genesis: Introduction, Translation, and Notes* (AB 1; New York: Doubleday, 1964) 126.

Michael Coogan, *The Old Testament: A Historical and Literary Introduction to the Hebrew Scriptures* (New York: Oxford University Press, 2006) Box 5.1.

Readers have already met Abram and Sarai in Terah's genealogy at the end of chapter 11. There the critical fact of Sarai's barrenness reveals that she can have no part in the fulfillment of God's promise of children to Abram. The story opens as the infertile couple moves with the extended family from Babylon around the Fertile Crescent to settle in Haran. They are probably among other tribal groups migrating in search of land and resources. [Fertile Crescent] Despite the family history of immigration, God's command for Abram to move again comes as a disruptive break from the past. [Continuity and Discontinuity in Abram's Departure] Without preparation and before offering identification or motivation, God simply demands that Abram leave everything he knows: "Go from your country and your kindred and your father's house to a land I will show you" (12:1). The staccato sound of the command in Hebrew, "Go"

Fertile Crescent

"The Fertile Crescent refers to the crescent-shaped area of fertile land extending from the Tigris and Euphrates Rivers, westward over Syria to the Mediterranean and southward through Palestine and the Nile Valley of Egypt" (Richards, 2:308). The crescent borders the Arabian desert and was important for commerce and its ability to sustain life.

Kent Harold Richards, "Fertile Crescent," *HBD*.

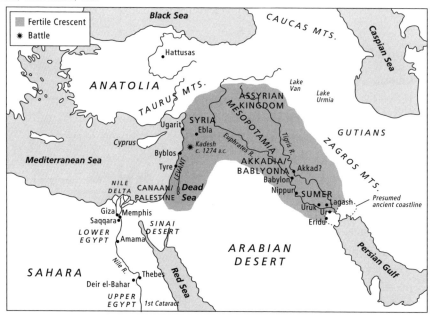

(*lek lĕkā*, lit., "go you"), conveys this abruptness. He must leave behind basic securities of daily life—land, kinfolk, and his father's house—and journey toward the unknown, "to the land that I will show you" (12:1). [The Father's House] Like exiles in Babylon considering the wrenching possibility of returning to Judah after the edict of Cyrus permits them to do so, Abram must begin again.

Because God summons Abram to a future about which God tells him little, the divine command places a heavy test of trust upon him.[1] The promises are vague. The land is geographically unspecified and "merely implicit."[2] Children are impossible. Blessings lack concreteness, and all the promises seem, on the face of things, to be utterly impossible. Yet their impossibility is the

> ### Continuity and Discontinuity in Abram's Departure
>
> The text uses the same language to present Abram's journey as it uses to tell of his father Terah's migration from Ur. Both "went forth to go the land of Canaan" (11:25; 12:5). Abraham merely finishes the move begun by Terah, who settled in Haran (Fretheim, 31). Despite the history of family movement, God's call for Abram to leave Haran signals a new beginning, a going forth toward an unknown future. At stake in both the continuation and disruption of the family story is Israel's claim upon the land. Terah was headed to Canaan to begin with and Abram fulfills those human intentions. In this chapter, however, the land comes as the gift of God to his offspring.
>
> Terence Fretheim, *Abraham: Trials of Family and Faith* (Columbia: University of South Carolina Press, 2007).

The Father's House

AΩ The father's house is not a parental homestead so much as it is an ancient reference to the extended family itself.

The nuclear family was the cornerstone of Israelite society in general and of village society in particular, but since the economy demanded large human resources the nuclear family joined with others in a bigger unit of the extended family (*bêt ab*), which sometimes included up to three generations. The family [or father's house] included the (grand)father, (grand)mother, their unmarried daughters, their sons (married and unmarried) and their wives and children. All these lived in one four-room house or in a complex made of several attached houses. In addition, the compound housed unrelated people who were considered part of the extended family, including slaves, hired hands, and others (see Judges 17-18). The population of a village could be made of one father's house or more. (Borowski, 22)

Every member of the household contributed to its well-being and had assigned roles.

Most households were self-sufficient economic units practicing subsistence agriculture. It was the workplace for all its residential members. From an early age children worked with same-gender parents, who transmitted life skills, household lore, and wisdom to their offspring. Spousal interactions were generally complementary, with the senior male representing the household in extra-household clan affairs and the senior female serving as household manager (e.g., Prov 31:10-31). Male dominance characterized sexual matters but not general household dynamics, making the designation "patriarchal household" problematic. The large number of people in a household meant that senior adults were vested with considerable authority to maintain order and assure that tasks were accomplished (see Exod 21:15, 17). (Meyers, 980)

In addition to "father's house" as a designation for the ancestral household, "mother's house" (*bêt 'ēm*) appears four times (Gen 24:28; Song 3:4; 8:2; Ruth 1:8) and several other texts allude to it (2 Kgs 8:1; Prov 9:1; 14:1; 31:21, 27). These references appear in passages focusing on women or providing a female perspective. Taken together, they suggest that the dominance of women in household management led to the identification of the household's internal dynamics with the senior female, whereas the predominance of "father's house" in the HB/OT reflects the identification of the senior male with the household in terms of its patrimony and its place in the larger socio-political structure (see Meyers, 981).

Oded Borowski, *Daily Life in Biblical Times* (ABS 5; Atlanta: SBL, 2003).

Carol Meyers, "Father's House," *EBR*.

point because, for the book's audience, a reconstituted nation is impossible.

God gives Abram little reason to depart from his present life beyond offering indeterminate blessings. [Blessings] Abram neither questions nor complains; he says nothing. Maybe the sparseness of this divine-human encounter results from the passages' literary intention—to introduce major themes of the ancestral stories that unfold in the rest of the book. Because Abram is silent, these verses also imply his immediate and trustful obedience, an obedience given in the dark in the midst of barrenness, impossibility, and un-knowing. Perhaps absence of detail in this opening scene seeks to inspire similar trust from the book's ancient audience. Although God's promises are not very specific, they invite a vision of a different future, of blessings enough to motivate departure and beginning again:

> I will make of you a great nation
> And I will bless you
> I will make your name great so you will be a blessing
> I will bless those who bless you and curse the one who curses you
> And in you [or by you] all the families of the earth shall be blessed (12:1-3). [Blessings as the Glue]

Both first-person speech and language of blessing saturate God's promises:

Blessings

People in the ancient world believed that divine powers shaped the fate of individuals and nations. In this view, life is neither accidental nor self-directed. Outside actions of spiritual beings determined its course, and blessings or curses could influence life. Blessings and curses derive their power from the authority of the one who utters them. In the Old Testament, YHWH, the God of Israel, is the one who ultimately controls good and evil. The Hebrew root meaning "bless" (*brk*) can convey many meanings. It refers primarily to the power of uttered speech that brings about good for someone or refers to the good that comes from that speech. It can also mean a form of prayer or of praise for the benefits received.

In an article in *Opportunity for No Little Instruction*, Old Testament interpreter Christopher Frechette has observed that "blessing belongs in contexts of ancient Near Eastern customs regulating interactions between rulers and their subjects. Multiple biblical traditions depict YHWH as a king and the Israelites as his subjects." Even though such relationships are not between equals, according to Frechette, they were "personal, favorable, and reciprocal." In other words, to bless means to be in personal, mutual, and kindly relationship. In biblical Hebrew and other Semitic languages, "to bless" can also mean "to greet" in a formal "recognition of and commitment to the relationship."

The most important aspect of God's blessing of Abram may well be God's formal announcement of this relationship not only in speaking to him but also in promising blessing. Besides indicating commitment to the relationship, "God's activity of blessing entails creating and giving life, health, progeny, and the means to sustain a harmonious life as a society." In this sense, blessing can also be material (see Frechette, "Why Bless God?" 114).

Christopher G. Frechette, "Blessing the LORD with the Angels: Allusion to *Jubilees* 2.2 in the Song of the Three Jews," in *Opportunity for No Little Instruction: Studies in Honor of Richard J. Clifford, S.J. and Daniel J. Harrington*, ed. C. Frechette, C. Matthews, and T. Stegman (New York: Paulist Press, 2014).

Christopher Frechette, "Why Bless God?" in *Reading the Old Testament: Pastoral Essays in Honor of Lawrence Boadt*, ed. C. Carvalho (New York: Paulist, 2013).

- "I will show you"
- "I will make of you"
- "I will bless you"
- "I will bless those"
- "I will curse those" (vv. 1-3)

Divine promises establish that events to follow in the ancestors' lives flow from God no matter how things might seem. What happens to them is not the work of chance or other gods or through human effort. The Hebrew root "to bless" (*barāk*) appears five times across two verses (vv. 2-3), establishing a major theological claim: God is the agent who will bring forth a future of blessing. Whatever transpires will ultimately work for the good of Abram and his family because God promises blessings.

From Abram's small, childless family, God promises to create a great nation, to bless Abram and make him a blessing, to bless his friends and curse his enemies. [Curses] Remarkably, these blessings are not for Abram's family alone; they are for all the peoples of the earth who will be blessed on account of their relationship to him. Abram's call has global ramifications. [Challenges of Hebrew Syntax in 12:3] Whether other peoples are blessed by Abram's passive example or, as I prefer, through his active efforts to extend blessings to them, his vocation is to benefit the whole world. With this calling comes responsibility. "Abraham is assigned the role

Blessings as the Glue

The list of promises and blessings that occurs first in 12:1-3 reappears with slight alterations at four important times in chapters 12–36:

1. When Abraham receives three angelic guests before Sodom is destroyed (Gen 18:17-18)
2. When Abraham prepares to offer Isaac (22:16-18)
3. When God appears to Isaac (26:2-4)
4. When Jacob encounters God at Bethel (28:10-14)

Although individual blessings appear elsewhere, the repetition of the full list emphasizes "how Abraham and his descendants are to live in the world" (Cotter, 91). The story of Joseph (chs. 37–50), by contrast, lacks explicit reference to the list of blessings. I think that is because the Joseph story captures the plight of the broken people of Judah when they are being encouraged by Genesis to reunite as a people in the land (see chs. 37–50).

David W. Cotter, *Genesis* (Berit Olam; Collegeville MN: Liturgical, 2003).

Curses

Curses are just the opposite of blessings, the results of the pronouncement of evil. The Hebrew language for cursing includes several verbs whose meanings can be summarized this way: "to curse is to predict, wish, pray for, or cause trouble or disaster in a person or thing. One means by which God enforces the covenant is by threatening to send curses upon those who failed to keep covenant. The curses are warnings against infidelity and sin (Lev 26 and Deut 28-32)" (Stuart, 1:1218–19).

For further reading, see Kent Harold Richards, "Bless/Blessing" *ABD* 1:753–55.

Douglas Stuart, "Curse," *ABD*.

Challenges of Hebrew Syntax in 12:3

AΩ Hebrew syntax is unclear at the end of v. 3 and raises questions about how Abram relates to other people and nations. Does the verb "to bless" take a reflexive or passive form? Does God promise, "Through you shall bless themselves all the communities of the earth"? When the verb is translated as a reflexive form (*hithpael*), it means that all the nations of the world will bless themselves when they see Abram. Abram's role is ideal believer, an example of

goodness who inspires others but does not actively work to bless them (Speiser, 85–86). When the verb "to bless" is translated as a passive form (niphal), Abram is responsible for blessing others: "In you [or by you] all the families of the earth shall be blessed" (NRSV). Abram has responsibility to extend blessings beyond himself and his family to the whole earth.

E. A. Speiser, *Genesis: Introduction, Translation, and Notes* (AB 1; New York: Doubleday, 1964).

Chosen for What?

Wrenching problems of the inclusion and exclusion of others on the basis of their identity emerge again and again in American political and social life. Jewish scholar Jon Levenson has insisted that God's choice of Abram and the Israelite people from all the peoples of the world is neither an act of exclusion nor can it support exclusion.

Genesis 12:1-3 explicitly connects his [Abram's] call and commission to the possibility of a wider blessing, one that involves "all the families of the earth." It is thus a capital error (though sadly a familiar one) to treat the biblical and rabbinic theology of chosenness as encompassing only two categories, the chosen and the unchosen, like the intensely exclusivistic stream in Christian theology that speaks only of the elect and the damned. It is much more accurate to follow the lead

of Joel S. Kaminsky, who speaks of three categories: the elect, the non-elect, and the anti-elect. The last—and they alone—are the enemies of Israel and her God. (Levenson, 34)

Outsiders need not be identified with impurity and the like, and the blessings of a particular identity are not restricted to those defined by it but can extend generously outward (see Levenson, 34). Such is the biblical sense of chosenness.

For further reading, see Joel S. Kaminsky, *Yet I Loved Jacob: Reclaiming the Biblical Concept of Election* (Nashville: Abingdon, 2007).

Jon D. Levenson, *Inheriting Abraham: The Legacy of the Patriarch in Judaism, Christianity, & Islam*, Library of Jewish Ideas (Princeton: Princeton University Press, 2012), quoting Regina M. Schwartz, *The Curse of Cain: The Violent Legacy of Monotheism* (Chicago: Chicago University Press, 1997) 34.

---

of mediator of blessing in God's saving plan for 'all the families of the earth.'"[3] These blessings take a variety of concrete forms in the stories that follow. [Chosen for What?]

Holy Pilgrimage through the Land, 12:4-9

At first glance, the second scene appears to be no more than a transition passage to move the family across the land of Canaan toward Egypt where they arrive in the third unit (12:10-20). Yet Abram's travels introduce the "the land I will show you" as a place of worship (12:1). Throughout Genesis and the Pentateuch, the land remains elusive and out of reach. It is, however, the sought-after home and sacred place for Abraham's offspring, and for the book's Judean audience, it is the place that has been lost.

At the chapter's beginning God says "Go" (*lek lĕkā*, 12:1), and now three verses later, "he (Abram) went" (*wayyēlĕk*, v. 4).[4] If the repetition of the verbal root is too subtle to convey Abram's prompt obedience, the next clause declares it openly: Abram went "as the LORD told him and Lot went with him" (v. 4). [Lot] With few words, the narrator reports the haste with which Abram complies with the divine command. Still, challenges appear again when the narrator notes Abram's age. He is seventy-five years old, facing an arduous journey to an unspecified land, and unlikely to beget children. From a logical perspective, the promises are hardly likely to be realized.

Despite God's directions that Abram leave his country, his kinfolk, and his father's house, he does not depart alone. He brings his wife Sarai, his nephew Lot, all his possessions, and "all the persons whom they had acquired in Haran" (v. 5). In other words, Abram is the patriarch of an extended family that includes workers and slaves. [Slavery] God's harsh command to leave everything signifies the disruption involved in beginning again.

Only after Abram has set out on his journey does he discover the land of promise. In a large geographical sweep, he passes through Canaan as if on a holy pilgrimage, a kind of ritual procession into the future. He traverses land that will belong to the nation of Israel, but at present others occupy it. Verbs of motion tell of the departure of Israel's first family, migrants without a home except in the form of a promise—wandering, traveling people, displaced persons:

> **Lot**
>
> Lot plays an important role in Genesis. The son of Abram's deceased brother Haran (11:28), he accompanies Abram on the pilgrimage through the land (12:4-9). When the two face conflict over the land, Abram separates from him (13:1-8). Abram rescues Lot from mysterious kings (14:1-16) and from the rioting crowd in Sodom and Gomorrah (19:1-29). Lot becomes the father of neighboring nations, Moab and Ammon, through drunken incest with his daughters (19:30-38).
>
> Lot's presence in the narrative does more than create plot complications. His very existence as Abram's nephew highlights the childlessness of the first couple and places Lot in line to be Abram's true inheritor. Since Lot is the forefather of neighboring and not always peaceful nations, Ammon and Moab (Gen 19:30-38), the stories about his relationship with Abram convey ancient tensions among neighboring peoples and show Abram acting as a blessing to the nations.
>
> For further reading, see Frank Anthony Spina, "Lot," *ABD* 4:373–74.

Abram Leaves Haran
Abram, Sarai, and Lot leave Haran at the direction of an angel (Genesis 12).

Julius Schnorr von Carolsfeld (1794–1872). "Abram Leaves Haran." From *Die Bibel in Bildern* (1853). (Courtesy of the Richard C. Kessler Reformation Collection, Pitts Theology Library, Candler School of Theology, Emory University)

Slavery

Slavery is an economic and social institution in the Bible that is never questioned in either the Old or the New Testament. People became slaves in the ancient world as captives from war, as conscripts of kings, or due to extreme poverty within an economic system that had no safety net whatsoever. Agricultural production was unstable, affected by wars, droughts, and bad harvests. When families had exhausted their capacity to produce food or other goods for their own consumption or for markets, they could sell their land and then daughters and sons into indentured servitude and, finally, sell themselves as well. Lenders of money and goods could demand repayment at any moment and at any interest rate, while unscrupulous lenders could bankrupt a family, forcing them into servitude. This form of indenture is known as debt slavery (Dandamayev, 4:62–65). In Israel, such slaves could not be sold to a third party but worked until their debts were paid off. The ancestors in Genesis own slaves. Hagar is an Egyptian slave; Jacob is an indentured servant of Laban; and Joseph becomes a slave in Egypt.

Prisoners brought back as booty from war could be enslaved permanently, although there were some legal provisions to recognize slaves as human beings. The Pentateuch includes laws providing for the care of Hebrew slaves and their release after six years (Exod 21:12; Deut 15:12; Lev 25:29-41). Sometimes slaves might be purchased from foreigners or foreign nations. This may have been how Hagar came to be Abram's concubine.

Such ancient forms of slavery must be distinguished from slavery in the Americas in the seventeenth to nineteenth centuries. Israel's slavery was not racially driven, though it was still dehumanizing and deeply violent.

For further reading, see Stephen R. Haynes, *Noah's Curse: The Biblical Justification of American Slavery* (New York: Oxford University Press, 2002).

Muhammed A. Dandamayev, "Slavery (OT)," *ABD*.

Abram went,
Lot went,
he departed (v. 4).
They set forth to go,
when they had come (v. 5).
Abram passed through (v. 6).
He moved on (v. 8).
He journeyed by stages (v. 9).

This long march through the land answers the "question of why the land belongs to Israel":[5] because God gives it to them. Abram's symbolic journey includes another barrier to the promises of land, for "Canaanites were in the land." (See [The Canaanites].) The divine promise of land both obscures and interprets harsh historical struggles that lie ahead in Israel's story (Josh 1–12; Judg 1–12). [Struggles Over Land] At the narrative level, the unit anticipates the outcome of those struggles before the fact and claims the land as divine gift, given at the very beginning of Israel's life. For the book's audience, Abram's journey calls forth memories of their homeland occupied by others and implicitly encourages return and restoration.

Place names on the journey map out key locations in a line from north to south. [Place Names on Abram's Pilgrimage] At two of these sites, Abram builds an altar, and during the construction God appears to him. His first stop is Shechem, a city that later becomes a center of worship in Israel. There God appears (*rāʾāh*) to him (12:7). [Divine Appearance] The Hebrew verb forms a frame around the verse, centering on God's promise of land. In a peculiar omission, God does not promise the land to Abram himself but "to your offspring I will give this land" (v. 7). The land will belong to his seed in some undetermined future, but at present Abram has no offspring. When Genesis ends, the people still have no land, except for two symbolic plots—Sarah's grave (Gen 23) and a bit of land Jacob purchases

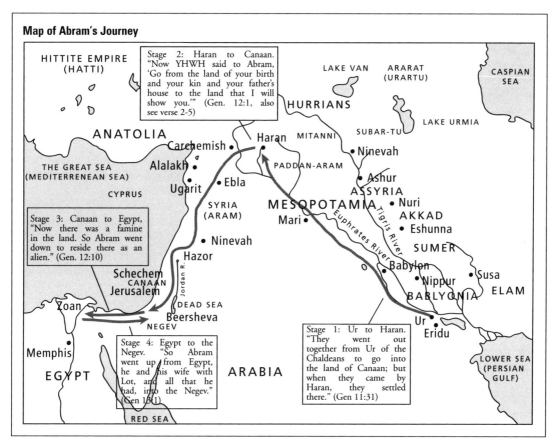

Map of Abram's Journey

Stage 2: Haran to Canaan. "Now YHWH said to Abram, 'Go from the land of your birth and your kin and your father's house to the land that I will show you.'" (Gen. 12:1, also see verse 2-5)

Stage 3: Canaan to Egypt, "Now there was a famine in the land. So Abram went down to reside there as an alien." (Gen. 12:10)

Stage 4: Egypt to the Negev. "So Abram went up from Egypt, he and his wife with Lot, and all that he had, into the Negev." (Gen 13:1)

Stage 1: Ur to Haran. "They went out together from Ur of the Chaldeans to go into the land of Canaan; but when they came by Haran, they settled there." (Gen 11:31)

(33:18-20). The attention to the offspring shifts the focus to the book's ancient audience, the Judean recipients of this promise of land.

Moving on through the hill country, Abram pitches his tent between Bethel and Ai, both also later sites of worship. He builds a second altar and invokes "the name of the LORD" (v. 8). [Bethel] This is the name Yahweh revealed later to Moses at the burning bush (Exod 3:13-15) and the name already spoken by Eve (Gen 4:1) as well as the narrator (4:26). Then "Abram journeyed on by stages toward the Negeb" (12:9). He has traveled down the spine of the land, has seen it, worshiped on it, and thereby staked out a symbolic claim over it.

As if surveyed by an ancient cartographer, the land is a place in which to pitch tents, build temples, and meet God. This sacred journey foreshadows Israel's history and claims the future land as a place of worship, of divine encounter, and as home for the worshiping people. For the book's audience, occupied and displaced, the text proposes that the land is still promised to them. Abram's journey would likely be for them a cause for astonishment, a word of hope, and a call to trust in divine promises. Restoration of the nation in the land probably seemed impossible to them.

Struggles Over Land

A major issue in Old Testament interpretation is the struggles over the land of Canaan. Whose land is it? How did Israel take possession of it from the native Canaanites (12:7)? This is an historical question made exceedingly complicated by conflicting accounts in the biblical texts themselves.

According to the Bible's first six books, after escaping from Egypt, receiving the Torah at Mt. Sinai, and wandering in the wilderness, Abram's descendants crossed over the Jordan River and invaded Canaan. There, under the leadership of Joshua, they swiftly embarked on three military campaigns, conquering the Canaanites and taking possession of the land (Josh 1–12). Yet later in the books of Joshua and Judges it becomes clear that much land, many cities, and several tribal groups were neither captured, removed, nor quieted. Many Canaanites remained in control of their home territories and were not subjected to Israel's rule even as David became king in Israel.

Contradictory biblical testimonies have prompted a search by biblical scholars and archaeologists to discover what really happened. Some have accepted the story in Joshua 1–12 at face value, marshaling evidence from archaeological sites that show destruction during the period of the 12th to the 11th centuries BCE. Others have relied more heavily on the latter parts of Joshua and the book of Judges to argue that Israel came into the land from the wilderness and, through a series of small military skirmishes and slow assimilation, gradually took possession of the land.

More recently, a group of interpreters and archaeologists have proposed other theories about how Israel gained possession of Canaan. Israelites who came into the land intermingled and intermarried with local Canaanites, so that Israel emerged from within native communities. These Canaanites were attracted to join the religious newcomers because of their stories of escape from slavery in Egypt at the hands of their liberating God, YHWH. This theory maintains that Israelites and Canaanites are essentially the same people who gradually intermarry, worship Yahweh, and then find themselves in opposition to other Canaanites who did not join the emerging society and continued to worship local Canaanite deities.

Archaeologists recognize that some of the cities that the book of Joshua claims were destroyed did not come to ruin at the time that Israel emerged in the land. In addition, much cultural continuity at archaeological sites suggest that the two peoples were not greatly different in their pottery, house-building materials and structures, and other elements of material culture. If the people of Israel were an invading, dominant force, greater difference in their cultural and physical remains would be expected.

The last opinion has gained support among many biblical scholars but remains highly controversial. If one holds to the first view that Israel took over the land in a violent military conflict, then God's chosen people engaged in a land-grab endorsed by God. If Israel gradually assimilated with the natives, then Israel took over gradually from the inside through internal conflicts until Israel prevailed. If one supports the last view of Israel as emerging largely among the Canaanites themselves, then Gen 12 makes sense as a reflection of faith by Abram's descendants after the fact. The land is a gift of God to them as determined from the beginning of their life as a people.

For further reading or viewing, see William G. Dever, "Archaeology and the History of Israel," in *The Blackwell Companion to the Hebrew Bible*, ed. Leo G. Perdue (Oxford: Blackwell, 2001) 119–26.

Place Names on Abram's Pilgrimage

The primary importance of place names in this chapter is to show that God revealed the entire land of Israel to Abram in advance of Israel's possession of the land. It is a gift long ago promised. At the same time, these names draw connections between Abram's story and future events in Israel as well highlight the land as a place of worship from the beginning.

Archaeologists have discovered that the first three places through which Abram and his family traveled— Shechem, Bethel, and Ai—were already sites of Canaanite worship. Shechem is significant in the Jacob stories (Gen 33:18-20; 34; 35:4; 48:22). His daughter Dinah is raped there, and her brothers avenge her against the Shechemites (ch. 34). Later, Shechem is also where the twelve tribes of Israel join in covenant under Joshua (Josh 24).

Bethel is the location of Jacob's famous dream of angels going up and down a ladder (28:10-22). Finally, Ai appears later as one of the cities conquered by Joshua in the conquest of the land (Josh 8). The Negeb is not a city but a large, dry wilderness through which the Hebrews later wander for forty years after they escape from slavery in Egypt.

First Threat to the Promise, 12:10-20

The chapter's final unit presents another hindrance to the fulfillment of the promises: Sarai is abducted into the harem of the Egyptian Pharaoh. [The Abduction of Sarai] Although it is not yet clear to readers of Genesis that Abram's offspring must be born through his barren wife Sarai, her endangerment here gains added significance from that later revelation (17:15).

Sarai's story takes place during the family's continuing journey, this time to Egypt. They flee there because of still another threat to survival, famine. (See [Famines].) "Now there was a famine in the

Divine Appearance

AΩ The divine appearance (*rā'āh*) during Abram's journey frames the repeated promise of land:

Then the Lord appeared (*rā'āh*) to Abram and said
"To your offspring I will give this land."
So he built there an altar to the LORD
who had appeared (*rā'āh*) to him" (12:7)

By surrounding the promise and the altar building, God's appearance seals and confirms the promise and identifies the land itself is a place of divine-human communion.

Bethel

Bethel, located north of Jerusalem, may have been a Canaanite site of worship that became important in biblical tradition as a place of worship. In Gen 12, the narrator mentions it as a notable place on Abram's march through the land his descendants will inherit. Bethel's connections with future worship help to characterize the land as a hallowed place wherein to sanctify the name of God. Later in Genesis, Jacob awakes from his dream of angels going up and down the ladder to heaven and declares,

"Surely the LORD is in this place—and I did not know it!" He was afraid and said, "How awesome is this place! This is none other than the house of God, and this is the gate of heaven." (28:16-17)

After that he changes the site's original name Luz to Bethel. Yet in chapter 12, Bethel is the only name mentioned.

This name change may be related to the mixing of sources during the book's composition, but the new name adds mystery and

Gustave Doré (1832–1883). *Jacob's Dream*. 19th C. Engraving. (Credit: www.creationism.org/images/DoreBibleIllus/)

power to the land itself. In the land of Canaan, Abram and his descendants—especially the book's audience—can find the house of God and the gate to heaven. To the house of God they must return.

The Abduction of Sarai

The basic plot of Sarai's seizure by the Egyptians, usually called "the endangerment of the matriarch," occurs three times in Genesis (12:10-20; 20:1-11; 26:6-11). In each version, characters and places vary but the story remains essentially the same. Suzanne Scholz has summarized the basic plot and its variations:

A man, either Abram or Isaac, leaves his country with his wife, either Sarah or Rebekah. In the foreign land, either Egypt or Gerar, the husband is afraid that another man might want to sleep with his beautiful wife and kill him to get rid of the competitor. When the couple encounters the powerful representatives of the other nation, the fearful husband identifies his wife as sister. She is placed in the harem of the other nation (Pharaoh and King Abimelech) so that he has sexual access to her. At this crucial point the various versions tend to differ. In two narratives, the foreign ruler takes the woman into the harem (12:15; 20:2); in the third he does not (chap. 26). In all of them the king discovers quickly—through a plague, dream, or chance observation—that the presumed sister is the wife of the man. Thereupon, the king returns the woman to her husband, who is compensated with goods and money before the couple leaves. (Scholz, 86)

Triple repetition of the same plot might imply that the book's composers were careless in putting the book together or were so respectful of traditional variations that they included them all. Yet why did the final editors of the book not remove the replications? Scholz follows the psychological interpretation that the repetitions express male rape fantasies in which husbands learn to negotiate fear about losing control over their wives' bodies by repeating the story of control again and again (84–88).

Although neurotic fear about loss of sexual control over a wife may be an undercurrent of the stories, the mother stories have other purposes too. The three versions point repeatedly to the essential role of the chosen mother in the fulfillment of the promises and reiterate the threat to the promises in the threat to the woman. The ruler of the empires abducts the woman and each time the woman escapes due to divine intervention, repeatedly averting the threat. Following the pattern of other narratives in Genesis, these end with survival following divine intervention. The women's experiences embody the captivity, release, and survival in Israel's larger story (Exod 1–15). Empires are outwitted, God rescues the woman, and life begins again, expressing the main theme of Genesis in microcosm.

Suzanne Scholz, *Sacred Witness: Rape in the Hebrew Bible* (Minneapolis: Fortress, 2010).

J. Cheryl Exum, "Who's Afraid of the 'The Endangered Ancestress'?" in *The New Literary Criticism and the Hebrew Bible*, ed. J. Cheryl Exum and David J. Clines (Valley Forge PA: Trinity Press International, 1993) 91–112.

land. So Abram went down to Egypt to reside there as an alien (*lāgûr*) for the famine was severe in the land" (12:10). Abram and Sarai "go down" to Egypt where Abram emerges as a fearful man who cares more for himself than for his wife. [Going Down to Egypt] Abram goes to Egypt as an alien, a term not used of him in Canaan, clearly anticipating Israel in its captivity in the book of Exodus. [Exodus]

Because Sarai is beautiful, Abram fears that the Egyptians will kill him to take her for themselves. To protect himself he asks Sarai to lie about their relationship by saying she is his sister rather than his wife. His fears turn out to be right. When Pharaoh hears of her beauty, he takes her into his house and lavishes livestock and slaves upon Abram (12:15-16). Sarai has no voice in the story, but God intervenes and rescues the voiceless woman from what is essentially sex slavery.

Going Down to Egypt

Whenever the Hebrews travel to Egypt, Genesis uses a form of the verb meaning "go down" (*yārad*, 12:10; 42:1; 43:1, 15; 47:4, 13). Leaving Egypt to return to Canaan is always "going up" (*ālāh*, 13:1). Although Egypt is south of Canaan and of lower altitude, the verbs connote more than topography. "Going down to Egypt" anticipates descent into slavery, and "going up to Canaan" signifies escape and return.

God afflicts Pharaoh and his house-hold with great plagues, anticipating the exodus. When Pharaoh learns somehow that Abram is the source of the trouble, he interrogates him about his lie and sends them both away with more livestock. [Abram's Character and Sarai's Suffering] Abram's trickery wins the day over the powerful ruler of the empire and yields material blessings for the family. Thanks to divine intervention, Sarai escapes disappearance into the harem of the ruler.

> **Exodus**
>
> Israel's Egyptian sojourn during the time of Jacob and Joseph (Gen 37–50) finds echoes in Sarai's story. Famine threatens life in both and provides the reason for migrating to Egypt. Sarai and Joseph are both forcibly captured and enslaved, divinely sent plagues affect their release, and both incidents end in wealth for the escapees. These narrative lines, of course, appear in Israel's escape from slavery in Egypt (Exod 1–15). The three stories evoke experiences of the book's audience and their ancestors, captive and without a clear future, whether they remain in the land or live in exile, for they are not in control of their land.

CONNECTIONS

Chosen for the Sake of All

God's promises are not for Abraham and his family alone. By choosing him, God does not abandon other people. To this point in Genesis, God has created and interacted with all peoples of the earth and then has sent them all into exile (Gen 1–11). Against this background, God commissions Abram to "be a blessing" (12:2), not simply to receive blessing. The call is not for Israel alone. [The Chosen People]

The ancestors do not always succeed in blessing other peoples, but God's intention to bless the nations through them guides the

---

Abram's Character and Sarai's Suffering

Abram gets Sarai to lie about their relationship so that he can survive by clever trickery. The trickster is a literary figure who uses deceit to overturn the power of the oppressor against all odds, making the trickster a folk hero. God's promises to Abraham hang in the balance.

People who find—to their own cost—what power-lessness means, are very well aware of the fact that trickery often is the only, thus legitimate, option for survival. They sustain each other by telling stories about the inventiveness of their heroes and heroines. (van Dijk-Hemmes, 229)

Although Abram employs a clever ruse, it callously disregards the consequences for Sarai and her place in the divine promises. Her beauty makes her a tradable commodity in the ancient world. Today the situation would be called sex trafficking, for she is forcibly taken into Pharaoh's house where she becomes one among other women in his harem available for sexual service, while Abram is paid abundantly in the exchange. He becomes wealthy through this arrangement and survives by being willing to trade her for his benefit.

At the same time, the story presents Egyptian men as characters whose "behavior is predictable" when faced with female beauty. They want her, and they take her and foolishly trust the word of a foreigner regarding Sarai's identity (see Jacobs, 82 and, more generally, 73–89).

Fokkelien van Dijk-Hemmes, "Sarai's Exile," in *A Feminist Companion to Genesis*, ed. Athalya Brenner (Sheffield, UK: Sheffield Academic Press, 1993).

Mignon R. Jacobs, *Gender, Power, and Persuasion: The Genesis Narratives and Contemporary Portraits* (Grand Rapids MI: Baker Academic, 2007).

The Chosen People

Although Abraham's role is linked to the blessing of others, his tomb in Hebron has become a focus of conflict and bloodshed. Surely Abraham, by definition, cannot be the exclusive possession of any one of the Abrahamic faiths! The portrayal of Abraham in both Christianity and Islam emphasizes that he is "a god-fearer" (in Arabic, *hanif*), someone who instinctively worshipped the One God before the establishment of a specific creed or system. The Quran's comment is remarkable.

Ye People of the Book! Why dispute ye about Abraham, when the Law and the Gospel were not revealed until after him? Have ye no understanding? . . . Abraham was not a Jew nor yet a Christian; but he was truth in Faith and bowed his will to God's . . . and joined not gods with God (Surah 3.65, 67).

Clare Amos, "Genesis," in *Global Bible Commentary*, ed. Daniel Patte (Nashville: Abingdon, 2004) 10.

story's unfolding in the rest of Genesis. Each of the main figures encounters, struggles with, or symbolizes (see Introduction) the nations and peoples who are Israel's neighbors. Chapter 12 alone anticipates conflicts with Canaanites (12:6) and enacts later struggles with Egypt (12:10-20).

Always the impulse of genuine Christian faith is active generosity toward the neighbor, particularly the poor and the most vulnerable, no matter their national, ethnic, economic, or social identity. With equal fervor, the New Testament insists on right relationship with neighbor. We need only think of Jesus' summary of the law: "You shall love the Lord your God with all your heart and with all your strength and with all your mind; and your neighbor as yourself" (Luke 10:27). And when asked "Who is my neighbor?" Jesus replies with the parable of the Good Samaritan, about a man robbed, beaten, and left by the roadside. Religious people who pass ignore him, but the hated Samaritan saves him, accompanies him, and spends lavishly on his well-being (Luke 15:11-32).

None of the children of Abraham—Christians, Jews, or Muslims—receive grace and blessing for themselves alone. Yet God singles out one man and his descendants to be the means by which the promises are enacted among the peoples. (See [Chosen for What?].)

Immigrants

With special resonance in our times across the globe, Genesis puts in the forefront people on the move through forced displacements and wanderings. Adam and Eve are expelled from the garden, Cain wanders outside the community, Noah and family are displaced from land altogether, the people of Babel spread across the earth against their will. Here in chapter 12 alone, our ancestors in faith move three times.

Migration, dislocation, and exile are persistent but often overlooked themes of the stories of patriarchs and matriarchs in Genesis 12–50. Each generation travels to avoid enemies, to find refuge among relatives, to find work, food, and/or spouses, or to escape the enmity of their own family. Movement and instability characterize their lives. Like Syrians and Afghanis today, they leave their "father's house" and go to a land they do not know. They are wanderers, semi-nomads, landless people. When they get there, they cannot stay but travel again. Abram, Sarai, and Lot join the mass migration of many peoples across the ancient Near East.

Contemporary communities of faith often interpret the wanderings of the ancestors as metaphors for wanderings of the human heart, sojourns in search of God, spiritual departures that apply to everyone's life. It is not wrong to see the ancestral journeys this way. Like our ancestors in faith, we, too, move through stages of displacement from our own lives, have times of searching, experiences of wildernesses and endangerment. [Displacement] It is essential for individuals to embrace these inner experiences of displacement to find inner freedom and compassion for the sufferings and desperation of others.

Yet to see the migrations of the ancestors in Genesis in terms of spiritual and psychological wanderings alone is a partial seeing. It flattens the text and abstracts from the harsh physical and spiritual realities of immigrants and refugees. Exclusive personalization of the text can blind us to neighbors in our communities today. Even with the distance of centuries, present-day situations of Syrian, Somali, and Libyan refugees, as well as countless others, shed light on the journeys of the fathers and mothers of Israel. Their plight can awaken us to our privileged lives and our blindness to the economic inequities that contribute to massive displacements in the first place. None of these global and local matters are simple or have single causes, but faith commitments remind us that migrants and refugees are our brothers and sisters. They may have much to bring to us. When we welcome them, we welcome our sisters and brothers.

To be a migrant often requires wariness of natives, the "Canaanites in the land," not knowing whether they will receive or harm you. It means to be uncertain of food and safety. It means to

Displacement

Jewish teacher and thinker Avivah Gottlieb Zornberg has pondered the psychological and spiritual aspects of God's call to Abram.

Here begins the journey of *Lekh Lekha* (12:1)—with its strange order of abandonments—first land, the community ("Leave that which produced you as one possible realization of potential"), and finally, father's house. For the first time, a journey is undertaken not as an act of exile or diminution (Adam, Cain, and the dispersed generation of Babel), but as a response to a divine imperative that articulates and emphasizes displacement as its crucial experience.

For what is most striking here is the *indeterminacy* of the journey. What is left behind, canceled out, is defined, clearly circled on the map of Abram's being; but his destination is merely "the land that I will show you"; from "your land," the landscape of your basic self-awareness, to a place that you will only know when the light falls on it with a difference."

Avivah Gottlieb Zornberg, *The Beginnings of Desire: Reflections on Genesis* (New York: Doubleday, 1995) 74.

have "nowhere to lay one's head" (Luke 9:58) nor a way to care for the children. It means to struggle with language not one's own and to confront culture, practices, and beliefs different from one's own.

Immigration and how to regulate it is a highly fraught political issue in the United States and Europe, particularly in strained economic times when it seems as if there is not enough to go around or extend to strangers. Yet the US is a nation of immigrants. The vast majority of us descend from immigrants who suffered enormously to better their lives and the lives of their children. Immigrants to this land echo the unsettled lives of our ancestors in faith, yet the historical memories of those hard struggles are easily lost, denied, or set aside in fear of the strangers among us.

NOTES

1. Herman Gunkel, *Genesis*, trans. Mark Biddle (Macon GA: Mercer University Press, 1997) 163.

2. David Carr, *Reading the Fractures of Genesis: Historical and Literary Approaches* (Louisville KY: Westminster John Knox, 1996) 180.

3. Gerhard von Rad, *Genesis*, rev. ed. (OTL; Philadelphia: Westminster, 1972) 160.

4. The same Hebrew verb (*hālak*) with which God commanded Abram to go appears in a different form at the beginning of this unit.

5. Gunkel, *Genesis*, 165.

MIGRATION, STRIFE, AND PROMISES

Genesis 13:1-18

Genesis 13 is a story of migration, interrupted by a fight that divides the family (13:5-13). Expelled by Pharaoh, Abram and his family "went up from Egypt" (13:1), taking a reverse path from the one in the pilgrimage through the land in chapter 12. (See [Place Names on Abram's Pilgrimage].) [Biblical Narratives of Expulsion and Deportation] After the family separates, God reiterates the promises of land and offspring.

In this chapter, danger to the family's survival comes not from the foreigners but from within its own ranks. [Outline of Genesis 13]

COMMENTARY

Continuation of the Pilgrimage, 13:1-4

The cohort returning from Egypt forms a large, wealthy party, for Abram travels with "all that he had and Lot with him into the Negev. He was very rich in livestock, in silver, and in gold" (13:1-2). [Silver and Gold] Abram's wealth points in two directions. First, it looks backward to the financial gain he acquired from Pharaoh in exchange for Sarai, and second, it anticipates the strife soon to erupt between uncle and nephew on the return to Canaan. Wealth threatens this family, but it also foreshadows Israel's escape when Pharaoh sends them away with wealth (Exod 12:29-36). [Parallels with Israel's Escape from Egypt]

Biblical Narratives of Expulsion and Deportation

Biblical stories of expulsion and deportation abound. Robert P. Carroll has called them "paradigmatic" narratives. Although Carroll did not mention the casting out of Abram and family from Egypt, the journey that began in chapter 12 continues here and follows the pattern of many such narratives in Genesis:

The expulsion of Adam and Eve from the Garden of Eden, from which we may argue the case that the whole Bible takes exile as its clue to the normal condition of human existence, the stories of the movement of Abram's family, driven out (commanded by God), from Babylonia to the land of Canaan, Jacob's self-imposed exile from his homeland for his crimes against his brother Esau, and his son Joseph's deportation by his brothers (Jacob's other sons) from homeland to Egypt, followed by the consequent movement of all the sons of Jacob and of Jacob himself, to Egypt and then their descendants' expulsion from Egypt (back) to the land of Canaan.

Robert P. Carroll, "Exile, Restoration, and Colony: Judah in the Persian Empire," in *The Blackwell Companion to the Hebrew Bible*, ed. Leo G. Perdue (Oxford: Blackwell, 2001) 102–16.

Outline of Genesis 13

1. Continuation of the Pilgrimage, 13:1-4
2. Separation, 13:5-13
3. Promises Expanded, 13:14-18

Silver and Gold

Possession of silver and gold was an important security during times of famine and other difficulties for pastoralists who lived off the land, moved with animals, and occasionally planted crops. "Pastoral nomads would often supplement their resources by engaging in subsidiary gainful activities, including commerce" (Sarna, 97). Although the text does not identify the source of the silver and gold, the previous chapter suggests that the money came from Pharaoh's settlement with Abram. If so, the precious metals bear a taint of ambiguity, at least from a modern perspective.

However complicated the sources of the ancestors' wealth may be, its possession signifies the fulfillment of God's promise of blessings to Abram. Blessings include the material necessities of life. (See [Blessings].) Wealth involves material blessings required for survival but given in overflowing abundance. Like offspring in uncountable numbers, God's blessings come in enormous quantities, far beyond basic needs. They guarantee a thriving life beyond imagining to assure the people of Judah that they have a future.

Nahum M. Sarna, *Genesis* (JPS Torah Commentary; Philadelphia: The Jewish Publication Society, 1989) 97.

From the Negeb, the family again moves "on by stages," probably from one source of water to another in the dry wilderness (13:3, cf., 12:9). This time the narrator reports fewer details about the journey than were recounted on the sojourn down to Egypt (12:4-9). Yet the migrant group returns to the previous places of encampment and altar-building, "the place where his tent had been at the beginning," between Bethel and Ai. It was there that Abram called upon the name of the Lord and the promise of land was repeated (13:3-4; cf. 12:8). The return retains the worshipful nature of Abram's first journey through the sacred land and quickly brings readers to the family troubles.

Separation, 13:5-13

Migration comes to a halt near the chapter's center when shepherds of Abram and Lot compete for arable land for their flocks.[1] [The Burden of Wealth]

Now Lot who went with Abram, also had flocks and herds and tents, so that the land could not support both of them living together; for their possessions were so great that they could not live together and there was strife (*rîb*) between the herders of Abram's livestock and the herders of Lot's livestock. (12:5-7)

Parallels with Israel's Escape from Egypt

Abram and Sarai's sojourn anticipates in broad outline Israel's captivity in Egypt. In both cases, the family goes to Egypt because famine is heavy in the land. Both groups are captive and then released by a pharaoh after God afflicts the Egyptians with plagues. Both leave with wealth in livestock, silver, and gold to journey through the Negev in stages upon the return. Gunkel has called these connections no more than borrowed "colors" in the stories rather than historical imitation, yet similarities in the plot are too remarkable to dismiss (172).

These narrative parallels provide another example of how Genesis portrays the figure of Abram as larger than life, a character who already underwent the sufferings and deliverances of his offspring in the book of Exodus. For the book's audience, the narrative line of captivity and release provides another story of hope. The Persian Empire, too, may release its hold on the people of Judah, and new life in the land may still lie ahead.

Herman Gunkel, *Genesis*, trans. Mark Biddle (Macon GA: Mercer University Press, 1997).

Map of Return

This map provides an overview of the area the family traveled through (from Egypt to Canaan) and shows the possible location of Sodom near which Lot settles. The map sets the ancient cities next to modern place names.

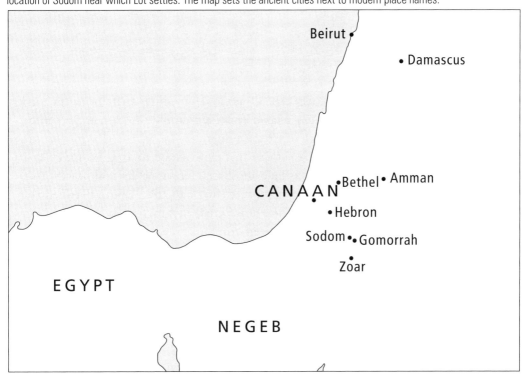

The Burden of Wealth

Wes Howard-Brook has reflected on the place of wealth in this story:

The crisis that follows the departure from Egypt is the inverse of famine, yet the basic choice (this time by Lot) remains the same. We hear that Abram is now "very rich (*kaved me'od*) in livestock, in silver, and in gold" (13:2). Hebrew *kabod* can mean both "heavy"/ "weighty" and "honorable"/"glorious." Here it means both. Abram and his entourage weigh heavily on the land because of their abundant possessions, so that the land teeters under the load (13:6). At the same time, the mention of silver and gold—of value only in an exchange between strangers—suggests that Abram is becoming honorable among other nomadic people as he journeys back from the Negev to the place of his first encounter with YHWH. The qualifier *me'od* is also doubly expressive, meaning both "very" and "powerfully." The extremity of wealth makes Abram powerful among the locals. The traveling band has become what to us seems an oxymoron: wealthy and honored homeless people.

The wealth and power, though, do not make for *shalom* but for *rib*, Hebrew for "strife" and "quarrelling."

Wes Howard-Brook, *"Come Out, My People!" God's Call out of Empire in the Bible and Beyond* (Maryknoll NY: Orbis, 2010) 56–57.

Violence among kinfolk is a strong possibility as strife (*rîb*) accelerates. [Topography and Climate Affect Events] The Hebrew word translated "strife" is multi-layered. It can refer to quarrels and conflict in general as well as to formal lawsuits or court battles among parties in a covenant relationship. Although the text makes no mention

Topography and Climate Affect Events

Topography, that is, the surface features of the land, as well as typical weather of the region, greatly affect events. Because the Negeb is a dry, barren, wilderness, a scrub land with few oases and about eight inches of rain per year, it is a stark place in which to keep people and animals alive. When the households of Abram and Lot arrive in the areas of Bethel, the topography changes from wilderness to rocky hill country, a difficult place for foraging livestock and agriculture (see Towner, 143). Competition for resources is nearly inevitable as a result.

W. Sibley Towner, *Genesis* (WBC; Louisville KY: Westminster John Knox, 2001).

of a covenant between Abram and Lot, their strife portrays a rift between intimately related kinfolk, bound by custom and common background in an implicit covenant.

Unlike Abram's actions in Egypt where he is at best a callous trickster, his actions here are those of a wise elder and peacemaker. Amicably, he proposes a settlement to the dispute between the families, confirms their close relationship, and announces, "Let there be no strife between you and me . . . for we are kindred" (13:8). Kinship matters more to Abram than acquiring the best land. "Is not the whole land before you?" (13:8) he says to Lot, with a spirit of confidence that there is enough land to go around, that blessings abound. Because Lot is not only his nephew but also the forefather of two nations, Moab and Edom, Abram's humble generosity models the divine call to be a blessing to the nations as God promised he would be (12:3). [Moab and Ammon] Abram the peacemaker proposes that the two families separate.

Moab and Ammon

Covenant overtones in the strife between Lot and Abram reflect the national identities of both parties. Lot is forefather of Moab and Ammon (Gen 19: 30-38) with whom Israel will have extremely difficult relations in the future. (See [Incest and Daughters].)

As the elder patriarch of the family, Abram should have first choice of land, but he steps back from customary privilege and invites Lot to choose his portion of land: "If you take the left hand I will go right; or if you take the right hand I will go left" (13:9). When Lot looks, he sees the "well-watered" plain of Jordan, "everywhere like the garden of the LORD, like the land of Egypt" (13:10).

In this etiological story that explains why things are the way they are, Lot, not Abram, decides who will settle where. Lot picks what looks like the best land, so it belongs to him and to his offspring, Moab and Ammon, because Abram allowed, proposed, and encouraged the choice. Symbolically, Abram brings blessing to the Moabites and Ammonites. Although Moab and Ammon become enemies of Israel, this story claims they are kindred. The enemy neighbors occupy their land because of the generosity of their relative Abram.

Yet the text says nothing of Abram's motivation. He may stand back to watch his foolish nephew chose the expanse of land that only looks superior on the surface. Elements of folklore infuse the portraits of Lot and Abram in these verses. Just as the story exalts the generosity of Abram and his cleverness in inviting Lot to choose first, it also makes fun of the neighbors. It insinuates that the forefather of Moab and Ammon fails to honor his elder uncle and reciprocate with deferential generosity. He grabs the more fertile land for himself and his family. These enemy neighbors possess their land only because of Abram's openhandedness. The story gives Abram the forefather of Israel the moral high ground as peacemaker and benefactor. Meanwhile, Moab and Ammon will become the objects of mockery later when Genesis portrays them as born from incest (19:30-38).

The narrator also reports that Lot settled near the wickedness of Sodom and Gomorrah, before "the LORD had destroyed" them, foreshadowing another disaster story (chs. 18–19) and hinting that Lot suffers from poor judgment (13:10). At this juncture, the narrator adds a further note of insta-bility. The Canaanites are still in the land along with another native group called the Perizzites (12:7). [Perizzites] With others occupying the land, the promise to Abram seems unlikely to be realized, a point that would not be lost by the book's audience during the Persian Period.

> **Perizzites**
>
> The Perizzites belong to the list of pre-Israelites who live in the land of Canaan. They appear fre-quently among lists of native peoples (Gen 15:18-21). It is not clear whether the name refers to a group of several peoples in the land or indicates an ethnic distinction.
>
> For further reading, see Stephen A. Reed, "Perizzite," *ABD* 5:231.

When the kinsmen separate, Lot settles "among the cities of the Plain and moved his tent as far as Sodom" (13:12). Abram settles in Canaan. Lot's location points to approaching trouble: "Now the people of Sodom were wicked, great sinners against the LORD" (13:13). Lot settled near them, either too naïve to realize his error or too foolish to know better. [Lot's Characterization]

Although God promised the land to Abram, it is curious that Abram chooses Canaan by default, almost accidentally. Only because Lot chose the right side of the land does Abram move to the left. The story implies that God is at work behind the veil of a human quarrel.

> **Lot's Characterization**
>
> Lot appears hasty and foolish, a "confused creature" (Cotter, 93). Fretheim has summarized the situation: "A significant disjunction exists between Lot's perception and the reality of things. His 'seeing' and his knowing are too limited. The narrator makes clear that Sodom is no Eden (verses 10, 13) . . . and the links to Sodom and Egypt suggest that Lot's ethical-theological perspective is questionable" (67). Lot's portrait serves to belittle Israel's enemies even as it simultaneously claims kinship with them.
>
> David W. Cotter, *Genesis* (Berith Olam; Collegeville MN: Liturgical 2003).
>
> Terence E. Fretheim, *Abraham: Trials of Family and Faith* (Columbia: University of South Carolina Press, 2007).

Promises Expanded, 13:14-18

Abram's family has been reduced to his immediate household, and now, after strife, separation, and the parceling out of land, God speaks to him with another command: "Raise your eyes now, and look from the place where you are" (13:14). God commands Abram to look in every direction according to the four points of the compass, "for all the land you see I will give you and your offspring forever" (13:15). In a mirroring of Abram's journey in 12:4-9, God again shows Abram the land's expansiveness. He walks through it in chapter 12, in chapter 13 he walks back, and now God adds to the promise of land the word "forever" (*ôlām*) (see [Land in Perpetuity]). The Hebrew term means a long time, beyond limitation. For the book's audience who had lost their land to Babylon and later to Persia, the promise of land forever would awaken hope that God still promises it to them. That others occupy it is not to be the end of the matter, for the gift of land is forever. The audience has a future even if they can barely imagine it.

The divine promises given in chapter 12 expand even further here. Not only will the land belong to Abram and his offspring "forever" but also the promise that he will have many children grows larger: "I will make your offspring like the dust of the earth; so that if one can count the dust of the earth, your offspring also can be counted" (13:16). Childless Abram will have so many children that counting them will be impossible. Like land given forever, uncountable offspring would have great resonance for a people facing extinction under foreign empires. With uncountable offspring, they can be a people again and avoid absorption through mixed marriages into Babylon and Persia; they have a future.

After enlarging the promises, God commands Abram a second time to walk through the length and breadth of the land: "Rise up and walk . . . for I will give it to you" (13:17). Again Abram cannot settle. He embarks on another pilgrimage, laying claim to "the length and breadth of the land" and again builds "an altar to the Lord."[2] All of Abram's actions make symbolic claims on the land. The land belongs to YHWH, God of Abram, not to the gods of the Canaanites or, by implication, the gods of Babylon or Persia. On the return, Abram travels on to Hebron rather than to Shechem and settles near different oak trees, this time at Mamre. Mamre anticipates both a visit from the angels who promise a child to Sarah (18:9-14) and the plot of land where she will be buried (23:17-19). [Oaks of Mamre]

Oaks of Mamre

The oaks of Mamre (13:18) are the second set of oak trees in the story. At the beginning of Abram's pilgrimage, he stopped at the oak of Moreh near Shechem. Oak forests were abundant in ancient Israel. Because the trees grew as tall as 60 feet and could live up to 500 years, the Canaanites venerated them and considered them sacred. When Abram builds altars near them, he claims them as sacred to his God.

For further reading, see Suzanne Richard, "Oak," *ABD*, 5:716.

Dawson Borrer. "Abraham's Oak." Plate from *A Journey from Naples to Jerusalem, by way of Athens, Egypt and the Peninsula of Sinai* . . . (London: J. Madden & Co., 1845) 481. (Credit: British Library, London; PD)

CONNECTIONS

A Behind-the-Scenes God

Lot's choice of the land in the plain of the Jordan, watered like a "garden of the LORD," left the promised land to Abram (13:8). That Abram gains the land only after Lot's choice points both to divine action behind the scenes and to an attitude of calm trust on the part of the deferential Abram. In this episode, at least, God influences events indirectly in the midst of messy human life. Rather than intervening directly or manipulating events miraculously, God works in unseen fashion behind the scenes.

Much, although not all, of God's portrait in Genesis is like this. Characters do encounter God through theophanies, dreams, and voices, but God performs few disrupting miracles on behalf of these ancestors. Instead, the ancestors struggle. Again and again, they make choices that threaten the promises. They endure long periods of confusion, captivity, and suffering. Somehow, though, they come through by using their wits, tricking, striving, and escaping. The course of events turns out to have been "providential" only after the fact.

Such indirect human experiences of the divine are closer to modern theological sensibilities in the West where doubt, wrestling with faith, and a sense of divine absence come along with glimpses and hints of divine presence. Most often, the experience of peace and wholeness becomes visible after the fact of struggles alone and in community. Often the distance of time shows a decision taken earlier and thought to be foolish, or a path chosen and then abandoned, appears as life-giving, trust-teaching, and love-producing. Surely this was so for the book's audience in the early Persian Period, severed from so much that had given meaning to their life and doubting God's care for them amid dispersion and displacement. This theological approach will become particularly clear in the Joseph cycle (Gen 37–50).

Land Struggles Today

People in urban societies can easily forget the importance of land for survival and well-being. Land for agriculture and animal herding remains a central cause of strife in modern times.

It is only a small step from Abraham and Lot's world of 3500 or so years ago into our own day and age. In so many areas of our world—for example, Brazil, Guatemala, India, and other places—similar questions of vital access to cultivatable land and control of the fruits of cultivation continue to be concerns, more often than not involving the question of life and death itself. (Cerekso, 306)

One need think only of timber wars in Brazil, demands for land for tourist resorts around the world, and, in the United States, conflicts among herdsman, farmers, and ecologists and the government in the Western states and mining interests in Appalachia, to name but a few prominent examples. Compounding these disputes is the ever-increasing need for water among farms, industries, and cities in California, Nevada, Arizona, Georgia, Alabama, and Florida.

Abram's magnanimous gesture of offering first choice to Lot models gestures of peacemaking. Lot himself is the quick decider who grabs what he thinks is best for his family without reference to the fate of his uncle's family. In our world of investment capital and international corporate business, his brash actions and self-focused choices invite reflection on cultural values, particularly during times of economic stress when our economic institutions are fraught by ethical failures.

For further reading, see Miguel A. De La Torre, *Genesis* (Belief; Louisville KY: Westminster John Knox, 2011) 154–57.

Anthony R. Cerekso, *Introduction to the Old Testament: A Liberation Perspective* (Maryknoll NY: Orbis, 1998).

Explosive Questions

The promise of land as a permanent gift to Israel remains to this day a highly explosive theological and political question. Some Christians and Jews continue to understand it as a literal statement of divine will for all time by which the Jewish people are divinely chosen owners of the land forever, God's eternal word. [Land Struggles Today] The basis for this position is a view that the biblical text always means the same thing without regard to the original context in which the text came to be and no matter how much cultures and political realities change. It understands the text as words God communicated directly with unchangeable meaning.

Yet the promises of land "forever" have a more particular purpose—to save the community from disappearing among the nations. The promise functions to revive hope of a possible future for Judah, to encourage those deported and those still in the land to gather again as descendants of Abram in the place of origin. It seeks to anchor them in a place still under the control of foreign empires. That place is sacred ground, the land on which they worship God, build altars, and meet God in unique ways. The promise urges them to rely on God who offers more than survival, offspring, and land in which to flourish as God's own people.

Many believing communities hold a different view of these shared Scriptures and understand them as a permanent template for all times. Yet God speaks through human words, human insights, human cultures. God chooses to speak through human limitations of time, place, and language.

[God's Particularity]

This means biblical texts require interpretation and reinterpretation from generation to generation. Such a view finds in the Bible a living word that takes on different nuances as time and place change. Meanings of texts are grounded in the realities of their original audiences, but those meanings require re-appropriation for our time. From this creative work of theologians, interpreters, preachers, pastors, poets, and other believers comes new light, a renewed word, for our time and place, our cultural reality, and our efforts to live as faithful believers. Many Christian faith communities see this as a process guided by the Holy Spirit at work among believers in the midst of their own struggles, disagreements, and creative reinterpretations.

This process of interpretation and reinterpretation occurs within the Bible itself. Second Isaiah, for one example among a great many, draws from Genesis 1–3 to speak of a new creation in the desert, and also from Exodus 1–15 to imagine a new exodus from slavery into new life.

From this interpretive perspective, the promise of land forever is not a political promise of land ownership into the twenty-first century; instead, it is a revelation of God's fidelity to be with the people, with both modern Israelis and Palestinians. God's promise to Abraham does not decide the issue of land in the dispute between them. At the root of the promise of land, of all the promises, is a call to trust God, a trust that does not come easily for the ancestors in Genesis.

God's Particularity

It is easier to read biblical texts as unchangeable and always true in the same way. Theologian R. R. Reno has written about God's choice of Abraham and his descendants in all complications of their existence and the temptation to understand the text as outside of time, as eternal.

Our natural instincts are gnostic. We prize the timeless, the disembodied, the universal, because we sense the fragility of the particular, as well as its unreliable arbitrariness. The ensuing story of Abraham and his descendants offers no metaphysical reassurances, accentuating instead the terrible narrow character of the divine invasion. The main source of drama of chapters 12–22 comes from the threat that infertility, paternal blindness, family conflicts, brotherly enmity, and foreign domination pose to the possibly fragile line of inheritance, culminating in the mysterious divine threat in the commandment to Abraham to offer his son as a sacrifice on Mount Moriah, a commandment that dramatizes the blind, inscrutable meaning of God's investment in the particular. Our natural and gnostic spiritual intuitions seem vindicated: no sensible religious person would invest all hope in something so vulnerable as Abraham and his clan's survival—or in a God so reckless. (32–33)

For further reading, see R. R. Reno, "Beginning with the Ending," in *Genesis and Christian Theology*, ed. Nathan MacDonnell, Mark W. Elliott, Grant Macaskill (Grand Rapids MI: Wm. B. Eerdmans, 2012) 26–42.

This call to trust God is everlasting and offered to Israelis and Palestinians alike. How can these two peoples turn toward each other and see the face of God in their brothers and sisters? How can there be justice in the face of competing claims? How can fear be moderated by faith and trust in God? These questions call forth creative openness to God at work in the world today and must be answered within the Jewish and Palestinian communities within Israel. Reinterpretation of the biblical promise of land must include justice as well as care for the oppressed, afflicted, and displaced of both communities.

NOTES

1. Nahum M. Sarna, *Genesis* (JPS Torah Commentary; Philadelphia: The Jewish Publication Society, 1989) 97.

2. Terence E. Fretheim, "Genesis" (*NIB* 1; Nashville TN: Abingdon, 1994) 434; and Sarna, *Genesis*, 99–100.

RELATIONS WITH THE NATIONS

Genesis 14:1-16

After Abram's journey in chapter 13, chapter 14 changes the subject. It plunges readers into the middle of a war among various kings of city-states and transforms Abram from peacemaker to warrior. His relationship with Lot, however, eventually returns to central focus because Abram must rescue Lot and family from captivity during the war. When the battles end, a king and priest named Melchizedek mysteriously comes forward not to fight but to bless Abram. [Outline of Genesis 14] Besides presenting Abram as a hero of military strategy and rescuer of Lot and his family, Abram is a blessing to the king of Sodom and, in turn, receives a blessing from Melchizedek, king of Salem.

Outline of Genesis 14

1. Lot Becomes Plunder in War, 14:1-12
2. Abram Rescues Lot, 14:13-16
3. Abram Meets Melchizedek, 14:17-24

COMMENTARY

Lot Is Captured in War, 14:1-12

The first literary unit of chapter 14 is dense with names of ancient kings from strange places who do battle with one another (14:1-12). Some of these are known figures, peoples, and places, but most remain opaque to interpreters. Understanding the basic situation requires knowledge of the feudal-like system of governance that prevailed among tribes and peoples in ancient times. [City-state Loyalties]

Even more confusing in the first unit is a plot line that gets

City-state Loyalties

The kings named in chapter 14 are not modern monarchs presiding over large national states with standing armies. They are leaders of groups of people, of tribes or collections of tribes, often joined to one another through covenant arrangements for protection and security from marauders, mercenaries, and other tribal groups loyal to other kings. The kings often preside over city-states—that is, urban enclaves sometimes enclosed behind fortress-like walls. Social and economic arrangements among them could be fluid. When a king or overlord promised protection to a vassal in a covenant arrangement, he expected complete loyalty in return. The overlord provided protection in return for military service and demanded tribute (taxes) from the tribe. Often the tribute placed onerous burdens on the subject people, who sometimes rebelled by refusing to pay tribute. That may be the case in Genesis 14, where several kings and their tribes rebel against Chedorlaomer and his coalition of kings.

For further reading, see Ze'ev Herzog, "Cities," *ABD* 1:1031–43.

lost among lists of people and places involved in battle. Events can be clarified only slightly. First, a contingent of kings appears, among whom Chedorlaomer of Elam is most important (vv. 1-2). Although he comes third in the list, he is first in power, the imperial overlord, the main man who controls his allies, neighboring kings, and tribes. He and his fellow kings make war against five other kings who had served as vassals to Chedorlaomer for twelve years but now rebel against him (vv. 2-4).

Of the rebels, the most important are the kings of Sodom and Gomorrah whose cities are later destroyed for their wickedness (Gen 19). Yet this group of rebels is confusingly left aside in the next verses while Chedorlaomer and his supporters battle other groups and subdue them (vv. 6-7). Chedorlaomer's forces turn back and subdue two additional groups, the Amalekites and the Amorites (v. 7). The imperial overlord's widespread invasions are probably an act of intimidation to quell the rebel kings mentioned at the chapter's beginning (vv. 1-2), but the text does not provide any motives for the assault against these other peoples.

After Chedorlaomer and his allies (v. 1) conquer the long list of peoples (14:4-7), the five rebellious kings from v. 2—kings of Sodom, Gomorrah, Admah, Zeboim, and Bela—finally join forces against them (v. 8). As if the book's editors realize the problem created by these multiple lists, they simplify the situation for us by counting the warriors as "four kings against five" (v. 9). The rebels lose the battle, seemingly because the kings of Sodom and Gomorrah fall into bitumen pits and others flee to the hills (v. 10). These battles occur in the valley of Siddim (vv. 3, 8). [Literary Oddities of the Story]

Only at the end of the military clashes does the war of kings and city-states narrow down to Abram's family. Chedorlaomer and his cohort have sacked Sodom and Gomorrah, taken their provisions, and captured Lot who resided there (13:10-13). Although we have already met Lot several times in the book (11:27; 12:4-5; 13:1-18), the text reintroduces him, calling him the "son of Abram's brother" (14:12). An important element of this chapter is the threat to Lot. As Abram's nephew, he is first in line to inherit Abram's promises. His abduction threatens the family and makes God's promises to form Abram and his offspring into a great nation appear to be impossible. Lot will not be Abram's heir, but at this point in the book, he is the only candidate for the role.

Literary Oddities of the Story

The story of Abram and the kings has puzzled many interpreters for its catalogue of names and confusing account of wars among peoples and kings. Explanatory details to clarify military actions are missing, such as why Chedorlaomer does not attack the rebels directly but instead subdues another list of peoples without mentioning the names of their kings. At the same time, the story adds clarifying comments after names of kings and places, found in parentheses in the NRSV, as if even the original audience also needed help to understand the events (vv. 2, 3, 8). Then the narrator over-identifies Lot, who is already known to readers (vv. 12, 16). Compared to his cowardly stance as he entered Egypt with Sarai (13:10-20), Abram becomes a significant player on the international scene, a fearless warrior and strategist. Then the king/priest Melchizedek appears out of nowhere and acts in surprising fashion (14:17-24). For these reasons, interpreters have been nearly unanimous in seeing the episode as from a different literary source than those woven together in Genesis (Alter, 58). So why include it?

The chapter portrays the patriarch Abram as a hero of war, a liberator of people, and an honest and generous diplomat in relation to the people of Sodom. It creates a contrast between his treatment of Sodom and their future treatment of Lot (ch. 19).

Thomas Brodie has interpreted the chapter in musical terms:

This story of war and peace (chap. 14) contains great color and musicality. The initial list of names and campaigns has a once-upon-a-time quality, which when read aloud hovers between the frightening and the humorous (14:1-12)—a story that is truly fabulous. When all seems lost Abram daringly turns the tables on the invaders at night (14:13-16), and in the peaceful denouement, in dealing with the kings of Salem and Sodom, he shows himself strongly as a man of graciousness and principle (14:17-24). (220)

Despite the fact that the story cannot be pinned to any historical events, Clifford has seen similarities to reports of military campaigns in the ancient Near East. "In genre the verses are an adapted report of a campaign" drawn from parallels in the Old Testament and the royal annals of Babylon and Assyria (Clifford, 2:23, 30; also see Westermann, 187–95).

Robert Alter, *Genesis* (New York: W. W. Norton, 1996).

Thomas L. Brodie, *Genesis as Dialogue* (New York: Oxford University Press, 2001).

Richard J. Clifford, *NJBC* 2:23, 20; Claus Westermann, *Genesis 12–36: A Commentary* (London: SPCK, 1981).

Abram Rescues Lot, 14:13-16

Comparatively speaking, the rescue that follows is a straightforward narrative, for the complicated catalogue of kings and peoples from the previous unit disappears (14:13-16). While living at the oaks of Mamre, Abram learns the news of Lot's captivity from an escapee and organizes a response. For the first time, the narrator calls Abram a "Hebrew," perhaps because it is a war scene (v. 13). [Hebrews]

Mamre is not simply a place in this chapter (cf. 13:18); it is also the name of a person, an Amorite, presumably from the peoples conquered by Chedorlaomer's coalition (v. 7). Mamre's two brothers happen already to be allies of Abram. The text does not say that they joined him in the rescue of Lot, although that is implied, but instead gives the glory to Abram himself. He musters his retainers—318 "trained men"—divides his troops, attacks by night, routs the enemies, retrieves the booty, and rescues Lot and all his goods and people. The narrator mentions Lot's rescue only

Hebrews

AΩ In English, "Hebrew" is often considered a synonymous epithet for "Jew," but in the biblical text the term is more complex and usually refers to the whole people of Israel, not just to the people of Judah. When Genesis 14 calls Abram a Hebrew, it may be referring to an ethnic group, but the term probably had an earlier life as a reference to a social group in the Late Bronze Age (155–1200 BCE). The Akkadian term transliterated either *Habiru* or *Hapiru* referred to an underclass of people who dropped out of the city-state system, some to avoid debt slavery, and regrouped as gangs of fugitives. They would have been among the poorest groups who lived on the margins of the city-states, not often accorded high honor in

the ancient world. Typically they survived by serving as mercenary soldiers for kings of city-states or by raiding city-states. Ancient documents, especially the administrative documents from the period of Egyptian control of Palestine called the Amarna Letters, mention them as troublesome outlaws.

The Old Testament uses the term for "Hebrew" only rarely—in the story of Joseph (Gen 37–50), in the story of the escape from Egypt (Exod 1–15), and in a few individual texts that refer to the people as foreigners or slaves. David is called a Hebrew when he joins up with the Philistines after abandoning King Saul (1 Sam 29:3).

after the booty retrieved from Sodom, suggesting a certain distance between the two kinsmen.

Whatever the source of this peculiar story, it portrays Abram as a blessing and a liberator of Canaanite peoples, especially of Lot, the forefather of the future nations of Ammon and Moab. Abram's tactical role in these international conflicts brings blessings to some nations when he defeats the tyrant and destroys his imperial control over many peoples. Most notably, Abram achieves these things after five kings have failed to do so. His good relationship with many Canaanite groups may overturn Noah's condemnation of his grandson Canaan to slavery among his brothers (9:20-27). Abram "conquers the conquerors" to reverse the curse in solidarity with Canaanites.[1] The last scene of the chapter adds further details to Abram's positive portrait (14:21-24).

Abram Meets Melchizedek, 14:17-24

The chapter's final unit is nearly as opaque to interpretation as the events surrounding the kingly battles, but its narrative line is clearer. The most puzzling features of the scene involve Melchizedek, his god, and his relationship with Abram. Melchizedek is a priest/king who appears out of nowhere in the company of the king of Sodom—either a new king of Sodom or the old one who survived his fall into the bitumen pit (v. 10). After Abram's successful war of liberation against Chedorlaomer, both kings honor him, for he has liberated the city-states and peoples around them. To honor Abram, the king of Sodom goes out to greet him (v. 17), and Melchizedek accompanies the king, bringing bread, wine, and blessing (vv. 18-20). Melchizedek, whose name means "my king is righteous" or "righteous king," comes from Salem, another name for Jerusalem, meaning "peace."

Melchizedek's encounter with Abram resembles a liturgy that comments on Abram's role in the war.[2] The priest/king comes in peace and brings bread and wine as a gift or offering for Abram. Then he reverses roles with Abram by solemnly blessing him in the name of the God Most High:

> Blessed be Abram by God Most High,
> maker of heaven and earth;
> and blessed be God Most High
> who has delivered your enemies into your hands (14:19-20).

El Elyon, translated "God the Most High," is a title for Israel's God, but Melchizedek is a Canaanite. Although it is true that *El* and *Elyon* have roots in Canaanite religion, Melchizedek's use of these names is puzzling.[3] [God the Most High] Priestly composers of Genesis may have added the ritual scene simply to set an account of the priestly role very early in Israel's origins. Although the Hebrew—"He gave him"—is unclear, Abram appears to give Melchizedek a tithe, perhaps modeling support for the priesthood or giving Melchizedek a tithe of the spoils of war traditionally owed to a king in the ancient Near East.[4] Alternatively, God may be giving Abram a tenth of everything. Yet Melchizedek, priest/king, stands for the nations and Israel's neighbors when he acknowledges Abram and the Creator God. He does this in a formal liturgical role, blessing and offering food and wine.

The chapter ends on another heroic note. Abram generously refuses to take any booty in payment for his success in battle, "not a thread or a sandal thong or anything that is yours" (14:23). Fretheim has proposed that the tithe is an act of worship and is given as part of a ritual meal.[5] Perhaps, though, it is not generosity that motivates Abram but a desire to have nothing more to do with Sodom. At the same time, he makes certain that his allies receive their share. Abram seems exceedingly generous,

---

God the Most High

ΑΩ "God the Most High" is the common translation of the Hebrew *El Elyon*. In the Old Testament *El Elyon* is a title, used here by Melchizedek (14:18-20). The term *Elyon* is the name given to the highest god in the Canaanite religion. It refers to the god above all gods, the chief god in the pantheon. It should not surprise us that Israel drew language to speak of God from its neighbors since they did not live in cultural isolation.

The term appears as one of Israel's titles for God (Deut 32:8-9; 2 Sam 22:14; Pss 7:17; 97:9). Some interpreters have disputed how much the borrowed title was accepted within Israel, but it does appear in poetry and liturgical passages, in Daniel, and in intertestamental texts where it emphasizes divine transcendence (Schmidt, 4:992). The only other place in the Bible where the two terms, *El* and *Elyon*, "God the Most High," appear together is Ps 78:35, although *Elyon* appears alone or with YHWH in other poetic and liturgical texts (Sarna, 381).

The title "God the Most High" emphasizes the transcendence and universality of the deity. The God on whom Melchizedek calls to bless Abram in this liturgical prayer is the One God above all gods and, by implication, the God of all nations.

Frederick W. Schmidt, "Most High," *ABD*.

Nahum M. Sarna, *Genesis* (JPS Torah Commentary; Philadelphia: The Jewish Publication Society, 1989).

scrupulously honest, and concerned about other peoples who have joined with him. These actions establish a contrast to future actions of the people of Sodom, who will be the opposite of generous in stories still to come (Gen 18–19).

CONNECTIONS

The less interpreters are able to make clear sense of a text or a biblical figure, the more vigorous are the interpretive traditions that grow from that text or figure. The stories of the sons of God and the daughters of humans (Gen 6:1-4) and Noah's blessings and curses upon his offspring (Gen 9:18-27) provide examples similar to the interpretive process that surrounds Melchizedek. Religious imagination has found much significance in his cameo appearance and enigmatic character. Ancient Jewish writers like Philo and Josephus saw his gifts of bread and wine as evidence of Melchizedek's generosity.[6] Other interpreters stressed his role as righteous king and priest. Still others found a foreshadowing of the Jewish office of divinely appointed high priest, and, among some Christian communities, readers have found an understanding of ordained priesthood as an irreversible calling of the priest. [Melchizedek, Priest/King]

In Psalm 110:4 the psalmist says, "The LORD has sworn and will not change his mind, 'You are a priest forever according to the order of Melchizedek'" (Ps 110:4). Christians apply this interpretation directly to Jesus (Heb 5:6-10; 6:20; 7:1-3), seeing him as the high priest appointed forever according to the order of Melchizedek (7:1-3). Both Melchizedek and the Christ offer sacrifice, and both use bread and wine in rituals. Melchizedek's offering anticipates the Last Supper and Eucharistic practices of Christians.[7]

Melchizedek, Priest/King

Genesis tells us almost nothing about Melchizedek. Although he makes only a brief appearance there, his place in later interpretation grows large indeed. The Old Testament may allude to him when it says, "You are a priest forever according to the order of Melchizedek" (Ps 110:4). This story about Abram and Melchizedek may validate one group of priests in Israel. Zadok was a priest during the reign of King David; his descendants were one line of priesthood in Israel (2 Sam 8:17; 15:24-35; see Fretheim, 439).

The New Testament letter to the Hebrews develops from there an understanding of Melchizedek as a prototype of Christ. He anticipates Christ because neither figure has antecedents and because both are priests "forever." He plays a prominent role in Hebrews (5:6-10; 6:20; 7:1-17). The author of Hebrews wants to establish that Jesus replaces the levitical priesthood of the Old Testament by claiming that Christ existed before the Old Testament priesthood (Backhaus, 79). This is because of another verse from Psalm 110 that assures the king of victory over his enemies: "The Lord has sworn and will not change his mind, 'You are a priest forever according to the order of Melchizedek'" (110:4, NRSV; see Johnson).

Later, Cyprian, an early church father and Bishop of Carthage during the third century, sees Melchizedek as a prefigurement of Christ on slightly different grounds:

. . . in the priest Melchizedek, we see the sacrament of the sacrifice of the Lord prefigured according to what the divine Scripture testifies and says "And Melchizedek, king of Salem, brought out bread and wine, for he was a priest of the most high God, and he blessed Abraham." But that Melchizedek portrayed a type of Christ, the Holy Spirit declares in the Psalms, saying in the person of the Father to the Son: "Before the day star . . . I have begotten you. . . . You are a priest forever according to the order of Melchizedek. . . ." For who is more a priest of the most high God than our Lord Jesus Christ, who offered sacrifice to God the Father and offered the very same thing that Melchizedek had offered, bread and wine, that is actually his body and blood? (in Sheridan, ed., 2:26)

Terence E. Fretheim, "Genesis" (*NIB* 1; Nashville: Abingdon, 1994).

Knut Backhaus, "Before Abraham was, I Am," in *Genesis and Christian Theology*, ed. Nathan Mac Donnell, Mark W. Elliott, Grant Macaskill (Grand Rapids MI: Wm. B. Eerdmans, 2012).

E. Elizabeth Johnson, *Ecclesiology in the New Testament* (Core Biblical Studies; Nashville: Abingdon, 2018).

Cyprian, *Letters* 63.4, in *Genesis 12–50*, ed. Mark Sheridan (ACCS, Old Testament II; Downers Grove IL: Intervarsity, 2002).

Peter Paul Rubens was a counter-reformation artist of the sixteenth century. Rubens's style was baroque with strong color and movement presented in a monumental style with lots of action. In this painting, *The Meeting of Abraham and Melchizedek*, the encounter of the two men forms a broad horizontal line across the center of the canvas. Rubens por-

trays Abraham in metal armor typical of warfare of his period. Melchizedek is the old wise king handing bread to Abraham, while wine urns rest on the steps and in the arms of a servant in the foreground. Most striking about the painting is the intimate exchange between the two figures, depicted by their face-to-face contact. Abraham is lower on the steps, signifying his reception of blessing from the wise, kingly figure. The two stand out against the darker clothing of the other figures as angelic cherubs oversee the scene. Melchizedek may be in the role of God who blesses his servant. The painting highlights the one who is the righteous king who comes suddenly to nourish and bless.

Sir Peter Paul Rubens (†577–1640). *The Meeting of Abraham and Melchizedek*. c. 1626. Oil on paneling. Gift of Syma Busiel. (Credit: National Gallery of Art, Washington, DC)

NOTES

1. David Carr, *Reading the Fractures of Genesis: Historical and Literary Approaches* (Louisville KY: Westminster John Knox, 1996) 164.

2. See Terence E. Fretheim, "Genesis" (*NIB* 1; Nashville: Abingdon, 1994) 439.

3. See Robert Alter, *Genesis* (New York: W. W. Norton, 1996) 61, notes 19, 20.

4. Num 31:25-41 tells of the division of spoils, some of which are shared with the Levites. See Nahum M. Sarna, *Genesis* (JPS Torah Commentary; Philadelphia: The Jewish Publication Society, 1989) 110 n. 20.

5. Fretheim, "Genesis," 440.

6. James L. Kugel, *The Bible As It Was* (Cambridge MA: Belknap Press of the Harvard University Press, 1997) 149–62.

7. Mark Sheridan, *Genesis 12–50* (ACCS, Old Testament 2; Downers Grove IL: InterVarsity Press, 2002) 25.

DIALOGUE IN THE DARK

Genesis 15:1-21

This chapter is about Abram's profound fear that his family will not survive. Despite God's promises of becoming a great nation (12:1-3), Abram has seen little progress toward their fulfillment. He and his household have journeyed to Egypt and back, encountered an angry pharaoh and hostile armies, and then settled in Canaan, but still he has no children and no hope of land because others occupy it. The entire chapter concerns darkness about the future, and this darkness becomes the backdrop for the luminous presence of the divine.

COMMENTARY

Genesis 15 takes the form of a vision in which Abram and God speak to one another. The dialogue between them, formal and emphatic, draws attention to the chapter's importance in Genesis. The subject of the dialogue is fear about Abram's survival and, by implication, the survival of the ancient Judean audience. Will there be children and land in the future? Despite divine assurances, Abram voices doubt in the face of unknowing and so encodes the uncertainty and fear of the book's audience during the Persian Period.

God twice offers Abram reassurance in the vision (vv. 1 and 7), but these words of comfort simply provoke doubting questions from Abram (vv. 2, 8) that, in turn, prompt further divine assurances. [Outline of Genesis 15] In the second part of the vision (vv. 7-21), dialogue about the land takes place within a covenant ritual that surrounds God's words about the future. Abram wants to "know" what will happen (v. 8), but God tells him that his knowledge, what he will "surely know," involves dark days ahead (v. 13). Finally, God's definitive response to Abram's doubt is to make a covenant with him (v. 18).

> **Outline of Genesis 15**
> 1. First Divine Assurance, 15:1
> 2. Dialogue about Children, 15:2-6
> 3. Second Divine Assurance, 15:7
> 4. Dialogue about Land, 15:8-18

First Divine Assurance, 15:1

Genesis 15 opens with a temporal phrase that connects this chapter to the previous one: "after these things." After Abram's battle with the warring kings, Lot's rescue, and the meeting with Melchizedek, God comes to Abram in a vision. The first words that God speaks in the vision—"Do not be afraid"—are surprising in light of Abram's recent success in warfare. For what does Abram require divine protection now that the fear-inducing armies no longer threaten (ch. 15)?

> "Do not be afraid,
> I am your shield,
> your reward will be very great." (15:1)

With God as his shield, Abram will survive new assaults on his well-being and gain a great reward, but the perils he faces here come from within him. [God as Shield]

Like the book's audience, Abram fears that he has no future because he has no prospect of getting all that he needs to be a "great nation," namely, children and land. God assures him that "his reward will be very great," for "the word of the Lord" guarantees it. [Word of the Lord]

Dialogue about Children, 15:2-6

Despite God's protection, Abram asks, "O Lord God what will you give me, for I continue childless, and the heir of my house is Eliezer of Damascus?" (15:2) (English translations use "Lord" in small capitals to honor the personal name YHWH, while "God" is a generic term for a deity in the ancient Near East). [Eliezer of Damascus] Abram is looking for God's promised offspring, but the primary candidate to inherit the promises is a household

---

God as Shield

The Psalms often refer to God as a shield, that is, a protection from injury and death in battle like a soldier's instrument of defense. Psalm 115, for example, repeats a refrain calling for trust in God, who is Israel's shield:

O Israel, trust in the Lord!
He is their help and their shield,
O house of Aaron, trust in the Lord!
He is their help and their shield
You who fear the Lord, trust in the Lord!
He is their help and their shield. (Ps 115:9-11)

Three times, the psalmist asserts that God helps and shields Israel, including priests of Aaron and all people who set their trust in God. Just as God seeks to evoke a response of trust from Abram in chapter 15, the psalm calls for trust in God among all worshipers.

Word of the Lord

Occurring two times in this dialogue between God and Abram, the phrase "word of the Lord" adds solemnity and authority to the divine speech in this unit (15:1, 4). If human words can make things happen merely by being uttered, if they have the power to construct the world, all the more so is the word of the Lord a force that makes things happen, builds reality, and creates and recreates the world (Gen 1:1–2:4a). The Bible is often referred to as the "word of God," but in the Old Testament the phrase usually refers to special communications of God's own being, divine self-revelation, or the divine will—similar ways to speak of divine presence. The word of the Lord is nearly equivalent to God's own being, God's self-expression to Israel. The word is powerful and brings everything into being (Gen 1:1–2:4a). In the New Testament Jesus preaches the word (Mark 2:2) and Jesus is himself the Word, "and the Word was with God" (John 1:1, 14). Hebrews 1:1-2 confirms Jesus' identification with the word: "Long ago God spoke to our ancestors in many and various ways by prophets, but in these last days, he [God] spoke to us through a son."

For further reading, see Dwight Moody Smith, "Word," *HBD* 1221.

servant from another people; "You have given me
no offspring, so a slave born in my house is to be
my heir" (15:3). Abram challenges divine inac-
tion with impatience and lack of trust. Yet how
could he reasonably expect that he and Sarai could
conceive their own child? He will ensure his own
future by adopting a son from among his foreign
slaves. He sets his hopes on Eliezer.

God's response to this plan is a quick and
firm: "No." The divine reply begins with *hinnēh*,
the Hebrew interjection meaning "behold" or "look" (v. 4). (See
["Look!"].) Although not translated in the NRSV, the term calls for
attention and emphasizes what follows. "Look," that is, "pay attention: Eliezer will not be your heir but one of your own 'issue' will
be your heir." The verse puts it clearly; the child will come from
Abram's own body and will be his own flesh and blood, but that
seems impossible. Abram's fears express the fears of the destroyed
nation of Judah, the book's audience who are in grave danger of
disappearing into the dominant empire.

Responding to Abram's fears, God offers
something like a visual parable that enacts
the promise and amplifies its impossibility. The Creator of the cosmos brings
him outside to look at the heavens and
orders him to count the stars, if he can,
but of course he cannot. God's command
is polite, using a Hebrew term that means
"please" or something like "if you would
be so kind." Fox has translated the phrase
"Pray look toward heavens and count the
stars."[1] Like the uncountable stars, "so
shall your descendants be" (15:5). [Abram
and Job]

The stars present Abram with a nearly
unthinkable future. By their multitude,
they ask this old, childless man with a
post-menopausal wife to imagine descendants beyond counting, beyond human
expectation, a whole nation of people. Yet
even with the stars as sign and promise,
the situation appears unthinkable
according to any reckoning. Somehow,
remarkably, the sight of the heavens leads

Eliezer of Damascus

In Hebrew, the name Eliezer means "God is my help." Eliezer's social role in Abram's house is uncertain, but ancient Near Eastern laws of inheritance provide for the adoption of a servant as an inheritor who gains the privileges of a son.

See Nahum M. Sarna, *Genesis* (JPS Torah Commentary; Philadelphia: The Jewish Publication Society, 1989) 113.

Abram and Job

Thomas Brodie has noticed similar literary and theological patterns in God's responses to questions from Abram and Job. Job also doubts, loses faith, and questions God.

Instead of remaining within Abram's knotted world, within his doubt and his frame of reference, Yhwh "brought him outside," and he challenged him to look at the heavens and count the stars. A similar drama occurs in Job, but at far greater length. The answer to Job's questioning—insofar as there is an answer—does not come from within the frame-work of Job's thinking, but through the voice from the whirlwind, which effectively puts Job in another world (Job 38-42). (228)

Brodie continued with the observation that for Job the problem is not solved intellectually. Abram's second ques-
tion to God clearly seeks intellectual knowledge: "How am I to know that I will possess it?" (15:8). Even though God takes Abram's doubts and fears seriously and honors them with replies, God does not provide intellectual confirmation to Abram either.

Thomas L. Brodie, *Genesis as Dialogue* (New York: Oxford University Press, 2001) 228.

Abram to believe, "and the LORD reckoned it to him as righteousness" (15:6)." Abram's immediate trust, after first doubting (15:3),

Abram's Faith

📖 The letter to the Hebrews (11:8-12) reflects on the promise to Abram that he might have more children than the stars of the heavens. Hebrews grasps the human impossibilities of the situation and sees in Abram's life a model of faith and the hope to live in the heavenly city and quotes the divine promise of children in the process.

By faith Abraham obeyed when he was called to set out for a place that he was to receive as an inheritance; and he set out, not knowing where he was going. By faith he stayed for a time in the land he had been promised, as in a foreign land, living in tents, as did Isaac and Jacob, who were heirs with him of the same promise. For he looked forward to the city that has foundations, whose architect and builder is God. By faith he received power of procreation, even though he was too old—and Sarah herself was barren—because he considered him faithful who had promised. Therefore from one person, and this one as good as dead, descendants were born, "as many as the stars of heaven and the innumerable grains of sand by the seashore."

gains God's praise and possibly astonishes the book's audience, who surely reside in doubting darkness themselves. Walter Brueggemann has observed "that Abraham is now abruptly *designated* as one well pleasing in God's sight. The text announces afresh what it means to be the human creatures we are created to be, that is, to be righteous"[2] (cf. Rom 4; Gal 2–4; Jas 2:22-24). God stands with Abram in this scene, honors his fear and doubt, listens to his questions, attends to his complaints, and praises his belief. Clearly these events invite the Judean audience to similar trust in the face of enormous barriers to their own hope of rebuilding the nation. [Abram's Faith]

Second Divine Assurance, 15:7

Again, God initiates a conversation that provokes doubt from Abram, this time on the subject of land: "I am YHWH who brought you from Ur of the Chaldeans to give you this land to possess" (15:7). At the chapter's beginning God announced his role as Abram's shield, his protection from attack (15:1). In this verse, by contrast, divine assurance takes a more intimate form: the revelation of Israel's particular name for the divine and later revealed to Moses at the burning bush (Exod 3:13-15). [The Name YHWH] God's name, possibly the untranslatable form of the Hebrew verb "to be," simultaneously reveals and conceals the Holy One. Its content emerges from God's actions: "I am the LORD who brought you from Ur of the Chaldeans to give you this land to possess." From the family beginnings in Ur, their migrations reveal God's presence and intention (cf. 11:31).

To understand who God is and how God relates to him, Abram must look to his family's past. The God appearing before him in this vision is the same God who led him and his ancestors around the Fertile Crescent to Haran and now to Canaan. All along, the divine intention hidden in their migrations has been to "give you a

The Name YHWH

AΩ The name YHWH is the name that God reveals to Moses at the burning bush (Exod 3:13-15). The name contains four consonants in Hebrew often called the "tetragrammaton," or the four letters. This name is an etymological enigma; neither its exact translation nor its original pronunciation is known. It may be an imperfect form of the Hebrew verb "to be" and is often interpreted to mean "I am who I am" or "I will be who I will be." Some interpreters connect it to the verb "to be," meaning "he is," while others find a causative form in the Hebrew meaning, "he who causes to be." Still others draw meaning from the short form Yah (Exod 15:2) as an exclamation, "Behold, it is him" (see Römer, 32–33).

In the tenth century, Jewish scholars called the Masoretes added vowels for the title *Adonai* in substitution for the sacred name since many Jews do not pronounce God's name.

Thomas Römer, *The Invention of God*, trans. Raymond Geuss (Cambridge MA: Harvard University Press, 2015).

Ryan P. Bonfiglio, "God and Gods," in *The Oxford Encyclopedia of the Bible and Theology*, ed. Samuel E. Balentine (New York: Oxford University Press, 2015) 1:412–26.

Claude Mellan (1598–1688). *Moses before the Burning Bush.* Engraving. 1663. (Credit: Metropolitan Museum of Art, Harris Brisbane Dick Fund, 1953, PD)

land to possess." At the heart of this statement lies God's fidelity to Abram's family. For a second time in the chapter, however, words of assurance have the opposite effect on doubting Abram.

Dialogue about Land, 15:8-18

Far from satisfied with God's plan to give them the land, Abram demands information: "O Lord (YHWH) GOD how am I to know I shall possess it?" (v. 8). He wants proof, certainty, knowledge of the unfolding future. He is not content to dwell safely in Canaan as he does now because fear rules him; he insists upon knowing that the land will belong to him in the future. Again, God honors Abram by replying to his fears, but the reply is not a direct intellectual response. God involves Abram in an action parallel to contemplating the stars, this time the performance of a liturgical ritual. [Covenant Ritual] In response to Abram's doubt, God instructs him to gather animals, including a heifer, a goat, a ram, and two birds—all traditional animal offerings in later legal texts (vv. 8-11).[3] By contrast to chapter 14 where Abram receives a blessing and offerings from the priest Melchizedek, here Abram assumes the priest-like role himself (15:8-18).

As Abram faces an opaque future, his doubts take the form of mental and spiritual darkness that increases across the ritual. He obeys divine instructions immediately, cuts the animals in half, and lays them on the ground. Suddenly, "birds of prey" swoop down

---

Covenant Ritual

A covenant or contract agreement between two parties often involved a ritual to solemnize it. Because there are no exact parallels to this ceremony—Jer 34:17-20 comes the closest—some interpreters have preferred to understand Abram's ritual as an enactment of an oath and not a full covenant rite (Westermann, 228–29). Yet the text uses the common term to describe covenant making, that is, to "cut a covenant" (15:18; Jer 34:17-20). Cutting language arises from the fact that cutting up animals was often part of covenant or treaty-making ceremonies. The ritual places responsibility on the covenant partners who call down upon themselves the fate of the spliced-open animals should they violate the covenant. In this ceremony, God alone "passes through" the cut-up animals, taking sole responsibility for the fulfillment of the covenant. This covenant, then, is a unilateral gift to Abram for which he is required to do nothing in return.

The ritual performed by Abram may represent common practice to seal a covenant in the ancient Near East. Here God is the suzerain or overlord who would exact punishment upon any violator of the covenant, including enemies who might interfere between the two parties (15:13-14). The covenant ritual responds to Abram's question by sealing and confirming the promise of land (vv. 7 and 18). The words and the ritual together comprise the divine response.

God makes a covenant with Abram two more times in Genesis, in chapter 17 and again in chapter 22 after the sacrifice or binding of Isaac (vv. 22:15-18).

For further reading, see Pauline A. Viviano, "Covenant," in *The Oxford Encyclopedia of the Bible and Law*, ed. Brent A. Strawn (Oxford and New York: Oxford University Press, 2015) 1:130–38.

Claus Westermann, *Genesis 12–36: A Commentary* (London: SPCK, 1981).

This engraving depicts Abraham sleeping (right), as the presence of God (symbolized by a smoking firepot and a blazing torch) passes between the carcasses and so seals the covenant between God and Abraham that his descendants will be as numerous as the stars in the sky.

Jan Goeree (1670–1731) and A. de Blois. "God's Covenant with Abraham." From *Historie des Ouden en Nieuwen Testaments* by David Martin (1639–1721). 1700. (Courtesy of the Pitts Theology Library, Candler School of Theology, Emory University)

upon the carcasses, but Abram drives them away (v. 11). This image of attacking birds gives a certain verisimilitude to the story because it is easy to imagine vultures, hawks, or falcons pouncing upon cut-up meats on the open ground. The preying birds also add an ominous threat to the scene, followed by the setting of the sun and deepening darkness (v. 12). In the dark Abram falls into a deep sleep, and that brings further terrors upon him. The intensifying darkness marks the passage of time toward night, of course, but it also signals the opaque and terrifying nature of the future that awaits him (15:13-16) as well as the overwhelming fear and awe that God's presence provokes. God's answer to his questions about land deepens the gloom rather than lifts it.

Abram's sacrifice and acts of worship create a literary frame (15:8-11, 17-21) around God's words at the center (15:12-16). God replies to Abram's desire to "know" that he will possess the land. An idiomatic construction that uses two forms of the Hebrew verb "to know" (*yādoa tēda*ʿ)—"knowing you will know" or "you will know surely" (15:13)—expresses certainty. Abram "will know for certain," know emphatically and without doubt. What he will know is the reverse of what he expects. He expects to know when they will possess the land, but what he will know is their absence from it and the suffering that lies ahead for his offspring. They will be "aliens in a land that is not theirs"; they will be slaves, oppressed for four hundred years (15:14). The four hundred years of suffering ahead refer to the story of Israel's exodus from Egypt after 430 years of servitude (Exod 12:40), but they also bring to mind the captivity of the book's audience to foreign empires. [400 Years] God reports that Abram's offspring will be foreigners, captives, oppressed people, not residents of their own land—the conditions facing the book's audience. Rather than reassuring Abram about the promise of land, God foretells a long time of darkness and pain.

When the ritual resumes, God returns to the subject of the present, assuring Abram again of his own safety (15:15). He will live to a ripe old age and go in peace to his ancestors; he will have a peaceful death. Quickly, however, the spotlight shifts from Abram to his offspring, that is, to the implied audience of the book. In the fourth generation they will return (v. 16). Four generations do not

400 Years

Exodus places the Israelites in Egypt for 430 years (Exod 12:40), while the reference to return in the fourth generation (v. 16) might add up to 100 years in some biblical calculations (Gen 6:3; Ps 90:10; Isa 65:20). Even if some people managed to live that long in those days, such an achievement of age would have been much less likely than in modern times. Fretheim has proposed that the fourth generation may refer to the "fourth generation" in Genesis, the sons of Jacob who return from Haran (48:22; see Fretheim, 446). This makes sense since in this commentary, I propose that the fourth generation in the Joseph stories most clearly engages the conditions of the Judean audience. (See Gen 37–50.)

Terence E. Fretheim, "Genesis" (*NIB* 1; Nashville: Abingdon, 1994).

add up to the 400 years mentioned in v. 13, so the meaning of this verse is not entirely clear, but it may suggest to the book's audience that they soon will resume life together in the land.[4] God's words to Abram continue to call forth the circumstances of the book's Judean audience. His descendants will return to the land after the fourth generation—in far less than 400 years—"for the iniquity of the Amorites is not yet complete" (15:16). [The Amorites] The time difference from return after 400 years, referring to the exodus, and return by the fourth generation, probably the book's audience, extends the promise of land into the future in two different ways. One way looks ahead to the narrative of Israel's beginnings, and the second refers to the future of the book's readers whose realities find particular expression in the fourth generation of Abraham's descendants in Genesis, that is, the stories of Joseph and Jacob's other sons (see chs. 37–50). The next verse promises "judgment on the nation that they serve" and that they "will come out with great possessions" (v. 14). This too points to Egypt as well as to Babylon and Persia.

The Amorites

The word "Amorite" underwent a long historical development. As far back as the third millennium BCE, it referred to a large swath of people in Mesopotamia, but by biblical times the term seems to have referred to linguistically specific peoples who lived in the mountains and east of the Jordan River (Pardee, 151–52). There is little mention of them or their specific iniquity in Genesis, leading to the likelihood that they function here symbolically. They are people living in the land and possibly stand in for occupiers in the time of the book's audience.

Dennis Pardee, "Canaan," in *The Blackwell Companion to the Hebrew Bible*, ed. Leo G. Perdue (Malden MA: Blackwell, 2001).

By now the sun has gone down and the darkness is even thicker, for it takes on dimensions beyond the absence of physical light. The darkness also signifies Abram's fearful mental state and forms a dramatic backdrop for the smoking pot and flaming torch that pass between the pieces of the sacrificed animals. The bright flame of the torch manifests God's presence in profound darkness and provides the most direct answer to Abram's question of how he will know he will possess the land (v. 8). The light in this bleak chapter comes from God, who is light in the midst of the most opaque darkness. The chapter conveys hope at the point of deepest hopelessness.

"On that day the LORD made a covenant with Abram saying, 'To your descendants I give this land'" (v. 18). In v. 7, Abram asks how he will know that he will possess the land. Here in v. 18, however, God moves away from Abram to his descendants. It is they who will inherit the land, they who are the recipients of the promise. At the narrative level of the Old Testament, Abram's descendants gain possession of the land five books later in the book of Joshua. Yet the descendants who matter most in the book of Genesis are its historical audience, displaced from their own land that is still occupied by other people whose "iniquity is not yet complete" (v. 16).

Abram knows that they will possess the land because of the covenant God makes with him, a covenant to which God will be loyal, for it is sealed in a ritual and God himself initiates it. God affirms the promise with this ceremony and further lays out the boundaries of the land that his descendants will possess. [Boundaries of the Land] Returning to the difficulties and impossibilities of the present, the promise comes with a list of the land's current occupants. [List of Occupants]

CONNECTIONS

One aspect of Abram's character in Genesis is that he believes quickly. In this chapter, God reckons him as righteous "because he believed the LORD" (v. 6) who promises him descendants more numerous than the stars of the sky. Believing surely means trusting, seeing the world afresh in a way that opens confidence for the future. Two verses later, however, Abram resides in darkness, asks for evidence, and wants to know how he will "know" that he is to receive the land. He wants intellectual content, concrete information, a way to gain confidence in the promise, and he does not know how to find it. He cannot see the future and everything looks impossible. In this chapter, his faith is anything but stable, marked by questions and demanding proof.

Abram believes the way many of us do, trusting one day, fearful and doubting the next. Faith does not stand against reason, but neither is it based on intellectual knowledge, insight into the future, or certainty that things will turn out as hoped. It is based on relationship with God, trust in the Lord, and hopeful confidence that there will be new life, no matter the form it takes.

Underneath Abram's anxiety in this family narrative lie the profound doubts and fears of the book's audience during and after the Babylonian Period. Like Abram, Judean survivors of the Babylonian invasions fear that they have no future. They require children to replenish the decimated population (cf. Jer 30:18-24).

Boundaries of the Land

The expanse of land promised in this covenant ceremony is at first glance enormous. It does not begin with the Nile as implied by "the river of Egypt." The Nile appears with a different word for river in other Old Testament texts (Gen 41:1; Exod 2:3, 5). Sarna has proposed that the phrase refers instead to a wadi or a dry riverbed "that marks the boundary between the settled land and the Sinai desert" (117). The other boundary, "the great river," has no clear referent in the topography. Perhaps the boundaries function to assure the people of a future in a land that will be more than adequate for them, beyond typical renderings of the land's boundaries.

Nahum M. Sarna, *Genesis* (JPS Torah Commentary; Philadelphia: The Jewish Publication Society, 1989).

List of Occupants

There are seventeen lists of pre-Israelite peoples in the historical books of the canon, but they exhibit a huge variety, featuring different numbers of peoples and only some repetition of names. "For seven nations see, Deut 7:1; Josh 3:10; 24:11. For six, see Exod 3:8, 17; 23:23, 33:2; etc. For five, see 13:5; I Kings 9:20; 2 Chron 8:7. For three, see Exod 23:28. For the Jebusites, see Josh 15:8; 18:28; Judg 19:10-11" (Sarna, 259, n. 23). The list of ten in Genesis 15 is the most comprehensive, but four of them appear nowhere else; the Kenites the Kennizzites, the Kadomites, and the Rephaim. The Jebusites who appear last refer to the people whom King David conquered to acquire Jerusalem.

Nahum M. Sarna, *Genesis* (JPS Torah Commentary; Philadelphia: The Jewish Publication Society, 1989). See also pp. 114–17..

They, too, doubt that their children will again have a nation of their own. Abram embodies an unsteady faith, and, as the stories unfold, he does not always seem to deserve divine approval for it. The design of Genesis 15 has rhetorical purposes beyond interest in the ancestral past. It seeks to persuade later generations to put aside their own real doubts and fears about the future and to trust God to bring them children and land. It mirrors to them the darkness and difficulties of the present, the questions that reflect hopelessness about the future, and provides a steady assurance from only one place: the presence of God who relates to them in covenant loyalty.

Contemporary readers may ask if such trust is even possible for human beings who live in fear, doubt, and uncertainty in its many manifestations. To me, it is a comfort that Abram's trust is not very solid. Strong at one moment, weak at the next, his doubt-filled faith wobbles and shakes. We never learn if his fears abate as the startling events of the covenant ceremony unfold in chapter 15, but we later see that he and Sarai keep trying to settle matters on their own, as if their trust was shallow and haunted by doubt.

For these reasons the chapter's presentation of darkness as a state of mind that is also a backdrop for divine presence has pointed significance. The darkness itself becomes the place where God's presence is manifested. In such spaces, all human constructions fail, proofs and intellectual knowledge are not up to the task, and powerlessness takes over. Yet it is exactly when human resourcefulness fails and powerlessness seems to control us that we can be most acutely able to receive help from beyond and become open to God and joined with other broken humans. In these conditions of fear and doubt, Abram meets God. That is the point at which we, too, are most open to the flaming torch of divine presence in our lives. [Darkness Is Pain]

Darkness Is Pain

The poet Christian Wiman received a diagnosis of aggressive cancer that, among other things, profoundly disrupted his life and plunged him into a form of spiritual darkness. That darkness he calls his "bright abyss," for the darkness, the pain, and the repeated prospect of oblivion became slowly and unsteadily an abyss that was illuminated from somewhere or someone beyond.

There is a sense in which love's truth is proved by its end, by what it becomes in us and what we, by virtue of love, become. But love, like faith, occurs in the innermost recesses of a person's spirit, and we can see only inward in this regard, and not very clearly when it comes to that. And then, too, there can be great inner growth and strength in what seems, from the outside, like pure agony or destruction. In the tenderest spots of human experience, nothing is more offensive than intellectualized understanding. "Pain comes from darkness / And we call it wisdom," writes Randall Jarrell. "It is pain." (Wiman, 19)

Yet for Wiman, this pain, this spiritual darkness itself, becomes a place to live, to search, to expand in consciousness to touch the divine fire.

Despite all that I have gone through, and despite all that I now face, I am still struck by the singular nature of the pain in the weeks after my diagnosis. It was not simply the fact itself searing though all the circumstances of my life, nor was it, as many people might suspect, the full impact of meaninglessness, the arbitrary nature of our existence, the utter illusion of God. No, it was an excess of meaning for which I had no context. It was the world burning to be itself beyond my ruined eye. It was God straining through matter to make me see, and to grant me peace of simple praise. (Wiman, 156)

By setting these two quotes from Wiman's "great abyss" next to each other, I do not mean to diminish the pain or depth of the migration through darkness or to suggest that the process of coming to praise is inevitable. I mean to say that living in the pain of darkness, the terror or doubt, and the sense that there is no future is a frequent path in religious life. I mean to suggest that we do not know the larger meanings of our individual lives or of our lives together, and, like Wiman and Abram, we too must learn to trust.

For further reading, see Christian Wiman, *My Bright Abyss: Meditation of a Modern Believer* (New York: Farrar, Strauss, and Giroux, 2013).

NOTES

1. Everett Fox, *The Five Books of Moses: Genesis, Exodus, Leviticus, Numbers, and Deuteronomy* (Schocken Bible; Dallas: Word, 1995) 65.

2. Walter Brueggemann, *Genesis* (Interpretation; Atlanta: John Knox, 1982) 145.

3. Claus Westermann, *Genesis 12–36: A Commentary* (London: SPCK, 1981) 225.

4. Nahum M. Sarna, *Genesis* (JPS Torah Commentary; Philadelphia: The Jewish Publication Society, 1989) 117.

FAMILY CONFLICTS

Genesis 16:1-16

When God declared that Abram's heir would be one of his own seed (15:4), Abram did not seem to realize that his own wife was included in the promise. Chapter 16 shifts the focus from him and his concerns to his two wives. Within the domestic arrangements of his household, Abram appears less heroic than in some previous chapters (except for 12:10-20). The main figure in chapter 16, however, is neither Abram nor Sarai but an Egyptian slave woman named Hagar. The chapter revolves around her treatment by Abram, Sarai, and God. Like Abram, she will become a recipient of divine promises and the foreparent of a great nation. At the chapter's beginning, however, that seems impossible. [Women in the Household]

The chapter divides into three units: the first takes place in Abram's household (16:1-6), the second occurs in the wilderness (16:7-14), and the last occurs back in the household (16:15-16). [Outline of Genesis 16] (Genesis 21 duplicates both the family conflicts and Hagar's escape from slavery into the wilderness, but it is not identical to it, for the later chapter advances the plot in important ways.)

> **Women in the Household**
>
> Particularly striking about this story is its repetitious vocabulary regarding the roles of the women. The text calls Hagar "slave girl" (*šiphah*) six times in vv. 1-8. It identifies her in a variety of ways as Sarai's own particular slave ("Sarai had an Egyptian slave girl," "my slave girl," "your slave girl," "slave girl of Sarai," vv. 1, 2, 3, 6, 7), and twice the chapter calls her an "Egyptian," that is, a foreigner, an outsider, not a full member of this family (vv. 1, 3). This linguistic insistence underscores Hagar's lowly status, Sarai's power as slave owner, and her privilege as Abram's wife (v. 1 and twice in v. 3), even though her relationship to Abram has been reported repeatedly since chapter 11. These domestic relationships are typical of hierarchical arrangement in the extended family in the ancient world. Abram is head of the family, Sarai is head of the household, and Hagar is enslaved to both.

> **Outline of Genesis 16**
>
> 1. The Women's Predicaments, 16:1-6
> 2. God Sees and Hears, 16:7-14
> 3. Hagar Returns, 16:15-16

The Women's Predicaments, 16:1-6

The fate of God's promise that Abram will become a great nation is the chapter's principal concern, but Abram and Sarai continue to face a childless future. Sarai decides to take matters into her own hands. Both she and her African slave Hagar face profound afflictions. Hagar could not be more powerless. She is of the lowest social status and has control over neither her body nor her life. Her mistress faces the hopeless but less horrible dilemma of being barren in a society that values women primarily for their childbearing capacities. Without a male child, she also faces the possibility of no one to support her in old age.

The opening verse reminds readers of what we already know: "Sarai, Abram's wife, bore him no children," and it introduces the second woman, "an Egyptian slave girl whose name was Hagar" (16:1). Despite their unequal roles as mistress and slave, the verse sets the two women next to each other as competitors in the events to follow.

Sarai's words and actions unleash subsequent events. She commands Abram to "go into my slave girl," that is, have intercourse with her, because "the LORD has prevented me from bearing children" (16:2). Consistent with ancient culture, Sarai interprets her childlessness as the action of God who opens and closes the womb. Not to bear a child was considered a form of curse or at least of exclusion from divine blessings. Because Sarai believes God has prevented her from becoming pregnant, she gives Hagar to her husband. "It may be that I shall obtain children by her" (16:2). [Surrogacy] This course of action, available in the ancient world where a slave can serve as surrogate, might produce a child who will legally belong to Sarai and bring the divine promise to fulfillment by force.

Surrogacy

Perhaps in an effort to exonerate Sarai and Abram, scholars have long pointed to parallel arrangements regarding surrogacy through slaves in ancient legal texts, including the Code of Hammurabi and a text from the Nuzi Tablets discovered at the beginning of the twentieth century. Legal parallels suggest that a woman may give her slave girl to her husband to bear his child who then becomes hers. Both of Jacob's wives, Rachel and Leah, give their slaves to Jacob to produce children for the family (ch. 30).

For further reading, see Claus Westermann, *Genesis 12–36: A Commentary* (London: SPCK, 1981) 238–39.

Although in the previous chapter God declared Abram righteous for his belief that he would have more children than the stars of heaven, he "listen[s] to the voice of Sarai" (16:2) and complies with her plan. To listen to someone's voice is an idiomatic expression in Hebrew that means "to obey." Does Abram obey Sarai because his faith is wobbling and her plan seems as good as any, or because he does not believe Sarai is part of the promise, or for his own sexual satisfaction? Of course, the text does not say, and, as often happens in Genesis, the situation appears all the more intriguing for its understatement. Perhaps the couple's ten years in Canaan without a child explains their mutual impatience to add a child to the family and take control of the promise. [Polygamy]

Even if we acknowledge that the practice of using slaves to gain children was accepted in the ancient world and in any world that practices slavery, the chapter depicts deep family tensions that act

Polygamy

Polygamy was an accepted form of marriage in ancient Israel.

The bond between the man and the woman in Gen 2:24 suggests a monogamous family in contrast with the polygamous families of Abraham (two wives, one slave, Hagar, belonging to Sarah), Esau (six wives) and Jacob (two wives, two slaves belonging to his wives) later in Genesis. These polygamous types of family structures appear as legitimate alternatives to monogamy . . . . Polycoity—a form of marriage in which a man takes other women who are of lower status—reflects the circumstances of Abraham, married to one legal wife, Sarah, and to one slave/concubine. (Steinberg, 282–83)

The legal wife brings money and/or property to the marriage, whereas lesser wives do not. The arrangements focus on the production of male heirs to ensure the passage of inheritance from one generation to another. The well-being of the family from generation to generation is the primary concern, not the fulfillment of the individuals involved.

For further reading, see Naomi A. Steinberg, "The World of the Family in Genesis," in *The Book of Genesis: Composition, Reception, and Interpretation*, ed. Craig W. Evans et al. (Boston: Brill, 2012).

Van Dyck's painting depicts the drama intensely, but he turns Hagar from an African slave to a Caucasian one to reflect his own Dutch audience.

Philip van Dyck (1680–1753). *Sarah Presenting Hagar to Abraham.* Oil on copper. Louvre, Paris, France. (Credit: © RMN-Grand Palais / Art Resource, NY)

as a critique of these arrangements. [Slave Girl and Rape] The violence appears in the verbs. Sarai "*took* Hagar, the Egyptian, her slave girl, and *gave* her to her husband Abram as a wife" (16:3). Sarai does not ask Hagar or even tell her; instead, she "takes" and "gives" her to Abram. To emphasize the force imposed on Hagar, the sentence varies the usual Hebrew order. The subject usually follows the verb—"Sarai took," as in the English translation—but this verse puts "took" (*lāqaḥ*) first ("took Sarai Hagar"). There are further indications of violence in the family arrangement. The verse repeats that Hagar is an "Egyptian, her slave girl," and it reminds readers that Abram is Sarai's husband. Yet Hagar too serves as a wife to Abram (16:3).[1] Her relationship with him lifts her status from Sarai's maid to second wife, a detail that will be important later in identifying Hagar's child as a legitimate son of Abram.[2]

Soon events take a happier turn. Hagar conceives a child and immediately rises in stature above her mistress. The NRSV translates Hagar's attitude toward Sarai this way: "she looked with contempt (*qālal*) upon her mistress" (16:4), but the Hebrew admits of a less hateful translation. The verb may mean to "treat lightly," that is, not to accord the proper honor due to her, i.e., "her mistress was light in her eyes" (16:4). Yet "contempt" may be exactly right to express Hagar's view of her mistress. Sarai's treatment of her was contemptible and, at the very least, gave her no choice in the matter. Now that she has conceived, Hagar resists returning to former arrangements, and the relative value of the two women in this patriarchal culture turns topsy-turvy. As mother-to-be of Abram's heir, Hagar can feel superior to her elderly, barren mistress Sarai who is using Hagar for her own ends.

It cannot be surprising, then, that Sarai is affronted, disturbed, and deeply jealous of Hagar. How could it be otherwise between them? Sarai's own husband has made love to her slave girl, and now that "uppity" slave threatens to displace her in his affections and the divine promises. [Lamin Sanneh on Polygamy] Meanwhile, in this dysfunctional family triangle, Sarai puts the burden of responsibility completely on Abram. "She has looked on me with contempt," she tells him and then curses him: "May the wrong done to me be upon you" (16:5). Moreover, if that were not enough retaliation against her husband, she wants the Lord to judge between her and him. (See [Curses].)

Even though Sarai initiated the plan herself, she believes Abram is at fault. He, in turn, responds to his wife's fury by refusing to step in and protect Hagar: "Your slave girl is in your power; do to her as you please" (16:6). He obeys his wife, as if domestic conflict were not his concern. "Then Sarai dealt harshly with her and she ran away from her" (16:6). Hagar has taken all she can bear and runs away into the wilderness. The Hebrew makes it clear that Hagar is not merely escaping the oppressive household but is running away "from her."

Lamin Sanneh on Polygamy

Yale professor of world Christianity Lamin Sanneh has described the challenges of growing up in a polygamous household in Gambia. His description mirrors some of the family dynamics in Genesis:

In traditional Gambia the social code allows a man up to four wives at any one time, and if they are of early childbearing age as is often the case, these wives among them can produce several dozen children, united in a common father and divided by having different mothers. The very ideas of unity and difference take on the peculiar complexity of polygamy. Sibling rivalry is rife among children of the same father, whereas children of the same mother observe a uterine pact that prescribes collaboration and mutual bonding . . . .

A husband of many wives may pretend to be above the fray but in truth the male ego is no match for the jealousy of women unsheathed for battle. . . . The man wishes strife away and when he meets it in his wives he flails in this and that direction, unsure of which way to turn. . . . It is easy enough to appreciate the husband's weakened influence: individually or in concert, the co-wives are the prime movers in the domestic sphere, with the man bobbing in and out of his wives' lives on a rotation dictated by the women's natural cycles. (27–28)

Lamin Sanneh, *Summoned from the Margin: Homecoming of an African* (Grand Rapids MI: William B. Eerdmanns, 2012).

Rembrandt's Interpretation of Abram's Family

Rembrandt's pen and ink drawing of the scene in Gen 16:1-6 captures the moment when Sarai accuses Abram of wronging her. Abram stands before both wives—the tall, stately, youthful Hagar with the beautiful face and the bent-over elderly Sarai with the cane and line-blotched face. Sarai extends her hand as if to speak to Abram, but Abram is clearly in charge and impatient with the situation. He has his back to viewers with one foot pointing forward on the path on which he is traveling and the other pointing toward the women, as if impatiently waylaid from more important activities. He appears to chide Sarai as he gives away authority to her and acknowledges her unlimited power in domestic matters.

Rembrandt interprets the family conflict in ways slightly different from the text itself. The famous Renaissance artist adds a peacock to the scene. In the history of art, the peacock can refer to arrogance and pride, but who is the prideful one in the painting? All three figures seem to behave with pride that harms others. The peacock, however, also signifies the figure of Jesus in paintings from Western art, not as a symbol of pride but of beauty and resurrection on the belief that the peacock's flesh did not decay after death (Jordan). If this is Rembrandt's intention, then the inclusion of the peacock connects both testaments and recognizes Jesus as offspring of Abram.

Elaine Jordan, "The Symbolism of the Peacock," traditioninaction.org/religious/f023_Peacock.htm (accessed 19 March 2018).

Rembrandt van Rijn (1606–1669). "Sarah Complains of Hagar to Abraham." Pen and brown ink. (Credit: © Bayonne, Bonnat-Helleu Museum/photo A. Vaquero)

God Sees and Hears, 16:7-16

When Hagar flees to the wilderness, she heads for her native land on the road to Shur.[3] The decision to run means probable death, but death must seem better than her present situation. A pregnant woman alone in a hostile terrain with little food, no shelter, and in danger of assault is in great peril. Yet in the Old Testament

Wilderness

The wilderness refers to dry desert places and to open grazing land for animals that is sparsely populated by humans. Within the Bible, the wilderness is a place of encounter with the divine. It is sacred space wherein basic revelation takes place. God's appearance to Hagar in the wilderness signals God's choice of the Egyptian slave woman, the ultimate outsider, as one to whom God is faithful in the grimmest circumstances, so "the place of peril becomes a safe haven for the nurturing . . . of life" (Dempsey, 69). It also reveals choice and inclusion of other peoples in the divine plan, for in Genesis God is God of all peoples.

For further reading, see Carol J. Dempsey, "The Wilderness: Sacred Space, Endangered Homeland, Hope for Our Planet," in *Turning to the Heavens and the Earth: Theological Reflections on a Cosmological Conversion, Essays in Honor of Elizabeth A. Johnson* (Collegeville MN: Liturgical, 2016) 61–80.

Camille Corot (1796–1875). *Hagar in the Wilderness*. 1835. Oil on canvas. (Credit: Rogers Fund, 1938, Metropolitan Museum of Art, PD)

the wilderness is often a place of divine encounter, and so it is for Hagar. [Wilderness] In this remarkable scene, the "Angel of the LORD" finds her by a spring of water. [The Angel of the LORD]

What follows is a dialogue between Hagar and the angel whom readers slowly discover is actually God. The angel finds her, speaks to her, and expresses full knowledge of her situation. "Hagar, slave girl of Sarai, where have you come from and where are you going?" (16:8). This question has long tentacles. She replies to the first part: "I am running away from my mistress, Sarai." The second part, "where are you going?" is unknown to her. Left unanswered, it foreshadows her return to Abram's family and her future when she will no longer be a slave but mother of her own people. [Hagar, Mother of Islam]

The Angel of the LORD

ΑΩ "The Angel of the LORD" translates a Hebrew phrase meaning "messenger of YHWH." The messenger performs a variety of tasks in the Old Testament, such as announcing births, giving reassurances, commissioning people, communicating with prophets, and speaking with individuals. Carol Newsom has pointed out that these figures may communicate divine promises or reveal the future, but they are not necessarily unique figures with any qualities that distinguish one from another. Instead, they are paradoxical, at one moment seeming distinct from God and at the next manifesting divine presence and indistinct from God. Such is the case in this scene with Hagar. In the wilderness the angel or messenger appears to be a separate from but then merges into "the God who sees," while messenger language falls away.

For further reading, see Carol A. Newsom, "Angels," *ABD* 1:248–53.

Hagar is running away from her mistress, but surprisingly, instead of rescuing her from enslavement and abuse, the angel sends her back to "submit to her" (16:9). [Return to Slavery] Along with the shocking command to return to her house of pain, the angel makes promises to her: "I will so greatly multiply your offspring that they cannot be counted for multitude" (16:10). The promise of uncountable offspring in Genesis is reserved for the patriarchs of Israel. Like them, Hagar will be the foreparent of many children, more than can be enumerated, but for this to happen, her child must survive. She must have the protection of a family and live in relative safety, not alone in the wilderness. Her return reestablishes her place as a second wife of Abram and her child's status as Abram's firstborn son. For these reasons, she has to go back.

Yet the promise of multiple offspring is a prologue to even more astonishing events. The One who hears her cry, the angel of the LORD who speaks to her in the wilderness, is not merely a divine messenger but God. In a burst of poetry, the angel reveals divine identity, tells her of her child's future life, and speaks of special

---

Hagar, Mother of Islam

Although Hagar does not appear in the Quran, she is depicted as the mother of Islam in pre-Quranic lore.

God's promise to Hagar indicates that God is not limited to the Hebrews. In this passage God promises to create another people who will be numerous. (Miguel, 176)

Miguel A. De La Torre, *Genesis* (Belief; Louisville KY: Westminster John Knox).

Return to Slavery

That God sends Hagar back into a household of enslavement seems appalling, leading Delores Williams to declare that in this text, God is "no liberator God" (20). Yet she further points out that the issue here seems to be first and foremost survival. A woman alone (or with a child, ch. 21) in the wilderness, without the protection of a family or food and shelter that they offer, is open to all kinds of peril. Returning to harsh treatment and afflictions might preserve life. The command to return has the larger purpose of keeping Hagar and her son within the family of Abram and to remind readers that she and Ishmael are also the family of Abraham.

Rodney S. Sadler, Jr., has put the matter differently. He has noticed that in the two accounts of Hagar, chs. 16 and 21, and in the stories of Jacob's wives, God treats the male offspring of slaves with concern for their welfare, a concern that does not extend to the mothers.

So what do we as children of disenfranchised, enslaved, raped, and otherwise abused Africana peoples have to do with texts that assume the commonplace nature of such behavior [misogynistic treatment of women]? How can we sing "Father Abraham" without examining his exploitation of Hagar? . . . How is it that we have traditionally identified with the protagonists of these narratives who have perpetrated the patterns of oppression, the legacy of which we ourselves suffer? (76)

Sadler has provided no answers but urges critical attention to what the texts say about family and God. His questions invite all readers of these texts to consider their larger purposes and to struggle not only with what they say about the lives of our ancestors in faith but also how the texts can continue to affect lives of contemporary believers.

For further reading, see Delores S. Williams, *Sisters in the Wilderness: The Challenge of Womanist God-Talk* (Maryknoll NY: Orbis, 1993) 15–33.

Rodney S. Sadler, Jr., "Genesis," *The Africana Bible: Reading Israel's Scriptures from Africa and the African Diaspora* (Minneapolis: Fortress, 2010).

relationship with her. God has seen her suffering. [The Annunciation in Luke]

> "Now you have conceived and shall bear a son;
> you shall call him Ishmael,
> for the LORD has given heed to your affliction." (16:11)

Within prose narratives of Genesis, poetry works as a device to draw attention to significant words. This poetic piece is no exception. In it, the angel addresses the Egyptian slave woman to announce that she will give birth to a son and name him "Ishmael." The name derives from the Hebrew verb "to hear" (*šāmaʿ*) and means "God hears." What God hears or gives "heed to" is the affliction of this abandoned, dehumanized, and harshly abused slave woman.

God hears her pain in all its concreteness and, hearing it, provides a future for her that no one could anticipate. Ishmael, child of Abram, will be "a wild ass of a man," at war with everyone and at odds with his own kin, notably Abram's future children. The angel's poetic anticipation of Hagar's future reminds readers that she stands not only for this one Egyptian woman but also for all her offspring. In Islamic lore, she will become the foremother of

---

The Annunciation in Luke

The first chapter of the Gospel of Luke contains two annunciations by angels that parallel the announcement to Hagar in some details. An angel of the Lord appears to Zechariah in the temple and tells him his barren wife, Elizabeth, will give birth to a son who will be named John (Lk 1:11-13). In Luke, the angel is clearly a messenger of God with his own name, Gabriel, who provokes fear and disbelief in Zechariah rather than the wondrous amazement of Hagar in Genesis. Mary, too, receives word from an angel that she will conceive and bear a son whom she will name Jesus (Lk 1:31). The angel reassures her, and she believes the angel and the angel's report to her that her cousin has also conceived, because "nothing is impossible with God" (Lk 1:37). The annunciation of Hagar is a likely source not only for Luke's accounts but also for the presence of God, who creates life from impossible circumstances. Elizabeth will conceive despite old age and barrenness, and Mary will conceive by the power of the Holy Spirit.

Giovanni Francesco Barbieri (Guercino) (1591–1666). "The Angel of the Annunciation." c. 1638/1639. Drawing. Pen and brown ink with brown wash. (Credit: Julius S. Held Collection, Ailsa Mellon Bruce Fund, National Gallery of Art, Washington, DC)

the Ishmaelites, and ultimately of Muslims. Hagar responds to her encounter with God as a theologian who dares to name God from her own experience. She calls God "El Roi," that is, "the God who sees" (16:15). Elsewhere in the Old Testament, God tells others the divine name, or human speakers use given names for God already known in the community. Hagar finds her own name for God. It is intimate, personal, and a witness to God's work in her life. God alone in this story sees her, and what God sees is her affliction. Then, in a play on words, she reflects on the reciprocity of that seeing. God sees her and she sees God. "Have I really seen God and remained alive after seeing him?" (16:13). [Seeing God]

Seeing God

The Hebrew of 16:13 is not entirely clear, but whether Hagar sees God as in a vision or encounters God in some other fashion, she does have some sort of transcendent experience of the divine. She knows that God witnesses her in her danger and is present to her so that she can name the place in relation to that experience. There is a tradition in ancient Israel that a direct sight of God face to face would be so overwhelming that a person would die. In Exod 33:20-23, God appears to Moses but sets him in the cleft of a rock and places the divine hand over him to protect him from the sight of God's face: "you shall see my back, but my face shall not be seen."

In this chapter, God is the only One who actually sees Hagar's suffering. Neither Abram nor Sarai see her, hear her, speak to her, or call her by name. Only God does that. This God stands with the enslaved and afflicted, the vulnerable and invisible members of society. Hagar names God from her realization of God's intimate presence in the deprived conditions of her life. Along with learning that this is a God who hears her affliction, she knows now that God perceives her and that she has met God. Seeing, hearing, and speaking are mutual exchanges between God and Hagar. At this point, the language "angel of the LORD" disappears completely, and she identifies the one with whom she has been conversing as the "God who sees."

Next comes a "therefore," a reason for telling the story. These events are so important that a place gains its name on account of them. The well where this encounter with God took place is called Beer lahairoi, meaning "well of the living one who sees me." It happened between two places in the Negeb. [Stories about Place Names]

Stories about Place Names

A long history of interpretation maintains that stories that end with the naming of a place may have arisen as a kind of explanation of the place itself, the way the story of Lot's wife turning to a pillar of salt explains a topographical phenomenon. These are called etiological stories (11:1-9) because they explain origins of places or things. But another way to think about stories of place is to reverse their interpretation. The events in the story are so important that they give name to a place, nailing down and underlining the revelatory event by attaching them to a place. It may be that Hagar's theophany is what mattered more to the storyteller, who punctuated its importance by connecting it to a place.

Hagar Returns, 16:15-16

The chapter concludes without reporting the kind of reception Hagar received when she returned to slavery, but it does report that she bore a son to Abram.[4] Abram does the naming, not Hagar, perhaps legitimating the child as his own firstborn son,[5] and he names their child Ishmael just as the angel of the LORD proclaimed in the wilderness. The sentence mentions Hagar's name three times so that readers do not miss the fact that this African slave bore Abram's firstborn. Her son is his child as much as Sarai's son Isaac will be. Then we hear of Abram's age, eighty-six years old when Hagar bore Ishmael. A barely imaginable conception and birth have happened.

CONNECTIONS

To be seen in one's suffering is to receive a most basic form of compassion. For another to see you as you are, to recognize your pain, shame, and dehumanization and reflect it back to you, is to have your humanity restored. To have such a witness means that you are no longer isolated; someone sees you in your present unbearable reality, recognizes you behind your illness or your loss, your humiliation or your terror, and forms a bond of common humanity, even if nothing else can be done to help. You can realize that you are neither absolutely isolated nor crazy. Your circumstances may have destroyed the usual marks of human dignity, but you remain a human being.

God sees and hears in this chapter, but the one seen, heard, and addressed is neither Abram nor Sarai. God attends to the foreigner, the captive woman, the sex slave, and the surrogate mother who has no voice in the matter. Even the fact that motherhood was considered the crowning achievement for women in ancient Israel does not take away from the violence inflicted upon Hagar. The text shows no one recognizing her human dignity but God alone. God sees her affliction and God hears her cry. This is a profound revelation of the God who sees and hears the afflicted ones, the invisible, the disregarded and displaced.[6]

Hagar's encounter with the angel/Lord also reveals with special clarity that Israel's God is the God of all peoples, not merely of chosen Israel, but God even of Israel's opponents and enemies. The testimony of this chapter is that Israel's future opponents are Abram's family, kinfolk. They share a claim to common blood among them and an equal claim to divine protection.

Contemporary members of the three Abrahamic faiths—Judaism, Christianity, and Islam—are only now beginning to recognize the implications of these relationships and of the biblical insistence that we are all children of Abram and of Abram's God.

We are one family, dysfunctional, yet united as members of the family of the One God. [Three Monotheistic Faiths]

Each of these Abrahamic communities has its own preferred names for God. Following in the tradition of Hagar, they speak of God from their own experiences of the divine. Jews often avoid saying the Divine Name, YHWH, and may instead call God Adonai or the Name (*Ha Shem*) or the Holy One. Many Christian names for God derive from the roles of men in ancient societies: Father, Judge, Lord, and Redeemer (i.e., the one who buys back the slave, the property, or the debt). Muslims refer to God primarily as Allah, but each of these traditions also has a long list of other names. When Hagar names God from her own experience as the God who sees, she shows the way forward. All three faiths hold that God is beyond every name, not containable by any

---

Three Monotheistic Faiths

Judaism, Islam, and Christianity trace their origins to Abraham. Genesis presents Isaac and Ishmael as brothers, descendants of the same father and inheritors of the promise. Abraham is thus the source of the three monotheistic faiths, of believers in the One God. Old Testament scholar Jon Levenson has pointed out, however, that the three faiths have their own unique understandings of Abraham that conflict with one another and support the particular identity of each group (173–214).

Ulrich Rosenhagen has summarized these differences:

For Jews, the biblical patriarch Abraham is chosen by God. Through him the people of Israel are also chosen as his descendants. God made a covenant with Abraham, who dutifully passed all tests of faith, showing his willingness to sacrifice his own son if required by God. In rabbinical literature, Abraham is represented as the exemplary Jew who faithfully follows the commandments of the Torah.

For Christians, the biblical patriarch is a central link between the Old and the New Testament. He serves as illustration of St. Paul's notion of justification by faith, and as an exemplar of faith he is somewhat of a Christian ideal type. No longer is he the one who observes the Torah; instead he's the one who is justified because of his faith in God. Thus Abraham is the "father of all Christians," and anyone who believes in Christ is a true descendant of Abraham.

For Muslims, Abraham belongs to the 21 biblical prophets mentioned in the Qur'an. He is an iconoclast who repeatedly passes God's muster, and even shows willingness to sacrifice his son. Abraham is the arche-

type of complete submission to God. He also initiates the cult at Mecca. (30–33)

Despite these differences, however, Rosenhagen believes that Abraham is a rich point of unity among the three faiths and a resource for civic conversation in the United States: "What some see as a problem for Abrahamic civic discourse . . . [may be] its greatest asset. Perhaps it even provides a fresh opportunity to reflect more profoundly on interreligious dialogue and otherness" (32).

Faithful interaction among them [the three faiths] would encourage a theology of difference that offers a much improved sense of their own particularity as well as a theologically enriched language to engage and interact with each other. Equipped with a theology of otherness and difference created under the Abrahamic paradigm, Americans would have a way to negotiate between the Protestant canopy of the founding, the unifying appeal of Judeo-Christianity, and the growing religious pluralism of the 21st century. Even though we cannot draw on a neutral UR-Abraham [original Abraham] as grand metaphor for peace, the paradigm does offer a new point of reference for the American marriage between faith and democracy. The discourse of the children of Abraham can spearhead efforts to define mutual ideas and values we share as Americans while we better appreciate our commonalities *and* differences. (33)

Jon Levenson, *Inheriting Abraham: The Legacy of the Patriarch in Judaism, Christianity, and Islam* (Princeton NJ: Princeton University Press, 2012).

Ulrich Rosenhagen, "One Abraham or Three?" *Christian Century*, 9 December 2015.

name, ultimately not fully nameable. This God has many names, and Hagar provides one: the God who sees.

NOTES

1. The Hebrew *ʾiššâh* means both " woman" and "wife."

2. Mignon R. Jacobs, *Gender, Power, and Persuasion: The Genesis Narratives and Contemporary Portraits* (Grand Rapids MI: Baker Academic, 2007) 146.

3. Nahum M. Sarna, *Genesis* (JPS Torah Commentary; Philadelphia: The Jewish Publication Society, 1989) 120.

4. Hagar's life and her naming of God have received attention from many women scholars. See especially Phyllis Trible, *Texts of Terror: Literary Feminist Readings of the Old Testament* (Philadelphia PA: Fortress, 1984) 30; Elsa Tamez, "The Woman Who Complicated Salvation History," in *New Eyes for Reading: Biblical and Theological Reflections by Women from the Third World*, ed. John S. Pobee and Bärbel von Wartenberg-Potter (Oak Park IL: Meyer-Stone, 1987) 5–17; Delores S. Williams, *Sisters in the Wilderness: The Challenge of Womanist God-Talk* (Maryknoll NY: Orbis, 1993) 15–33; and Suzanne Scholz, *Sacred Witness: Rape in the Hebrew Bible* (Minneapolis: Fortress, 2010) 57–63.

5. Sarna, *Genesis*, 122.

6. For further reading, see Kathleen M. O'Connor, *Lamentations and the Tears of the World* (Maryknoll NY: Orbis, 2002) 96–109.

COVENANT AGAIN

Genesis 17:1-27

As an account of the origins of God's covenant with Abram, chapter 17 has features in common with chapter 15. [Two Stories of the Covenant] Both covenant-making narratives take place within the context of worship, and both address Abram's continuing doubts about the promises. Chapter 17, however, proceeds as if chapter 15 had never happened and differs from it in significant ways.[1] It assumes Ishmael's birth (ch. 16), identifies Sarai alone as covenant matriarch, and depicts the covenant as a two-way agreement between God and Abram. Even liturgical rituals differ in chapter 17. In response to divine initiative, Abram prostrates himself rather than sacrificing animals as he does in chapter 15. In addition, God makes male circumcision the sign of membership in the covenant community and gives Abram and Sarai new names.

   These differences raise the question of how the two chapters relate to one another. The usual interpretive answer is that the two versions of covenant-making come from different sources,[2] but the chapters also serve different purposes in Genesis. Chapter 17 moves the promises closer toward fulfillment. Its center is a speech in which God announces covenant obligations that involve both divine and human covenant partners (17:1-21). Then God exits the scene as Abraham enacts his responsibility to circumcise all the men of his household (17:23-27). [Outline of Genesis 17]

COMMENTARY

Repetitive language expresses the chapter's special interests. In particular, it emphasizes the extension of the promises from Abraham to his offspring "after you" (vv. 7 [two times], 8, 9, 10, 19), and to subsequent "generations" (vv. 9, 12). By implication, these generations necessarily include the book's ancient audience. The chapter also insists that the covenant with Abraham is eternal like the covenant with Noah (9:8-17). For the audience, the ancestral covenant remains intact even though historical circumstances indicate otherwise. Despite the covenant's apparent demise in the nation's fall to

Two Stories of the Covenant

Doublets, two versions of the same story, occur regularly in Genesis. For example, Hagar departs for the wilderness twice (chs. 16 and 21), Abram abandons Sarai to a ruler's harem twice (12:10-20 and 20:1-18; a third version involves Isaac), and twice God makes a covenant with Abram (chs.15 and 17). While these doublets repeat the same or similar events, the two stories are not identical. The second version of the covenant, for example, advances the plot toward fulfillment of the promises.

Although both covenant-making chapters incorporate dialogue, promises, and worship, an outline of events shows how the two are different.

Chapter 15

The covenant account in chapter 15 emphasizes Abram's fear and, by implication, fear among the book's ancient audience. The chapter takes the form of a dialogue between God and Abram. Abram's questions bring fear to the forefront. God addresses the fear by promising children, land, and a return to the land, even though others occupy it.

God tells Abram not to fear.
Abram challenges God because he has no child.
God promises him his own child.
Abram believes and God declares him righteous.
Abram challenges God to tell him how he will know he will have land.
God orders a liturgy of animal sacrifice.
God tells Abram he will know that his offspring will be aliens.
God promises a return of his offspring in four generations.
Darkness and terror dominate and deepen across the scene.
At the end of the chapter, God makes a covenant, appears as fire, and reiterates the promise of land to Abram.

Chapter 17

Chapter 17 emphasizes mutuality of the covenant "between you and me," its eternal nature, the perpetual gift of land, and the practice of male circumcision as a sign of the covenant. Its form combines a divine speech (vv. 1-16), dialogue (vv. 17-22), and a narrative of action (vv. 22-24). Like chapter 15, it addresses the book's audience but in different ways. By stressing covenant mutuality, its eternal nature, and the sign of circumcision, God assures them of a future bound to God in the land. Disruption of their national life under the Babylonian Empire has not permanently ended their life. The sign of circumcision imprints this upon male bodies forever.

God orders Abram to walk before him and be whole (blameless).
God announces the covenant "between me and you" and reiterates the promise of offspring.
Abram falls on his face.
God changes Abram's name to Abraham.
God promises that nations shall come from Abraham.
God declares that the covenant "between you and me" will be everlasting.
God will be "God to you and to your offspring after you."
God promises the land as a "perpetual holding."
God commands Abraham to keep the covenant throughout the generations by circumcising every male.
God gives instructions about circumcision.
God reiterates the promise of offspring and promises that Sarai, now Sarah, will be mother.
Abraham falls on his face laughing.
Abraham puts forth Ishmael as heir, but God insists on Sarah's child.
God promises to give Ishmael numerous offspring.
God promises that Isaac will be heir of the covenant.
Abraham circumcises all the males of the household.

Chapter 17 is exceedingly important in assuring the people of Judah that although their life as God's people in the land has been ruptured, it is not over. This version of the covenant's origins builds hope and encourages confidence that Judah has a future in the land, even if their present situation seems to make national reconstitution appear impossible, even laughable.

Babylon, it is still active, still in effect, and still includes them, for it is eternal. This story teaches them that God is still their covenant partner because God declared it so to Abraham at their foundation as a people. His offspring will continue to grow and will again possess the land.

God Promises to Make a Covenant with Abram, 17:1-3

The narrator continues to remind readers of the difficulties that stand in the way of the promises. Abram is ninety-nine years old, far too old to father vigorous children needed to become a great nation. Amid this deep cavern of impossibility, God speaks: "I am God Almighty" (*El Shaddai*, perhaps meaning "God of the Mountains," 17:1). [El Shaddai] Self-identifying with this mysterious title, God commands Abram to "walk before me and be blameless" (*tāmîm*). To be *tāmîm* is to live rightly with God and all creation. It involves more than being "blameless" (NRSV) or free of offense. *Tāmîm* means to be whole, to have integrity and right orientation to God and to all that is. Fox's translation has captured the nuances of the Hebrew: "Walk in my presence! And be wholehearted!"3 Of course, such a wholehearted person lives an ethical life but is not simply blameless. To walk in God's presence means to live with God, to walk through life in divine presence. This relationship is the essential meaning of covenant, and from it flow responsibilities as a response to it and an expression of it. Living rightly in God's presence (*tāmîm*) is the proper response to God's invitation to covenant, not its origin.

El Shaddai

AΩ The meaning, origins, and etymology of *El Shaddai* are uncertain. *Shaddai* turns up in many poetic texts, leading Sarna to conclude that the term might be very ancient but later lost its vitality. Some interpreters have noted the relationship of *Shaddai* to an Akkadian word for mountain, identifying Israel's God as the God of the mountain. Others have pointed to similarities with the Hebrew word for "breast" and suggest that the term lends female connotations to the biblical portrait of God. *El Shaddai* was translated as "Almighty" in both the Septuagint (Greek) and the Vulgate (Latin), and the practice has "continued in modern translations, if only for want of one that is more precise" (Sarna, 384–85). The title conveys strength, mystery, and power and perhaps did not need explanation (Cotter, 108).

Nahum M. Sarna, "Excursus 11," *Genesis* (JPS Torah Commentary; Philadelphia: The Jewish Publication Society, 1989).

David Cotter, *Genesis* (Berit Olam; Collegeville MN: Liturgical Press, 2003).

The next verse lays out the formal framework of this divine-human relationship. It will be a covenant "between me and you," an agreement of intimacy and mutuality, not a one-sided gift from God as in the covenant with Noah and all creation or like the covenant with Abram in chapter 15 (15:18). Although God is still the one who initiates the relationship, this covenant involves two parties, "you and me," each with obligations to the other. [Covenant as a Root Metaphor] God's self-imposed responsibilities begin with the promise of children: "I will make you exceedingly numerous." This promise, reiterated from Abram's first encounter with God (12:2), is now solemnized in a formal contract, a covenant. The ritual of the covenant assures Abram that the impossible will happen. In response, Abram prostrates himself ("falls on his face") in a liturgical act of obedience, submission, and awe (v. 3).[4] [Types of Covenant]

Covenant as a Root Metaphor

Covenant is a major metaphor to speak of God's relationship with Israel and the cosmos in the Old Testament.

Closely related to promise, perhaps even an alternative version of it, is *covenant* (vv. 2-7 [italics original]) . . . the covenant is the primary metaphor for understanding Israel's life with God. It is the covenant which offers to Israel the gift of hope, the reality of identity, the possibility of belonging, the certitude of vocation. (Brueggemann, 154)

Borrowed from ancient political, commercial, and treaty arrangements, covenants involve formal agreements or contracts wherein one party or two "promise to perform or refrain from certain actions stipulated in advance" (Mendenhall and Herion, 1:1185).

In chapter 15, God provides the terms and alone declares faithfulness to the promises of children and land. Chapter 17 places requirements upon Abraham and his household, and the requirements will be two-directional. The covenant will be "between me and you" (vv. 3, 7, 9), and it extends to Abraham's offspring.

Covenant is a particularly popular way of speaking of relationship with God among many Protestant communities today. It condenses into one word the divine-human relationship in both its fidelities and responsibilities, and it joins the old and new testaments of Christian faith. In my experience, the term is less central among contemporary Roman Catholics and Orthodox Christians. Instead, the language of popular spirituality among them often focuses on the Eucharist, the sacrament of the new covenant. Although the approach is different, Eucharistic language draws from the same connections between Old and New Testament and articulates the intimate relationship of God and humans in New Testament terms. Both covenant and Eucharist express faith in God's grace-giving relationship with believers. Both begin with divine grace, God's free gift of life and love. Both involve good works and righteous living as a free and loving response to God's grace. Humans do not win grace; they receive it as a gift.

Walter Brueggemann, *Genesis* (Interpretation; Louisville: Westminster John Knox, 2010).

George Mendenhall and Gary A. Herion, "Covenant," *AB*.

"As for Me," 17:4-8

The chapter's second unit lays out covenant stipulations that bind both parties. God's words stress divine commitment. The emphatic Hebrew uses the first person independent pronoun and the by now familiar exclamation "look" or "behold" (*hînnēh*) that often signals important speech in Genesis. "As for me (*'ănî hînnēh*), this is my covenant with you." The Hebrew phrase means something like "Look, I, I will covenant with you." The next sentence repeats the promise of offspring but with significant expansion, for Abram will not only beget many children; he will be the father of nations. "You will be ancestor of a multitude of nations" (17:4). [Father of Many Nations]

As part of the covenant-making event, God changes Abram's name to Abraham, probably meaning the "father of many." Then God repeats the promise in a slightly altered fashion: "I have made you (*nětîkkā*) the ancestor of a multitude of nations" (17:5). This time the promise of offspring is no longer a simple future event such as "I will make you the ancestor." Here it is completed or past tense: "I have made you the ancestor of multitudes." It is already done; the future is certain and all that remains is for events to come to pass.

Types of Covenant

Involving complex understandings of how God relates to people and creation, biblical covenants fall into two general types, conditional and unconditional. Old Testament interpreter, Safwat Marzouk has provided an overview and also connected covenants with the crisis of Babylonian Period and its aftermath:

> While all of the covenants found in the Hebrew Bible are initiated by God and thus all of these covenants are expressions of God's grace, some of the formulations of the covenant highlighted its conditional nature: if . . . then. If the people obey the laws of the covenant, then they would receive blessings and if they disobey, then they bear the consequences. Other formulations of the covenant between God and the people present the covenant as a grant from God with no conditions attached to it. The former, the conditioned covenant, i.e. the covenant at Sinai, helped to explain the exile as a just divine punishment because the people have breached the covenant. The latter, the unconditional covenants with Noah, Abraham, David along with the New Covenant of Jeremiah and the Covenant of peace in Ezekiel, these covenants played a significant role in offering hope to the people who suffered from the alienation of the exile, proclaiming that God is faithful and is loyal to God's people. The Old Testament does not have one covenant but multiple ones. Interestingly, however, the writers of the New Testament were able to see a fundamental connection between these covenants and the divine covenant with all humanity through Jesus Christ.
>
> The events that surrounded the exile of the people of Judah around 587 BCE brought to question all of the institutions and beliefs that the people of God relied on for a few centuries. The collapse of walls of Jerusalem, and the temple, and the monarchy left the people disoriented and dismayed. This disaster tested the glue that held the people together as the discourse of blame dominated the relationship between the different groups among the people. Who was more righteous? Those who were exiled to Babylon or those who remained in Jerusalem? Who was more righteous? Those who remained outside of the land or those who returned to the land after the exile ended? Theologically speaking, the suffering and pain, the shame and despair left the people wondering about what has gone wrong: whose fault is it? Has God abandoned us, has God forgotten God's covenant? Or is it our sin and unfaithfulness that has brought all of this upon us? A disaster like the exile has generated a complex set of theological engagements with the Israelite traditions including the theme of the covenant.

Safwat Marzouk, "The Paradoxes of the Covenantal Relationships," paper presented to the Mennonite Church of Canada Assembly 2016, Saskatoon, 6–10 July 2016.

God returns to the future or incomplete form of the Hebrew verbs, perhaps to include the audience who await a future:

> "I will make you exceedingly fruitful:
> and I will make nations of you,
> and kings shall come from you." (17:6)

The promise of future progeny extends forward through history and includes nations and kings who will descend from Abraham. The composers and editors of this text live among Abraham's descendants and know that nations and kings and many peoples have descended from him. These words of assurance address the later generations, probably the book's audience in the Persian Period. The eternal covenant and the promise of many children in the midst of barrenness and impossible odds concern them. The next verse confirms this connection between Abraham's time and that of the audience:

Father of Many Nations

📖 That Abraham becomes "an international figure, the father of a multitude of nations and an ancestor of kings may signify the fulfillment of the promise that all the families of the earth will be blessed through Abraham (12:3)" (Levenson, 49–54). Yet who are these many blessed nations? Various faith traditions have approached this question differently.

In Christian interpretation, all who have faith through Christ Jesus (Rom 4:11; Gal 3:14), that is, the children of father Abraham, make up different ethnic groups in the Church (Levenson, 52). Jewish interpretation similarly has held that all the ethnic groups making up Judaism are the multitude of nations of whom Abraham is father.

Within the book of Genesis, however, Jewish scholar Jon Levenson has proposed more specifically that the Abraham is father of different nationalities around Canaan at the time, not all the people of the world. Genesis explicitly connects Ishmaelites, Edomites, and offspring of the six sons of Abraham, including Midian, to father Abraham. Levenson's interpretation makes historical sense since the

composers of Genesis would likely have had immediate neighbors in mind. Theologically, however, the text implies that Abraham's role as father of many nations establishes family connections among the three monotheistic faiths. All people are his descendants.

Islamic interpretation, by contrast to the views of Judaism and Christianity, finds in Abraham a father who is an example of true faith for all people, including Mohammed, yet it assumes that all people must identify with Islam. "There is no hint of the biblical notion of a chosen people set apart to enjoy a special relationship with Allah. In the Muslim view, Allah does not play favorites but desires all people to embrace Islam and thereby establish an intimate and special bond with the deity" (Kaltner, 94).

Abraham's descendants are connected in the same "family" of the one God.

Jon D. Levenson, *Inheriting Abraham: The Legacy of the Patriarch in Judaism, Christianity, and Islam* (Princeton: Princeton University Press, 2012).

John Kaltner, *Ishmael Instructs Isaac: An Introduction to the Qu'ran for Bible Readers* (Collegeville MN: Liturgical, 1999).

"I will establish my covenant between me and you
And your offspring after you throughout their generations,
For an everlasting covenant
To be God to you and to your offspring after you." (17:8)

The covenant is not finished, not broken, not forgotten. It embraces the whole of Israel's history from Abraham to the book's ancient audience. Despite the profound disruption of their history, despite invasions, displacements, and exile, despite the fall of the nation to the Babylonian Empire, the Abrahamic covenant remains alive for it is everlasting. That it endures means that the people of Judah and their relationship with God will continue to exist. The promises are still in place and belong to them even now. God will also again give Abraham's "offspring after" him the land. Members the book's audience are, like him, aliens in their own land. To them, God gives the "land of Canaan," not temporarily, not only for Abraham's generation, not only until Babylon destroys the nation, but for "a perpetual holding" (17:8). (See [Struggles Over Land].)

Chapter 17 reasserts the terms of Abraham's call in the most ironclad of ways (12:1-3). The promises are still operative, but now they are legally binding upon God and Abraham. The obligations of this covenant, however, flow in two directions. Abraham, his family, and his offspring also have responsibilities in this covenant agreement.

"As for You," 17:9-14

As for Abraham, his responsibility is to keep the covenant, but the responsibilities fall upon his descendants as well. It is a covenant "between me and you and your offspring after you: Every male among you shall be circumcised" (17:10). "Throughout your generations," circumcision shall be the sign of the covenant inscribed upon the flesh of the males of the community. [Circumcision] God commands that Abraham circumcise all the male babies in his household when they are eight days old and all male members of his household, including slaves and foreigners, those purchased and those born within the household. A permanent cutting of the flesh of the male organ of reproduction, circumcision becomes a sign of God's everlasting covenant relationship with Abraham and his offspring. A wordplay makes this clear. The failure to cut the foreskin will cut off the uncircumcised from the people. [Circumcision: A Gender Issue]

"As for Sarah and Isaac and Ishmael," 17:15-22

Although circumcision excludes women from primary covenant membership, Sarai, too, has a place in the covenant promise. God also changes her name from Sarai to Sarah, marking her status as the mother of Israel. Her new name suggests a new beginning or at least clarifies her vocation for the benefit of her husband. God will bless her and through her give him the son of the promise. Her blessing is fertility, for she too shall give rise to nations and kings of peoples with Abraham. In response to this announcement addressed to Abraham, about her but not to her, he falls on his face a second time, now laughing out loud in response to this news (17:17). [Laughter] The narrator tells us what makes him laugh. "Abraham said to himself, 'Can a child be born to a man who is a hundred years old? Can Sarah, who is ninety years old, bear a child?'" (17:17). The answer to both questions is "no, of course not." The situation is impossible, truly absurd, barely imaginable. The only way such a thing could happen is through the creative action of God.

Considering the biological impediments, Abraham again proposes the obvious alternative: "O that Ishmael might live in your sight" (17:18). To this, God simply repeats the impossible:

Circumcision

Although male circumcision was practiced in the ancient Near East among Egyptians and Western Semitic groups in Syria and Palestine, its origins are not clear. The ritual may have been connected with hygienic or fertility practices, marriage rites, or covenant sacrificial offerings. Old Testament stories about circumcision do not clarify its original meanings (Gen 34; Exod 4:24-26). The World Health Organization today, for example, has concluded that the practice of male circumcision has had a strong beneficial effect in the prevention and spread of HIV infections in parts of Africa (Hargreave, 628–38).

Editors of Genesis may have learned of circumcision from ancient fertility practices. Before Abraham's circumcision, Sarah cannot conceive; afterward she can. Before circumcision, Abraham has only Ishmael; afterward he also begets Isaac. At least at the level of narrative, fertility follows circumcision.

Whatever might be the ancient origins of circumcision, however, the blessings of fertility come about in Genesis because of God's promises. Rather than causing fertility, circumcision is a response to God's promises and a sign of the covenant. It symbolizes ineradicably in male flesh that Abraham and his descendants are God's covenant partners.

Strangely, however, the sign is a hidden one, covered by clothing. Rather than being visible to the general population such as might be achieved by facial markings or tattoos, only the individual and the community know it as a mark of identity. The practice's hidden nature may suggest a need for cultural secrecy in the midst of foreign rule.

Among Jews, the practice of male circumcision underwent many interpretations. Several Old Testament texts treat it as a spiritual metaphor, such as "circumcision of the heart" (Exod 6:16, 30; Deut 10:16; 30:6; Lev 26:41; Jer 4:4; 6:10; 9:25-26; Ezek 44:7-9). To have a circumcised heart means to be committed to God and to participate in the spiritual communion between God and Israel. Physical circumcision is not enough if one's whole being is not properly dedicated.

Among early Christians, the matter of circumcision was a cause of dissension. Was it necessary for Jewish Christians or for non-Jewish Christians? How are Christians to receive the divine blessings promised to Abraham if not through circumcision? Some held that circumcision was necessary for believers to be saved (Acts 15:1); others thought that God saved Abraham before circumcision so that it is only a sign (Rom 4:9-12). Faith in Christ rather than circumcision assures acceptance by God (Gal 4:21-5:1). Still others argued that Christ included everyone in the body of Christ, so circumcision could be and was abolished as a requirement of membership (Eph 2:13-22). For further reading, see John G. Hall, "Circumcision," *AB* 1:1025–31.

Tim Hargreave, "Male Circumcision: Towards a World Health Organisation Normative Practice in Resource Limited Settings," *Asian Journal of Andrology* 12 (2010).

Christoph Weigel (1654–1725). "The Covenant of Circumcision." *Biblia ectypa: Bildnussen auss Heiliger Schrifft Alt und Neuen Testaments . . .* (1695). (Courtesy of the Pitts Theology Library, Candler School of Theology, Emory University)

"Your wife Sarah shall bear a son, and you shall name him Isaac." Abraham, the ancient one, will have two sons, and God shall establish the covenant with Sarah's son alone, Abraham's second-born (17:19).

The next four verses alternate attention between the two sons on an equal basis: Ishmael (v. 18a), and Isaac (v. 19), Ishmael (v. 20)

Circumcision: A Gender Issue

If there is any religious practice in Israel that excludes women, it is circumcision as the external sign of the covenant. That such a practice is ascribed to Abraham and the time of the ancestors implies that membership in the covenanted community was always the provenance of men alone. Women participated indirectly through their connection with circumcised men in their family. In ancient Israel it was not likely that women would have questioned the practice, since they, too, may have believed in male fertility as a sign of divine blessing upon the whole people. Even when Deuteronomy and Jeremiah implicitly include all members of the community through circumcision of the heart or of the lips, the language remains focused on male bodies in covenant membership. Male circumcision contributes to gender inequality in a hierarchy of male importance, but since it involves mutilation of the body with more serious consequences for women, extending the practice to women is not desirable.

Sarah, and through her the women of Israel, however, are not completely excluded from participating in the covenant. Today some Jewish communities welcome female babies with a ritual of anointing and naming to mark the incorporation of girls into the community.

and Isaac (v. 21). Although firstborn Ishmael is not included in the covenant, God does not cast him off. In a wordplay on Ishmael's name ("God hears"), God hears Abraham's plea on his behalf ("I have heard you"). God will make Ishmael fruitful like Isaac's own future son, Jacob. He will be father of "twelve princes," and, as God promised his mother Hagar, he will become a great nation. Yet only Isaac and his offspring after him will inherit the covenant. Within a year Sarah will bear him the sole heir of God's covenant with Abraham.

Laughter

ROFL is a social media acronym for "rolling on the floor laughing." It seems an apt phrase to describe Abraham's response to the news that Sarah will give birth to the child of promise. He laughs because he is 100 years old and she is 90. How can they conceive a child? Her barrenness and their status as ancients of days make birth impossible by human standards. Laughter is another motif highlighting the absurdity and impossibility of the situation of the characters in the text and in the life of the audience. Abraham falls on his face laughing (17:17), Sarah will laugh when the angels announce that she will conceive (18:12-15) and again when the child is born (21:6), and they name the child Isaac (*yiṣḥaq*), a name related to the Hebrew word "to laugh" (*ṣāḥaq*). The laughter around Sarah's motherhood and Isaac's birth expresses incredulity, impossibility, and joy beyond imagining.

Now that covenant relationships among the parties are clear, God departs and leaves Abraham to execute his duties.

"As for All the Men," 17:23-27

"On that very day" (17:23), Abraham obediently executes his responsibility to circumcise all the males of his household, beginning with his firstborn son Ishmael and then his slaves. He circumcises himself when he is ninety-nine years old and Ishmael is thirteen.

CONNECTIONS

Names have power. Names create relationships, establish linkages, and join people and things with one another past and present. The giving of names has more than one meaning. [Cultural Differences] In some traditions, names express the essence or character of the thing or person being named (1 Sam 25:25). To name does not necessarily mean to subject or exploit. To name is to honor communal identity and to confirm a unique relationship. (See [Naming].)

To be addressed by name is another matter. It means to be seen, noticed, recognized, and set apart for good or ill. In American culture, personal and group names matter. Individuals and communities want to be, and have the right to be, named accurately according to their own choice and not with slurs or demeaning nicknames.

In Genesis, God addresses some ancestors by name directly—Abram, Hagar, Isaac, and Jacob—clearly singling them out and recognizing a special relationship with them. In chapter 17, however, God changes the names of both Abram and Sarai. Although interpreters have proposed that the new ancestral names result from linguistic changes that took place during the long development of the text over centuries, the name changes have an important theological function in Genesis whatever linguistic shifts might be involved. [Name Changes] The changes signify a new moment in the vocation of Abraham and Sarah. They are now formally bound as participants in the covenant with their God. The name changes formalize their new identity as recipients of the promise of offspring and of land. They live in a new reality, a covenant "between you and me," and from this their future will follow. They walk with God.

Cultural Differences

Samson Olusina Olanisebe has written about the importance of names in African Yoruba tribal culture and the impact of the Pentecostal practice of name change upon that culture in Nigeria.

> To the Africans, names are very important. There is much in a name. A name is a mark. To be nameless is to be without identity. A name identifies a person. A name, according to Oduyoye [61–63], is the linguistic symbol by which you remember an individual. To the Africans in general and to the Yoruba in particular, nothing is said to exist until it is named. Names are not just abstract terms couched in indefiniteness, they are not mere labels, but they are pregnant with meaningful and symbolic import.

Traditional names in Yoruba society often derived from the circumstances of the child's birth, from festivals or events at the time of the birth, from patron deities or from religious feeling.

Pentecostals, however, are leaving these traditional sources of names behind in favor of names derived from literal interpretations of Scripture, names teaching proper behavior, such as patience, charity, etc., and names compounded with the Yoruba equivalent for "Lord." Often the new names or changed names seek to create a distance from traditional deities and possible harmful influences of the ancestors. Names are powerful in Yoruba culture whether they are traditional or newly inspired.

Mercy Amba Oduyoye, *Yoruba Names: Their Structures and Meanings* (Ibadan: Sefer, 2001).

Samson Olusina Olanisebe, "Change of Names in Gen. 17.1-22 and Among Yoruba Pentecostals: A Comparative Investigation," *AsJT* 25/2 (2011): 288–313.

Name Changes

The chapter gives neither a reason for the changes of the ancestral names nor their significance. Interpreters have seen them as a result of alterations in the language over the long course of the text's transmission, or from the blending of literary sources in the book, but others have contested these views (Westermann, 84–85). From a literary perspective, the changes imply a change in status like a king or queen acquiring a new throne name and beginning a "new era in life that separates it out from the past" (Westermann, 261). Abraham and Sarah live in a new reality whereby the promise of offspring makes them parents of the nation.

For further reading, see Claus Westermann, *Genesis 12–36* (Minneapolis: Fortress, 1995).

The prophet of the exile known as Second Isaiah (Isa 40–55) depicts God calling the nation of Israel by name, assuring the people of divine presence and redemption (Isa 43:1-7). [God Calls Israel by Name, Isaiah 43:1-7] People receive names from their family or community, but God has a unique name, a name that marks special belonging and intimate connection. Names given at baptism in Christian communities and Hebrew names given to Jewish children in Jewish communities have similar purpose. They clarify calling and identify the individual with a community of believers. If God has a name for each individual, then everyone has unique dignity known to God. To think like this is to see in a different way that we are humans made in the divine image, each special and particular in God's eyes.

NOTES

1. For further reading, see David Carr, *Reading the Fractures of Genesis: Historical and Literary Approaches* (Louisville KY: Westminster John Knox, 1996) 82–85.

2. See Claus Westermann, *Genesis 12–36* (Minneapolis: Fortress, 1995) 217, 256.

3. Everett Fox, *The Five Books of Moses: Genesis, Exodus, Leviticus, Numbers, and Deuteronomy* (Schocken Bible; Dallas: Word, 1995) 71.

4. Nahum Sarna, *Genesis* (JPS Torah Commentary; Philadelphia: The Jewish Publication Society, 1989) 123.

God Calls Israel by Name, Isaiah 43:1-7

Writing after the nation's fall to Babylon, Second Isaiah reflects on the importance of God's name for Israel. The nation's whole identity is connected to the name given to them by the Creator who protects, cherishes, and lives with them.

But now thus says the LORD,
    he who created you, O Jacob,
    he who formed you, O Israel:
Do not fear, for I have redeemed you;
    I have called you by name, you are mine.
When you pass through the waters, I will be with you;
    and through the rivers, they shall not overwhelm you;
when you walk through fire you shall not be burned,
    and the flame shall not consume you.
For I am the LORD your God,
    the Holy One of Israel, your Savior.
I give Egypt as your ransom,
    Ethiopia and Seba in exchange for you.
Because you are precious in my sight,
    and honored, and I love you,
I give people in return for you,
    nations in exchange for your life.
Do not fear, for I am with you;
    I will bring your offspring from the east,
    and from the west I will gather you;
I will say to the north, "Give them up,"
    and to the south, "Do not withhold;
bring my sons from far away
    and my daughters from the end of the earth—
everyone who is called by my name,
    whom I created for my glory,
    whom I formed and made." (Isa 43:1-7)

HOSPITALITY, LAUGHTER, AND LOOMING DISASTER

Genesis 18:1-33

God's promise of offspring to Abram (12:1-3) continues to thread across the chapters. The promise has been slow of fulfillment and seems increasingly unrealizable as Abraham and Sarah age, but a visit by three mysterious strangers renews the promise and specifies against all likelihood that Sarah will be the matriarch of Israel. Yet chapter 18 delays the promise's fulfillment to tell of another catastrophic disaster, namely, the destruction of Sodom and its aftermath (chs. 19–20).

COMMENTARY

[Outline of Genesis 18] The first unit takes place at the couple's tent by the oaks of Mamre (vv. 1-15; see [Oaks of Mamre]) and, like the previous chapter (17:15-22), continues to insist that Sarah will bear a son. The second unit moves from events at the tent to a journey toward Sodom and Gomorrah (18:16-32). God appears to Abraham in this chapter, first in the guise of three strangers (18:1-15) and then as a direct presence in a strong debate between the two (18:16-32). Although the chapter begins with an announcement that "the Lord appeared to Abraham," that appearance unfolds slowly with particular ambiguity. There is no immediate exchange between God and Abraham after the narrator announces the appearance. Instead, three visitors arrive whose identity is far from clear. They seem to be three human visitors on the one hand, and on the other they represent the Lord as announced by the first verse and confirmed by the events that follow.

Abraham's character differs from previous chapters. Here he is nervous, rushing and scurrying about before his mysterious visitors (18:1-15). Later he stands up to argue stubbornly with God. He is an insistent advocate who demands that the Just Judge of the world do justice (18:16-33).

Outline of Genesis 18

1. Laughter, 18:1-15
   a. Hospitality, vv. 1-8
   b. A Favor in Return, vv. 9-15
2. Looming Disaster, 18:16-32

The Three Visitors in Artwork

The Russian iconographer Andrei Rublev created this famous interpretation of Abraham's three visitors in the fifteenth century. The visitors here are clearly angels, messengers of the divine, rather than ordinary men because they have wings and halos. This Christian interpretation of Gen 18 represents the three visitors in terms of the Christian doctrine of the Trinity. Although the Genesis passage does not and could not make such an association, Christians have found in the strangers' visit an anticipation of later Christian understanding of God as one God in three persons. For Orthodox Christians, icons emerge from the artist as sacred revelations of divine presence. Iconographers understand the process of producing icons as a form of prayer in which artists "write" what is revealed to them in a creative and inspired process.

From the perspective of Genesis itself, the interpretation of the angels as the Trinity is a form of midrash, an extension of the meaning of a text for a later time, in this case in the context of Christian belief. The three angels sit in close relation to one another, in peaceful harmony, gathered around a chalice that suggests the Eucharist. Thus, this artistic scene of Abraham's ordinary hospitality takes on additional meaning about strangers as emissaries from God and then as God's own self.

Andrei Roblev (?–1428). *The Trinity* (also *The Hospitality of Abraham*). Tempera on panel. Tretyakov Gallery, Moscow. (Credit: Wikimedia Commons, PD-1923)

Laughter, 18:1-15

Confusion about the divine presence begins immediately. The narrator reports that Abraham is sitting at the entrance to his tent at Mamre when the Lord appears (*rāʾāh*) to him (v. 1). Yet when Abraham lifts up his eyes, "behold" (*hinnēh*), he sees (*rāʾāh*) three men standing nearby. (See ["Look!"].) The Hebrew uses the same verbal root (*rāʾāh*) for both God's appearance and Abraham's seeing, creating the expectation that he will see the Lord, but instead he sees three men suddenly standing before him. When he sees them, he jumps into action to provide elaborate hospitality as expected in the ancient Near East whenever strangers come to one's home (vv. 2-8). [Hospitality]

Hospitality, vv. 1-8

Abraham shows the wayfaring strangers every courtesy. He runs from the tent to meet them, bows down, and addresses them respectfully. Yet strangely, he speaks to the three of them with the singular form of address as if they were one person: "My lord, if I find favor in your [singular] eyes, do not pass me by" (v. 3). Perhaps Abraham speaks in the singular to the most prominent of the three men, or perhaps he recognizes the three as messengers of God and one manifestation of the divine, as readers soon will. The next verse adds to the confusion when Abraham invites them (plural) to "rest under the tree" (v. 4) and to eat bread, "since you have come to your [plural] servant" (v. 5). His deferential forms of address suit the situation of a host in the presence of august visitors, although it is not clear whether he knows who

Hospitality

Oded Borowski has studied daily life in biblical times and writes,

Hospitality was one of the most important customs observed throughout Israelite society. Actually one might look at hospitality as a cornerstone institution of Israelite culture. There is no reason to assume that this was uniquely Israelite, but other cultures did not leave records of this practice. (22)

In desert traditions such as those of Bedouins and others in ancient and contemporary worlds, local people have a duty to feed and protect strangers in the hostile environment. That Abraham's hospitable actions occur in the heat of the day suggest the travelers' need for water and nourishment. Often hospitality offered to the stranger garners a return favor or gift for the host. Possibly the strangers' reiteration of the divine promise of a son to Sarah may serve as the return gift. Something similar happens when Abraham's servant goes to Mesopotamia to obtain a wife for Abraham and Sarah's son, Isaac (Gen 24:1-49).

Yet the ancient tradition of hospitality to strangers also involves the recognition that visiting strangers may be other than they appear (Westermann, 276–77). Such is the belief in the New Testament book of Hebrews that reminds readers, "Do not neglect to show hospitality to strangers, for by doing that some have entertained angels without knowing it" (Heb 13:2). We never know who strangers might be or from where they come. In Homer's *Odyssey*, for example, old people, peasants, and strangers appear suddenly on the road and turn out to be gods in human disguise. Even Odysseus returns to his own household in the guise of a foreigner after twenty years of war, travel, and adventure. An old servant woman sees scars on his leg as she washes his feet in welcome and recognizes him as the master of the house. These stories share insights with the visit of the three strangers to Abraham and Sarah. Welcome everyone because, no matter how wounded and decrepit or healthy and beautiful, strangers might carry the light of God to us. So it may be with immigrants and homeless people, with refugees and wanderers. Who knows how they may reveal God to us?

For further reading, see John Koenig, "Hospitality," *AB* 3:299–301.

Oded Borowski, *Daily Life in Biblical Times* (ABS 5; Atlanta: SBL, 2003).
Claus Westermann, *Genesis 12–36: A Commentary* (London: SPCK, 1981).

is before him or whether he is showing customary hospitality to strangers. [The Three Visitors in Film]

When Abraham offers to feed them, the three accept his hospitality. The narrator accentuates Abraham's prominent role in organizing his household to provide a prodigious welcome. He gives precise commands to Sarah to prepare bread for the guests. She should use "choice flour," knead it, and make cakes from it. Then he obtains curds and milk and a calf from the herd, orders a servant to prepare it, serves the guests, and watches them eat as if he were a servant at the ready to supply any need. [Meals]

None of this behavior is unusual considering ancient Near Eastern customs of hospitality. Yet words expressing urgency stress Abraham's thoroughness in arranging details of the welcome. He *hastens* into the tent, tells Sarah to prepare the cakes *quickly*; he *runs* to the herd to find a tender and good calf, and the servant *hastens* to prepare it (vv. 6-7). Abraham's hospitality is intentional, designed to provide for every aspect of his guests' needs. This may be because he senses who the visitors are, even as it surely establishes him as an exemplary host. His alacrity and thoroughness in receiving strangers sets a high bar of hospitality and contrasts

The Three Visitors in Film

The text's ambiguous presentation of God in the guise of three visitors receives different interpretations in a film from 1966 and in a television miniseries from 2013. Biblical interpreter Rhonda Burnette-Bletsch has observed in her study, "God at the Movies," that just as the Bible anthropomorphizes God (presents God with human qualities), film often does the same in effective visual ways:

For example, Abraham's meal with three angelic visitors (Gen 18) is depicted naturalistically in John Huston's *The Bible: In the Beginning . . .* (1966). That one (or possibly all) of these angels is actually God is indicated by their unnaturally slow and deliberate movements, the ghostly way that they fade into and out of frame, and the fact that all three of them are played by Peter O'Toole. The pleas of Abraham (George C. Scott) for "the judge of the all the earth" to "do what is right" followed by violent destruction of Sodom raise questions of theodicy and violent divine retribution—topics that Huston neatly sidesteps (at least in this scene) . . . .

The intentionally reverential television miniseries, *The Bible* (prod. Mark Burnett/Roma Downey, 2013) indicates the otherness of Abraham's visitors via sound effects and character reactions. Here, however, one of the three angels is clearly singled out as God. Unlike the other two, who defer to him, his face remains hidden; he is hooded, turns his back to the camera, and stands in shadow. He also seems to have the supernatural ability to occupy two spaces at one; outside the text with Abraham (Gary Oliver) and inside with Sarah (Josephine Butler) . . . . It is God/angel who stays behind to converse with Abraham as the other two angels proceed along their way. (301–301)

For further reading, see Rhonda Burnette-Bletsch, "God at the Movies," in Rhonda Burnette-Bletsch, ed., *The Bible in Motion: A Handbook of the Bible and Its Reception in Film*, part 1 (2 parts; Handbooks of the Bible and Its Reception, vol. 2; Boston: Walter de Gruyter, 2016) 299–326.

Meals

Biblical meals are often occasions of divine revelation. In Gen 18, the meal Abraham prepares for his visitors expresses customary hospitality, but he offers it with unusual energy and care. The meal itself becomes a sacred setting for Abraham's encounter with the divine. The three visitors are present to receive nourishment from him, but it is Abraham who gains nourishment from them.

Isaiah invites the people of Israel to come to a meal that echoes this one. At this meal, the one who eats will hear the voice of God and gain life:

Ho, everyone who thirsts come to the waters; and you that have no money, come, buy and eat! Come, buy wine and milk without money and without price. Why do you spend your money for that which is not bread, and your labor for that which does not satisfy? Listen carefully to me, and eat what is good, and delight yourselves in rich food. Incline your ear, and come to me; listen, so that you may live. (Isa 55:1-3)

God meets the guests, speaks to them, makes an everlasting covenant with them, and assigns them a mission to the nations. The meal is a sacred occasion where the Holy One becomes present.

In Proverbs, Woman Wisdom herself is the host who slaughters animals, mixes wine, and sets the table. She sends out her servant girls to invite everyone to her table: "Come, eat of my bread and drink of the wine I have mixed. Lay aside immaturity and live, and walk in the way of insight" (Prov 9:5-6).

The meal as place of revelation and life-altering communion appears again in the New Testament in the meal known variously as the Lord's Supper, the Eucharist, or Holy Communion. To many Christians, the New Testament meal is a sign, a sacrament, or a place where God is uniquely present and encountered. The meal of the disciples as they stop along the road to Emmaus presents this reality in clear terms, for there, after the Lord blesses the bread and wine, the disciples recognize the divinity of their table companion and their lives change (Lk 24:13-35).

sharply to the inhospitable behavior of the men of Sodom in the next chapter (19:4-10).

A Favor in Return, vv. 9-15

When the three visitors speak, they heighten the mystery of their identity because they ask about Abraham's wife by name: "Where is your wife Sarah?" (18:9). How do they know her name, and why do they act so audaciously as to inquire about his wife in a culture where women generally belong in the private sphere? [Women's Place] More cause for consternation follows. The voice of one declares in the first-person singular, "I will surely return to you in due season, and your wife Sarah shall have a son" (18:10). Twice the speaker promises to return in due season (*kāʿēt ḥayyāh*, vv. 10, 14).1 The same phrase occurs again only in 2 Kings 4:16, 17 when Elisha promises that the Shunamite woman will also bear a son. The unique expression with *ḥayyāh*, a noun from the root "to live," as in the time of living or living anew, highlights the unexpected quality of the pregnancy, but it may also point to the situation of the reading community who need assurance that life is reviving soon.

Sarah, meanwhile, is inside listening to this announcement, and she laughs at the news. (See [Laughter].) Her laughter reminds readers again of the great ages of the couple and the post-menopausal status of eavesdropping Sarah. "It had ceased to be with Sarah after the manner of women" (v. 11). [Suffering of Barren Woman] Naturally,

---

Women's Place

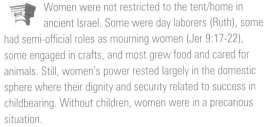
Women were not restricted to the tent/home in ancient Israel. Some were day laborers (Ruth), some had semi-official roles as mourning women (Jer 9:17-22), some engaged in crafts, and most grew food and cared for animals. Still, women's power rested largely in the domestic sphere where their dignity and security related to success in childbearing. Without children, women were in a precarious situation.

Juliana Claassens has reported that some contemporary women in Zimbabwe live in situations constrained in ways that echo ancient expectations. Here she quotes Dora Mbuwayesango:

The importance of child-bearing is . . . demonstrated in Shona society by the practice of *kudgadzs mapfihwas* in which a married woman is only given her own cooking place . . . after bearing her first child. Prior to that she is regarded and treated as a child and her mother-in-law is her overseer. The giving of a cooking place to a woman

is accompanied by celebration when she cooks her first meal in her own cooking place. A woman childless is regarded and treated as a child who is told what to cook by her mother or mother-in-law. To be considered a mature woman, a woman has the right to select daily meals. (115)

In the Zimbabwean situation, the woman's role as mother and then preparer of meals limits and defines her place. In Sarah's situation in Genesis, she is a preparer of meals under Abraham's direction or encouragement, and her place is in the tent while the men meet outside it and travel beyond it. That the mysterious strangers know her name is surprising and points further to their divine identity.

Dora Mbuwayesango, "Childlessness and Woman-to-Woman Relationships in Genesis and in African Patriarchal Society: Sarah and Hagar from a Zimbabwean Woman's Perspective (Gen 16:1-16; 21:8-21)," in *Reading the Bible as Women Perspectives from Africa, Asia, and Latin America*, ed. Phyllis A. Bird et al. (*Semeia* 78; Atlanta: Scholars Press, 1997) 28, quoted in Juliana M. Claassens, *Claiming her Dignity: Female Resistance in the Old Testament* (Collegeville MN: Liturgical, 2016).

Suffering of Barren Woman

Sarah says, "After I have grown old ["after I am worn out"], and my husband is old, shall I have pleasure?" (18:12). According to Jeansome, Sarah's question about pleasure can mean a number of things: perhaps Abraham has not "responded to Sarah sexually," or "her barrenness has made her life so bleak that pleasure is not possible," or she cannot imagine pleasure because the social stigma of her barrenness has depleted her of life (23). I think that Sarah's words serve to emphasize further the impossibilities involved in God's promises. The two ancestors are so old that sexual pleasure and the conception of a child require a miracle. Similarly, only a miracle can bring the people of Judah back to life after the devastation of land and people resulting from the disasters of the Babylonian Period.

Sharon Pace Jeansome, in *The Women of Genesis* (Minneapolis: Fortress, 1990).

she laughs to herself like her husband before her (17:17), for the promise is preposterous. "After I have grown old, and my husband is old, shall I have pleasure?" she wonders, as if turning to speak directly to readers to let us in on the joke.

After the laughter, the three visitors merge into one figure. They are either messengers of God or a manifestation of God: "The LORD said to Abraham, 'Why did Sarah laugh, and say, "Shall I indeed bear a child now that I am old?" Is anything too wonderful for the LORD?'" (18:13-14). With this reiteration of the promise to Sarah, the narrator clarifies the meaning of the first verse of the unit, "The LORD appeared to Abraham" (18:1). The Lord asks Abraham, not Sarah, why his wife laughed and repeats the thrust of her question: "Shall I indeed bear a child now that I am old?" When this mysterious visitor inquires about Abraham's wife, it not only reminds readers that this is a patriarchal society where husbands have final authority and interpretive power in a household but also draws attention to the doubt that pervades the situation. All the more astonishing then is the major point of the scene: "Is anything too wonderful for the LORD?" (18:14). Clearly, Abraham, Sarah, and the book's audience need to be persuaded that the barren woman can bear a child and that Abraham and his descendants have a future they cannot yet grasp. Jon D. Levenson has noted that the question, "Is anything too wonderful for the LORD?" serves as proof of divine ability "to work miracles" and therefore "of the miraculous nature of the nation to descend from the promised son."[2] Only a miracle can produce a child and offspring more numerous than the stars of the heavens and the sands of the sea.

Again the divine speaker promises to return in "due time" when Sarah will have a son. [Birth Oracles] But the chapter will not let the difficulties of this promise fade from sight. Sarah denies that she laughed, "for she was afraid," but God insists, "Yes, you did laugh" (18:15). The Hebrew verb "to laugh" (*ṣāḥak*) occurs four times in this scene (vv. 12, 13, 15 [two times]). Surely God's promises appear risible, ridiculous, worthy of guffaws. Only a miracle can change the situation, but no one expects that nor, it seems, can

Birth Oracles

Birth oracles are promises given to barren women (Gen 17:19; 18:10, 14; Judg 13:3, 5, 7; 1 Sam 1:17; 2 Kgs 4:16) or to pregnant women whose lives are in danger (Gen 16:11; 25:23). Priests, prophets, or strangers deliver the promises, and sometimes the ones delivering the oracle of birth turn out to be heavenly beings or messengers (Gen 18:1-6 and Judg 13:15-21). The women's husbands have no control over these promises, as is the case with both of Abraham's wives, Sarah and Hagar. The birth oracle may point to women's spiritual experiences or, at the least, highlight lack of patriarchal control over pregnancy and birth (Albertz and Schmitt, 273–75). In Genesis, pregnancy and birth are under God's control alone.

Women in the ancient world gained their identity, their place in society, and their security in old age from mother-hood, especially from the birth of sons. Without children, women had little standing with their husbands. Rachel (30:1-3) and Hannah (1 Sam 1) have husbands who love them above other wives despite their failure to bear children, but the women yearn mightily for children. Without children, women are endangered in old age and widow-hood because they may have no one to care for them. They are failed women in the eyes of society and their own. Indeed, a widow is not merely a woman who has lost her husband but also one who has no sons to protect her.

Although modern Western women have many other ways to gain status, self-respect, and protection from poverty, the inability to bear children can remain a most painful and private suffering. The fertility industry has helped, but there are still women and couples who cannot have children. Biblical reversals from barrenness to birth can cruelly build hope for a miracle, and many will still not become mothers. In the biblical text, the subject of barren women is a metaphor, a symbolic and literal condition of lifelessness transformed by the acts of God. It may not be comforting to women unable to conceive that God's work of transformation does not always take shape in physical ways for everyone who desires it. This reality means that preachers, teachers, and pastoral caregivers are best advised to treat the subject of biblical births to barren women with the gentle recognition that among their people may be women who long for children with deep intensity. These leaders must find words that will not deepen the wound.

Rainer Albertz and Rüdiger Schmitt, *Family and Household Religion in Ancient Israel and the Levant* (Winona Lake IN: Eisenbrauns, 2012) 273–75.

they believe it when God promises it. Sarah's laughter does not make her "a negative figure" who contrasts with the goodness of Abraham, as Cotter and von Rad have argued.[3] She is a character whose human response to the impossible draws attention to divine graciousness, even as she echoes the laughter of her husband (17:17). The couple's laughter captures the incredulity of the book's readers, for, humanly speaking, she cannot bear a child. Her denial that she laughed sharpens the fearful difficulties of believing in God's promise.

Looming Disaster, 18:16-32

The second unit of chapter 18 moves the male figures away from Abraham's tent toward the city of Sodom, and it changes the subject. Abraham departs with the three visitors, referred to simply as "men," and in a further act of hospitality he "sets them on their way" (v. 16). "The men," now distinguished from God, veer off toward Sodom, but Abraham "remained standing before the LORD" (18:22). At this moment, the Lord is thinking out loud about whether Abraham should or should not be let in on "what I am about to do" (18:17-21). An accumulation of reasons motivate God to make Abraham his confidante:

- "Abraham shall become a great and mighty nation,
- all the nations of the world shall be blessed in him . . .
- I have chosen him, that he may charge his children and his household after him to keep the way of the LORD by doing righteousness and justice;
- so that the LORD may bring about for Abraham what he promised him." (18:18-19).

This complicated divine self-reflection summarizes the promises to Abraham and adds a new element to his role. Justice will be the hallmark of "his children and his household after him," and Abraham himself will be the teacher of justice. Because he will instruct those "who come after him," God finally decides to let him in on the decision-making process.

God tells him of an ominous but unspecified plan prompted by hearsay. An outcry from an unidentified source about the "very grave sins of Sodom and Gomorrah" has drawn divine attention (18:20, see 11:5, 7). Echoing the story of Babel, God intends to come down to see whether or not the gossip is true (18:21). Abraham somehow knows that God's plan involves complete annihilation of the cities, although the narrator does not reveal it. To forestall the disaster in advance of its happening, Abraham interrogates God like a prosecutor in a law court.

An unrelenting defender of the innocent and a resister of injustice, Abraham asks the central question of the scene: "Will you indeed sweep away the righteous with the wicked?" (18:23). So far, God has said nothing about destroying anyone, only that the outcry about the behavior of the two cities requires investigation. Abraham's worry is not whether God should punish the wicked but whether the obliteration of everyone will destroy innocent people the way a storm indiscriminately destroys everything in its path. To prevent such a disaster, Abraham sets an imagined set of events before God: "Suppose there are fifty righteous people within the city; will you then sweep away the place and not forgive it for the fifty righteous who are in it?" (18:24). To prevent God from even considering such an action, Abraham presumes to answer his own question: "Far be it from you to do such a thing, to slay the righteous with the wicked, so that the righteous fare as the wicked! Far be that from you!" (v. 25).

Twice Abraham expresses how unthinkable it would be for God to destroy the innocent along with the wicked. Surely God is the one with the responsibility, wisdom, and insight to judge justly. By appealing to divine righteousness, Abraham coaxes God to do the right thing: "Shall not the Judge of all the earth do what is just?" If God is not just, then by implication there is no justice upon the earth. [Arguing with God]

Abraham has made his argument. He wants to restrain divine violence, to dissuade God from destroying the good along with the wicked, to persuade God to do justice, and his rhetoric works! God complies and agrees not to destroy Sodom as long as there are fifty righteous people within it: "I will forgive the whole place for their sake" (v. 26). Because God is a just and forgiving God, the very presence of some righteous people can save the wicked.

Abraham, however, is still worried about the fate of the innocent (18:27-33). He remembers his lowly position, uses submissive speech, and steps out of his creaturely place again to argue with God. "Let me take it upon myself to speak to the LORD, I who am but dust and ashes" (v. 27, cf. 2:7; 3:19). He knows he is a mortal standing before the Lord of Life, but still, as a seeker of justice for the people of Sodom and Gomorrah, he dares to involve himself in negotiations with the divine. Again he persists:

> "If five are lacking, will you destroy the city?" "No, I will not," answers God.
> "If there are only forty?" "No."
> "Do not let the LORD be angry if I speak. If there are only thirty?" "No."
> "Let me take it upon myself to speak. If there are only twenty?" "No."
> "Do not let the LORD be angry if I speak just once more. If there are only ten?" "For the sake of ten I will not destroy it." (vv. 28-32, paraphrased)

This is God's final word—end of conversation. Abraham is satisfied that God is just and will not destroy a whole city when there are a mere ten innocent people in its midst. With the battle over, the Lord goes away and Abraham returns to his tent (18:33).

Arguing with God

Arguing with God is a deeply rooted biblical tradition, practiced by Abraham, Jeremiah, Job, the psalmist, and others. When Abraham asks, "Shall not the Judge of all the earth do justice?" he dares to urge God to perform the divine role of doing justice. Arguing with God is a tradition of prayer that protests, resists, and challenges God, even as it simultaneously holds fast to relationship with God.

No one has written more eloquently about biblical arguments with God, perhaps, than Old Testament scholar Walter Brueggemann: "Disputatious questioning . . . constitutes a major dimension of Israel's life of faith." The questions "how long?" "why?" and "where?" again and again challenge Israel's "core testimony," that is, the central claims of the Old Testament that anticipate decisive action by God "to intervene and transform unbearable circumstance" (319).

Walter Brueggemann, *Theology of the Old Testament: Testimony, Dispute, and Advocacy* (Minneapolis: Fortress, 1997) 318–58.

This divine-human tug of war interprets the coming destruction of the city of Sodom in advance of the story of the events. Abraham's debate with God has set up a situation where the city's destruction in the next chapter must mean there were not even ten innocent people to be found within its population, for God has promised not to destroy the innocent (ch. 19). The city deserves to be punished because God is just and does not destroy whimsically.

The catastrophe debated here falls upon the city of Sodom (ch. 19). The debate occurs before the fact to interpret what follows; it directs readers toward one understanding of the catastrophe ahead. [Two Disasters] At stake is how the audience is to understand God's relationship to overwhelming cataclysm and the traumatic destruction of a city. In this text, Sodom will be obliterated because the people are wicked. For the audience of the book, however, the city in question and the disaster that haunts their

---

Two Disasters

The story of the destruction of Sodom that begins here (18:16) has connections with the destruction of Babel and its tower. Both concern the destruction of a city and survival by inhabitants. Both tell of God coming down to see what is going on (18:21; 11:5, 7), and God is the agent of the disaster. Both involve puzzling destruction without satisfactory explanations. Behind both catastrophic accounts lies the invasion of Judah and Jerusalem. These disaster stories (see Introduction) function to reframe and interpret the historical collapse of the nation of Judah in a different narrative dimension. The destructions are not reported in factual "history" but in a mythic account about an ancient and distant world where cataclysm happens to other people. These trauma narratives embedded in Genesis, along with story of the flood and of God's command for Abraham to sacrifice Isaac, encode in a literary realm the traumatic history of Jerusalem and the fall of Judah to Babylon. Besides indirectly connecting the surviving nation with its traumatic past and reframing it, they continue to raise unsettled and unsettling theological questions that follow from it. Where was God? Why did it happen? Is there a future?

Camille Corot (1796–1875). *The Burning of Sodom*. 1843; revised 1857. Oil on canvas. (Credit: H.O. Havemeyer Collection, Bequest of Mrs. H. O. Havemeyer, 1929; Metropolitan Museum of Art, PD)

lives is the city of Jerusalem destroyed by the Babylonian Empire in their past. (See Introduction.) How could a just God cause or even allow such a cataclysm to happen to God's beloved city? This dramatic story has profound significance for the Judean audience of Genesis as they struggle to understand God's role in their own disaster. Why did it happen if their God is a just God?

CONNECTIONS

The Justice of God

Any community, nation, family, or individual that has had their world destroyed through the death of one person or the catastrophic deaths of many lives, places, or the environment faces the burning question of God's role in overwhelming loss. In theological language this question is called "theodicy," from the combined Greek roots for God and justice. Is God just? The question of divine justice is not an abstract theological discussion in this chapter. The catastrophe that lurks behind Sodom's ruin is the destruction of Jerusalem, the beloved city, the dwelling place of God, the central place of Israel's worship. For the book's audience, the fall of Jerusalem exists as a parallel disaster, a similar shocking event that requires theological explanation and interpretation. The conversation about Jerusalem takes place in the guise of a conversation about another city—a distant, mythic one. The distance enables the people of Judah to continue questioning God's role in their own losses. It legitimizes actual memories of Judah's catastrophe refracted through a new narrative that helps them remember, forget, and integrate the horrible past into the present.[4]

Abraham's debate with the Just Judge of all the earth unequivocally asserts that God is just because God agrees to protect the innocent. But then why was Jerusalem, God's special dwelling place, destroyed by an invading empire? That Sodom disappears under fire and brimstone despite God's promise to protect the innocent "explains" why destruction happened. Everyone in the city must have been wicked. [Jeremiah Searches the City for the Innocent]

For many modern readers this is a frightfully inadequate interpretation of horrors, a theology of a violent God who deliberately brings ruin and pain upon the people. Trauma and disaster studies help us understand it, even if we do not adopt it wholeheartedly. To interpret a disaster as divine punishment for sin means that God is still in relationship with the people. God has not abandoned or

Jeremiah Searches the City for the Innocent

The book of Jeremiah addresses the fall of the nation to Babylon. It portrays Jeremiah as one commanded by God to search the city for one person who acts justly to avert catastrophe:

Run to and fro through the streets of Jerusalem,
    look around and take note!
Search its squares and see
    if you can find one person
who acts justly
    and seeks truth—
so that I may pardon Jerusalem. (Jer 5:1)

God's command to the prophet functions like Abraham's argument with God. It interprets the coming disaster in advance of the Babylonian attack, even though the book actually addresses the survivors of the invasion. Here God wants to pardon the people of Jerusalem and sends the prophet as the emissary to find even one good person in order to pardon the whole city, but there are none. God sends the Babylonian army because there is no just and truthful person to prevent the invasions.

turned away from them, but instead God punishes them to bring survivors back into relationship with the divine in the future.

After disasters, trust in God, the world, and other people typically collapses. To rebuild trust requires explanation, a new way of thinking, a new story that places the disaster into a larger narrative and gives a sense of meaning and safety. As Louis Stulman has written, "Prose no less than poetry shifts the worst of circumstances to bearable distance. It removes the trauma of war from ground zero to the symbolic world of language, thus making it not only manageable but also intelligible."[5] In this theology, the composers of Genesis contribute to the survival of Judah. But is the violent, punishing, disaster-causing picture of God an adequate theology or a satisfying explanation of horrible events?

At the historical level, for example, this interpretation of disaster fails. While human factors always contribute to disasters, the fall of the city from universal sin omits other causes, including failed leadership, military and financial malfeasance, and imperial aggression on the part of the invading empires. On the theological level, arguing that disasters occur because God punishes wickedness affirms God's justice and, of most importance, keeps God in connection with the people, but it also sets all the responsibility on human sin. What did we do to make awful things happen? How could we have prevented it? [Is It Our Fault?]

Hope

When communities sink into doubt or individuals face despair, hope for a different reality becomes unthinkable, unimaginable, beyond comprehension. We cannot hope for new beginnings if we are held captive by preprogrammed determinations about what is possible. Assessing loss through the lens of past experience and intellectual efforts alone can be fruitless. Yet biblical testimony tells us otherwise. The crisis facing the audience of Genesis is their

---

Is It Our Fault?

After disaster, loss, or traumatic violence, survivors want to know why it happened. It is essential to find an explanation to help one go on with life. Without an interpretation, a new narrative about the disaster and displacement, complete chaos seems to rule the cosmos. This is because disasters destroy trust and confidence in God, the world, and other people. Everything that held life together, that gave meaning and stability to life, has proved false. Theology and faith collapse. Inconceivably, God did not protect the poor or stop the violence or save the child. Why? Is God powerless? Has God abandoned us? Or is God punishing us and teaching us?

Taking the blame for terrible loss upon oneself is a theological survival strategy, an instinctive response of people who survive traumatic events. It gives meaning to situations that defy meaning. As a survival strategy, it is a way to get through impossible circumstances that both keeps God in relationship with us and gives us a sense that we can prevent such terrifying events from occurring again. We will behave better. We will be good.

Using words of Robert Frost about the function of poetry, this theology can be called a "temporary stay against confusion" (49). It makes some sense of the situation but does not reveal it all. It helps for the time being, but it is not a theological absolute about our God.

For further reading, see Sam E. Balentine, "Legislating Divine Trauma," in Elizabeth Boase and Christopher G. Frechette, eds., *The Bible through the Lens of Trauma* (Semeia Studies 86; Atlanta: Society of Biblical Literature, 2016) 161–76.

Robert Frost, "The Figure a Poem Makes" (1939), quoted by Christophe Benfey, "The Storm over Robert Frost," *New York Review of Books*, 4 December 2008. See Kathleen M. O'Connor, *Jeremiah: Pain and Promise* (Maryknoll NY: Orbis, 2011) 149, n. 34, and pp. 56–57.

---

own survival as the people of Judah after a series of disasters. Will they grow as a people or be absorbed by intermarriage among the Babylonian and Persian peoples?

Abraham and Sarah can gain a future only by a miracle. The ancient audience as well as contemporary readers can see in this childless couple both doubts and the beginnings of hope. A new beginning arrives out of the blue with the surprising, mysterious visit of the three strangers. Sarah's laughter underscores how ridiculous the whole thing seems to the human eye. Neither she nor her husband can contain their amusement and perhaps their scorn because the promise contradicts visible reality. Yet a miracle awaits, for "Is anything too wonderful for the LORD?" (v. 15). [A Miracle of New Life]

The Old Testament insists on God's involvement in human life in ways that imperceptibly or dramatically alter human expectations. Again and again, the community of Israel rises from the grave, dead bones take on flesh (Ezek 37:1-14), the people escape from slavery (Exod 1–15), and the desert blooms so that the people can pass through it to return home (Isa 41:17-20). The New Testament continues, magnifies, and personalizes these claims through Jesus, whom God raises from the dead. The hope for new life that God gives is our heritage, our call as Jews and Christians and Muslims to anticipate new beginnings after collapse.

A Miracle of New Life

"Sarah's laughter may provoke God to finally transform her impossible situation: 'Is anything too wonderful (extraordinary) for God?' God promises one final time that God's return, in the spring, will give Sarah a son. The reference to spring (literally 'at the time when it is reviving') symbolizes the new life that God will bring in this woman's impossible situation of barrenness."

Juliana M. Claassens, *Claiming Her Dignity: Female Resistance in the Old Testament* (Minneapolis: Liturgical, 2016) 117.

The emergence of hope does not mean the fulfillment of our dreams, expectations, or even human needs. It does not enable us to avoid suffering. Consistently, hope arises after the fact in the discovery of the goodness and love of the Creator to bring all things to life. Hope is less a decision than it is a grace in the midst of suffering. Our difficulties in hoping, our weak and wobbly confidence that God will make things new, should not discourage us. After all, Sarah and Abraham laughed at the preposterous thought of a child.

NOTES

1. Sharon Pace Jeansome, in *The Women of Genesis* (Minneapolis: Fortress, 1990) 22–23, has translated the phrase "the time when it is revising," that is, the spring.

2. Jon D. Levenson, *Inheriting Abraham: The Legacy of the Patriarch in Judaism, Christianity & Islam* (Princeton: Princeton University Press, 2012) 60.

3. David W. Cotter, *Genesis* (Berit Olam; Collegeville MN: Liturgical, 2003) 118, n. 51, and Gerhard von Rad, *Genesis* (OTL; Philadelphia: Westminster, 1972) 208.

4. Ingeborg Löwisch, *Trauma Begets Genealogy: Gender and Memory in Chronicles* (Sheffield UK: Sheffield Phoenix Press, 2015) 32.

5. Louis Stulman, "Reflections on the Prose Sermons in the Book of Jeremiah: Duhm's and Mowinckel's Contribution to Trauma Readings," in *The Bible through the Lens of Trauma*, ed. Elizabeth Boase and Christopher B. Frechette (Semeia Studies 86; Atlanta: Society of Biblical Literature, 2016) 133.

DISASTER AND ESCAPE AT SODOM AND GOMORRAH

Genesis 19:1-38

With its assault on strangers, the fiery destruction of cities, and a woman turned into salt, the story of Sodom and Gomorrah is among the better-known biblical tales. [Operation Gomorrah] Chapter 19 continues the narrative thread of hospitality begun in chapter 18. [Law Codes about Foreigners] There Abraham's hospitality to the mysterious strangers brings new life in the midst of barrenness. Here Abraham's nephew Lot offers hospitality to visitors with equally high standards of hospitality. The customary welcome to the foreigners shown by Abraham and Lot contrasts sharply with the aggressive assault on the angelic visitors by the men of Sodom. Shocking behavior, however,

---

Operation Gomorrah

"'Operation Gomorrah' was the name of the week-long attack on Hamburg, Germany, July 1943 that killed 40,000 civilians and destroyed nearly the entire city" (Hirsch, 10). The attack's title, Operation Gomorrah, borrows from Genesis 19 a view of total destruction and, in popular thinking, elicits moral evaluation of the people of Hamburg as the wicked who deserve destruction. In a review of books about World War II, the so-called "good war," Adam Hirsch has asked if Americans can maintain our sense that we were the innocent warriors against wicked enemies in the face of atrocities like the destruction of Hamburg during Operation Gomorrah. The review invites a reconsideration of the moral implications of our memo-

ries of that war, not to reconsider the horrors of the Nazi regime but to show how expansive was the cruel destruction of civilians on both sides.

Adam Hirsch, "The Battle for History," *The New York Times Book Review*, 29 May 2011.

J Dowd (Fg Off), Royal Air Force official photographer. "Royal Air Force Bomber Command, 1942–1945." Oblique aerial view of ruined residential and commercial buildings south of the Eilbektal Park (seen at upper right) in the Eilbek district of Hamburg, Germany. These were among the 16,000 multi-storeyed apartment buildings destroyed by the firestorm that developed during the raid by Bomber Command on the night of 27/28 July 1943 (Operation GOMORRAH). The road running diagonally from upper left to lower right is Eilbeker Weg, crossed by Rückertstraße. (Credit: Wikimedia Commons, United Kingdom Government, PD-pre1957)

Law Codes about Foreigners

Part of what makes the Bible so bizarre in its ancient context is its repeated insistence on hospitality for the foreigner. There are lots of ancient law codes from the ancient Near East (Hammurabi's famous code is merely one of them), and none of them have laws that protect foreigners, and none of them say anything at all about welcoming foreigners. This is because foreigners had absolutely no rights in anybody else's land: they posed a threat to everyone else's scarce resources, and they could always be a scouting party for a foreign enemy. So, it is best to shut them out unless they are beneficial to your people in some way. Foreign dignitaries and rich merchants were always welcome; people fleeing oppression never were.

Ancient Israel, though, is an odd duck because their law codes say over and over again that you *have* to welcome the wandering foreigner and you *have* to help them, you *cannot* oppress them: "You shall not wrong or oppress a resident alien, for you were aliens in the land of Egypt" (Exod 22:21).

Published on Facebook by Old Testament scholar Brennan Breed, Columbia Theological Seminary, Decatur, Georgia, as an informal aid for preachers. See also Brennan Breed, "'Love the Alien as Yourself': Trump's Refugee Ban and the Bible," *HuffPost*, 30 January 2017, http://www.huffingtonpost.com/brennan-breed/love-the-alien-as-yoursel_b_14480198.html.

does not end with the men of Sodom. Lot himself shows utter disregard for the well-being of his daughters who, in turn, trick their father into incestuous sex at the chapter's end.

Chapter 19 has both etiological and theological purposes. Theologically, it presents the events over which God and Abraham were arguing in the preceding chapter. Etiologically, it explains why the Moabites and the Ammonites turn out to be less than excellent neighbors, why the ancient cities of Sodom and Gomorrah are no more, and why a pillar of salt resembles the figure of a woman. [Outline of Genesis 19] The gradual unfolding of the divine identity of the visitors repeats itself here. The narrator calls them "angels" (19:1), men (19:5, 10, 12, 16), "he" (19:21, 25), and finally the "LORD" (19:24). Only two angels, not three, come to Sodom (v. 1), for the Lord had remained behind to speak with Abraham (18:22-33).

Outline of Genesis 19

1. Layers of Wickedness, 19:1-11
2. Destruction of the Cities with a Surviving Remnant, 19:12-29
3. The Ingenuity of Lot's Daughters, 19:30-38

COMMENTARY

Sodom and Gomorrah and "all the land of the Plain" (v. 29) come to ruin in this chapter, but the story depicts a closeup of events in only one city. Those events provide narrative evidence of the city's wickedness and "justify" God's destruction of it. Perhaps the focus on one city also reminds the book's audience of the destruction of their own city, Jerusalem. The destruction of Sodom and Gomorrah is an earth-shattering, cosmic event: "The LORD rained on Sodom and Gomorrah sulfur and fire from the LORD out of heaven" (19:24). Rape threatens women and men and the population is largely killed, but, as in all the disaster stories of Genesis, survivors escape to begin life again. (See Introduction.) Even though this story concerns the remote past, it encodes the traumatic history of the people of Judah and points tentatively toward new life.[1]

Layers of Wickedness, 19:1-11

The opening scene echoes and continues the previous chapter (18:1-8). Two strangers approach Lot, who sits at the gate of Sodom just as Abraham sat at the door of his tent when three strangers appeared before him (18:2; 19:1). Lot follows Abraham's exemplary protocols of hospitality. He rises to meet the strangers and bows to the ground. He implores them with deference: "Please (*nāʾ*) my lords, please (*nāʾ*) turn aside to your servant's house" (19:2). When the angels at first refuse his invitation, he urges them more strongly to stay with him. Finally, he prepares a feast and bakes unleavened bread for them. [Parallels with Judges 19] Lot omits no customary ritual of welcome.

Perhaps because Lot is a relative stranger in Sodom himself (13:12; 19:9), he knows the importance of hospitality. Among the citizenry he alone welcomes the visitors, but readers already know that the people of Sodom "were wicked, great sinners against the LORD" (13:13). The people of Sodom threaten the strangers and reverse the warm welcome that Lot provides to his guests: "The men of the city, the men of Sodom, both young and old, all the city to the last man, surrounded the house" (v. 4). All—every man of every age to the last one—demand that Lot send out the strangers so that they may "know them" (v. 5). Noteworthy in this verse is its insistence that all the men of Sodom storm Lot's house. Suddenly, Abraham's stubborn arguments with God on behalf of the innocent in the previous chapter have become moot (18:22-32). There are no innocents among them, not even a meager ten prevent the city's destruction (18:32). The blanketing of blame over all the people interprets the destruction of the city. This understanding of human sinfulness as the cause of the disaster is a theological way to make sense of horrible events. It insists that God is not whimsical and unjust; instead, humans bring destruction upon themselves and God rightly punishes them (see [Is it Our Fault?]).

When the men of Sodom demand that Lot send out his visitors that they may "know" (*yādaʿ*) them, they use a Hebrew verb that

Parallels with Judges 19

Events in Genesis 19 resemble events in another terrible story of sexual assault in Judges 19. There a Levite travels to Bethlehem to win back his concubine, who, for unexplained reasons, has returned to the home of her father. After much delay the father gives his daughter back to the Levite, who sets out very late in the day to bring her back to his home in Ephraim. They stop overnight in an Israelite town called Gibeah. No one offers them hospitality except for another man of the same tribe as the Levite. The men of the city pound on the door and demand that the host send out the guest so that they may "know him" (*yāda*') just as the men of Sodom do at Lot's house. Like Lot, the host protests and protects his guest, saying, "Since this man is my guest do not do this vile thing" (Judg 19:23). Again the violation is against the custom of hospitality to strangers. Then the Levite, not the host, takes his own concubine and throws her out to the men, who rape her all night. She dies on the threshold of the house.

In both Gen 19 and Judg 19, the natives of the city violate hospitality and attempt to sexually assault visitors. The hosts defend the male guests and proffer women as a substitute. In the case of Judges, the woman is not rescued but dead on the threshold in the morning. Yet the violation of the concubine's body does not end with her death. Her "husband" chops up her body to serve both as a symbol of the broken tribes of Israel and as a rallying cry for unity among them (Judg 19:27-30). In the passage from Judges, it is not foreigners who perpetrate the violation but Israelites themselves. Provoking outrage is the clearly a purpose of the Judges text in its larger concern for unity and kingship in Israel.

Both are outrageous accounts in their disregard of the safety, bodily integrity, and human dignity of women. Women simply do not count as valuable humans in their own right. To a certain extent, women's lack of humanity, of control over their bodies, and of autonomy were a given in the ancient world, even though the texts are designed to provoke dismay and repulsion on the part of readers. In both cases, the intended sexual offenses against men have less to do with homosexual relationships than with inhospitality expressed in the most egregious attacks on the human bodies of strangers.

Cherubino Cornienti (1816–1860). *Levite of Ephraim's Wife*. 1845–1846. Oil on canvas. Pinacoteca di Brera, Milan, Italy. (Credit: Mondadori Portfolio / Art Resource, NY)

frequently conveys sexual knowing. [What Is the Sin of Sodom?] The men do worse than fail to welcome strangers; they reject the visitors and try to abuse, shame, and violate them sexually.[2] Like a lynch mob, they attack the house of strangers who come from somewhere else.

Another layer of wicked behavior in this chapter, however, goes without explicit notice in the text. Lot's response as host is to protect the strangers. He offers the crowd a substitute in the strangers' place, his *own* virginal daughters! "Look (*hînnēh*)," he says, "I have two daughters who have not known men. Let me

What Is the Sin of Sodom?

The text, as well as the history of interpretation, leaves the nature of the sin of Sodom in a cloud of uncertainty. There is no precision in identifying the sin of Sodom because the text itself does not allow it. Instead, like the sin of the sons of God and the daughters of humans (6:1-4) and the equally vague offense by Noah's son who sees his father's nakedness (9:18-28), the larger purposes of Gen 19 are to provide another example of a disaster and to explain it as the consequence of human behavior. The story of Sodom and Gomorrah aims squarely at the book's audience, which continues to struggle with the theological consequences of its own destroyed city of Jerusalem. (See Introduction.)

When "the sin of Sodom" comes up in the rest of the Old Testament, it receives a variety of interpretations, none of which concern homosexuality. For example,

• Isaiah addresses the people of Israel and their rulers as "people of Sodom and people of Gomorrah" (Isa 1:9-10), referring to the near destruction of Zion. Oppressive rulers make the people like Sodom, a collapsed city (3:9).
• in Ezekiel, the sin of Sodom involves a charge against people who lived with "pride, excess of food and prosperous, but did not aid the poor and the needy" (16:49). This interpretation is possible because Gen 19 leaves the nature of the sin of Sodom unclear.
• in Jeremiah, the prophets have become like Sodom and Gomorrah because "they commit adultery, walk in lies, and strengthen the hands of evildoers" (Jer 23:14).
• in Deuteronomy, Israel's enemies come from poisonous vines, like Sodom and Gomorrah (Deut 32:32).

The sin of Sodom symbolizes various forms of wickedness in many texts, but, primarily, most biblical references to Sodom and Gomorrah view them as symbols of massive destruction rather than examples of particular sins.

Amos refers to the Sodom and Gomorrah as places that frighten by their very collapse, examples of terrible ruin (Amos 4:11, similarly Deut 29:22; Zeph 2:9; Lam 4:6; Jer 49:18; 50:40).

The New Testament yields similar interpretations of Sodom and Gomorrah as horrifying places of destruction, places of terror and shocking ruins.

When Jesus speaks of Sodom and Gomorrah in Matthew's Gospel, he shows compassion for the two cities. Their inhospitality to the two visitors (angels) pales in comparison to the sins of cities of his own time that reject his disciples and the word of life they bring. He advises the disciples to shake the dust off their feet of cities that reject them. The sin of Sodom and Gomorrah is again inhospitality: "Truly I tell you, it will be more tolerable for the cities of Sodom and Gomorrah on the day of judgment than for that town" (Mt 10:15; see Lk 10:10-12). Jesus continues, "If the deeds of power [miracles] done in you had been done in Sodom, it would have remained unto this day" (Mt 11:23).

Sodom and Gomorrah live in the biblical tradition primarily as exemplars of catastrophe, while the sins thought to provoke destruction are never identified, much less understood to be sexual, as some insist in modern times. The fact that daughters are offered as substitutes for the guests shows that this is not about homosexuality but about using sexuality for terrorizing purposes. The crime involves intimate assaults on strangers, Lot's offering of his daughters for abuse, while the men of Sodom "attempt to harm Lot even more viciously than the visitors" (19:9; Fischer, 273).

Interpreting the sin of Sodom as acts of male-with-male sex seems to have come into the Christian tradition through the writings of ancient Jewish historians. Philo (50 CE) and Josephus (96 CE) interpreted the sin of Sodom as pederasty (sex with children). Both writers were rejecting Hellenist (Greek) special regard for the male body, nudity, and general unbridled sexual openness.

Irmtraud Fischer, "On the Significance of the 'Women Texts' in the Ancestral Narratives," in *Torah*, ed. Irmtraud Fischer and Mercedes Navarro Puerto, vol. 1 of The Bible and Women: An Encyclopedia of Exegesis and Cultural History (Atlanta: Society of Biblical Literature, 2011).

Philo, Qu'est ce Salut, iv:31-37.

bring them out to you, and do to them as you please. Only do nothing to these men, for they have come under the shelter of my roof (v. 8)." The use of "look" (*hinnēh*) draws attention to Lot's cavalier attitude. (See ["Look!"].) When he begs the men of the city, whom he calls "brothers," not to act so wickedly, he highlights the value of his male guests over his own female flesh and blood.

"Do nothing to these men, for they have come under the shelter of my roof" (v. 8). He provides no protection for his daughters, prepares to cast them out to the rioting crowd, and even invites the attackers to abuse them as they please. The one from whom the daughters need protection before all others is their own father.

Although the text does not directly challenge Lot's betrayal of his daughters, the writers are not blind to his shocking treatment of them. The rest of the chapter consistently depicts him as a fool. The last scene even provides the daughters with a form of "poetic justice"[3] that subtly critiques his behavior here (19:30-38).

Meanwhile, the rioters reply to Lot with scorn and heightened aggression: "This fellow came here as an alien, and he would play the judge!" (19:9). In their view, Lot remains a foreigner who has overstepped his bounds. In just the nick of time, however, the two angels reach out from the house and grab Lot and then blind the natives so that they cannot find the door. When the angels save Lot, they also save his daughters, but we only learn of their survival because they continue to appear in the story (v. 15). Although all the men of Sodom are guilty in their treatment of strangers, Lot himself is anything but a sterling character. [Obligation to Protect Daughters]

Destruction of the Cities with a Surviving Remnant, 19:12-29

After foiling the mob, the angelic visitors inquire about Lot's family, as if they do not know about his daughters' existence. "Have you anyone else here, sons-in-law, daughters, or anyone? Bring them out of this place, for we are about to destroy this place," they command (19:12-13). At this moment the angels distinguish themselves from God. They announce that the Lord has sent them to destroy the city because of the "outcry against the people" of Sodom that initiated the debate between God and Abraham in the first place (18:20-21).

The destruction of the city unfolds in slow motion with a series of delays and confusions. In the first delay, Lot goes to convince his sons-in-law, not yet married to his daughters, to get up and go because "The LORD is about to destroy the city" (19:14). Lot's

---

Obligation to Protect Daughters

One of the obligations of males of the household is to protect the virginity of daughters and sisters. "In ancient Israel, as other village-based traditional societies, shame stains the entire household. For an unmarried woman, shame reflects directly on parents and brothers, especially unmarried ones, who did not protect or avenge her" (Peristiany, 182).

When Lot offers his daughters to the men of Sodom, he places hospitality over his duty to protect his female offspring. "He preserves his honor as host but is stained with shame as father. His speech makes the gender hierarchy clear: . . . 'but to these men, do not do anything.' This is a heightened example of the inner contradictions of the patriarchal value system, which are exposed in a moment of crisis" (Hendal et al., 85–86).

J. G. Peristiany, "Honour and Shame in a Cypriot Highland Village," in *Honour and Shame: The Values of Mediterranean Society*, ed. J. G. Peristiany (Chicago: University of Chicago Press, 1966).

Ronald Hendal, Chana Kronfeld, and Ilana Pardes, "Gender and Sexuality" in *Reading Genesis: Ten Methods*, ed. Ronald Hendal (Cambridge: Cambridge University Press, 2010).

potential sons-in-law—presumably as wicked as the rest of the city—disrespect him. They do not believe him, though it is easy to see why, since he almost ruined their marriage plans by callously offering his daughters for the other men of the city to despoil.

Lot causes the second delay himself when he carelessly lingers in the city even after the angels urgently tell him to leave with his wife and daughters. Again the angels have to rescue him; they take him and the women by the hand, "the LORD being merciful to him" (19:16). When the escapees arrive outside the city, the angels continue to urge them, "Flee for your life, do not look back . . . or you will be consumed" (v. 18).

In yet a third delay, Lot argues with the angels because he does not want to flee to the hills where they have directed him for fear he will not make it in time. The angels comply and agree to let him go to the little city called Zoar because Lot believes it is closer and safer. Only now in the depth of this crisis do the angelic visitors emerge again as God: "I will grant you this favor and will not overthrow the city of which you have spoken" (19:21). Lot must hurry because the divine hands are tied until he arrives at his destination. Adding to the dramatic frenzy, God expresses powerlessness to postpone the disaster until Lot gets to the mountains. These delays in escaping the city help to characterize Lot as a fool and the situation as chaotic.

When Lot and his daughters finally escape to the city of Zoar, the Lord rains sulfur and fire upon the cities from out of the heavens. [An Earthquake?] All the cities and the plain are destroyed. [Did Sodom and Gomorrah Exist?] The narrator uses a matter-of-fact tone to tell of another disruption after the escape. Against the angels' instruction, Lot's wife looks back on the burning the city and turns into a pillar of salt (19:26). [The Story's Traumatic Details] Her demise removes her from the story and opens the way for the next scene between the daughters and their father in the cave. Her petrified body also serves etiological purposes, explaining why a rock formation in the desert has the shape of a woman. Her curiosity kills, or, more likely, the shock from the violence at her back paralyzes and destroys her. [Lot's Wife]

After the cataclysm, Abraham goes out early in the morning to the same spot where he and the Lord had spoken (18:26-21), and he sees the smoke "going up like the smoke in chimney" (19:27). When God destroys the cities, God remembers Abraham and therefore saves Lot in a blessing to future nations that descend from him. On account of Abraham, two neighboring nations receive the blessing of existence (12:1-3).

The Destruction of Sodom and Gomorrah

John Martin, an English romantic painter, rendered this interpretation of Genesis 19 in 1852. Martin's painting captures the moment of destruction. To the right of the painting is a streak of lightning, presumably representing the fire of God sent down to destroy the city. Lot and his daughters are at the top of the hillside, and Lot's nameless wife follows along behind in the valley. The tip of the lightning bolt points to her as if she is the special object of divine punishment along with the city. In the fiery center of the painting, buildings are shown collapsing into the flames. The destruction appears as a magnificent inferno orchestrated by an invisible, punishing God. Martin interprets the wife's transformation into a pillar of

salt as divine punishment, but he also presents her as a forgotten family member left behind by the others.

Although Martin painted many biblical scenes with operatic imagination, he does not seem to be commenting on any particular catastrophe of his own time, but his personal history could be another matter. This work, however, may simply reflect interest in landscape painting that prevailed among artists in the 1800s.

John Martin (1789–1854). *The Destruction of Sodom and Gomorrah*. 1852. Oil on canvas, Laing Art Gallery, Newcastle upon Tyne. (Credit: Wikimedia Commons, PD-1923)

An Earthquake?

Von Rad has proposed that an ancient tradition underlying the text may preserve the memory of an actual earthquake: "Perhaps a tectonic earthquake released gases (hydrogen sulphide) or opened up the way for asphalt and petroleum." Speculation continues that an entire mass of air could become ignited. The areas of the Dead Sea where these cities were said to have existed have many deposits of asphalt and sulfur that could catch fire. (von Rad, 220)

By contrast, Westermann has argued that fire and brimstone is a "fixed image of God's judgment"(p. 306; cf. Ps 11:6; Ezek 38:22; Isa 30:33; Isa 34:9; Deut 29:22). It is not meant to describe accurately an individual event. There may be ancient memories of physical destruction behind chapter 19, but in this commentary scientific explanations are not as important as the disaster's function as a narrative to help Judah survive their own destruction.

Gerhard von Rad, *Genesis*, rev. ed. (Philadelphia: Westminster, 1973).

Claus Westermann, *Genesis 12–36: A Commentary* (London: SPCK, 1981).

The Ingenuity of Lot's Daughters, 19:30-38

Despite divine protection through several rescues of Lot and his daughters, fear continues to motivate Lot as it does most survivors of trauma. Afraid of life in Zoar, he chooses to live alone with his daughters in a cave. The two daughters quickly realize that there are no eligible male partners available to them to produce offspring, so they concoct a plan to "preserve offspring through our father" (19:32). For two nights in a row they get him drunk,

Did Sodom and Gomorrah Exist?

No remains of ancient cities have yet been found in the plain near the Dead Sea. It is likely that the story arose from the ruins of destroyed cities from ecological or military disasters. Fretheim has summarized recent conversation about the possible location of the cities:

We do not know where these cities were located, but some now place them southeast of the Dead Sea (rather than under the southern part of the sea). The area lies in a geological rift, extending from Turkey to East Africa, the Dead Sea being its lowest point (1,305 feet below sea level). The area has extensive sulfur and bitumen deposits and petrochemical springs, which the text points out (14:10; 19:24; cf. Deut 29:23; Zeph 2:9). An earthquake associated with fires (brimstone is sulfurous fire) may have ignited these deposits, producing an explosion that "overthrew" the cities.

The tradition has taken up tales of some such ecological disaster and woven them into the story of Abraham and his family. (473)

Terence E. Fretheim, "Genesis" (*NIB* 1; Nashville: Abingdon, 1994)..

The Story's Traumatic Details

There can be no question about the traumatic nature of this disaster story. Besides the descent of fire and brimstone from the sky to take down the city and the ones around it on the Plain, the human character Lot acts with confusion, doubt, and uncertainty. He cannot think straight. He has confusing ideas about how to escape. He denies the urgency of taking action. His wife turns into an ossified pillar of human flesh.

each in turn has sex with him, and each becomes pregnant by him. [Parallels with Noah's Sons]

The daughters' motivation for arranging sequential acts of incest with their father has many possible interpretations. The narrator provides preserving offspring as a noble motive (19:32). Whether the daughters act in desperation to keep the family line alive or to retaliate against their father for offering them to the angry crowd, or whether the story is a cover-up to protect Lot by blaming the daughters for the incest is not clear. The fruit of these incestuous unions are the patriarchs of two neighboring nations, Moab and Ammon, who become enemies of Israel (cf. Deut 23:3-4). [Incest and Daughters] Foolish Lot is presumably oblivious of the conception of sons/grandsons in a cave outside civilization. His offspring are blood relatives of Abraham, but in this folkloric narrative they emerge as less-than-worthy cousins, born in incest to a foolish, frightened man. Their birth provokes scorn and laughter as it explains the perceived failures of their neighbors.

The chapter's etiologies or origin stories interpret the behavior of neighbors, the existence of a salt rock formation in the desert, and the destruction of ancient cities and their environs.[4] Despite possible etiological purposes, however, it also echoes Judah's own history in the post-Babylonian Period. Like other disaster stories in Genesis, it does not tell history in a direct account of events. Rather, it presents a narrative of another catastrophe set in the distant past but bearing elements typical of traumatic violence

Lot's Wife

Despite the divine command not to look back (19:17), turning to see the catastrophe seems like a normal human response to fire falling from the sky. The transformation of Lot's wife from a human woman into a pillar of salt has often been interpreted as punishment for "looking back" at the destroyed city when God prohibited looking (v. 26). Origen, an early Christian theologian (185–254 CE), has a sympathetic but dualistic interpretation of this "little statue of salt." Like most thinkers of the time, Origen divided humans into separate spheres of flesh and spirit. For him, women represented the flesh with a propensity toward evil:

> What great crime was it, if the concerned mind of the woman looked backward when she was being terrified by the excessive crackling of the flames? But because the law [God's command] is spiritual and the things that happened to the ancients "happened figuratively," let us see if perhaps Lot, who did not look back, is not the rational understanding and the courageous soul. For it is the flesh which always look to vices . . . the flesh looks backward and seeks after pleasures. . . . [Jesus said,] "No man putting his hand to the plow and looking back is fit for the kingdom of heaven" and he adds, "Remember Lot's wife" (Lk 9:62). (Origen in Sheridan, ed., 79)

Women interpreters have pointed to the text as another story intended to keep women in their place, in this case by prohibiting curiosity. Perhaps, though, the petrified body of Mrs. Lot signifies the life-destroying, body-and-spirit-paralyzing impact of disaster upon victims and witnesses. Maybe it is the terrors of viewing the destruction of the cities and all their inhabitants, her home, the near miss for her and her family, the traumatic mutilation of earth that turn her to stone. Perhaps this is what the command not to look back means, a way to protect Lot and his wife and daughters from being frightfully overcome by the massive destruction. Maybe looking back too intently to the Babylonian disaster has turned some survivors and their offspring into mute and half-alive people resembling a pillar of salt. The wife's representation as a pillar of salt also works as an explanation of salt formations in the area around the Dead Sea (Jeansome, 41). Finally, her actions function as a plot device to remove her from the family in order that the daughters' plans are not hampered by their mother.

Origen, 19.26, "Lot's Wife Looks Back," in *ACCS II: Genesis 12-50*, ed. Mark Sheridan (Downer's Grove IL: Intervarsity, 2002).

Sharon Pace Jeansome, *The Women of Genesis* (Minneapolis: Fortress, 1990).

Hilda Katz (1909–1997). *Lot's Wife*. Print. Smithsonian American Art Museum. Gift of the artist in memory of her parents, Max and Lina Katz. (Credit: Smithsonian American Art Museum; http://edan.si.edu/saam/id/object/1978.109.12)

Parallels with Noah's Sons

Like Noah's sons in the aftermath of the flood story (9:18-28), Lot's daughters deal with a drunken father following a catastrophe (19:30-38). Both accounts also encode relationships with other peoples. When one of Noah's sons looks upon his naked father, Noah curses his grandson. Although it is not mentioned in the passage, some interpreters think sexual intercourse may be implied. See [Nakedness]. By contrast, Lot's daughters make their father drunk and engage in incestuous sex to preserve life. Ironically, in the case of Lot, "the man who offered to have his daughters sexually brutalized is now manipulated sexually" (Jeansome, 41). Lot remains a foolish character who never provides for his family and who does not even know what happens to him in the cave in which he chooses to hide.

Sharon Pace Jeansome, *The Women of Genesis* (Minneapolis: Fortress, 1990).

Orazio Gentileschi (1563–1639). *Lot and His Daughters*. 1628. Oil on canvas. Bilbao Fine Arts Museum, Bilbao, Spain. (Credit: Wikimedia Commons, PD-US)

and its aftermath. Confusion, delays, and illogic characterize the escape that happens miraculously, through the mercy of the Lord. Lot's wife freezes in shock and dies when she sees the devastation. Lot and his daughters survive and are constricted by fear, even though they are safe in Zoar. Abraham's questions about God's justice that introduce the story heighten the pressing theological question that still haunted Judah in the post-Babylonian Period: How could Jerusalem and its environs be destroyed like Sodom and Gomorrah? (cf. Jer 5:1-7). Abraham, the father of the nation,

Incest and Daughters

Do Lot's daughters exact a form of revenge against their father when they trick him into having sex with them? Do they perform heroic deeds to save the family line? Are they acting to protect their future by ensuring children for themselves in old age? Or is this story, as some interpreters suggest, a cover-up to protect an incestuous father?

At the narrative level, this text pictures the two daughters raping their father, since he is drunk and unaware of what is being done to him. Yet incest typically arises from the fathers' initiative in assaults on their daughters. Susanne Schulz and Cheryl Exum have insisted that daughters do not initiate sex with their fathers. They propose that the text does not describe incest as it occurs but instead expresses male fantasy about incest. Irmtraud Fischer has agreed that the scene is a classic story of repression of the truth by an incestuous father such as can often be found in court transcripts today:

Alcohol was involved, the daughters wanted intercourse or even provoked it, and the mothers are not available to call upon for help. Even the story surrounding Lot's daughters can only partially cover up evidence of the crime. The incestuous names of the children Ammon ("of my people") and Moab ("from my father") speak volumes. (274)

These insights are of great pastoral importance, for they expose circumstances of a cover-up that may exist behind the text and that surely exist today. The biblical text cannot be used to reinforce patterns of abuse and incest.

Yet the folkloric and etiological qualities of the story add other dimensions. It uses sexuality to make larger etiological points and provide accounts of the origins of enemies. The daughters' focus on survival of the people and their clever plan for that to happen bring literary satisfaction. The father, who callously proffered their bodies to assaulting strangers, becomes the shamed, drunken object of their efforts to provide a future for themselves.

Susanne Scholz, *Sacred Witness: Rape in the Hebrew Bible* (Minneapolis: Fortress, 2010) 172.

J. Cheryl Exum, "Desire Extorted and Exhibited: Lot and His Daughters in Psychoanalysis, Painting, and Film," in *A Wise and Discerning Mind": Essays in Honor of Burke O. Long*, ed. Saul Olyan and Robert Culley (BJS 325; Providence RI: Brown Judaic Studies, 2000) 83–108.

Irmtraud Fischer, "On the Significance of the 'Women Texts' in the Ancestral Narratives," in *Torah*, ed. Irmtraud Fischer and Mercedes Navarro Puerto, vol. 1 of The Bible and Women: An Encyclopedia of Exegesis and Cultural History (Atlanta: Society of Biblical Literature, 2011).

witnessed this disaster, and his nephew's family survived because God remembered Abraham. "As Abraham gazes in silence over the scene of the disaster (vv. 27-28), he looks beyond himself and his experience into the history of his people and the history of the peoples of the earth."[5]

CONNECTIONS

For too long the story of Sodom has been treated as an excuse to harm, abuse, and exclude people who are sexually different (known sometimes by the acronym LGBTQ), despite biblical evidence that the sin of Sodom is the violation of hospitality to strangers. The abuse and rejection of people of different sexual identities actually reenacts the sin of Sodom. Rejecting, terrorizing, and failing to welcome those who are different from the dominant clan, is, in von Rad's terms, "a frightful violation of the law of hospitality."[6] [Xenophobia]

Hospitality—a virtue that stands at the center of Christian discipleship—is the opposite of xenophobia. Hospitality is a way to stand before God, the world, and oneself. It manifests itself in multiple dimensions of life, in our welcome of new ideas, in our openness new ways of being, and in material and social care for individuals, peoples, and cultures that we meet in our neighborhoods local and global. Hospitality involves curiosity, radical receptivity, and the letting go of defensiveness before those who are "not from here, not like us, not from our tribe." Hospitality includes and maybe even starts with openness to the strange elements of our own beings, the alien parts of ourselves we wish to shame and drive away.

To be hospitable is to live confidently with God, who takes away fear. It is to put on "the mind of Christ," as Paul urges the Philippians to do. It means to be rooted in love, to do nothing from selfish ambition or conceit, in humility to regard others as better than one's self. "Let each of you not look to your own interests, but to the interests of others" (Phil 2:4; see vv. 1-5).

Xenophobia

 Burton Visotzky has reflected on the Bible and "zenophobia" (alternate spelling):

Zenophobia [fear of strangers] is something the Bible legislates against, and the story of Sodom and Gomorrah is a grim reminder of how poorly God looks upon those who would be cruel to strangers. The destruction of Sodom and Gomorrah is the most terrible act of destruction God wreaks following Noah's flood. It seems God wants to make a clear point about the inviolability of sanctuary and the sacredness of hospitality.

To be fair the biblical book of Leviticus is replete with exclusivist themes . . . [but] by the time the Bible gets to the book of Ruth, it is a Moabite, Ruth herself, who mothers the grandfather of King David, ancestor to the Messiah. A complex moral is being taught here. Yes, there are exclusivist tendencies—don't we all have them, in our nations, in our own communities, in our own families? In the end hospitality must overturn our dislike of the other, our fear of the stranger. Unless we know we live in one global village, all the cities of the plain may yet be overturned. (78)

Burton L. Visotzky, *The Genesis of Ethics: How the Tormented Family of Genesis Leads us to Moral Development* (New York: Three Rivers Press, 1996).

Although Paul's admonitions to empty ourselves like Jesus need some qualification—such as one must first have a self to empty— he invites the community to take on the mind of Christ in fearless, universal hospitality. Paul captures the sense of Jesus' parable that separates the sheep and the goats on the basis of hospitality:

"For I was hungry and you gave me food, I was thirsty and you gave me drink, I was a stranger and you welcomed me, I was naked and you gave me clothing, I was sick and you took care of me, I was in prison and you visited me." Then the righteous will answer him, "Lord, when was it that we saw you hungry and gave you food, or thirsty and gave you something to drink? And when was it that we saw you a stranger and welcomed you, or naked and gave you clothing? And when was it that we saw you sick or in prison and visited you?" And the king will answer them, "Truly I tell you, just as you did it to one of the least of these who are members of my family, you did it to me." (Matt 25:35-40)

Jesus' identification with the stranger, the cast off, the weak, and the despised is so central to the revelation of God that treatment of the least of these becomes the identifying mark of Christian discipleship. [Hospitality] The practice of hospitality and welcome can benefit the recipients by enabling their survival in the face of menacing regimes, bringing them into safety and community from choppy seas, or giving them an opportunity to live with dignity. For certain, the practice of hospitality heals and enriches the ones who offer it.

Hospitality

Reginald Brantley, minister in the United Church of Christ and President of the New York Metropolitan Association (UCC), has called Christians in the United States to welcome immigrants and refugees:

Whether immigrants or brought here in chains, were we not once strangers in this land which for some held the promise of being a city on a hill shining forth brightly as a beacon of Christianity and civilization? The command to the Hebrews was to remember their former status as aliens in Egypt. The injunction to us in the 21st century western nations of luxury is to reflect prophet Jeremiah's words to the king of Judah: "Do justice and righteousness . . . . Also do not mistreat or do violence to the stranger . . ." (Jer. 22:3). This is a call to not only refrain from committing harm, but to assertively promote justice. We can do that if our own hearts are dwelling places for God's grace and mercy. Then, we will be compelled to be people who care about what happens to others, who demonstrate that concern by proactively taking up the cause of the immigrants among us.

We are the people in whose hearts God has pitched a tent (Jn. 1:14). The God who pitches a tent in our hearts in John's gospel is the same God who sojourned with the patriarchs and matriarchs of faith. If God travels with us as with them, does not God expect us to care for the living Aylan Kurdis, the ones still out there trying to find a dwelling place far from tyranny? [Aylan Kurdi is the Syrian child who died in the Mediterranean when his family was trying to flee to safety in Europe.]

Would not the discomfort of making room in our hearts for them be an act of sacrificial love and worship as we become conduits of love and grace? Would not that be a joy, privilege, and a fulfillment of Christian love and human compassion? Or do we limit our exercise of compassion only to those whose ancestors snuck into this country on the Mayflower who were immigrants as well, ones who would have perished had it not been for the selfless kindness and grace of the indigenous people who showed compassion.

Reginald Brantley, "God's Heart: A Dwelling Place for Strangers," *The Living Pulpit* 25/2 (Summer–Fall 2016): 7–8.

NOTES

1. See Louis Stulman and Hyun Chul Paul Kim, *You Are My People: An Introduction to Prophetic Literature* (Nashville: Abingdon, 2010) esp. 1–23, for insights into prophetic literature as artistic mediations for survival after the destruction of warfare.

2. See Lynn M. Bectel, "A Feminist Reading of Gen 19:1-11," in *Genesis: A Feminist Companion to the Bible* 1 (Second Series) (Sheffield UK; Sheffield Academic Press, 1998) 108–28.

3. Mark G. Brett, *Genesis: Procreation and the Politics of Identity* (OTR; New York: Routledge, 2000) 68.

4. See Herman Gunkel, *Genesis*, trans. Mark Biddle (Macon GA: Mercer University Press, 1997) 206–18.

5. Claus Westermann, *Genesis 12–36: A Commentary* (London: SPCK, 1981) 309.

6. Gerhard von Rad, *Genesis*, rev. ed. (Philadelphia: Westminster, 1973) 218.

THREATENED AND EXONERATED

Genesis 20:1-18

Chapter 20 tells a parallel version of the endangered matriarch story (12:10-20; see 26:6-11 for a third version). The versions are similar. Abraham passes Sarah off as his sister, a foreign ruler "takes" her, and God intervenes to rescue her, thereby preserving her, the promise, and the bloodline. Chapter 20 expands the chapter 12 story, providing motivations to exonerate all the characters of any wrongdoing and restoring their honor. [Type Scenes] Despite the change of subject from the destruction of cities (chs. 18–19) to Sarah's predicament, this chapter continues to question God's justice, especially regarding the punishment of the innocent. [Outline of Genesis 20]

Type Scenes

A type scene is a basic narrative plot repeated with variations. Genesis 12:10-20; 20; and 26:6-11 follow the same pattern. A patriarch and his wife are migrating in a foreign land; he passes her off as his sister; a ruler wants her and then lets them both go. While the narrative frame is similar, the stories serve different purposes in the book. The first two involve Abraham and Sarah and the third concerns Isaac and Rebekah. What joins them further in each case is the threat to the matriarch and hence to the fulfillment of the promise. The story encodes the possible disappearance of the people into foreign empires, prevented in every case by God, who preserves the woman and sets the couples free. Once again, the stories have layers of meaning for the characters alone and for the book's audience. They can find echoes of their predicament in the situation of the characters or see their own serious doubt about their future as a people and cultural entity.

Outline of Genesis 20

1. Abimelech's Innocence, 20:1-10
2. Abraham's and Sarah's Innocence, 20:11-13
3. Sarah's Exoneration, 20:14-18

COMMENTARY

Questions that haunt Genesis and its Judean audience come subtly to the fore in chapter 20. Do the Judean survivors of the nation's fall have a future as a people? Will they bear children or disappear into other empires as Sarah almost does here?

Abimelech's Innocence, 20:1-10

Abraham and his family continue their migratory lives, going "out to the land of the Negeb," a desert region in the south. They settle in a

Map of Abraham's Journey

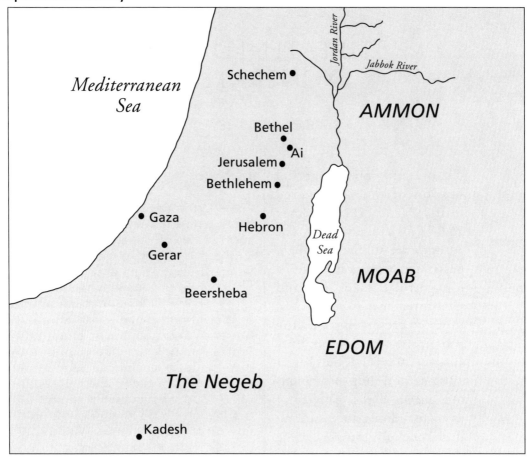

place called Gerar. The Hebrew makes a point of Abraham's alien status because the verb translated "settle" (*gûr*) indicates temporary rather than permanent residence. Abraham still resides as a stranger or alien in the land promised to him as a possession (20:1). [Foreigners]

After establishing the family's new location, the narrator shrinks the story presented more fully in chapter 12. Abraham, for example, announces for no evident reason that Sarah "is my sister," and with no intervening explanation, "Abimelech of Gerar sent and took Sarah" (v. 2; see 12:11-16). [Abimelech] Missing is any reference to Sarah's beauty that motivated Pharaoh to take her and that put her husband's life in danger in

Foreigners

The experience of displacement is the foundation of the book of Genesis. Our ancestors in the faith in Genesis live as foreigners no matter who or where they are. The foreigner (*ger*) searches for a home to protect his family and himself. Reasons for moving about as foreigners include warfare and famine. The Old Testament has extensive legislation concerning the welfare of foreigners. Because the foreigners are often associated with the poor, widow, and orphan, the *ger* foreigner probably refers to a social group rather than to ethnic groups. The root of justice and protection for the foreigner lies in the memory of Israel's own oppression in Egypt (Exod 20:22-26).

For further reading, see Anselm C. Hagedorn, "Foreigner," in the *Oxford Encyclopedia of Bible and Theology*, vol. 1, ed. Samuel E. Balentine (New York: Oxford University Press, 2015) 368–71.

Egypt (12:11-12). Yet here as in chapter 12, the danger to Sarah creates a similar barrier to the fulfillment of the promises. Were she to disappear from the family, God's promise that she will bear Abraham's son would be thwarted (18:9). She and the promise would vanish among a foreign people.

Sarah's release from King Abimelech's harem also happens quickly, but this version of the story shows more interest in her escape than in retelling the plot of earlier events. She avoids absorption into the king's empire through divine intervention, not due to a plague upon Pharaoh's household but because God sends a dream to Abimelech, who heeds it. Dreams are common revelatory events in Genesis. [Dreams] In this one, God warns Abimelech directly that he is about to die because the woman he has taken is "married." [A Married Woman, *bě'ulat bā'al*] Pointedly, the narrator discloses the fact that the king had "not approached her,"

Abimelech

Abimelech is either a name or possibly a title of the king of Gerar. It means "My father is king," namely, my god is king. It has an ironic relationship to the story. Abimelech is the figure who trusts God in this chapter. The foreign king acts with justice, honors Sarah, obeys God promptly, and overflows with generosity.

He is the ruler who takes Sarah into his household in Gen 20 and who later takes Rebekah, Isaac's wife, in Gen 26. This latter account is the third version of the wife-sister type scene that takes place in Genesis. In it, Abimelech is called the king of the Philistines, but that connection is uncertain since the Philistines or Sea Peoples seem not to have occupied the area around Gerar in the western Negev (Matthews).

Victor Matthews, "Abimelech," *AB* 1:20–21.

Abimelech returns Sarah to Abraham and confronts him after discovering that Sarah is not only his sister but also his wife.

Nicolas Fontaine (1625–1709). "Abraham and Abimelech." *L'histoire dv Vieux et dv Nouveau Testament*. 1670. (Courtesy of the Pitts Theology Library, Candler School of Theology, Emory University)

although the reason for his restraint appears only at the end of the chapter (v. 18). What matters here is that Abimelech is innocent of meddling with Sarah; there was no adultery, and any child to be born will be Abraham's own.

Remaining within the world of his dream, Abimelech asks a question that explicitly affirms his innocence: "Lord, will you destroy an innocent (*sadîq*) people?" (20:4; cf. 18:23-28 [6 times]).[1] He echoes Abraham's inquisition of God about saving Sodom for even ten innocent people (18:22-33): "Should not the Judge of all the earth do what is just?" (18:25). Abimelech knows, like Abraham, that the individual is not fully separable from the community. His innocence or his guilt will have consequences for all, but he and the whole people of Gerar are innocent. He

Dreams

Belief in the significance of dreams was widespread in the ancient world and prevalent in Genesis. The dreams in Genesis play important roles in the plot development and signify that God directs events from behind the scenes. Dreams were considered a way to receive divine messages, as in the case of Abimelech's dream encounter with God. Jacob dreams of a ladder extending from heaven to earth (28:12), a numinous event that propels the action of the divinely orchestrated story of Jacob's future. Some dreams include commands from God as here, and others require interpretation as happens in the story of Joseph, the last long section of Genesis (chs. 37–50). Joseph has his own dreams (37:5-11) and then becomes an interpreter of the dreams of the cupbearer and baker (40:1-23). Finally, he interprets Pharaoh's dreams to result in saving his own family, Egypt, and the peoples of the world (41:1-57). Some of the prophets challenge dreams as false claims of revelation offered by false prophets (Jer 27:9-10; 29:8-9; see the provisions for evaluation in Deut 13:2-6).

A Married Woman, *bĕʿulat bāʿal*

AΩ The Hebrew terms used here to speak of married women are significant because they provide a linguistic insight into ancient understandings of marriage. The root meaning of *bĕʿulat* means both "to rule over" and "to marry." The noun from the same root (*bāʿal*) means "lord," "owner," and "husband." For a woman to be married is to be ruled over by her lord/husband. Such an asymmetrical understanding of marriage relationships was not unique to Israel in the ancient world, nor is it absent from the modern world. The use of this phrase in Gen 20:3 implies that Sarah cannot rightly become one of Abimelech's concubines because her lord/husband Abraham already owns her. The offense of taking her is less against her than against her husband, but Abimelech surprises readers later in the story by speaking to Sarah directly and assuring her that she will not be shamed for what he has done to her (v. 15). He shows her surprising respect.

fears that God will destroy the people of Gerar on account of an offense that he might have committed unwittingly. [Corporate Identity]

Unlike the citizens of Sodom, Abimelech is innocent (*sadîq*). He has not touched Sarah, and he reminds God that he was tricked. Abraham and Sarah misled him by declaring themselves to be brother and sister. Even if he had succeeding in having sex with her, he would have been innocent, but he did not. "I did this in the integrity of my heart and the innocence of my hands"; that is, his motives and his actions were pure (20:4). Settling the case, God also declares Abimelech to be innocent: "Yes, I know that you did this in the integrity of your heart." Besides, "It was I who kept you from sinning against me"; in other words, God says, "You did not touch her because I prevented it" (20:6) [Emphatic Speech]

At stake in the overwhelming proof of Abimelech's innocence is more than the safety of the people of Gerar or the reputations of the characters. Sarah's sexual integrity lies at the heart of the story. The king's failure to approach her means that the child about to be born in the next chapter is not Abimelech's but the proper offspring of Abraham. Since

Corporate Identity

Corporate identity is the concept that traditional cultures derive identity from the family, tribe, or nation rather than from primary focus on the role or qualities of individuals. Modern Western societies focus on the individual more than some cultural groups in modern Africa and Asia, for example. Ancient Israel was community oriented, and Genesis reflects this. It presents main characters who not only represent individual beings but also stand for the people who descend from them. In chapter 20, King Abimelech understands his actions as encompassing and representing his whole people.

For further reading, see Anselm C. Hagedorn, "Corporate Identity," *EBR* 5:798–99.

Sarah remained chaste in Abimelech's house, Abraham's paternity is beyond question. Furthermore, both God and Abimelech declare the king's innocence in the matter, an innocence assured by a form of divine intervention that does not unfold until the chapter's end (20:17-18).

As the dream continues, God orders Abimelech to return Sarah to her husband, not for her sake but because Abraham is "a prophet (*nābī*) and he will pray for you" (20:7).[2] Although the term *nābī* refers most prominently to the preaching prophets of later biblical books, here it refers to an intermediary between God and the people. Why does God commission Abraham to pray for Abimelech? Abraham started the trouble in the first place by claiming Sarah as his sister to protect himself, whereas the

Emphatic Speech

AΩ Both Abimelech and God use emphatic speech forms during the dream encounter (20:5-6). Hebrew often expresses personal pronouns as verbal suffixes, but here both characters use independent personal pronouns separate from the verbs (I, me, he, her) to underscore the absence of sexual activity between Sarah and Abimelech. Abimelech, for example, declares his innocence: "Did not he (*hû*) say to me, my sister is she (*hiw'*) and she (*hî'*) also she (*hî'*)[Is this repetition correct?] said, 'my brother is he . . .'?" (v. 5). God replies in the same emphatic style: "Indeed I (gam *ānokî*) know you did this in the integrity of your heart ; indeed it was I (gam *ānokî*) who stopped you from sinning against me; therefore I did not let you touch her (*'ēleyāh*)" (20:6, my translation). This emphatic style of speaking draws attention to the nonevents in the harem. Notably, too, God holds Abimelech back from sinning against God, not from sinning against either Sarah or her husband. (Note that variations in the spelling of the Hebrew pronoun "she" (*hiw'* and *hî'*) occur in Genesis.)

See *BDB* 215b.

guiltless Abimelech merely trusted his words. As an intermediary for Abimelech, however, Abraham assumes his role to be a blessing to the nations (12:2).

Again God threatens Abimelech with death if he does not return Sarah to her husband. God speaks very harshly to Abimelech to stress the importance of Sarah's role. Although the king is innocent according to the standards of the culture, failure to comply with God's command will provoke the death penalty, for Sarah's freedom is critical to the fulfillment of the promises. Immediately Abimelech complies with the divine command, rising "early in the morning" to tell his servants about the situation. The servants comply too, for upon hearing this news, the servants "were very much afraid" (20:8). Their "fear" shows how obedient to and reliant on God these strangers are. Fear may include simple human dismay, but in light of Abraham's remarks (v. 11), fear here expresses the religious attitude known as "fear of God." [The Fear of God] Like their king, they, too, are both innocent and righteous (*sadîq*).

The Fear of God

Fear of God or fear of the Lord is the "awe that a person ought to have before God" (Prov. 5:7; Eccl 12:13). Fear of God is a broad term that expresses a variety of responses to an encounter with the deity. These include feelings of terror as well as reverence and awe that give rise to praise and worship. The fear of God or fear of the Lord is often associated with divine greatness and transcendence, beyond humans. The idea of the fear of God occurs most often in Psalms, Wisdom, and Deuteronomistic literature (Lasater, 1:350–51). Job is the quintessential biblical figure who fears the Lord (Job 1–2). Because fear of God includes a variety of responses to the experience of God, it is sometimes inclusive of "true religion" (Ps 34:11). The "fear of the Lord" is represented by the "fear and trembling" with which Paul exhorts the Philippians to work out their salvation (Phil 2:12). It describes the piety of the growing church in Acts 9:31. However, it may carry overtones of judgment (2 Cor 5:11; 1 Pet 1:17; see Bosman).

For further reading, see Phillip Michael Lasater, "Fear," in the *Oxford Encyclopedia of Bible and Theology*, vol. 1 (2 vols., ed. Samuel E. Balantine; Oxford and New York: Oxford University Press, 2015) 344–51.

Hendrik L. Bosman, "Fear of God," *EBR* 8:1022–23.

David P. White, "Fear of the Lord," *HBD* 305

Abraham's and Sarah's Innocence, 20:11-13

Abimelech then calls Abraham before him and demands an explanation. "How have I sinned (*ḥāṭā*) against you that you have brought such guilt (*ḥāṭā*) upon me and my kingdom?" (20:9). Abraham's false words have produced great troubles, and Abraham admits as much. He spoke as he did because he was prejudiced against Abimelech's people. He believed that there was no "fear of God in this place" (20:11).[2] Readers have just learned the contrary: the fear of God is alive among the people, the servants, and their king who obey God immediately. Abraham has come among the people of Gerar with distrust and suspicion, for he could not believe that they live righteous lives.

Abraham's biased judgment is hardly a compelling self-defense for his actions. His character appears weak at best, but he adds new information about his relationship to Sarah that suggests he is not the complete swindler he first appears to be. She really is his sister, he says, his half-sister by the same father and a different mother. "This is a ruse that does not entail literal incest," some interpreters have pointed out, "but the scene is not innocent of incestuous innuendo,"[3] or perhaps it is a further cover-up of an outright lie. Still, Abraham defends Sarah's honor, explaining that he is the one who persuaded her to do him a favor by complying with his half-truth. The chapter excuses both Abraham and Sarah from the charges that they are bold-faced liars, but it also reveals them, and particularly Abraham, as schemers who omit crucial information for the sake of survival. He readily risks his wife's life and well-being to protect himself. At the same time, he is a trickster figure who survives in a foreign land by manipulating the king and those around him for the sake of survival, and in this case the injuries are survivable.[4] (See [Folkloric Influences].)

Sarah's Exoneration, 20:14-18

When he exceeds God's command to restore Sarah to her husband, Abimelech's righteous nobility becomes even more apparent. First, he gives Abraham animals and slaves as a form of restitution for the potential harm to Sarah; then he invites Abraham to settle in the land anywhere he wishes. He becomes God's instrument in fulfilling the promise of blessing, in this case, gracious material provisions for life and well-being. Second, he turns to speak to Sarah directly in surprising concern about her reputation: "Look, I have given your brother 1,000 pieces of silver; it is your exoneration before all who are with you; you are completely vindicated" (20:16). When Abimelech speaks to her as if she is an independent, dignified woman in her own right, he breaks with ancient culture, and he even accepts Abraham's designation of her as his sister. The story stresses the king's goodness and establishes Sarah's innocence. It also underscores the goodness of other people for whom Abraham is to be a blessing, but here they bless him.

The chapter ends with Abraham in a new role as prophet/mediator praying for Abimelech. Only now do we learn why Abimelech refrained from having sex with Sarah. He and all his household required healing in the sexual realm. Abimelech could not have sex with her, for God prevented it. Healing becomes possible through Abraham's prayer for him. God heals the king, his wife, and his female slaves, all of whom had been unable to conceive children. The Lord "had closed fast all the wombs of the house of Abimelech because of Sarah" (20:18). Clearly, the God of Abraham and Sarah is the One who provides offspring and gives people hope for the future. [Fertility] The

Fertility

"At the heart of biblical conceptions of infertility—either as divine punishment, or more often as a state that God has the power to change—is a basic sense of the unknown. In an age long before fertility treatments, before pregnancy tests, indeed, even before the fundamental manner in which sperm fertilizes an egg was known, the entire process of conception was a mystery. Of course it should be remembered that much of that mystery remains to this day; we are not always able to identify why a couple is unable to conceive. . . . In the biblical world, these mysteries were both broader and deeper. . . . In the absence of almost any—not to mention accurate—biological information about conception, those in the ancient world put the responsibility for fertility on the ultimate unknowable entity: God." (53)

Candida R. Moss and Joel S. Baden, *Reconceiving Infertility: Biblical Perspectives on Procreation and Childlessness* (Princeton: Princeton University Press, 2015).

Relief, allegory of fertility. Personification of Mother Earth: Tellus holding two infants between a cow and sheep. 2nd C. Carthage. Marble relief. (Credit: © RMN-Grand Palais / Art Resource, NY)

God of Israel keeps the mother safe so the impossible will become possible in the next chapter.

CONNECTIONS

This chapter could be a contemporary stage play on the workings of prejudice, fear, and the beginnings of something different. Abraham fears for his life from the strange, different, and foreign people among whom he is living. He distrusts his neighbors who differ from him. He believes they do not "fear God." He thinks they plan to harm him, actually to murder him. He lies or at least omits the critical truth that he and Sarah are husband and wife because he is fear-filled and closed-minded. His self-protecting deceit endangers her life as well as God's promises and plans for them. His fear dominates him and builds distrust of God and the neighbors around him. In his prejudice, he assumes the worst about his strange neighbors. Abraham is us.

Abraham's relationship to the people of Gerar fails to bless the nations and comes closer to cursing the nations. He sojourns among them and lives in their midst, assuming the worst about them, expecting them to be killers, and completely misperceiving their relationship with God and God's deep involvement with them. His prejudice guides his actions and brings near catastrophe upon both of them. [Pre-judging Others]

Wonderfully, however, chapter 20 turns Abraham's assumptions upside down. He is completely, utterly, and emphatically wrong about the people of Gerar, and his behavior stands in stark contrast with theirs. They are more honorable than he, more faith-filled, more obedient to God, and they trust Abraham, the stranger in their midst, accepting his excuse at face value.

Yet Abraham models hope for the beginnings of communion and reconciliation among disaffected groups, oppressed victims of colonialism, racism, sexism, and heterosexism, and other matters that make some people afraid of those who are different. He acknowledges his prejudice. He explains his motivation. He confesses his doubt, distrust, and fear, and he admits that he was terrified of these people. Perhaps that admission is what enables Abimelech to be so generous to him and Sarah in response.

The first step against prejudice, the first move toward peace and reconciliation, is to admit prejudice, to lay it out in the open, to recognize our own limitations, and to bring them into the light. This may be true in most human relationships from marriage

Pre-judging Others

Abraham's fear of others different from himself nearly derails the promise. He makes negative assumptions about people different from himself, assumptions that chapter 20 undermines emphatically at every turn.

American journalist Ta-Nehesi Coates writes about this experience from the side of those consistently pre-judged: African Americans and people of color in white America. His book, written in the first person, is a letter to his son to bring him to consciousness about racism in America, to armor him, and to lead him to fullest humanity in this broken world.

And I am afraid. I feel the fear most acutely whenever you leave me. But I was afraid long before you, and in this I was unoriginal. When I was your age, the only people I knew were black, and all of them powerfully, adamantly, dangerously afraid. I had seen this fear all my young life, though I had not always recognized it as such. (14)

Coates names that fear in the African-American community, in its music, street styles, fights, in "brutal language and hard gaze," in his parents, and before the law and its executioners. The fear comes from the violence against black bodies and the history of dehumanization and continuing threats to people of color.

Ta-Nehesi Coates, *Between the World and Me* (New York: Spiegel & Grau, 2015).

Ta-Nehisi Coates at the University of Virginia during the MLK Celebration 2015. (Credit: Wikimedia Commons, Eduardo Montes-Bradley, CC BY-SA 4.0)

to friendships to business relationships, but admission of our failed seeing and self-protecting fears are a major step toward the improvement of race relationships in churches, neighborhoods, and our nation. Shame and defensiveness like Abraham's prevent us from telling the truth about our lives, sometimes even to ourselves. But it is the truth that makes us free. Maybe that is why Abimelech and Abraham can meet again in honor and respect (21:22-33). Abimelech intervenes on Abraham's behalf and the two make a covenant.

NOTES

1. It might be worth noting that the NRSV translates this word not as "LORD" but as "Lord," perhaps highlighting that Abimelech is an outsider who doesn't know Abraham's God but still respects this God.

2. Terence Fretheim has called this use of "prophet" anachronistic, but it may be used because prophets engage in intercession ("Genesis" [*NIB* 1; Nashville: Abingdon, 1994] 482).

3. Ronald Hendal, Chana Kronfeld, and Ilana Pardes, "Gender and Sexuality," in *Reading Genesis: Ten Methods*, ed. Ronald Hendal (Cambridge: Cambridge University Press, 2010) 90.

4. See Susan Niditch, "Genesis," in *The Women's Bible Commentary: Revised and Updated*, ed. Carol Newsom, Sharon Ringe, and Jacqueline Lapsley (Louisville KY: Westminster John Knox, 2012), who finds more evidence of Abraham as a trickster and underdog in the chapter 12 version of the scene (p. 36).

LAUGHTER, TROUBLES, AND COVENANT

Genesis 21:1-34

After the conflict with King Abimelech (ch. 20), chapter 21 returns to the subject of Abraham's family and the birth of a second son who leads to further family troubles. King Abimelech reappears at the chapter's end, thereby framing frightful family events with relational troubles in the international political arena. God appears explicitly only in the family scenes. Although modern Western readers typically separate private and public domains and human and non-human spheres, all are places of divine interaction, intense struggle, and new life that cannot be easily separated in Genesis. Family events and the lives of individual ancestors encode national events in overlapping narrative threads.

COMMENTARY

Chapter 21 forms a doublet with the story of Hagar's escape from slavery in chapter 16. For the second time, Sarah's African slave finds herself facing death in the desert, only this time the family expels her. Again God speaks to Hagar directly, makes promises to her, and rescues her. Yet this version of the story also differs from the previous one because here God fulfills promises to both wives of Abraham. [Outline of Genesis 21]

Outline of Genesis 21

1. Born amid Laughter, 21:1-7
2. Divided by Laughter, 21:8-21
3. Covenant with Abimelech, 21:22-24

Born amid Laughter, 21:1-7

Nine chapters after God promises to make Abraham into a great nation (12:1-3) and four chapters after God promises to give Sarah a son (17:15-19; 18:9-15), the child is finally born. Many obstacles have prevented the couple's shared parenthood to this point: extreme old age, Sarah's barrenness, and danger from her abduction by foreign kings. Both Sarah and Abraham have tried separately and successfully to acquire a legal heir through their own schemes. Abraham

The Bloodline

The insistence that the promised child be born to Sarah expresses an attitude that favors genetic purity. It prefers one's people, one's kind, one's kin above anyone from a different community. It encourages endogamous marriage where spouses come from within the community (see Steinberg, 5–81).

This firm stance about the choice of the wife from within the family gains importance from the circumstances of the ancient audience. It is not a universal instruction to stick to your own kind. It does not teach racism, at least not explicitly. Instead, it tells the ancient audience that Abraham's descendants will not disappear among the empires that have conquered them. The survival of the Judean people as God's own after their fall to the Babylonian Empire is the urgent issue that prompts the formation of Genesis. The author of Genesis writes for a new generation when Persia rules, and he points the way toward home. The people of Judah must survive by not marrying the native people and not settling down into exile as Jeremiah had directed (Jer 29). They will not be absorbed into the empires and God will not be displaced by the gods of the empires.

That Genesis does not understand prohibition of intermarriage as a universal teaching becomes pointedly clear in the story of Joseph (chs. 37–50). Jacob's son Joseph marries the Egyptian woman Asenath, who is included by name in the census of Israelites in Egypt (46:8-27, v. 20). Jacob further includes her by blessing and adopting her foreign-born sons as if they were his own (ch. 48). Surely these passages, along with the book of Ruth where the foreign wife proves more faithful than any of the book's Israelite characters, dispute Ezra's dictum to cast out foreign wives.

Naomi Steinberg, *Kinship and Marriage in Genesis: A Household Economics Perspective* (Minneapolis: Fortress, 1993).

substituted Eliezer of Damascus (15:2-6), while Sarah provided herself with a surrogate when she gave her Hagar to Abraham to be his concubine (ch. 16). Now, after a long, frustrating delay, God gives them a son.

That God is the source of life and provider of the child is the point of the chapter's first verse: "The LORD dealt with Sarah as he had said, and the LORD did for Sarah as he had promised" (21:1). After all this time and failed efforts, nobody should mistake the child's birth for an ordinary human event. Twice the verse asserts in slightly different ways that what is about to happen is God's doing, for God is reliable and faithful to the promises. Although the parents have been impatient and despondent, God overturns the tangled string of impossibilities that made the birth so unlikely. The family bloodline continues. [The Bloodline]

The narrative buildup to the birth extends from chapter 12, but the narrator reports the conception and birth succinctly: "she conceived and she bore" (21:2), and "Abraham gave the name Isaac to his son whom Sarah bore him" (v. 3). (See [She Conceived and She Bore].) The name "Isaac" ("he laughs") derives from the Hebrew verb "to laugh" ($ṣāḥaq$), a linguistic connection that underscores the surprise, joy, and impossibility of his birth. Laugh with Abraham, because even though he is 100 years old, he has the promised son. Laugh with Sarah who proclaims in joy, "God has brought laughter for me; everyone who hears will laugh with me" (21:6). Laugh out loud, laugh heartily, for the impossible has happened; the barren woman is mother to the promised child. Astonished by this turn of events, Sarah knows that surprise must extend to everyone who learns of it. "Who would ever have said to Abraham that Sarah would nurse children? Yet I have borne him a son in his old age" (21:7). It is impossible, risible. Even when Abraham's three mysterious visitors promised her a son, she laughed (18:9-15); nor could she believe it when God assured Abraham that she was to be the mother with more offspring than the stars of the heavens and the sands of the sea (17:18-19). [Prayer of a New Mother]

The laughter connects with Isaac's birth and the derivation of his name, and his mother's joy contrasts vividly with the long hope for a child. Above all, the laughter expresses delight and surprise that God is faithful to the promises. Genesis presses the laughable nature of events to assure the book's ancient audience that they, too, have an unimaginable future of offspring extending beyond their imaginings, of offspring more numerous than the sands and stars, for God creates new life even for the collapsed nation.

Divided by Laughter, 21:8-21

In this dysfunctional family, however, laughter and joy are not long-lived, for laughter among sons becomes its undoing. The problems emerge during a party. After Isaac grows and is weaned, Abraham celebrates with a feast that occasions further conflicts. [Breastfeeding and Weaning] During the celebration, Sarah sees "the son of Hagar the Egyptian whom she bore to Abraham, playing (*měṣāḥēq*) with her son Isaac" (21:9). The word "playing" also comes from the root meaning "to laugh" (*ṣāḥaq*).[1] Ishmael is "laughing" with his half-brother, whose name means "laughter."[2] The family wounds from chapter 16 remain painfully alive. Sarah expresses as much when she avoids calling Ishmael by name and identifies him instead by his mother's foreign status and sexual relationship to Abraham. Laughter between Abraham's sons provokes bitterness, not joy, and threatens Sarah again.

Because Sarah fears for Isaac's future, she commands Abraham, "Cast out your slave woman, for the son of the slave woman shall not inherit along with my son Isaac" (21:10). Although Hagar was her slave, she calls her "your slave woman." Jealousy and denial of

Prayer of a New Mother

The late Hebrew Bible scholar and mother Tikva Frymer-Kensky wrote a prayer to celebrate the birth of a child. In this excerpt, she draws from Psalms as well as from the joy of pregnancy and motherhood.

from "Covenant of Creation"

In my womb You formed the child, (Ps. 139:13)
in my womb, I nourished it, (Ps. 139:16)
You formed and numbered the baby's limbs,
I contained and protected them.
You who could see the child in my depths, (Ps. 139:15)
. . . .

From Tikva Frymer-Kensky, *Motherprayer: The Pregnant Woman's Spiritual Companion* (New York: Riverhead, 1995).

Berthe Morisot (1841–1895). *Le Berceau (The Cradle)*. 1873. Oil on canvas. Musée d'Orsay, Paris. (Credit: Wikimedia Commons, US-PD)

Breastfeeding and Weaning

Weaning meant that a child had survived infancy to age two or three. Abraham celebrates Isaac's survival with a feast (Gen 21:8). Nursing children would have been an important aspect of childbearing. Children were probably breast fed until the age of two or three years. This may have contributed "to relatively low rates of childbirth in ancient Israel." Women nursed their own children except in the case of the mother's death or of insufficient milk supply. An ironic story in Exod 2:9 finds Pharaoh's daughter paying Moses' mother Jochabed to nurse her own son.

For further reading, see Jennie R. Ebeling, *Women's Lives in Biblical Times* (New York: T & T Clark International, 2010) 116–19.

Mary Cassatt (1844–1926). *Maternité*. 1890. Pastel.
(Credit: Wikimedia Commons, PD-US)

responsibility drive events. At stake for Sarah is inheritance for her and her child alone. Abraham responds with great distress, whether from love, duty, or both—he does not want to divide his family no matter how fractious it is. His two sons belong together; the two peoples of Israel and Ishmael belong together. Surprisingly, however, God takes Sarah's side, for "it is through Isaac that offspring will be named for you" (21:12).

In this version of Hagar's departure from the family as compared to chapter 16, God shifts the focus from her to her men, Abraham and Ishmael: "As for the son of the slave woman, I will make a nation of him also because he is your offspring" (21:13). Even though God endorses the family separation, this statement keeps the connection between the two peoples firmly in place, for Ishmael is as much Abraham's son as is Isaac, and Ishmael, too, will be the father of a nation. Yet he is not the chosen son of the covenant promised since chapter 12.

The expulsion of Hagar and Ishmael presents a sorrowful tableau of separation and danger. Abraham promptly obeys the divine command to listen to Sarah. Rising "early in the morning,"[3] he provides bread and water for his concubine and their son, places a water skin and the child on Hagar's shoulder, and sends her away (21:14). With the barest provisions, mother and child depart for the wilderness to face great danger and probable death. The story's restrained style underlines its poignancy. Like so many other narratives in Genesis, it makes no direct mention of anyone's feelings as the two are exiled from the family, but in actions fraught with tension and hidden pain, it implies them. Narrative understatement depicts the relationships between two peoples represented by

Abraham's kin, divided from one another by fear and jealousy yet joined by blood. The story is an etiology of connection and fracture. [Hagar in African-American Interpretation]

Hagar and Ishmael wander about the wilderness, where survival depends on access to water and shelter. With neither of these, the foremother of the Ishmaelites is forsaken in a desert without resources, support, or kinfolk. Soon the water runs out, death approaches, and, in immense pain, Hagar succumbs to despair. She "casts off" her child, puts him in a shaded spot under a bush, and sits opposite from him, for she cannot bear to watch her only child die. She sits the distance of a bowshot away from him. The archery reference hints at Ishmael's future as a warrior. "Do not let me look on the death of the child," she cries out, and then she weeps (21:16). All seems lost, but it never really is in Genesis.

Again God calls to her in the wilderness: "What troubles you? Do not be afraid" (21:17). When God invites her to take action, everything changes. Just at the moment of no hope, God urges this desperate single mother to assume her proper role as her child's protector: "Come, lift up the boy and hold him fast with your hand, for I will make a great nation of him" (v. 19). In this place of deep impossibility, God expands the promise made to her in 16:7-13, a promise similar to those given to Abraham, Isaac, and Jacob. She will be the foremother of a great nation.

Only now does God open her eyes to show her the well of water that will enable survival of mother and son. Again, a basic narrative pattern in Genesis overturns expectations. When all seems lost, God creates life anew. Not only will Hagar and Ishmael survive but a great future also lies ahead. Twice God intervenes on behalf of this Egyptian slave woman. Mother and son live; Ishmael becomes

---

Hagar in African-American Interpretation

African-American feminists—often known as "womanists" to highlight the distinct experiences of African-American women—have found in Hagar both a model of their history as descendants of slaves and survivors of racial oppression as well as a figure of courage and survival.

Renita Weems has pointed to Hagar as a victim of ethnic prejudice combined with economic and social exploitation in relationship to Sarah, her abusive and jealous mistress. Wilma Bailey has noted Hagar's strength and survival skills, while Delores Williams has shown how Hagar's story has "has been validated as true by suffering black people." Hagar and Ishmael represent many black American families in which a lone mother struggles to hold the family together despite the poverty to which the ruling economic class consigns it. Hagar is a hero because, like many black women, she scrapes and struggles to make a living for herself and her child despite hatred from others, with only God by her side. Too often their men are caught in the massive incarceration of African-American males.

For further reading, see Delores S. Williams, "Hagar in African-American Biblical Interpretation," in *Hagar, Sarah, and Their Children*, ed. Phyllis Trible and Letty M. Russell (Louisville KY: Westminster John Knox, 2006) 171–84.

Renita J. Weems, *Just a Sister Away* (San Diego CA: LuraMedia, 1988) 1–21.
Wilma Bailey, "Hagar: A Model for an Anabaptist Feminist," *Mennonite Quarterly* 68/2 (1998): 219–28.

an expert with the bow, and she finds him a wife like a patriarch of any ancient family.

As her son grows to adulthood, Hagar's story comes to an end in Genesis, but she lives on in the New Testament, herself a symbol of the Old. [Hagar in the New Testament] In the lore of Islam, she is a distant foremother of the Prophet Mohammed. [Hagar, Ishmael, and Islam]

Covenant with Abimelech, 21:22-24

King Abimelech, whose connection with Abraham is not yet on firm ground, returns to the forefront of the narrative. He arrives in a show of military power with Phicol his general by his side, but he comes in peace. "God is with you in all that you do," he says to Abraham, presumably referring to their dealings over the abduction of Sarah (ch. 20). Yet Abimelech remembers that Abraham failed to tell the full truth about his wife, so he requires Abraham to "swear by God" not to deal falsely with him or his offspring. The king offers himself as a model of right behavior: "As I have dealt loyally with you, you will deal with me and with the land

---

Hagar in the New Testament

Paul presents the story of Sarah and Hagar in very different ways from the story in Genesis. In the letter to the Galatians, he turns the women's situations into an allegory or symbolic account in which each figure acquires new meaning. The women stand for covenants, Hagar for the old covenant with Moses and Sarah for the new covenant in Jesus. Paul's larger point is that Christians need not keep the Jewish law (Torah) in all its commands and prohibitions in order to be Christian, despite claims of some in the Galatian community.

Tell me, you who desire to be subject to the law, will you not listen to the law? For it is written that Abraham had two sons, one by a slave woman and the other by a free woman. One, the child of the slave, was born according to the flesh; the other, the child of the free woman, was born through the promise. Now this is an allegory: these women are two covenants. One woman, in fact, is Hagar, from Mount Sinai, bearing children for slavery. Now Hagar is Mount Sinai in Arabia and corresponds to the present Jerusalem, for she is in slavery with her children. But the other woman corresponds to the Jerusalem above; she is free, and she is our mother. For it is written, "Rejoice, you childless one, you who bear no children, burst into song and shout, you who

endure no birthpangs; for the children of the desolate woman are more numerous than the children of the one who is married." Now you, my friends, are children of the promise, like Isaac. But just as at that time the child who was born according to the flesh persecuted the child who was born according to the Spirit, so it is now also. But what does the scripture say? "Drive out the slave and her child; for the child of the slave will not share the inheritance with the child of the free woman." So then, friends, we are children, not of the slave but of the free woman. (Gal 4:21-31)

Rather than strictly following the law, Christians must be open to grace in Jesus, for Jesus fulfills the law. To follow Jesus is to keep the law, to listen to the law itself. The law means not only the commands and prohibitions but also more broadly "instruction" for daily living in right relationship with God that Jews followed. Besides drawing from the story of Sarah and Hagar as an allegory or symbolic tale to make his point, Paul also mentions Isaiah's reference to the barren woman who bears many (Isa 54:1-3).

For further reading see Letty M. Russell, "Twists and Turns in Paul's Allegory," in *Hagar, Sarah, and Their Children*, ed. Phyllis Trible and Letty M. Russell (Louisville KY: Westminster John Knox, 2006) 71–97.

Hagar, Ishmael, and Islam

The Qur'an presents the story of Abraham's family with important differences from the accounts about them in Genesis. Whereas Genesis suggests that the rift between Sarah and Hagar and the expulsion of Hagar and Ishmael from the family left the two sons alienated from one another, the Qur'an presents a far more harmonious picture. John Kaltner has summarized the Qur'anic version. The Qur'an

gives no hint of this fractured family history. Later Islamic tradition and commentary does discuss the expulsion of Hagar but with an interesting twist. Abraham does not send her and Ishmael into the wilderness alone, but accompanies them as far as Mecca where he leaves them in order to return to his family obligations. These sources go on to report several subsequent visits to Mecca by Abraham, including one in which he and Ishmael erect the Ka'ba.

Kaltner reports that the Mecca traditions arise from Jewish sources and are not found in the Qur'an. Hagar does not appear in the Qur'an nor does it report any estrangement between Ishmael and Isaac, and there is neither ethnic nor religious division. "The two brothers are united by their common faith and family identity." In Genesis God chooses Isaac over Ishmael, but in the Qur'an the individual must choose. "Abraham is sent as a leader for all humanity and each person must freely choose to accept his message and surrender to the divine will." Islam makes membership a matter of faith alone.

The words in quotation marks above are John Kaltner's, and all the ideas are from his discussion in John Kaltner, *Ishmael Instructs Isaac: An Introduction to the Qur'an for Bible Readers* (Collegeville MN: Liturgical Press, 1999) 120–21.

where you have resided as an alien" (21:23). The king is using covenant language to set forth a legal relationship between them.

[*Ḥesed* and Kinship]

Only by Abimelech's generosity is Abraham living in the king's land where he and his family are resident aliens. Abraham immediately agrees to be loyal: "I swear it" (21:24). Abraham's God will preside over this covenant arrangement as its witness and enforcer. The arrangement establishes peace between the leaders but not for the people. Abimelech's servants have seized a well of water presumably dug by Abraham and his household. When Abraham complains about it, the king declares his innocence in the matter: "I have not heard it until today" (21:25).

Abraham responds with a covenant ritual to seal their relationship. [The Covenant and the Nations] He takes sheep and oxen, gives them to Abimelech, and the two "cut a covenant." (See [Covenant Ritual].) When Abimelech asks Abraham the meaning of the seven lambs that Abraham "has set apart," Abraham replies that they are the witness that "I dug this well." The public giving of the gift testifies that he is telling

Ḥesed and Kinship

AΩ Abimelech's request for kindness (*ḥesed*) with Abraham asks for a return of favor that the king extended to Abraham in the previous chapter. He invited Abraham to sojourn in his land, and he was patient with Abraham's lies about Sarah (Kennedy, 184). Abraham swears he will act with kindness toward Abimelech and in the process establishes a close covenant relationship with him and his people.

"Kindness" is the loyalty one shows to one's kin in a given situation. . . . It has been observed that the covenant relations arise as a form of substitute kinship relations. That is, covenant relations formally extend kin ethics beyond the range of kin relations, implicitly exploring the possibility that different kinship communities may treat one another within the horizon of common human kinship under God. (Janzen, 247)

Elisabeth Roberston Kennedy, *Seeking a Homeland: Sojourn and Ethnic Identity in the Ancestral Narratives of Genesis* (Bible Interpretation Series; Leiden: Brill, 2011).

Gerald J. Janzen, *Abraham and All the Families of the Earth: A Commentary on the Book of Genesis 12-50* (ITC; Grand Rapids MI: Wm. B. Eerdmans, 1993), cited in Kennedy, *Seeking a Homeland*, 185.

The Covenant and the Nations

So far in Genesis, God's has made a covenant with Noah and the cosmos (9:8-17) and twice makes a covenant with Abraham (chs. 15 and 17). Here, however, Abraham's covenant is not with God but with another human and national leader. According to Mark

Brett, the human covenant expands God's exclusive relationship with Abraham to include concern for a larger family of nations, such as the Moabites, Ammonites, Ishmaelites, and the Philistines, all blessed through Abraham as promised (12:2).

Mark G. Brett, *Genesis: Procreation and the Politics of Identity* (OTR; New York: Routledge, 2000) 72.

---

the truth, and it probably obliges the king to Abraham in return. By receiving the gift, Abimelech acknowledges Abraham's right to the well.[4] The scene concludes with an etiology that explains the name of the place where these events occur: "The place was called Beersheba because there both of them swore an oath" (21:31). [Beersheba]

Beersheba

Abraham seals the covenant in a ritual offering of seven lambs. Beersheba acquires its name from this event. The Hebrew name plays on the words for the number seven and for making an oath, probably referring to the covenant oath that Abraham swears to Abimelech (21:23-24). Hagar is wandering there when God repeats the promise to her and shows her a well that enables life to resume (v. 8), perhaps the same well that is the cause of dispute with Abimelech's people. Beersheba serves as a home for Abraham (22:19) and Jacob (28:10), and Isaac builds an altar there (26:23-25), as does Jacob (46:1, 6).

For further reading, see Sharon Pace, "Beersheba," *The New Interpreter's Dictionary of the Bible*, ed. Katherine Doob Sakenfeld (Nashville: Abingdon, 2006) 1:419.

After sealing the covenant, Abimelech and Phicol return to the land of the Philistines. [Land of the Philistines] There Abraham plants a tamarisk tree to mark the place, and then he calls on the name of the eternal God. He dwells in the land of the Philistines as an alien for "many days."

CONNECTIONS

Sacredness of Domestic Spaces

In Genesis, everything in existence is potentially a place of revelation. Divine presence and involvement are not limited to the broad

---

Land of the Philistines

Abimelech is the king of Gerar, not of the land of the Philistines. When Abimelech returns to the Philistine land, the text may be using an anachronism, that is, setting a more contemporary reality in earlier times. If so, Abimelech represents Israel's important Philistine neighbors with whom they engaged in war (Judges), but in this episode, Abimelech respects and admires Abraham. The land of the Philistines refers primarily to the city-states of Gaza, Ashdod, and others along the Mediterranean coast, not to the desert land of Gerar in the extreme south of the Negeb. The chapter ends with the notice that Abraham lived as an alien in the land of the Philistines for many days.

Isaac and Rebekah go to Gerar in the land of the Philistines in the third version of the endangerment of the matriarch story; Isaac calls Rebekah his sister and a water dispute arises between Abimelech, Pichol, and Isaac (ch. 26). Gunkel has suggested that Gerar of the Negeb has been confused by later writers with another Gerar in the area of Gaza (219).

For further reading, see H. J. Katzenstein, "Philistines," *AB* 5:326–28.

Herman Gunkel, *Genesis*, trans. Mark E. Biddle (Macon GA: Mercer University Press, 1997).

scope of cosmic creation, to public events, religious rituals, politics, military events, or matters of empire and economy. Of equal importance is the domestic realm, the life of the family, and the struggles of women, slaves, and children. All are arenas of divine-human interaction. In chapter 21, God's actions are as evident in the life of the family as in the exchanges between Abraham and Abimelech. By its attention to the domestic lives of women, Genesis encourages recognition of the sacredness of daily life, even as it also points toward social strictures that continue to bind women, especially poor women in our time. [God Sees]

Juliana Claassens has written about the "feminization of poverty," the burden that women in her country of South Africa carry for the sick and the dying, and women's particular vulnerability to rape and to HIV-AIDS. Yet she finds in their lives and in Old Testament texts profound resources and energy for resistance, and "myriad ways" to survive.[5]

Yet in modern Western societies, domestic life is often an afterthought. The result is a diminishment of attention to the mundane and the daily, a lessening of value given to work traditionally assigned to women, including care of children, the elderly, and the ill, the preparation of food, and the labor and love involved in the making of a home. Of course, this is changing, especially among younger generations. The loosening of gender roles is due, in large part, to feminist Euro-women's theology, womanist, and especially *mujerista* discourse.

In her ethical and theological reflections, the late Latina theologian Ada Maria Isasi-Diaz gave particular attention to the sacredness of the daily and to embodied struggles to keep families alive and together. There she found a source for understanding divine engagement with human life. Isasi-Diaz used the Spanish expression *lo cotidiano*, the dailyness of life, to highlight the burdens and challenges facing grassroots Latina women seeking survival and liberation. She has insisted that the daily upkeep of life in its material and relational aspects is an overlooked but key domain of divine revelation. "*Lo cotidiano* constitutes the immediate space of our lives, the first horizon in which we have our experiences, experiences that in turn are constitutive elements of our reality. . . . It is the simple world, a world where one has to take care along the surface minute by minute."[6] The precariousness of life among poor people and

God Sees

Miguel de la Torre has raised important contemporary questions in relation to this chapter:

Why send Hagar and Ishmael into the wilderness in the first place? Was it to pacify an ungrateful and ungenerous Sarah? We can rejoice that God saves mother and child in the desert, but how many other mothers and children (as well as fathers and brothers) who are of Hispanic descent are presently dying in the U.S. Sonoran Desert (on the southern border) due to unjust immigration laws? Are they less worthy than Hagar and Ishmael? Does the God who sees not "see" them?

Miguel A. De La Torre, *Genesis* (Belief; Louisville KY: Westminster John Knox, 2011) 214.

Migrant Mother

Dorothea Lange (1895–1965) for U.S. Farm Security Administration, February/ March 1936. *Migrant Mother*. Destitute pea pickers in California, mother of seven children, age 32, Nipoma, California. Photograph. (Credit: Wikimedia Commons, US-PD)

women in particular creates virtues of creativity, strength, and courage. It produces a kind of wisdom that arises from living on the edge in the struggles for survival. The basic activities and chores that humans face every day should not be relegated to a separate "private sphere" as if they were not important for the well-being of society. Isasi-Diaz's theology invites everyone to live more fully and consciously in our bodies and spirits.

Essentially, *lo cotdidiano* means to become aware of and to live in the midst of reality, rather than in abstract ideas about how we should live. It is to live with more consciousness of the immediate challenges in our physical and relational lives, to participate in a spirituality or way of life that is highly incarnational, an embodied search for God that is a school of love and freedom. Often a place of pain, anxiety, and struggle, attending to the daily struggles of poor women and to our embodied lives brings an awareness that awakens compassion and enables resistance to oppressive forces in our families and societies. This theological approach honors the poor and encompasses everyone. It invites all of us to radical changes in awareness, and it calls for structural societal changes to benefit women and men who struggle simply to live. [New Narratives]

New Narratives

"People do not live or die for a creed or a belief. They need narratives that arise from their reality, that not only convince but motivate. That is to say, the descriptions of reality that are based on and fed by *lo cotidiano* have the capacity to move hearts in a way that laws, authoritarian dictates, and arbitrary exigencies do not have. There is a need for narratives that echo our reality, for it is through them that we learn to know ourselves, our lives, and their moral aspects, and the relation that exists between the morality of human behavior and happiness or unhappiness."

Ada Maria Isasi-Diaz, *La Lucha Continues: Mujerista Theology* (Maryknoll NY: Orbis, 2004) 99.

Sending away Foreign Wives

The attempt to cast out foreign women and their children under Ezra and Nehemiah provides a haunting parallel to the expulsion of Hagar and Ishmael by Sarah and Abraham. The books of Ezra and Nehemiah present events that take place when exiles return to Judah and begin to rebuild during the Persian Period in the mid-fifth century BCE. Judah's leaders appointed by Persia during that time, Ezra and Nehemiah, demand that the community send away foreign women and children (Ezra 10). A list of men who had foreign wives follows the decree against intermarriage (10:16-44), but there are no biblical stories about its enforcement. The decree may have been forced upon them by the Persian Empire in relation to land tenure, or it may have expressed Judean desire to preserve their cultural and religious identity. Or the women labeled "foreign" may simply have been Judeans who had not been deported to Babylon and so were considered to be outsiders by returnees.

Old Testament scholar Harold C. Washington has noted that Judean identity comes at a high cost: the bereavement of foreign women and their children and the grief of the "very great assembly of Judean men, women, and children, who are presented weeping bitterly, and stand exposed in the rain trembling because of this matter" (Ezra 10:9).[7] Genesis both supports and critiques Ezra's decree in some ways. On the one hand, wives of the patriarchs must preserve Abraham's bloodline. On the other, God miraculously protects Hagar and Ishmael, who remain part of Abraham's family, and Ishmael attends Abraham's burial. Later Joseph marries an Egyptian; Jacob himself blesses and adopts his two Egyptian grandsons, and the census of Israelites in Egypt includes Joseph's foreign Egyptian family (see ch. 47). [How to Treat Foreigners]

How to Treat Foreigners

Theologian Grace Ji-Sun Kim has reflected on her experience of being held in suspicion because Americans perceive her to be a foreigner: she is Korean-American. Frequently people ask if she speaks English because she is not a white European American even though her English is fluent.

Then she reminds readers that God tells us how to treat foreigners: "When an alien resides with you in your land, you shall not oppress the alien. The alien who resides with you shall be as the citizen among you; you shall love the alien as yourself, for you were aliens in the land of Egypt. I am the LORD your God" (Lev 19:33-34).

Even though King Abimelech is not Judean and does not worship Abraham's God, he loves the strangers.

For further reading see Grace Ji-Sun Kim, "'Do you Speak English?': Racial Discrimination and Being the Perpetual Foreigner," in *Here I Am: Faith Stories of Korean-American Clergywomen*, ed. Grace Ji-Sun Kim (Valley Forge PA: Judson Press, 2015) 51–57.

NOTES

1. Hebrew omits the phrase "with her son Isaac," but the Septuagint includes it.

2. For other possible meanings, see Wes Howard-Brook, *"Come Out, My People!" God's Call out of Empire in the Bible and Beyond* (Maryknoll NY: Orbis, 2010) 67; and Terence E. Fretheim, *Abraham: Trials of Family and Faith* (Columbia: University of South Carolina Press, 2007) 100.

3. The righteous King Abimelech similarly rose early in the morning to obey a divine command (20:8).

4. Claus Westermann, *Genesis 12–36: A Commentary* (London: SPCK, 1981) 349.

5. For further reading, see Julianna M. Claassens, *Claiming her Dignity: Female Resistance in the Old Testament* (Collegeville MN: Liturgical, 2016) 102–36.

6. Ada Maria Isasi-Diaz, *La Lucha Continues: Mujerista Theology* (Maryknoll NY: Orbis, 2004) 95.

7. Harold C. Washington, "Israel's Holy Seed and Foreign Women" *BibInt* 11/3–4 (2003): 427–37.

NEAR DISASTER ON THE MOUNTAIN

Genesis 22:1-24

Chapter 22 contains the repellent and heartbreaking story of God's command to Abraham to offer his son Isaac as a "burnt offering" (v. 2). This chapter has been deeply contro-
versial as well as influential in the three Abrahamic faiths, though in different ways. [Divergent Readings] The heart of the problem is the divine command to kill a child, any child, but in this case the promised child whose birth has been anticipated for ten chapters. How can sense be made of this portrait of God as cruel, mercurial, and murderous?

Divergent Readings

Christians name events in this chapter "the sacrifice of Isaac"; Jews refer to it as the Aqedah or "the binding of Isaac"; and, although Muslims have no special title for it, they leave open the identity of Abraham's son to be offered on the mountain. For them, the child might be Ishmael. Differences in interpretation relate to subsequent traditions of the three communities who emphasize divergent aspects of the story.

For further reading, see John Kaltner, *Ishmael Instructs Isaac: An Introduction to the Qu'ran for Bible Readers* (Collegeville MN: Liturgical, 1999) 122–31.

Trauma and disaster studies provide a helpful lens for interpreting this narrative. I group it with the other disaster stories in the book, including the expulsion from the garden, the flood, and the destruction of Babel and of Sodom and Gomorrah, along with many others that depict near catastrophes. (See Introduction.) All of these present a narrative that heads in the direction of the traumatic end of life, but the major characters survive. In each case, the portrait of the Holy One is problematic. God appears as the divine executioner who enacts punishment or arbitrarily sends the cataclysm.

Genesis 22 takes Judah's fall to Babylon and the seeming end of the nation and relates the disaster symbolically in a micro version of events like the other disaster stories. The chosen family and the chosen child face extinction, but at the very end of life, divine inter-
vention enables survival. Like the other stories, this one implies that God has imposed the terrible suffering for a purpose. In this instance, the purpose is to test Abraham rather than punish him. Understanding these horrible events as a test is a common response to tragedy, for it keeps God alive and helps survivors understand themselves as having successfully passed through trials.

COMMENTARY

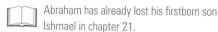
The main narrative of chapter 22 is highly stylized and structured around three call-and-response expressions, as if in a liturgy. Three times a voice calls to Abraham and three times he replies, "Here I am" (vv. 1, 7, 11). [Outline of Genesis 22]

Commission and Preparation for the Burnt Offering, 22:1-8

The chapter opens with the common connecting phrase "after these things," meaning something like "as time goes by" or "sometime later." Vague and innocuous enough, the phrase links this chapter with events in the previous one, where another child nearly dies. [Sacrifice of Two Sons] The neutral opening tone soon becomes ominous: "After these things, God tested Abraham" (Gen 22:1). The verse interprets what is to follow right at the chapter's beginning; events on Mount Moriah test Abraham, his right motives, and his loyalty to God. At the same time, the test raises excruciating questions about God.

Sacrifice of Two Sons

Abraham has already lost his firstborn son Ishmael in chapter 21.

Following the near sacrifice of Ishmael, the narrative soon moves to the near sacrifice of Isaac (Gen 22:1-9). In both stories, children are objects: God orders their abuse . . . only in time to prevent their deaths. But the differences between the stories contend with their similarities. Most significantly, Sarah is absent from the second story. She who demanded the expulsion of her surrogate son plays no role in the departure of her natural son. God, who supported her cruel treatment of Ishmael, does not even tell her what is to happen to Isaac.

Phyllis Trible, "Ominous Beginnings for a Promise of Blessings," in *Hagar, Sarah, and Their Children: Jewish, Christian, and Muslim Perspectives,* ed. Phyllis Trible and Letty M. Russell (Louisville KY: Westminster John Knox, 2006) 50.

The first call-and-response exchange starts the action. God calls, "Abraham," who responds promptly, "Here I am" (*hinnēnî*). ["Here I am"] Abraham's answer is more than a simple "yes"; it expresses his prompt and complete obedience, for he is putting his whole being at the service of the one who addresses him. After Abraham steps forward in full readiness, God presents him with a command that is unthinkable under any circumstances but particularly in the context of this story. From the moment God calls him in chapter 12, God has promised to give him, and ultimately Sarah, innumerable

"Here I am"

The Hebrew word *hinnēnî* combines *hinneh* ("Behold" or "Look") with the first person singular ending. Abraham's trifold response to calls to him could be translated literally as "Look me" or "Here I am." The word expresses his absolute readiness to respond to the calls upon him, to gather himself up, and to give himself totally. It gives voice to a full-throated, wholehearted connection to God. We can borrow the word to express our own desires to serve God and others with full and open spirits no matter how afraid and broken we might be.

offspring. Now the long-awaited child has at last been born (Gen 21:1-7), and God tells him to kill that child:

Take your son, your only one, Isaac, whom you love
And go you (*lek lĕkā*) to the land of Moriah,
And offer him there as a burnt offering on one of the mountains that
I will mention. (my translation, 22:2)

The divine command piles up vocabulary about Abraham's relation to the child about to be sacrificed—"your son, your only one, Isaac, whom you love." The list of descriptors highlights the father-son relationship, making it impossible for readers to miss the pain and loss entailed by obedience to the command. Isaac is not Abraham's only son, of course, but he is the only son of the promise, the one whose birth, after numerous parental missteps and misdirections, turns out to be miraculous in character. Abraham has already "sacrificed" his other son Ishmael by sending him and his mother away to face great danger (ch. 21). Now he will be left with no child. [Child Sacrifice]

God's verbs of command are clear and sharp: "take," "go," and "offer." The middle term, "go" (*lek lĕkā*), repeats God's first

---

Child Sacrifice

Child sacrifice was frequently condemned in ancient Israel, and some texts accuse neighboring Canaanite peoples of this heinous crime (Deut 12:31; 18:10; 2 Kgs 17:17; 23:10; Jer 7:31; 32:35; Ezek 16:20; Ps 106:37-38). There are stories of Israelites and others offering children in sacrifice (1 Kgs 16:34; 2 Kgs 3:27; 16:3; 21:5; 2 Chr 28:3; 33:6). One occurrence in the book of Judges is particularly chilling, especially for women (Judg 11:29-40). An Israelite Judge named Jepthah, a local tribal chieftain, vows that if God gives him victory in battle he will sacrifice the first person in his household who meets him upon his return. His joyous daughter runs out to greet him, and after she goes to the mountains with her girlfriends to lament her virginal, childless fate, she returns to be sacrificed.

This narrative of child sacrifice is one of a series of stories in Judges that serves as political propaganda for kingship in ancient Israel, as opposed to rule by the judges. Jepthah's crime is one among many illustrations of the refrain, "Every man did as he pleased, for there is no king in Israel" (17:6; 18:1; 19:1; 21:25). The story condemns him and the practice of child sacrifice. At the root of this view is a terrible theology of a God who demands to be appeased by the offering of human blood from the most innocent.

For further reading see Carol L. Meyers, Toni Craven, Ross Shepard Kraemer, eds., *Women in Scripture: A Dictionary of Named and Unnamed Women in the Hebrew* (Winona Lake WI: Wm. B. Eerdmans, 2001) 224–25.

Alexandre Cabanel (1823–1889). *The Daughter of Jephthah*. 1879. Oil on canvas. Private Collection. (Credit: Wikimedia Commons, PD-US)

Burnt Offerings

The term translated "burnt offering" appears six times in this passage (vv. 2, 3, 6, 7, 8, 13). The first five occurrences help build the unbearable tension in the story; only the last mention occurs after the ram has been substituted (v. 13). A burnt offering involved an animal killed and burned on an altar (Lev 1; Num 28–29). The most common of ancient Israelite sacrifices, the animal was understood as a gift to God to win favor. In liturgical practice, the animal was male and entirely burned. Cattle, sheep, goats, doves, and pigeons could be offered in sacrifice (Rattray). The term was applied during the twentieth century to describe the massacre of European Jews under the Nazis. The term connects the catastrophic death of millions of Jews in gas chambers and in other ways in Europe during World War II to the binding of Isaac; but for the Jews, there was no divine intervention.

Susan Rattray, "Worship," *HBD* 1143–47.

emphatic charge to Abraham: "Go (*lek lěkā*) from your country and your kindred and your father's house to a land I will show you" (12:1). You, go, obey my order to destroy the very gift that I promised and provided in the midst of the most impossible conditions. Destroy all your hopes and leave everything behind again. Offer Isaac as a "burnt offering." [Burnt Offerings] This is the test announced to readers in v. 1.

Like the obedient Abimelech (20:8), Abraham, too, rises early in the morning to begin his preparations for the sacrifice. Literary critic Eric Auerbach has observed that the details of Abraham's preparation are painstakingly and slowly described, told without emotional comment yet laden with frightful deliberation.[1] Abraham saddles his donkey, takes two servant boys and "his son Isaac," cuts wood, and goes to the place that God has appointed. He does these things to prepare for the "burnt offering." It is hard to imagine a more horrible command or to understand why a loving father would comply with it.

The small party travels for two days, and on the third, Abraham lifts up his eyes and sees the place from far away (22:4). [The Third Day] As the destined mountain comes into view, double verbs— "lifts up his eyes and sees"—offer a cameo moment of extreme terror. Readers can imagine Abraham's first glimpse of that mountain where the one he most loves must die at his hand, but the narrator tells us nothing of his feelings. To arrive within sight of the place of sacrifice involved a long, heavy-footed journey under an extreme burden of divine command.

The Third Day

The number three is symbolic in the Bible and, like the number seven, indicates completeness. In this case, the dread, terror, and focused efforts reach their apex as the little group arrives at the place of sacrifice. Jesus is raised from the dead on the third day.

Joel F. Drinkard, "Numbers," *HBD* 711–12.

Before proceeding to the mountain, Abraham leaves his two young servant men behind, but first he assures them that he and Isaac will go to worship, "and then we will come back to you" (22:5). There is much ambiguity in this statement. Why does he say "we" will come back? Is he trying to forestall possible interference from his servants by lying to them, or does he still hope that both he and Isaac will return? Does he trust God so much that he expects a last-minute intervention? The narrator does not fill in the gap because the point of the description is that no matter what Abraham is thinking or feeling, he obeys the awful command.

The journey's relentless drumbeat resumes as Abraham gives Isaac the wood to carry, while he himself takes the deadly elements of fire and knife, and "the two of them walked on together" (22:6). Isaac breaks the silence and calls out, "Father." Abraham responds just as he responded to God in v. 2: "Here I am (*hinnēnî*) my son" (v. 7). He answers Isaac's call with wholehearted presence, like any father reassuring his child. Isaac has noticed that elements for sacrifice are ready, but he asks, "where is the lamb for burnt offering?" (22:7). Abraham's answer adds further ambiguity: "God himself will provide the lamb for burnt offering, my son" (22:8). Abraham's confidence in divine provision may cover up his intentions to make his son into the lamb of sacrifice, or it may express trust that God will find a way to alter the expected outcome. "So the two of them walked on together," father and son, one trusting his father, the other planning to kill his son (22:8).

The Burnt Offering, 22:9-13

As they arrive at the place that God "mentioned to him," Abraham continues to follow the divine command with slow, purposeful pacing. Only the barest details tell the story. He builds an altar there, lays the wood "in order," binds his son, and lays him on the altar on top of the wood (22:9). Missing are sounds, shouts, struggles, gasps of fear, cries of sorrow, screams of resistance. In the silence, Abraham "reached out his hand and took a knife to kill his son."

Only at the last possible minute, survival comes for Isaac and Abraham as in the other disaster stories. When Abraham raises the knife to murder his son, the angel of the Lord calls him by name twice, "Abraham, Abraham." Doubling his name magnifies the urgency and intervenes as if saying, "Stop, Stop." Again Abraham, fully present, focused, and ready, answers, "Here I am" (*hinnēnî*).

Do not lay your hand on the boy
or do anything to him
for now I know that you fear God,
since you have not withheld your son, your only son. (22:12)

Abraham has passed the gruesome test. [Reading with Abraham] He has been willing to destroy the son whom he loves along with the hope for the future given to him by God's promises. He again obeys the God who called him in the first place. If hopes of children and

Renaissance Interpretations in Conversation

Between 1598–1603, Renaissance painter Caravaggio is thought to have created two somewhat different artistic versions of *The Sacrifice of Isaac*. The first one below is disputed as to the artist, but it is the gentler of the two. Whether by Caravaggio or not, it uses light and dark contrasts to highlight the composition, a technique called *chiaroscuro*. The light leads the eye through the composition, beginning with the angel's brightly lit face and moving to Abraham's bald head across his shoulder down to his hand that holds Isaac's head in place. From there the light leads across Isaac's shoulder to Abraham's other hand that holds ready the knife, and finally it lands on the ram that is held by the hand of the angel. Both Abraham and Isaac turn toward the angel, who is the focus of the picture—drawing the viewer's attention to the miraculous intervention that saved the father and the child together. This painting is held at the Princeton University Museum of Art.

Caravaggio (Michelangelo Merisi da) (1571–1610) (disputed). *Sacrifice of Isaac*. c. 1603. Barbara Piasecka Johnson Collection, Princeton, New Jersey. (Credit: Wikimedia Commons, PD-old-100)

The second *Sacrifice of Isaac* by Caravaggio can be found at the Uffizi in Florence Italy and appears below. It, too, uses *chiaroscuro* techniques to highlight the same three figures. Here, however, the light moves differently, and the composition, though essentially the same, exhibits striking differences from the painting above. The light begins at Abraham's bald head, traveling across his shoulder to the pointing finger, then to the shoulder and back of the angel, whose face is shaded. From there the light leads again to the angel's hand, which is staying Abraham's hand and knife. Isaac's arm and face follow next in the circle of light that ends with the ram's face. In this painting the light leads viewers to the dramatic terror of Isaac's face as his father's hand clamps his neck in place, and his shriek can almost be heard. The violence of the scene becomes unavoidable in this rendition. In the background on the upper right, typical of Renaissance interest in visual perspective, lies a distant set of buildings and light in the sky. Perhaps Caravaggio alludes to the importance of the scene to the whole world.

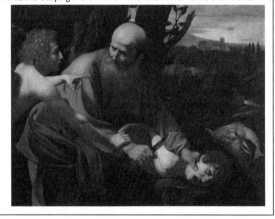

Caravaggio (Michelangelo Merisi da) (1571–1610). *The Sacrifice of Isaac*. c. 1603. Uffizi Gallery, Florence, Italy. (Credit: Wikimedia Commons, PD-old-100)

land motivated Abraham's obedience to God's original charge to "Go you" (*lek lĕkā*) (the narrator never says), when God calls this time, "Go you" (*lek lĕkā*) and make a burnt offering of your son," he responds from a different motivation.[2] His obedient relationship with God takes priority over everything.

When he lifts up his eyes again, what he sees this time alters everything (v. 13). Like Hagar who sees the well at the last moment (21:19), Abraham sees a ram trapped in the thicket. God shows him a way out, and he knows now that his son will survive and so will the promises. The overbearing dread that has haunted the

Reading with Abraham

A Jewish Midrash imagines Abraham's response to God's command to offer his son on the altar: "His eyes shed tears that fell into Isaac's eyes because of his fatherly compassion; nonetheless his heart rejoiced to do the will of his Creator" (quoted in Levenson, 68). Yet this midrash does not question God's command for Abraham to kill his son, a question of paramount importance in more modern times and with our awareness of how we often claim divine approval for our own wicked ways.

Jewish and Christian interpretations of Genesis 22 have been largely positive until the time of Enlightenment philosopher Immanuel Kant, when he and later Danish thinker Soren Kierkegaard begin to resist this view of an abusive God.

In the "Dispute between the Philosophical and Theological Faculties," he [Kierkegaard] remarks: "There are certain cases in which man can be convinced that it cannot be God whose voice he thinks he hears, when the voice commands him to do what is opposed to the moral law . . . he must count it as deception. . . .The myth of the sacrifice of Abraham can serve as an example: Abraham, at God's command, was going to slaughter his own son—the poor child in his ignorance even carried the wood. Abraham should have said to this supposed divine voice: that I am not to kill my beloved son is quite certain; that you who appear to me are God, I am not certain, nor can I ever be, even if the voice thunders from the sky."

In a similar vein, New York City's Temple Emanu-El put Abraham on trial on the counts of child endangerment and attempted murder of his son. The trial was performed as a play by former New York governor Eliot Spitzer in the role of Prosecutor. Harvard Law Professor Alan M. Dershowitz served as Abraham's defense

For further reading, see Terence E. Fretheim, *Abraham: Trials of Faith and Family* (Columbia: University of South Carolina Press, 2007) 132–39.

Genesis Rabah, 56:8, quoted in Jon Levenson, *Inheriting Abraham: The Legacy of the Patriarch in Judaism, Christianity & Islam* (Princeton NJ: Princeton University Press, 2012).

Appendix to von de Boor's German translation of S. Kierkegaard's *Furcht und Zittern* [Eng., *Fear and Trembling*], 1949, 160–61, quoted in Claus Westermann, *Genesis 12–36: A Commentary* (London: SPCK, 1981) 354.

Vivian Yee, "At Educational Event, a Modern Legal Interpretation of a Biblical Story," *New York Times*, 16 November 2014, https://www.nytimes.com/2014/11/17/nyregion/at-educational-event-a-modern-legal-interpretation-of-a-biblical-story.html.

journey to the mountain dissipates as he substitutes the ram for the burnt offering in place of his son.

An etiology that names the place underscores the story's main theme: "So Abraham called that place 'The LORD will provide,' as it is said to this day" (22:14). The mountain's new name reinforces trust and obedience in the God who provides amid impossible conditions and in the direst of circumstances. The place name and the story invite the ancient audience to trust God as Abraham did, for this God will provide for them too. [Reading with Sarah]

Abundant Blessings, 22:14-19

The relationship between God and Abraham deepens through this crisis. God swears formally and declares solemnly to bless Abraham and his offspring, as if now their mutual loyalty could be made official and permanent.

"By myself I have sworn," says the LORD: "Because you have done this, and have not withheld your son, your only son, I will indeed bless you and make your offspring as numerous as the stars of the

Reading with Sarah

Phyllis Trible has noted that in Genesis 21, Sarah speaks of "my son Isaac," language of connection and relationship never heard from Abraham (44). Chapter 22 makes no mention whatsoever of Sarah, and, in accord with the patriarchal society, she has no voice to challenge her husband or her God regarding the attempt on the life of the miracle child who was born to her so late in her life. In the ancient world, the father had full authority to do as he pleased. Still, Sarah's imagined response reveals how difficult women's lives were and how powerless she would have been. She is no model of moral living herself, having abused and cast out Hagar and her son out of jealousy and fear, but as women readers have pointed out for decades, both Sarah and Hagar are subordinate to a misogynistic system that creates extreme although not equivalent difficulties for the two women (Sadler, 75)

Phyllis Trible and Letty M. Russell, eds., *Hagar, Sarah, and Their Children* (Louisville KY: Westminster John Knox, 2006).

Rodney Sadler, "Genesis," *The Africana Bible: Reading Israel's Scriptures from Africa and the African Disapora* (Minneapolis: Fortress, 2010).

heaven and the sands that are on the seashore." (Gen 22:16-17a)

God swears to keep providing, to bless Abraham, and to make his offspring too numerous to count. Because Abraham has obeyed the divine command, his children in later generations will receive additional blessings. They will "possess the gates of their enemies, and by your offspring shall the nations of the earth gain blessings for themselves" (Gen 22:17b-18). Abraham's obedience echoes through the generations, and, like him, his offspring will become God's instruments to bring blessings to "all the nations of the earth." Primary among these blessed children is the book's ancient audience who, like Abraham, has lost its future.

After the narrow escape on the mountain, Abraham returns to the two servant boys who are waiting for him, but the chapter never refers again to Isaac. He disappears from view, leaving another gap in the telling. Although Isaac does not disappear from Genesis, chapter 22 does not mention him again. [Reading with Isaac] The relationship between father and son is gone from attention. This might imply permanent trouble between them, as surely it does from a modern perspective, but the composers are simply not concerned about it. Their focus is Abraham, who has passed the test because of his obedient trust in a God who provides. In the process, they invite the book's audience to trust God as well.

Rebekah's Family, 22:20-24

Chapter 22 ends by returning to the genealogical threads that weave Genesis together into multi-textured fabric. This genealogy of Rebekah's family anticipates Isaac's future, highlighting fertility, offspring, and the fulfillment of blessings. The phrase "after these things" introduces it and connects it narratively to the events on Mount Moriah. Abraham receives news that Milcah, wife of his brother Nahor, has birthed a number of children. Nahor has not been mentioned since their father Terah's genealogy (11:27-29), although his line has been represented by his foolish son Lot.

Reading with Isaac

In both midrashic and Qu'ranic interpretations, Isaac participates willingly in Abraham's obedient response to God's command to sacrifice his son. *Genesis Rabah* 56:8 depicts Isaac asking his father to bind him lest his body "flinch because of his fear of the knife" and render Abraham's sacrifice invalid (Levenson, 79). The Qu'ran portrays the son submitting to the divine will without protest and participating fully in his father's obedience (see [A God Who Tests?]). In these interpretations, Isaac is not an abused child but a willing partner in his father's fidelity.

Tracing post-biblical traditions of interpretation, Bruce Chilton has rightly asserted that what God asks Abraham to do in Genesis 22 is "monstrous" (27). And so it is. When readers position themselves as Isaac, they find a frightful depiction of psychological and physical child abuse. The absence of reference to Isaac when Abraham returns to the young men at the end of the scene raises questions about whether or not Isaac and Abraham ever recover the sense of togetherness.

Terence Fretheim has written with particular eloquence on this subject. He notes that the silence of interpretation on the matter has been broken open by increasing attention to the vulnerability of children. The scandals in the Catholic Church in the United States and abroad are only one dimension of the problem. Efforts to locate the text in a historical-cultural world where child sacrifice was not unthinkable does not solve the problem for modern readers. It is clear that the text does not authorize child abuse, not only because God provides a substitute but also because many other texts condemn it.

Jon Levenson, *Inheriting Abraham: The Legacy of the Patriarch in Judaism, Christianity & Islam* (Princeton: Princeton University Press, 2012).

Bruce Chilton, *Abraham's Curse: Child Sacrifices in the Legacy of the West* (New York: Doubleday, 2008).

Terence E. Fretheim, "God, Abraham, and the Abuse of Isaac," *Word & World* 16 (1996): 49–57; *Abraham: Trials of Family and Faith* (Columbia: University of South Carolina Press, 2007) 121–32.

Of note is the genealogy's attention first to Milcah (cf. 11:29).[3] Her importance comes from her relatives; she is grandmother to Rebekah and Laban through her son Bethuel Both feature prominently in the Jacob stories. Rebekah becomes Isaac's wife and Jacob's mother, and Laban will be Jacob's father-in-law. A concubine named Reumah also gives birth to children of Nahor. The attention to mothers by name shows that the whole of Abraham's extended family is blessed with fertility and a future.[4]

CONNECTIONS

The End of Civilization

The story of the aborted sacrifice on the mountain is about catastrophe averted, the near extinction of the life of Israel. Abraham and Isaac stand for the whole people facing its end. Although Ishmael survives in the wilderness after also being sacrificed, if Isaac is sacrificed, Abraham's family of promise ceases to be. Abraham's offspring, the book's audience, are in danger of becoming extinct themselves after the Babylonian destruction and occupation of their nation. They face the end of life together as a people absorbed among the empires.

By boiling down the collective historical experience of disaster into a family narrative, this chapter, with its pathos and focused

A God Who Tests?

For many modern believers, a God who tests is just as troubling as a God who punishes, yet people who have suffered individual or collective disaster often voice both theological interpretations of tragedy of many kinds. This is, first, because to survive requires interpretation. Humans are meaning-makers, interpreters who must make sense of the world, particularly when chaos seems to prevail. Without meaning, there is nothing but desolation and nihilism. Second, after surviving terrible events, people can sometimes realize that they are resilient, have gotten through, and are participating in life together again. They are agents who act in the world, rather than powerless victims.

Human benefits from this viewpoint may be hidden here, but then along comes the matter of God. Is our God testing us? How can a testing God be a loving God? Can we be safe from God? The parental notion of a God who punishes and tests us to make us better has merit, but this chapter, as much as any in the Bible, portrays the testing God as uniquely cruel and vicious, even though the killing never happens.

This biblical text is not trying to present a full-blown theology; it is not offering insight into the essence of the deity; it is not a systematic theology trying to tell us about the whole of the divine character. It is, instead, telling us one principal thing about God: God never abandoned the people. The testing God, like every other biblical portrait of God, offers a partial glimpse, a historically conditioned insight aimed at keeping Judah and their relationship with God alive after the seeming end of everything. Seeing it as a test is an imaginative work of resilience.

For further reading, see Robert J. Schrieter, "Reading Biblical Texts through the Lens of Resistance," in *The Bible Through the Lens of Trauma*, ed. Elizabeth Boase and Christopher B. Frechette (Atlanta: Society of Biblical Literature, 2016) 193–207.

terror, works as a biblical survival strategy. It offers the audience a glimpse of their own national disasters from a narrative and historical distance. Through it, survivors can see their past and continue to come to terms with it, give it a narrative form, and find meaning in it. Without such slow processes of interpretation, the people cannot begin life again. Here, rather than interpreting the nation's fall as punishment, the disaster is a test that Abraham passes. The people too have come through and survived because God has never left them but instead solemnly deepens relationship with them. [A God Who Tests?]

To this broken community, Genesis 22 says in the starkest terms, "God will provide; God has sworn fidelity to you through Abraham; live intimately with God, trust God, obey God. The promises will be fulfilled in you." Abraham meets the challenge and passes the test that saves his son from a horrible end because he is utterly obedient to God's will. If the book's audience lives with their eyes on God, they too may see offspring "as numerous as the stars of the heavens and as the sand that is on the seashore" (22:17). They too may have a future. [A Mirror of Israel's Later Life]

Three Abrahamic Faiths

There is neither a uniform portrait of Abraham nor of Genesis 22 to be found among the three Abrahamic religions. Although Judaism, Christianity, and Islam mutually claim Abraham as an honored ancestor of faith, they each interpret his life and role differently. There is not one Abraham but three, according to Hebrew Bible scholar Jon Levenson. In this he is correct, for each tradition interprets the story within the context of its own developments and traditions. [The Binding of Isaac: Reading with Jews] [The Sacrifice of Isaac: Reading with Christians] [The Son Supports the Father: Reading with Muslims] Levenson has worried that, in the interest of interfaith conversation, interpreters will obliterate

A Mirror of Israel's Later Life

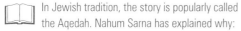 Terence Fretheim has also seen a reflection of Israel's history after the Babylonian Period in the events on Mount Moriah:

Once again, an Abrahamic text mirrors a later period in Israel's life. Israel, God's firstborn, had been sentenced to death *by* God in the fires of judgment. But exilic Israel remains God's firstborn (as Jeremiah affirms, 31:9), the carrier of God's purposes into the future. As Isaac was saved from death, so was Israel delivered from the brink of annihilation. But what of the future? Out of this matrix the Israelites developed an understanding that a sacrifice was necessary to assure Israel's future, shaped most profoundly in Isaiah 53. . . . Israel's redemption was not without cost. At the same time, Israel's faithfulness was not an optional matter as it moved into the future shaped by God's promises. The emphasis on descendants in v. 17 also connects well with these exilic concerns.

Terence E. Fretheim, "Genesis" (*NIB* 1; Nashville: Abingdon, 1994) 1:499.

The Binding of Isaac: Reading with Jews

In Jewish tradition, the story is popularly called the Aqedah. Nahum Sarna has explained why:

The Hebrew stem k-d, "to bind," in verse 9—is organically connected to the previous chapter. Abraham has lost one son and now seems about to lose the other. In both narratives, the child is saved by divine interventions at the critical moment, the only two biblical instances of an angel calling from heaven to human beings. In both cases there is a fortuitous discovery: a well of water in the earlier story, a ram in the thicket here. (150)

Still more is involved in the choice of the title "the Binding of Isaac" than its loose connections with the previous chapter. The text plays an important role in Jewish liturgy of the Passover and New Year. Levenson has pointed out that Isaac's binding gains little attention in the rest of the Hebrew Bible, but that it is important in post-biblical literature and commentaries. Mt. Moriah appears in "Chronicles where it is the name of the mountain on which King Solomon builds his temple in Jerusalem. The implication is clear; the Aqedah has become a foundation legend for the Jerusalem Temple" (89).

After the destruction of the Jerusalem Temple by the Romans, the rabbinical midrash about the Aqedah foreshadows the loss of the practice of sacrifice that accompanied the destruction (Levenson, 90). A post-biblical book known as Jubilees makes Abraham the founder of Passover and its sacrifice. In both, a sheep is substituted for the firstborn son. The Aqedah also becomes the root of reflection in the book of Jubilees on Israel's slavery in Egypt as a test of Israel akin to Abraham's test on the mountain (Exod 12:13).

Genesis 21 and Genesis 22 became the readings for the first and second day of Rosh Hashanah, respectively. It is on those days that Abraham's great test, always at the heart of religious Jews' relationship to God, becomes central to worship as well—a recurring and unforgettable note in the rhythm of Jewish life. (Levenson, 96)

Within Judaism Abraham's role is keeper of Torah in the book of Jesus ben Sira:

He [Abraham] kept the law of the Most High
And entered into covenant with him;
He certified the covenant in his flesh,
And when he was tested he proved faithful (Sir 44:20). (Levenson, 72)

Nahum M. Sarna, *Genesis* (JPS Torah Commentary; Philadelphia: The Jewish Publication Society, 1989).

Jon Levenson, *Inheriting Abraham: the Legacy of the Patriarch in Judaism, Christianity & Islam* (Princeton: Princeton University Press, 2012) see esp. 68–112.

differences among faith communities or let one view dominate in a false effort at tolerance and cooperation. Indeed, the call of interfaith relationships is not to build a pseudo-unity but to accept

The Sacrifice of Isaac: Reading with Christians

The story of Abraham's test on the mountain has played a large role in the development of Christian understandings of the life and death of Jesus. Christians see Jesus as the new Isaac, the lamb that was slain, the one who died in obedience to the Father and who, by doing so, has willingly saved the world.

For further reading on Abraham and the New Testament, see See Terence E. Fretheim, *Abraham: Trials of Family and Faith* (Columbia: University of South Carolina Press, 2007).

The Son Supports the Father: Reading with Muslims

The Qu'ran alters the story of Genesis 22 in significant ways. It never names Abraham's son, allowing for the later interpretation that he is Ishmael. Action begins when Abraham tells the son about a dream in which he is to sacrifice him. The son urges his father to comply with the divine command; together both father and son submit to the will of Allah, a ram is provided, and then comments appear about the blessedness of Abraham as a doer of good and one of the believers. Isaac is a prophet whose offspring are not the people of Israel but are all those who do right.

Jon Levenson, *Inheriting Abraham: The Legacy of the Patriarch in Judaism, Christianity & Islam* (Princeton: Princeton University Press, 2012).

John Kaltner, *Ishmael Instructs Isaac: An Introduction to the Qu'ran for Bible Readers* (Connections; Collegeville MN: The Liturgical Press, 1999).

and appreciate differences, while simultaneously holding fast to the unique traditions of one's own faith.[5]

While I applaud Levenson's emphasis on the importance of recognizing the specificity of each faith community, I do not think we should lose sight of our common claim of origins as children of Abraham. To hold together our own identities with profound respect and love for each other is one of the most difficult challenges facing people today, whether among faith communities or among cultural, ethnic, racial, and gender groups. [My God and Your God] That the three major monotheistic religions affirm a common ancestor and worship the one God provides a common floor on which to build the house of mutual respect, honor, and acceptance. We are kinfolk, according to Genesis, born of one father in faith, and no matter how different our development may be, we are one family under God. To live in such a way is a great balancing act, a slippery plank from which it is easy to fall, but it is the place toward which we must struggle if we and the world are to survive. ["The Parable of the Old Man and the Young"]

My God and Your God

"Nothing has proved harder in the history of civilization than to see God, or good, or human dignity in those whose language is not mine, whose skin is a different colour [sic], whose faith is not my faith and whose truth is not my truth. There are, surely, many ways of arriving at this generosity of spirit, and each faith must find its own. The way I have discovered, having listened to Judaism's sacred text in the context of the tragedies of the twentieth century and the insecurities of the twenty-first, is that the truth at the beating heart of monotheism is that God is greater than religion: and that He is only partially comprehended by faith."

Jonathan Sacks, *The Dignity of Difference: How to Avoid the Clash of Civilizations* (New York: Continuum, 2002) 65.

"The Parable of the Old Man and the Young"

"The Parable of the Old Man and the Young," by English poet Wilfred Owen, follows Genesis 22 closely but alters it at the end. Owen joined the British army during World War I, was injured and hospitalized, and then returned to battle in France. He won the military cross for bravery in the Battle of Amiens, but he died in battle just before Armistice Day, which marked the end of the war. He wrote many of his poems during his hospitalization. His poems countered the idealization of war and patriotic fervor associated with it. Owen has been popular among pacifist groups and war resisters throughout the twentieth century and into the present one.

So Abram rose, and clave the wood, and went,
And took the fire with him, and a knife.
And as they sojourned both of them together,
Isaac the first-born spake and said, My Father,
Behold the preparations, fire and iron,
But where the lamb, for this burnt-offering?
Then Abram bound the youth with belts and straps,
And stretched forth the knife to slay his son.
When lo! an Angel called him out of heaven,
Saying, Lay not thy hand upon the lad,
Neither do anything to him, thy son.
Behold! Caught in a thicket by its horns,
A Ram. Offer the Ram of Pride instead.

But the old man would not, but slew his son,
And half the seed of Europe, one by one.

From *The War Poems of Wilfred Owen*, Chatto & Windus, London. Wilfred Owen, American Academy of Poets, http://www.poets.org/poet.php/prmPID/305.

Wilfred Owen (1893–1918). plate from *Poems by Wilfred Owen*. 1920. (Credit: Wikimedia Commons, US-PD)

NOTES

1. Eric Auerbach, "Odysseus' Scar," *Mimesis: The Representation of Reality in Western Literature* (Princeton: Princeton University Press, 1953) 3–23. Auerbach has compared the literary style of Abraham's sacrifice of Isaac with that of Homer's *Odysseus*. He finds the Genesis story "fraught with 'background,' that is, told within layers of history and traditions, whereas the Odysseus presents characters, gods, and actions as if all were taking place in the present, in the foreground of the story. Everything is externalized, nothing is left out. The Genesis story, by contrast, creates a world that incarnates doctrine and claims absolute authority. The past and present are inseparable and expressed not only in divine intervention but in psychological elements, left untouched and in the background. God remains a hidden God always left in the background, merely glimpsed and left incomplete" (14–15).

2. Nahum M. Sarna, *Genesis* (JPS Torah Commentary; Philadelphia: The Jewish Publication Society, 1989) has pointed out that the phrase *lek lĕkā* that I have translated "Go you" does not occur again in the Bible, showing its importance for Abraham's story as it frames his call to obey in chapter 12 with his final call to obey in chapter 22 (p. 150).

3. Mignon R. Jacobs, *Gender, Power, and Persuasion* (Grand Rapids MI: Baker, 2007) 109, n.14, has noted that the mention of Milcah by name may enhance Rebekah's suitability as a marriage partner for Isaac in chapter 24.

4. Matthew A. Thomas, *These are the Generations: Identity, Covenant, and the 'Toledot' Formula* (London: T & T Clark, 2011) 50.

5. For further reading, see Jon Levenson, *Inheriting Abraham: the Legacy of the Patriarch in Judaism, Christianity & Islam* (Princeton: Princeton University Press, 2012).

LAND

Genesis 23:1-20

Sarah's death and burial frame chapter 23 (23:1-2, 19-20), but the chapter gives primary attention to Abraham's purchase of a burial plot for her. The purchase of the land—a cave in a field in Canaan that belongs to the Hittites—fulfills in a limited way God's promise of land to Abraham. [The Hittites] Although the patriarch gains no more than a toehold in Canaan, his purchase is legal and obtained with the full cooperation of the native people. The bulk of chapter 23 concerns a legal exchange marked by high formality, cordiality, and manipulation between Abraham and the Hittite owners of the land. [Outline of Genesis 23]

The Hittites

The Hittites who own the land are sons of Heth, probably a group among the local Canaanites. Heth is Canaan's second son (Gen 10:15). Later, Rebekah will be greatly disturbed that her son Esau marries Hittite women, and Isaac forbids Jacob from doing the same (27:46–28:1). It is likely that Hittite becomes a common name for the Canaanites (cf. Judg 1:10). The Hittites were probably among the "people of the land" who lived in Canaan before the Israelites (Fretheim, 1:503). They were a ruling group known in Syria and Palestine in the second millennium and later reduced to a name for the native peoples (von Rad, 247).

Terence E. Fretheim, "Genesis" (*NIB* 1; Nashville: Abingdon, 1994) 1:503.
Gerhard von Rad, *Genesis*, rev. ed. (OTL; Philadelphia: Westminster, 1972).

Outline of Genesis 23

1. Sarah Dies, 23:1-2
2. Land for a Burial Plot, 23:3-18
3. Sarah Is Buried, 23:19-20

COMMENTARY

Sarah's burial plants the body of the foremother of Israel in the soil of the motherland. This symbolic union points to the land of Canaan as the place of birth, nurture, and homecoming to which exiles must return and reunite with all Sarah's children who remained in the land.

Sarah Dies, 23:1-2

Sarah dies at the advanced age of 127 years, in keeping with the exalted life spans of ancestors in the primeval history (Gen 5). [127 Years] Although her life span comes closer to ordinary limitations on the length of human life, she still exceeds them, signifying that she was specially chosen by God. Her burial place is

127 Years

Sarah's age is the only life span of a woman reported in the Bible, showing this mother's importance (Fox, 97). Her age plus details of her death evoke fullness of life:

As well as achieving the full span of 120 (as set by God, 6:3; and fulfilled in Moses, Deut 34:4), she has an extra seven, itself a symbol of fullness. And the unnecessary-looking repetition of the reference to her years of life ("the years of the life of Sarah," 23:1b) heightens further the sense of a full life. The effect is still greater because she was once described as barren.

Not only in time but also in space or geography there is a fullness about her death. Her place of death, Hebron, is preceded by a new designation, the City of the Four (Kiriath-arba), and followed by the unnecessary-looking information that Hebron was "in the land of Canaan." Just as seven has a general sense of fullness, so, when dealing with space, does four (four corners of the earth; four rivers in Eden, Genesis 2; four directions around the tabernacle Num 2:3, 10, 18, 25). And the land of Canaan is not just an address; it has been associated in various ways with God's great promise. Sarah, therefore, does not shrink away in a corner of nothingness. Her death, however quiet, has evocations of great life and of a broad land. (Brodie, 274–75)

Everett Fox, *The Five Books of Moses: Genesis, Exodus, Leviticus, Numbers, and Deuteronomy* (Shocken Bible; Dallas: Word, 1995).

Thomas L. Brodie, *Genesis as Dialogue* (New York: Oxford University Press, 2001).

Kiriatharba—meaning "four quarters"—the original name for the city of Hebron. [Map of Hebron]

Sarah may have died alone, for Isaac does not appear in the death scene, and Abraham may also be missing, for he "went to mourn for Sarah and to weep for her" (23:2).[1] [Did Sarah Die Alone?] Fittingly, he does mourn and weep for her, but she receives little attention in the chapter; the motherland matters more than the mother.

Map of Hebron

The ancient Canaanite city of Hebron plays an important role in Genesis. Abraham lived there previously (13:18; 14:13; 18:1), Jacob visits Isaac there (25:9), and Joseph leaves there to search for his brothers (37:14). Abraham, Sarah, Isaac, Rebekah, and Leah are also buried there (49:29-31), and Jacob is buried there, too (50:13).

For further reading, see Jeffrey R. Chadwick, "Hebron," *EBR* 11:694–68.

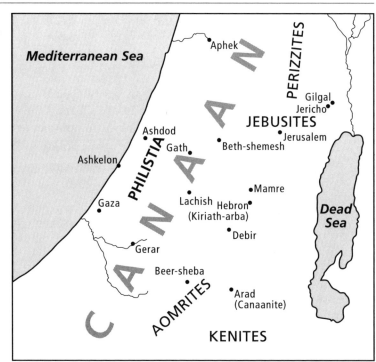

Did Sarah Die Alone?

Where had Abraham been that he "went" to mourn his wife, Sarah? Had the family, dysfunctional at best, fully disintegrated after the frightful events on Mount Moriah? Or did he go "in" to mourn her as the NRSV translates, implying that he was already outside her tent (23:2)? The text leaves another gap.

Some rabbinical traditions believe she [Sarah] had a heart attack when she heard that Abraham took off with Isaac in order to sacrifice the child to God. Other traditions have her dying as she heard Isaac recount what occurred to him during the father-son outing—the shock of almost losing him led to her death. Regardless of whether these events are connected, the fact remains that she died. According to the text,

Abraham mourned and grieved for her. As touching as his spilled tears may be, Sarah might have appreciated a display of such emotions if they were to occur before he pimped her to the Egyptian pharaoh of the king of Gerar. All too often we express emotions at the loss of persons we ignored and mistreated while they lived. (De La Torre, 223)

For further reading, see Phyllis Trible, "Ominous Beginnings for a Promise of Blessing," in *Hagar, Sarah, and Their Children: Jewish, Christian, and Muslim Perspectives*, ed. Phyllis Trible and Letty M. Russell (Louisville KY: Westminster John Knox, 2006) 32–69.

Miguel De La Torre, *Genesis* (Belief; Louisville KY: Westminster John Knox, 2011).

Perhaps Abraham respects her sufficiently by ensuring her proper burial, although he also seems to be an opportunist who uses his wife's death to acquire land. At the least, his success at the task brings the divine promise of land to fruition in miniature form. [Ancestral Tomb]

Land for a Burial Plot, 23:3-18

The scene opens on Abraham rising up from Sarah's dead body as he speaks to the Hittites, "saying . . ." (*lēʾmor*, v. 3). Usually when the Hebrew infinitive form (*lēʾmor*) follows another verb of

Ancestral Tomb

This ancestral tomb connects several generations of the family through a common burial site. The only main figure missing from it is Rachel, who was buried on the way to the land.

Irmtraud Fischer, "On the Significance of the 'Women Texts' in the Ancestral Narratives," *Torah*, ed. Irmtraud Fischer et al., in *The Bible and Women: An Encyclopedia of Exegesis and Cultural History* (Atlanta: SBL, 2011) 261–62.

Gustave Doré (1832–1883). *The Burial of Sarah*. 19th C. Engraving.
(Credit: www.creationism.org/images/DoreBibleIllus/)

speaking (saying, answering), the effect is something like quotation marks in English. This happens five times during the land purchase, marking direct quotes of both Abraham and the Hittites (vv. 3, 5, 8, 10, 13, 14). The grammar highlights the formality of the exchange as if the chapter were a court transcript recorded word by word to seal permanent ownership of the land for the future.

Adding to the legal tone of events is the location and style of the exchanges. Everything happens at the city gates, the traditional place in towns where judges, elders, and others conduct legal affairs and make judgments involving the citizens. The speeches are formal, respectful, and courtly as if honoring partners in a legal business transaction. The Hittites, for example, address Abraham with the highest forms of polite address, calling him "my lord" and "a prince of God among us"[2] (v. 6). Finally, witnesses to events play an important role in the chapter. Events occur within the hearing ("in the ears of") and sight of ("the eyes of") the whole Hittite community. Together these elements depict Abraham's land purchase as a choreographed piece of respectful, clever negotiations, a legal business exchange within a courteous communal relationship.

Abraham begins the interchange humbly and politely. Twice he identifies himself as a foreigner, an outsider in need of special consideration: "I (*'ānokî*)[3] am a stranger and an alien residing among you; give me property among you for a burying place, so that I may bury my dead out of my sight" (23:4). ["I am a stranger"] The NRSV translation "out of my sight" sounds like Abraham wants to get rid of his wife's corpse as quickly as possible. Yet because dead bodies were considered unclean—contact with them made one unsuitable for worship—"out of my sight" might be appropriate despite its unfortunate English nuances. Alter has proposed a less harsh translation with "from before me," since dead flesh is considered distant from God (cf. [Clean and Unclean Creatures]).

"I am a stranger"

AΩ Abraham identifies himself using the Hebrew term *gēr*, a word with a wide range of meanings, including "immigrant, non-citizen, or temporary resident" (Galambush, 150). The *gēr*, the non-resident, is, above all, landless. Within the Genesis narrative, no ancestor possesses land except for this small claim and a plot of land that Jacob will purchase in Shechem (Gen 33:18-20): "A very small part of the Promised Land—the grave—belonged to them; therefore, they did not have to rest in the 'Hittite earth'" (von Rad, 250). The sale of land to Abraham foreshadows the gift of the land to Abraham's descendants. For the book's audience who are aliens within an occupied land and in exile, the purchase of the cave is fraught with meaning. The promise of land, actualized in miniature here, is a promise for them, Abraham's offspring.

No longer will the land be simply a burial place. The text enacts symbolically the future return to the land of the landless people of Judah.

Julie Galambush, "Be Kind to Strangers, But Kill the Canaanites: A Feminist Biblical Theology of the Other," in *After Exegesis: Feminist Biblical Theology: Essays in Honor of Carol A. Newsom*, ed. Patricia K. Tull and Jacqueline E. Lapsley (Waco TX: Baylor University Press, 2015) see esp. 141–54.

Gerhard von Rad, *Genesis*, rev. ed. (Philadelphia: Westminster, 1973).

The Hittites reply with exaggerated respect, "saying, 'Hear us, my lord; you are a prince of God among us'" (23:6). They offer him the choicest of burial plots and announce in advance that none among them will refuse him his request. The Hittites seem eager to give Abraham everything he needs. Somehow this complete acquiescence by native owners of the land neither settles the matter nor satisfies Abraham, who continues to bargain with them. Perhaps Hittite generosity is a customary ploy to exact an exorbitant price for the land through clever manipulation.[4]

Abraham rises, bows politely to the Hittites, and says to them, "saying"—really he asks them—to entreat Ephron the land owner to sell him the cave of Machpelah. Abraham is willing to pay full price, but then he proposes that this should happen in a public setting: "Let him give it to me in your presence as a possession for a burial place" (23:9). Ephron the Hittite, who owns the land and happens to be among them, takes up the role of chief negotiator. In the hearing of the people, that is, of everyone at the gate of the city, he makes an astonishing offer, "saying, 'No, I will give you the field and I will give you the cave and the field in which it rests. I will give it to you in the eyes of my people'" (23:11). Ephron is giving his land to Abraham, refusing his money, and showing himself to be a generous and welcoming person.

Yet in this delicate negotiation, Abraham must respond with equal generosity. He bows again before the people and speaks to Ephron "in the ears of the people" "saying," no, no, no, "if only you will listen to me" (23:13). He insists that he must pay full price for cave and field, perhaps to gain respect among the Hittites. His refusal of the gift and stubborn firmness about paying full price results in an indisputable, permanent hold on the land. He cannot be accused of stealing the property.

Ephron concedes, "My lord, listen to me, a piece of land worth 400 shekels of silver, what is that between you and me?" (23:14). Only now does the clever Ephron mention the price of the land, 400 shekels, a small matter between two people who have such respect for one another. The price hardly counts, he says, and in the process he emerges as one reluctantly complying with Abraham's wishes to pay. The sale price of 400 shekels is huge compared with Jeremiah's purchase of a field for 17 shekels. That land sale, however, also highly symbolic, was made during the Babylonian invasion of Jerusalem when the land was worth very little indeed (Jer 32). [Jeremiah Buys Land] Abraham complies with Ephron's polite demand by publicly weighing out the silver shekels according to proper weights in the full sight of all.

Jeremiah Buys Land

📖 In the midst of one of the Babylonian invasions of the city of Jerusalem, when land is close to valueless, the prophet Jeremiah buys property there. He is in prison, and a divine command orders him to buy his cousin's land, for he has the right of redemption. The redeemer in ancient Israel was the kinsperson who rescued someone in the face of extremity such as loss of their land, unpayable debt, or indentured slavery of themselves or their families. With the assistance of his friend Baruch, Jeremiah engages in a belabored legal transaction to redeem his cousin's land. He pays 17 shekels for it and obtains the deed.

Jeremiah's purchase could not have occurred at a worse time; it is not a wise economic exchange. Rather, it is a symbolic action that communicates the hopeful fact that the Babylonians do not own all the land, although their armies are taking possession of it at that very moment. The deed is signed in the full sight of witnesses and then buried. Jeremiah's purchase, like Abraham's, reaches toward the future, for it points to a return, a repossession, a future time when the Judeans will regain their own land.

For further reading see, Kathleen M. O'Connor, *Jeremiah: Pain and Promise* (Minneapolis: Fortress, 2011) 69–79.

What he purchases are the field, the cave, all the trees in the field, and the whole area; these belong now to Abraham legally. He takes possession "in the eyes" of the Hittites, "in the eyes" of all who went to the city gates to witness the exchange of land from the Hittites to Abraham and his descendants—that is, to Israel. The deal is done. Abraham is the owner of the field formerly belonging to Ephron in Machpelah, to the east of Mamre where the angels appeared to him (18:1). The land purchase is a symbolic acquisition, a legal event that reaches toward the future. [Symbolic Guarantee] At the present time in the Genesis narrative, Abraham owns only a grave site.

For the book's ancient audience, the land itself might seem to be a sort of grave, a place where Babylonian invasions brought the deaths of people and of the Judean nation, but the purchase of Ephron's field is a promissory note toward the day when the whole land will be theirs again.

Symbolic Guarantee

📖 "It is possible that securing the grave with a clear legal title is a symbolic but concrete guarantee of possession of the whole land. . . . The memory of the transaction reassures exiles, those again made 'strangers and sojourners.' They do, in fact, have a secure place. This little piece of land signifies the whole land, certainly promised and undoubtedly to be possessed."

Walter Brueggemann, *Genesis* (Interpretation; Atlanta: John Knox, 1982) 196.

Sarah Is Buried, 23:19-20

The narrator's attention now returns to Sarah's dead body, and, in perfunctory fashion, Abraham buries her in the cave of the field of Machpelah facing Mamre, that is, Hebron. A primary concern of the chapter is to connect the matriarch and the family of Abraham to the land itself. The field and the cave that is in it have passed from the Hittites into Abraham's possession as a burying place and a sign that the wandering people will find a homeland. [Burial Plot for Familial and Political Reasons]

Burial Plot for Familial and Political Reasons

"The purchase of the cave gains a foothold in the Promised Land. Neither birth in native soil—'a natural rooted-ness'—nor military conquest, but mortality honored through burial provides the Israelites first title to the land. The nascent nation of Israel is thus tied to the land not by conquest or agriculture, and not even only by God's promise, but also by ancestral piety, by reverence for those who embarked on the new way in relation to God's promise. The land—more precisely a portion of it—becomes Israelite land because that is where their founding fathers and mothers are buried: the Holy Land is holy *first* because it is the land where my fathers (and mothers) died. Isaac and Rebekah will be buried in the cave at Machpelah; so too will Jacob and Leah. Moreover, during the four hundred years of slavery in Egypt the purchased cave at Machpelah, containing the remains of the patriarchs and three of the four matriarchs, will embody the Israelite presence in the land, past and future. Ownership of this small plot of earth will be the Children of Israel's sole legal claim in the Promised Land during their lengthy exile."

Leon R. Cass, *The Beginning of Wisdom: Reading Genesis* (Chicago: University of Chicago Press, 2003) 366–67.

Abraham offers to purchase Ephron's cave at Machpelah as a burial plot for Sarah.

Martin Bernigeroth (1670–1733) after the design of Samuel Bottschild (1641–1707). "Abraham Purchases a Tomb." Engraving. From Martin Luther, trans. (1483–1546), *Biblia: Das ist die gantze Heilige Schrifft, Alten und Neuen Testaments*. 1716. (Courtesy of the Pitts Theology Library, Candler School of Theology, Emory University)

CONNECTIONS

In the Saharan Desert on a trip to Morocco, I had the privilege of visiting the tent of a small family of nomads, headed by a widow who lived there with her young daughter. The woman's son had purchased property and wanted her and the daughter to live with his family, but she refused. The life of the desert nomad was what she knew. She owned sheep, a donkey, and a few camels, so she could support herself. She did not want the life of the settled people. It should not be assumed that ancient peoples or modern nomads crave land to possess when they have the necessary skills and traditions to live on the move, to have strong family lives and connections with the earth through movement across the seasons.

Abraham and his family appear to be nomadic or at least semi-nomadic people who move their flocks with the season and plant some produce during the growing season. If this is so, then why is the acquisition of land such an important theme in the book of Genesis? [Land and the Colonized]

Land and the Colonized

"For a colonized people the most essential value, because the most concrete, is first and foremost the land: the land which will bring them bread and, above all, dignity."

Frantz Fanon, *The Wretched of the Earth* (New York: Grove Press, 1963) 44, quoted in Miguel De La Torre, *Genesis* (Belief; Louisville KY: Westminster John Knox, 2011) 222.

Land matters greatly for the people who have lost it, are displaced from it, and whose land is now under the political and military control of a foreign empire. The book's audience has lost possession of its land and has again become a dispersed people. After the Babylonian invasions, some are displaced within Judah and others are exiled abroad. Even those who remain in Judah and Jerusalem have lost control of the land to their occupiers. That loss also means loss of identity. They had been attached to a specific geographical expanse of earth with the livelihoods it provided and the connection to God, who promised to dwell there with them on the holy mountain of Zion. Who are they now? Will they be absorbed into the conquering nations? Although they may have little hope for a future as God's chosen people, they have this narrative memory.

Abraham's purchase of the cave and the field is anticipatory, a foreshadowing of life again in the motherland. That they own land matters, and that what they own is a grave is a reminder of the former life entombed there, but in this book a grave site turns into a place of new beginnings, for it demonstrates that God is faithful to the promises made to Abraham.

NOTES

1. The Hebrew verb could be translated "went to" mourn her or "went in" to mourn her, following the NRSV translation. Alter (p. 23) translates "came to mourn her," while Fox (97) translates more loosely, "Abraham set about to lament for Sarah" (Robert Alter, *Genesis* [New York: W. W. Norton, 1996]; and Everett Fox, *The Five Books of Moses: Genesis, Exodus, Leviticus, Numbers, and Deuteronomy* [Schocken Bible 1; Dallas: Word, 1995]).

2. The NRSV translates the phrase "mighty prince," but the text reads literally prince of God or of the gods, an even higher honor among the ancient communities.

3. Abraham's use of the independent personal pronoun adds emphasis and formality to his request.

4. Meir Sternberg, "Double Cave, Double Talk: The Indirections of Biblical Dialogue," in *"Not in Heaven": Coherence and Complexity in Biblical Narrative*, ed. Jason C. Rosenblatt and Joseph C. Sitterson, Jr. (Bloomington: Indiana University Press, 1991) 28–57.

REBEKAH JOINS THE FAMILY

Genesis 24:1-67

Like successive births and deaths in real life, stories about the generations in Genesis braid across one another. Before Abraham dies (ch. 25), the narrative shifts attention to his son Isaac and the challenge of finding him a wife. [Obtaining a Wife] Placed near the center of Genesis, chapter 24 is the longest chapter in the book. It is a literary hinge that separates stories of life's beginnings and of Abraham's family from those of subsequent generations that bring the promise of uncountable offspring into fulfillment.

Obtaining a Wife

"Israelite marriage was essentially an arrangement between two families, usually initiated by a man and his parents (Judg 14:1-2; Gen 34:1-4, 8; Gen 24). The verbs and the actions that commonly describe the incorporation of the woman into the new household illustrate the male locus of the initiative; she is 'given,' 'taken,' 'sent for,' 'captured'—even purchased, in the case of a slave wife. Some texts suggest, however, that the woman's role was not wholly passive or lacking in initiative (2 Sam 11:25; 1 Sam 18:20), that she could refuse an 'offer' (Gen 24:5, 57-58) and make demands of her own (Judg 1:15). Though a woman could not divorce a husband, the mistreated wife might simply return to her father's house (Judg 19:2)."

Phyllis A. Bird, *Missing Persons and Mistaken Identities: Women and Gender in Ancient Israel* (OBT; Minneapolis: Fortress, 1997) 39.

For further reading, see Sarah Shectman, "Marriage and Divorce, *Ancient Near East*," and Annalisa Azzoni, "Marriage and Divorce, *Hebrew Bible*," in *The Oxford Encyclopedia of the Bible and Gender Studies*, ed. Julia M. O'Brien, 2 vols. (New York: Oxford University Press, 2014) 1:479–88.

COMMENTARY

This long chapter is filled with dialogue, repetition, complicated plans, divine speech, and prayers for help. It portrays the selection of the proper wife for Isaac as a complex and dramatic quest. To ensure that he marries a woman of his own blood and not a native Canaanite, Abraham exercises immense care and foresight. The challenge is how to continue bloodlines begun with Abraham's father Terah (11:27-32) and to show that the marriage was really "made in heaven." [Outline of Genesis 24]

One odd element of the quest is that Abraham will not allow Isaac to leave the land for any reason, neither to participate in nor approve of the choice of his own wife. Instead, Abraham commissions his servant to find a suitable woman for his son

Outline of Genesis 24

1. A Suitable Wife for Isaac, 24:1-9
2. Plea for *Hesed*, 24:10-14
3. Encounters, 24:15-28
4. Successful Negotiations, 24:29-60
5. Union, 24:61-67

Repetition

Literary critic Meir Sternberg has noted that serialization (repetition in a sequence) is imperative "where God works from behind the scenes." How else can God's intentions be made clear if not by presenting a "series of marvels too regular for the operations of chance?"

Meir Sternberg, *The Poetics of Biblical Narrative: Ideological Literature and the Drama of Reading* (Indiana Studies in Biblical Literature; Bloomington: Indiana University Press, 1985) 113.

Arranged Marriages

Arranged marriages are the norm in biblical stories, and the father or older men in the family are the primary arrangers. The matriarch Hagar, however, acts as patriarch when she finds a wife for Ishmael (21:21).

Johanna Stiebert has observed that there are a "number of father-daughter references in the Hebrew Bible that pertain to marriage alliances. The exchange of daughters among men contributes to the development of culture and of social stability because the exchanges connect the men, creating alliances and networks of relationships. In several of these cases, the daughter is highly valued as a gift and a reward" (38–39).

See Phyllis A. Trible, *Bird, Missing Persons and Mistaken Identities: Women and Gender in Ancient Israel* (OBT; Minneapolis: Fortress, 1997) 39.

Johanna Stiebert, *Fathers and Daughters in the Hebrew Bible* (Oxford: Oxford University Press, 2013) esp. 38–50.

(Gen 24:6-7). [Repetition] The chapter provides no reason for this restriction, but in the rich symbolic world of Genesis, the requirement that Isaac remain within the geographical boundaries of Canaan evokes experiences of Judeans who remain in the land under Babylonian occupation.

A Suitable Wife for Isaac, 24:1-9

A brief summary of God's gifts to Abraham follows Sarah's death. Abraham is "well advanced in years and the LORD had blessed Abraham in all things" (24:1).[1] Before he dies, he has one major challenge remaining: to find for Isaac a wife who comes from his own kinfolk. Perhaps because the distance back to the land of his father is too great to undertake in old age, Abraham sends his servant as his duly empowered emissary. [Arranged Marriages] For this solemn responsibility, he selects his oldest servant who "had charge of all he had" (24:2). The servant oversees his household as Joseph will do for Pharaoh. The servant, who is the principal actor in the chapter, works with utmost loyalty and fidelity to his master, yet he has no name. Some interpreters believe him to be Eliezer of Damascus whom Abraham wanted previously to be his heir (15:1-6),[2] but the text does not make that connection. His identity matters less to the narrator than his role as Abraham's surrogate in the quest for the right woman.[3]

Abraham underscores the seriousness of the search by requiring his servant both to take an oath and to perform a ritual act: "I will make you swear by the LORD, the God of heaven and earth." The God of heaven and earth, that is, the Creator of all things, is guarantor of the oath concerning this solemn task. Abraham emphasizes the oath's importance by stating it in both negative and positive terms: "You will not get a wife for my son from the daughters of the Canaanites," and you "will go to my country and to my kindred to get a wife for my son Isaac" (24:3-4). [Endogamous Marriage] The oath has one point: the wife must come from Abraham's family. Taking the oath is not enough,

Endogamous Marriage

That sons of the patriarchs are to marry wives of their own kin group is a requirement of Abraham for his son Isaac and then of Isaac and Rebekah for their son Jacob. Jacob's twin brother Esau makes both parents unhappy by marrying Canaanite women. Elisabeth Robertson Kennedy has found many parallels in the telling of courtship stories about Isaac and Jacob. Both patriarchs obtain wives from Padam Aram in Mesopotamia; divine guidance directs both courtships, and, of most importance, the chosen wives follow calls similar to those of the men. They too must leave their father's land and sojourn to Canaan in a process of divine election. In this way they add their own stories to Israel's myth of origins. Kennedy explained,

The women relatives in Padam-aram are the divinely chosen wives for the patriarchs not simply because of a quality inherent in the area or kin group, but because of the overarching logic of the promise which will call them to that precise land and kin group, following the same path as their male counterparts. Sojourn is so important a part of the ethnic myth that the narrative gives not only to the group of Israel's ancestors, but also to each individual within it, a moment of decision in which they too commit to it. (136–37)

In addition, symbolic overtones for the book's audience during the Persian Period add significance to the endogamous (within a certain group) marriages. The composers of Genesis connect the women to the land by divine selection and thereby heighten the ancient audience's own attachment to the land. When the women choose to come to the land, they implicitly invite the exiles to choose to return with their own wives from foreign parts to be part of God's people.

Elisabeth Robertson Kennedy, *Seeking Homeland: Sojourn and Ethnic Identity in the Ancestral Narratives of Genesis* (*BibInt*; Boston: Brill, 2011) see esp. 77–139.

---

however; the servant must seal it with a ritual in which he puts his hand under "Abraham's thigh and swear[s] concerning this matter," for this is a life-or-death search. [Hand Under the Thigh] This commission is fraught with importance, as if everything depends on it.

Anticipating possible resistance from the unknown woman, the servant wonders what he should do if she will not "follow him." Should he take Isaac to that land of the ancestors to continue

---

Hand Under the Thigh

"An oath is a statement by which people give assurance that they have spoken the truth or by which they obligate themselves to perform certain actions," as is the case here (Saldarini, 716). The enactment of the oath by placing the hand "under the thigh," that is, on or near the genitals, occurs again in Genesis when Jacob demands that his son Joseph swear to return his bones to Canaan when he dies (Gen 47:29-31).

Although the extreme solemnity of the occasion is obvious, the exact meaning of the act is unclear. Alter has noted that this solemn oath-taking is known in other ancient sources (eg., Ibn Ezra in the twelfth century; Alter, 113, n.2), but Speiser has proposed that the act might involve the threat of infertility if the oath is not carried out (178, n.2). Gunkel has referred to similar practices in Babylonian sources and proposed that it means simply "one vouches for another," even while it also points to the "unusual sacredness" of the male organ (249). Westermann's suggestion is the clearest:

"The rite of touching the generative organ when taking an oath occurs elsewhere only in Gen. 47:29 where the circumstances are the same, namely, imminent death. The one who is facing death secures his last will by 'an oath at the source of life'" (384).

It seems likely that in this story about the continuation of Abraham's family and the passing along of his seed through the marriage of his son to Rebekah, the rite of placing the hand under the thigh surely conveys a symbolic representation of the story line. Abraham's last will and testament will continue to create new generations through the choice of this woman.

Anthony J. Saldarini, "Oath," *HBD*.

Robert Alter, *Genesis* (New York: W. W. Norton, 1996).

E. A. Speiser, *Genesis: Introduction, Translation, and Notes* (AB 1; New York: Doubleday, 1964).

Herman Gunkel, *Genesis*, trans. Mark Biddle (Macon GA: Mercer University Press, 1997).

Claus Westermann, *Genesis 12–36: A Commentary* (London: SPCK, 1981).

Women's Choices

Recent interpreters have observed that women in ancient Israel clearly lived under a system of patriarchy that gave power and authority to males, particularly fathers, yet they also had some liberties. Patriarchy was not equivalent to misogyny, that is, hatred of women. In this chapter, for example, Abraham's servant anticipates a possible refusal of marriage by the woman that he is sent to fetch for Isaac, and later in the passage, despite plans established by her family, Rebekah is consulted about whether she will go immediately with the servant to marry Isaac or follow their plan to delay ten days longer or perhaps indefinitely.

It is possible that rather than reflecting typical cultural treatment of women, the chapter's attention to Rebekah's wishes is a literary device to show her eagerness for the marriage and willingness to cooperate with God's designs to fulfill the promises to Abraham. She becomes a model for exiles to choose the land of promise.

See Johanna Stiebert, *Fathers and Daughters in the Hebrew Bible* (Oxford: Oxford University Press, 2013) 228–29; Carol Meyers, "Contesting the Notion of Patriarchy: Anthropology and the Theorizing of Gender in Ancient Israel," in Deborah Rooke, ed., *A Question of Sex? Gender and Difference in the Hebrew Bible and Beyond* (Hebrew Bible Monographs 14; Sheffield: Phoenix, 2009) 84–105.

Simeon Solomon (1840–1905). *Isaac and Rebekah*. 1863. Watercolor. Victoria & Albert Museum, London. (Credit: V&A Images, London / Art Resource, NY)

the search for a suitable wife himself? [Women's Choices] In reply, Abraham is adamant that Isaac should not leave the land. Whatever the reason for this restriction, Abraham's instructions to his servant are clear: "See to it that you do not take my son back there" (24:6, 8).

Abraham elevates the task's importance even further by assuring his servant that God will assist him in his search, for God's promises are at stake in the mission:

> "The LORD God of heaven, who took me from my father's house and from the land of my birth, who spoke to me and swore to me, 'To your offspring I will give this land,' he will send his angel before you, and you shall take a wife for my son from there." (24:7)

It should be clear by now that this is no ordinary search for a mate, even in ancient times. Although many marriages may be "made in heaven," as the modern expression goes, this one will occur because of explicit divine intervention. The God of heaven who called Abraham from his father's house will send an angel to guide the selection process. One more time, Abraham repeats the command not to take Isaac "back there" (24:9, 2). Finally, the servant takes the oath and performs the ritual act with which his commissioning began.

Abraham has been relentless in insisting that Isaac cannot leave Canaan under any circumstances whatsoever. Why does this matter so much? Will the family lose possession of the land purchased for Sarah's burial in the previous chapter if the heir leaves? Might Isaac be lured into staying in the land of his grandfather? Some interpreters assume that the patrilineal promises demand that Abraham's heir live in Canaan, and that Lot is not a candidate for the role of heir because he chooses Moab for his inheritance in chapter 13,[4] or that Abraham "subjects the terms of his own vocation upon his son."[5] Yet the requirements for Isaac to remain in the land are singular, for all the other ancestors leave the land or come from another place. Abraham goes to Egypt, Jacob goes to Padam-aram, and Joseph will be taken to Egypt. Rebekah, Leah, Rachel and Zilpah come from Mesopotamia. Only Isaac must remain where he is for symbolic and literary reasons. He serves as a unifying figure for the book's audience by representing the people who never leave after the invasions, even though their lives too are greatly disrupted.

Plea for *Ḥesed*, 24:10-14

The servant's journey to Aram takes up only one verse, for the narrator's primary attention now falls on the careful preparations for this mission. The servant begins by gathering a show of Abraham's wealth, ten camels and choice gifts, and then proceeds to Aram-naharaim, the city of Nahor, Abraham's brother. [Camels] To build up expectation, the narrator presents the place where the servant will discover the woman. It is outside the city by a well of water, the place where women come in the evening to collect water for their families. [Wells of Water] Then, having positioned himself at a location where he can meet the women of the neighborhood, the most important aspect of preparation happens: the servant prays for a successful outcome: "O LORD, God of my master Abraham, please grant me success today and show steadfast love (*ḥesed*) to my master Abraham" (24:12).

Appealing to the God of Abraham, the one Abraham called the God of heaven and earth, the servant asks for a successful

Camels

 "Archeological and extrabiblical literary evidence indicates that camels were not adopted as beasts of burden until several centuries after the Patriarchal Period, and so their introduction into the story would have to be anachronisitic." This should not surprise readers in view of the long history of composition of the book and its probable audience living after the Babylonian Period. Alter has postulated that the camels had become such a customary feature of desert travel that they are inadvertently assumed to have existed in the time of Abraham.

Robert Alter, *Genesis* (New York: W. W. Norton, 1996) 114.

Wells of Water

Many biblical stories occur at wells and springs of water. In segments often called "type scenes," the setting at the well is a conventional place for betrothals where a "girl" meets a stranger. The story type has its roots in desert countries where women to this day meet at wells, streams, and springs to gather water and do washing for their families. The location reflects the reality of life in dry lands where water is a most precious requirement and women are charged with the task of transporting it to the home (Alter, 115).

This chapter speaks first of a well and then of a spring. The change in terms may reflect a synonymous understanding of springs and wells since both are vital sources of water. Or the change may indicate a story composed from more than one preexisting version of the story. Probably the term "spring" has symbolic implications of fertility.

Robert Alter, *Genesis* (New York: W. W. Norton, 1996).

mission as evidence of God's steadfast love, of divine *ḥesed*. His prayer repeats elements of the narrative. He tells God about his location by the spring of water and that it is an advantageous spot where women come to draw water. He tells God how to orchestrate the search successfully. He even audaciously scripts the dialogue that should unfold between him and the woman to signal to him that he has found the right one. He plans to ask a "girl" for a drink from her jar of water. She will agree and then go beyond his request by offering water for his camels. When that exchange takes place, then the servant will know that God has shown *ḥesed* to his master. Although a marriage partner for Isaac is at stake here, the primary beneficiary is Abraham, for this is how the promise of uncountable offspring will be fulfilled.

Rebekah at the Well by Phillip Ratner

Artist Phillip Ratner has sculpted a tall, thin, young Rebekah carrying her water jug on her shoulder. The starkness of her figure evokes the first vision the servant has of her at the well and attends to the literal dimensions of the story, but the water jug also suggests her larger role as a foremother of Israel, a source of fertility and a spring of life. The S-curve of her figure echoes the typical S-shape of madonnas in sculpture and painting in later art history, further interpreting Rebekah as an important mother of Israel.

Phillip Ratner. *Rebekah at the Well*. Sculpture. (Credit: Image used by gracious permission of the artist.)

Encounters, 24:15-28

It comes as no surprise that before the servant finishes his prayer "Look (*hinnēh*), there was Rebekah before him with her water jar upon her shoulder"! The NRSV translation omits the Hebrew marker of important speech, "Look," the exclamation that occurs at significant moments across Genesis. The narrator supplies readers with key information about Rebekah. She is the daughter of Bethuel, who was the son of Milcah, who was the wife of Nahor, Abraham's brother. That means Rebekah and Isaac are cousins, a fact readers already know (cf. 20:20-24). She is beautiful and a virgin according to the omniscient narrator. Obviously, the servant has found the right woman and not by accident, but he does not yet know this, for he is ignorant of her identity, and she may still refuse him as he suggested to Abraham (v. 5).

The scene is lively, like a film speeding up, with much scurrying and hurrying by the participants. The servant runs to meet her. She hurries to lower her jar of water to comply with his request and to add the unasked-for water for the camels, "until they finished drinking." She empties her jar quickly into the trough and runs to draw more water for the animals.

In the midst of this running about, the servant "gazes at her to see if the Lord had made his journey successful" (24:21). He seems to think so because he gives her a gold nose ring and two gold bracelets weighing ten gold shekels, perhaps in gratitude for her hospitality to his animals but surely to impress her with the wealth he has brought. He asks about her parentage and whether there is room in her father's house for his party to spend the night. She tells him what the narrator has already told the reader, that she is the "daughter of Bethuel, son of Milcah, whom she bore to Nahor" (24:24). After she assures him that there is room for the humans and fodder for the animals, he bows his head and worships the Lord with a prayer of thanksgiving: "Blessed be the Lord, the God of my master Abraham, who has not forsaken his loving kindness (*ḥesed*) and his faithfulness to my master. As for me, the Lord has led me on the way to the house of my master's kin" (24:27).

Rebekah runs again, this time to tell her mother's household about her encounter at the well. [Mother's House]

Mother's House

AΩ "'Mother's house' (*bêt 'ēm*) is found four times (Gen 24:28; Song 3:4; 8:2; Ruth 1:8) and is alluded to in several other texts (2 Kgs 8:1; Prov 9:1; 14:1; 31:21, 27). These references appear in passages focusing on women or providing a female perspective. Taken together, they suggest that the dominance of women in household management led to the identification of the household's internal dynamics with the senior female, whereas the predominance of 'father's house' in the HB/OT reflects the identification of the senior male with the household in terms of its patrimony and its place in the larger socio-political structure."

Carol Myers, "Father's House: Hebrew/Old Testament," *EBR* 8:981.

Successful Negotiations, 24:29-60

Although the servant has managed to arrive at the right household and to locate the chosen daughter, his work is not complete. Now he must both convince the family that Abraham's son Isaac is a suitable match for their daughter and persuade her to come with him. These negotiations comprise the remainder of the chapter and report with more detail events that have already been told.

When Rebekah's brother Laban hears what happened at the well and sees the valuable jewelry that the visitor has given to his sister, he runs out to meet the man. The quick dash outside ends in another startling encounter. "[Look], there he was standing by his camels at the spring" (Gen 24:30). Laban welcomes the servant with every form of desert hospitality. "Come in, O blessed of the LORD. Why do you stand outside when I have prepared the house and a place for the camels?" As the servant enters, Laban himself cares for the animals and provides foot washing for the servant's entourage, followed by food.

The servant, though, focuses intently on his mission, refusing food until he can explain his important errand. His elaborate explanation retells and slightly expands the entire story thus far (vv. 34-48). The retelling has the purpose of persuading Laban and family that God arranged this betrothal and the family should cooperate with it. He declares that the Lord has blessed Abraham (v. 1) with wealth, described in all-inclusive pairs: flocks and herds, silver and gold, slaves male and female, camels and donkeys. He reports that Sarah gave birth to Isaac in her old age, that Abraham required an oath of him not to take a wife from the Canaanites for Isaac but to go to his father's house to find a wife for Isaac. He reports his fears that the chosen woman might not agree and again tells of Abraham's insistence that Isaac remain in the land. He relates his encounter with Rebekah at the well. He even retells his prayer that the Lord would show *hesed* and also keep him utterly focused on his mission (v. 49), to remind readers that this is God's doing.

Other members of Rebekah's family appear on the scene to make this decision about the servant's proposal. Her father Bethuel joins brother Laban. This looks to them like the Lord's doing, and they have neither good nor bad to say in reply. "There is Rebekah," they say, "take her and go and let her be Isaac's wife as the LORD has spoken" (v. 51). The servant recognizes that his prayer has been answered, and he bows to the ground and worships. More valuable gifts are given, first to Rebekah and then to her brother and mother. Finally, they eat and depart "early in the morning," but not so fast; negotiations are still not finished.

Rebekah's mother and brother appear to renege on the plan, offering a delaying tactic. The servant should leave without her and she can join him after ten days. This effort to stall the marriage may simply reflect the family's desire to have time for proper good-byes and to help Rebekah prepare for her married life in a faraway land, or it may be a ruse to break the arrangement and keep her. Most certainly, however, it is a way to reveal Rebekah's character and to portray her whole-hearted response to her own call. Like Abraham, she must choose to leave her land and her father's house for a husband and a land that God will show her. The servant refuses to accept this delaying option because "the LORD has made my journey successful" (24:56), and he urges them for a second time them to "send me to my master."

Only now does anyone think about consulting Rebekah. "Will you go with this man?" they ask, and without hesitation she responds, "I will" (24:58). The servant has persuaded her that this venture is worth the risk, and she accepts the challenge. Her motives are not clear. Is she merely compliant with her family's arrangements for her, is she a practical woman seeing the opportunity to make a good marriage, or is she convinced that God has shown steadfast love and truth in his plan, or perhaps a mix of these? The family accepts her decision and sends her away with a blessing of fertility:

> "May you, our sister, become
> thousands of myriads;
> may your offspring gain possession
> of the gates of their foes." (24:60)

This family blessing echoes across Genesis, highlighting the promise of uncountable children, more than the stars of the heaven and the sands of the sea. The hope for Rebekah is also the hope for her descendants living under imperial occupation and uncertain of any future at the gates of their foes.

Union, 24:61-67

Rebekah's willingness receives further expression as she mounts the camels, rides along with her maid, and "follows the man," Abraham's surrogate who prayed for her compliance. Meanwhile, Isaac himself finally appears in the story. He has settled in his own place in the Negeb and is walking out in the evening, like God in the Garden of Eden, when he sees the servant's entourage approaching. Rebekah in turn sees him. She dismounts from the camel, for she suspects that he is the one, and asks the servant, "Who is this man?" The servant calls Isaac his master, after which she covers herself with a veil in accord with bridal custom. Then the servant tells Isaac all he has done, but, happily for readers, he does not repeat the proceedings again. Immediately Isaac brings her into his mother's tent and is so happy with his new wife that he forgets his sorrow over his mother's death.

Isaac's role in Genesis is minor, so minor that there is little attention to his character and interpreters have understood him to be a mere cipher, the object of an aborted sacrifice, passive recipient of a search for a wife, and a trickster who, like his father, passes his wife off as his sister. He seems to have no substance of his own compared to the other patriarchs in the book. He is a bridge between generations in the unfolding of the book's narrative. His minor role may also relate to his symbolic status as representative of the Judeans who never leave the land after the nation's destruction, for the people of the land are largely subsumed under the powerful leadership of the returnees when the Persians allow some to return to rebuild the nation. The deportees are the more educated, privileged, and powerful elites whose offspring take control of the narrative during the nation's rebuilding. Isaac's role is significant primarily as a figure to include the ones who remained in Judah.

CONNECTIONS

Behind the Scenes

The search for a wife for Isaac expresses a theology of divine guidance underlying normal human activities. In this chapter, as in the other stories in Genesis including particularly the Joseph narrative (chs. 37–50), humans rely on God, but God neither directly speaks nor intervenes. The human activity of finding a spouse, exalted and solemnized as it is here, is nevertheless not driven by divine appearance, divine speech, or direct command. First Abraham and then his servant, who actually gives God directions, engineer it.

A theological belief that God acts indirectly in human affairs but nevertheless directs events behind the scenes drives the story. Many people of faith hold such a theological view. It creates problems when people assert that God directly controls and engineers their own desires, convictions, and plans. Yet often when people of faith look back at their lives, it seems that God has truly been directing them, whether they had been aware or not. Choices made in the dark that turned sour, decisions that caused precipitous ends to hopes and dreams, turns in the wrong direction that seemed like colossal mistakes can appear in the light of faith to have been preparations for later callings, a later life of creativity and wholeness. It is not always so, of course. Faith provides no guarantee that the paths we take will bring life.

Yet faith is often an over-the-shoulder realization that God had been there all along, leading us, accompanying us through hard times, tragedies, and our own traumas. Genesis 24 is certain that the servant's choice of Rebekah was the right one, significant for the nation's life, the result of divine calls to Abraham, the servant, and finally to Rebekah herself. God was with them, leading them to life and to a future of blessing. [God's Providential Care]

Our Own Kind?

Abraham's rejection of women from the Canaanites and his insistence on a wife for Isaac from his own family creates problems for contemporary readers. Although his relationship with the Hittites and other Canaanites has been respectful and generally peaceful, his demand for a wife of Isaac's own kind embodies prejudice against an entire group of people. Although this stance may be understandable for the Judean community, broken, scattered, and in danger of disappearance from history, communal identity must not be built by means of exclusion. Old Testament texts reflecting the Persian Period argue about this. Genesis incorporates Joseph's Egyptian wife and sons formally into the family (ch. 47). The book of Ruth portrays the Moabite woman as the most faithful character in the book. The God of Genesis does choose one people, but this God is also the God of all the nations from whom none are excluded. [Foreign Wives]

God's Providential Care

Does God in fact lead and guide humans in such a way? Walter Brueggemann considered that question:

The answer will not emerge directly from the text. This text does not stress the leadership of Yahweh as much as it emphasizes the faithful following of the actors. The principal characters accept a reading of reality related to Yahweh. They interpret events accordingly. For its seeming naiveté, this narrative is a mature reflection on faith. It asks people not first of all to anticipate the faithfulness of God, but to read it in retrospect. We do not always know the gifts of God in advance. But given a perspective of faith, we can in subsequent reflection discern the amazing movement of God in events we had not noticed or which we had assigned to other causes. Thus we are like the servant of this narrative (v. 21) who must study to draw a conclusion.

Walter Brueggemann, *Genesis* (Interpretation; Atlanta: John Knox, 1982) 201.

Foreign Wives

This text does not send native women away, but it does eliminate them as candidates for marriage to the patriarchs. Other biblical texts plan to send foreign wives away (Neh 10). "Given the sending away of wives recommended in the Persian Period, one wonders whether the editors of Genesis have repeated this plot in order to explore the motives for such actions," according to Mark G. Brett. Brett points to Abraham and Sarah's two wife-sister stories, first in Egypt (12:10-20) and second in Gerar (20:1-18), as examples of Abraham's fear and suspicion of foreigners that turns out to be groundless.

It is possible, though, that stories of Rebekah and then Rachel and Leah deliberately choosing to come to the land seek to depict them responding independently to the call of Abraham and Sarah. Their origins in Padam-aram where the family began ensures that they will follow Abraham's God, but it also presents them as models for exiles living in Mesopotamia to make similar courageous decisions to live in the promised land. The women's place of origin may say more about their willing participation in the life of Abraham's family than about common blood.

Mark Brett, *Genesis: Procreation and the Politics of Identity* (OTR; London: Routledge, 2000).

NOTES

1. Paul D. Vrolijk, *Jacob's Wealth: An Examination into the Nature and Role of Material Possessions in the Jacob-Cycle (Gen 25:19-35:29)* (SVT; Leiden; Brill, 2011) 316–17, has argued that the meaning of God's blessings upon Abraham "in all things" is multifaceted. It includes material possessions, descendants, a great name, links to the nations, happiness and success, and spiritual blessings.

2. Gerhard von Rad, *Genesis*, rev. ed. (OTL; Philadelphia: Westminster, 1972) 254; Terence E. Fretheim, "Genesis" (*NIB* 1; Nashville: Abingdon, 1994) 509.

3. Claus Westermann, *Genesis 12–36: A Commentary* (London: SPCK, 1981) 384.

4. See Naomi Steinberg, *Kinship and Marriage in Genesis: A Household Economics Perspective* (Minneapolis: Fortress, 1993) 84, n.106.

5. Fretheim, "Genesis," 510.

THE FIRST GENERATION DIES

Genesis 25:1-18

The genealogical buttresses that support the Genesis narratives express fulfillment of the promise of offspring. With their compressed notices of the lives and deaths of ancestors, genealogies erect structural walls for the book. They portray creation and recreation from generation to generation. Into their rhythmic patterns are embedded stories about particular ancestors that have the effect of slowing down history through portrayals that exemplify life, death, and life again. [Outline of Genesis 25] Volume 1 of this commentary ends midway through chapter 25 before the birth of Jacob and Esau. Their dramatic story begins at 25:19 and appears in volume 2 as life begins again.

> **Outline of Genesis 25**
> 1. More Life and Death for Abraham, 25:1-11
> 2. Abraham's Death, 25:7-11
> 3. Descendants of Ishmael, 25:12-18

COMMENTARY

Chapter 25 is a genealogical chapter, the first part of which completes the account of Abraham and Sarah's generation (25:1-18) and concludes the first half of Genesis. The second part of the chapter introduces the book's second half. It tells of Isaac and Rebekah's descendants in narrative form (25:19-34) to lead into accounts of Jacob and his many descendants who will constitute the family of Israel (chs. 25–50). [Family as the Basic Social Unit] Isaac and Rebekah, the second generation, receive short shrift in Genesis, skipped over except as parents keenly involved in the lives of their twin sons, Jacob and Esau. (See volume 2, *Genesis 25B–50*.)

> **Family as the Basic Social Unit**
> The family is the dominating form of community in the patriarchal (and matriarchal) stories. According to Westermann, the emphasis falls on the "family bond far and away beyond political and national divisions and in accordance with the programmatic pronouncement in Gen 12:3" (400). Yet this statement overlooks the symbolic important of the families in Genesis as representative of Israel and neighboring nations.
>
> Claus Westermann, *Genesis 12–36: A Commentary* (London: SPCK, 1981).

More Life and Death for Abraham, 25:1-11

Despite his greatly advanced age, Abraham takes yet another wife. Her name is Keturah, and we know little about her except that she

Concubines

A concubine is not a prostitute or whore but holds the status of a second wife in a polygamous marriage. Hagar was a concubine of Abraham, and now Keturah takes that role.

These arrangements not only create hierarchical relationships among wives but also provide some protection for the concubine because she is attached to a family, although she has no freedom and may be readily subject to abuse of all kinds. Nevertheless, the primary importance of Keturah's concubine status probably arises from the question of who among Abraham's many children will inherit the promise.

For further reading see Mignon R. Jacobs, *Gender, Power, and Persuasion* (Grand Rapids MI: Baker, 2007) 144–46.

Biblical Numbers

The number twelve is among those recurring numbers of the Bible with symbolic significance. Others include three, four, seven, and ten. The number twelve refers to the number of tribes or nations in a political confederation. Here Ishmael has twelve sons as will Jacob, and the sons become the eponymous ancestors of the tribes of Israel. Jesus calls twelve disciples in the New Testament to symbolize the nation of the new Israel.

For further reading, see "Numbers and Counting," *ABD* 4:1139–46.

is one of Abraham's concubines (v. 6, cf. 1 Chr 6:32) and the mother of six sons. [Concubines] By this time, Abraham may be too old to have children, and so perhaps this genealogy of Keturah should have been inserted into the narrative in an earlier chapter.[1] Yet by ordinary human standards, Abraham was too old even when Ishmael was born, so such realistic biological assessments are not meaningful in Genesis, where God alone creates life. The chapter does not specify the time of Keturah's entry into the family, but its narrative placement after Sarah's burial suggests "serial monogamy" rather than polygamy,[2] although Abraham had two wives simultaneously with Sarah and Hagar.

Abraham's marriage to Keturah is but a footnote to his story, but it does portray him as a vital begetter of children, not simply of Ishmael and Isaac but also of half a dozen more. God continues to intervene in the face of the impossible for this ancient man. [Biblical Numbers] Keturah's sons establish Abraham as forefather of many related peoples, namely those in the trans-Jordan region and the Arabian Peninsula.[3]

Keturah bears six sons of whom only three have been identified with known tribes or groups.[4] Of the six, additional genealogical details name sons for three of them, Dedan, Midian, and Shuah (25:3-4). It is not clear whether the names are personal or tribal,[5] but it seems likely that they represent groups in neighboring nations, as do so many characters in Genesis. If so, they establish family connections between Israel and its neighbors, a point further elaborated in Ishmael's genealogy below (25:12-18). Abraham again is a blessing to the nations.

Whoever the sons and grandsons of Keturah are, their presence creates a potential crisis of inheritance that further isolates Isaac. He alone is the child of the promise, and the text makes clear that Abraham gave all he had to him (v. 6). Yet Abraham is still a good father who does not fail his other offspring. To the sons of his concubines, presumably Hagar and Keturah, he gives gifts "while he was still living." Just as he insisted to his servant in chapter 24 that Isaac not leave the land in search of a wife, he again prevents Isaac from interacting with other peoples. Abraham sends Isaac's half-brothers away from him, "eastward to the east country" (v. 6). Separation may be necessary to protect Isaac from jealousy and competition for inheritance at the narrative level, but sending Keturah's sons away also connects neighboring peoples to Abraham's family, even though they do not hold the same status as Isaac.

At the symbolic level, Isaac's isolation from other members of Abraham's family relates to the book's audience. His repeated separation from others signifies the Judeans who remain in the land throughout the Babylonian Period. They are the poor of the land who survive under the rule of foreign empires and are separated from their deported Judean sisters and brothers, the wealthier, elite leaders exiled in Mesopotamia. Like Isaac, they are overlooked and largely powerless as the nation begins to rebuild. They do not assume leadership, take much initiative, or engage in many great adventures. Still, the figure of Isaac includes them in the national narrative. Although less visible, he is an honorable man, blessed by God, and, as father to Jacob and Esau, he gives birth to Israel. [Isaac and Jeremiah]

Isaac and Jeremiah

In a complex portrait, the book of Jeremiah depicts the prophet Jeremiah as figure who is repeatedly captured and released by the Babylonians and by leaders of his own people (Jer 26–38). During one of the Babylonian assaults of Jerusalem, he undergoes in his own individual life the suffering of his people. In particular, he does not go to Babylon with the exiles but remains in the land like the poor who are not deported (Jer 37–38). Yet the prophetic book also identifies him with the exiles when he is carted off to Egypt against his will (Jer 41–44). The book manages to portray Jeremiah as both one of the remnant left in the land during the Babylonian occupation and as an exile—although to Egypt, not Babylon. In this way, Jeremiah is a unifying figure in the disaster's aftermath, gathering up the experiences of both groups of Judeans (see O'Connor).

The book of Genesis does something similar but uses two figures to achieve a unifying effect. Isaac is not allowed to leave the land and Jacob is forced to do so. His story will evoke experiences of exiled Judeans in the second part of Genesis.

Kathleen M. O'Connor, *Jeremiah: Pain and Promise* (Minneapolis: Fortress, 2011) 69–79.

Abraham's Death, 25:7-11

After 175 years of life, Abraham, father of Isaac, dies full of years and is "gathered to his people" (25:7). [Death Is Part of Life] Isaac and his half-brother Ishmael, who has not returned to the family since he and Hagar were expelled (Gen 21), bury their father together. Their joint performance of the duties of sonship at Abraham's grave displays neither animosity nor sibling rivalry between them. Perhaps both have forgiven their father for "sacrificing" them, one to the jealousy and fear of Sarah (ch. 21) and the other to God's frightful command to make of him a holocaust on Mount Moriah (ch. 22). Genesis leaves readers to speculate about motivations among family members by telling of their actions, not their feelings. The text, however, gives no indication that forgiveness was ever needed, because family relationships in Genesis serve larger symbolic purposes. In this chapter, Abraham's burial

Death Is Part of Life

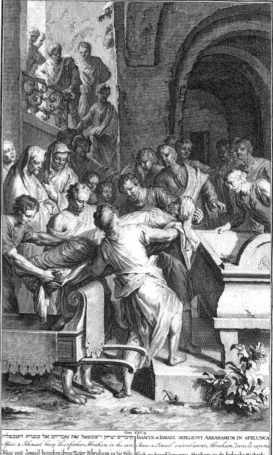

"Abraham died at the ripe old age of 175, a nice round 100 years after he responded to the divine call (12:4). The writer describes his death in quite matter-of-fact ways. Death appears not to be an enemy, but simply as the end of a good life (see 15:15; cf. 47:9)."

Terence E. Fretheim, "Genesis" (*NIB* 1; Nashville: Abingdon, 1994) 515.

Gilliam van der Gouwen, engraved from the design of Gerard Hoet (1648–1733). "Abraham's Burial." From *Taferelen der voornaamste geschiedenissen van het Oude en Nieuwe Testament en andere boeken, bij de heilige schrift gevoegt.* 1728. (Courtesy of the Pitts Theology Library, Candler School of Theology, Emory University)

takes place in peace among his sons, the ancestors of Israelites and Ishmaelites.

The narrator reminds readers that Abraham owns a small piece of land, the cave of Machpelah where Sarah is buried and where he is buried too. Formerly this land belonged to Ephron the Hittite (ch. 23), but now the grave site fulfills the divine promise in miniature fashion. Sanctified by the bones of Israel's foreparents, the land is a promise of future life, a seedbed of hope for the future, but at present the land of future life is a grave.

Abraham's death concludes with a summary remark by the narrator: "After the death of Abraham God blessed his son Isaac" (v. 11). When the phrase "After the death of" occurs elsewhere, it ends one era of leadership and points toward another in regard to the death of great leaders, including Moses (Josh 1:1), Joshua (Judg 1:1), and Saul (2 Sam 1:1). Perhaps like the English expression, "The king is dead, long live the king," the verse passes leadership from Abraham to Isaac.[5] Geography again joins the lives of the two brothers, for Isaac settles at Beer-lahai-roi, the well where God promised Hagar a great future through her son Ishmael (16:14). The well's name translates as "well of the Living One who sees me." God sees both Isaac and Ishmael.

Underneath the story of Abraham's burial by the two brothers lies the question of birth order. The firstborn male is the traditional heir in a family, but the second-born Isaac is indisputably in that role; yet Abraham's story ends with a genealogy of Ishmael. [Election of the Second Born]

Descendants of Ishmael, 25:12-18

The promise given by the angel of the Lord to Hagar in the desert reaches fulfillment through her son: "I will so greatly multiply your offspring that they cannot be counted for multitude" (16:10). God has seen and heard Hagar (16:11-14), and God has been with the boy. Ishmael becomes the father of twelve sons equivalent in the number to the sons of Jacob, grandsons of Isaac. A dozen sons make each patriarch into a great nation.

Unlike the multiple generations of Keturah's genealogy, however, Ishmael's list does not extend beyond the first generation, for his line comes to an end here in the Bible. Ishmael's genealogy lays out equivalence of offspring between of Ishmael and Isaac, who will be the grandfather of Jacob's twelve sons (21:20). [Ishmael and Isaac in the Qur'an] Even as the non-chosen child, Ishmael knows divine protection, and the blessing of fertility promised to Abraham has been extended to him as well, but neither he nor Keturah's sons are the chosen heirs.[6]

The generations (*tôlĕdoth*) of Ishmael include the sons' names "in order of their birth" (25:13). Twelve names follow (vv. 14-15), but the narrator reports that they are named according to "their villages, by their encampments, twelve princes according to their tribes" (v. 16). Further geographical detail places them near Egypt in the direction of Assyria. Westermann has suggested that the

---

Election of the Second Born

"Election in the HB/OT is the notion that God favors some individuals and groups over others, an idea that finds fullest expression in the affirmation that Israel is God's chosen people" (Kaminsky).

In Genesis, God repeatedly chooses the second-born son over the first, such as favoring Abel over his brother Cain, Isaac over Ishmael, Jacob over Esau, and Joseph over ten older brothers. The motif of unexpected election appears in other Old Testament texts like God's choice of David to be king of Israel over ten older brothers (1 Sam 9:1–10:15).

Genesis gives no reason for God's election of the second born, but the choice implies divine overturning of human custom and law, since the firstborn is the expected heir. God elects the least likely candidate, suggesting that human status and social expectations are neither important nor determinative in God's call, nor can humans control God. Perhaps Israel's election functions in the same way in Genesis. Who would expect God to favor a destroyed nation and a scattered people?

For further reading, see Nathan Mac Donald, "Did God Choose the Patriarchs?" in *Genesis and Christian Theology*, ed. Nathan MacDonald, Mark W. Elliott, and Grant Macaskill (Grand Rapids MI: William B. Eerdmans, 2012) 245–66.

Joel S. Kaminsky, "Election," *EBR* 7:611–12.

latter refers to the semi-nomadic existence of the Ishmaelites and names various locales according to the grazing seasons.[7] Ishmael's death notice comes between the locations of his sons (v. 17).

Although the genealogy contains multiple ways to describe Ishmael's sons, its overriding purposes are to show that God has been faithful to the promises made to Hagar and that the neighboring peoples are part of Abraham's family, connected to him by blood, blessed by God, and made fruitful, even if not included in the covenant. Yet Abraham circumcises his son Ishmael (17:23-15). Ishmael participates in the sign of the covenant in accord with God's command, even if he is not the chosen one. Thomas has noted that Ishmael's genealogy spreads across one generation rather than going forward to future offspring to preserve the ancestral lines that will no longer be a focus of the story. The sons are honored as "princes" (cf. 17:20), but now the narrator can turn attention to Isaac, the son of the promise.[8]

The second half of Genesis (chs. 25B–50) is organically connected to the first half by the genealogical structures and by the promises to Abraham. Those promises come to further realization in the stories of Jacob's family. He is the father of the nation, for his sons form the twelve tribes of Israel. His squabbling children end up in Egypt away from the land, and, although they prosper there, return remains a distant hope.

CONNECTIONS

Abraham is rightly known as the father of faith because when God says, "Go you," he goes (12:1-4 and 22:1). His obedience is full and trusting when God demands the impossible of him. But what if we thought about him as the father of doubt, a model of the struggles there are in living a life of faith? Abraham's doubts and fears appear with equal clarity in the text and ricochet through the lives of many modern Western believers. Although he travels to an unknown land as God commands, his trip to Egypt is marked by self-protective doubt (12:10-20). He so fears for his life that he risks his wife Sarah's life to save his own when Pharaoh wants her for his harem. He learns little from this incident and risks her life again in Gerar when Abimelech desires her (ch. 20). He does not believe that God will provide him with an heir, so he attempts to substitute Eliezer of Damascus (15:1-6) and implicitly Hagar's son Ishmael (ch. 16).

In the process of taking control of the promises rather than trusting God, he participates in Sarah's harsh sexual abuse of Hagar, and then casts her out (ch. 21). He agrees to "sacrifice" his own firstborn son, Ishmael (ch. 21). When he finally grows to fully trust God, his obedience to the command to slaughter his son Isaac with no protest to the Just Judge whom he begged not to destroy Sodom is, at best, an act of hope against hope that God will not really require it of him and, at worst, a disregard for his son's life in some fatalistic decision bordering on fanatic belief (ch. 22). In the end, Abraham has mistreated everyone in his family except for his nephew Lot who separates from him (13:1-13).

Abraham's doubts, his moral dubiousness, and his efforts to take matters into his own hands are immensely comforting. They give us an ancestor in faith who does not know what he is doing, whose broken humanity prevents deifying him, and whose doubt and hesitant faith closely resembles the lives of most of us. Yet his doubts do not destroy his relationship with the God who calls him. They do not hinder the fulfillment of divine promises. Each failed effort to take control yields some new moment of hope and fulfillment for him and his family despite their deeply frail humanity.

Conclusion to Genesis 1–25A

The first twenty-five chapters of Genesis (1:1–25:18) prepare the ground for the book's second half, where promises to Abraham reach some fulfillment, but, like the book's audience, the family still does not reach the land that God will show them (25:19–50:26). Chapters 1–25A set Israel's formation and identity within the spectacular birth of the cosmos and all living things. These are brought into being by the potent word and bursting creativity of God. The creative power of God must be the theological starting point of Genesis, the foundation of the entire enterprise. [Creator God] Only such a God can recreate the fallen nation. God's creative power is not merely introduction or prologue to the creation of Israel; it is the *sine qua non* of all that follows. Only the recognition that God has the transcendent and unlimited capacity to create again and again can anchor hope amid the impossible conditions facing the destroyed nation, dispossessed of and displaced from its land and unable to imagine a future under the control of foreign empires. Only the Creator God who speaks life into being can bring them back to life. Only the Creator God can overcome the impossibilities that the book's ancient audience confronts. Genesis tells about beginnings to encourage and empower the remnant of Judah to begin again. It promises them that, like their ancestors, they too have a future as God's chosen people because Genesis is the story of God personally recreating "a people as God's own—a story in progress."[9]

To be continued . . .

NOTES

1. E. A. Speiser, *Genesis: Introduction, Translation, and Notes* (AB 1; New York: Doubleday, 1964) 189; Herman Gunkel, *Genesis*, trans. Mark Biddle (Macon GA: Mercer University Press, 1997) 256.

2. Naomi Steinberg, *Kinship and Marriage in Genesis: A Household Economics Perspective* (Minneapolis: Fortress, 1993) 85–86. Nahum Sarna, in *Genesis* (JPS Torah Commentary; Philadelphia: The Jewish Publication Society, 1989) 172, has argued that Abraham had described himself as too old to sire children over forty years earlier, "so it is unlikely that he had six sons after the age of one hundred and forty." In his view, this report, therefore, must come from an earlier time, but composers of the book may not be so concerned about precise chronology. The marriage to Keturah marks Abraham as a fertile father of peoples.

3. Gunkel, *Genesis*, 257; Robert Alter, *Genesis* (New York: W. W. Norton, 1996) 124.

4. Sarna, *Genesis*, 172–73.

5. Claus Westermann, *Genesis 12–36: A Commentary* (London: SPCK, 1981) 396.

5. Sarna, *Genesis*, 174.

6. Jon D. Levenson, *Inheriting Abraham: The Legacy of the Patriarch in Judaism, Christianity & Islam* (Princeton NJ: Princeton University Press, 2012) 55.

7. Westermann, *Genesis 12–36*, 399.

8. Matthew A. Thomas, *These Are the Generations: Identity, Covenant, and the 'Toledot' Formula* (London: T & T Clark, 2011) 115–16.

9. Words adapted from William P. Brown, "Manifest Diversity: The Presence of God in Genesis," in *Genesis and Christian Theology*, ed. Nathan MacDonald, Mark W. Elliott, and Grant Macaskill (Grand Rapids MI: William B. Eerdmans, 2012) 21.

BIBLIOGRAPHY

Commentaries

Bandstra, Barry. *Genesis 1–11: A Handbook on the Hebrew Text*. Waco TX: Baylor University Press, 2008.

Blenkinsopp, Joseph. *Creation, Un-Creation, Re-Creation: A Discursive Commentary on Genesis 1–11*. London and New York: T & T Clark, 2011.

Brett, Mark. *Genesis: Procreation and the Politics of Identity*. Old Testament Readings. London: Routledge, 2000.

Brodie, Thomas L. *Genesis as Dialogue: A Literary, Historical, & Theological Commentary*. New York: Oxford University Press, 2001.

Brueggemann, Walter. *Genesis*. Interpretation. Atlanta: John Knox, 1982.

Cass, Leon R. *The Beginning of Wisdom: Reading Genesis*. Chicago: University of Chicago Press, 2003.

Clifford, Richard J. *Genesis*. New Jerome Biblical Commentary. New York: Prentice Hall, 1990.

Cotter, David W. *Genesis*. Berit Olam. Collegeville MN: Liturgical, 2003.

De La Torre, Miguel A. *Genesis*. Belief. Louisville KY: Westminster John Knox, 2011.

Gowan, Donald E. *From Eden to Babel: a commentary on the book of Genesis 1–11*. Grand Rapids: Eerdmans, 1988.

Gunkel, Herman. *Genesis*. Translated by Mark Biddle. Macon GA: Mercer University Press, 1997.

Janzen, Gerald J. *Abraham and All the Families of the Earth: A Commentary on the Book of Genesis 12–50*. International Theological Commentary. Grand Rapids MI: Eerdmans, 1993.

Niditch, Susan. "Genesis." *The Women's Bible Commentary: Revised and Updated*. Edited by Carol Newsom, Sharon Ringe, and Jacqueline Lapsley. Louisville KY: Westminster John Knonx, 2012.

von Rad, Gerhard. *Genesis*. Old Testament Library. Philadelphia: Westminster, 1972.

Sarna, Nahum M. *Genesis*. Philadelphia: The Jewish Publication Society, 1989.

Towner, W. Sibley. *Genesis*. Westminster Bible Companion. Louisville KY: Westminster John Knox, 2001.

Westermann, Claus. *Genesis 1–11*. Minneapolis: Augsburg, 1984.

———. *Genesis 12–36*. Minneapolis: Fortress, 1995.

Additional Works

Albertz, Rainer, and Rüdiger Schmidt. *Family and Household Religion in Ancient Israel and the Levant*. Winona Lake IN; Eisenbrauns, 2012.

Alter, Robert. *Genesis*. New York: W. W. Norton, 1996.

Altmann, Peter. "Tithes for Clergy and Taxes for the King: State and Temple Contributions in Nehemiah." *Catholic Biblical Quarterly* 76/2 (2014): 21–229.

Amit, Yairah. *Reading Biblical Narratives: Literary Criticism and the Hebrew Bible.* Minneapolis: Fortress, 2001.

Anderson, John E. *Jacob and the Divine Trickster: A Theology of Deception and YHWH's Fidelity to the Ancestral Promise in the Jacob Cycle.* Siphrut 5. Winona Lake IN: Eisenbrauns, 2011.

Ascalone, Enrico. *Mesopotamia.* Translated by Rosanna M. Gianmmanco Frongia. Berkley: University of California Press, 2005.

Attridge, Harold W. "Sin, Sinners." In volume 5 of the *New Interpreter's Dictionary of the Bible,* edited by Katharine Sakenfeld, 263–79. Nashville: Abingdon, 2009.

———. "Word (LOGOS)." In volume 2 of *The Oxford Encyclopedia of the Bible and Theology,* edited by Samuel E. Balentine, 434–38. Oxford and New York: Oxford University Press, 2015.

Auerbach, Eric. "Odysseus' Scar." In *Mimesis: The Representation of Reality in Western Literature.* Translated by Willard R. Trask, introduction by Edward W. Said, 50th Anniversary Edition, 3–23. Princeton: Princeton University Press, 2003.

Augustine, Saint, Bishop of Hippo. *On Genesis.* The Works of Saint Augustine, Part 1, Volume 13. Translated by Edmund Hill, edited by John E. Rotelle. Hyde Park NY: New City Press, 2002.

Azzoni, Annalisa. "Marriage and Divorce, *Hebrew Bible.*" In volume 1 of *The Oxford Encyclopedia of the Bible and Gender Studies,* edited by Julia M. O'Brien, 483–88. New York: Oxford University Press, 2014.

Backhaus, Knut. "Before Abraham was, I Am." In *Genesis and Christian Theology,* edited by Nathan MacDonald, Mark W. Elliott, and Grant Macaskill. Grand Rapids MI: Eerdmans, 2012.

Baden, Joel S. *The Promise to the Patriarchs.* New York: Oxford University Press, 2013.

Balentine, Samuel E. *The Torah's Vision of Worship.* Overtures to Biblical Theology. Minneapolis: Fortress, 1999.

———. "Legislating Divine Trauma." In *Bible through the Lens of Trauma,* edited by Elizabeth Boase and Christopher G. Frechette. Semeia Studies 86. Atlanta: Society of Biblical Literature, 2016.

Barton, John. "Theodicy: II. Old Testament." In volume 12 of *Religion Past & Present: Encyclopedia of Theology and Religion,* edited by Hans Dieter Betz et al., 593. Leiden; Boston: Brill, 2012.

Becker, Eve-Marie, Jan Dochorn, and Else Kargeland Holt, editors. *Trauma and Traumatization in Individual and Collective Dimensions: Insights from Biblical Studies and Beyond.* Studia Aarhusiana Neotestamentica 2. Göttingen: VandenHoeck & Ruprecht, 2014.

Berquist, Jon L. "Family Structures: Hebrew Bible." In volume 1 of *The Oxford Encyclopedia of the Bible and Gender Studies,* edited by Julia M. O'Brien, 199–205. Oxford and New York: Oxford University Press, 2014.

Biddle, Mark E. *Missing the Mark: Sin and Its Consequences in Biblical Theology.* Nashville: Abingdon, 2005.

Bird, Phyllis. *Missing Persons and Mistaken Identities: Women and Gender in Ancient Israel.* Overtures to Biblical Theology. Minneapolis: Fortress, 1997.

Boase, Elizabeth and Christopher G. Frechette, editors. *Bible through the Lens of Trauma*. Semeia Studies 86. Atlanta: Society of Biblical Literature, 2016.

Borrowski, Oded. *Daily Life in Biblical Times*. Archaeology and Biblical Studies 5. Atlanta: Society of Biblical Literature, 2003.

Bosman, Hendrik L. "Fear of God, Hebrew Bible/Old Testament." In volume 8 of *The Encyclopedia of the Bible and Its Reception*, edited by Dale Allison et al., 1022–23. Boston, Berlin: DeGruyter, 2014.

Brown, William P. *A Handbook to Old Testament Exegesis*. Louisville KY: Westminster John Knox, 2017.

———. "Manifest Diversity: The Presence of God in Genesis." In *Genesis and Christian Theology*, edited by Nathan MacDonald, Mark W. Elliott, and Grant Macaskill. Grand Rapids MI: Eerdmans, 2012.

———. *The Seven Pillars of Creation: The Bible, Science, and the Ecology of Wonder*. New York: Oxford University Press, 2010.

———. "Whatever Your Hand Finds to Do: Qoheleth's Work Ethic." *Interpretation* (July 2001): 271–84.

Brueggemann, Walter. *An Unsettling God: The Heart of the Hebrew Bible*. Minneapolis: Fortress, 2009.

———. "Of the Same Flesh and Bone, Gn 2:23a." *Catholic Biblical Quarterly* 32/4 (October 1970): 532–42.

———. *Theology of the Old Testament: Testimony, Dispute, Advocacy*. Minneapolis: Fortress, 1997.

Burnette-Bletsch, Rhonda. "God at the Movies." In *The Bible in Motion: A Handbook of the Bible and Its Reception in Film*, edited by Rhonda Burnette-Bletsch, 299–326. Berlin/Boston: de Gruyter, 2016.

Carr, David. *Holy Resilience: The Bible's Traumatic Origins*. New Haven CT: Yale University Press, 2014.

———. "Reading into the Gap: Refractions of Trauma in Israelite Prophecy." In *Interpreting Exile: Displacement and Deportation in Biblical and Modern Contexts*, edited by Brad E. Kelle, Frank Richtel Ames, and Jacob L. Wright, 295–308. Ancient Israel and Its Literature 10. Atlanta: Society of Biblical Literature, 2011.

———. *Reading the Fractures of Genesis: Historical and Literary Approaches*. Louisville KY: Westminster John Knox, 1996.

Carroll, Robert P. "Exile, Restoration, and Colony: Judah in the Persian Empire." In *The Blackwell Companion to the Hebrew Bible*, edited by Leo G. Perdue, 102–16. Oxford: Blackwell, 2001.

Cavanaugh, William T. *Torture and the Eucharist*. Challenges in Contemporary Theology. Oxford and Malden MA: Blackwell, 1998.

Cerekso, Anthony R. *Introduction to the Old Testament: A Liberation Perspective*. Maryknoll NY: Orbis, 1998.

Chadwick, Jeffrey R. "Hebron (Place), Hebrew Bible/Old Testament, archaeology." In volume 11 of *Encyclopedia of the Bible and Its Reception*, edited by Dale Allison et al., 694–68. Boston, Berlin: DeGruyter, 2014.

Chilton, Bruce. *Abraham's Curse: Child Sacrifices in the Legacy of the West*. New York: Doubleday, 2008.

Clifford, Richard J. *Creation Accounts in the Ancient Near East and in the Bible.* Catholic Biblical Quarterly Monograph Series 26. Washington DC: The Catholic Biblical Association of America, 1994.

Coates, Ta-Nehesi. *Between the World and Me.* New York: Spiegel & Grau, 2015.

Coffin, William Sloan. *Letters to a Young Doubter.* Louisville KY: Westminster John Knox, 2005.

Cooley, Jeffrey L. *Poetic Astronomy in the Ancient Near East: The Reflexes of Celestial Science in Ancient Mesopotamia, Ugaritic, and Israelite Narrative.* Winona Lake IN: Eisenbrauns, 2013.

Craine, Renate. *Hildegard, Prophet of the Cosmic Christ.* New York: Crossroad, 1997.

Davis, Ellen F. *Scripture, Culture, and Agriculture: An Agrarian Reading of the Bible.* Cambridge UK; Cambridge University Press, 2007.

Day, Peggy L., editor. *Gender and Difference in Ancient Israel.* Minneapolis: Fortress, 1989.

Dempsey, Carol J. "The Wilderness: Sacred Space, Endangered Homeland, Hope for Our Planet." In *Turning to the Heavens and the Earth: Theological Reflections on a Cosmological Conversion. Essays in Honor of Elizabeth A. Johnson,* edited by Julia Brumbaugh, 61–80. Collegeville MN: Liturgical, 2016.

Diamant, Anita. *The Red Tent.* New York: Picador, 1997.

Dozeman, Thomas B., and Konrad Schmid, editors. *A Farewell to the Yahwist? The Composition of the Pentateuch in Recent European Interpretation.* Symposium. Atlanta: Society of Biblical Literature, 2006.

Ebeling, Jennie R. *Women's Lives in Biblical Times.* New York: T & T Clark International, 2010.

Exum, J. Cheryl. "Desire Extorted and Exhibited: Lot and His Daughters in Psychoanalysis, Painting, and Film." In *"A Wise and Discerning Mind": Essays in Honor of Burke O. Long,* edited by Saul Olyan and Robert Culley, 83–108. Brown Judaic Studies 325. Providence RI: Brown Judaic Studies, 2000.

———. *Song of Songs: A Commentary.* Louisville: Westminster John Knox, 2005.

Fergusson, David. "Interpreting the Story of Creation: A Case Study in the Dialogue between Theology and Science." In *Genesis and Christian Theology,* edited by Nathan MacDonald, Mark W. Elliott, and Grant Macaskill, 155–74. Grand Rapids MI: Eerdmans, 2012.

Fischer, Irmtraud. "On the Significance of the 'Women Texts' in the Ancestral Narratives." In *Torah,* edited by Jorunn Okland, Irmtraud Fischer, and Mercedes Navarro Puerto, with Andrea Taschle-Erber, 251–93. The Bible and Women: An Encyclopedia of Exegesis and Cultural History 1. Atlanta: Society of Biblical Literature, 2011.

Fishkin, Shelley Fisher, editor. *The Diaries of Adam and Eve.* New York: Oxford University Press, 2010.

Fox, Everett. *The Five Books of Moses: Genesis, Exodus, Leviticus, Numbers, and Deuteronomy.* Schocken Bible. Dallas: Word, 1995.

Frechette, Christopher G. "Blessing the Lord with the Angels: Allusion to *Jubilees* 2.2 in the Song of the Three Jews." In *Biblical Essays in Honor of Daniel J. Harrington, SJ, and Richard J. Clifford, SJ: Opportunity for No Little Instruction,* edited by Thomas Stegman, Christopher G Frechette, and Christopher R Matthews. New York: Paulist Press, 2014.

———. "Why Bless God?" In *Reading the Old Testament: Pastoral Essays in Honor of Lawrence Boadt, C.S.P.*, edited by Corrine Carvalho, 111–19. New York: Paulist, 2013.

Fretheim, Terence E. *Abraham: Trials of Family and Faith*. Columbia: University of South Carolina Press, 2007.

———. *Creation Untamed: The Bible, God, and Natural Disasters*. Theological Explorations for the Church Catholic. Grand Rapids MI: Baker, 2010.

———. "Genesis." In volume 1 of *The New Interpreter's Bible*, edited by Leander Keck. Nashville: Abingdon, 1994.

———. "God, Abraham, and the Abuse of Isaac." *Word & World* 16 (1996): 49–57.

———. *The Pentateuch*. Interpreting Biblical Texts. Nashville: Abingdon, 1996.

Galambush, Julie. "Be Kind to Strangers, But Kill the Canaanites: A Feminist Biblical Theology of the Other." In *After Exegesis: Feminist Biblical Theology: Essays in Honor of Carol A. Newsom*, edited by Patricia K. Tull and Jacqueline E. Lapsley, 141–54. Waco TX: Baylor University Press, 2015.

Garber, David G., Jr. "Trauma Theory and Biblical Studies." *Currents in Biblical Research* 14/1 (October 2015): 24–44.

Gerstenberger, Erhard S. *Israel in the Persian Period: The Fifth and Fourth Centuries B.C.E.* Translated by Siegfried S. Schatzmann. Leiden, The Netherlands: Brill, 2012.

Gossai, Hemchand. *Barrenness and Blessing: Abraham, Sarah, and the Journey of Faith*. Eugene OR: Cascade Books, 2008.

Grabill, Rhiannon. "Male-Female Sexuality: Hebrew Bible." In volume 1 of *The Oxford Encyclopedia of the Bible and Gender Studies*, edited by Julia M. O'Brien, 445–50. Oxford and New York: Oxford University Press, 2014.

Greenblatt, Stephen. "If You Prick Us: What Shakespeare taught me about fear, loathing, and the literary imagination." Annals of Culture. *The New Yorker* (10 and 17 July 2017): 34–39.

Habel, Norman C. *Readings from the Perspective of Earth, The Earth Bible*. Volume 1. Sheffield: Sheffield Academic Press, 2000.

Hanks, Gardner C. *Capital Punishment and the Bible*. Scottsdale PA: Harald, 2002.

Haynes, Stephen R. *Noah's Curse: The Biblical Justification of American Slavery*. Oxford and New York: Oxford University Press, 2002.

Hays, Christopher B. *Hidden Riches: A Sourcebook for the Comparative Study of the Hebrew Bible and the Ancient Near East*. Louisville KY: Westminster John Knox, 2014.

Hendel, Ronald, editor. *Reading Genesis: Ten Methods*. Cambridge: Cambridge University Press, 2010.

———, Chana Kronfeld, and Ilana Pardes. "Gender and Sexuality." In *Reading Genesis: Ten Methods*, edited by Ronald Hendal, 71–91. Cambridge UK: Cambridge University Press, 2010.

Herzfeld, Noreen L. *In Our Image: Artificial Intelligence and the Human Spirit*. Theology and the Sciences. Minneapolis: Fortress, 2002.

Herzog, Ze'ev. "Cities, Cities in the Levant." In volume 1 of the *Anchor Bible Dictionary*, edited by David Noel Freedman, 1031–43. New York: Doubleday, 1992.

Hiebert, Paula. "Whence Shall Help Come to Me?: The Biblical Widow." In *Gender and Difference in Ancient Israel,* edited by Peggy L. Day, 125–43. Minneapolis: Fortress, 1989.

Holladay, William L. *A Concise Hebrew and Aramaic Lexicon of the Old Testament.* Grand Rapids MI: Eerdmans, 1971.

Howard-Brook, Wes. *"Come Out, My People!" God's Call out of Empire in the Bible and Beyond.* Maryknoll NY: Orbis, 2010.

Isasi-Diaz, Ada Maria. *La Lucha Continues: Mujerista Theology.* Maryknoll NY: Orbis, 2004.

Jacobs, Mignon R. *Gender, Power, and Persuasion.* Grand Rapids MI: Baker, 2007.

Janzen, Waldemar. "The Theology of Work from an Old Testament Perspective." *The Conrad Grebel Review* 10 (1992): 121.

Jesurathnam, K. "Am I my brother's keeper?: Corruption from an Old Testament perspective." *Bangalore Theological Forum* 47/1 (June 2015): 22.

Kaltner, John. *Ishmael Instructs Isaac: An Introduction to the Qur'an for Bible Readers.* Collegeville MN: Liturgical Press, 1999.

Kaminsky, Joel S. "Election, Hebrew Bible/Old Testament." In volume 7 of the *Encyclopedia of the Bible and Its Reception,* edited by Dale Allison et al., 611–15. Boston, Berlin: DeGruyter, 2014.

Kelle, Brad E., Frank Ritchel Ames, and Jacob Wright, editors. *Interpreting Exile: Displacement and Deportation in Biblical and Modern Contexts.* Ancient Israel and Its Literature 10. Atlanta: Society of Biblical Literature, 2011.

Kennedy, Elisabeth Robertson. *Seeking a Homeland: Sojourn and Ethnic Identity in the Ancestral Narratives of Genesis.* Bible Interpretation Series. Leiden: Brill, 2011.

Kessler, John. "Persia's Loyal Yahwists." In *Judah and the Judeans in the Persian Period,* edited by Oded Lipschits and Manfred Oeming, 91–121. Winona Lake IN: Eisenbrauns, 2006.

Kim, Grace Ji-Sun. "'Do you Speak English?' Racial Discrimination and Being the 'Perpetual Foreigner.'" In *Here I Am: Faith Stories of Korean-American Clergywomen,* edited by Grace Ji-Sun Kim, 51–57. Valley Forge PA: Judson Press, 2015.

King, Phillip J., and Lawrence E. Stager. *Life in Ancient Israel.* Library of Ancient Israel. Louisville KY: Westminster John Knox, 2001.

Kugel, James L. *The Bible as It Was.* Cambridge MA: Belknap Press of the Harvard University Press, 1997.

———. *In Potiphar's House: The Interpretive Life of Biblical Texts.* Cambridge MA: Harvard University Press, 1994.

LaCocque, André. *Onslaught against Innocence: Cain, Able and the Yahwist.* Eugene OR: Cascade, 2008.

Lakoff, George and Mark Turner. *More Than Cool Reason: A Field Guide to Poetic Metaphor.* Chicago: The University of Chicago Press, 2004.

Lee, Archie Chi Chung. "When the Flood Narrative of Genesis Meets Its Counterpart in China." In *Genesis: Texts @ Contexts,* edited by Athalya Brenner, Archie Chi Chung Lee, and Gale A. Yee, 81–97. Minneapolis: Fortress, 2010.

Lemche, Niels Peter. "Habiru, Hapiru." In volume 3 of *The Anchor Bible Dictionary,* edited by David Noel Freedman, 6–10. New York: Doubleday. 1992.

———. "Hebrew." In volume 3 of *The Anchor Bible Dictionary*, edited by David Noel Freedman, 95. New York: Doubleday, 1992.

Levenson, Jon D. *Inheriting Abraham: The Legacy of the Patriarch in Judaism, Christianity & Islam*. Princeton: Princeton University Press, 2012.

Lipka, Hilary. *Sexual Transgression in the Hebrew Bible*. Hebrew Bible Monographs 7. Sheffield: Sheffield Phoenix, 2006.

Lipschits, Oded. *The Fall and Rise of Jerusalem*. Winona Lake IN: Eisenbrauns, 2005.

———, and Manfred Oeming, editors. *Judah and the Judeans in the Persian Period*. Winona Lake IN: Eisenbrauns, 2006.

Louth, Andrew, editor. *Genesis 1–11*. Ancient Christian Commentary on Scripture, Old Testament 1. Downers Grove IL: InterVarsity Press, 2000.

Löwisch, Ingeborg. *Trauma Begets Genealogy: Gender and Memory in Chronicles*. Sheffield UK: Sheffield Phoenix Press, 2015.

MacDonald, Nathan. "Did God Choose the Patriarchs?" In *Genesis and Christian Theology*, edited by Nathan MacDonald, Mark W. Elliott, and Grant Macaskill, 245–66. Grand Rapids MI: Eerdmans, 2012.

McEntire, Mark. *Struggling with God: An Introduction to the Pentateuch*. Macon GA: Mercer University Press, 2008.

McKenzie, Steven L. *Covenant*. Understanding Biblical Themes. St. Louis MO: Chalice, 2000.

Mellish, Kevin. "Edom, Edomites." In volume 7 of the *Encyclopedia of the Bible and Its Reception*, edited by Hans-Jospeh Klauck et al., 403–11. Berlin, Boston: DeGruyter, 2012.

Meyers, Carol. "Contesting the Notion of Patriarchy: Anthropology and the Theorizing of Gender in Ancient Israel." In *A Question of Sex? Gender and Difference in the Hebrew Bible and Beyond*, edited by Deborah Rooke, 84–105. Hebrew Bible Monographs 14. Sheffield: Sheffield Phoenix, 2009.

———. *Rediscovering Eve: Ancient Israelite Women in Context*. New York: Oxford University Press, 2013.

———, Toni Craven, and Ross Shepard Kraemer, editors. *Women in Scripture: A Dictionary of Named and Unnamed Women in the Hebrew*. Winona Lake WI: Eerdmans, 2001.

Miller, Robert D. II. *Oral Tradition in Ancient Israel*. Biblical Performance Criticism 4. Eugene OR: Cascade, 2011.

Moore, Megan Bishop. "Historical Criticism: Hebrew Bible." In volume 1 of the *Oxford Encyclopedia of Biblical Interpretation*, edited by Steven McKenzie, 391–400. Oxford and New York: Oxford University Press, 2013.

Moss, Candida R., and Joel S. Baden. *Reconceiving Infertility: Biblical Perspectives on Procreation and Childlessness*. Princeton and Oxford: Princeton University Press, 2015.

Murray, Robert. "The Cosmic Covenant." *The Ecologist* 30/1 (Jan/Feb 2000): 25–29.

Neusner, Jacob. *The Genesis Rabbah: The Judaic Commentary on the Book of Genesis: A New American Translation*. Brown Judaic Studies 104–106. Atlanta: Scholars Press, 1985.

Niditch, Susan. "Folklore and Biblical Interpretation." In volume 1 of the *Oxford Encyclopedia of Biblical Interpretation*, edited by Steven McKenzie, 313–21. Oxford and New York: Oxford University Press, 2013.

————. *A Prelude to Biblical Folklore: Underdogs and Tricksters*. Urbana: University of Illinois Press, 1987.

Noll, K. L. *Canaan and Israel in Antiquity: A Textbook on History and Religion*. Second edition. London: Bloomsbury T&T Clark, 2013.

Nossiter, Adam. "Young and Alone in France's Migrant Jungle." *New York Times*. 22 October 2016.

O'Brien, Julia M., editor. *The Oxford Encyclopedia of the Bible and Gender Studies*. 2 volumes. Oxford and New York: Oxford University Press, 2014.

O'Connor, Kathleen M. "The Feminist Movement Meets the Old Testament." In *Engaging the Bible in a Gendered World: an introduction to feminist biblical interpretation in honor of Katharine Doob Sakenfeld*, edited by Linda Day and Carolyn Pressler, 3–24. Louisville KY: Westminster John Knox, 2006.

————. *Jeremiah: Pain and Promise*. Minneapolis: Fortress, 2011.

Penchansky, David. "Good and Evil." In volume 1 of *The Oxford Encyclopedia of the Bible and Theology*, edited by Samuel E. Balentine, 426–32. Oxford and New York: Oxford University Press, 2015.

Person, Raymond F., Jr. "Orality Studies and Oral Tradition: Hebrew Bible." In volume 2 of the *Oxford Encyclopedia of Biblical Interpretation*, edited by Steven McKenzie, 55–63. Oxford and New York: Oxford University Press, 2013.

Pilch, John J. "Honor and Shame." In *Oxford Bibliographies* in Biblical Studies. http://www.oxfordbibliographiesonline.com/view/document/obo-9780195393361/obo-9780195393361-0077.xml (accessed 8 August 2016).

Provan, Ian. *Discovering Genesis: Content, Interpretation, Reception*. Discovering Biblical Texts. Grand Rapids MI: Eerdmans, 2015.

Reno, R. R. "Beginning with the Ending." In *Genesis and Christian Theology*, edited by Nathan MacDonald, Mark W. Elliott, and Grant Macaskill, 26–42. Grand Rapids MI: Eerdmans, 2012.

Römer, Thomas. *The Invention of God*. Translated by Raymond Geuss. Cambridge MA: Harvard University Press, 2015.

Rooke, Deborah, editor. *A Question of Sex? Gender and Difference in the Hebrew Bible and Beyond*. Hebrew Bible Monographs 14. Sheffield: Sheffield Phoenix, 2009.

Rose, Jenny. "The 'Persian' Period." In *Oxford Bibliographies* in Biblical Studies. http://www.oxfordbibliographiesonline.com/view/document/obo-9780195393361/obo-9780195393361-0194.xml (accessed 16 February 2017).

Rosenhagen, Ulrich. "One Abraham or Three?" *Christian Century* 13/25. 9 December 2015. 30–33.

Russell, Letty M. "Twists and Turns in Paul's Allegory." In *Hagar, Sarah, and Their Children*, edited by Phyllis Trible and Letty M. Russell, 71–97. Louisville KY: Westminster John Knox, 2006.

Sacks, Jonathan. T*he Dignity of Difference: How to Avoid the Clash of Civilizations*. London and New York: Continuum, 2002.

Sadler, Rodney. "Genesis." In *The Africana Bible: Reading Israel's Scriptures from Africa and the African Diaspora*, edited by Hugh R. Page, Jr., 70–79. Minneapolis: Fortress, 2010.

Saliers, Don, and Emily Saliers. *A Song to Sing, A Life to Live: Reflections on Music as Spiritual Practice*. The Practices of Faith Series. San Francisco: Josey-Bass, 2005.

Saneh, Lamin. *Summoned from the Margin: Homecoming of an African*. Grand Rapids MI: Eerdmans, 2012.

Sarna, Nahum M. *Understanding Genesis: The Heritage of Biblical Israel*. New York: Shocken, 1986.

Schmidt, Brian. "Canaanites, I-III." In volume 4 of the *Encyclopedia of the Bible and Its Reception*, edited by Hans-Jospeh Klauck et al., 871–73. Berlin, Boston: DeGruyter, 2012.

Scholz, Susanne. *Introducing the Women's Hebrew Bible*. Introductions in Feminist Theology 13. London: T & T Clark International, 2007.

———. *Rape Plots: A Feminist Cultural Study of Genesis 34*. Studies in Biblical Literature 13. New York: Peter Lang, 2000.

———. *Sacred Witness: Rape in the Hebrew Bible*. Minneapolis: Fortress, 2010.

Schrieter, Robert J. "Reading Biblical Texts Through the Lens of Resistance." In *The Bible Through the Lens of Trauma*, edited by Elizabeth Boase and Christopher B. Frechette, 193–207. Atlanta: Society of Biblical Literature, 2016.

Schwartz, Regina M. *The Curse of Cain: The Violent Legacy of Monotheism*. Chicago: University of Chicago Press, 1997.

Shectman, Sarah. "Marriage and Divorce, Ancient Near East." In volume 1 of *The Oxford Encyclopedia of the Bible and Gender Studies*, edited by Julia M. O'Brien, 479–83. Oxford and New York: Oxford University Press, 2014.

Shemesh, Yael. "Vegetarian Ideology in Talmudic Literature and Traditional Biblical Exegesis." In *Genesis: Texts @ Contexts*, edited by Athalya Brenner, Archie Chi Chung Lee, and Gale A. Yee, 107–27. Minneapolis: Fortress, 2010.

Sheridan, Mark. *Genesis 12–50*. Ancient Christian Commentary on Scripture, Old Testament 2. Downers Grove IL: InterVarsity Press, 2002.

Shore-Goss, Robert E. "Gay Liberation." In volume 1 of *The Oxford Encyclopedia of the Bible and Gender Studies*, edited by Julia M. O'Brien, 257–64. Oxford and New York: Oxford University Press, 2014.

Smith-Christopher, Daniel L. "Trauma and the Old Testament: Some Problems and Prospects." In *Trauma and Traumatization in Individual and Collective Dimensions: Insights from Biblical Studies and Beyond*, edited by Eve-Marie Backer, Jan Dochhorn, and Else K. Holt, 223–43. Studia Aarhusiana Neotestamentica 2. Göttingen: VandenHoeck & Ruprecht, 2014.

Smith, Dwight Moody. "Word." In *The Harper-Collins Bible Dictionary*, edited by Paul D. Achtemeier, 1221. San Francisco: HarperSanFrancisco, 1985.

Smith, Mark S. *How Human Is God? Seven Questions about God and Humanity in the Bible*. Collegeville MN: Liturgical Press, 2014.

Spencer, John R. "Levi (Person), 1." In volume 4 of the *Anchor Bible Dictionary*, edited by David Noel Freedman, 294. New York: Doubleday, 1992.

Steinberg, Naomi. *Kinship and Marriage in Genesis: A Household Economics Perspective*. Minneapolis: Fortress, 1993.

———. "The World of the Family in Genesis." In *The Book of Genesis: Composition, Reception, and Interpretation*, edited by Craig, W. Evans, Joel N. Lohr, and David L. Petersen, 279–300. Leiden and Boston: Brill, 2012.

Sternberg, Meir. "Double Cave, Double Talk: The Indirections of Biblical Dialogue." In *Not in Heaven: Coherence and Complexity in Biblical Narrative*, edited by

Jason C. Rosenblatt and Joseph C. Sitterson, Jr., 28–57. Bloomington: Indiana University Press, 1991.

Stiebert, Johanna. "The Construction of Shame in the Hebrew Bible: The Prophetic Contribution." *Journal for the Study of the Old Testament* Supplement Series 346. Sheffield: Sheffield Academic Press, 2002.

———. *Fathers and Daughters in the Hebrew Bible.* Oxford: Oxford University Press, 2013.

Stuart, Douglas. "Curse." In volume 1 of the *Anchor Bible Dictionary*, edited by David Noel Freedman, 1218. New York: Doubleday, 1992.

Stulman, Louis. "Reading the Bible Through the Lens of Trauma and Art." In *Trauma and Traumatization in Individual and Collective Dimensions: Insights from Biblical Studies and Beyond*, edited by in Eve-Marie Backer, Jan Dochhorn, and Else K. Holt, 177–92. Studia Aarhusiana Neotestamentica 2. Göttingen: VandenHoeck & Ruprecht, 2014.

———. "Reflections on the Prose Sermons in the Book of Jeremiah: Duhm's and Mowinckel's Contribution to Trauma Readings." In *The Bible through the Lens of Trauma*, edited by Elizabeth Boase and Christopher G. Frechette, 125–39. Semeia Studies 86. Atlanta: Society of Biblical Literature, 2016.

———, and Hyun Paul Kim. *You Are My People: An Introduction to Prophetic Literature.* Nashville: Abingdon, 2010.

Thomas, Matthew A. *These are the Generations: Identity, Covenant, and the 'Toledot' Formula.* London: T & T Clark, 2011.

Thompson, Trevor W. "Punishment and Restitution." In volume 2 of *The Oxford Encyclopedia of the Bible and Law*, edited by Brent Strawn, 183–93. Oxford and New York: Oxford University Press, 2015.

Trible, Phyllis. "Genesis 22: The Sacrifice of Sarah." In *Not in Heaven: Coherence and Complexity in Biblical Narrative*, edited by Jason Philip Rosenblatt and Joseph C. Sitterson, 170–91. Bloomington: Indiana University Press, 1991.

———. *God and Rhetoric of Sexuality.* Overtures to Biblical Theology. Philadelphia: Fortress, 1978.

———, and Letty M. Russell, editors. *Hagar, Sarah, and Their Children.* Louisville KY: Westminster John Knox, 2006.

Tull, Patricia K. "Jobs and Benefits in Genesis 1 and 2." In *After Exegesis Feminist Biblical Theology: Essays in Honor of Carol A Newsom*, edited by Patricia K. Tull and Jacqueline E. Lapsley, 15–29. Waco TX: Baylor University Press, 2015.

Vanderhooft, David. "Babylonian Strategies of Imperial Control in the West: Royal Practice and Rhetoric." In *Judah and the Judeans in the Neo- Babylonian Period*, edited by Oded Lipschits and Joseph Blenkinsopp, 104–14. Winona Lake IN: Eisenbrauns, 2003.

Visotzky, Burton L. *The Genesis of Ethics: How the Tormented Family of Genesis Leads us to Moral Development.* New York: Three Rivers Press, 1996.

Vrolijk, Paul D. *Jacob's Wealth: An Examination into the Nature and Role of Material Possessions in the Jacob-Cycle (Gen 25:19–35:29).* Supplements to Vetus Testamentum 146. Leiden; Brill, 2011.

Washington, Harold C. "Israel's Holy Seed and Foreign Women." *Biblical Interpretation* 11/3–4 (2003): 427–37.

Weems, Renita J. *Battered Love: Marriage, Sex, and Violence in the Hebrew Prophets.* Overtures to Biblical Theology. Minneapolis: Fortress, 1995.

Williams, Delores S. *Sisters in the Wilderness: The Challenge of Womanist God-Talk.* Maryknoll NY: Orbis, 1993.

Wilson, J. Christian. "Tithe." In volume 6 of the *Anchor Bible Dictionary*, edited by David Noel Freedman, 578–80. New York: Doubleday, 1992.

Wiman, Christian, *My Bright Abyss: Meditation of a Modern Believer.* New York: Farrar, Strauss, and Giroux, 2013.

van Wolde, Ellen. "Facing the Earth: Primeval History in a New Perspective." In *The World of Genesis: Persons, Places, Perspectives*, edited by Philip R. Davies and David J. A. Clines, 22–47. Sheffield: Sheffield Academic Press, 1998.

Yee, Gale A. "What is Culture Criticism of the Old Testament?" In *Pastoral Essays in Honor of Lawrence Boadt, CSP: Reading the Old Testament*, edited by Corrine L. Carvalho, 43–55. Mahwah NJ: Paulist, 2013.

Zakovitch, Yair. "Inner Biblical Interpretation." In *Reading Genesis: Ten Methods*, edited by Ronald Hendel, 92–118. Cambridge UK: Cambridge University Press, 2010.

Zornberg, Avivah Gottlieb. *The Beginnings of Desire: Reflections on Genesis.* First Image Books edition. New York: Doubleday, 1995.

Zsolnay, Ilona. "Gender and Sexuality: Ancient Near East." In volume 1 of *The Oxford Encyclopedia of the Bible and Gender Studies*, edited by Julia M. O'Brien, 275–87. Oxford and New York: Oxford University Press, 2014.

INDEX OF MODERN AUTHORS

INDEX OF SCRIPTURES

INDEX OF SIDEBARS AND ILLUSTRATIONS

Illustrations

INDEX OF TOPICS